Public Papers of
the Secretaries-General of
the United Nations

VOLUME VI

U THANT
1961–1964

Public Papers of
the Secretaries-General of
the United Nations

VOLUME VI

U THANT
1961–1964

Selected and Edited with Commentary by

ANDREW W. CORDIER
AND
MAX HARRELSON

COLUMBIA UNIVERSITY PRESS

1976

NEW YORK AND LONDON

ANDREW W. CORDIER served as Dean of the School of International Affairs at Columbia University from 1962 to 1972 and as president of the university from 1968 to 1970. From the beginning of the United Nations until 1962 Dr. Cordier was Executive Assistant to the Secretary-General with the rank of Under-Secretary. During the entire period he also had the top Secretariat responsibility for General Assembly affairs.

MAX HARRELSON served as a United Nations correspondent from 1946 until 1972, the last twenty-two years as chief correspondent of the Associated Press. Later he became a research associate in the School of International Affairs, Columbia University.

Library of Congress Cataloging in Publication Data (Revised)

Cordier, Andrew Wellington, 1901-1975 comp.
  Public papers of the Secretaries-General of the United Nations.

  Bibliographical footnotes.
  CONTENTS: v. 1. Trygve Lie: 1946-53—v.2. Dag Hammarskjöld: 1953-1956.—v.3. Dag Hammarskjöld: 1956-1957. [etc.]
  1. United Nations—Collections. I. Foote, Wilder, joint comp. II. Harrelson, Max. III. Lie Trygve, 1896-1968. IV. Hammarskjöld, Dag 1905-1961. V. Thant, U, 1909-1974. VI. Title.
JX1977.C62   341.23'08   68-8873
ISBN 0-231-03966-2

86403

Editors' Note on the Series

THE ROLE OF THE Secretary-General in the political life and constitutional development of the United Nations since 1945 has far exceeded the expectations of those who wrote the Charter. This has enhanced the historical significance of their public papers. These include many texts that are valuable and often indispensable as source materials in study of the Organization as a whole, of the office of Secretary-General in particular, and of the place of both in world affairs.

It is important that such papers be readily available to scholars and specialists in international affairs. In practice their accessibility has been severely limited. Some of the public papers of the Secretaries-General are included in the official documentation and some are not. In the former category are periodic and special reports to United Nations organs, proposals, and statements at meetings of the General Assembly, the Security Council, the other councils, committees, and commissions, and certain communications to governments. Not included in the official records are various other communications to governments, the Secretary-General's addresses outside the United Nations, statements to the press, press conference transcripts, radio and television broadcasts, contributions to magazines and books. Most of the texts in this second category were issued as press releases, none as official documents.

More or less comprehensive collections of the official documents are maintained by depository libraries designated by the United Nations and located in most of the countries of the world. After more than twenty-five years it is not surprising that the volume of this documentation is immense. The record of what successive Secretaries-General have spoken or written in the official proceedings is widely dispersed throughout a great mass of records. Furthermore, it is necessary to go to the press releases for the public papers in the second category described above. The Dag Hammarskjöld Library at United Nations Headquarters maintains a comprehensive collection of press releases but it has not been the practice to include them in the deposit of official documentation in the depository libraries. Yet the press releases are usually the only source of a very important part of the public record—the Secretary-General's speeches to other groups and organizations and his press statements and press conferences. Successive Secretaries-General have frequently used these for historically significant and revealing statements.

Thus the present series of volumes of the public papers of the Secretaries-General has been undertaken to meet a real need. The project has been made possible by a grant from the Ford Foundation to the School of International Affairs of Columbia University. The series will include all texts believed by the editors to be essential or most likely to be useful in study and research about the United Nations. These have been assembled from official, semiofficial, and nonofficial sources. The texts selected for the printed series are reproduced in full except where otherwise indicated. The styles of spelling and capitalization, which were variable in the official documents and press releases, have generally been reproduced as they were in the originals. Dates have been conformed throughout to the month-day-year style. The texts are arranged for the most part in chronological order corresponding to the sequence of events to which they are related. Commentary recalling the contemporary context and giving other background for the texts is provided whenever this seems useful. The full collections at Columbia University and the Dag Hammarskjöld Library are open to scholars wishing to consult them.

It should also be explained that the official records of the United Nations include many reports issued in the name of the Secretary-General that may more correctly be classified with the records of the organs requesting them. Such reports are factual accounts of developments or programs without personal commitments of policy or principle by the Secretary-General. There are a few borderline cases, but in general reports of this nature have not been considered as belonging with the public papers of the Secretaries-General.

Acknowledgments

PUBLICATION of the *Public Papers of the Secretaries-General of the United Nations* was made possible by a grant from the Ford Foundation to the School of International Affairs of Columbia University. The editors are deeply grateful for this financial assistance.

Our editorial and research assistant, Charlotte Carpenter, and her predecessor, Alice Smith, rendered indispensable and devoted service in assembling texts, researching the background of events for use in the commentary, finding and checking sources and references, reading proof, and supervising the reproduction of both texts and commentary.

The task of collecting the papers of U Thant included in this volume was greatly facilitated by the cooperation of the United Nations Secretariat, especially officers of the Dag Hammarskjöld Library and the Public Inquiries Unit at United Nations Headquarters.

The editors are especially grateful for the personal assistance of the late U Thant and other officials close to him in providing background material essential for the commentary. They also wish to acknowledge with appreciation the help given by the late Wilder Foote, former Research Associate in the School of International Affairs and coeditor of the preceding volumes in this series. His comments and suggestions were invaluable.

Contents

Public Papers of
the Secretaries-General of
the United Nations

VOLUME VI

U THANT

1961–1964

Note

IN THE course of the decade following the events recorded in this volume, European names of places and a number of persons in the Congo were changed to African names. Thus, the Republic of the Congo itself was renamed the Republic of Zaïre, Leopoldville became Kinshasa, Elisabethville Lubumbashi, and General Joseph Mobutu (who became President in 1965) Mobutu Sese Seko. All names in this volume are given only as they appeared in the official records of the time.

Introduction to This Volume of the Public Papers of U Thant

I

The death of Dag Hammarskjöld not only raised the question of who would be the next Secretary-General of the United Nations, but in the minds of many it posed a much more serious question: Would there be another Secretary-General? This was by no means a rhetorical or a fanciful question. The United Nations was in the midst of a serious crisis both internally and externally. The Hammarskjöld tragedy could not have occurred at a more inopportune time.

It was not enough that the Organization was faced with grave problems of finance and with major differences on the Congo military operations; the concept of the Organization, as accepted by the majority of Member states, was being challenged. The office of the Secretary-General itself was under attack. The Soviet Union was attempting, somewhat recklessly it seemed at the moment, to halt the evolution of the office which had taken place under Lie and Hammarskjöld.

Between 1945 and 1961, the office of the Secretary-General had assumed responsibilities beyond those contemplated by some of the founders of the Organization, and the two Secretaries-General had witnessed a gradual and significant expansion of their roles. Although both Lie and Hammarskjöld accepted the concept of a dynamic rather than a static United Nations and a flexible interpretation of the Charter regarding the office of Secretary-General, neither had sought deliberately an aggrandizement of personal power. Both were innovators; both were exponents of a diplomatic role for the Secretary-General; both were ready and willing to accept executive responsibility in addition to their administrative duties. Many of the responsibilities they assumed under the Charter were assigned to them by the Security Council, the General Assembly and other United Nations organs. This trend and the success attained became so pronounced during Hammarskjöld's administration that "Leave it to Dag" became a common phrase. In addition to Hammarskjöld's diplomatic successes, he created peacekeeping forces in the Middle East and the Congo which were of great value to his total efforts. By the time of his death, the United Nations was engaged in major peacekeeping operations, with some 25,000 soldiers under the United Nations flag and—what was more important—under the command of the Secretary-General.

While these developments stemmed from actions approved by a substantial majority of the Member states, some countries still clung to the belief that the United Nations should be fundamentally a conference-type organization limited to providing the machinery and facilities for international meetings, and that the Secretary-General should be an administrator only. This group was small, but it was not to be ignored because it included the Soviet Union. It had not come as a complete surprise when Nikita Khrushchev launched his "troika" plan in 1960, proposing that the office of the Secretary-General be replaced by a three-man committee made up of representatives of the socialist world, the West and the non-aligned countries. This plan found no support outside the socialist states, but the Soviet Union had never withdrawn it as a policy. In fact, it had been restated as late as five months before Hammarskjöld's death when Khrushchev told columnist Walter Lippmann that there was no such thing as a neutral man and added, "we cannot have another Hammarskjöld, no matter where he comes from among the neutral countries." A major question, therefore, after the September 18 tragedy was whether the Soviet Union would accept anyone as Hammarskjöld's successor.

The problem turned out to be less difficult than expected. The Soviet Union did not use the occasion to press for the troika idea, but instead it proposed a modified plan under which the Secretary-General would have a three-man advisory group or, perhaps, a double troika with a six-man advisory group. For a time it seemed that the task of selecting a Secretary-General might become enmeshed in endless delays because of these demands, but it soon became apparent that the Soviet Union was trying to back away as gracefully as possible from the troika proposal, which had found no Third World support.

Despite the uncertainty over Soviet thinking, private discussions began on the problem immediately after Hammarskjöld's death. The main attention was focused on talks between United States Ambassador Adlai Stevenson and Soviet Ambassador Valerian Zorin, but consultations on other fronts were also in progress. Discussions were going on, for example, among three friendly small-power ambassadors who constituted themselves an informal committee to seek a new Secretary-General. This group consisted of Sievert Nielsen of Norway, Frederick Boland of Ireland, and U Thant of Burma. These three were members of a larger group along with representatives of India, Mexico, the United Arab Republic, Venezuela and Yugoslavia.

There were no avowed candidates, but the names mentioned most frequently were those of the Irish ambassador, who had just completed a term as president of the General Assembly, and Mongi Slim of Tunisia, who had been elected president of the sixteenth session three days after Hammarskjöld's death. Boland took himself out of the picture because of his feeling—shared by many—that the new Secretary-General should not be another European. By this time the Organization had begun to sense the need for greater geographic recognition to take into account its new Asian and African Members. Although Slim met this requirement, both he and his government were considered to be pro-Western and this would have made it difficult for him to win Soviet approval. Slim never actively sought the job, but simply signified that he was prepared to accept it if he were drafted.

While public attention was directed at Boland and Slim, the man who began to attract the notice of Stevenson and Zorin was U Thant. They had known him as a colleague since 1957, but they were impressed anew during the private discussions. Furthermore, Thant came from a country that was geographically correct and, equally important, politically neutral. Within ten days after Hammarskjöld's death, Thant had been assured privately that he was acceptable to both the United States and the Soviet Union. Agreement on Thant was confirmed by Stevenson in a television broadcast on October 15.[1]

"There will be a Secretary-General," he said, "And, by the way, I should say we have agreed upon him. Ambassador U Thant of Burma is acceptable to the Soviet Union and highly acceptable to the United States."

The election of Thant was delayed, however, by Soviet efforts to restrict his authority. Stevenson said in his October 15 statement that final agreement was being held up by a dispute over how many principal advisers Thant would have and from what geographic regions they would come. French Ambassador Armand Bérard confirmed that agreement on Thant had been reached rapidly but that a dispute had developed "related to methods of his designation, definition of his mandate and his

[1] WABC TV, Adlai Stevenson Reports, October 15, 1961.

relations with his collaborators." Under normal conditions, a new Secretary-General would have been appointed for the customary five-year term, but because of the Soviet Union's distrust of the office a compromise had to be devised. The Soviet Union finally agreed to the appointment of Thant as Acting Secretary-General for the remaining eighteen months of Hammarskjöld's term rather than choosing him outright as Secretary-General for a full term.

Thant refused to accept any restrictions on his authority, but his friends did prevail upon him to make a declaration agreeing to name an unspecified number of advisers, including Ralph Bunche of the United States and Georgy Arkadev of the Soviet Union. Such an arrangement had always existed since the assistant secretaries-general and the under-secretaries had been consulted on important questions within their jurisdiction. Thant's statement in the General Assembly after his appointment on November 3 enabled Zorin to retreat from the troika proposal without an acknowledgement of defeat. Zorin referred to Thant's appointment as "a temporary solution." The selection of a group of principal advisers, he said, "leads us to hope that . . . genuine international cooperation will be ensured in the United Nations machinery and practical steps will be taken to eliminate one-sidedness in the functioning of the executive organ of the United Nations, exclude the possibility of the United Nations Secretariat acting in the interests of any particular group of states, remove discrimination against individual states and ensure fair geographical distribution in the staff of the Secretariat, as required by the United Nations Charter."[2] This interpretation was accepted neither by Thant nor by most delegates to the Assembly. Adlai Stevenson, for example, said the integrity of the office of Secretary-General had been fully protected. Stevenson added: "There will be no veto in the Secretariat and no weakening of the office. The principles contained in Articles 100 and 101 of the Charter have been fully preserved. He will have the full powers and responsibilities of that exalted office."[3]

Events proved Stevenson to be right. Thant conducted the office of Secretary-General without any veto, or attempted interference, by his principal advisers. The troika episode came to an end—at least for the time being—when Thant won unanimous approval a year later for a full term as Secretary-General and the word "Acting" was dropped from his title.

[2] General Assembly Official Records, Sixteenth Session, 1046th plenary meeting.
[3] Ibid.

II

Anyone who has examined statements made by Thant before November 3, 1961, can only marvel at the ease with which he was accepted by the five permanent members of the Security Council. After four years as Burma's permanent representative, his views were known to all. Some of them obviously could not have been pleasing to one or another of the big powers. His acceptance by the Soviet Union must have been especially difficult in view of Thant's outspoken opposition to the Kremlin's efforts to neutralize the office of Secretary-General. Thant had vigorously defended Hammarskjöld against Soviet attacks and had fully endorsed Hammarskjöld's concept of "quiet diplomacy" as well as the right of the Secretary-General to take diplomatic initiatives without prior authorization by other United Nations organs.

In a speech before the fifteenth session of the General Assembly on October 10, 1960, Thant not only insisted that Hammarskjöld had never exceeded the authority granted him by the Security Council in dealing with the Congo problem, but that he had acted properly in the discharge of other functions assigned to him. This was a direct challenge to Khrushchev's position. Thant said further that he saw no need in the circumstances to modify either the office of Secretary-General or to reorganize the Secretariat. "Any such course is not only bound to retard the efficiency of the United Nations operations," he said, "but is sure to weaken the Organization itself" (p. 48).

During the weeks immediately preceding his appointment, Thant had removed any remaining doubts as to his views on the office of the Secretary-General. In an interview[4] after the disclosure of the United States-Soviet agreement on his appointment—but two weeks before the Security Council acted—Thant said that in his opinion the functions of the Secretary-General could be classified in four categories: "(1) administrative functions, (2) organization of conferences, (3) implementation of the decisions of the principal organs of the United Nations and (4) diplomatic initiatives—or if you wish, political initiatives—which I consider to be very important." He went on to say by way of elaboration: "If there is any prospect of disturbance of the peace in any particular area, I think the Secretary-General should take appropriate measures to prevent this from breaking out." He noted that Hammarskjöld on several occasions had taken such initiatives. Five days before his appointment, in a televi-

[4] Interview with William N. Oatis of the Associated Press, October 15, 1961.

sion interview with Stevenson,[5] Thant said there could be no moral neutrality. "Whoever occupies the office of the Secretary-General," he said, "must be impartial, but not necessarily neutral . . . I think the judges of the . . . Supreme Court must be impartial. . . . But they are not neutral as regards who is the criminal and who is the person on whom the crime has been committed. . . . There are many men not only in the United Nations but outside the United Nations who are impartial, who are imbued with the spirit of service, who can override their national and ideological considerations."

Thant's views on France's Algerian policy were equally frank. As Burma's permanent representative, he had been a leader in the Asian-African effort for Algerian freedom and had actually been chairman of a working group set up to back the Algerian independence movement. What might have been more damaging was his personal criticism of President Charles de Gaulle, whose handling of the Algerian problem he called "far from gratifying."[6] He said the French president had "emptied the word 'self-determination' of all its meaning." "It is certainly regrettable," he said, "that the French government is now engaged in two wars, both equally far from glorious. In Algeria, it fights the Algerian nationalists. In France, it is fighting French editors, writers and intellectuals. And so far it has won more victories on the second front."

Thant had frequently criticized United States policy not only on China, but on broader questions such as its relations with Asia and its attitude toward communism. It would have been difficult to object if he had simply supported the seating of the People's Republic of China in the United Nations, since in this case he would have been reflecting the policy of his government. It was apparent, however, that he was voicing his personal convictions as well in speeches both inside and outside the United Nations. As early as 1957, he described United States policy toward China as "unreal,"[7] and declared it needed "a thorough examination and reappraisal." In this same speech, he said: "By excluding the Peking government, one damages not Peking but the United Nations, which is thereby ruled out as an effective instrument of international conciliation. I believe this is not the intention of United States policy, but it is its unhappy

[5] WABC TV, Adlai Stevenson Reports, October 29, 1961.
[6] General Assembly Official Records, Fifteenth Session, 897th plenary meeting.
[7] Address before United States National Commission for UNESCO, San Francisco, November 8, 1957, U Thant, *Toward World Peace: Speeches and Public Statements, 1957-1963*, edited by Jacob Baal-Teshuva, Thomas Yoseloff, 1964.

consequence." He said further: "The United States has, of course, sufficient power to be able to buy the friendship of a few Asian states who
need its military protection, but it is generally true to say that no one in
Asia except two or three leaders comes anywhere near to sharing the
American attitude to Peking."

Thant spoke out plainly on United States Asian policy. For one thing,
he expressed the belief that fear of Soviet communism had led the United
States to take a distorted view of the world situation, confusing nationalism with pro-communist or anti-American feeling. "On many occasions,"
he said, "we Asians feel that leaders of American life and thought . . . fail
to make a distinction between nationalism and communism. You are
vigorously supporting certain of these régimes in spite of the fact that
they are undemocratic, corrupt, and discredited. The effect on some
Asian minds has been to build up the impression that America is against
change and that it wishes to preserve the status quo."

Some of these statements may well have been reviewed—perhaps, with
considerable misgivings—in the capitals of the world when Thant was
being considered for the post of Secretary-General, but they obviously
were outweighed by other factors. These included the desirability of selecting a non-European, Burma's position of neutrality and Thant's high
personal standing among his colleagues.

III

Because of Hammarskjöld's brilliant intellect, some observers of the international scene have been too ready to underrate the mind of Thant.
Although the two men differed in personality, philosophy, background
and manner, Thant's public statements both before and after his appointment as Acting Secretary-General reflect a keen grasp of world problems
and their causes. Like his predecessor, Thant was a skilled diplomat eager
to continue the development of the office of the Secretary-General as an
agency of conciliation and mediation.

Although Thant had never left Burma until 1951, he traveled widely
during the following years as secretary to Prime Minister U Nu. Together
they visited all the major countries. He met such world leaders as Nikita
Khrushchev, Leonid Brezhnev, Alexei Kosygin, Mao Tse-tung, Chou En-
lai, Ho Chi Minh, Tito, Nehru, Nasser, John Foster Dulles, Richard
Nixon, Adlai Stevenson and David Ben-Gurion. On his first visit to the
United States in 1952, as a member of the Burmese delegation to the

United Nations General Assembly, Thant traveled to some twenty states. Another memorable event for him was the Bandung Conference of non-aligned states in 1955. Thant had helped U Nu plan the meeting along with the prime ministers of Ceylon, India, Indonesia and Pakistan, and during the conference he had the opportunity to meet most of the leaders of the twenty-nine Asian and African countries participating.

As one can see in his statements in later years, Thant remained a firm believer in the merits of neutrality and of peaceful coexistence between the communist and noncommunist worlds. While choosing democracy and the fundamental freedoms over dictatorship, he advocated a live-and-let-live approach toward those who disagreed with him. Thant frequently stated his belief in the Hegelian concept that human society is moving toward eventual synthesis, with the dictatorships becoming less and less rigid and the so-called free societies turning more and more toward state regulation and control of individual initiative. In addition to this political synthesis, Thant was also convinced that there was a trend toward a synthesis of Eastern and Western concepts of culture and education. In the technological societies, including the Soviet Union, the stress was primarily on the development of the intellect, he stated on several occasions, while in the East the main emphasis has been on the development of moral and spiritual qualities. In a statement before the annual conference of Non-Governmental Organizations on May 28, 1964, he said: "My feeling is that a pure intellectual development, unaccompanied by a corresponding moral and spiritual development, is sure to lead humanity from one crisis to another. At the same time, pure moral and spiritual development, without corresponding intellectual development, will be just another anachronism, in this second half of the twentieth century."

He believed that, just as the great religions now exist side by side in amity, the day will come when communist societies, capitalist societies, socialist societies and possibly others will collaborate peacefully. He liked to talk about making the world safe for diversity. "Human beings come in all sizes and shapes and in a variety of colors," he once said. "We are thrown together on this planet and we have to live together. That is why the Charter imposes the imperative on all human beings to practice tolerance and live together in peace with one another as good neighbors. To my mind this is the simplest definition of coexistence" (p. 503).

Thant was a deeply religious man, a devout Buddhist. He saw a close parallel between the tenets of the great religions and the United Nations

Charter. The principle of nonviolence, for example, is found in the Charter and in the credos of most religions. As a result of his beliefs, he found himself in agreement with the Roman Catholic Church in many of the Vatican's international political efforts. And, like his predecessors, he maintained a friendly contact with the Vatican. This is reflected both in personal visits with Pope John XXIII and Pope Paul VI and through exchanges of messages with them. Thant was particularly impressed by Pope John's encyclical Pacem in Terris, noting that its contents were in complete harmony with the purposes and objectives of the United Nations (p. 318).

Thant was fully aware that religion also could come into conflict with the principles of the Charter and at times become a complicating factor in international relations.

In a speech before the General Assembly in 1958, Thant said:

> As an Asian, let me confess that a major weakness of Asia is religion employed as a weapon for political ends, and the existence of politics of community or language, or a combination of all. These undesirable forces corrode within, and foul relations between nations. Asia has to overcome these forces in order that the potential strength of the masses for a more peaceful and good-neighborly feeling may be fully developed.[8]

He did not elaborate on this thesis, but it was clear from the context that he was suggesting that religion would be a factor in the composition of a proposed military stand-by force for the Middle East, then under discussion, because of the religious differences between Israel and her Arab neighbors.

"The most effective weapon to fight this malady," he continued, "is to develop and encourage democratic institutions and legitimate national aspirations, and to combat prejudice and ignorance. The United Nations, in the view of my delegation, has a significant role to play in this fight."

IV

Before his appointment as Acting Secretary-General was formally confirmed, Thant had made it clear that his concept of the office was similar to that of his predecessors and that he intended to continue in the same direction. This he did. From time to time he discussed his views of the

[8] General Assembly Official Records, Third Emergency Special Session, 740th plenary meeting.

functions and weaknesses of the United Nations itself. Many of these views will be found in statements in the following pages. In his first press conference on December 1, 1961, he enunciated what some observers called the "Two-Thant" doctrine. Originally, he applied the doctrine to distinguish between statements made by U Thant the permanent representative of Burma and U Thant the Acting Secretary-General. Later, however, he was to extend it to permit himself temporarily to divest himself of his official role and assume the role of a private individual. He made this distinction, for example, in dealing with some phases of the Vietnam conflict. Because North Vietnam was not a member of the United Nations, he communicated with Hanoi on several occasions not as Secretary-General, but as a fellow Asian. There were other occasions on which Thant put aside his mantle of office to express his personal opinion.

Like Lie and Hammarskjöld he applied the broadest possible flexibility to his interpretation of his functions and limitations under the Charter. His yardstick was not whether the Charter provided for the performance of a function, but whether the authority to perform it was implicit in his broad general mandate. Proceeding under this interpretation, he undertook a number of initiatives during his first months in office that were not specifically provided for in the Charter. Several personal interventions were undertaken at the invitation of Member states and not as a result of action by the Security Council or the General Assembly.

Alistair Cooke, the journalist, noted in an interview with Thant in September, 1963 (p. 429), that suggestions had been made that he had exceeded his authority in some cases. Thant replied that he had no knowledge that any Member state had questioned his actions, even though there may have been some criticism in the press and by the public. Thant added that in the performance of his duties he had to be "sensitive to the views of Member states," not to a section of the population or a section of the press. Cooke pointed out that Hammarskjöld had come under criticism from some Member nations because of his initiatives and asked whether the same thing might happen to Thant. "One cannot rule out such a prospect," Thant replied.

Thant saw it as his duty not only to implement decisions of the principal United Nations organs, but to help explain them to the public and to uphold them against criticism, even when the critic happened to be a Member state. It was under this interpretation of his responsibilities that he delivered sharp rebukes to Belgium and other countries he believed were undercutting United Nations efforts to expel mercenaries from the Congo. He was convinced that, because the Assembly and the Security Council had repeatedly denounced the *apartheid* policies of South Africa, he himself had the authority and the obligation to speak out against these policies even though South Africa was a Member government. Thant even protested on occasion against nuclear tests by the United States and the Soviet Union after the Assembly had condemned the continuation of such tests. In a more general way, quite apart from United Nations resolutions, Thant was convinced that many people believed the Secretary-General was the conscience of the world and that he had a duty to speak out.

From the time he took office Thant spoke his mind about the shortcomings of the United Nations. At his first press conference, he asserted that "so far the United Nations has not been able to achieve much in the political field." He also voiced vigorous opinions on specific issues such as proposals for weighted voting, universality of membership, and the trend toward increased use of regional machinery. Thant insisted there was no cause for alarm over the flood of new Members from Asia and Africa. Their membership was good for the United Nations, he said, because it created a more realistic and balanced structure.

As for weighted voting, Thant held that a truly representative organization could be based only "on the principle of the sovereign equality of its Members, whatever their size." "The world is an untidy place," he said in a speech at the University of Denver on April 3, 1964, "but it is hard to imagine another system by which the voting in the United Nations could be more equitably arranged."

Thant was convinced that the strength and effectiveness of the United Nations could not be improved by sudden structural changes and sweeping innovations because basically what was involved was the whole question of relations between sovereign states. Summing up, he said:

We have to fashion, from the elements now at hand, some form of world authority, however rudimentary, to mitigate the anarchy implicit in the concept of absolute freedom of action of sovereign states. Such an authority cannot merely consist of a paper constitution and must be based on a certain degree of power. . . . It is to be hoped that eventually the powers of the great states, now precariously held in balance by nuclear armament, will be shifted to supporting, in all ways, the United Nations, which will only then become a true world authority (p. 562).

V

Upon assuming office, Thant assigned top priority to the problem of completing the Congo operation which had engulfed the United Nations in what seemed to be almost insurmountable political and financial difficulties. This task was to demand most of his time and energy during his first two and a half years as Acting Secretary-General and Secretary-General. Before the withdrawal of the last United Nations military contingents in mid-1964, the Congo operation had cost a total of 126 United Nations troops killed in action and $433 million in military and civilian aid expenditures.

Although Thant was deeply concerned by the drain on the United Nations, which had brought it to the verge of bankruptcy, he was determined from the beginning that there could be no cessation of United Nations involvement until the territorial integrity of the new African nation had been assured and a reasonable level of internal order attained. In a speech in the General Assembly more than a year before he became Acting Secretary-General, he warned that this was a test case for the United Nations and that the Organization must assert its authority forcefully or go the way of the League of Nations. "My delegation," he said, "considers it essential that the present enterprise should not be allowed to break down."[9]

Thant was convinced that part of Hammarskjöld's problem had been a lack of authority to assist the Congo Central Government in restoring and maintaining law and order. During the weeks immediately after Hammarskjöld's death, the breakdown of internal order had become so serious that it was threatening the safety of United Nations forces which, at that time, had no mandate beyond the expulsion of mercenaries and the prevention of the secession of Katanga Province. The Security Council shared Thant's concern over the deteriorating situation. On November 24, just three weeks after Thant became Acting Secretary-General, the Council broadened the mandate of the United Nations Congo command, authorizing it not only to employ the requisite measure of force for the expulsion of mercenaries but pledging "firm and full support" to the Central Government. Thant welcomed the expanded authority and promised to carry out the provisions of the resolution with vigor. No member

[9] Ibid., Fifteenth Session, 897th plenary meeting.

of the Council objected when he read into the record his interpretation of the resolution, which he said, in his opinion, implied "a sympathetic attitude on the part of ONUC toward the efforts of the government to suppress all armed activities against the Central Government" in addition to halting the Katanga secessionist movement.

One of the immediate results of the new tough policy was an acceleration of the fighting both in Katanga and elsewhere as United Nations forces sought to defend and maintain their lines of communication and to attack sniper sanctuaries. This, in turn, brought Thant into a diplomatic conflict with Paul-Henri Spaak, foreign minister of Belgium, who challenged the legality of the United Nations military operations and, in addition, accused United Nations forces of violating the Geneva Convention by attacking civilians. Thant denied the latter charge and defended the actions of the United Nations forces as necessary (p. 54).

"The United Nations Force," he told Spaak, "is a peace force; but because of the hostile attitude of certain Katangese and, I must add, of certain non-African civilians, including Belgians, it was obliged to resort to force in self-defense. I sincerely hope that the fighting will not last long; but at the same time, I am determined to take all necessary action to implement the mandate entrusted to me by the Security Council and the General Assembly."

Two years later Thant was to note that the same elements which had been critical of the United Nations command for "the exercise of the requisite measure of force" were the leading advocates of keeping United Nations forces in the Congo for an additional six months—a proposal to which Thant agreed with reluctance.

"I wonder," he said at a press conference on September 12, 1963, "if they want the United Nations forces in the Congo to perform the functions of Boy Scouts or Sunday school teachers—a proposition, of course, which I cannot accept" (p. 446).

By this time the secessionist threat and the major fighting had long since ended. What Prime Minister Cyrille Adoula wanted the six-month extension for was to help preserve law and order.

From the time Thant took office he and his aides had continued to press forward with the peace efforts initiated by Hammarskjöld. Thant deserves major credit for the eventual settlement which was based on his Plan of National Reconciliation. This plan was submitted to Adoula and Katanga President Moïse Tshombé in August, 1962, on a take-it-or-leave-it option, and was finally accepted by both leaders.

The question has often been asked whether this largest and costliest United Nations peacekeeping operation was a success. From the standpoint of achieving its objectives in the Congo, the evidence seems clearly on the affirmative side. Not only was the territorial integrity of the Congo preserved, but the country was enabled to achieve internal stability, which in 1960 appeared to be beyond attainment. From the standpoint of its impact on the United Nations and the financial and political difficulties it created for the Organization, the final assessment cannot yet be made. The United Nations is still struggling with the aftermath. Not only does the burdensome deficit remain, but the Organization has failed so far to reach agreement on a formula for financing future peacekeeping operations and thus averting a repetition of the Congo experience.

Personally, Thant came through the experience with his prestige enhanced, despite some criticism. He shouldered the enormous responsibility that had originally been placed upon Hammarskjöld and he stood his ground when challenged. Although he did have full authority to implement the Security Council's mandate in his own way—and he did take numerous initiatives both in directing the military operations and in seeking peace—this was primarily a task of executing a decision of the Council as distinguished from some other initiatives which he undertook on his own responsibility.

Also in this category was the United Nations peacekeeping operation in Cyprus, which was undertaken in March 1964, just as the last United Nations forces were leaving the Congo. Although the Cyprus intervention was on a smaller scale, Thant's responsibilities were broader and in some ways more vexing. In this case the Security Council not only gave the Secretary-General the responsibility for determining the size and composition of the United Nations force, the appointment of its commander and its over-all supervision, but also the task of raising money for financing it through voluntary contributions. In addition Thant was asked to appoint a mediator who would report directly to him.

This was the first large-scale peacekeeping operation for which no financing was provided for through assessments on the Member states. As early as September 1964, Thant reported that the financing of United Nations peacekeeping operations by the method of passing the hat was most unsatisfactory. He had found that the burden was being borne by a handful of Member states and that, even though the Security Council had voted unanimously to create the Cyprus force, six of its eleven members contributed nothing during the first year of its operation. The noncontributors included three of the permanent Members—China, France, and the Soviet Union.

VI

Thant's first major initiative was a proposal for a $200 million bond issue to ease the Organization's financial crisis. Although the Member states sponsoring the draft resolution [10] in the General Assembly did not identify the plan as Thant's, he himself acknowledged that he had participated in formulating it. The idea originally was advanced by the United States, but the Acting Secretary-General accepted it and became its sponsor in private consultations. Details were worked out by the United Nations Comptroller, Bruce Turner, and by Thant himself. The resolution was submitted to the Fifth Committee on December 16, 1961, and was approved by the Assembly on December 20, but by a vote that made it all too apparent that many Member states were not happy about it. The vote was 58 to 13, with 28 abstaining. Both the Soviet Union and France criticized the proposal and voted against it, but did not publicly link the Acting Secretary-General with it. The sale of bonds totalling $154.7 million relieved the financial pressure for the moment, but the response to the plan was disappointing. Only sixty-five states, including five nonmembers, made purchases. The United States bought half of the total.

From the beginning of his administration, Thant demonstrated that he would be an activist Secretary-General in the sense that he would use his office as an agency for settling disputes—often without awaiting a directive from the Security Council or the General Assembly. His first intervention of this sort came on December 14, 1961, when he sent messages to the governments of India and Portugal appealing to them to use restraint in their dispute over the Portuguese territories of Goa, Damao and Diu which were situated along the coast of Bombay. The appeal failed, however, and Indian troops seized the territories four days later.

In another early personal intervention, he appealed to the Netherlands and Indonesia on December 19, 1961, to seek a peaceful solution to their dispute over West Irian—or West New Guinea, as it was known to the Dutch. This was the first of several measures initiated by the Acting Secretary-General in this controversy, culminating in a settlement of the

---

[10] Canada, Denmark, Ethiopia, Federation of Malaya, Netherlands, Norway, Pakistan, Tunisia, and Yugoslavia.

problem through his own mediation and that of his personal representative, Ellsworth Bunker. Under his direction and with the approval of the General Assembly, the United Nations actually administered the territory of West Irian during a brief transition period between the withdrawal of the Netherlands authorities and the take-over by the Indonesians. This was the first time such an operation had ever been undertaken by the Organization. It also was the first time the parties to a dispute had paid the complete costs of a United Nations intervention.

Up to the end of 1964, the period covered in this volume, Thant took a number of peacekeeping initiatives. One of the most important, from the standpoint of world peace, was in connection with the Cuban missile crisis of October 1962. Thant's personal intervention was in the form of urgent appeals to President Kennedy and Premier Khrushchev proposing that the Soviet Union agree to a voluntary suspension of all arms shipments to Cuba for a period of two or three weeks and that the United States suspend for a like period the proposed quarantine measures involving the search of ships bound for Cuba (pp. 240-42). His action came as the Security Council debated the threatened confrontation. Many believe that the timely appeal by the Secretary-General provided a convenient way out for both the super powers. At any rate, they seized upon his proposal as the formula for a backdown and later both thanked him for his intervention.

Another example of the exercise of independent initiative, although not comparable in importance, was Thant's appointment on October 19, 1962, of a personal representative to Thailand and Cambodia, at the request of the two governments, to help solve their border dispute. A similar action had been taken by Hammarskjöld in 1959, but his representative, Johan Bech-Friis, had made only a brief visit. Thant appointed Nils G. Gussing, a Swedish diplomat, who remained in the area until the end of 1964. Gussing's expenses were paid by the two governments, so no mandate from the Security Council was necessary. Thant did, however, report to the Council on his decision and on subsequent developments.

The fall of 1962 was indeed a busy time for the Acting Secretary-General, who was on the verge of being appointed to a full term as Secretary-General. It was at this time that he intervened quietly in the Yemen civil war which had developed into an international struggle between Saudi Arabia and the United Arab Republic. Saudi Arabia was supplying military aid to the royalist forces of the Imam and the United Arab Republic was backing the new republican government. Thant's role was revealed by him in a report to the Security Council on April 29, 1963 (p. 328). By that time, the parties to the dispute had agreed to disengage their troops and to have impartial observers check on the implementation of the agreement. In subsequent reports, he told the Council he was planning to send a force of two hundred men to the area to act as observers, under the command of Major General Carl von Horn, Chief of Staff of the United Nations Truce Supervision Organization in Palestine, and that Saudi Arabia and the United Arab Republic would bear the cost. At this point, the Soviet Union requested a meeting of the Security Council to consider the situation. In a letter to the Council President, Soviet Ambassador Nikolai T. Fedorenko said the Secretary-General's reports contained proposals on which only the Council had the authority to act. Fedorenko made it clear in the subsequent proceedings that he would not oppose the observer mission, but he stressed the point that the Council was the only United Nations organ competent to take decisions relating to United Nations action for the maintenance of international peace. At the end of a two-day debate on June 12, the Council adopted a resolution "noting with satisfaction" the initiatives taken by the Secretary-General and formally requesting him to establish the observer mission as already defined by him. The vote was 10 to none, with the Soviet Union abstaining. The Yemen mission began operating on July 4, 1963, and ended in September 1964.

During the summer of 1963, Thant undertook another mission at the request of the governments of the Federation of Malaya, Indonesia, and the Philippines. This involved sending a survey team to North Borneo (Sabah) and Sarawak to ascertain whether the people of those territories wished to join the proposed expanded Federation of Malaya. Thant appointed Laurence V. Michelmore, a member of the United Nations Secretariat, to head the eight-man mission. The Michelmore team spent just under three weeks making the survey. The Secretary-General, in a report which he made public on September 14, concluded that a majority of the people in the two territories wanted to join in the new federation (p. 402). The findings were challenged by both Indonesia and the Philippines, but the establishment of the Federation was nevertheless proclaimed on September 16. The stage was thereby set for a prolonged controversy, which included armed conflict between Indonesia and the Federation of Malaya and eventually led to Indonesia's withdrawal from the United Nations for twenty-one months.

It is of interest, perhaps, to note that Thant's own appraisal of his actions up to September 1963 listed his intervention in the Cuban missile crisis as the one that gave him the greatest measure of satisfaction up to that time. He said further in an interview (p. 436) that next to this came the successful conclusion of the Congo operation. Referring to the temporary relief provided by the United Nations bond issue, he added that "the gradual easing of the financial crisis which confronted the United Nations when I took office has also been a very reassuring development." There was no cause, however, for any lasting cheer over the financial situation which was to remain a major preoccupation to the end of his administration.

VII

Over and above the day-to-day problems of dealing with United Nations peacekeeping operations and administrative matters, Thant from the beginning had placed high priority on the restoration and maintenance of cordial relations with all the big powers. The most pressing need was to patch up the split between the Soviet Union and the office of Secretary-General. France's attitude toward the United Nations was also a matter of concern because of President de Gaulle's disenchantment with the Organization. Thant's immediate efforts, therefore, were directed at Moscow and Paris.

One of the first signs of success was an invitation in the summer of 1962, while he was still Acting Secretary-General, to visit Moscow. This was the first of three visits by Thant to the Soviet Union during his first three years in office. He came away empty-handed as far as a financial contribution was concerned, although this was discussed at length, but more important, perhaps, was the friendly welcome he received. This in itself was a major step forward after the freeze which had existed for a year before Hammarskjöld's death. Thant was received both by Leonid Brezhnev, president of the Presidium of the Supreme Soviet, in Moscow and by Khrushchev at Yalta. The Acting Secretary-General said the subject of his reelection had not come up in his talks with the Soviet leaders, but they apparently were pleased with his performance since they agreed a few months later to support him for a full term as Secretary-General.

Thant was cordially welcomed in Moscow again when he was invited to attend the signing of the three-power treaty banning the testing of nuclear weapons in the atmosphere, in outer space, and underwater. On this occasion, he was also received by Khrushchev for a private talk. By the time he visited Moscow next, in July 1964, it was apparent that he was on excellent terms with the Soviet leaders despite disagreements now and then. Both he and Soviet officials described their conversations as having been very cordial. Thant said he was convinced that Khrushchev sincerely wanted to see the United Nations strengthened. He added: "His concept as to how this may be done is in some respects different from concepts of other Members. . . . I am optimistic, and I feel sure that some consensus will eventually emerge."[11] All but forgotten was the troika plan when Khrushchev proposed a toast to the good health of "U Thant, the man and the Secretary-General of the United Nations."

Thant's efforts to end President de Gaulle's coolness toward the United Nations were equally productive. At one point France had reduced its participation in United Nations activities to a token representation, but it was clear by the time of Thant's visit to Paris in July 1964 that all was well again. De Gaulle personally paid tribute to him for fulfilling his duties "with dignity, wisdom, and an awareness of reality." He noted further that, though it had stayed apart from some undertakings of the United Nations in the past France continued to have great confidence in the Organization's future, especially in view of the functions with which the Secretary-General was invested and of the general trust which he so justly enjoyed. Maurice Couve de Murville, Minister for Foreign Affairs, stated during this same visit that France was gratified by the cooperation that existed between his country and the Secretary-General.

With the rapprochement between him and the governments of France and the Soviet Union, Thant had added greatly to the usefulness of the office of Secretary-General and had opened channels of communication which had previously been clogged, if not closed. This was one of his primary goals. In accepting appointment to a full term on November 30, 1962, he told the Assembly: "If I accept this extended term, it is because I do believe that I may be able to play a role, however humble, in the easing of tensions and in bridging the gulf between the major powers." By the end of 1964, he had indeed laid the foundation which was to keep the channels of communication open throughout his ten years in office with all Member states, large and small.

ANDREW W. CORDIER
and MAX HARRELSON

May 15, 1975
[11] UN Press Release SG/SM/129, July 30, 1964.

✲ *1961* ✲

ACCEPTANCE OF OFFICE

As PERMANENT REPRESENTATIVE OF BURMA, U Thant had worked closely with Dag Hammarskjöld for four years and held him in high regard. He had defended him when he was under attack by Soviet Premier Nikita Khrushchev and had more than once endorsed Hammarskjöld's concept of the office of Secretary-General. Something of Thant's own personality and thinking is reflected in the eulogy he delivered three days after Hammarskjöld's death—and long before Thant had any inkling that he might be chosen to fill the post of Secretary-General. He praised Hammarskjöld, for example, both for the exceptional courage with which he faced his critics and for his skill in holding his own against those who challenged his views. Another point stressed by Thant was the fact that Hammarskjöld held strong convictions and that he never swerved from them. These were qualities which appealed to him.

Thant's first statement as Acting Secretary-General was delivered from the same podium on November 3 immediately after he took the oath of office. He began by pledging an attitude of objectivity in the pursuit of his duties, without regard to ideologies. More significant, however, was a segment of the speech dealing with his plans to appoint a number of principal advisers. Although he did not mention it, much of the backstage discussion preceding his selection revolved around this issue. The Soviet Union at first had attempted to back away from the so-called troika plan, which would have replaced the Secretary-General with a three-man executive group, by proposing a "double troika" of six under-secretaries from the three main political divisions of the world to serve as principal advisers to the Secretary-General. The discussions turned into a "numbers game." Every number from one to fifteen was eventually proposed, but the deadlock remained. Thant persistently refused to accept any control or restraint by any group of under-secretaries. The Russians finally agreed to a U.S. proposal to take Thant on approval by naming him "acting" Secretary-General to serve out the remaining year and a half of Hammarskjöld's five-year term. As indicated in his acceptance speech, Thant agreed to name an unspecified number of under-secretaries, selected on a geographic basis, to serve as principal advisers. These would include Ralph J. Bunche of the United States and Georgy P. Arkadev of the Soviet Union, the others to be named later. Thant promised to "work together with these colleagues in close collaboration in a spirit of mutual understanding"—a formula agreed upon in advance. He would not commit himself to accept any proferred advice and, further, he reserved the right to make any future organizational changes "as experience may reveal to be necessary." Thant did name some additional "principal advisers" a few weeks later, but there is no evidence that he ever considered their advice any more binding than had his predecessors.

Thant's statement dedicating the Dag Hammarskjöld Library came two weeks after he took office. It was an emotional occasion for Thant and for the many who had worked with Hammarskjöld personally on plans for the new building.

---

1. From Statement in the General Assembly as Permanent Representative of Burma, after the Death of Dag Hammarskjöld

NEW YORK   SEPTEMBER 20, 1961

. . . . The death of Mr. Hammarskjöld brings with it three thoughts from my delegation. There is a very wide appreciation of his work as Secretary-General of the United Nations, purely from the recognition of his exceptional abilities and of his dedication to the set task of strengthening the world Organization. Second, there is the increasingly clear image of a man who had come to be identified with the very purposes and principles set forth in the United Nations Charter. Who else could implant in one's mind more forcefully the symbol of a man relentlessly dedicated to the maintenance of international peace and security? Third, there is universal admiration for the exceptional courage with which he faced his critics.

Did his achievements really rest on his quality as an expert, or as a politician, or as a statesman? Mr. Hammarskjöld was clearly a very great expert in foreign affairs. Knowledge of the subject and his abiding interest in it were never in doubt. He was also a remarkable politician, for, despite the difficulties, he held his own with the critics of his views. If it is a test of world statesmanship decisively to influence the broad trend of affairs, Mr. Hammarskjöld passed this test.

Like all great men, he held strong convictions. This strength of belief gave him a broad consistency. He never swerved from the wide course

General Assembly Official Records, Sixteenth Session, 1010th plenary meeting.

dictated to him by his convictions. I knew him for more than four years and I am convinced that he was essentially a man of peace. Nothing was more paramount in his thoughts than to fulfil the essential objectives of the United Nations, namely, the prevention and removal of threats to peace. Despite the fact that there were some human errors of judgment in his pursuit of peace, he drove himself and pursued his policies with a steady singleness of purpose.

Who could be more deserving of a Nobel Peace Prize than Mr. Dag Hammarskjöld, who fell in his unrelenting fight for peace, even though the award would be posthumous? I would also heartily endorse the suggestion just made by the representative of the United States of America to perpetuate the memory of Mr. Hammarskjöld by a fitting memorial in the United Nations.

In conclusion, on behalf of my delegation, allow me to extend our heartfelt condolences to the Government and the people of Sweden and to the Swedish delegation, to the United Nations in their bereavement, as well as to the families of Mr. Wieschhoff and of the others who perished in the tragic disaster.

---

2. Statement in the General Assembly after Taking the Oath of Office as Acting Secretary-General

NEW YORK   NOVEMBER 3, 1961

SPEAKING FOR THE FIRST TIME in this hall, not in my familiar role as the representative of Burma but in the new role as Acting Secretary-General of the United Nations, my first thought is to thank my fellow representatives for the honour they have done me and the confidence that they have placed in me in electing me to this high office. May I at the same time thank the President for his very gracious words of welcome, and also the President and members of the Security Council for unanimously recommending my name to the General Assembly for election as Acting Secretary-General.

General Assembly Official Records, Sixteenth Session, 1046th plenary meeting.

Most of my colleagues present in this hall know me personally. They know that I come from a relatively small country in Asia. They know also that my country has steadfastly pursued over the years a policy of non-alignment and friendship for all other nations, whatever their ideologies. In my new role I shall continue to maintain this attitude of objectivity and to pursue the ideal of universal friendship.

Having been the permanent representative of my country to the United Nations for the last four years and more, I am not unaware of the heavy responsibilities I am undertaking today. The debates in the General Assembly have already shown that the international climate can hardly be described as sunny. The Organization is also facing a serious financial problem. In the Congo operation, which is one of the major undertakings in the history of the Organization, we continue to encounter serious difficulties which clamour for an urgent solution.

If I am to discharge these responsibilities, surmount these difficulties and resolve these problems I shall need, in the first instance, the whole-hearted support, friendly understanding, and unstinting cooperation of all my colleagues. I have enjoyed such friendly cooperation from you all for so long as a representative that I would fain hope that in my new role I shall receive it in even greater measure. For my part I shall endeavour to cooperate with you all in every possible way. In addition to your cooperation I shall need also the loyal support of my colleagues in the Secretariat.

I know how hard the Secretariat has had to work during the last sixteen months, especially in connection with the Congo operation. The Secretariat has shown itself capable of meeting all demands made on it so far, and I count on the continued assistance and team spirit of my colleagues in the Secretariat, especially in the difficult days ahead that we shall face together.

In particular it is my intention to invite a limited number of persons who are at present undersecretaries, or to be appointed as undersecretaries, to act as my principal advisers on important questions pertaining to the performance of functions entrusted to the Secretary-General by the United Nations Charter. In extending this invitation I am fully conscious of the paramount consideration of securing the highest standards of efficiency, competence and integrity, and with due regard to the importance of as wide a geographical basis as possible, as laid down in Article 101 of the Charter. I intend to include among these advisers Mr. Ralph J. Bunche and Mr. Georgy Petrovich Arkadev. It is also my intention to work together with these colleagues in close collaboration and consulta-

tion in a spirit of mutual understanding. I am sure that they will seek to
work with me in the same manner. Of course, this whole arrangement is
without prejudice to such future organizational changes as experience
may reveal to be necessary.

Once again I thank the President, my fellow representatives in this hall,
and the President and members of the Security Council for entrusting me
with these heavy responsibilities. In discharging these responsibilities I
shall count on the support of all men and women of good will all over the
world, whose overriding interest in the peace, security, and progress of
the world it will be my task to reflect and serve.

---

3. From Statement at Ceremonies Dedicating the Dag Hammarskjöld Library

NEW YORK   NOVEMBER 16, 1961

THE LAST TIME Dag Hammarskjöld visited the old United Nations Headquarters Library he said to the staff in parting, "I hope that when we
meet again I shall find you in more appropriate quarters."

Fate denied him that appointment, but today we are gathered to dedicate a splendid new library building which I am sure would satisfy him as
"appropriate." That it should be named for Dag Hammarskjöld is not in
the circumstances an unusual action. Buildings often are named in memory of men who have contributed brilliantly and uniquely to the cause for
which they labored, although the completion date of an appropriate
building less commonly follows so closely the death of one in whose name
it is dedicated. But how rarely is a building named for a man who by
choice and temperament was wholly sympathetic with the purpose for
which that building was constructed, and who himself had worked for its
creation and overseen every detail of its planning.

That is the possibly unique distinction of this dedication, for Dag
Hammarskjöld was a man of learning and a poet of the breed for whom

UN Press Release SG/1066—HQC/199.

books and libraries are necessary delights. He was an intellectual whose training and daily work embraced history, economics, and the law, and whose private pleasures included philosophy and poetry. He read Kierkegaard and Sartre and Buber, Eliot and Perse, as he listened to Bach and looked at Picasso; they delighted his mind and gave flight to his imagination.

For such a man, architecture's combination of precise physical and mathematical principles with the most subtle aesthetic harmonies was a most congenial combination. It is not surprising, therefore, that the late Secretary-General took a close personal interest in every detail of the Library's design, from its general outline to the texture of the fabric on a single chair. He looked at plans, drawings, models, samples of wood and marble and leather; he requested construction of model rooms to display alternate lighting fixtures and flooring materials; he expressed opinions and took final decisions on such questions as the curve of the roof, the color of the draperies, the dimensions and design of a mural. And he did these things with delight, as a relaxation from the daily responsibilities of his office, and with such good humor and evident taste that, far from annoying the professionals—the architects, designers, engineers, artists— he won their immediate respect and their admiring cooperation.

As the building neared completion, he began planning its dedication and gave to this, too, his earnest consideration. It was his intention, as it had been from the very beginning of the discussions with the Ford Foundation, that the Library should become a great center for the study of international affairs, and he wished in dedicating the building to emphasize its function as a library designed, equipped and staffed to contribute to the rule of law in the world. Accordingly, he proposed that the dedication be marked by a gathering of librarians from all over the world for the purpose of discussing their general professional concerns and the specific role of the United Nations Library as a member of the global family of libraries.

With the agreement of the Ford Foundation a portion of the building grant was set aside to make this possible, and in the summer of 1961 preliminary plans were made for a two-day library symposium to be held in connection with the library's dedication. To this symposium Mr. Hammarskjöld invited the leading librarians of about forty countries, a number of whom were further asked to prepare papers to be read at the symposium or to participate in panel discussions of library problems, the emphasis of their papers and their discussions to be upon the United Nations Library itself.

His hopes for this library and his plans for its dedication to the cause of peace in the world deserve our respect and our pledge of fulfillment. His plans have remained unchanged, and we have among our guests today those librarians whom he invited to share his hopes and to counsel him on this library's mission. They will meet together tomorrow and on Saturday, as he had planned, and I am sure that they and all of you will share with me the conviction that this dedication of a splendid building to the memory of an exceptional human being of rich talents and dedicated effort, is not only appropriate but is an expression of the faith we all must have in the ultimate triumph of truth—that flame which libraries help to keep alight.

It is in that spirit that we now dedicate this new library building as the Dag Hammarskjöld Library, not as a monument but as a center of research and learning inspired by his zest for knowledge and his earnest search for truth. It will serve delegates to the Assembly and to other principal organs, the members of the permanent missions of member countries, the staff of the Secretariat, research scholars and others who are seriously concerned with the work of the Organization and the problems which it now confronts and which it will face in the years ahead. The rows upon rows of books, its facilities and quiet atmosphere for reflection and research provide an ordering of the experience of mankind as it has found expression in books, and an offering of that collective experience to all who seek it. . . .

STAFF PROBLEMS

When u thant took over the office of Secretary-General, morale in the Secretariat was unbelievably low. The staff had not fully recovered from the shock of Dag Hammarskjöld's death and the general uncertainty which had followed in the wake of Nikita Khrushchev's efforts to replace the Secretary-General with a troika arrangement. There also was a depressing uncertainty about the possible effects of the proposed wider geographic distribution of personnel upon those already in the Secretariat. Another negative factor was the salary level and its failure to keep pace with the pay in private industry. Thant was fully aware of the morale problem and the need ro reassure the staff as soon as possible. One of his first acts was to appear before the Fifth Committee to express his concern and to urge that top priority be given to consideration of salary increases.

1. Statement in the Fifth Committee

NEW YORK   NOVEMBER 7, 1961

Thank you for your very warm words of welcome. I can best respond by assuring you, and through you all the distinguished representatives who are serving on this Committee, that the vital matters for which you are responsible have, and will continue to have, top priority on my time and attention. Conscious as I am, not alone of the very high honor of having been selected as your acting Secretary-General, but even more importantly, of the challenging administrative and budgetary responsibilities associated with that Office, it will be my policy always to look first to the guidance of the Fifth Committee in regard to the right road to follow in the weeks ahead.

I would like to think that the four years or more that I have been privileged to spend in close and friendly collaboration with so many of those present will make my task easier to some extent. But I am also

UN Press Release SG/1062. The summary record is given in General Assembly Official Records, Sixteenth Session, Fifth Committee, 873rd meeting.

aware that, however close one's identification as a representative of one's country with the United Nations and its manifold activities, the responsibilities entrusted to me for the next seventeen months are so different in character, so much more comprehensive and complex, that I will need to draw unreservedly on your patience, your cooperation, and your good will.

Above all, I will have to ask for a little time fully to familiarize myself with many of the basic issues relating to personnel, budgetary, and financial policy which confront the Organization today. I have no panaceas to offer, no simple and ready-made solutions to propose. As I have stated, these problems will receive my immediate study and attention, in consultation with those of my colleagues who are directly concerned, as also those whose views may help me formulate constructive proposals for your ultimate approval.

I shall approach my task, however, in the knowledge that these problems have been, and are at this moment, a matter of deep and serious concern to each and every delegation here represented. We in the Secretariat share with you a confident conviction that the issues at stake are too great to contemplate the possibility of failure. I am therefore optimistic enough—perhaps even simple enough—to believe that where there is a will there is a way, and that despite the apparent differences or divisions that seem temporarily to beset this or that vital sector of United Nations affairs, there is no lack of real desire to effect reasonable reconciliations.

May I venture to express the conviction, which I am sure members of this Committee share, that the decisions reached by this Committee will affect the Organization's strength and vitality, no less than the decisions taken in other Assembly forums, because it is so clear that the Organization will inevitably be weakened, and seriously so, if its administrative and financial integrity is not zealously maintained.

That, Mr. Chairman, very simply, is the reason why, as your Chief Administrative Officer at present, I shall follow the proceedings of this Fifth Committee with the closest attention, and happily make myself available whenever the Committee might judge my personal participation to be helpful.

2. *Statement in the Fifth Committee*

NEW YORK   NOVEMBER 10, 1961

WHEN I MADE a statement before this committee the other day I told you something that must have been fairly obvious to you, namely, that it would take me some time to get a thorough grasp of the many problems with which the Organization is faced. If, therefore, I venture to address you again today on the question of staff salaries, it is certainly not because I feel that a thorough study of that question should be given absolute priority before all others: I realize very well that we have many other important problems before us.

At the same time, I must tell you that I received, a day or two ago, a telegram signed by all the executive heads of our sister organizations in the United Nations common system, stressing their conviction—and I quote—"that the proposed improvements in salaries are essential if we are to recruit and retain competent headquarters and field staffs." I think that I have a duty to put that unanimous view before you.

Secondly, I have received from the staff council a memorandum on the subject which impressed me with its reasoned tone. One cannot, of course, form final conclusions from such a document, but it gave me the impression that the staff had a good case.

And lastly, although I cannot pretend to have examined all the evidence given to the International Civil Service Advisory Board of my predecessor, I have taken a quick look at the Board's report, and I must say that it seems convincing to me. Indeed, the language is quite forceful, and I conclude that the Board itself had strong convictions over its recommendations. The members of the Board are all people of very great experience, and they come from countries with a very wide spread of salary ranges. None of them could be said to have had extravagant ideas about salary scales. When, therefore, they say, as they emphatically do,

UN Press Release SG/1063. The summary record is given in General Assembly Official Records, Sixteenth Session, Fifth Committee, 877th meeting.

that their proposals are essentially moderate, I think we must all give very great weight to that opinion. Indeed, I do not see how I could substitute my own judgment for that of the Board.

It seems an indisputable fact that since the present conditions were established by the intergovernmental Salary Review Committee in 1956, there has been a marked worsening of United Nations conditions of service in comparison with outside conditions, both in civil services and elsewhere. That is bound to cause me concern because quite clearly we must, we absolutely must, be in a position to recruit the best people for the enormously complex tasks we have to carry out. And apart from recruiting needs, I am sure that morale in any organization is bound to suffer if the staff feel that they, and they alone, are constantly dropping in status in terms of their relative position in the salary structure generally.

Therefore, insofar as I have been able to form a judgment in the last few days, I feel that you should, and I very much hope that you will, approve the proposals which my predecessor made. I am sure that such approval will materially help me in the very beginning of my tenure of an office which is difficult enough in any case.

Transcript of His First Press Conference

NEW YORK   DECEMBER 1, 1961

FOR U THANT the press conference was an enjoyable experience. He had a natural warmth toward journalists and was never uncomfortable with them. Long before he became Acting Secretary-General, he made it a practice to drop in on friends in the press area of the Secretariat building. He liked to think of himself as a former journalist and he recognized that an enlightened information program was essential for the success of the United Nations. When he talked with correspondents, either privately or at news conferences, he used language that could be understood by the man-on-the-street. He met questions head on. He often employed words that seemed unnecessarily blunt. Yet he never showed anger and he was rarely, if ever, flustered by a question. He almost never replied "no comment" when asked a question. If he could not, or did not wish to answer a question he usually explained the reason. It generally was a case in which the matter was before a United Nations organ, or one in which delicate negotiations were in progress or one to be dealt with in a forthcoming report. He often invited individual correspondents to his office for private talks. On these occasions he would talk with candor about current problems and about his own thinking on world affairs. He was a great admirer of several American commentators, including Walter Lippmann and James Reston, whom he saw occasionally for private conversations.

The fact that Thant had been in office almost a month when he held his first press conference on December 1 in no way implied that he intended to downgrade this device as a major channel for his views. He was to use the press conference, as his predecessors had done, to make important declarations and to communicate both with the public and the United Nations diplomatic missions.

The delay, he explained, did not mean that he was unaware of the need for keeping the press informed. This was essential for an organization whose strength "primarily depends upon the support it gets from enlightened public opinion all over the world." He said that even now he was breaking a "tradition of the House" that the Secretary-General does not hold a press conference while the General Assembly is in session. The meeting would have been earlier, he said, had it not been for the critical problems, particularly the need for urgent action in the Congo, which faced him upon his election.

The December 1 press conference, like his many future meetings with the press both at Headquarters and elsewhere, demonstrated his readiness to speak out. In replying to a question, for example, about Moïse Tshombé, President of Katanga Province, the Acting Secretary-General expressed the belief that Tshombé was "a very unstable man." His impatience with Tshombé was to be reflected on numerous occasions in the future. Even after a month in office, Thant had concluded that Tshombé's word could not be relied upon and he was publicly accusing him of failing to comply with agreements. In a report to the Security Council in August, 1962, he asserted that Tshombé's "evasive tactics . . . are dangerous and cannot be indefinitely tolerated either by the United Nations or by the Central Government."

A substantial part of the press conference was devoted to the Congo question and the related problem of United Nations finances. In response to a question as to possible conditions for the withdrawal of United Nations forces from the Congo, Thant cited three contingencies which would govern a decision to withdraw: (1) when United Nations resolutions are satisfactorily implemented; (2) irrespective of the stage of implementation, if the Security Council decides the forces should be withdrawn; and (3) when the United Nations has not sufficient resources to give effect to the United Nations resolutions. As Acting Secretary-General, he said, it would be his duty to report the latter situation in time and leave the question for the Security Council to decide.

It was here that he disclosed he was engaged in private discussions on proposals to ease the growing financial difficulties piling up as a result of the huge costs of the Congo operation. These proposals materialized on December 16 as a resolution calling for a $200 million United Nations bond issue. Thant also revealed that during his brief time in office, he had initiated talks with "some of our more recalcitrant Members" in an effort to get them to pay up their arrears in peace-keeping assessments. "I am quite optimistic," he said.

Near the end of the conference, Thant dealt with the Vietnam question for the first time as Acting Secretary-General. He was asked whether the United Nations could do anything to alleviate "the tense situation in Southeast Asia, particularly in Laos and Vietnam." Up to now, he replied, the question had not come up for discussion in the General Assembly and "I do not know whether it will ever come up." In the absence of any action by Member states to inscribe the item on the agenda, he said, "I do not think that I should make any observation."

On the question of Chinese representation, he made it clear that he had not renounced the views he had expressed as representative of Burma in favor of seating the People's Republic of China, but that as Acting Secretary-General he did not think it proper to voice opinions on matters pending before United Nations bodies. To explain his position, he introduced his often-used "Two-Thant" theory in which he suggested "it would be proper to bear in mind two U Thants, U Thant as the permanent representative of his country and U Thant as the Acting Secretary-General."

THE ACTING SECRETARY-GENERAL: Ladies and Gentlemen of the Fourth Estate, I am very glad indeed that I have at last had an opportunity to meet with you. In view of my own background, no one could be more conscious of the need for keeping all of you informed of the manifold

United Nations Note to Correspondents No. 2430.

activities of the United Nations, and by that I mean not exclusively the work of the Secretariat. The United Nations is an Organization whose strength primarily depends upon the support it gets from enlightened public opinion all over the world; and you, Ladies and Gentlemen, are in the best position to make it possible for that opinion to be not only enlightened but also well informed.

I had planned to have this meeting with you even earlier but, in view of the many exciting things that have been happening in the Organization, I regret I had to postpone it until now. Anyhow, better late than never.

I know it has been a tradition of the House that the Secretary-General does not hold a press conference while the General Assembly is in session. However, I felt that I should have this meeting with you even while the Assembly was in session because I have not had a chance to meet with you since my election as Acting Secretary-General. I would also hope that once the Assembly has completed its work, we might meet more regularly.

During this period I have spent much time to get better acquainted with the work of the House, which I knew fairly well from one side but not so well from this side. In particular, I have devoted very great attention to the problems of the Congo operation and I have also given much thought to the speedy and effective implementation of the latest resolution of the Security Council. My preoccupation with the Congo has, to some extent, prevented me from giving sufficient time to some of the other important problems which I have to tackle. I hope, however, in the course of the next two or three weeks to deal with these problems, and you will be kept informed of the decisions I may take on some of them from time to time.

One question relating to the Congo, however, seems to me to merit mention on this occasion. You are all aware that one of the major problems confronting the Organization has arisen directly out of the Congo operation, and that is the financial problem. Yesterday, there were some newspaper reports in regard to certain proposals that had been suggested to deal with this problem. I must inform you straightaway that these proposals are highly tentative and intended to serve more as a basis for discussion. They are in no sense the proposals of the Secretary-General for dealing with the financial problem. As you all know, such problems must be dealt with by the General Assembly, and my intention is just to present some ideas to facilitate such discussion. In the circumstances, I hope you will understand that until the round of consultations I am undertaking with the delegations mainly concerned is complete, it will not be possible for me to disclose the details of the tentative proposals under consideration. In any event, this is a matter for the General Assembly to decide, perhaps the week after next.

There is the latest Security Council resolution of November 24 and, in the statement I made to the Council after the resolution was adopted, I drew attention to the need for providing the Secretariat with resources to carry out the tasks imposed on it by the Security Council. However, the issue is before the General Assembly and—as I said a moment ago—the Assembly will have to decide how the needed resources are to be found.

I have followed with interest the progress made in recent weeks by our world Organization in the direction of universality of its membership. Since the sixteenth session of the General Assembly began, we have gained a new member from Asia and two new members from Africa. Tanganyika has been able to advance its independence day to December 9, so that there will be enough time for Council and Assembly action to enable it to become our 104th Member before the Assembly concludes its present session.

This Assembly has also confirmed the recommendation of the Trusteeship Council that Western Samoa should become independent on New Year's Day. You will agree with me, I am sure, that this is a happy way indeed to start the New Year. And while Western Samoa has indicated that it is not yet ready to apply for membership in the world Organization, I would hope that it would wish to participate in the economic, social, and technical assistance work of the United Nations.

This last remark leads me to say a few words about the work of the United Nations in what I may call the "nonpolitical" field. I am one of those who believe that no activity of the United Nations is more important than that of meeting the pledge given in the Charter "to promote social progress and better standards of life in larger freedom." In this context, I have noted that the economic and social goals of our common work have been given new significance by the unanimous adoption by the Second Committee, last Tuesday, of the resolution designating the present decade as "the United Nations Development Decade." I also note that, under this resolution, we have been asked "to develop proposals for the intensification of action" to promote economic and social development. This is a directive which my colleagues and I accept with humility, and shall discharge to the best of our ability.

In this task, we are fortunate in having available to us not only our own resources but the rich and extensive experience of the specialized agencies of the United Nations and the International Atomic Energy Agency. The work of these agencies, mainly in the field of preinvestment and technical assistance, as well as the work of the International Monetary Fund and the World Bank and its affiliates, is well known.

Not so well known is the fact that, of the total of approximately 18,000 staff members working in the United Nations family all over the world, some 16,000 are working in the economic and social fields and in the area of technical assistance. It is also not so well known, especially at a time when the Organization has extraordinary expenses to meet on account of operations like the Congo, that during ordinary times nearly 85 per cent—I repeat, 85 per cent—of all the funds expended by the United Nations and specialized agencies are invested in work in these fields.

You will also agree that, while the political work of the United Nations attracts the headlines in the newspapers all over the world, very little space is given to its fruitful but unobtrusive activities for economic and social development. I am sure that in the present United Nations Development Decade many new and interesting programs for economic and social development will be initiated and that many good and newsworthy stories will emerge from these programs, so that you may be able to give a better and more balanced coverage to this side of our work.

In conclusion I have just one word to say. The United Nations can be only what its Member countries choose to make it. At present, especially in the discharge of its political functions, it is weak and inadequate but it is still the best hope for getting out of our intolerably dangerous thermonuclear jungle and for creating the beginnings of a civilized international community.

Ladies and Gentlemen, now the floor is yours.

MR. STANLEY BURKE (President of UNCA): Mr. Secretary-General, I do not know whether we can welcome you to your own press conference, but many of those here might recall that Mr. Hammarskjöld on many occasions referred to the press as almost an organ of the United Nations, and perhaps we might call this a meeting of the "Seventh Committee." Knowing as we do, Sir, your interest in the press and the communication of ideas, we appreciate very deeply this interest, and I am sure our association will be a very fruitful one in the "Seventh Committee." May I ask our colleagues to remember that we are pressed for time, to make their questions as brief as possible and to identify themselves.

May I ask you this, Sir? The *raison d'être* for the Congo operation is to prevent the conflict there from becoming internationalized. Is this danger becoming less? If so, at what point would you visualize the whole of the force might be withdrawn?

THE ACTING SECRETARY-GENERAL: The question of withdrawal of the United Nations forces from the Congo depends, as I see it, on three contingencies. First, when the United Nations resolutions are satisfactorily implemented. Of course, in such an eventuality we would have to withdraw our forces from the Congo. Second, irrespective of the stage of implementation of the resolutions, whenever the Security Council decides that the United Nations forces should be withdrawn, they will be withdrawn. Third, when the United Nations has not sufficient resources to give effect to the United Nations resolutions, then I feel that it is my duty to report to the Security Council in time. Then the Security Council will decide on the line of action to be taken.

QUESTION: President Tshombé of Katanga is charging this morning that what he calls enemies of Katanga, as well as Mr. Smith[1] and Mr. Urquhart,[2] helped to provoke the attack on them the other night to try to change Senator Dodd's opinion from Katanga being a civilized state to a state of savagery. What comment do you have on that?

THE ACTING SECRETARY-GENERAL: I would say that, as you are no doubt aware, Mr. Tshombé is capable of making any statement. I have a feeling, after consultations with many who know Mr. Tshombé, that he is a very unstable man.

QUESTION: Sir, I have two brief questions. First, would you care to comment on Mr. Zorin's communication of today in reference to the so-called illegal act involving a cease-fire in the Congo? Second, why has the United Nations not sent a personal representative to the nuclear testing conference in Geneva so far?

THE ACTING SECRETARY-GENERAL: About the legality or otherwise of the cease-fire agreement in the Congo, of course there are various opinions. I do not think I should pass judgment on the legality or otherwise of such an agreement, which took effect before I assumed office.

I am not very clear about your second question. Will you please repeat it?

---

[1] George Ivan Smith.
[2] Brian Urquhart.

QUESTION: At the nuclear testing conference in Geneva there is no representative of the United Nations present. I was wondering why he is here at Headquarters and not there in Geneva at the present time.

THE ACTING SECRETARY-GENERAL: The nuclear conference in Geneva is being covered by a United Nations representative now.

QUESTION: Mr. Secretary-General, it is held by a number of persons that bilateral and regional disputes and threats to the peace should be subjected to regional and bilateral negotiation before they are submitted to the United Nations. Do you believe that such questions as disarmament or the alleged intervention in the Dominican Republic should be discussed, respectively, by the great powers or the Organization of American States before they are submitted to the world as a whole?

THE ACTING SECRETARY-GENERAL: I do not think that the Secretary-General should make any remarks on such issues. As you know, the matter of the Dominican Republic came up for discussion in the Security Council some time ago, but the Security Council did not come to any conclusion. And I do not think it would be proper for me to make any observations on this.

QUESTION: Mr. Secretary-General, could you tell us what progress has been made toward reorganizing the Congolese Army or the United Nations effect or influence on the Congolese troops?

THE ACTING SECRETARY-GENERAL: The Security Council, of course, passed its latest resolution last Friday afternoon, less than a week ago, and since then I have been giving very close attention to the best means of implementing this resolution. I hope to finalize these steps or, if I may say so, programs some time next week. Of course, it is my intention, first of all, to present my views to the Congo advisory committee. I propose to have a meeting of this advisory committee some time late next week, and I will try to get the benefit of its advice. Of course, in due course I will make this plan known to the press.

QUESTION: Mr. Secretary-General, I remember that you said that you consider the question of the Congo your most important problem—in fact, your number one problem—immediately after your nomination. I wonder whether you still think so.

Also, could you tell us what other important problems you have in mind by now? I believe that you must have quite a few.

THE ACTING SECRETARY-GENERAL: Of course, I am sure every one of you will agree with me that the Congo is just at the moment the most important problem facing the United Nations. One other important problem before us is the financial problem. This involves the financing of the Congo operations, our regular operations, the Middle East operations, and so on. And as I have stated earlier, I am giving very serious attention to the financial aspects and am in consultation with the various delegations primarily concerned. I would say that the financial problem is the second most important problem facing the United Nations today.

I might also say that the reorganization of the Secretariat, in terms of the resolutions adopted by the General Assembly, is also a very important problem before us. When I say "reorganization," of course it involves equitable geographical distribution, too.

QUESTION: Mr. Secretary-General, there have been widespread reports about a U Thant Congo plan whereby you would instruct the United Nations forces in Katanga, after having informed the Katangese authorities, you would use force on land and in the air in order to force the mercenaries out of the country. Could you comment on that and say whether such a plan is being envisaged and whether it is nearly at an implementation stage?

THE ACTING SECRETARY-GENERAL: As I have just explained, I am working on a plan in the context of the latest Security Council resolution, as well as in the context of the previous resolutions. The next steps to be adopted in regard to our Congo operations will first of all be presented before the advisory committee on the Congo, perhaps some time next week. Then I will make this known later on, after getting the benefit of the advice of the committee.

QUESTION: Mr. Secretary-General, in your opening remarks you referred to the United Nations increasing membership. Would you have any comment for us today on the question of Chinese representation?

THE ACTING SECRETARY-GENERAL: On such issues I think it would be proper to bear in mind two U Thants, U Thant the permanent representative of his country and U Thant as the Acting Secretary-General. Of course U Thant in his first role had certain ideas regarding not only this question but other questions, too, and U Thant in his second role is not supposed to express any definitive views on any item apart from the implementation of the United Nations resolutions.

QUESTION: Mr. Secretary-General, first, on behalf of over one hundred members whom you know in the correspondents circle, I wish to assure you, in regard to your statement, of their moral cooperation. My question is this: When do you expect to have your general staff, so to speak, completed? I refer to your statement when you took the oath of office before the Assembly in regard to the constituting of your staff.

THE ACTING SECRETARY-GENERAL: As you no doubt remember, Mr. Gabriel, when I made that statement, immediately after the acceptance of office, I did not set any deadline for the appointment of my principal advisers. All I said on that occasion was that it is my intention to invite a limited number of persons who are at present under-secretaries, or to be appointed as under-secretaries, to act as my principal advisers on important questions pertaining to the performance of functions entrusted to the Secretary-General by the Charter.

So it involves certain processes. As I see it, I must have some additional under-secretaries, to comply with the requirements of equitable geographical distribution. In the second place, certain adjustments might be necessary in the Secretariat setup. Then in the third place, I have to invite some of them to serve as my principal advisers. I propose to implement this idea in the course of this month, before the year is out.

QUESTION: Mr. Secretary-General, you are the only Secretary-General who has also served as an ambassador here. Did you bring from your experience some ideas not only about the running of the Secretariat but also of the Assembly, and are you hoping to put these into effect? Are you hoping to put into effect such ideas as you brought concerning the reorganization not only of the Secretariat but also of the Assembly? "Reorganization" is too large a word. But you have had experience as an ambassador; have you brought with you ideas on ways in which the place can be better run?

THE ACTING SECRETARY-GENERAL: When I spoke of reorganization, I was thinking primarily in terms of the reorganization of the Secretariat; I was not thinking in terms of the reorganization of the Assembly, which I do not think I am competent to do.

QUESTION: On every major occasion in the past when the United Nations has been called upon to play a role, there has been a marked lateral collision of views among big and small powers alike. This situation is likely to continue in the future. Under these circumstances, Sir, what is your basic philosophy? Should the United Nations keep away from involvements, at the cost of diminishing influence and effectiveness, or should it endeavor to be a factor at the risk of grave political and financial dangers to its very existence?

THE ACTING SECRETARY-GENERAL: This, of course, is essentially a question to be answered by the General Assembly. My own feeling is that so

QUESTION: I know that there are more important issues, but I am chiefly interested in my own welfare and health, and that of my colleagues, and even of the delegates. Here is my question. When will this terrible session be closed, and are we really threatened with a second part of the sixteenth session?

THE ACTING SECRETARY-GENERAL: The matter will be discussed by the General Committee early next week.

From Statement in the Fifth Committee Preceding
the Proposal for a Bond Issue

NEW YORK   DECEMBER 11, 1961

U THANT began private consultations on the critical financial problems of the United Nations immediately after taking office. At his first press conference, held on December 1, he acknowledged that he was engaged in talks on "certain proposals," but he said the proposals were "highly tentative and intended to serve more as a basis for discussion." He went on to say that "they are in no sense the proposals of the Acting Secretary-General." What he was referring to was the still-secret plan for a United Nations bond issue. The plan, in the form of a working paper at the time, was to emerge a fortnight later as a resolution sponsored by Denmark, Ethiopia, the Federation of Malaya, Netherlands, Norway, Pakistan, Tunisia, and Yugoslavia. Later Canada joined as the ninth sponsor.

The following statement by the Acting Secretary-General in the Fifth Committee was intended as a curtain-raiser for the introduction of the bond issue proposal on December 16 by Zouhir Chelli of Tunisia, who made the formal presentation on behalf of the sponsors. Thant's speech made no reference to a bond issue, but simply stressed the urgency of the problem and the need for extraordinary measures. In submitting the draft resolution, Chelli told the Fifth Committee that the sponsors' action was a response to the Acting Secretary-General's appeal. It was no secret, however, that the proposal not only had Thant's support but that it also had been drafted under his auspices. A United Nations press release stated that the resolution was introduced after "extensive informal discussions in the early part of December between the Acting Secretary-General and most of the delegations in the United Nations." It also said Thant had consulted with Eugene Black, President of the International Bank for Reconstruction and Development, "who gave support and valued advice concerning the possible issuance of the United Nations bonds."

Although Ambassador Philip M. Klutznick, United States representative in the Fifth Committee, at the time denied Soviet charges that the United States was an unavowed sponsor of the bond issue plan, it was known that the bond concept originated in Washington and that after Thant accepted it, United States experts worked with United Nations Comptroller Bruce Turner, a New Zealand national, in drafting the resolution. One of these was Albert Bender, United States member of the Advisory Committee on Administrative and Budgetary Questions. The plan, as finally approved, called for issuance of $200 million in United Nations bonds, bearing interest at 2 percent and repayable in twenty-five equal annual installments. They were to be offered to Member states, United Nations specialized agencies and, if the Secretary-General so decided, to private nonprofit organizations.

The Soviet Union opposed the bond issue as a dangerous precedent, which it said would involve a change in the nature of the United Nations. Soviet Representative A. A. Roschin declared that adoption of the proposal would be tantamount to mortgaging the Organization and would place the "shareholders" in a position to influence its policies. He said the resolution obviously was inspired by the United States and that the United States also was responsible for the fact that it had been sprung on the Fifth Committee without advance warning. Klutznick recalled that the Acting Secretary-General had discussed the problem at length with many delegations and had issued an aide-mémoire setting forth the bond issue as one possible solution.

The bond issue was finally approved by the General Assembly on December 20, 1961, by 58 votes to 13, with 28 abstentions. Both the Soviet Union and France were among those voting against the proposal. Despite a pledge by President John F. Kennedy that the United States would match the total purchases by other countries, the bond sale was disappointing. Total sales finally reached $154.7 million out of the $200 million authorized. Purchases were made by sixty-five states, including five which were not members of the United Nations. The bonds were never offered to nongovernmental investors.

. . . ON THE ASSUMPTION that the Organization's expenses will continue during the first half of 1962 at the rate of approximately $17 million per month and that the collection of contributions during that period will total approximately $40 million, the gap between the debts of the Organization and its available net cash resources will have increased to approximately $170 million by June 30, 1962.

In view of the present situation and the prospects for the immediate future, I consider it imperative that the General Assembly take appropriate action at the present session to reestablish the financial solvency of the Organization and to provide it with the financial resources necessary to carry out its continuing responsibilities. In the absence of adequate and assured long-term arrangements looking to the Organization's immediate as well as prospective financial needs, the consequences of insolvency will have to be faced seriously and soon.

It is estimated that by December 31, 1961, the United Nations will have unpaid bills amounting approximately to $82.5 million. In addition, depletion of the Working Capital Fund (plus temporary loans from other United Nations accounts) is likely to account, as of that date, for a fur-

General Assembly Official Records, Sixteenth Session, Annexes, agenda item 54, document A/C.5/907. The summary record is given in ibid., Fifth Committee, 899th meeting.

ther $26 million. Thus, financial arrangements must be made at this session of the General Assembly which will not only ensure the provision of some $107.5 million for meeting these obligations and needed fund restorations but will provide also for the payment of the continuing costs of other authorized activities.

Against total current liabilities as indicated above (i.e., unliquidated obligations plus advances from the Working Capital Fund and other special or trust accounts) it is calculated that year-end financial statements will show some $86 million in unpaid assessments.

Despite some relative improvement in the course of 1961, the Organization's cash position can be said to be equally critical, with the virtual certainty of its rapid and progressive deterioration during the first half of 1962, and the prospect that all reserves will shortly be exhausted. It is also clear that exclusive reliance on the short-term borrowing expedients used so far would no longer be possible or desirable.

In short, Mr. Chairman, the United Nations will be facing imminent bankruptcy, if, in addition to earliest possible payment of current and, particularly, of arrear assessments, effective action is not promptly taken for the purpose of enabling outstanding obligations to be settled; improving the cash position and providing needed financing for approved continuing activities.

I therefore venture to express the hope that, before it concludes its present session, the General Assembly will devote thought and attention to this continuing financial crisis, and agree upon ways and means by which it could be resolved.

The situation requires that all Member states assist us, not only by alleviating the present crisis, but also by providing sound and longer-range financing. This applies to activities for which provision is made under the regular United Nations budget, as also to separately financed operations specifically approved. It was in anticipation of such a spirit of cooperation, and in the confident expectation that all Members share a common interest in preserving the Organization they have built up as a going concern, that I undertook my present responsibilities. The tasks that have been entrusted to me, however, can be successfully accomplished only if pledges of goodwill are accompanied by a readiness to provide the financial support and resources essential for their fulfilment.

THE SITUATION IN THE CONGO
NOVEMBER AND DECEMBER

DURING THE FORTY-SIX days between the death of Dag Hammarskjöld and the election of U Thant as Acting Secretary-General, the situation in the Congo seriously deteriorated. By September 17 it had already sunk to a level which placed the entire United Nations Congo operation in jeopardy. Not only had UN forces failed in their efforts to expel mercenary troops and other non-Congolese elements from Katanga province; they themselves were threatened in other provinces by mutinous units of the Central Government's military force, the Armée Nationale Congolaise (ANC). Some commanders had lost control of their troops, or had actually encouraged their rebellion. Influential political leaders, including Vice-Premier Antoine Gizenga, were playing games that imperiled the authority of the Central Government. Gizenga had gone to Stanleyville, capital of Orientale province, on October 4 and had failed to return, even when urgently and repeatedly summoned by Premier Cyrille Adoula.

At the time of his death, Hammarskjöld was en route to a rendezvous with Moïse Tshombé, president of Katanga province, at Ndola, Northern Rhodesia, to negotiate a cease-fire in the expanding United Nations-Katanga fighting. The unfinished mission fell to Stüre Linnér, Officer-in-Charge of the United Nations Operation in the Congo (generally known as ONUC, its French acronym). During the evening of September 18, it was decided that the negotiations would be carried on by Mahmoud Khiari, chief of ONUC civilian operations. Khiari met Tshombé at Ndola on September 19 and at 3:45 p.m. on September 20 a provisional agreement was reached for a cease-fire to come into force at midnight that same day.

It appeared for some days that the cease-fire would be successful. Only a few isolated shots were fired on UN positions in Elisabethville on September 21. Unfortunately, however, the cease-fire was destined to be short-lived. The Katanga authorities failed to comply fully with the provisions of the agreement and those of a protocol signed on October 13. On November 2, Linnér reported that the Katanga government had not met its obligations under the protocol, particularly its undertaking to get rid of foreign military personnel and mercenaries. He also reported that Tshombé had resumed a violent propaganda campaign against the United Nations.

This was the situation faced by Thant when he took the oath of office on November 3. Despite Security Council resolutions of July 14, 1960, and February 21, 1961, calling for the withdrawal of all foreign paramilitary personnel and mercenaries, some 237 were reported by the Officer-in-Charge to be still in Katanga province. Many were operating under the cover of civilian employment by the immensely wealthy Union Minière du Haut-Katange, whose Belgian and other foreign owners were the private source of funds for the secessionist movement.

Having served for four years as Burma's permanent representative at the United Nations, Thant was familiar with the Congo problem, On October 10, 1960, a few months after the UN intervention in the Congo, Thant told the General Assembly that "the United Nations must, in some sense, assert its legitimate authority in the Republic of the Congo, or lapse into humilitating passivity." He staunchly defended Hammarskjöld's handling of the Congo operations, at that time under attack by the Soviet Union, asserting that he "is sincerely and efficiently discharging his functions assigned by the United Nations." Part of the problem, he said, was that the UN forces did not have a mandate broad enough to cope with the growing internecine strife among the Congolese, which "from time to time assumed the character of civil war." Later on, when he had become Acting Secretary-General, he did get a more sweeping mandate and he welcomed it, as we shall see in the text of his first statement before the Security Council (pp. 51–54).

From the time he took office, Thant relied upon the same group of advisers who had served under Hammarskjöld. At Headquarters those mainly concerned with the Congo problem included Andrew W. Cordier, executive assistant to the Secretary-General; Ralph J. Bunche, under-secretary for Special Political Affairs; Brigadier Indar Jit Rikhye, military adviser; and Robert Gardiner. In the Congo, the principal United Nations representatives were Linnér, Khiari, and George Ivan Smith, special representative in Elisabethville. Most of them had been involved in the Congo problem from the beginning. At Headquarters, Thant also received help and guidance from the Advisory Committee on the Congo, made up of ambassadors from the states contributing military contingents to ONUC. He himself, at the suggestion of Hammarskjöld, had been chosen as chairman of a seven-member Commission of Reconciliation, established by the General Assembly on April 15, 1961.

Although the Advisory Committee was an informal group set up by the Secretary-General to assist him in the direction of United Nations forces, the committee held six private meetings between the time of Hammarskjöld's death and the appointment of his successor. Bunche and other top staff members represented the office of Secretary-General at these sessions. The first meeting of the committee under Thant's leadership took place on November 17, just two weeks after he took office. In his initial statement he informed the group that he was planning decisive action to eliminate mercenaries from Katanga once and for all. He said he had been advised by his aides, both at Headquarters and in the Congo, that this objective could be attained with the existing forces at his disposal.

On the very day that Thant became Acting Secretary-General the representatives of Ethiopia, Nigeria, and the Sudan—the African members of the Security Council—formally requested that the Council be convened to consider the situation in Katanga. The Council began a series of meetings on November 13, almost simultaneously with the massacre of thirteen Italian crew members of a United Nations aircraft at the Kindu airport in Kivu province. The Council debate culminated in the adoption of a resolution on November 24 authorizing the Security-General to take vigorous action, including the requisite measure of force, for the apprehension, detention, or deportation of all foreign mercenaries and other hostile elements as specified in the resolution of February 21, 1961. This authorization is contained in paragraph 4 of the resolution, a paragraph referred to in some of the texts below. Another mentioned by Thant in his statement to the Council is paragraph 5 which "further requests the Secretary-General to take all necessary measures to prevent the entry or return of such elements under whatever guise and also of arms, equipment, or other material in support of such activities." Paragraphs 8 and 9 broadened the mandate of ONUC by declaring all secessionist activities in the Congo to be illegal and by pledging "the firm and full support" of the United Nations for the Central Government.

In a brief statement in the Council, reproduced in full below (pp. 51-54), Thant promised to carry out its provisions with determination and vigor and to do everything possible to avert a civil war. He further told the Council that, according to his interpretation of the resolution, it implied "a sympathetic attitude on the part of ONUC toward the efforts of the government to suppress all armed activities against the Central Government" as well as the Katanga secessionist movement.

Tshombé's response to the resolution was a wave of attacks on United Nations personnel, attempts to isolate UN troops and a barrage of anti-UN propaganda. Four days after the Council's action, taken by a vote of 9 to none (with France and the United Kingdom abstaining), George Ivan Smith and Brian Urquhart, both of them senior UN officials in the Congo, were seized and brutally beaten by Katangese "paracommandos" and gendarmes while attending a reception in Elisabethville in honor of U.S. Senator Thomas J. Dodd. Tshombé later apologized for the incident, but rejected a UN charge that the attack had been provoked by the propaganda campaign conducted by the Katangese authorities. The situation was aggravated by the erection of roadblocks by the gendarmerie in Elisabethville and elsewhere in an effort to impede United Nations communications. In some instances, UN personnel were molested at the roadblocks. A number of UN soldiers were killed. The conflict suddenly broadened to include bombings and strafing from the air. A Katanga airplane dropped three bombs near UN positions at the Elisabethville airport and UN planes responded by attacking airports at Jadotville and Kolwezi.

All this happened within the first month after Thant took office. On December 10, 1961, the Acting Secretary-General issued a statement saying that military action had been forced on the United Nations by a series of deliberate attacks on UN personnel and positions and by the impeding of the freedom of movement in Elisabethville. The spreading violence had its diplomatic correlatives. Thant became engaged in a hot exchange of messages with Belgian Foreign Minister Paul-Henri Spaak, a veteran UN figure who had served as president of the General Assembly and at one time had been considered for the office of Secretary-General. Among other things, Spaak questioned the legal basis for the UN military actions and denied allegations that the Union Minière was permitting the use of its installations for sniping at United Nations troops. Thant's replies to Spaak's messages are among the texts below. Thant also engaged in strongly-worded exchanges with the president of the Congo (Brazzaville), Abbé Fulbert Youlou, who notified the United Nations that UN aircraft transporting men and supplies for ONUC would be denied landing and overflight rights by the Brazzaville government. Up to mid-December the fighting appeared to be spreading rather than subsiding. The UN forces by then had fifteen jet fighters and had shown their readiness for full-scale counteraction. It was at that time that the tide began to turn. The Acting Secretary-General informed the Advisory Committee on the Congo on December 16 that he had received appeals for a cease-fire from the representatives of the United Kingdom, Belgium, and Greece and from the president of Madagascar. He stated that he was always ready to consider reasonable proposals for a cease-fire provided that the UN objectives were safeguarded. At the same time, President John F. Kennedy passed the word to Thant that he had received a message from Tshombé indicating a desire to negotiate with Premier Adoula. Fighting gradually ended except for small pockets in areas controlled by the Union Minière, where mercenaries continued to direct mortar fire on UN forces.

Adoula and Tshombé arranged a meeting, with assistance from United Nations and United States representatives, on December 19 at Kitona, a former Belgian military base under ONUC command. On December 21, an agreement was reached based on a declaration from Tshombé which seemed at the time to offer some promise for the future. The text of the Kitona declaration is brief. It says:

> The president of the Government of the province of Katanga: (1) accepts the application of the *Loi fondamentale* of May 19, 1960; (2) recognizes the indissoluble unity of the Republic of the Congo; (3) recognizes President Kasavubu as head of state; (4) recognizes the authority of the Central Government over all parts of the Republic; (5) agrees to the participation of representatives of the province of Katanga in the governmental commission to be convened at Leopoldville on January 3, 1962, with a view to study and consideration of the draft constitution; (6) pledges himself to take all necessary steps to enable deputies and senators of the province of Katanga to discharge from December 27, 1961, their national mandate within the government of the Republic; (7) agrees to the placing of the Katanga gendarmerie under the authority of the President of the Republic; (8) pledges himself to ensure respect for the resolutions of the General Assembly and the Security Council and to facilitate their implementation.

The texts included in the next few pages reflect something of the atmosphere in which Thant began his first months as Acting Secretary-General.

1. Statement in the Security Council

NEW YORK   NOVEMBER 24, 1961

MR. PRESIDENT, in this, my first intervention in the Security Council as Acting Secretary-General, I have no need to take up very much of your time. Indeed, I ask to speak even briefly only because I think the members of the Council and all interested parties are entitled to know without delay what they may expect from me with respect to those provisions of the resolution just adopted which call for action by the Secretary-General. In this regard, I may refer particularly to paragraphs 4 and 5 of the resolution.

The subject of the activites of mercenaries in Katanga is one on which we are all entitled to have strong views. For it is intolerable that efforts to prevent civil war and to achieve reconciliation in the Congo should be persistently obstructed and thwarted by professional adventurers who fight and kill for money. I intend, therefore, to discharge the responsibilities entrusted to me in paragraphs 4 and 5 of the resolution with determination and vigour. It will be my purpose to employ toward that end, and to the best advantage, as much as possible of the total resources available to the United Nations Operation in the Congo.

I am sorry in this connection, however, to have to utter a word of realistic caution. It would be highly desirable, in fact, to be in a position to focus all of our resources on the elimination of mercenaries and hostile elements in Katanga, for that objective is of major importance and I believe its realization could lead to decisive results. But the recent tragic events in Luluabourg, Albertville, and Kindu—or more important, the causes underlying those events—carry implications of the most serious nature for the United Nations Force. It is clear that the need for continuing United Nations assistance in the maintenance of law, order, and security in many parts of the Congo is still critical. Moreover, recent performances by Congolese troops, as pointedly indicated in addendum 13 to

Security Council Official Records, Sixteenth Year, 982nd meeting.

document S/4940, certainly are not encouraging as to the capability of the Central Government, at this stage, to assume an increased responsibility in the vital sphere of law and order. It may be necessary, therefore from time to time to establish temporary, short-range priorities in the continuing efforts to achieve the various objectives.

All the United Nations responsibilities flowing from past resolutions on the Congo continue with new emphasis, since these resolutions have all been reaffirmed in the action just taken. Assistance must be given to the Central Government in the maintenance of law and order. Everything possible must be done to avert civil war, even by the employment of force, should this prove necessary as a last resort. This, I believe, necessarily implies a sympathetic attitude of a part of ONUC toward the efforts of the government to suppress all armed activities against the Central Government and secessionist activities. Supporting the territorial integrity of the country, the United Nations position, it seems to me, is automatically against all armed activities against the Central Government and against secessionist forces. This, of course, is reinforced by our confidence in Mr. Adoula and his government. More determined and effective steps must be taken with regard to the training and reorganization of the Congolese armed forces under the terms of the previous resolutions adopted by this Council. The United Nations program of technical assistance should be steadily expanded, particularly as conditions in the country permit the military assistance to be reduced.

It is true that at the present critical stage in the Congo, there is actually an acute need for more troops and I must make a strong appeal to Member states, and particularly the African states, for added contingents or for increases in existing contingents. Nevertheless, once the current phase of disorder and secessionist threat is over, I feel that there will be a real possibility for undertaking a gradual reduction in the size of the Force, beginning, I hope, in early 1962.

Above all, I may assure you that the United Nations will continue and even redouble its attempts to achieve reconciliation, by peaceful means of course, of the sharp differences which now seriously endanger the unity of the country. Much skill and effort have already been employed by the United Nations in this direction. It might be a further useful step for me to designate a special representative of high standing to devote his energies exclusively to the purpose of national reconciliation for a limited time, if the Government of the Republic of the Congo so desires. I am

pondering over this since, in my view, national reconciliation should figure in our attempts to restore law and order in the Republic of the Congo.

My duty now, as I see it, is to do all that can be done to give full effect
to the resolutions of the General Assembly and of this Council relating to
the Congo, including the one just adopted. I shall devote myself steadfastly to that purpose.

Before concluding, I feel impelled to say a word or two about Kindu.
There, on November 11, 1961, a horrifying crime was committed by Congolese troops against thirteen brave Italian men serving the United Nations. This was an act of bestiality, and I assure you that ONUC, on my
orders, is taking all possible measures to see to it that all who are guilty of
the crime will be severely punished. But I must point out that the Kindu
tragedy is not a new experience for the United Nations in the Congo, nor
is it necessarily an indication of any new condition. There has been a long
and very painful series of such experiences at the hands of Congolese
soldiers which ONUC personnel, both civilian and military, have suffered
with patience and fortitude, beginning in August 1960. This includes the
savage beatings of American, Canadian, and Indian air-crew personnel at
the Leopoldville and Stanleyville airports; the ambush of the Irish in
Niemba, North Katanga, with eight casualties; the massacre of the forty-
two Ghanaians and two Swedes at Port Francqui; the assault on the
Sudanese at Matadi; and the besieging of the Irish at Jadotville. It will be
noted from this recital, incidentally, that these attacks follow no pattern
with regard to the race, colour, or nationality of the victims. Undisci-
plined but heavily armed troops who do not respect their officers are a
threat to the security of everyone, Congolese and non-Congolese alike.

I must also say, without opening up any new debates or entering into a
defence of the United Nations Secretariat—for I think it needs none—
that I welcome constructive criticism of the Secretariat and that I will be
the first to admit its faults and errors and try to do all possible to correct
them. Without specific reference to persons or events and without admit-
ting any particular charge, I would grant that mistakes have undoubtedly
been made in the Congo; no operation of that scope and complexity
could be free of them. But to allege discrimination is quite a different
matter, for it is a harsh and ugly charge. I am sorry that it has been made
at all, and especially that it should be done publicly without any prior
reference to me. I do not think that that charge is justified.

Finally, I need not stress that the task of guiding the Congo operation is a difficult and complex one, under any circumstances. It becomes possible of achievement only if I can count on the goodwill of Member governments and especially on their readiness to provide the resources, and particularly the financial support, that is essential for its successful accomplishment.

There is, unfortunately, no reason to anticipate in the next few months an order of expenditure appreciably different from that being incurred at present. I am confident, however, that ONUC will fulfill all of its responsibilities if the necessary resources are made available.

---

2. Message to Paul-Henri Spaak, Foreign Minister of Belgium

NEW YORK   DECEMBER 8, 1961

I HAVE JUST received your telegram of December 8, 1961. You seem to imply that United Nations troops do not respect the obligations of the Geneva Convention and do not take the necessary measures to safeguard the lives and properties of the civilian population. I must most vigorously refute this charge.

United Nations troops have received strict orders to do everything possible to protect and safeguard the lives and properties of the civilian population and I am satisfied that they have obeyed these orders to all extent possible. Indeed, their discipline and their behavior give me very great pride.

But there is evidence that since the beginning of the operation certain non-African civilians have participated in the fighting against the United Nations troops and, in particular, many non-African civilians have sniped at United Nations troops from the shelter of private houses and buildings.

In self-defense, United Nations troops had to take action against these civilians. But in general, they have endeavored to safeguard the lives and properties of the civilians even to the extent of prejudicing the military operations.

Security Council Official Records, Sixteenth Year, Supplement for October, November and December 1961, document S/5025, part B, sect. I.

With regard to the telecommunication installations of the Union Minière it is true that ONUC has warned that, in case the Katangese gendarmerie should use the system of telecommunications of that company, it would have to consider these installations as military objectives. ONUC is aware of the consequences which might result from the destruction of these installations and will endeavor not to take action against then. But if these installations are used for military purposes by the Katangese gendarmerie, military considerations must of necessity prevail.

In this connection, surely you must be aware of the extent of the assistance the Union Minière has given to secessionists in Katanga. According to unimpeachable sources, officials of the Union Minière have proudly admitted the manufacture of gendarmerie armored cars and of bombs which have been dropped on the airport and ONUC headquarters in Elisabethville. It is also a well-known fact that the Union Minière has never denied having made it possible for the mercenaries to go underground by putting them nominally on their payroll.

In your telegram you drew attention to the fact that if the installations of the Union Minière are not protected by ONUC, it would be impossible for this company to oppose their requisition by the Katangese gendarmerie. I can assure you that ONUC will willingly assure the protection of the installations of the Union Minière provided the Union Minière officials seek such assistance and also stop their hostile actions against ONUC.

I cannot conclude this message without expressing my surprise at your attitude regarding the recent events in Katanga. While you readily give credence to unfounded allegations against ONUC, you seem to ignore the circumstances which have led to the present hostilities in Katanga.

It may be useful, therefore, to recall once again the campaign of violence launched by Tshombé and his associates immediately after the adoption of the Security Council resolution of November 24; the brutal and unprovoked assault by Katangese gendarmes on two senior ONUC officials on the evening of November 28, when the Katangese gendarmes went so far as to invade a private home and brutally assaulted a Belgian civilian at the same time; the cold-blooded murder of an Indian soldier and the abduction of an Indian major during the night of November 28 and 29; the abduction on December 3 and 4 of a number of United Nations personnel, thirteen of whom are still held as hostages by the Katangese gendarmerie; the attack on December 4 on three United Nations personnel, one of whom died while the other two were severely wounded; and the setting up of roadblocks by Katangese gendarmes to prevent the movement of United Nations personnel.

It is a matter of pride for me that, despite all these provocations, ONUC representatives have shown remarkable restraint and made every possible attempt to obtain by peaceful negotiation the release of the abducted personnel and the removal of roadblocks. It was only when ONUC discovered a plan for a full-fledged attack by Katangese gendarmes against its vital positions that it decided on December 5 to remove the roadblocks by force. I feel it not only fair to ONUC but highly desirable for all concerned if your government could explain the true situation to the Belgian people who, as you said, were following the current events in Katanga "avec une vive émotion."

The United Nations Force, as you know, is a peace force; but because of the hostile attitude of certain Katangese and, I must add, of certain non-African civilians, including Belgians, it was obliged to resort to force in self-defense. I sincerely hope that the fighting will not last long; but, at the same time, I am determined to take all necessary action to implement the mandate entrusted to me by the Security Council and the General Assembly.

---

3. *Message to the Foreign Minister of Belgium*

NEW YORK   DECEMBER 8, 1961

I HAVE JUST received your second telegram of December 8 which charges that action by ONUC in Katanga has been carried out in violation of its mandate. I greatly regret that the reports received by your government have resulted in such a profound misunderstanding of the bases and reasons for United Nations action in Katanga.

In my reply to your previous telegram of today's date, I have recalled in detail the series of hostile acts by Katangese gendarmerie, including violent assaults on United Nations personnel and the setting up of roadblocks to prevent the movement of United Nations personnel. Even more

Security Council Official Records, Sixteenth Year, Supplement for October, November and December 1961, document S/5025, part B, sect. II.

serious was the discovery of plans for a full-fledged attack by Katangese gendarmerie against vital United Nations positions.

This left no alternative to ONUC but to use the force necessary in self-defense to ensure the security of its communications, as also its freedom of movement. I fail to see how such measures, undertaken in response to outright and deliberately planned attacks on ONUC forces, could be re-garded as outside of its mandate.

Moreover, I should like to repeat that ONUC has been under strict instructions to use only such force as was absolutely necessary in the circumstances to defend itself and to restore public order. In particular, as I pointed out today, the troops were enjoined from firing on civilian persons, vehicles or buildings unless they themselves were fired upon.

Reports which have reached me indicate that they have carried out this instruction to safeguard lives and properties of the civilians, even to the extent of jeopardizing necessary military operations. Measures are also being taken for the evacuation of civilians in danger areas and to give assurances that military operations will not be directed against noncombatant personnel.

4. Statement on United Nations Operations in Katanga

NEW YORK DECEMBER 10, 1961

MY ATTENTION has been drawn to statements in the press alleging that the aim of the present United Nations operations in Katanga is to force a political solution of the Katanga problem by smashing the military strength of the present political leadership there, as also the political leadership itself; that instructions to this end have been given to the officials of ONUC; and that I have given them carte blanche or a com-pletely free hand in order to achieve the above-mentioned aim.

I wish to state categorically that the above description of the aim of the present Katanga operations is false. It is equally false to say that I have

UN Press Release SG/1086.

given the ONUC officials a free hand in the pursuit of such an objective. All Member governments of the United Nations have been informed of the genesis and purpose of the present military operations in Katanga in two reports to the Security Council, S/4940/Add. 16 and 17. The military action was forced on the United Nations by a series of deliberate attacks on United Nations officials, soldiers, and military officers in Katanga, and particularly Elisabethville, involving wanton and brutal assault, cold-blooded murder, and seizure of such personnel; the setting up of road-blocks impeding the freedom of movement in Elisabethville; and attacks in strength on positions held by the United Nations elsewhere in Katanga, all of which were clearly part of a plan.

This military action was undertaken with the greatest reluctance, and only when it became obvious that there was no use in continued negotiations, which were marked by repeated instances of bad faith and failure to implement agreed measures on the part of the political leaders of Katanga, who indulged in a violent and inflammatory campaign against the United Nations over the press and radio even while they were engaged in negotiation with our representatives.

The purpose of the present military operations is to regain and assure our freedom of movement, to restore law and order, and to ensure that for the future the United Nations forces and officials in Katanga are not subjected to such attacks; and meanwhile to react vigorously in self-defense to every assault on our present positions, by all the means available to us. These military operations *will* be pursued up to such time, and *only* up to such time, that these objectives are achieved, either by military or by other means, and we have satisfactory guarantees in this regard for the future, not only in Elisabethville but over the whole of Katanga. We shall also need to be satisfied that we shall be able to go ahead with the implementation of the Security Council and General Assembly resolutions, and especially the latest Security Council resolution of November 24, 1961, without let or hindrance from any source. We have endeavored to make our objectives known to the people of Katanga, as also the rest of the Congo, by pamphlets, broadcasts and public announcements. I shall welcome any initiative which would enable us to achieve our aims as peacefully and as speedily as possible. In this connection I am fully aware of the need for reconciliation and pacification, and I recall that I stated in the Security Council on November 24, 1961 that "in my view national reconciliation should figure in our attempts to restore law and order in the Republic of the Congo."

Our long-term mandate is stated and restated in the various resolutions of the Security Council and the General Assembly, which it is my responsibility to implement. I shall continue to strain every nerve, and to use all the resources available to me to execute this mandate in the spirit of the Charter.

5. *Letter to Sir Patrick Dean, Permanent Representative of the United Kingdom*

NEW YORK   DECEMBER 14, 1961

YOU HAVE EXPRESSED to me certain anxieties of your government as to the aims and objectives of the United Nations in the Congo.

In reply, I would reaffirm that my aim and objective, and that of the United Nations civil and military authorities in the Congo, is to achieve the solution of the differences between the Central Government and the provincial authorities in Katanga, in accordance with the resolutions of the Security Council and the General Assembly.

I would remind you that, in interpreting the authority placed in my hands by the Security Council on November 24, 1961, I said, among other things, ". . . in my view, national reconciliation should figure in our attempts to restore law and order in the Republic of the Congo." Earlier in the same statement I said, "Above all, I may assure you that the United Nations will continue and even redouble its attempts to achieve reconciliation, by peaceful means, of course, of the sharp differences which now seriously endanger the unity of the country."

I reaffirm what I said then, and to this end I have sent to Leopoldville two of my colleagues who have been most closely associated with the United Nations Operation in the Congo to seek to achieve the objectives outlined above.

UN Press Release SG/1089.

6. Letter to the Foreign Minister of Belgium

NEW YORK   DECEMBER 15, 1961

I HAVE STUDIED with the greatest attention your message of December 9, 1961.

With reference to the remarks concerning the necessity of ensuring strict observance of the Geneva Convention, let me first reply to the three questions you have put to me.

(1) ONUC never refused to evacuate civilians when it was physically possible and safe to do so. Indeed, around ONUC headquarters Colonel Maitra of ONUC has spent a large amount of his time comforting and feeding civilians and arranging, if they so wished, for the evacuation of those who were endangered by the mortar fire to which ONUC headquarters has been periodically subjected. Indeed, those civilians have expressed gratitude for what our troops have done for them.

As regards the so-called "new hospital" (which is not and has never been used as a hospital and in which there are no doctors, nurses, or patients), very severe fighting took place around it because it was a mercenary stronghold and indeed had a mercenary observation post on its roof, as it commands a very good view of the entire Elisabethville area. As soon as it was safe and possible for civilians to be evacuated from the "hospital," they were evacuated with the help of ONUC troops.

(2) The "hospitals" you referred to are probably the "new hospital," already mentioned, and Prince Leopold Hospital. The latter is only about 200 metres from Camp Massart, which was the main base and headquarters of the gendarmerie. On the night of December 7 and early on the morning of December 8, Camp Massart was subject to mortar fire from the Swedish camp, and the hospital, which is in the direct line of flight of mortar shells and within mortar zone, was unfortunately hit by some shells. Two persons in the hospital were reported to be wounded, but there was considerable damage to the building. ONUC greatly regrets

Security Council Official Records, Sixteenth Year, Supplement for October, November and December 1961, document S/5025, part B, sect. III.

this incident and has taken all precautions against the recurrence of similar incidents despite the military disadvantage involved.

(3) It may well be true that uninvolved civilians have been wounded or even killed in mortar and machine gun fire. It is known, for example, that much of the mortar firing directed on ONUC headquarters by the Katangese gendarmes has gone wide in the surrounding residential area.

No one regrets more than I do the casualties suffered by civilians, and indeed by all others as well, in the present hostilities. Strict orders have been given and repeated to ONUC troops to safeguard to all extent possible the lives and properties of the civilian population, Congolese and non-Congolese alike.

I am satisfied that ONUC troops have done so, sometimes even to the extent of prejudicing the military operations and often at the risk of their own lives. But it must be pointed out that their efforts have been impeded by the brutal methods of non-Congolese mercenaries, and the Katangese gendarmes acting under their orders, who often use the civilian population as a shield during their attacks against ONUC troops. Leaders of the mercenaries and Katangese politicians have openly declared that they do not want the non-Congolese population to leave. Mr. Tshombé and Mr. Munongo have ordered roadblocks to be set up at exit routes controlled by the gendarmerie in order to prevent the evacuation of civilians. Moreover, gendarmerie units have deliberately occupied positions in private houses and gardens and in the immediate vicinity of schools and hospitals, which they know that ONUC would hesitate to attack. These units have also used a great number of vehicles bearing false insignia of the Red Cross, from which they have fired at ONUC positions, and Mr. G. Olivet, the delegate of the International Red Cross at Elisabethville, has made many protests on the subject.

The ONUC authorities, in close collaboration with the Red Cross, have spared no efforts, in difficult circumstances, to protect civilians from the dangers to which the gendarmerie and mercenaries deliberately expose them. ONUC armoured cars with loudspeakers have gone around residential areas, where sniping has taken place, announcing that civilians will have nothing to fear provided they do not fire on ONUC troops or do not give shelter to isolated snipers and to mercenaries or gendarmes firing at ONUC positions. However, when ONUC troops are exposed to attacks coming from civilian houses, as has occurred many times in the past days, they are evidently obliged to riposte in self-defense.

With regard to the Union Minière, you said that that company had refuted most categorically my affirmations, but I suppose that you referred to the directors of the company in Brussels, not its officials in Elisabethville. According to the reports of my representatives in Elisabethville, in whom I have full confidence, these officials have openly boasted that aerial bombs and heavy armoured cars (one of which was knocked out by ONUC at the Jadotville road junction on December 8) have been made in workshops of the Union Minière. Civilian sources in Elisabethville have also given evidence to this effect and a Rhodesian paper has carried an article and a photograph about the manufacture of armoured cars. It is also common knowledge in Elisabethville that a number of mercenaries have been recruited through the representatives of the Union Minière outside Katanga and that a number of mercenaries now carry working papers giving them the status of workers on the Union Minière payroll. As an example, one may cite the case of Captain Brown, a notorious mercenary who, after being expelled by ONUC, has now returned on the Union Minière payroll. The assistance given by the Union Minière to the secessionist movement in Katanga has been confirmed by many persons or groups concerned with the question. I wish only to recall here the findings of the United Nations Conciliation Commission for the Congo which went to the territory at the beginning of 1961 and which stated in its report (A/4711) that "it is also recognized that the Union Minière du Haut Katanga finances the Katanga authorities to an appreciable extent." Since you have put a number of questions to me, may I in turn ask you whether you sincerely believe that Mr. Tshombé could have provided the Katangese gendarmerie with its modern and heavy weapons, could have created an air force with modern planes, including jets, and could have proceeded with the intensive recruitment of highly paid mercenaries without the financial and material assistance of the Union Minière and other foreign firms operating in Katanga?

As regards the request to protect the telecommunications installations of the Union Minière, I have insisted that protection could be given by ONUC troops provided that the Union Minière ceases its hostile activities against ONUC. If I have set this condition, it is because we have had a rather sad experience during the September events, when a company of 155 Irish soldiers, who had been retained in Jadotville against the wishes of our military advisers in order to protect non-Congolese population there, was attacked and surrounded by a far superior number of gendarmerie under non-Congolese leadership. In this connection I would draw your attention to your telegram of September 2, 1961, to the late Secretary-General and his reply of September 4. The Union Minière telecommunications installations are in Union Minière grounds next to Cité Lubumbashi. This area is at present not in United Nations control, but under gendarmerie control and my representatives in Elisabethville have informed me that the local officials of the Union Minière have not asked for United Nations protection. However, after receipt of your message of December 9, I have instructed ONUC to take measures to ensure the protection of the installations, subject to military considerations.

With regard to the genesis and purpose of the present hostilities, you asked me to publish the plan of full-fledged attack prepared by the Katangese gendarmerie. For obvious military reasons I cannot disclose the plan immediately, but I assure you that I will, in due course, release all the information available to me. But let me tell you right now that the main objectives of the plan were to seize the airport and ONUC headquarters in Elisabethville and cut off ONUC forces in South Katanga from their bases with a view to weakening their effectiveness and ultimately to destroying them.

I cannot agree with you when you suggest that what I said in my message of December 8 indicates that it is the discovery of the plan of full-fledged attack, and not the "few incidents which had taken place befire," that has set off the ONUC action of December 5. The plan must be linked with the incidents which took place before December 5 as well as with the campaign of violent and inflammatory speeches unleashed by Mr. Tshombé immediately after the adoption of the Security Council resolution of November 24. The events which have led to the outbreak of December 5 are described in some detail in the report of the Officer-in-Charge of ONUC (S/4940/Add. 15 to 17) and have been briefly recalled in my message of December 8. I shall not repeat them here, but I wish to stress once again that, in the face of all the provocations, involving wanton and brutal assault, cold-blooded murder and abduction of its personnel and the setting up of roadblocks which impeded its freedom of movement and endangered its lifelines, ONUC endeavored for days to settle the crisis by peaceful negotiations. It was only when it became evident that in the face of the bad faith displayed by Katangese authorities no negotiations were possible, that while pretending to negotiate these Katangese authorities were preparing for more assaults and that they had a plan the purpose of which was the very destruction of ONUC, that it decided to take action to regain and assure its freedom of movement. I ask if in your view such action is not covered by the normal right of self-defence?

If the action taken on December 5 has assumed proportions which go beyond those of a purely defensive action, it is because shortly after ONUC troops removed the roadblocks between the airport and ONUC headquarters in the town of Elisabethville they were attacked by gendarmes and mercenaries with increasing violence. These aggressive actions included an attack by a Katangese airplane which dropped three bombs at the airport on the night of December 5 and 6. This first air attack, it may be pointed out, was undertaken by Katangese, not by ONUC.

As I stated publicly on December 10, the purpose of the present military operations is to regain and assure our freedom of movement, to restore law and order, and to ensure that for the future the United Nations forces and officials in Katanga are not subjected to such attacks; and meanwhile to react vigorously in self-defense to every assault on our present positions, by all the means available to us. The military operations will be pursued up to such time, and only up to such time, that these objectives are achieved, either by military or by other means, and we have satisfactory guarantees in this regard for the future, not only in Elisabethville but over the whole of Katanga. We shall also need to be satisfied that we shall be able to go ahead with the implementation of the Security Council and General Assembly resolutions, and especially the latest Security Council resolution of November 24, 1961, without let or hindrance from any source. In my statement of December 10, I also said that I should welcome any initiative which would enable us to achieve our aims as peacefully and as speedily as possible. In this connection, I added that I was fully aware of the need for reconciliation and pacification, and I recalled my statement in the Security Council on November 24 that "in my view national reconciliation should figure in our attempts to restore law and order in the Republic of the Congo (Leopoldville)".

That is what I said on December 10 and that is what I stand on today. I do not want to do more than that, and I have no right to do less.

7. *Statement to the Advisory Committee on the Congo*

NEW YORK   DECEMBER 16, 1961

AT THE LAST MEETING of the Congo Advisory Committee I promised to consider, in consultation with you, the next steps to be taken in implementation of the Security Council resolution of November 24. We finally worked out such a plan of implementation, which I intended to discuss with you, after consulting with our colleagues in Leopoldville and Elisabethville as also with the Central Government.

You are, however, aware of the campaign of violent and inflammatory speeches unleashed by Tshombé and his collaborators from the time that the Security Council resolution was adopted. You are also aware of the subsequent outrages, murders, and ambush of United Nations personnel, and of the plan to capture the airfield at Elisabethville and to prevent ONUC forces from communicating freely with each other.

These events forced the United Nations to take defensive action, regarding the progress of which General Rikhye will report to you shortly. To that extent the plan that we had in mind for implementation of the Security Council resolution has been overtaken by events.

The objectives of the present operations were set out in my public statement of December 10, and especially in the penultimate paragraph thereof:

> The purpose of the present military operations is to regain and assure our freedom of movement, to restore law and order, and to ensure that for the future the United Nations forces and officials in Katanga are not subjected to such attacks; and meanwhile to react vigorously in self-defense to every assault on our present positions, by all the means available to us. These military operations *will* be pursued up to such time, and *only* up to such time, that these objectives are achieved, either by military or by other means, and we have satisfactory guarantees in this regard for the future, not only in Elisabethville but over the whole of

UN Press Release SG/1094.

Katanga. We shall also need to be satisfied that we shall be able to go ahead with the implementation of the Security Council and General Assembly resolutions, and especially the latest Security Council resolution of November 24, 1961, without let or hindrance from any source.

Since the present operations were initiated, the propaganda not only in Elisabethville but elsewhere to misrepresent the present activities and exaggerate the loss of life and property suffered by civilians, has gathered momentum. We have tried our best to brief the newspapers at this end and to keep them informed of the true facts and of the progress of the operations. Some of the newspapers and wire service agencies seem to have particularly biased reporters at the Congo end, and print their dispatches without any verification. I am amazed at the lack of, or disregard for, the normal standards of journalism by these newspapers.

Two days ago we received information that the radio station in Usumbura in Ruanda-Urundi was also broadcasting some of these atrocity stories and we have taken action to lodge an urgent protest with the Belgian authorities. There have also been many efforts to secure a cease-fire, especially now that it seems likely that the United Nations may succeed in achieving its short-term objectives.

I am sure I am speaking for all of you when I say that we do not want one unnecessary casualty to be suffered or one superfluous round of ammunition to be fired. To that extent I am always ready to consider reasonable proposals for a cease-fire, provided that our objectives are safeguarded. At the same time, I am sure that you will all agree that for us to stop short of our objectives at the present stage, would be a serious setback for the United Nations. In this connection I am having circulated to you a copy of a letter dated December 14 from Prime Minister Adoula to Mr. Linnér. I should also mention that recent statements by Tshombé, Kibwe, and others indicate that there is no eagerness on their part to have a cease-fire.

In regard to the cease-fire, you are aware, of course, of the position taken by the Government of the United Kingdom, because their attitude has been made public. I should also inform you that similar appeals for a cease-fire have been received from the representatives of Belgium and Greece, and yesterday the President of the Congo (Brazzaville) sent a communication to me and to the President of the Security Council calling for an urgent meeting of the Security Council with a view to deciding on an immediate cease-fire. The President of Malagasy Republic has also appealed for a cease-fire.

In the same connection, you must be aware of the exchange of letters on December 8 by which the Government of the United Kingdom indicated their willingness to make a certain number of bombs available to us for use with the Canberra jets. You must also be aware of my subsequent letter addressed to the Government of the United Kingdom in which I withdrew the request for these bombs. The reasons for my decision, which had to be taken without consultation with members of the advisory committee, in view of the information I had that a governmental crisis was imminent in the United Kingdom over this bomb issue, have also been made known in my letter to Sir Patrick Dean. While on the same subject, I must inform you that Tshombé sent a telegram to President Kennedy in regard to which I was consulted. My attitude was that we would do everything in our power to facilitate a meeting between Prime Minister Adoula and Tshombé, provided it was held at a venue which was acceptable to the prime minister. My present thinking is that such a meeting might take place at Kitona, and once again we have given assurances in regard to the personal security and safe conduct of Tshombé for the duration of these negotiations.

I know that you must be extremely anxious to have news about the progress of the operations and the assessment of the resources available to us. I will ask General Rikhye to give such an appreciation. You are all aware that I addressed a special appeal to all African countries to help us with additional troops at this critical juncture. So far I have received a favorable response only from Tunisia—which has so generously agreed to send us a contingent of three hundred troops. I have already thanked President Bourguiba for this. I have still received no reply from the President of Indonesia, to whom also I addressed a special appeal for troops some days ago.

8. Cable to Abbé Fulbert Youlou, President of the Congo (Brazzaville)

NEW YORK   DECEMBER 17, 1961

I HAVE NOTED with the most profound concern your telegram of December 16, 1961, in which you declare that your government has decided to forbid the landing on, and overflight of, the territory of the Republic of the Congo (Brazzaville) by aircraft engaged in transporting men and supplies for the United Nations operation in the Congo.

As you are no doubt aware, the transit and overflight facilities which your government has hitherto placed at the disposal of ONUC have been and continue to be essential for the effective pursuit of the operation which the United Nations, in pursuance of repeated decisions of the Security Council and General Assembly and in response to the request of the Government of the Republic of the Congo (Leopoldville), has carried out for the purpose of restoring law and order in that country and ridding it of foreign intervention.

Since in your telegram you refer erroneously to the "Opérations de guerre menées au Katanga par l'ONU," may I assume that at the time of dispatching it you had not yet received my telegram of yesterday in reply to your telegram of the same date? In my message I clearly delineated the purpose, scope, and limits of the self-defense operations which United Nations Forces in Katanga have been compelled to carry out in order to put an end to assaults, ambushes, murder, and concerted military attacks to which they have been exposed, to restore vital communications cut by the Katangese gendarmes led by mercenaries, and to continue the implementation of the Security Council and General Assembly resolutions.

I would hope that a careful study of my message will not fail to convince you that the present defensive moves by the United Nations Force are the very least that had to be done if ONUC was to fulfill the tasks

Security Council Official Records, Sixteenth Year, Supplement for October, November and December 1961, document S/5035.

assigned to it by the Security Council and the General Assembly, tasks which a group of non-Congolese mercenaries and adventurers, having misled certain figures in the Katanga provincial administration, have attempted to frustrate by violence and murder.

It is further my duty to draw your attention to the fact that the measures apparently contemplated by your government would, if they were actually introduced, constitute a grave hindrance to the fulfilment of the purposes of the United Nations and would by that token be in manifest conflict with the provisions of Article 105 of the Charter.

They would flagrantly contradict the provisions of Articles 25 and 49, under which the Members of the United Nations agree to accept and carry out the decisions of the Security Council, and to join in affording mutual assistance to that end. Moreover, they would constitute a clear violation of the provisions of the Security Council and General Assembly resolutions on the Congo in which states Members are called upon to refrain from any action which may directly or indirectly impede the policies and purposes of the United Nations in the Congo. I am referring especially to paragraph 11 of the resolution of November 24, 1961, and part A, paragraph 5, and part B, paragraph 3, of the resolution of February 21, 1961.

I would find it inconceivable that a state which only so recently was, upon the attainment of its independence, admitted to membership of the United Nations should now act in a manner which would inevitably have to be described as in contradiction with its declaration of being able and willing to fulfill its obligations under the Charter.

I would further draw attention to the fact that the disabilities which your government seems to be planning to impose on the United Nations operation would chiefly affect many other states Members of the Organization which are loyally assisting the United Nations in discharging its responsibilities in the Congo as laid down by its principle organs. These measures would accordingly constitute an attempt to hinder these states Members in carrying out their obligations under the Charter.

It is therefore my profound and heartfelt hope that the measures contemplated by your government will, upon further study of all the facts, especially as set out in my telegram to you of yesterday's date, not be instituted, and that the specific prohibitions announced in your cable will be rescinded.

9. *Cable to the Foreign Minister of Belgium*

NEW YORK   DECEMBER 18, 1961

I HAVE THE HONOR to acknowledge receipt of your cable of today's date in which certain reports, most of them unverified, about the behavior of UN troops in Katanga are brought to my attention.

I can assure you that ONUC troops are under the strictest orders to protect lives and property of innocent civilians and have done so despite grave provocations. I am proud of the standards of behavior established by the ONUC forces of many nations in the most onerous circumstances. Such isolated reports of misconduct as have been brought to the notice of ONUC authorities are, of course, being investigated. I have given orders that prompt corrective action, including, where appropriate, severe punishment of men found guilty of misbehavior should be taken.

On the other hand, it is my duty to draw your attention again to the reprehensible comportment of non-Congolese mercenaries and civilians who have led and instigated gendarmerie units into senseless combat against the UN forces. Fully reliable and verified reports indicate that these individuals have followed a consistent pattern of sniping at and shelling UN personnel and positions from civilian homes, and from the immediate vicinity of hospitals, schools, and similar institutions. They know that the ONUC forces would be extremely reluctant to fire at such targets, even in self-defense—but the mercenaries felt no such inhibitions. While it was in the end necessary for ONUC forces to respond to such tactics, strict measures were taken to ensure that ONUC action should be directed only at military objects from which firing had actually been sustained by the UN.

To my profound regret, I am not aware that the tactics of the mercenaries and civilian snipers, many of them Belgian nationals, have earned them any reprimand from Brussels. For its part, ONUC will redouble its efforts to ensure that its troops will continue to show self-restraint in the

UN Press Release SG/1097.

face of provocation, and confine their self-defense action to the strict minimum required to put an end to the murderous assaults of the merce-nary-led gendarmes. This will continue to be the UN policy until law and order and UN freedom of movement have been restored, and the imple-mentation of the Security Council and General Assembly resolutions completed.

---

10. Cable to the Foreign Minister of Belgium

NEW YORK   DECEMBER 19, 1961

As ALWAYS, I have examined your message of December 18 with great attention.

It is true that for compelling military considerations ONUC planes had to strike at Union Minière installations. But I must reject most categori-cally the assertion that these installations contain no military objective and, therefore, it was an operation of "pure reprisals."

In recent days not only were the Union Minière telecommunications installations being used by the Katangese gendarmerie and mercenaries in their fight against ONUC forces, but also continued firing, even by mortar and machine guns, was directed on ONUC positions from the Union Minière main office building as well as from Union Minière educa-tional institute and houses on the fringe of the Union Minière camp.

Indeed, my representatives in Elisabethville have conclusive evidence of organization of mercenary activities and of concentration of gen-darmes in and around these buildings. According to their report, the deputy manager of Union Minière, Mr. Urbain himself, admitted that he could not control elements which were firing from Union Minière build-ings although he had made every effort to evict them. He also admitted he knew that they were extremist elements and in particular that they were responsible for the opening of fire by mortar and machine guns from Union Minière buildings on December 18 at precisely the moment when Mr. Tshombé was leaving the Palace for Ndola, while ONUC troops had been ordered to hold fire.

UN Press Release SG/1099, December 20, 1961.

The severe fire coming from the Union Minière buildings has caused many casualties among our Ethiopian troops; in particular during the two days preceding the airstrike six Ethiopians were killed and at least five wounded. This inevitably made these buildings a military target. ONUC command had therefore no alternative but to take action to neutralize this dangerous center of resistance, and it did so with great reluctance and confined its action to the minimum military requirement.

It may be useful to point out that Union Minière installations had been spared for twelve whole days despite evidence of the hostile action which was taking place therein against ONUC troops. My representatives in Elisabethville had repeatedly warned Union Minière authorities that if firing from Union Minière buildings did not stop, ONUC would be obliged to use its right of self-defense. But these warnings were made in vain.

All the air attacks ONUC had been compelled to carry out in Katanga were made in the same conditions. They were made with great reluctance and because they were absolutely dictated by military considerations, and they were all directed at military objectives. I can assure you that ONUC troops have no "passion for fight," but as I told you in my message of December 15, they must react in self-defense to every assault and attack on them.

---

11. *Note Verbale to Vasco Vieira Garin, Permanent Representative of Portugal*

NEW YORK   DECEMBER 30, 1961

THE ACTING SECRETARY-GENERAL of the United Nations presents his compliments to the Permanent Representative of Portugal to the United Nations and has the honor to request the Permanent Representative to bring the following matter to the attention of the Government of Portugal.

In order to ensure that mercenaries and other foreign elements referred to in the Security Council resolutions of February 21, and November 24,

UN Press Release SG/1106, January 2, 1962.

1961, as well as arms, equipment, and other materials in support of the secessionist activities of the provincial administration of Katanga, are not entering that region from or through Angola, the Acting Secretary-General proposes, in agreement with the Government of Portugal, to station United Nations observers at a few selected airports and roads from or through which transit from Angola into Katanga might commonly take place.

This proposal carries no implication at all that the authorities in Angola are giving assistance to secessionist activities in Katanga. It is a general measure contemplated by the Acting Secretary-General in order to implement the mandate entrusted to him by the Security Council and the General Assembly, and especially the provisions of paragraph 5 of the Security Council resolution of November 24, 1961. A request for the stationing of United Nations observers on the territory of the Federation of Rhodesia and Nyasaland has been similarly submitted by him to the Government of the United Kingdom of Great Britain and Northern Ireland.

The Acting Secretary-General would be grateful if the Government of Portugal could be so kind as to let him know at an early date if it will be possible for the United Nations to station such observers on the territory of Angola.

Text of Identical Cables to Jawaharlal Nehru, Prime Minister of India, and Antonio de Oliveira Salazar, Prime Minister of Portugal

NEW YORK   DECEMBER 14, 1961

THE UNITED NATIONS found itself faced with an unexpected crisis in December, 1961, over the Portuguese territories of Goa, Damao, and Diu. These territories, situated along the coast of Bombay and known as Portuguese India, were claimed by India and tension had been mounting for some time. The question was brought to the attention of the Security Council in a series of letters from Portugal between December 8 and 16, charging that India was massing forces in order to carry out its declared intention of annexing the territories. India, in turn, accused Portuguese forces of attacking Indian villages. On December 14, U Thant intervened personally in an attempt to head off a military conflict. He appealed to both sides to use the utmost restraint and to seek a negotiated settlement. The text of his brief appeal is reproduced below. Although the appeal proved to be in vain, it is worth noting as an example of the personal role he was to play in many later controversies. The issue was settled four days later, when Indian troops took over the disputed territories.

HAVING BEEN APPRISED of the serious situation which has recently developed at the border of India and Goa, Damao, and Diu, as revealed in letters addressed to the President of the Security Council by the Permanent Representatives of India and Portugal, I respectfully and urgently appeal to Your Excellency and to your government to ensure that the situation does not deteriorate to the extent that it might constitute a threat to peace and security. I would urge immediate negotiations with a view to achieving an early solution of the problem. I would naturally hope that such negotiations would be in accordance with the principles embodied in the Charter and formulated by the United Nations.

UN Press Release SG/1095, December 17, 1961.

THE QUESTION OF WEST IRIAN

DECEMBER 1961—FEBRUARY 1962

WHEN THE REPUBLIC OF INDONESIA attained its independence in 1949, one of the questions left unsettled was the future status of West New Guinea or, as the Indonesians called it, West Irian, at the eastern extremity of the 3,125-mile string of islands in the Netherlands East Indies. The transfer agreement provided that the future of the territory should be determined within a year through negotiations between Indonesia and the Netherlands. No such agreement was reached, however, and the issue continued for the next decade as a source of continuous friction between the two governments.

Two proposals advanced by the Netherlands were turned down: one that sovereignty be invested in the short-lived Netherlands-Indonesian Union; the other, that the issue be submitted to the International Court of Justice. Indonesia, on the other hand, brought the question to the General Assembly in 1954, 1955, and 1957, but it failed to obtain a two-thirds majority for its draft resolutions urging settlement through negotiation and assuming that sovereignty had already passed to Indonesia. The situation became critical in December 1961. President Sukarno, losing patience, ordered a total mobilization of his armed forces and declared that he was prepared to take the territory by force.

Thant, in office only a month, decided to make a personal effort to head off the threat of violence. On December 19, he dispatched messages to the leaders of the two countries expressing deep concern and urging a peaceful solution. The situation became urgent in mid-January when Dutch and Indonesian naval vessels clashed off the shores of the disputed territory. Thant lost no time in sending off new appeals and in launching private talks with the United Nations representatives of the two governments. Meanwhile, he asked the Netherlands, as a humanitarian gesture "which might help ease tension," to release Indonesians taken prisoner during the naval clash. Prime Minister Jan de Quay promptly agreed and at the same time accepted a proposal by the Acting Secretary-General that a United Nations representative be sent to West Irian to arrange for the release and repatriation of the prisoners. It was from these invitations that serious negotiations eventually developed.

1. Text of Identical Cables to Jan de Quay, Prime Minister of the Netherlands, and Achmed Sukarno, President of Indonesia

NEW YORK   DECEMBER 19, 1961

IT IS WITH deep concern that I have learned of the possibility of a serious situation arising between the Republic of Indonesia and the Netherlands. I therefore urgently appeal to Your Excellency and to your government to take no action which could give rise to a threat to peace and security. It is my most sincere hope that the parties concerned may come together to seek a peaceful solution of the problem and I would therefore respectfully urge that Your Excellency and your government take steps to this end.

UN Press Release SG/1098.

2. Text of Identical Cables to Prime Minister de Quay and President Sukarno

NEW YORK   JANUARY 15, 1962

I HAVE LEARNED from news reports this morning of an incident involving a clash between Dutch and Indonesian naval vessels in connection with the dispute over West Irian (Netherlands New Guinea).

I am deeply concerned to hear this news and I reiterate my appeal of December 19, 1961, to Your Excellency and your government to seek a peaceful solution of the problem.

UN Press Release SG/1116.

3. *Text of Identical Cables to Prime Minister de Quay and President Sukarno*

NEW YORK   JANUARY 17, 1962

THIS IS IN continuation of my telegram to your Excellency of January 15.

I earnestly appeal to your Excellency and your government to refrain from any precipitate action following the clash of naval vessels which took place on January 14. I would also request that your permanent representative in New York be instructed to discuss with me the possibilities of a peaceful settlement of the whole question in conformity with the purposes and principles of the Charter of the United Nations.

Would be grateful for very urgent consideration of this appeal by Your Excellency and for an early reply.

UN Press Release SG/1118.

4. *Exchange of Communications with Prime Minister de Quay*

FEBRUARY 1, 1962

Message to Prime Minister de Quay

I am grateful to Your Excellency for your cable of January 18 in which you have informed me that the "Netherlands government are determined to continue in the attitude of utmost restraint." I have been discussing with your permanent representative in New York the possibilities of a peaceful settlement of the whole question of Netherlands New Guinea.

UN Press Release SG/1128.

Meanwhile, I would like to make an appeal in regard to the prisoners that are now held in Netherlands New Guinea, following the incidents of January 15. I shall be very grateful if, as a humanitarian gesture which might help in easing tensions all round, your government would agree to the release of these prisoners and to their repatriation to Indonesia. If the response of Your Excellency and your government to this appeal were to be favourable, I shall discuss with your permanent representative modalities of actual transfer of these prisoners from Netherlands New Guinea to Indonesia.

What I have in mind is to send to Netherlands New Guinea a United Nations representative who would meet the prisoners, discuss mutually satisfactory arrangements for their repatriation, and also accompany them on their return to Indonesia.

Message from Prime Minister de Quay

I have the honor to acknowledge the receipt of your message of January 29, in which you directed an appeal to the Netherlands government for the release of the Indonesian prisoners who are held in Netherlands New Guinea, following the incident off the coast of the territory between Netherlands and Indonesian naval units which occurred on January 15.

In the same spirit which animated Your Excellency's appeal the Netherlands government are prepared to release these prisoners through the intermediary of the United Nations Organization, in the hope that this voluntary gesture may contribute to easing the present tension and thus to improve the climate for negotiations between the parties under your auspices.

I welcome your suggestion to send to Netherlands New Guinea a United Nations representative who would meet the prisoners, discuss mutually satisfactory arrangements for their repatriation and who would also accompany them on their return to Indonesia. Instructions will be sent to the civilian and military authorities in Netherlands New Guinea to give every assistance to your representative. Our permanent representative in New York has been instructed to assist the members of your staff in making the necessary arrangements.

❧ 1962 ❧

STATEMENTS AND MESSAGES ON THE CONGO QUESTION

JANUARY   1962

As HE PROMISED in his statement to the Security Council (p. 51), U Thant proceeded with vigor to implement the mandate given him in the November 24 resolution. Two major developments in December led him to believe that progress was being made as the year ended. One was the Kitona agreement (p. 50) and the other was the United Nations military successes in Elisabethville. In a statement to the advisory committee on the Congo on January 9, the Acting Secretary-General reported that some of the provisions of the Kitona agreement were being carried out, but that Tshombé had not kept his pledge to get rid of his mercenary forces. Thant also reported his failure to get permission from the United Kingdom and Portugal to station observers along the frontiers of Rhodesia and Angola to control illicit traffic in arms and military equipment for the Katangese authorities. Despite what he called "the improved situation" in the Elisabethville area, Thant appealed for additional troops to reinforce the United Nations command. In a message dated January 22 to the ten governments with combat contingents in the Congo, he said "more assistance may be temporarily needed" and would be welcome. He also urged the ten to use their influence to persuade African states not already contributing contingents to do so.

In a surprise move on January 25, the Soviet Union asked for an urgent meeting of the Security Council to consider the implementation of the November 24 resolution. The Soviet representative, Ambassador Nikolai T. Fedorenko, said ONUC had abandoned its efforts to expel the mercenaries. In a cable dated January 28, Prime Minister Adoula said he was opposed to a Council meeting at a time when the situation was showing a substantial improvement. The following day the conference of heads of African and Malagasy states, meeting at Lagos, Nigeria, expressed the view that any uncalled for intervention by the Council would be prejudicial to the interests of the Congo. On January 30, the Council took the unusual course of adjourning without adopting the agenda, which consisted solely of the Soviet complaint. The vote was 7 to 2, with 2 abstentions. The action was generally interpreted as a vote of confidence for the Acting Secretary-General and his handling of the Congo problem.

Another development at this time was an announcement by Thant on January 26 that Stüre Linnér had asked to be relieved as Officer-in-Charge and that Robert Gardiner had been appointed to succeed him.

---

1. Statement to the Advisory Committee on the Congo

NEW YORK   JANUARY 9, 1962

I HAVE ASKED you to come to this meeting for three main reasons:

(a) I wish to consult you about the replies I have received to my request to the governments of the United Kingdom and Portugal that observers be stationed along the frontiers of Rhodesia and Angola for the purpose of controlling illicit traffic into Katanga, about which you have already seen something in the press;

(b) there are a couple of matters on which there appears to be need for some explanation on my part since some questions have been raised; and

(c) it is desirable to bring you up to date on developments in the Congo and particularly in Katanga, since we have not met since December 16.

You have before you copies of my letters to the United Kingdom and Portugal about the stationing of observers and of the replies which I have received from those governments. There is also before you a copy of a statement concerning this matter made by Sir Roy Welensky. This latter text, incidentally, has not been checked against delivery and I cannot, therefore, verify its accuracy.

You will note that the replies are negative, although the Government of the United Kingdom suggests an alternative in the form of an invitation to me to go to Salisbury, which I have been told informally would equally cover a representative of mine. It is not at all clear to me what, if any, constructive results might be achieved from such a visit.

It certainly does not cover what I had in mind in making the approach to the British government. Here I might say that this approach was made because we finally had some concrete evidence of illicit assistance to Katanga from the Rhodesian side, which we immediately presented to the

UN Press Release SG/1110.

British government and which Sir Roy Welensky has promptly denied in phraseology that could not be described as gracious.

In this regard, I might call to your attention that, though Sir Roy vigorously tried to explain away the crossing of the forty-eight jeeps at Kipushi, he has never made any public reference to the activities of the Dornier aircraft based at Ndola and piloted by one Mr. Wickstead— probably because the evidence we presented was too convincing for even Sir Roy to deny.

I would appreciate the views of the members, particularly on the British alternative proposal, since I must reply to it.

With regard to the situation in Katanga since the intense fighting in early December came to a halt, there have been frequent references to a "cease-fire." I wish to make it quite clear that since the cease-fire of last October broke down because of its wanton and repeated violation by the Katangese, leading finally to the fighting which began on the afternoon of December 5, there has not been, and there is not now, any cease-fire in effect.

There has been no approach by United Nations officials to the Katangese on this question, although Mr. Tshombé and some of his colleagues have frequently alluded to the subject and Mr. Tshombé tried to make a cease-fire a condition for his participation in the Kitona talks. This condition, as you know, was refused by ONUC.

There has been what might be called unilateral withholding of fire, or "hold fire," by ONUC since the achievement of ONUC's immediate military objectives in Elisabethville, which, in fact, coincided with the beginning of the Kitona talks. This has meant only that ONUC in Elisabethville would not initiate fire but would return fire if fired upon.

This was undertaken for a number of reasons. First of all, because with the collapse of gendarmerie resistance in Elisabethville and the capture of the Union Minière compound, which was the last stronghold of resistance, the ONUC task in Elisabethville consisted primarily of "cleaning up," that is, eliminating the last vestiges of sniping from private dwellings and other buildings, stopping looting by the Katangese—who alone were responsible for it and *not* ONUC troops, as was recklessly and maliciously alleged in some quarters—and generally restoring order in the city toward resumption of normal civilian pursuits.

With the necessity of thus consolidating itself in Elisabethville, requiring retention of major strength in that area, ONUC, in any case, could not for some time be ready to undertake a new operation against mercenaries in such other localities as Kaminaville, Jadotville, Kolwezi, and Kipushi, where, according to our information, the remaining mercenaries in Katanga are to be mainly found. A bit later on I will ask Brigadier Rikhye to give you the latest information about the mercenaries involved and taken captive and arms and ammunition captured by ONUC in the Elisabethville operation of December.

Moreover, it would have been highly inadvisable for the United Nations to initiate fighting which would have made the United Nations responsible for preventing the meeting at Kitona of Mr. Adoula and Mr. Tshombé, or for the United Nations now to undertake any action which would prevent the Kitona Declaration from being implemented, since, in fact, some of its points are in the process of being implemented.

We are pressing Mr. Tshombé on point 8 in this declaration concerning the implementation of Security Council resolutions, and particularly that relating to mercenaries. It is our hope that he will keep his promise to facilitate the elimination of mercenaries in such a way as to make it unnecessary for ONUC to employ further force toward that end. I must add, however, that our plans and preparations for further operations in areas of Katanga other than Elisabethville, with a view to achieving the total elimination of mercenaries, are going forward without delay.

---

2. Message from Deputy Prime Minister Gizenga and Message to Prime Minister Adoula

JANUARY 17, 1962

THE ACTING SECRETARY-GENERAL received a message from Antoine Gizenga from Stanleyville as follows:

Have the honour to alert world opinion represented by the international organization of the United Nations about the motion of censure which the Chamber has just passed on me. Know nothing whatever about the circumstances in which this motion was voted upon or its exact motives. The Chamber's decision of January 15 concerning me can have no validity until the Chamber has given me a hearing.

Security Council Official Records, Seventeenth Year, Supplement for January, February and March 1962, document S/5053/Add. 1, annexes VIII and IX.

Only then shall I be able to tender my resignation if that is necessary. World opinion has known since January 14 that I have arranged to return to Leopold-ville on January 20 in order to reply to the complaints made against me and that I have meanwhile asked the United Nations, through the Prime Minister, to provide the means for my transport in complete safety. I regard the decision of the Chamber as an artful and arbitrary manoeuvre for the purpose of gaining time in order to confront me with a *fait accompli,* with the preconceived intention of taking me prisoner as soon as I leave Stanleyville. During this period of joint national effort the higher interest of the country demands that all arbitrary meth-ods should be banned and that legality should be observed in all forms of proce-dure and in respect for fundamental freedoms. I take the liberty of holding the Secretary-General responsible for my safety.

ANTOINE GIZENGA
Deputy Prime Minister

* * *

The following message was then sent by the Acting Secretary-General to the prime minister, Cyrille Adoula:

You have been informed by Mr. Linnér of the message which has been ad-dressed to me by Mr. Gizenga. As you know, I have scrupulously avoided any intervention in the internal political and legal affairs of your country and I hold firmly to this position now. You will, however, permit me to express the hope, which I am sure is widely shared in world opinion, that all procedures employed in dealing with Mr. Gizenga will be entirely in accordance with the law of your land, that they will be consistent with due process of law, and that his rights under the law will be fully respected. Should there be any need for United Nations assistance toward ensuring Mr. Gizenga's security, the United Nations Force will respond without delay to a word from you.

---

3. Letter to Permanent Missions of Countries Having Combat Troops Serving with the United Nations Force in the Congo

NEW YORK   JANUARY 22, 1962

ACTING SECRETARY-GENERAL U Thant has sent the letter quoted below, dated January 22, to the permanent missions of those countries having

UN Press Release SG/1124.

combat troops serving with the United Nations Force in the Congo. Those countries are: Ethiopia, the Federation of Malaya, Ghana, India, Ireland, Liberia, Nigeria, Sierra Leone, Sweden, and Tunisia. (The letter to Tunisia was sent in French.)

The English text of the letter follows:

Dear Mr. Ambassador,

As you will have noted, there has been an apparent improvement in the situation in the Congo in the context of the relevant Security Council resolutions since the end of the December fighting in Elisabethville and the conclusion of the Kitona talks. I would, therefore, be very grateful if you would now convey to your government, as one of those providing contingents to ONUC, my hope that present indications pointing to the possibility of a new and constructive phase in the efforts of the United Nations in the Congo will prove to be soundly based. Should this be the case, it will be in large measure due to the persistent and courageous actions of the contingents comprising ONUC over the past year and a half. In this regard, I must point particularly to the actions of those contingents of ONUC which, with great restraint under severe provocation, dealt so effectively with the attacks against the United Nations in Elisabethville in the first half of December 1961. There can be no doubt that the success which the troops of ONUC had in Elisabethville in December has contributed vitally to the improved situation now prevailing in that area. The elements of the contingents of Ethiopia, India, Ireland, Malaya, and Sweden which were mainly responsible for carrying out that operation are due special praise for the role they played.

While it is hoped that this improvement will continue, in the meantime more assistance may be temporarily needed for the conduct of this operation which has received such generous and invaluable cooperation from your government. Should additional assistance be possible from your government, it would be highly welcome. I would also be very grateful if your government would use its influence and good offices, as opportunity may be afforded, to pursuade African states not now contributing to respond positively to this need.

Yours sincerely,
U THANT
Acting Secretary-General

From Transcript of Press Conference

NEW YORK   MARCH 27, 1962

U THANT's second press conference was held nearly five months after he had assumed office. As will be seen from the partial transcript below, things were not going well either in the Congo peace talks or in the private negotiations between the Netherlands and Indonesia on West Irian. In both cases there had been temporary suspensions, but the Acting Secretary-General believed the difficulties would be overcome. He used the press conference to announce plans for his first trip as Acting Secretary-General. His itinerary included visits to Norway, Finland, and the United Kingdom. In connection with the question of regional organizations (p. 88), it will be recalled that complaints involving both Guatemala and Cuba had been referred to the Organization of American States, the first in 1954 and the latter in 1960. There also had been an increasing demand among the new African states that they be given a greater voice in handling African problems. The question asked in the press conference was to be posed frequently over the next few years and Thant's reply was one that he stood by consistently. This was that reliance on regional organizations for the solution of some problems was in no way incompatible with the Charter and did not necessarily mean that the authority of the United Nations was being diminished.

THE ACTING SECRETARY-GENERAL: Ladies and Gentlemen of the press: I am happy indeed to meet with you once again after a long interval of more than three months. Of course, in the future I shall look forward to seeing you at shorter intervals.

To start with, I may say a word about the talks going on—and we believe that they are still going on—between Prime Minister Adoula and Mr. Tshombé in Leopoldville. As you know, on the basis of a full guarantee of his security given to him by ONUC, Mr. Tshombé finally accepted Prime Minister Adoula's invitation to go to Leopoldville for talks looking toward reconciliation of their differences.

He arrived in Leopoldville in an ONUC aircraft on the evening of March 15, but because of sudden difficulties that might be described as psychological in nature, the two leaders met only on March 18. The first

UN Note to Correspondents No. 2548.

meeting, however, was held in a friendly atmosphere, and from March 18 to March 23, Prime Minister Adoula and Mr. Tshombé, and their collaborators, met every day.

But, on March 23, the two delegations encountered their first major obstacle over the question of the mandate of the Katangese delegation. Over this obstacle, the discussions were suspended but not ended. They were scheduled to resume late yesterday afternoon in a private meeting between the two principals. We are awaiting word about that meeting.

ONUC has exerted its best efforts to bring about these discussions, but has studiously avoided interfering with them since they have started. Of course, ONUC will assist the delegations whenever United Nations assistance may be requested by the parties.

Moreover, Mr. Gardiner, my special representative there, has standing instructions to do all that he can to prevent an actual breakdown of the talks, should that be threatened. He did, in fact, talk with each of the parties last Friday, after the impasse had developed.

As you may already know, General Séan McKeown will be relinquishing his command of the United Nations Force in the Congo at the end of this month. In fact, he will be departing from Leopoldville, I understand, tomorrow. His original appointment expired at the end of last year, but in response to my appeal he agreed to extend his tour of duty for another three months. I am releasing this morning my message to General McKeown expressing my great appreciation for the distinguished service he has rendered to ONUC and to the United Nations.

General McKeown will be succeeded as commander of the Force by Lieutenant-General Kebbede Guebre of Ethiopia. The services of General Guebre, who is chief of staff in Ethiopia, have generously been made available to ONUC by the Emperor.

Until General Guebre arrives in Leopoldville to take up his command, the acting commander will be the present deputy commander of the Force, Major General Yacob, who is, of course, stationed in Leopoldville.

May I also add a few words regarding my travel plans, which have aroused some speculation. I have accepted invitations from the governments of Norway, Finland, and the United Kingdom to visit their countries some time toward the end of June and the beginning of July.

The floor is now open. I would like to give the floor first of all to Mr. Pierre Huss, the president of the United Nations Correspondents Association.

MR. PIERRE HUSS: Mr. Secretary-General, would you tell us also the status of the negotiations on the New Guinea question, in view of the stalemate, or the impasse, in Washington.

THE ACTING SECRETARY-GENERAL: As you all know, in the third week of December, I think it was, I sent out an immediate appeal to the president of the Republic of Indonesia and the prime minister of the Netherlands not to precipitate any action which might develop into a situation that could threaten international peace and security. And of course, in the course of the next few weeks, both the president of Indonesia and the prime minister of the Netherlands very kindly responded to my appeal, favourably, and they have instructed their permanent representatives in New York to keep in close contact with me, with a view to finding a peaceful solution of the whole problem.

Since the middle of January, I have been in close consultation with the two representatives, in secret and in informal talks. About two weeks ago it was agreed that the discussions should be staged in two phases; the first phase would be secret and informal, and the second stage would be formal.

It was also agreed that for the first phase, in order to avoid publicity and in order to avoid unnecessary speculation, somebody outside the United Nations should offer his good offices. With my knowledge and consent, as you all know, these preliminary, informal talks took place outside New York in the presence of Mr. Ellsworth Bunker, who of course reported to me on the developments in these exploratory talks. Mr. Bunker reported to me that after three meetings, in his presence, the discussions were adjourned so that the Indonesian representative, Ambassador Malik, would be able to go back to Jakarta to seek fresh instructions on the substance of the negotiations. According to information available to me, I had the impression that Mr. Malik would be back in Washington towards the end of this week, so that negotiations would go on.

But the news dispatches of yesterday and today reported certain developments which I am not in a position to confirm or deny. But I very much hope that these negotiations will go on as originally scheduled. As I have just said, the first phase of the negotiations will be secret and informal, in the presence of a third party represented by Mr. Ellsworth Bunker. After the successful progress of these preliminary talks, the formal negotiations will take place here in my presence. This procedure has been agreed to by both parties concerned.

QUESTION: Mr. Secretary-General, I have two questions relating to the bond issue. One is that, out of twenty-one subscribers so far, five are countries which are already in arrears on UNEF and Congo expenses. Do you or do you not feel that countries should first pay what they are in arrears with before they subscribe to bonds?

The second question is this. Latin American countries can be found among those in arrears both on regular and extra assessments, but not among those who have offered subscriptions to bonds. Could you change that situation?

THE ACTING SECRETARY-GENERAL: I am sorry I am not in a position to change this situation. As regards the figures just quoted, I have here the latest figures regarding the purchase of bonds.

So far, up till yesterday, the situation is as follows: three countries—Norway, Finland, and Denmark—have actually purchased bonds to the value of $5,780,000. In addition, seventeen countries have pledged subscriptions, subject, in some cases, to parliamentary approval, up to a total of $43,735,000.

Thus, not counting the United States, a total of twenty countries have undertaken to purchase a total of $49,515,000. If the proposal of the United States Senate Committee, with which you are all familiar, should ultimately be adopted, this would ensure, as of today, a total subscription of approximately $125,000,000.

It is expected that at least two further pledges will be announced within the next day or two, in addition to which a considerable number of countries have indicated definite interest.

QUESTION: Mr. Secretary-General, as you probably are aware, there is some public sentiment in various areas—not government sentiment—to the effect that more reliance should be placed on regional organizations of like-minded states, instead of on the United Nations. Would you comment on that attitude?

THE ACTING SECRETARY-GENERAL: On this, I find myself in complete agreement with President Kennedy, for instance, who maintains that reliance on regional organizations should in no way conflict with reliance on the United Nations. I do not see any reason why the two are incompatible. Of course, as far as this Organization is concerned, I feel very strongly that the United Nations has grown in strength, is growing, and that in the future its influence will not be diminished.

It is, of course, a question of influence and not exactly of power. The influence of the United Nations cannot be considered in terms of battalions, nor can it be considered as a purely moral force. I think it is the cumulative influence of massive public opinion, which cannot be disregarded by any country.

QUESTION: Would you care to tell us whether the new system of special advisers which you have appointed to represent the different trends in the United Nations has been helpful in the discharge of your functions and whether you are satisfied that this is a system which can be fruitfully continued in the United Nations and adopted in other international organizations?

Also, sir, now that you are planning to make a plane trip soon, will you tell us whether you have thought of something which will not put the United Nations in the contingency that it had to face—which I hope will never happen—when the late Mr. Hammarskjöld passed away in Africa?

THE ACTING SECRETARY-GENERAL: Regarding the first part of your question, so far the working arrangements in the Secretariat have been very satisfactory and the operation has been very smooth. Regarding the second part of your question, of course I do not know how to devise ways and means of averting the prospective disaster or catastrophe which you have in mind.

QUESTION: Mr. Secretary-General, coming back to New Guinea, could you tell us if you have taken or are planning to take any initiative to bring the parties back to the table? Secondly, if this does not materialize, do you see other means to further a peaceful solution of this dispute?

THE ACTING SECRETARY-GENERAL: Mr. Bunker only yesterday reported to me that he had sent out an appeal to the president of the Republic of Indonesia to permit his representative, Ambassador Malik, to come back to Washington. Of course we have to await further developments and I am afraid that I cannot say anything beyond that.

. . . . QUESTION: If the financial difficulties were to end the Congo and Middle East operations, do you think that the resulting atmosphere would hinder the expansion of United Nations economic operations, which also rest on voluntarily contributed funds?

THE ACTING SECRETARY-GENERAL: As I have indicated on previous occasions, the successful implementation of the Security Council resolutions with regard to our peacekeeping operations depends primarily on the availability of resources, men, money, and materials—if I may so put it, the three "M's." So at some stage, of course, we have to review the whole situation. My present thinking is that we shall get a much clearer picture of our financial resources in the next six to eight weeks—that is, some time in May. And by that time, on the basis of these developments regarding the financial situation, I have to report back to the Security Council, for a fresh mandate if necessary.

.... QUESTION: Turning again to the West Irian issue, I should like to know if you are still optimistic with regard to a peaceful settlement and, secondly, whether you would like to comment on the latest news reports reaching here to the effect that the Dutch will send reinforcements to West Irian by sending the destroyers which are now visiting San Diego?

THE ACTING SECRETARY-GENERAL: With regard to the first part of your question, I am not pessimistic. With regard to the second part, it would, of course, be rather difficult for me to comment on the press reports.

QUESTION: On the question of New Guinea I should like to ask you whether, if armed activities should continue around New Guinea, you would consider sending out a United Nations observer to that region, and whether you consider a United Nations presence there as a useful deterrent to the threats to peace?

THE ACTING SECRETARY-GENERAL: I have given some thought to this, and I do not feel that it would be helpful if I were to reveal at this stage my line of thinking.

QUESTION: I do not wish to get too theoretical but, in connection with your conclusion that the force of the United Nations was not battalions or other rather technical things, you said that it was, in the main, public opinion which cannot be ignored by any country. I am really curious as to your own feelings about or interpretations of certain spectacular times and events in which public opinion, as expressed in this building, has been ignored. How do you, as a diplomat, account for these events, and how do you feel about a recurrence of such events in the future?

THE ACTING SECRETARY-GENERAL: My point is that the United Nations has been growing and the influence of the United Nations will not be diminished in the future. That is my reading of the development of this Organization. When I say that the influence of the United Nations is not to be considered in terms of battalions—although, of course, it is performing peacekeeping operations in the Middle East and the Congo—I mean that the United Nations is not a military power in the strict sense of the term. Neither is the United Nations purely a moral force. It is somewhere in between. My concept of the growth of the United Nations is that it is now the cumulative influence of a very powerful and massive public opinion which, I think, it will be difficult for any nation to ignore. I think that is a fact, whether we like it or not. Of course, I am aware of the fact that certain sections of public opinion in some countries, especially in the West, have been showing unnecessary nervousness about the trend in the United Nations. I feel that this nervousness is not at all justified.

QUESTION: It is apparent that the success of the United Nations bond issue depends to a very large extent on the purchase by the United States of about $100 million worth of bonds. Should the Congress find itself unable to approve of United States purchase of $100 million worth of bonds, what alternative proposals do you have for the purchase of the remaining bonds, and, if there are no alternative proposals, do you hope to approach the General Assembly for a fresh mandate to help the United Nations solve its financial problems?

THE ACTING SECRETARY-GENERAL: As you know, the sale of the $200 million worth of bonds was authorized by the General Assembly. If the response of the Member states is not as satisfactory as was anticipated, that, of course, will affect the peacekeeping operations in the Congo and the Middle East. In that event, as I indicated earlier, it would be my duty to report back to the Security Council, perhaps in May, to seek a fresh mandate.

. . . . QUESTION: Mr. Secretary-General, you have had some experience now with the lonely job of Secretary-General. Would you be willing to accept a full term?

THE ACTING SECRETARY-GENERAL: Well, such a prospect is very far from my thoughts, for the moment.

From Speech at the Annual Luncheon of the United States Committee for the United Nations

NEW YORK   APRIL 17, 1962

ALTHOUGH U THANT himself was often highly critical of the United Nations, he rarely failed to defend the Organization when he felt others were criticizing it unfairly. He was particularly disturbed by criticism he believed to be based on misconceptions or misrepresentations. He felt it was the duty of organizations such as the United States Committee for the United Nations and the various national UN associations to refute unjust judgments on the Organization. In a speech to the United States Committee on April 17, 1962, he stressed a point he was to make many times in the future: that the real political decisions were being made by the two super powers and that the United Nations could not help but reflect the political realities that existed.

. . . . SO MANY of the criticisms one hears nowadays about the United Nations are based on misconceptions or misrepresentations, and it is fitting that the United States Committee should be so active in helping the people understand better what the United Nations *can do* and *has done* to help maintain international peace and security, and to promote the betterment of human beings all over the world.

In particular, I am glad that at the present time there has been a revival of interest in the economic, social, and human rights activities of the United Nations. The General Assembly has designated this decade as the United Nations Development Decade, thus highlighting the important role that the United Nations will play in this decade for the welfare of all human beings. It is our common experience that the smallest political wrangle attracts headlines in newspapers all over the world, whereas some of the most significant work of the United Nations in the economic and social fields is hardly ever mentioned. I hope that the United States Committee will give due importance to this aspect of our work.

On the political plane, it cannot be repeated too often that the United Nations can only be what its members make of it. It cannot help but

UN Press Release SG/1175.

reflect the political realities of the world today, but it would be unfair to blame the United Nations merely because it mirrors the imperfections of the world around us.

In these turbulent times we should well remember a few fundamental facts.

The first task of leaders of men all over the world is to find the first steps toward a world system of preventing war. Eighteen years ago three men, Roosevelt, Stalin, and Churchill, settled by themselves at Yalta the fate of Europe, Asia, Africa, and the Middle East. Now, the three most powerful men in the world cannot even decide in any positive way the fate of Europe.

But two of them are masters of the world in a sense that no two men before them have ever been. The president of the United States and the chairman of the Council of Ministers of the Soviet Union may not be able to make the world behave as they wish, but they have the power to destroy it. The United States and the Soviet Union control between them almost the whole of the world's nuclear arsenal. The process of stockpiling is still going on at a frightening pace. No sane person can believe that either the United States or the Soviet Union will wage a nuclear war deliberately, but there are good reasons to think that the risk of an unintended war is very great. This risk does not depend upon any supposed equality of power between East and West, but upon the risk of accident in the technical measures taken by both sides in the hope of preventing a surprise attack.

The process of replacing men by electronic devices in the complicated machinery of nuclear deterrence now brings new terrors into the so-called balance of terror. From time to time we have been hearing of a nuclear-tipped missile being nearly launched by accident or on false alarm, even by an electrical short circuit. It is common knowledge that both the American and Soviet missiles are at hair-trigger readiness and controlled by electronic devices.

What does this all mean? This means that some system must be found to limit and control the nuclear arms race before it gets out of hand.

Political or territorial disputes such as the future of Berlin or the uncertainties of the Middle Eastern situation, or the highly charged situation in certain parts of Asia, Africa, and Latin America, are serious and urgent, and it is extremely difficult to find solutions to these problems. But it is imperative that the seriousness of these situations does not develop to the point of application of this monstrous nuclear power. If no final solution can yet be found for these disputes, the most sensible and practical course is to insulate them as far as possible from war risks by temporary stand-still agreements, while an effort is made to build a more permanent war-free international system.

It is perhaps a utopian dream when we aspire to create a world in which major war is impossible. In the light of history, it is certainly a utopian dream, but today, when we live under the shadow of the nuclear bomb, nothing less than that kind of utopia will do.

. . . .

From Transcript of Press Luncheon Given by the United Nations Correspondents Association

NEW YORK   APRIL 24, 1962

IN RESPONSE to questions on April 24, 1962, at a luncheon of the United Nations Correspondents Association, U Thant made statements that reflected his thinking on the functions of the Secretary-General. The first was related to a formula presented by his special representative, Ellsworth Bunker, during the West Irian negotiations. Thant said he was aware of the content of the formula, but had advised Bunker not to solicit his reaction to it because of the risk involved. "If I am associated with any formula," he said, "and if that particular formula happens to be unacceptable to one party or the other, then it might even damage the office of the Secretary-General." This appeared to suggest rather severe self-restriction. He did not consider it an iron-clad rule, however. A few months later he was to submit his own Plan for National Reconciliation in the Congo, which he put forward on a take-it-or-leave-it basis. At the Correspondents Association luncheon Thant made another statement which appeared to be an acknowledgement of the limitations under which he must function. Asked about the possible use of his office to head off a new round of nuclear test explosions by the United States and the Soviet Union, he noted that the General Assembly had urged the parties concerned to refrain from nuclear tests. He added: "In my position, of course, I cannot go beyond that." This view also was to be changed later in the year, when he did intervene with a protest against the tests (see commentary on press conferences June-August 1962, p. 168).

.... I THINK it is not exactly right to say that I have been a journalist for the last forty years. Actually, I first tried my hand at journalism when I was fifteen. At that time, I contributed a small article to the organ of the Burma Boy Scouts Association, called *The Burma Boy*. It was simply a collection of school anecdotes. That was my first attempt at journalism. Then, of course, I kept up the practice, off and on. All my life, my ambition was to become a journalist—or, as we call it in Burma, a political journalist, just to distinguish that from the type of correspondent who

UN Note to Correspondents No. 2574.

deals with sports or movies or book reviews. All my life, I have had a greater interest in political developments, both domestic and international, than in other aspects of public life.

One of my favorite columnists, even when I was in Burma, was Walter Lippmann. I still retain a very high regard for that great man. In my view, he is one of the most perceptive analysts in the world of journalism.

I do not think I should take more of your time in discoursing on these generalities, and I am sure that many of you must have specific questions in mind. I do not want to focus attention deliberately on any particular issue at the moment, and therefore, as has been the practice in the past, I shall be very glad to answer any questions that you may wish to put.

.... QUESTION: In the light of today's meeting of the advisory committee on the Congo, can you tell us whether there is any change in the attitude of the United Nations toward the continuous refusal of Mr. Tshombé to accept a real integration of Katanga into the Republic of the Congo?

THE ACTING SECRETARY-GENERAL: The United Nations has not changed its policy as far as its operations in the Congo are concerned. Of course, the talks between Prime Minister Adoula and Mr. Tshombé have been temporarily suspended. My interpretation is that the talks have not broken down. There are definite indications that Mr. Tshombé will come back to Leopoldville to resume the talks. My special representative, Mr. Robert Gardiner, who is in New York today and who is leaving for Leopoldville tonight, will get in touch with Prime Minister Adoula as soon as he returns there and, if necessary, he will use his good offices to bring the two men together again. I am not pessimistic about the outcome of the talks.

QUESTION: Mr. Secretary-General, what do you think about a possible reduction of the United Nations forces in the Congo?

THE ACTING SECRETARY-GENERAL: I have not been thinking of a possible reduction of the United Nations forces in the Congo in the immediate future. Of course, it will depend on a variety of circumstances. One of them, of course, is the availability of resources, of funds. Another will be the attitude of the Central Government. A third consideration, of course, is the attitude of the Security Council. If the Security Council decides that I should take a certain line of action by way of reduction or by way of an increment, I shall, of course, have to abide by the decision of the Council. For the moment, however, I have not been thinking of any possible reduction of the ONUC forces in the immediate future.

QUESTION: What is Ellsworth Bunker doing to get the Dutch and the Indonesians together again to talk about their dispute over West New Guinea? What have they told him? How soon are they likely to meet again, and will they settle things?

THE ACTING SECRETARY-GENERAL: As you all know, the negotiations between the Netherlands and Indonesia went on outside the United Nations, informally and secretly, in the presence of Mr. Bunker, who represented me in these negotiations. The intention was that these informal and secret negotiations should proceed smoothly, without any chance of leaking out, and therefore Mr. Bunker organized these informal negotiations away from New York—in a place near Washington, as you know. The negotiations were interrupted for various reasons. Among these reasons was the fact that some of the representatives had a limited mandate, and, since their mandate was restricted, they felt that they had to seek a fresh mandate.

While the negotiations were suspended, Mr. Bunker was in constant touch with me, and at some stage he came up with his own formula, calculated to break the impasse. He presented his formula to me. In my present position, of course, I should not identify myself with any formulation because of the risk involved: if I am associated with any formula, and if that particular formula happens to be unacceptable to one party or the other, then it might even damage the Office of the Secretary-General. I therefore advised Mr. Bunker not to solicit my reactions to his formula. I encouraged him to present his formula to the two governments, which he did. Of course, I am fully aware of the substance of his formula, and my intention was and is that, if Mr. Bunker's formula is acceptable to both parties, formal negotiations can take place on the basis of that formula in my presence in New York. So far, I have not received any official communication from either party regarding its reactions to Mr. Bunker's formula. All I have been hearing—as you have been hearing—has been only through the press. I understand that Mr. Bunker is vigorously pursuing his efforts, bending all his energies to getting the two parties together as soon as possible. For the moment, of course, I have no means of knowing when the negotiations will be resumed.

QUESTION: If the United Nations is asked to play a role during an interim period in supervising the administration of the territory, could the Secretary-General take the necessary steps for that purpose, or would such a step require the authorization of the General Assembly?

THE ACTING SECRETARY-GENERAL: If Mr. Bunker's formula is accepted by both parties as a suitable basis for formal discussions, and if these formal discussions go through, then I shall have to request the convening of the General Assembly. Without the mandate of the General Assembly, I do not feel that the Secretary-General should assume full responsibility for the implementation of the agreement envisaged in this formula.

QUESTION: To your knowledge, are there any mercenaries still in Katanga Province, and if there are any, are any measures planned by the United Nations to deal with them in the spirit of the Security Council resolution?

THE ACTING SECRETARY-GENERAL: To our knowledge there are still mercenaries in Katanga, and the attitude of the United Nations toward this issue has not changed at all. But for the moment the United Nations is concentrating all its energies to implement the Security Council resolutions without resort to force—for the moment. Of course, as you know, the United Nations has been authorized by the Security Council to exercise force only in three situations. The first situation is to prevent civil war. The second situation is to retaliate when attacked, as self-defense. The third situation is to arrest the mercenaries. Of course, the United Nations has been authorized to use force to apprehend, arrest, and detain foreign mercenaries. But for the moment, as I have indicated, we are concentrating our energies on the nonmilitary aspects of the UN operations.

QUESTION: How serious is the crisis resulting from the failure of the United Nations so far to find a satisfactory basis of financing the peacekeeping operations? Is the method of raising bonds the first and last attempt of its kind?

THE ACTING SECRETARY-GENERAL: Just now, of course, it is perhaps a little too early to pass judgment on whether the idea of selling bonds to finance the United Nations peacekeeping operations is a success or a failure. As you know, several governments have indicated their readiness and their willingness to buy bonds. Apart from Washington, we have received assurances from several Member states and nonmember states to purchase $64 million worth of bonds, and we are expecting a few more replies from two or three other countries in the next week or so. Therefore, generally speaking, the result is not as unsatisfactory as I thought at one time. Perhaps we will be able to review the whole financial situation by the end of June when the picture will be more clear.

QUESTION: Has the Acting Secretary-General made, or considered making, use of the tremendous prestige of his office to try to dissuade the

United States and the USSR from engaging in a new round of nuclear test explosions?

THE ACTING SECRETARY-GENERAL: The General Assembly resolutions of the last session are very clear on this question of nuclear tests. It will be recalled that two resolutions were adopted by overwhelming majorities in the last session, urging the powers concerned to refrain from nuclear tests. So in my position, of course, I cannot go beyond that and I have simply to reflect the sentiment of the General Assembly, and I think it is quite proper for me to take this opportunity of appealing to all powers concerned to refrain from tests on the basis of the resolutions adopted at the sixteenth session of the General Assembly.

QUESTION: If the United Nations were to have a permanent army, would not the foreign legion be a convenient nucleus?

THE ACTING SECRETARY-GENERAL: I am not aware of any delegation or delegations thinking of starting a United Nations standing army, for the moment, although much thought has been given to this aspect. I propose to deal with this particular aspect in one of my speeches some time in the next few months. I am studying this problem from all aspects and for the moment I do not think I am competent to express any views on it. But if the United Nations decides to maintain an armed force of its own, of course the question of the foreign legion will be considered by the appropriate organs.

. . . . QUESTION: You have said that peacekeeping operations cannot continue without the three M's—the first being money. Taking the stated political stands into consideration, does it mean that the United Nations is virtually eliminated as a peacekeeper and vacuum-filler in any future Congo-like situations?

THE ACTING SECRETARY-GENERAL: In any future contingency, of course, it is common knowledge that without adequate resources the United Nations will not be able to undertake tasks similar to those in the Congo. I think it is known to everybody. Without the resources—and by resources I have made it clear that they connote men, money, and materials—without these resources, the United Nations will not be able to undertake a similar task, of the same magnitude as in the Congo, and I think it is not a secret and it is known to every delegation and every observer. Therefore, I think the attention of all of us, the attention of all Member states, and the attention of all delegations should be focused on the prevention of situations in other parts of the world similar to those which we have been witnessing in the Congo.

. . . .

Statement Dedicating the Hammarskjöld Room at the House of the New York City Bar Association

NEW YORK   APRIL 30, 1962

U THANT often spoke of the "two schools of thought" regarding the direction in which the United Nations should develop: whether it should be a debating forum or conference-type organization or whether it should have broad powers for conciliation and the maintenance of peace. He had made it clear even before he became Acting Secretary-General that he was a firm believer in the latter school. In his brief speech to the Association of the Bar of the City of New York on April 30, 1962, he noted that Dag Hammarskjöld had wanted the United Nations to become an "effective world authority" and he asserted once more that he himself endorsed the objectives of his predecessor.

FIRST OF ALL let me say how grateful I am to the Association of the Bar of the City of New York for the honor of the invitation extended to me to dedicate the Hammarskjöld Room in this House of the Association. I sincerely appreciate the opportunity of performing this task as a tribute to my distinguished predecessor.

Since his unexpected and tragic death on September 17, 1961, a deep appreciation of his work as Secretary-General of the United Nations has been shown by all sections of peoples all over the world. Even those who were critical of his actions, from time to time, expressed their admiration for his unswerving devotion to the principles he held dear and his dedication to the task of strengthening the world organization he headed with distinction for eight years. Today, we have the clearer image of Dag Hammarskjöld, who has come to be identified with the very purposes and principles of the United Nations Charter, and who has assumed the symbol of a man relentlessly dedicated to the maintenance of international peace and security.

He had exceptional courage of convictions, and never swerved from the set course dictated to him by his convictions. This gave him a broad

UN Press Release SG/1184.

consistency. He was convinced of the necessity of developing an international authority within the present world setup. He realized that anything capable of mitigating the present state of tensions would represent a valuable advance. He also realized that the objective of all peace-loving peoples should be an effective world authority like any other governmental system.

I want to take this opportunity of endorsing these convictions and these objectives which were cherished by my predecessor. The greatest problem of our age is to find a system of war prevention that works in our present circumstances. Basically, this is a problem that can be solved only by the willing cooperation of all countries. But many countries will not be brought to operate a limited form of world government unless there is everywhere a growing recognition of the unity of human society. We should therefore be united in our unprecedented need to find a system for living together in peace.

It is now my pleasure and privilege to dedicate this Hammarskjöld Room to the cause of world peace through world law not only for our generation but for all generations to come.

FIRST MAJOR SPEECHES ABROAD

U THANT had been in office six months before he made the first of his many trips abroad. Like his predecessors he was convinced that personal contacts with world leaders could and should be used to the utmost to win support for the United Nations and to channel problems to United Nations organizations. As secretary to U Nu, former Burmese chief of state, Thant had traveled widely long before he had come to the United Nations and had met many prominent political figures. On his first trip abroad as Acting Secretary-General, in May 1962, he visited Geneva, Stockholm, and Copenhagen where he not only talked with leaders but made major speeches.

In an address at Uppsala University in Sweden, he developed a theme to which he was to return many times in the future—the role of the small nations both as a bridge between the super powers and as an instrument through which the conscience of the world might be expressed. Thant believed, as Hammarskjöld did, that the small nations, rather than the great powers, need the protection the United Nations can give. He was convinced, as well, that the small countries had much to contribute to the Organization and that they must continue to speak out even when their views clash with those of their powerful friends. It was in his Uppsala speech that Thant also voiced the conviction that, if the United Nations is to have a future, it must assume some of the attributes of a state. It must have the right, the power, and the means to keep the peace, he said, and this can be achieved only if Member states are willing to give up the concept of the absolute sovereign state.

His Copenhagen address was his first major speech on the United Nations Development Decade. President John F. Kennedy had proposed, while addressing the General Assembly on September 25, 1961, that the 1960s be officially designated as the Development Decade. The Assembly had accepted the proposal and had called upon the Acting Secretary-General to develop specific proposals to coordinate and intensify United Nations and governmental efforts to promote economic growth. At the time of the Copenhagen speech, Thant was completing the proposals he would present to the Economic and Social Council in July. In Copenhagen he dealt with such broad questions as needs, capabilities, and available resources rather than with the specifics of his forthcoming plan. His message was that the main obstacle to development was ignorance of the scale of the world's resources and of the new techniques of growth and that during the 1960s "one of our great purposes must be to end the ignorance and liberate the generous and decent instincts of mankind."

Shortly after returning from Europe Thant went to Ottawa to deliver an address at Carleton University entitled "Education for Peace." Much of the world's trouble, he said, was caused by an obsession with the past, a belief in the "fallacious" assumption that history repeats itself. He asserted that the first task in education for peace is to allay this fear and mistrust. The essence of all great religions and possibly the key to solving many of our most pressing problems, he said, is "in a sharing of our beliefs, in civilized conduct and generous behavior, the spirit of tolerance, of live and let live, and of understanding the other man's point of view."

1. "The Small Nations and the Future of the United Nations"
Address at Uppsala University

UPPSALA, SWEDEN   MAY 6, 1962

SEVENTEEN YEARS AGO, when the statesmen of the world gathered at San Francisco and tried to work out a world organization to establish peace on secure foundations, the international situation was very different from what it is today. The conference was naturally dominated by the three greatest military powers, the United States, the Soviet Union, and Britain. There was a widespread belief at that time that, if only these Big Three could be brought together in an international organization, there would be no fear of another world war, and even small brush-fire wars could be banished. In the wake of the most catastrophic war in the history of mankind, humanity had a new vision: it saw the glimmer of dawn of a warless world. The tragic history of the League of Nations was still fresh in the minds of these statesmen who realized that the League failed because it did not have sufficient authority to act. There were many in San Francisco who were familiar with the circumstances leading to the collapse of the League of Nations, and who realized that the League failed not only because it was lacking in authority but also because it was lacking in will. The psychological climate in the spring of 1945 at San Francisco was one of hope and even optimism; there was general feeling that the statesmen had learned a bitter lesson of history; the Big Three had emerged victorious in the colossal war against the Fascist and Nazi

UN Press Release SG/1186.

dictatorships at tremendous cost; peace had been won, and that hard-won peace must endure with the continued cooperation of the allies.

That hope, that vision, and that belief speedily vanished in the years following the war. The causes of the deterioration in international relations which followed the Second World War were mainly political and psychological. After an all-too-brief period of harmony, the Big Three split among themselves. The United States and Britain were suspicious of Russian intentions and Russia was suspicious of Western intentions. In course of time, the West moved closer together and established "collective defense pacts." For her part, Russia too established a cordon of friendly states around herself and entered into similar "collective defense pacts." To ask which side started this process would be unprofitable, since this would generate ceaseless arguments. The relevant consideration in this context is that fear and suspicion on both sides generated tensions which came to be reflected in the United Nations. The big powers on the Security Council, which was originally designed as the chief instrument for maintaining peace and preventing war, have made it an arena of contention and conflict. The United Nations, like its predecessor the League of Nations, has had several impressive successes to its credit, but it has not been an unqualified success in its essential purpose to establish the rule of law everywhere. One fact clearly emerges out of the debates and discussions on major political questions in the United Nations: ordinarily the Security Council can take effective action only if the United States and the Soviet Union are in agreement.

It is impossible to conceive in our times of a world authority that could physically eclipse the giant states of the United States and the Soviet Union. All that seems possible is to employ the strength of the two giants to support a system of preventing war between other, weaker countries. But how is war to be prevented in disputes between the two giants themselves? This is *the* paramount question of today. In the last resort, there is only the so-called "balance of terror" between them. No doubt there is also a tacit recognition between them that their interest in world peace is greater than any of their other political interests. It is only on this premise that serious negotiations can be based. Herein comes the role of the smaller uncommitted countries like Sweden, which is to develop every means of strengthening this implicit understanding between the Americans and the Russians, thus making "the last resort" increasingly remote.

As far as the United States and the Soviet Union are concerned, the aim for the time being should be to stabilize and, if possible, to reduce arms stockpiles without disturbing the existing "balance of terror"; to eliminate as far as possible the risks of surprise attack or of war by accident; to check the development of new weapons, and the continuous stockpiling of existing ones. In short, the most hopeful approach is through disarmament, starting with the banning of tests under appropriate and effective control and an agreed system of inspection, as the United Nations General Assembly has repeatedly favored.

As far as all other powers are concerned, the aim should be to develop the peacekeeping authority of the United Nations. A Member state such as Sweden could greatly increase the usefulness of the United Nations— and I am indeed very glad to have this opportunity of stating from this forum that Sweden has been playing a very significant role in this direction. Although the moral authority of the United Nations could be built up by channelling international activities through this instrument, its efficacy will always require, ultimately, the supporting enforcement of both the United States and the Soviet Union. In the last analysis it must be a system in which the two giants must be increasingly involved. Such a development of the United Nations would also serve to add another brake to the danger of war between the two giants themselves, and forge a permanent link between them.

I said earlier that the political climate today is very different from that of 1945 when the United Nations was founded. There are still other important differences between 1945 and 1962. The first of these is the increasing use and, indeed, diversion of scientific and technological progress for military purposes. The atom bomb and the hydrogen bomb were not generally known in the spring of 1945. I do not know whether the scientists at that time who were engaged in this field of research realized that large-scale atomic warfare might so poison the world as to destroy our civilization. Certainly it did not enter into the minds of those planning a new order.

Looking back over the years one would have thought that by now these obvious risks in our present situation would have become apparent to everyone. The best hopes for peace are now placed in maintaining a "balance of terror" but this balance is beginning to look like an illusion. It is surely time to return to the common-sense conclusion that peace and security cannot be achieved without first reaching agreements between East and West to halt the arms race. The arms race not only feeds on itself but creates in every country an attitude of mind which makes agreements impossible. The time has come for statesmen to say firmly that they do not believe in an indefinite continuation of the delicate balance of terror. This balance seems to me to be purely a theoretical conception when considered in the light of political reality. The reality is that neither the United States nor the Soviet Union will deliberately seek a nuclear war, though they may be plunged into one by accident, and the sensible course is to try to prevent accidents by limiting the arms race and reducing the areas of dispute.

Neutralization of certain areas seems to be a welcome trend in international negotiations. In 1955, the great powers, including the Soviet Union, signed a treaty which neutralized Austria. In 1960, they signed a treaty neutralizing Antarctica. A year later they were prepared to guarantee the neutralization of Laos.

The importance of neutralization does not lie solely in the creation of buffer states, valuable though that is. Neutralization is a form of territorial disarmament, a partial dismantling of the great military machines whose destructive powers have now become so terrifying. Each act of neutralization, therefore, is a kind of pilot project for the comprehensive disarmament that alone can rid the world of fear and suspicion.

These are among the great issues of the 1960s which were never thought of when the United Nations was founded. Nor had the world's statesmen contemplated the tremendous advance in national self-consciousness first in Asia and then in Africa, the ending of colonialism and the long-existing hegemony of Europe. The world of 1945, like the world of the League of Nations, was essentially the world of Europe, and of the Americas. Asia and Africa were just mere appendages of Europe. Apparently no thought was given at that time to the prospect of emerging nations of these two continents. Today half of the Members of the United Nations are from Asia and Africa. One observes a growing nervousness in the West about the rise in membership of the Asian-Africans in the world organization. But surely the best interests of the West are ill-served by sour comments about newly independent countries in Asia and Africa. Such an attitude is a poor tribute to the generations of dedicated and idealistic Westerners who worked precisely toward the ultimate goal of independence, even if they did not know it was going to be reached so early. Nor is it fair to expect those countries at their present stage to express frequently and vociferously their gratitude for what the West did for them. Many newly independent countries still retain bitter memories of the past. In some cases independence was too long postponed, causing a mood of frustration and desperation among freedom fighters. If a country has to fight too long and too hard to win an independence which comes too late, then some extreme forces more hostile to their old masters come to the surface and become more dominant. But by and large these new states which now constitute half the membership of the United Nations generally share democratic ideas, including the liberal concepts of objectivity, tolerance, and the rule of law, and are rarely attracted by dogmas alien to their way of life. With just a little imagination both the East and the West could find in the building up of the United Nations authority a common platform with these newly emerging nations, for many of whom this would be the best guarantee of their independence. For the Western powers it would be the rational sequel in world politics to their renunciation of control over their far-flung empires. It would, moreover, pave the way for new techniques of international relationship within the framework of a growing United Nations.

A mature sense of responsibility was first demonstrated by the Asian-African countries in the historic Bandung Conference seven years ago. Nearly half of the twenty-nine countries attending that conference were not members of the United Nations at that time. Surprisingly enough, support for the United Nations was one of the first principles endorsed. The keynote of the Bandung Conference was moderation and a surprising degree of unanimity was achieved in the final declarations. Countries with different ideological and social systems went on record as favoring closer and friendlier relations.

I believe that all small countries everywhere have the same interest in the maintenance of peace and the development of a more effective international instrument for that purpose. The record of Sweden in the United Nations is an unmistakable demonstration of this attitude. Most of the small countries care passionately about peace. Many of them are aroused to furious protest against, say, racial discrimination as against *all* explosions of atomic and hydrogen bombs. For it is all part of the same compassion for humanity and the same commitment to a belief in the future of man. This philosophy which is increasingly in evidence all over the world is an affirmation of community of interest, a mass declaration that human beings must learn to understand one another even if they cannot agree with one another or like one another. It is a challenge to the conscience of the present society—a society characterized by fear, suspicion, frustration, and bitterness.

I am in complete agreement with my distinguished predecessor Mr. Dag Hammarskjöld when he said that it is the small nations, rather than the great powers, which need the protection the United Nations can give. If the West were to set about strengthening the United Nations authority upon the basis of this widely shared common interest, the possibility of effective United Nations intervention for the peaceful resolution of dangerous situations will be greatly increased. Disarmament provides an additional reason why the West should try to prepare the United Nations for a more positive role. Agreed disarmament, which all the major governments profess to want, requires as its inescapable condition the establishment of an international authority with substantial powers. To do so, the first requisite is mutual confidence. The build-up of confidence can be successful only if the United Nations is made to reflect adequately the interests and aspirations of all Members large and small. In this context the role of the small nations is still more significant. One of their functions in the United Nations should be to build bridges between East and West—to interpret the East to the West and the West to the East, and thus strengthen the very foundation on which this world organization is built.

Based on these premises let us consider the future of the United Nations.

First we must realize that the world is facing a situation which is entirely unprecedented. The situation of mutual deterrence which has preserved an uneasy peace during the past few years is not in itself likely to produce continuing stability. The more the two great powers struggle to perfect their deterrents, the less likely it is that they will dare to use them to deal with anything except a direct attack on themselves. Tension and the dangers of an accidental calamity will rise higher and higher. Lasting security cannot be produced by this policy.

Therefore, the development of the United Nations as a really effective instrument of preventing war is of primary importance to every one of us. Every man or woman should not only ask himself or herself what he or she is going to do in the world, but also ask, "Will there be a world in which I can live?"

The second great fact of our times is that the whole world is closely linked as never before in the history of mankind. It is not true to say that Russia and the West have no interest in common. Both have the one great overriding interest in preserving peace and avoiding total war. Once that fact is recognized, it may be possible to begin the slow, painful, and extremely difficult task of constructing some agreed system of disarmament, inspection, and control to replace the present international anarchy. It is not too much to hope that the small uncommitted nations will take the lead in this very necessary historic enterprise within the framework of the United Nations.

Another great fact of our times is the myth of the absolute sovereign state. Up to the First World War, Britannia ruled the waves with a very powerful navy. She was, in fact, more than an absolute sovereign state: she was also the nerve-center of a great empire. The United States, separated from possible aggressors by great oceans, was safe and could afford to be sovereign and isolationist. The same could be said of many other countries with varying degrees of strength and stability.

In San Francisco, seventeen years ago, the assembled statesmen of the world clung to this myth. They still conceived it possible to have a peaceful world consisting of a number of armed sovereign states clinging to their sovereign status without any thought of abandoning an iota of this sovereignty. If the United Nations is to grow into a really effective instrument for maintaining the rule of law, the first step must be the willingness of the Member states to give up the concept of the absolute sovereign state in the same manner as we individuals give up our absolute right to do just what we please, as an essential condition of living in an organized society. The individual has to submit to the rules laid down by the authorities, and every one of us has to pay this price as a condition of living. While the sovereignty of each of us is limited to what is necessary in the interest of the community, one retains the domestic rights for the purpose of regulating one's home life.

Similarly, in the community of nations it is increasingly important to restrict the sovereignty of states, even in a small way to start with. This restriction may involve the renunciation of the threat or the use of force as an instrument of policy, the reduction of armed forces and the undertaking to submit disputes to the arbitration of an international judiciary. Even where Member states of the United Nations have voluntarily agreed to such restrictions on their absolute freedom of action, the United Nations has no authority at present to enforce them. It seems to me that the United Nations must develop in the same manner as every sovereign state has done. If the United Nations is to have a future, it must assume some of the attributes of a state. It must have the right, the power, and the means to keep the peace. In this historic task the small countries have a significant role to play.

In fact, the small nations have more than one role to play in this regard. First of all, as I have already noted, they are to play the part of a bridge between the big powers, especially in issues which are of global interest. For example, the disarmament conference could not get going for many years, so long as its membership was confined to the principal protagonists in the armaments race. It will be generally agreed that the issue of disarmament is of interest not only to the major military powers but to the entire world; in fact, it is one of the central responsibilities of the United Nations under the Charter. This responsibility was ultimately reflected by the addition of eight countries—outside of the major power blocs—to the disarmament conference, and since then there is more hope of progress than there was before. The same is true of nuclear testing, because the effects of fall-out are universal. In all such issues the small nations have a legitimate role in trying to bridge the gap between the extreme positions which are too often taken—for the record, at any rate—by the major powers.

The other role of the small nations is to give expression, so to speak, to the still, small voice. More often self-interest, rather than conscience, "makes cowards of us all" and prevents us from speaking out the truth as we see it. It is again a proper role for the small nations to speak the truth as they see it, and let the chips fall where they may. This attitude was shown repeatedly by many of the small nations, and not necessarily the Asian-Africans alone, during the sixteenth session of the General Assembly. I hope that for the future too the small nations will not be either overawed by their more powerful friends, or cowed by threats into silence, and that they will continue to speak out when the occasion demands.

Both these roles—I might even say, functions—of the small nations were exemplified by my distinguished predecessor, the late Dag Hammarskjöld. Over the years his role as a bridge-builder was so successful that it became a common practice, when any difficult situation came along, for the major organs to say in so many words "Leave it to Dag." His "quiet diplomacy" was one of the most successful ways of bridging the gap between extreme positions, and in his own quiet and unobtrusive way he played the part of bridge-builder to perfection.

Even more significant was his role as the authentic voice of the conscience of humanity. Many times he had to speak out when others were inclined to be silent. Perhaps the most notable example was when he declared on October 31, 1956,

This afternoon I wish to make the following declaration: The principles of the Charter are, by far, greater than the Organization in which they are embodied, and the aims which they are to safeguard are holier than the policies of any single nation or people. As a servant of the Organization the Secretary-General has the duty to maintain his usefulness by avoiding public stands on conflicts between Member nations unless and until such an action might help to resolve the conflict. However, the discretion and impartiality thus imposed on the Secretary-General by the character of his immediate task, may not degenerate into a policy of expediency. He must also be a servant of the principles of the Charter, and its aims must ultimately determine what for him is right and wrong. For that he must stand. A Secretary-General cannot serve on any other assumption than that— within the necessary limits of human frailty and honest differences of opinion—all Member nations honor their pledge to observe all Articles of the Charter. He should also be able to assume that those organs which are charged with the task of upholding the Charter, will be in a position to fulfill their task."[1]

But this was not the only occasion. Increasingly during the last two years of his tenure, which was so cruelly cut short by a tragic fate, he spoke out on major issues and was listened to with respect, even by those who, by implication, disagreed with him. I wish, at this place where he studied and grew to manhood, to place on record this tribute to him and to his memory, and to his great contribution to the internal community.

[1] See volume III of this series, p. 209.

---

2. *"The Decade of Development"*
Address to the Students Association

COPENHAGEN   MAY 8, 1962

I AM VERY GLAD to be speaking to you on this occasion on the subject of the Development Decade. It is common experience that political news of any kind is reported fully by the news media while the most spectacular programs of economic development and social progress are hardly mentioned. While this is understandable, I feel at the same time that it should not be overlooked that such development and progress are one of the main purposes of the Charter of the United Nations. The Charter states that the peoples of the United Nations are determined "to promote social

UN Press Release SG/1194/Rev. 1.

progress and better standards of life in larger freedom." The States Members of the United Nations have accordingly pledged themselves, for these ends, "to employ international machinery for the promotion of the economic and social advancement of all peoples."

I also feel that it is particularly appropriate that I should be speaking on this subject from this forum. Denmark has been one of the advanced countries which has consistently taken great interest in the economic development of the less developed countries of the world. Within your own shores you have established a pattern of life with the conscious goal that few should have too much and none should have too little. I believe that social justice is one of the great stabilizing forces of the world today, and that it is a good thing if this concept of social justice can be enlarged in scope so that it is no longer national in character, but becomes a global concept.

This year we are beginning a wholly new experiment in human cooperation. Over the next ten years, the United Nations and its specialized and associated agencies are pledged to mobilize their past experiences and coordinate their present efforts in a sustained attack upon the ancient enemies of mankind—disease, hunger, ignorance, poverty—and to lay the foundations in all developing lands for a more modern and productive economy. This is the broad purpose behind the Development Decade—a coordinated program on which the Member governments of the United Nations have set their seal of approval and to which each of the United Nations agencies has pledged enthusiastic support.

Why is this experiment new? The enemies, we all know, are old enough. Throughout human history, men and women have toiled painfully and all too often vainly to give themselves and their children even the simplest elements of decent human living. The sad verdict of philosophers and historians on the general lot of mankind echoes in our ears— Hobbes' definition of the human condition as "nasty, brutish and short," Thoreau's picture of innumerable, anonymous lives lived "in quiet desperation." And in the past, the degree to which the basic sources of human want and misery could be alleviated did in fact remain strictly limited. The resources needed to counter suffering were desperately scarce. And men had not the technological means to expand them or use them better. How could famine be relieved if the oxen who drew the grain carts ate half the food before it could reach the people who were starving? Such were the iron limits of human productivity. And in generation after generation, all but a fortunate few lived in permanent want—undernourished, short-lived, victims of disease, watching their children die, ignorant, bound indeed to a "melancholy wheel" of incurable privation.

I wonder if we fully realize the immense revolution that has occurred in this regard—a revolution that has begun to put an end to the old hopelessness? In the last century, at an accelerating pace, humanity has begun to break out of the old bondage. Science and technology, applied to a wider and wider range of human activities, have unlocked the doors of production. There is food enough to feed all mankind. There is speedy transport to deliver the food to any potential famine area. There are advances in fertilizers, in improved seed, in insecticides which make it certain that tomorrow—or the day after tomorrow—other economies will follow in the wake of the Danish farmer and produce more grain, more meat, more fruit, more fibers from the same acres under cultivation. In energy, in addition to conventional sources, a vast expansion of atomic power hopefully awaits us. And all the time technologies are changing and evolving so that minerals and metals can be substituted for each other and, if one wishes to be fanciful, who knows when we may not mine the planets or, by new chemical formulas, extract our needs out of sun and air?

But there is no need to be fanciful. In most of the developed societies, abundance is not a dream. It is a fact. Otherwise, how can we explain the astonishing phenomenon that the advanced nations can spend upwards to $120 billion a year on their weapons—and yet achieve rising standards of living for their people, and on top of all that still have surplus industrial capacity lying idle—and some of them still face problems of unemployment at home? Even after all that wealth has been poured into armaments, I repeat, some of the most powerful of the world's economies still have spare labor, idle capacity, vast stockpiles of metals and minerals, and surplus food which can be, and is being, made available to feed needy men elsewhere. I cite these astonishing facts above all to illustrate the degree to which sheer abundance of available resources and *not* a narrow scarcity is the hallmark of this crucial economy, proving that the breakthrough to abundance is the profoundest achievement of the new technology in our day.

A transformation on this scale was bound to have far-reaching repercussions. And I would suggest that one of the most significant political and social changes in the last decade is the realization among more and more people that the relative abundance achieved by more developed nations is not a gift of destiny but a goal which should be available for all.

The contrast between rich and poor which used to be confined to domestic society is now impressing itself deeply upon the thinking of mankind as a whole. There are rich nations and poor nations. There is a gulf of poverty and affluence cutting right through the structure of world society. And beneath the surface-play of politics, it is possible that this gulf is the deepest and most vital fact with which we have to deal.

But *can* we achieve this goal? Is it perhaps determined by culture or climate, by the local endowment of resources, by profound causes—both material and historical—over which we have all too little control? Here I would like to point to another significant change which, almost unnoticed, has been overtaking our society since the Second World War. We have become steadily more interested in the *processes* of development and more and more of our trained minds have been devoting themselves to the problems of why development occurs, of what changes and social modifications are necessary to achieve it, of the techniques it requires, the blocks and difficulties it is likely to meet. A whole new field of theory and practice is opening up here and I suggest that although, clearly, we do not know all the answers to the problem of building up a nation's resources, we know more than we did—and I think we are beginning to know it in a more systematic way. Let me give one or two illustrations of this point.

First of all, few governments now ignore the fact that growth toward greater abundance involves sustained investment. If societies aim at a 5 per cent rate of growth each year—and when population grows by 2 per cent a year, they can hardly aim at less—then they must be prepared to increase domestic saving and investment up to a level of at least 15 per cent of national income. But, of course, an investment ratio tells us nothing about the kind of investments that have to be made, the order in which they should be undertaken, the balance that should be given to this or that sector of the economy, nor any of the deeper social implications of seeking larger savings. However, in all these fields we are beginning to know more.

A country can hardly devote more savings to the development of its resources if it does not know where those resources are to be found. Careful surveys of mineral reserves, of agricultural endowment, of resources in river and territorial waters must precede the formulation of programs for expansion. A "preinvestment" phase in which something like a resource map of the economy is pieced together is a vital tool in the new armory of development; and where such surveys can cover not simply a country, but a group of countries naturally linked by some common regional interests—such as a river valley—the survey can itself make a direct contribution to growth on a wider basis.

Again, investment in resources is inseparable from investment in men. We are in the midst, I believe, of new, pioneering work in studying the development of education—in the broadest sense—in its relationship to growth and development in the economy as a whole. The standards and aims laid down at the various regional conferences on education organized by the United Nations Educational, Scientific and Cultural Organization show, I think, a far more systematic grasp of the need to dovetail the training of human beings into the expanding needs of a developing society. The balance between primary and secondary education, the role of vocational and "on-the-job-training," the size and character of the university programs—all these issues are being studied much more clearly in the light of our growing experience and we are perhaps on the brink of a breakthrough in the science of linking human and capital development in an orderly scheme of growth.

This is, in fact, one more example of a wider assertion we can make— that a measure of balance between sectors is a precondition of successful growth. For instance, nearly all developing countries have to keep a careful eye on their systems of power and transport. Once an economy begins to grow, its demand for both is virtually insatiable and planners are all too often caught in a series of bottlenecks which have their origins in too many firms chasing too little electricity and too few railway wagons.

But perhaps the most dangerous imbalances occur when farming is neglected and allowed to lag behind growth in other sectors. Dynamic agriculture, producing more food for a growing urban world, releases workers to the cities, providing markets for manufactured products, affects the cycle of growth at every turn and societies which neglect it find themselves limping along with the leg of agriculture disastrously shorter than the leg of industry.

And industry too has its pitfalls and imbalances. Nowhere are the implications of indiscriminate programming more intense. Nowhere is it easier to imagine that ten enterprises, all running below capacity and working at a loss, are in some magic way contributing to development. The wrong factory in the wrong place for the wrong product is the besetting danger of every period of growth.

All these facts of imbalance—which our work in development is making steadily more clear—point to a wider need—the need to see developing economies as organic wholes, to devise their pattern of growth systematically through a series of country plans and to accept the disciplines of such a plan in all phases of the nation's economic and social life.

And I think it is at this point that the full significance of our proposed Development Decade begins to become more clear. For in essence it is an application to our own work, here among the agencies of the United Nations, of the principle of balance, coordination, and interdependence which I have been trying to describe. There is not a sector in the developing economies of our world which cannot call upon the work and experience of an international agency. The UN Special Fund, our technical assistance programs and our work directly under the Economic and Social Council are providing unique experience not only over the whole field of economic development but also specifically in such vital areas as preinvestment and the development of human resources. UNESCO is doing pioneering work in the central field of education and the World Health Organization is there to add the extra dimension of physical health. The Food and Agriculture Organization stands ready to fight hunger and to assist in all phases of a dynamic farming program. The World Bank has a magnificent record of supplying capital for power, transport, harbors, and highway development in the modernizing countries. It is also building up a corps of professional advisors in the critical field of resource planning. The International Development Association has a growing record of achievement in providing capital for the "infrastructure," for schools, hospitals, and communication systems. In addition to its traditional work in various fields the International Labour Organisation has expanded its operations and now has numerous training projects in the industrial and management fields. And since developing economies have wholly new problems in the sphere of their relations with other economies, we have the General Agreement on Tariffs and Trade to oversee their flow of trade and the International Monetary Fund to care for the imbalance and capital shortages which can arise in trade relations of such volume and complexity. I have already referred to the imminence of large-scale development of atomic power which is the special concern of the International Atomic Energy Agency. And almost at the grass-roots level, we have our UN regional commissions—in Asia, in Africa, in Europe, in Latin America—whose special responsibility it is to coordinate effort and correlate experience.

Clearly all these institutions represent a growing combination of immediate practical experience and longer-term research and analysis. And it is essential that their efforts should complement each other. Just as the developing economy itself needs to coordinate its programs and its resources and channel them through a rationally evolved country plan, so, too, it is our hope, during the Development Decade, to bring about a similar concentration of effort, close liaison, and sustained cooperative work among the agencies and thus to achieve our fundamental goal—a rate of growth among the millions of people who live in the developing world which will put them, ten years from now, on or over the threshold of self-sustaining growth.

I would like to remind you that such an effort has never been made before. The United Nations family of organizations has not hitherto proposed to itself any such broad set of goals, aiming, in a coordinated way, at human progress. And I believe that this attempt, in itself, reflects both our growing knowledge of the development process and the growing sense of urgency in dealing with the problems of development. Ten years ago, we probably did not have the experience to make such an attempt. Now the time is ripe, and by adding our efforts to each other's in a cumulative way, our assistance will be more effective, our rate of advance—in both growth and knowledge—will be speeded up, and all the while we shall be learning invaluable lessons on the types of *joint* work and effort which mankind has to undertake if our human experiment is to survive.

Shall we be able to make of this Development Decade the achievement in human solidarity we hope it will be? We must be realistic. Our agencies represent Member governments. In the last analysis, they can go no further and no faster than the nations of the world wish them to go. So it is not enough for us in the United Nations to dedicate ourselves to a Decade of Development. We have to take with us the governments to whom we are responsible and through them we have to reach out to the peoples whom these governments represent. Our Development Decade cannot ultimately succeed unless it is rooted in the wills and hearts of millions of citizens everywhere. It will not succeed unless it can win their sustained support. It will not succeed unless they see it as a great goal of human endeavor and one which they are prepared to make their own. What are our chances? What are the obstacles? How can we see to it that sustained development is among the aims upheld by "the decent opinion of mankind"?

I think our first task must be to come back to the point with which I opened my address—the availability of resources. I question whether men and women among the wealthier nations of mankind quite realize what abundance is at their disposal or how radically science and technology are transforming and expanding the resources available to man. I have spoken of the spending on arms. Let me repeat it. Something like $120 billion a year goes into the arms effort. Were we sane enough and wise enough to make progress toward disarmament—and I hope and pray we may be sooner or later—much of this vast accumulation of capital would ultimately become available to us for human betterment. The tanks could be beaten into tractors, the missiles into rockets for air transport, the metals wasted in mortar and cannon into power plants and laboratories, while the men in uniform could become the instructors, the technicians, the social workers, the artists of a new and richer life of all mankind.

But I would stress with all the vigor at my command that we do not have to wait upon disarmament. Even with armaments, many economies now operate below capacity. Many have growth rates half as great as the big expanders—who go ahead by 6 and 8 and 12 per cent a year. Even if we put the capital needed for the Development Decade at twice the level normally proposed—not at 1 per cent but at 2 per cent of annual national income among the richer states—the transfer would still represent no great or unbearable sacrifice.

The truth, the central stupendous truth, about developed economies today is that they can have—in anything but the shortest run—the kind and scale of resources they *decide* to have. If defense gobbles up $120 billion, the resources are provided and economies go on growing just the same. If it takes $40 billion to go to the moon, great nations will go to the moon, creating vast new electronics industries and millions of new jobs, products, and opportunities as they go. It is no longer resources that limit decisions. It is the decisions that make the resources. This is the fundamental, revolutionary change—perhaps the most revolutionary mankind has ever known.

For—make no mistake about it—the revolution brought by science and technology to the developed nations is a revolutionary extension in human freedom. Freedom is choice. Freedom is the ability to act. In the past, it has been wholly limited by the unavailability of so many of the means of action. I cannot feed my neighbor if there is no food and I cannot transport what food there is. Now those old and dreadful tyrannies of shortage are being overcome. A new freedom stares the wealthy nations in the face—the freedom to help or not to help their neighbors who still lie on the far side of abundance and who do not yet command the means to help themselves.

And so, at its profoundest level, the challenge of the Development Decade is a *moral* challenge. How is the new freedom of our resources to be used? Can our imagination match our abundance only when the ugly, destructive risks of war are at work? Is the only challenge we recognize the challenge of fear—in weapons, in outer space, in international rivalry? Is there no way in which the great constructive and peaceful purposes of man can so grip our heart and conscience that the spending needed to end starvation, to prevent the death of little children, to shelter the homeless and clothe the naked comes to have first priority in the purposes of the human race?

I believe our enemy here is ignorance—ignorance of the scale of our resources, ignorance of the new techniques of growth, ignorance of the possibility of a bold new crusade for humanity's physical liberation. And during this Development Decade one of our great purposes must be to end the ignorance and liberate the generous and decent instincts of mankind.

.This task cannot wait. It becomes more difficult, the longer it is postponed. The secret of getting the job done is to gain early momentum, not only to increase income but to build growth of a self-sustaining kind into the systems of the developing countries. This decade is a crucial time. If we cannot take a great step forward and bring down the number of human beings living in conditions of poverty, disease, hunger, and illiteracy, the outlook for all of us is not a happy one.

But I must end with a profession of faith. I am one of those who believe that development assistance to poorer countries is in the ultimate self-interest of the advanced countries themselves. But I would not want to rest my case mainly on that. I believe that ordinary men and women, once convinced of the ability to feed and succour and cherish their fellow men, will not rest until the task is done. The record of the human race is not all of war and horror. It has been sustained through generations by quiet compassion and all-encompassing love. Only the love has been limited by poverty. Today it can be as unlimited as its instincts dictate. There is no greater liberation than this and it is with this fundamental moral imperative that I would end and say, with the poet Auden, "We must love each other or we must die."

3. *"Education for Peace"*
Address at Carleton University

OTTAWA   MAY 25, 1962

A LITTLE WHILE AGO Carleton University honored me by conferring on me the degree of Doctor of Laws, *honoris causa,* and you have now honored me further by asking me to deliver an address to this convocation. I deeply appreciate this dual honor, as also this opportunity to say a few words on a subject with which all thinking men today are rightfully preoccupied.

I recall that the first honorary degree conferred on my distinguished predecessor, Dag Hammarskjöld, was by Carleton University in 1954. In your letter inviting me to accept the degree of Doctor of Laws, Mr. President, you mentioned that Carleton is a young and rapidly growing university in the capital of Canada. You also mentioned that my speaking on this occasion at your university in the capital of Canada would further strengthen the feelings that most Canadians have for the United Nations.

I feel therefore that it is appropriate for me not only to speak on the most crucial subject of this age, but also to address myself particularly to the younger generation. The Charter of the United Nations begins with a reference to determination of the peoples of the world "to save succeeding generations from the scourge of war" and "to unite our strength to maintain international peace and security." This preoccupation with peace is, however, not in any sense recent; it is in fact as old as recorded history. Throughout history men have fought and at the same time yearned for peace. All the great religions of the world have peace among men as their basic purpose.

At the same time I have often pondered, as I have no doubt many of you might have, on that truth which is so simply stated in the constitution of the United Nations Educational, Scientific and Cultural Organization, "since wars begin in the minds of men, it is in the minds of men that the

UN Press Release SG/1203.

defenses of peace must be constructed." Thus the teachers are the true architects of minds and the students are the true builders of peace. If the teachers instruct the younger generation in the ways of peace, not only will their work succeed, but the basic idea of peace in our time will triumph. If we lose the minds of men, no matter how hard we may propagate the idea of peace through the United Nations and through collective international action, the idea will fail, leaving us in a lawless and disorderly world, if indeed a world should continue to exist.

The burning issue today is this battle for the minds of men, and here we have the phenomenon that each of the major ideologies is convinced not only that it represents the true philosophy of peace, but that the other system is bound to fail. As a result of this preoccupation with ideology and dogma, and on the general assumption that history repeats itself, we have mistrust and fear which is the source of all our problems and the basic fact behind the cold war.

Historians have concluded that many wars in the past were inevitable, and from this they proceed to infer that, given a similar set of circumstances, wars in the future will similarly be inevitable. But nothing is more fallacious than the generally accepted assumption that history repeats itself. The plain fact is that history does *not* repeat itself.

It seems to me that historical developments are conditioned by a peculiar set of circumstances prevailing at a particular time and place. At Munich, British Prime Minister Chamberlain tried, with extraordinary patience and almost in desperation, not to repeat the events of 1914, with results which were worse. Disillusioned by the tragic failure of Mr. Chamberlain's policy of appeasement, another British prime minister, Sir Anthony Eden, eighteen years later, embarked on a tough Suez policy which ended in failure. There was a considerable body of opinion in Britain in 1956 that history would repeat itself and that a policy of appeasement would be disastrous. The thesis turned out to be false, with unfortunate consequences.

The same obsession with the past seems to me to govern the thinking of the big powers today. Russia's obsessive fear of encirclement probably has its roots in her memories of 1919, and leads her to think in terms which are no longer valid in this thermonuclear age. The United States of America, too, seems to me to be a prisoner of her past. She was rudely dragged into the center of the world stage, much against her will, by the unprovoked attack on Pearl Harbor. It seems to me that the fear that such a catastrophic surprise attack will be repeated dominates the thinking in Washington, and a surprise attack is seen in the United States as the supreme risk. This fear stems from the same assumption that history will repeat itself.

It is therefore our first task to allay, if not to remove, this fear and mistrust, and to do so we need two things. First we need to try and understand each other's point of view. We also need to realize that it is no longer true to say that there are two sides to every question; in fact, there are many sides. It is accordingly meaningless to present the problems of our complicated existence in simple terms of black and white and to overlook the infinite gradations in between, or the whole spectrum of colors outside of these two basic hues.

This need for mutual understanding is reinforced by the amazing technological progress of our time. We live in an age when men are not content to circle the globe in a matter of minutes, but are aiming literally at the stars. The fantastic developments in the methods of transportation and communication have reduced the universe to the size of a simple county. In such a world it is essential that we realize the identity of interest that binds us together and not exaggerate the issues that divide us, however big the issues and however deep the divisions. We have to think of the world as a unit in the same way that we think of a city or county as a unit whose inhabitants, as I said, have a complete identity of interest, and especially the interest of survival.

And that brings me to the next point, that the same technological progress which has shrunk the world is also responsible for the development and perfection of inventions with a capacity for destruction which no one could have dreamed possible a generation ago. Today the major powers have the power literally to extinguish all life on this planet. It is perhaps true that over any period of history, notwithstanding its catalogue of wars, nations have never waged war lightly but only when there seemed no other way out of national danger. Today the chapter of wars in the pages of history may have to be closed, not by the exercise of moral judgment that war is bad, but by sheer necessity—the imperative of self-preservation. Surely there can be no material stake so important as to lead one to undertake the total destruction of his enemy, especially if, at the same time and in the same process, his own destruction is involved.

I have said elsewhere, and I repeat, that the great danger to our world today is that peace is preserved by the precarious balance of terror, with the ever-present possibility of global nuclear war by accident.

The development of nuclear weapons, it seems fairly obvious, has added a new dimension to the concept of war. War itself loses its utility as a consequence of uncertainty. War is not just violence. It is the controlled use of violence for attainable ends. But how can anyone control a war when he has no means of knowing whether his first nuclear strike has been effective or not? The whole conduct of military operations, whether by land, sea or air, is based on getting back information on what has been achieved in the first stage of operations. All that one can be certain of with a nuclear strike is that it has killed a lot of people and destroyed a number of installations over a wide area.

But you cannot be certain that you have killed the right people and destroyed the right buildings or installations. All that is certain is that the object of the war—the defense of your own country or territory—will be foiled by the very operations undertaken to achieve it. What is called strategy will be a kind of chess game played blindfold. Quite literally, the players do not know what they are doing, for they have no previous experience of their moves. Disarmament, therefore, is not only a very desirable alternative to war, but it is the only possible alternative if the human race itself is to survive.

It is for this reason that I advocate that we discontinue the piling up of armaments, and the mistrust and fear which is as much a cause as a consequence thereof. In fact, if war is no longer desirable, one might well ask: why armaments? Why this astronomical expenditure on weapons of such terrible destruction that they are in fact stillborn because they can never be used? Let us hope that this is only a passing phase and a temporary paradox, and that before long we might see the first steps toward the halting of the arms race, beginning perhaps with nuclear disarmament.

I referred earlier to the fact that men are now aiming at the stars. I do believe that, while disarmament may come about in our time and nuclear engines of destruction may be dismantled, the exploration of space will proceed with increased momentum. Indeed, we may be on the threshold of adventures in the universe which go far beyond the navigation of uncharted seas and the discovery of new lands that our ancestors undertook only a few centuries ago. Let us hope, however, that the kind of national claims and counterclaims, colonialism and imperial wars which characterized the discovery of the earth will not mark the exploration of outer space. For this reason I attach great significance to the coordination of work in the development of outer space which is taking place within the aegis of the United Nations.

There is one other area where a better understanding of each other's point of view can mean increased prosperity for all. This is also the result of the same technological progress to which I referred earlier. I said in Copenhagen the other day that the basic fact of our time is the fact of abundance. This abundance, this embarrassment of riches in the advanced countries, exists side by side with deep unfulfilled needs elsewhere, so that the problem is not one of production, to use the language of the economists, so much as of distribution.

I am one of those who are distressed by the attempt of nations, as of human beings, to exploit each other because, truly, such exploitation is so unnecessary. I believe it is unnecessary because I do not think it is true any longer that one nation can become rich only by beggaring its neighbor. I believe that it is possible for the advanced countries, for example, to contribute to the economic development of the less advanced and in doing so to gain greater prosperity for themselves.

The concept of taxing the rich according to their capacity to pay, in order to cater to the poor according to their needs, is now well established as a simple canon of social justice in all democratic countries. It requires only a little imagination to lift this concept to a higher plane, namely the international plane, and to extend its scope from the country to the universe. Surely it is not too difficult for educated people to raise their sights a little in economic matters, as they do so easily when they turn their minds skywards into outer space.

This is the century of the common man and it is at the United Nations, through governments big and small, strong and weak, politically mature and inexperienced, that the common aspirations of mankind find a voice and an expression. Our task in the United Nations is thus to bring about a real international democracy so that the common man everywhere may live free from fear and want. But nations are made up of human beings and, as I said at the beginning, the real task is to build peace into their minds.

If this task is to be successful, then our young and educated men must have minds which are independent and objective, detached and inquiring. It quite often happens that an issue arises in a country, or even in a neighborhood, which is deemed vital to its security or prosperity, and at that point pressures develop which make it doubly important for people to preserve an independent, objective, detached, and inquiring attitude of mind.

One of the ways of preserving these attitudes is the search for the basic concepts and the underlying principles from which men of various races and creeds draw their inspiration in the pursuit of the higher life and the ultimate goal of human endeavor. Such a search is most likely to end in a sharing of our beliefs, in civilized conduct and generous behavior, the spirit of tolerance, of live and let live, and of understanding the other man's point of view. This is the essence of all great religions and I believe that it holds the key to the solution of the most pressing problems of our time.

The young men and women who are here with us today have the opportunity, and the responsibility, to help in developing and maintaining such an attitude of mind, so that we might have a world which is made up of societies whose doors are as open as their hearts and, most important of all, societies which are made up of people with open minds.

THE QUESTION OF WEST IRIAN

MAY AND JUNE

As a result of U Thant's efforts, Indonesia and the Netherlands entered into negotiations early in 1962 on the West Irian dispute. A key figure in the talks was United States diplomat Ellsworth Bunker who had been named by Thant as mediator. It was Bunker who laid the foundation for a settlement by his plan for a phased transfer of West Irian from the Netherlands to Indonesia. However, Thant himself followed the negotiations closely and intervened personally when they broke down. The following exchange of messages helped bring about a resumption of the talks and the eventual agreement on August 15, 1962 (p. 194).

---

1. Text of Identical Cables to the Prime Minister of the Netherlands and the President of Indonesia

NEW YORK   MAY 23, 1962

In view of the serious developments during the past few days, I urgently appeal to Your Excellency to resume urgently the discussions which had been undertaken through the good offices of Ambassador [Ellsworth] Bunker. I am certain that you will agree with me that it would be most regrettable if the situation were allowed to deteriorate further, particularly as it is my firm belief that the question is capable of an acceptable solution at an early date, on the basis of the proposals already communicated to Your Excellency by Ambassador Bunker. I would be most grateful for very urgent consideration of this appeal by Your Excellency and for an early reply.

UN Press Release SG/1204.

2. Text of Identical Cables to Prime Minister de Quay and President Sukarno

NEW YORK   MAY 29, 1962

I AM MOST GRATEFUL to Your Excellency for responding to my appeal to resume negotiations on the basis of the Bunker proposals. I would now urgently appeal to Your Excellency to order the immediate ending of all hostilities in West New Guinea so that the negotiations on the future of the territory on the basis of the Bunker proposals may take place under the most favorable conditions. I sincerely hope that, in view of the excellent chances for a peaceful settlement of the problem, this appeal will be heeded.

UN Press Release SG/1209.

3. Cable to President Sukarno

NEW YORK   JUNE 17, 1962

I WISH TO REFER to my cable to Your Excellency dated June 6, 1962. I have since been informed by the permanent representative of the Netherlands that his government accept in principle the proposals of Ambassador Bunker. In the circumstances, I hope there will be no further delay in the resumption of negotiations between the representatives of the two governments under the auspices of Ambassador Bunker.

I would reiterate the hope that there could be an ending of hostilities on both sides once the negotiations have been resumed. I am publishing the contents of this cable immediately in view of the public interest in this matter.

UN Press Release SG/1227.

4. *Cable from President Sukarno*

JUNE 20, 1962

I THANK YOU for your message of June 17, 1962. I certainly regard the acceptance of the Bunker proposals in principle as has been conveyed to Your Excellency by the permanent representative of the Netherlands government as a step forward toward the resumption of negotiations between the Netherlands and Indonesia.

In order to avoid any misunderstanding between Your Excellency and my government, I would stress that "the acceptance of the principles of the Bunker proposals" as we have phrased it and the wording conveyed to you by the permanent representative of the Netherlands, "the acceptance of the Bunker proposals in principle," should stipulate the sequence of actions constituting the solution of the West Irian problem.

This means that the free choice for the West Irian people will be executed after transfer of administration of West Irian to Indonesia.

I hope Your Excellency will excuse me, if I am rather insistent to get this basic interpretation of the Bunker proposals. This is based upon our experiences with so many agreements we had with the Netherlands in the past which after debate in the Netherlands Parliament became modified from their original interpretation.

Next to the communication I received from Your Excellency, may I draw your attention to press reports from which we learned about the official statements issued in the Netherlands as a reaction to your message. The spokesman of the Government Information Service in the Netherlands stated that "the Netherlands Government is still prepared to resume negotiations on the basis of the proposals." Since the debate in Parliament about the West Irian issue, "there has been no change in the attitude of the Netherlands Government." This statement on Sunday, June 17, has been followed by a statement of the spokesman of the Netherlands Ministry of Foreign Affairs: "Minister Luns has instructed his

UN Press Release SG/1228.

permanent representative of the Netherlands to the United Nations, Mr. Schurmann, to convey the message to the Acting Secretary-General that the Netherlands Government does not see any difference in the phrases used by the Netherlands and Indonesia for the preparation of the discussions of the Bunker proposals."

I have instructed Ambassador Sukardjo Wirjopranoto to get further clarifications of the basic understanding of the principles of the Bunker proposals we should arrive at before the final decision for an early resumption of talks. Your Excellency can rest assured about my full cooperation and support in your efforts for an early settlement of the West Irian issue.

5. *Cable to President Sukarno*

NEW YORK   JUNE 20, 1962

I HAVE THE HONOR to acknowledge receipt of your message of June 20. My understanding of the Bunker proposals is that they constitute a phased operation under which, as outlined in their third paragraph, by the end of the second year full administrative control will be transferred to Indonesia and under which, as indicated in their fourth paragraph, at a certain date still to be determined, arrangements will be made by Indonesia, with the assistance and participation of the Acting Secretary-General of the United Nations and UN personnel, to give the people of the territory the opportunity "to exercise freedom of choice."

The Government of the Netherlands, having signified their acceptance of the Bunker proposals, without any qualification or reservation, have, in my judgment, accepted the principle of the phased operations as envisaged in the Bunker proposals and I therefore have the honor to reply to your inquiry in the affirmative.

UN Press Release SG/1229.

6. *Exchange of Messages with President Sukarno*

(a) Cable from President Sukarno, June 27, 1962

I thank you very much for your message of June 26. I am very gratified for your reply in the affirmative to my inquiry as contained in my message of June 20. The understanding between us has been established about the phased operation as contained in the Bunker proposals, the transfer of administration to Indonesia, followed after so many years by the arrangement made by Indonesia, with the assistance and participation of the Secretary-General and the United Nations to give the people of the territory of West Irian the opportunity to exercise freedom of choice.

In fact, upon this understanding I do not see any reason for further delay in the resumption of negotiation. On the other hand, to be frank, even up till now it is not yet clear to me about the public attitude of the Netherlands government.

Whereas you mentioned in your message, the Netherlands government having signified their acceptance of the Bunker proposal without any qualification or reservation, in your judgment, implying the acceptance of the phased operation envisaged in the Bunker proposal, there has been no official public confirmation yet from the Netherlands government regarding this interpretation. On the contrary the spokesman of the Ministry of Interior in The Hague said on June 25 that "Secretary Bot[1] had stated only that the Netherlands government are prepared to talk on the Bunker plan without any reserves."

Thus, the statement made earlier by Secretary Bot whilst in Washington to the effect that the Netherlands government has accepted the Bunker proposal without any reservation or qualification, has been refuted by the Netherlands government in The Hague.

UN Press Release SG/1233.

[1] T. H. Bot, Secretary of State for New Guinea Affairs in the Netherlands Ministry of the Interior.

I sincerely hope that the Netherlands government will give its public affirmation to the content of your message you sent to me on June 21, so that the negotiation can be resumed soon.

(b) Cable from the Acting Secretary-General, June 28, 1962

I have the honor to acknowledge receipt of your message of June 27, the contents of which I conveyed to the permanent representative of the Netherlands that very same day.

Today I received from Ambassador Schurmann a reply confirming my interpretation as follows: "The Netherlands government confirms once more that, as was already apparent from its previous statements, it accepts the sequence of events as laid down in the Bunker proposals on condition that it will receive, equally in accordance with the Bunker proposals, adequate conditions and guarantees for the rights and interests of the Papuans."

Regarding the statement by a spokesman of the Netherlands Ministry of the Interior, mentioned in your telegram, the permanent representative of the Netherlands was authorized to inform me that no such statement exists and that neither the aforementioned ministry nor any other government authority had made such a statement.

In view of the above, I feel it appropriate to reiterate my request, made to Your Excellency earlier this month, to expedite the designation of your plenipotentiary for the discussions envisaged.

TWO SPEECHES ON NEW NATIONS

AS BURMA'S PERMANENT REPRESENTATIVE, U Thant was known for his militant stand against colonialism. His own country had won its independence only in 1948, nine years before he came to the United Nations. It was not surprising, therefore, that on many occasions he undertook the task of interpreting the role of the new states and defending them against critics. He dealt with several aspects of this subject in speeches at Williams College on June 8, 1962, and at the Lord Mayor's luncheon in London on July 6. In the Williams College speech he noted the impact of the newly emerged states on the United Nations and the apprehensions of some older countries that the Afro-Asians were "now running the United Nations, in fact, running away with it." One of the results, he said, was talk about weighted voting. He spoke out strongly against such proposals, as he was to do on other occasions. In the London speech he called for patience and understanding in appraising the lack of parliamentary government in many Asian and African countries. It would be a mistake, he stated, to expect these countries to have the same type of political institutions as those prevailing in the United Kingdom. He expressed the belief that powerful nationalist movements would control many of the new governments without any serious challenge. "The notion that democracy requires the existence of an organized opposition to the government of the day is not valid," he said. "Democracy requires only freedom for opposition, not necessarily its organized existence."

1. *"The United Nations and the Birth of New Nations" Address at Williams College*

WILLIAMSTOWN, MASSACHUSETTS   JUNE 10, 1962

I AM MOST GRATEFUL to Williams College for honoring me with the degree of Doctor of Laws *honoris causa* and also for giving me this opportunity to say a few words at the end of the commencement exercise.

UN Press Release SG/1216, June 8, 1962.

Only three days ago the General Assembly of the United Nations resumed its sixteenth session in order to deal with the question of Ruanda-Urundi and I feel that it might be appropriate for me to say a few words on this occasion on the role of this world organization in bringing new nations into being.

The principle of equal rights and self-determination of peoples is one of the basic principles and purposes of the Charter. The Charter contemplates that non-self-governing territories may gradually emerge as full members of the international community, and has emphasized that those administrations in charge of non-self-governing territories should "recognize the principle that the interests of the inhabitants of these territories are paramount, and accept as a sacred trust the obligation to promote to the utmost . . . the well-being of the inhabitants of these territories and to this end . . . to develop self-government . . . and to assist them in the progressive development of their free political institutions. . . ."

In addition, as you are no doubt aware, the United Nations established, under its own authority, an international trusteeship system with the basic objective of promoting "the political, economic, social, and educational advancement of the inhabitants of the trust territories and their progressive development toward self-government or independence as may be appropriate. . . ."

As a result of this preoccupation by the United Nations with the attainment of self-government by non-self-governing and trust territories, we have seen a remarkable expansion of the membership of the United Nations during its history of sixteen years. Thus, the membership of the United Nations, which was fifty-five in 1946, stands today at the figure of 104, with the prospect of at least five or six new Members joining us before the end of the year.

In this connection I would like to recall that my own country, Burma, emerged as an independent and sovereign state only in January 1948 and became a Member of the United Nations in the same year. The 1950s may well be called the decade of Asia because the number of Asian countries who were Members of the United Nations at the beginning of the decade was nine and the number at the end of the decade was fifteen. Similarly the 1960s will surely go down in history as the decade of Africa, because, of the twenty-two new Members who have joined the United Nations since January 1, 1960, nineteen are from the African continent and it also seems fairly clear that in the future the majority of our new Members will be African states.

I could, of course, be more specific and describe in detail the role of the United Nations in the birth of new nations, but the facts are too well known to need repetition. It is mainly in the field of trusteeship that the United Nations has direct responsibility, and a number of trust territories which were former mandates of the League of Nations have been guided toward independence under the watchful eyes of the Trusteeship Council and the General Assembly.

Ruanda-Urundi is the latest instance of a trust territory gradually emerging toward independence and before long we will probably have two new independent nations born out of this trust territory.

In addition to such direct assistance, the debates in the General Assembly and in the Trusteeship Council have generally created a climate which is favorable to the emergence of independent nations, after long periods of colonial rule. I am almost certain that, without the pressure of international public opinion which was thus created and developed, many of these newly independent countries might still be only on the road to self-government and would not have arrived at nationhood so quickly. This process will, I am sure, continue.

While on this subject I would like to refer very briefly to certain aspects of colonialism. A great debate has been going on for decades as to whether the imperialist method has morally justified itself: whether the impact of Western civilization has brought more blessings than disadvantages to the subject peoples. The colonial record can claim, with some justification, to have controlled or eliminated some of the worst aspects of primitive life in certain parts of the world. It has introduced hospitals and better sanitation. It has attempted to combat ignorance as well as disease. It has brought improved methods of transport and communication. Many other material accomplishments can be enumerated.

Nevertheless, against these substantial benefits must be reckoned many features and tendencies which have counteracted these progressive influences. Chief among them is the fact that, in the past at any rate, the primary motive of the colonial power in developing the natural resources of a colony was its own commercial profit. Consequently, the greater part of the wealth obtained from the colony went into the pockets of the colonial investors. Further, the colonies remained essentially as primary producers, with little industrial development.

There is still another disturbing feature of colonialism. Whatever advantages may have been gained by native societies consequent on the impact of a new civilization, they were offset by the fact that the colonizers often kept themselves aloof from native society. Very few of them bothered to learn the language of the people, or made a real effort to understand the indigenous culture. Wherever it existed, this aloofness and cultural exclusiveness created resentment, particularly in the minds of the educated subject peoples.

One very significant feature of independence movements is that, when independence is too long delayed, a mood of frustration and desperation sets in, and then some extreme forces come to the surface and gain the upper hand. This certainly does not help the cause of healing old wounds, or bridging the gulf between the past and the future. The role of the United Nations therefore should be not only to help expedite the emergence of new nations, but also to create conditions which will help establish friendly relations between the new nations and their former masters as also with other fellow Members of the world organization.

While the United Nations can look back with satisfaction on the important role it has played in bringing these new nations into being, this historic process has had important effects on the structure and functions of the world organization. In the first place the emergence of these new countries has placed an additional responsibility on the United Nations in regard to their economic development. These countries, having become masters in their own house, have had to face serious economic problems and have turned for assistance to the United Nations and the international community. It is a heartening feature that in the last decade there has been a greatly increased sense of responsibility on the part of the international community and, especially, the economically advanced countries. During this decade we have witnessed a tremendous increase in the volume of international aid, some of it channeled through such multilateral institutions as the United Nations and its family of specialized agencies including the International Bank, but most of it has been bilateral. Recently the General Assembly adopted resolutions calling upon the advanced countries to set aside 1 per cent of their national income for the economic advancement of the less developed countries. The sixteenth session of the General Assembly also decided to designate the next ten years as the United Nations Development Decade and you will hear a great deal more about what we plan to do to assist the less developed countries in stepping up their economic development at the summer session of the Economic and Social Council.

Apart from the increase of such constructive activity, especially in the economic and social field, the United Nations has been called upon to assume tremendous political responsibilities as a result of the birth of some of these new nations. I have in mind particularly the Congo, which has become one of our most important operations during the last two years. The responsibilities entrusted to the United Nations in regard to the Congo, beginning with the Security Council resolutions in July 1960, were completely novel besides being extremely onerous.

While this is not the occasion for me to deal at any length with the Congo problem, I think it will be generally conceded that the United Nations has played a significant part in preserving the sovereignty, independence, unity, and territorial integrity of this new republic located in the very heart of Africa. The Congo is one of the hotly debated issues both within and outside the United Nations and it occupies a great deal of my time and energies, as also that of my colleagues. To those who are dissatisfied with the slow pace of progress in the Congo I would like to say only this: let us just look at the Congo picture today, with the possibility of the peaceful integration of the last of the secessionist provinces, and compare it with the situation this time last year, when practically two-thirds of the country was outside the control of the Central Government and in fact we had no legitimate Central Government to deal with. Today we have a legally constituted Central Government under the able leadership of Prime Minister Adoula, and we have only one province out of six still striving to maintain some form of separate identity. But it is a matter for congratulation that, during the last twenty-two months, not one Member government of the United Nations has recognized this secessionist state, and there are now good prospects that this secession will be ended by peaceful negotiation between the provincial president and the prime minister.

One consequence, of course, of the emergence of these new countries, especially from Africa and Asia, has been that the United Nations has made greater progress toward universality during the last decade than would have been considered possible ten years ago. This, I am sure you will agree, is a good development. At the same time it has led to all kinds of complaints that the Afro-Asians are now running the United Nations, in fact, running away with it; and there are certain proposals for weighted voting. It seems strange to me that some of these suggestions about weighted voting come from countries which in their own domestic politics attach the greatest importance to democratic principles including the principle of one vote per adult human being, be he rich or poor, strong or weak, learned or ignorant.

It also seems strange that these critics of the United Nations should ignore one of the fundamental principles of the Charter, which states that "the Organization is based on the principle of the sovereign equality of all its Members" as also the principle of "equal rights of nations, large and small." I hope that this criticism of the United Nations is only a passing phase and before long even the critics will realize that the interests of humanity are best served by a universal organization practicing the true principles of democracy on the international plane.

2. From Speech at Lord Mayor's Luncheon

LONDON   JULY 6, 1962

. . . . THE IMPACT of Western civilization on the rest of the world has brought a mixture of blessings and evils. One of the great blessings brought to Asia and Africa by Britain is education in parliamentary democracy. In your country, Parliament has enjoyed a recorded history for more than six centuries. Of course, its origin springs from traditions of far greater antiquity. It has changed much and is always changing. It has reached its present powerful and independent position after a long series of struggles, setbacks, and sometimes open violence.

It is not perhaps surprising that, so far, little advance has been made in parliamentary democracy in many Asian and African countries. The popular theory that every community that is struggling toward political independence must immediately assume the robes of parliamentary democracy has been exploded in many parts of the world. Our traditional belief in the universal applicability of representative government is likely to be put to severe strain for some time to come.

It is a mistake to assume that the political institutions and forms of democracy in most of the newly independent countries will be of the same type as those prevailing in Britain, or that there will necessarily be two main parties competing against each other for the votes of the people. The notion that democracy requires the existence of an organized opposi-

UN Press Release SG/1240.

tion to the government of the day is not valid. Democracy requires only freedom for opposition, not necessarily its organized existence.

In many newly independent countries, it is most unlikely that there will be a two-party system for many years to come. The nationalist movements are powerful indeed. They will control governments without there being any effective challenge to them from within. And any challenge from the outside would only strengthen them. As was the case in many European countries, it might take some time before it would be possible for political opposition to be expressed in constitutional forms. Moreover, it is worth bearing in mind that the democratic system of government, though most desirable, is perhaps the most difficult form of government to operate.

It is most important that countries like Britain, which have successfully developed this form of government, and which have done so much to establish it in other lands, should show patience and understanding over the difficulties which the newly emerging countries will undoubtedly encounter in developing their political systems along democratic lines.

The transformation of an empire into a commonwealth of free nations has been one of the most inspiring developments in human history. But the world's need for inspiration is not exhausted, and I do not doubt that the worldwide family of free nations which must come into being if we are not to perish, will owe much to the political wisdom, to the creative imagination and to the practical helpfulness of the British people.

THE DEVELOPMENT DECADE

THE UNITED NATIONS Development Decade, later known as the First Development Decade, coincided roughly with U Thant's ten years in office. As mentioned previously (p. 102), it was President Kennedy who originated the idea in a speech before the General Assembly on September 25, 1961. On December 19, six weeks after Thant became Acting Secretary-General, the Assembly unanimously endorsed the suggestion and requested him to "develop proposals for the intensification of action in the fields of economic and social development" and to present them to the Economic and Social Council at its thirty-fourth session.

It was obvious from the detailed specifications laid down in the resolution that a comprehensive plan was expected. He was given a list of ten questions to look into and, further, he was asked to take into account the views of governments and international agencies in making his recommendations. Even with the full machinery of the United Nations at his command, it was a Herculean task to turn out the required report in the six months available.

The Acting Secretary-General completed the report on time, flew to Geneva and presented it personally in a major speech on July 9, 1962, opening the Economic and Social Council's debate on the subject. The voluminous document, circulated to members of the Council, was entitled "The United Nations Development Decade: Proposals for Action." Much of the subsequent thinking in the Council and the General Assembly was strongly influenced by the Acting Secretary-General's recommendations.

Thant based his proposals for action on his conviction that the psychological climate was favorable for a concerted attack on the problem of underdevelopment and on his belief that the United Nations, even with its modest resources, was a natural agency to focus international efforts on the problem. He proposed a number of priority objectives. One was to help developing countries formulate sound development plans. Another was to assist them in mobilizing their national resources and still another was to help in creating sources of supplementary external aid. There were others, such as improving the quality of the labor force by assisting in vocational education and technical training. The report also contained proposals for action in the fields of food and agriculture, trade, housing, health, transport, communications, and science and technology.

"The main economic objective for the decade," Thant said in the foreword to the report (p. 141), "is to create conditions in which the national incomes of the developing countries not only will be increasing by 5 per cent yearly by 1970, but will also continue to expand at this annual rate thereafter. If this can be done, and if the population of the developing countries continues to rise at its present rate of 2 to 2-½ per cent yearly, personal living standards can be doubled within twenty-five to thirty years."

The proposals for action were discussed for almost a month by the Economic and Social Council and also came before the General Assembly at its seventeenth session. Both bodies expressed appreciation for the work done by Acting Secretary-General and both called on him to carry out follow-up studies and reports. The Council outlined a number of objectives, based on his report, and asked him, with the cooperation of the regional economic commissions and other United Nations agencies, to draft "a program consisting of detailed phased proposals of action" and to submit a progress report covering achievements up to March 31, 1963. The Assembly requested Thant to study the desirability and feasibility of establishing a UN institute for training of personnel for developing countries. This idea had been advanced by the Acting Secretary-General in his proposals for action. The requested study resulted in the creation by the eighteenth session of the Assembly of the United Nations Institute for Training and Research, which since then has trained thousands of personnel from developing countries for administrative, diplomatic, and operational assignments and has conducted scores of seminars to give advanced or specialized training for persons already serving in such posts.

---

1. Foreword to the United Nations Development Decade: Proposals for Action

JUNE 1962

IT IS AN extraordinary fact that at a time when affluence is beginning to be the condition, or at least the potential condition, of whole countries and regions rather than of a few favored individuals, and when scientific feats are becoming possible which beggar mankind's wildest dreams of the past, more people in the world are suffering from hunger and want than ever before. Such a situation is so intolerable and so contrary to the best interests of all nations that it should arouse determination, on the part of advanced and developing countries alike, to bring it to an end. The United Nations has recognized the need for action by designating the current decade as the United Nations Development Decade. We can say with confidence that the means can be found if only there is the will to achieve the end.

The United Nations Development Decade: Proposals for Action (United Nations publication, Sales No. 62.II. B.2).

At the opening of the United Nations Development Decade, we are beginning to understand the real aims of development and the nature of the development process. We are learning that development concerns not only man's material needs, but also the improvement of the social conditions of his life and his broad human aspirations. Development is not just economic growth, it is growth plus change. As our understanding of development deepens, it may prove possible, in the developing countries, to compress stages of growth through which the developed countries have passed. It may also be necessary to examine afresh the methods by which the goals of development may be attained.

During the past decade we have not only gained greatly in understanding of the development process and what it requires, but we have also achieved much. In particular, we have now at our disposal such instruments of effective action as the International Bank and the International Monetary Fund (with their newly strengthened resources), the International Development Association and the International Finance Corporation, the United Nations Special Fund, the Expanded Programme of Technical Assistance, special programmes such as the World Food Programme and the United Nations Children's Fund, and the regular programmes of the various United Nations agencies and of the United Nations itself. The resources of these various channels of proven effectiveness should be strengthened as an essential precondition for the success of the development decade. As new problems and new opportunities emerge, the instruments will evolve with them, as has been the case in the past.

The United Nations itself, quite apart from its own operational activities, has also proved its value as an international forum for discussion. A number of the developments, broadly described in chapter I, following, which have helped to create the conditions for the launching of the development decade, had their origin in discussions and in the gradual change of attitudes made possible by the exchange and confrontation of views in United Nations organs.

The basic problem in the present situation is to find ways in which the express desire of the advanced countries to help the developing countries can be translated into effective action. New methods of technical cooperation, added to those already well tried, will have to be found to take full advantage of the new economic and technological possibilities which have emerged in recent years.

The main economic objective for the decade is to create conditions in which the national incomes of the developing countries not only will be increasing by 5 per cent yearly by 1970, but will also continue to expand at this annual rate thereafter. If this can be done, and if the population of the developing countries continues to rise at its present rate of 2 to 2-½ per cent yearly, personal living standards can be doubled within twenty-five to thirty years. If, however, the growth of population should be even more rapid by the end of the decade than it is now—and there are indications that in a number of countries the annual rate of increase is already 3 per cent or higher—it will take correspondingly longer to double living standards.

This objective for 1970 is within our reach, given a greater willingness among both the developing and the advanced countries to make the efforts and sacrifices required. And yet it is ambitious, for if achieved it would open up for a significant number of underdeveloped countries the prospect of a real improvement in their conditions of life. In particular, it offers hope for the younger generation of today.

A better understanding of the nature of development has resulted in the clarification of a number of issues as being irrelevant to the fundamental problems of development; for example, the demarcation of the public and private sectors in economic life, agricultural development *versus* industrial development, and education *versus* vocational training. There has perhaps been less progress in recognizing the nature of the relationship between aid policies and trade policies, but even here there are signs that a more enlightened view may be making headway.

Meanwhile, there has been increasing appreciation of the need for a number of new approaches. These include:

1. The concept of national planning—for social as well as for economic development. This is central to all the proposals for intensified action by the United Nations system during the development decade outlined in this report. Former objections to planning, based largely on a misunderstanding of the role envisaged for the private sector in most development plans, have died away. It is now generally appreciated that the purpose of a development plan is to provide a programme of action for the achievement of targets based on realistic studies of the resources available. Planning is proving to be a potent tool for the mobilization of existing and latent resources—human and material, public and private, domestic and external—available to countries for the achievement of their development aims. It has been shown that vigorous efforts are more likely to result if national and sectoral objectives are defined and translated into action programmes.

2. There is now greater insight into the importance of the human factor in development, and the urgent need to mobilize human resources. Economic growth in the advanced countries appears to be attributable in larger part than was previously supposed to human skills rather than to capital. Moreover, the widening of man's horizons through education and training, and the lifting of his vitality through better health, are not only essential preconditions for development, they are also among its major objectives. It is estimated that the total number of trained people in the developing countries must be increased by at least 10 per cent a year if the other objectives of the decade are to be achieved.

3. One of the most serious problems facing the developing countries is increasing underemployment and unemployment. This increase is not confined to countries already experiencing population pressures, although rapidly rising population is undoubtedly a major aggravating factor. Far-reaching action will be required if the fruits of economic progress are to benefit all the inhabitants of the world.

4. The disappointing foreign trade record of the developing countries is due in part to obstacles hindering the entry of their products into industrial markets, and in part to the fact that production of many primary commodities has grown more rapidly than demand for them. It is appreciated that "disruptive competition" from low-income countries may be felt by established industries in high-income countries. Yet, precisely because they are so advanced, the high-income countries should be able to alleviate any hardships without shifting the burden of adjustment to the developing countries by restricting the latter's export markets. A related problem to be solved is that of stabilizing the international commodity markets on which developing countries depend so heavily. Progress could certainly be made if the main industrial countries were to devote as much attention to promoting trade as to dispensing aid.

5. The acceptance of the principle of capital assistance to developing countries is one of the most striking expressions of international solidarity as well as enlightened self-interest. If such assistance increases to, and maintains, a level of 1 per cent of the national incomes of the advanced countries during the development decade, as suggested by the General Assembly, this will represent yet another essential contribution to the success of the decade. At the same time, there is a need for pragmatism and flexibility in determining the forms of capital flows and aid, in rela-

tion both to the needs of the developing countries and to the shifting balance-of-payments position of assisting countries.

6. Toward the end of the fifties the importance of laying an adequate groundwork for large-scale investment programmes came to be widely recognized. Many developing countries lack any detailed knowledge of their resources. However, even where potential investment opportunities can be identified, it may be impossible to implement them in the absence of one or more of the necessary factors of production—labor, capital, and entrepreneurial and technical skills. Within the United Nations, the Special Fund has concentrated on preinvestment work, paying special attention to surveys and feasibility studies of natural resources, technical and vocational training, and the establishment of institutions for applied research. It is estimated that total expenditure on preinvestment work must rise to a level of about $1 billion a year by 1970, if the objectives of the decade are to be reached. This is about double the present rate of expenditure.

7. A crucial area for intensified preinvestment activity is the surveying and development of natural resources, including water, minerals, and power. In the development of water resources, in particular, the United Nations system may have a significant part to play. Nearly all the world's great rivers flow through several countries, and their development is a problem requiring regional and international cooperation.

8. The potentialities of modern technology and new methods of research and development for attacking the problems of the developing countries are as yet only dimly perceived. Since the Second World War it has become clear that new techniques permit the solution of most scientific and technical problems once they are correctly posed. However, too little effort has been directed toward posing or solving the problems of the developing countries, although many of them would appear to present no insuperable difficulties; for example, the problems involved in developing a sturdy piece of mechanical equipment which can be kept running with very little maintenance should be less than those involved in designing and launching a permanently operating space satellite. It also seems desirable to stimulate research on the social problems of developing countries entering upon a period of rapid social change.

9. If the skills of the advanced countries are to be successfully adapted to the problems and conditions of the developing countries, the former must be willing and able to make available the necessary resources of skilled personnel. Indeed, it may be that the shortage of such highly skilled personnel, rather than a shortage of material resources or finance,

will be the greatest obstacle to action in the development decade unless new steps are taken. Technical cooperation field workers or field teams should no longer be isolated but work in close contact with those institutions in the advanced countries which have the most knowledge of the problems they will encounter. Ways must also be found for the foreign experts to participate in setting up institutions which will take over and carry forward their work when they leave.

The success of the United Nations Development Decade in achieving its objectives will depend in large part on the application of such new approaches. Precisely because they are new, all their implications cannot yet be fully seen. They may be expected to change many existing attitudes and approaches.

The report which follows contains a number of suggestions for the intensification of the existing activities of the United Nations system, together with proposals for new departures. These range over a wide area of development problems. But an attempt has been made, in every case, to identify those areas in which action by the United Nations system might be expected to have the maximum leverage effect on development as a whole, and the maximum linkage effect in promoting advances in other sectors.

U THANT
Acting Secretary-General

2. Statement in the Economic and Social Council Opening the Debate on the United Nations Development Decade

GENEVA   JULY 9, 1962

IT IS FOR ME a privilege to attend this summer session of the Economic and Social Council—a privilege enhanced by the occasion to present to you my proposals for the United Nations Development Decade.

UN Press Release SG/1263, July 16, 1962. The summary record is given in Economic and Social Council Official Records, Thirty-fourth Session, 1214th plenary meeting.

This question is indeed more than a broad agenda item. It is, I believe, a program of such significance that, if dealt with appropriately, with vision and resolution, it might make the thirty-fourth session of the Council a historic one.

Since the adoption of the resolution by the General Assembly last winter, the United Nations Development Decade has been a major preoccupation in our minds. It has prompted much reflection and soul-searching among us and two months ago I could not refrain from addressing Danish students on this theme, during my visit to Copenhagen (pp. 111–19). I hope that I shall be forgiven if, in opening your debate on the Decade, I go back to some of the thoughts which I then expressed. This hope rests on the perhaps daring assumption that, when it comes to sharing deep convictions on fundamental issues, the language spoken to government representatives need not be altogether different from that used in addressing a nonofficial audience.

The basic fact, the basic circumstance, which warrants and indeed demands a bold, world-wide approach to enconomic and social development, is the now demonstrated possibility for mankind at large to create resources rather than depend on them. Endowed as our planet is, and able to take advantage of its riches as we have become, it is no longer resources that limit decisions. It is decisions that make resources, just as, in an economy where growth has acquired enough impetus, acceleration of such growth becomes mainly a matter of effective demand.

As I am not a professional economist, I might perhaps be candid about that notion of effective demand. It evokes the illustration of Keynesian theories inviting us to reflect on the possible stimulating effects on a depressed economy of a mobilization of workers for burying empty cans which could then be dug out, or any other modern version of Penelope's web. I wonder what Lord Keynes would say if he lived in our world of today, in which 1.5 billion people suffering from hunger or malnutrition have become pressingly vocal in international forums. Across frontiers he would see, on the one hand, demand for more necessities and greater opportunities; on the other hand, competition for more and deadlier weapons, which I can only conceive as a highly dangerous substitute for the empty can exercise.

In this respect, it is good, and significant of the United Nations' approach, that at the time when the Economic and Social Council is breaking new ground for a momentous long-term program of economic and social development, it is also seized for the first time with the problem of economic and social consequences of disarmament. This may be historically a coincidence, but we should turn it into an opportunity for a broader and deeper reflection on the major problems of our day. Armaments—or disarmament—are a major determinant of the pace, nature, and scope of economic and social progress, and they bear in more than one way on the debate which is opening today. At the threshold of the 1960s it is of great importance that a report of the quality of that which is before you should do justice in a decisive way to an alleged and invidious relationship between armaments and prosperity, which may be lingering in the minds of many. By stating categorically, and on the basis of a unanimous finding, that the disappearance of military budgets should not result in the collapse, nor even a serious dislocation of the economies of the industrialized countries, the experts have strengthened our belief that the trend toward increasing armaments is not irreversible and that disarmament, our only durable insurance against the risk of annihilation, is not beyond the reach of the international community. The experts have at the same time drawn attention to the fact, very relevant to this debate on a decade of development, that action should be planned ahead, and preparations made in the economic and social field, for the advent of disarmament. And it is good that we can have confidence that this is being done.

At the same time, I should like to emphasize my conviction that we cannot wait upon disarmament. Mobilizing resources for economic and social progress is an effort which can and must go forward, whatever happens to military budgets. If the latter were to dwindle or disappear in a near future, as we so keenly hope, the less developed world should, of course, share the savings with the taxpayers of the big powers and additional billions would be available to speed up development all over the world. But let us not make fuller international cooperation contingent upon a particular manifestation of it, however crucial the latter may be.

Is our imagination going to be spurred only by the fear of an international rivalry? Or will the idea that man can change and better his lot become the most powerful driving force of mankind in this century? The latter proposition is the one which we must make come true. What would be the significance, otherwise, of the current process of decolonization bringing to independence so many countries which immediately acquire membership in the Organization by unanimous vote? Political freedom can only render more intolerable the coexistence between the rich and the poor, in the international context just as in any national one.

It is gratifying to see that financial and technical assistance from high-income to low-income countries have become an accepted feature of the international economy, with former colonial powers often accounting for a decisive share in the foreign financial and human resources placed at the disposal of the newly independent countries. But the problem of increasing external assistance and of maximizing its effectiveness becomes every day more acute. In a world shrunken by the progress of communication media, the pressure of underprivileged citizens against national inequalities in levels of living becomes the impatience of entire populations with subnormal standards of nutrition, shelter, education, and medical care while billions are spent on, say, space research. I say this because, if everybody is not assured a share in the benefits of the scientific progress which leads us into space, if the fast-growing investment capital and technical know-how which are applied to push further the present boundaries of the kingdom of man are not also fully used to bring better life to all within such boundaries, then the fate of mankind itself is in serious jeopardy. And while, on the plane of tactics, this explosive situation might still allow the interplay of political considerations, on the plane of global strategy it has come to assume the proportions of a compelling moral challenge, in terms of human dignity and human kinship.

It is now a recognized fact that, with present population trends, the widening of the gap between affluent societies and low-income economies can only be countered by self-sustaining and accelerated growth in the latter. To achieve such growth in minimum time, efforts must, of course, proceed in the most coherent manner toward predetermined objectives. In recent years, the will to get more for more people at a fast pace has led governments to frame their major lines of action in the economic and social field in development plans and today we see the emergence of this approach on the international scene.

In 1960, the General Assembly requested industrialized countries to devote at least 1 per cent of their global national product to international aid. In 1961, it has set as a target a 5 per cent annual rate of growth in the aggregate national income of less developed countries. Those figures are very modest ones, and purely indicative of a desirable minimum. They evidence, however, a definite desire to project, to organize and phase the work in relation to clearly defined and quantified targets—an approach typical of that adopted by an increasing number of governments for their national economies.

The United Nations Development Decade is a pressing invitation to Member governments to increase their social and economic investments in a most forward-looking, purposeful, cooperative and integrated fashion. But it is also, and as much, a development plan for the United Nations family of organizations. In my report, a prospective presentation has been attempted which aims at determining how the current efforts of our organizations—as distinct from the sum of those of their members—could best be pursued and stepped up for a greater effectiveness of our response to the development challenge. For the numerous fields of activity and many areas of work in which projects have been undertaken under the aegis of the United Nations family, indications are given on the ways in which the secretariats concerned see a possibility to increase their catalytic role and usefulness to the community of nations, on the basis of past experience and present expectations.

The analogy with planning exercises conducted in national contexts is not yet carried very far, as attempts to detail our proposals in quantitative terms encounter obvious limitations at this stage. We have endeavored to determine targets, however. Thus, we envisage that the total resources available for United Nations programs in the field of preinvestment and technical cooperation, including Special Fund activities (but leaving aside extraordinary undertakings such as our civilian operations in the Congo) should grow at a minimum yearly rate of $25 million, from the level of $150 million for the year 1962—a level which, we must note, is not yet reached.

One of our most important undertakings in this regard is the United Nations Conference on Science and Technology to be held early in 1963. A glance at the agenda of the Conference evokes the breadth and span of man's imagination and inventiveness which have brought us from subsistence economy to the atomic age. But as we now enter the space age, while entire nations still have to make their industrial revolution, the real challenge for that imagination and inventiveness is to render advanced theory and modern practices valid and effective in less developed contexts. The purpose of the Conference is precisely to assess possibilities and stimulate efforts in that direction. The confrontations, discussions and exchanges which are to take place in these very halls among scientists and experts from many countries at all stages of development should have far-reaching effects.

In sharing ideas and experience about specific development problems, industrialized countries may receive from less-developed ones as much as they will give to them. Also, less-developed countries will learn one from another in the true spirit of United Nations cooperation, which is characterized by an increasing proportion of expert and training services provided to less-developed countries by countries which are themselves underdeveloped. The work of the Conference and the dissemination of its documents should open up new vistas for investment projects. They should stimulate interest in a lasting manner for adjusting different methods and processes to different operating conditions, for modifying concepts, schemes and procedures as required by given changes in milieu. They should inspire scholars as well as foster among experts the desire and ability to diversify their experience and to try out abroad a "know-how" so far proven only at home. And all this should increase the availability of persons professionally and mentally prepared for international service, the human resources on which United Nations programs of technical cooperation are so dependent.

The importance of the human factor is so overriding that the success or failure of our efforts in the course of the United Nations Development Decade may well depend on our success or failure to carry out properly the training activities which we propose to undertake in the various sectors of the economic and social life of less-developed countries. Over the years past, much progress has been made in training methods and techniques. The distinctions between academic and vocational training, between adult and child education, between teachers and students, have become ancillary to the urgent task of enabling every human being to assert himself as an individual and as a productive citizen to the best of his capacities. As if the need for education as an essential support of the dignity of man was not compelling enough in moral terms, we now see, in economic and social terms, that no breakthrough will be possible for less-developed countries unless they add fast to their resources in skilled manpower. While training abroad, with its special value from the point of view of international understanding, continues to be of importance, emphasis has been placed on training within the less-developed regions and countries themselves. The time is now ripe for an all-out effort. Training on the spot, training on the job, training of the teachers who will train the teachers—everything must be done to achieve the maximum multiplier effect inherent in the dissemination of knowledge and know-how. Without more schools and more institutes such as those on which the United Nations Special Fund spends much of what my colleague Paul Hoffman so aptly calls its "seed money," less-developed countries will not be able to turn their population growth from a curse into a blessing.

The United Nations Development Decade is an appeal to our faith in the preservation and in the continuation of economic and social progress by investing in the younger generations who, in addition to education and training, require help to fight malnutrition and disease. Together with investment in industry, large and small, in natural resources and in transport, investment in less-developed countries during the Decade must provide for the construction of more than twenty million dwellings in less-developed areas and for an increase in food supplies of 50 per cent; in those same countries, expenditure for public health services must double over the period and expenditure on education must rise to an annual rate of 4 per cent of the national product by the end of the Decade—all this in order to meet minimum requirements so interrelated that failure to reach one target in time may jeopardize advances on all other fronts. The complexities of the processes of balanced economic and social development are great, and available techniques for comprehensive planning are far from perfect. But enough knowledge and experience have accumulated already to give our efforts a decisive momentum. We will correct and improve as we go but we must forge ahead in all sectors with mutually supporting programs and projects. For we have passed the time of rising expectations to enter the era of achievements counted upon by billions of people who do not yet enjoy full rights as producers and consumers, or simply as human beings living in the twentieth century.

One very important field in which concrete progress is eagerly awaited is that of international trade. However unfamiliar he may be with the intricacies of its many problems, even the ordinary layman realizes that the possibility to sell more and buy more abroad is a crucial test of international cooperation. The momentum gathered by the work of your Commission on International Commodity Trade, the initiation of intergovernmental action for the development of international compensatory schemes taking into account long-term trends in the demand and supply of primary commodities, carry us well beyond the mere discussion of the compatibility of regional groupings. Encouraging steps have already been taken. Let us hope that, during the Decade, the expansion of international trade will be significant enough for its beneficial effects to be felt in the budget of every household.

So much for the tasks ahead of us. They will no doubt impose a vast additional burden of responsibility on the Secretariat, which over the last few years has already shouldered a significant increase of work in the economic and social field.

To these new tasks I am determined to devote fully all the resources available to me, both in Headquarters and in the four regional economic commissions of the United Nations. The heads of the agencies will no doubt similarly devote the energies of their respective secretariats to the tasks falling within their fields of competence.

The efforts of the organizations of the United Nations family cannot, however, be isolated from the sum of the efforts of their members. For it remains true that the United Nations family can mobilize and utilize no more than the human and financial resources put at their disposal by governments. The extent to which our targets and proposals will acquire value as setting minimum standards of progress depends on the extent to which they can be implemented, and this again depends on the decisions and pledges of our membership. This Council, for its part, should play a decisive role not only in the formulation of our ten-year development plan but also in its implementation, responsibile as it is for evaluating progress from year to year and for seeing that all activities proceed at the right pace and in proper balance in the economic and social field. I am convinced that your discussions and resolutions will contribute much to translating the proposals for the United Nations Development Decade into integrated programs for practical action unfolding gradually and effectively. And may our endeavors be a true reflection and a useful complement of the efforts of individual nations to help each other and, in so doing, to make for a more prosperous and safer world for all.

THE SITUATION IN THE CONGO

JUNE—SEPTEMBER

MOÏSE TSHOMBÉ arrived in Leopoldville on March 15, 1962, to carry out his agreement to negotiate a settlement with the Central Government of the Congo. During the next month the two delegations held fifteen meetings. Tshombé left on April 18 for Elisabethville after stating that he would return to Leopoldville for further talks. The meetings were resumed on May 16 and forty-one more sessions were held. The two delegations parted again on June 26 without any agreement on major issues. In a statement to the Advisory Committee on the Congo, on June 29, U Thant reported the breakdown. The Acting Secretary-General sent a communication to all Member states on July 31 appealing to them to use their influence to persuade the principal parties concerned that it was in their own long-term interests to find a peaceful solution. He added that he might ask them to apply economic pressures if all else failed.

Perhaps the most important development during the summer of 1962 was the Secretary-General's "Plan of National Reconciliation" which was submitted to Prime Minister Adoula on August 20 and to the Katangese authorities four days later. Thant outlined the proposals to the Security Council in a report dated August 20. The main provisions were: elaboration of the federal constitution, the division of revenue and foreign exchange earnings between the central provincial governments, the unification of the currency, integration of all military and paramilitary units, the withdrawal of all provincial representatives and diplomatic and consular missions abroad not serving under authority of the central government, the proclamation of a general amnesty, the reconstitution of the central government to provide representation for all political and provincial groups, and cooperation by all Congolese authorities in the execution of United Nations resolutions. It was made clear to the parties that the plan was to be accepted or rejected in its entirety and that it was not negotiable. Adoula accepted the plan on August 23 "as a token of good will." Tshombé accepted it on September 2. In a statement issued in New York on September 5, Thant said he was encouraged by the responses but that the true significance "will be revealed only as the specific provisions of the plan are put into effect." He said the parties could be assured "that I will afford them all possible assistance and extend every effort to ensure its [the plan's] implementation."

Another important development took place in August 1962. The Acting Secretary-General, at the request of Adoula, appointed four experts in constitutional law from Canada, India, Nigeria, and Switzerland to draft a federal constitution which would give the provinces greater autonomy. The draft of what later became the constitution of the Congo was completed and submitted to Adoula on September 27. Neither the Plan of National Reconciliation nor the constitution brought peace to the Congo, but both were significant steps in this direction.

---

1. Statement to the Advisory Committee on the Congo

NEW YORK   JUNE 29, 1962

I CALLED THIS MEETING in order to bring the members up to date on developments in the Congo, particularly with regard to the Adoula-Tshombé talks in Leopoldville. Since issuing the call for this meeting, those talks, as you know, ended early in the morning of June 26 without agreement, thus creating a new critical phase for the UN operation in the Congo.

You will have seen by now the text of Mr. Gardiner's[1] report on the Adoula-Tshombé talks, which I have distributed as Security Council document S/5053/Add.10. The annexes, however, which are voluminous, are still being processed and have not yet been circulated.

Mr. Rolz-Bennett, the ONUC Representative in Elisabethville, who sat with Mr. Gardiner in the second phase of the talks, has returned and I intend to call upon him to give you first-hand information supplementary to the written report about the talks.

It is, I think, a bit early to attempt to draw any conclusions as to the significance of the failure of the Leopoldville talks to end in agreement. There is no provision for their resumption but we will press for them to do so.

The decisive question, of course, will be whether Mr. Tshombé and his lieutenants in Katanga will now undertake to resume their secessionist efforts. They may or they may not.

As you know, Mr. Tshombé, at Kitona and on other occasions since then, has renounced secession, but what he will actually do now remains to be seen, particularly since some of his colleagues, most notably Mr. Kimba, have increasingly evidenced a lack of sympathy with Mr.

UN Press Release SG/1234.

[1] Mr. Robert Gardiner, Officer-in-Charge of ONUC.

Tshombé's participation in the talks and with the so-called "conciliatory" line he was pursuing at Leopoldville.

I might add that while we were hoping that the Leopoldville talks might end in agreement, we were always prepared for their likely failure, despite the fact that Mr. Gardiner was exhibiting great skill and doing everything humanly possible to keep them going and to achieve fruitful results from them.

I have suggested to Mr. Gardiner that he come here for consultations in the next few days, since I would wish to have the benefit of his analysis in giving thought to the immediate future. You may be sure that our people in the Congo have been told to be very much on the alert for any contingency as a consequence of the breakdown of the talks.

It is quite possible that in the light of developments in the few weeks ahead I would find it necessary to consult you about courses of action and even to invite the Security Council to review the entire Congo situation and to consider the advisability of clarifying and strengthening existing mandates and providing certain new ones.

You may be sure, of course, that in the meantime we will continue the policy of giving all possible assistance under the Security Council resolutions to the government in its efforts to achieve unity and protect the territorial integrity of the country. In this respect, I may read to you the text of the message which I am sending today to Leopoldville in connection with the second anniversary of independence of the Congo which will be celebrated on Saturday, June 30.

I may also inform you that the Katangese authorities some time ago informed our people in Elisabethville of their intention to celebrate "Katangese independence" on July 11 and to bring a thousand or more Katangese gendarmes from places outside Elisabethville to participate in the parade on that date.

Our people have taken a firmly negative position against bringing in any additional gendarmerie to Elisabethville for this or any other purpose and, indeed, we have informed the Katangese authorities of our strongly negative view of any so-called independence celebration at all by them.

I think it might now be advisable to call upon Mr. Rolz-Bennett and after his statement to invite discussion about the situation in general.

2. *From Speech to the United Nations Association of the United Kingdom*

LONDON   JULY 5, 1962

. . . . Of the many practical challenges facing the United Nations, the situation in the Congo is perhaps the most complex, and has, in the past, at any rate, been one of the most urgent. The complexity and difficulty of the Congo situation, and of the efforts to alleviate or control it, are in proportion to the number and variety of the interests involved in that large and fascinating country. In the Congo one finds conflicting interests and opinions at every level—at the levels of world power politics, high finance, and the political interests of emerging Africa and, internally, at the level of national political competition and tribal rivalry. Also competing on this overcrowded stage are adventurers of various kinds attracted by the natural wealth of the country, by the possibility of making a quick gain from confusion and disorder, or even by the exotic and exciting nature of the scene.

The role of the policeman, protector, and adviser is not always a happy one, as a distinguished English song-writer has pointed out. It is small wonder, therefore, that many harsh things have been said over the past two years—sometimes, perhaps, even with a certain justification—about the United Nations Operation in the Congo. But when I think of these strictures and criticisms, I take courage from two considerations: One is that they have come from many opposing sides, and especially from people of extreme views or with special interests. This gives me the feeling that United Nations efforts at objectivity and impartiality have been, on the whole, successful. Secondly, the enormous interest in the United Nations Operation in the Congo illustrates very clearly both the vital nature of that work and the unique problems which have to be faced, and can only be faced, by the world organization. I do not for a moment suggest that mistakes have not been made and that, especially in the light of

UN Press Release SG/1239.

hindsight, some parts of the operation could not have been better conducted. But I must also say very frankly that the nature both of the situation in the Congo and of the problems and the position of the United Nations there has more often than not been seriously misunderstood, and therefore criticised for the wrong reasons.

The United Nations position in the Congo, quite apart from the complex and often confused nature of the local scene, is a difficult and unusual one. It is there to advise and assist the Government of the Congo, but not to usurp its power or authority. Nonetheless, its eminence as an organization and the essential role it plays at the present time in the affairs of the Congo give it, in the public mind, a responsibility for whatever happens, which is quite out of proportion to the limited nature of its authority, resources, and powers vis-à-vis the Congolese authorities. Thus, the United Nations is liable to be blamed for whatever happens, and to be asked to take responsibility for many eventualities which are, in fact, within the domain of the Government of the Congo. One of the most important roles of the United Nations in conflicts or difficulties is that of a lightning conductor or, perhaps more accurately, of the old English institution of the Aunt Sally—the large and conspicuous figure at which things can be thrown both with impunity and with an almost complete certainty of hitting the target.

There can be no doubt that in this strange and unprecedented operation the United Nations has from time to time been jostled or abused or found itself in an undignified position. Lives have been lost, including that of my great predecessor, Dag Hammarskjöld; there has been violence, and from time to time remarks and accusations have been made in various quarters, including some with strong vested interests in the Congo, which have hardly been suitable either to the dignity of the world organization or to the gravity of the task it faces in the Congo. But this situation has attracted so much attention perhaps primarily because it constitutes the most striking current example of the problems of rapid historical change, and the United Nations, as the elected moderator of those consequences, must inevitably accept the risks and insults involved.

It is hard to think of a working alternative to the United Nations operation in the Congo. In 1960 the world faced, in that vast and newly independent country, a desperate danger, compounded of internal chaos and potential external intervention. It faced an almost classic example of rapid change overtaking all those concerned and leaving them helpless and confused—Africans and Europeans alike.

I therefore feel impelled to list, if only briefly, some of the successes which I believe the Government of the Congo and the United Nations have together achieved in these past two years.

Despite the initial mutiny of the army and the nation-wide breakdown of confidence, law and order now exist again in the Congo, even if they may be disturbed occasionally in some areas by political and tribal differences. Despite the departure in July 1960 of many key European workers, essential public and private services have been preserved and kept working, even though sometimes temporarily on a reduced scale; and in recent months the Europeans have been returning.Despite the extreme confusion of the political situation in the early days of independence, the Parliament was finally reconvened in July 1961, through United Nations effort and its protection, and approved the Constitution of a Central Government universally recognized and now gaining daily in strength and experience.

In spite of various secessionist tendencies or movements, there is now a steady trend toward national reconciliation. Especially, the vexed question of Katanga, which has raised, as I well know, much honest, though not always well-informed, interest and indignation in this country, has been discussed intensively and practically by Prime Minister Adoula and Mr. Tshombé in Leopoldville. Although the talks are now suspended, great efforts are being made for their resumption.

In this effort at conciliation, we are also beginning to see at last a new comprehension by the outside interests involved of the great issues at stake and a new willingness on their part to use every influence in the direction of a united and stable Congo. This is, indeed, an encouraging development. The famine among 300,000 Baluba refugees in Kasai in the winter of 1960–1961 was dealt with successfully by a great international humanitarian effort. The United Nations and its affiliate agencies are also wrestling with the economic and fiscal problems of the Congo.

Finally, the great basic problem of the Congo—lack of training, experience, and qualifications—is being tackled. It is a long and arduous job to equip a country, roughly the same area as India, with all the public and private professional people and know-how which it requires to secure its future, and, unfortunately, two years ago such people and training scarcely existed at all among the Congolese population. Political tension and pressures from outside have not made the task any easier, but, nonetheless, the first results are now beginning to show, and the program of training and assistance, so essential to the successful future of the Congo, has, under United Nations auspices, gathered considerable momentum.

I would like to conclude by asking you to view the United Nations role as the agent and moderator of historic change in the world in general, and in the Congo in particular, in the light of some of the things I have said. The English way of thought and your tradition of administration, and the bringing of peoples to self-government provide the inhabitants of this country with an inherited basis for a sound judgment in such matters. Despite the revolutionary changes that have taken place and are still taking place in this world, I believe this basis for judgment, and the talents that go with it, can be immensely valuable both to the United Kingdom and to the world community, always provided that it is turned toward the future and not toward the past. There are, no doubt, very difficult times ahead in Africa and elsewhere in the world. But there is also, as never before, a growing feeling of international solidarity, which finds its most practical expression in some of the programs of the United Nations. It is in this spirit that I hope you will understand the brief remarks that I have made, and in this spirit also that you will continue your efforts on behalf of the United Nations in particular and international cooperation and understanding in general.

3. *Letter to Prime Minister Adoula*

NEW YORK   JULY 30, 1962

I HAVE IN RECENT DAYS been giving a great deal of thought to the role and problems of the United Nations in its program of assistance to the Government of the Congo. While my representative in the Congo, the officer-in-charge, Mr. Gardiner, will be discussing with you in detail some possible future developments in the program of assistance which the United Nations is affording to your government, I would like especially to reaffirm at this time two points relating to this assistance.

Security Council Official Records, Seventeenth Year, Supplement for July, August, and September 1962, document S/5053/Add.11, annex XXIX.

In the first place, it is my intention, under the mandate given to ONUC by the Security Council and the General Assembly, to assist the Government of the Congo in maintaining law and order, and to help the government by all possible peaceful means to exert its authority and to perform the legitimate functions of the government throughout the entire Congo, as it was defined on June 30, 1960.

Secondly, on the assumption that in some areas, such as the province of Equateur, the government may now soon be ready, with the assistance of the Armée nationale congolaise, to assume full responsibility for maintaining law and order, I should like to reaffirm that the United Nations for this purpose will give all possible assistance to the ANC in making available to it transport, equipment and training, as needed and requested.

In conclusion may I express my hope that the Government of the Congo, with the assistance of the United Nations, may find early and satisfactory solutions to its major problems and particularly that of Katanga, so that the country as a whole may look to the future with confidence.

---

4. *Appeal to Members of the United Nations*

NEW YORK   JULY 31, 1962

THE SITUATION in the Congo has been, and is now perhaps more than ever, a very serious problem for the United Nations. It is true, of course, that much constructive work has been done in the Congo since the disastrous state in which that country found itself in July 1960. Nevertheless, after more than two years of intensive effort to assist the Government of the Congo, the stability and territorial integrity of the country remain far from established, and the purpose of the United Nations in it, therefore, far from realized. This situation is particularly crucial in view of the lives, effort and money already expended and currently being expended by the

Security Council Official Records, Seventeenth Year, Supplement for July, August, and September 1962, document S/5053/Add.11, annex XXVII.

United Nations and the financial crisis into which this unprecedented drain on its resources has brought the Organization.

Although there are many contributory causes to this state of affairs, there can be no doubt that the main cause is the continuing attempt at secession by the province of Katanga. Until a satisfactory and constructive solution to this issue is found, it will be very difficult for the Congolese government to face successfully its responsibilities and problems, or for the United Nations to assist it very effectively. I assure you that no one can be more desirous than I am to see this solution brought about by peaceful means through processes of conciliation and consultation, and the United Nations continues to employ its very best endeavours to this end. Unfortunately, these endeavours so far have not produced fruitful results, and the situation becomes more and more distressing.

I therefore feel impelled to appeal to all Member states to use all the influence and exert all the effort which they can bring to bear to achieve a reasonable and peaceful settlement in the Congo. I do not claim that the blame for the abortive talks in the Congo is altogether on one side. But I do assert that secession of any province is no solution for the Congo's ills, that it would serve no interests other than, possibly, those of the mining companies and certain neighbours, and has neither historical nor ethnic justification. I strongly believe that only a unified Congo can give hope for peace and prosperity in Central Africa. In this connection I note with satisfaction the latest proposals of the prime minister of the Congo, Mr. Adoula, for the drafting of a federal-type constitution with the assistance of international experts.

The situation in the Congo has been aggravated and confused by an intensive and skillfully waged propaganda campaign on behalf of Katanga which has never failed to portray the situation in a false light. This campaign, having both money and ability behind it, makes it all the more important to see and portray the Congo-Katanga problem in its true perspective.

The United Nations is very much concerned with the cultivation of useful economic activity everywhere. Indeed, much of its effort in the Congo has been devoted to the protection of the personnel and property of the enterprises which are vital to the Congo's economy. But the situation becomes immensely complicated when one of these great enterprises is found involved, whether intentionally or unintentionally, in disruptive political activities which can be carried on only because of the very large sums of money available. This is a highly undesirable activity, both for the good of the Congo and of the enterprises themselves. Moreover, the overriding importance, both for Africa and for the world community, of the stability of the Congo and the conciliation of the conflicting parties in that country cannot be compared with the short-term and short-sighted interests and ambitions, both economic and political, of a relatively very small group of people. Moreover, I have no doubt that, in the long run, the best safeguard for the interests of all concerned, including those I have just mentioned, is the successful establishment of stability and peace in a united Congo.

I appeal, therefore, to all Member states to use their influence to persuade the principal parties concerned in the Congo that a peaceful solution is in their own long-term interest, as well as in the interest of the Congolese people. If such persuasion should finally prove ineffective, I would ask them to consider seriously what further measures may be taken. In this context, I have in mind economic pressure upon the Katangese authorities of a kind that will bring home to them the realities of their situation and the fact that Katanga is not a sovereign state and is not recognized by any government in the world as such. In the last resort, and if all other efforts fail, this could justifiably go to the extent of barring all trade and financial relations. I also appeal to all governments to do everything in their power to ensure that bad advice, false encouragement, and every form of military and nonmilitary assistance be withheld from the authorities of the province of Katanga. Such efforts should include all possible attempts to control the entry into Katanga of adventurers who sell their services to the Katangese provincial authorities and whose reckless and irresponsible activities have contributed much to the worsening of the situation.

In making this appeal I wish to make it clear that the United Nations in the Congo, as in the rest of the world, is particularly anxious to preserve and strengthen the economic life of the country. This applies as much to Katanga as to the rest of the Congo. I need hardly add that this appeal is in strict conformity with the resolutions adopted by the Security Council and the General Assembly.

5. *From Report to the Security Council Presenting His Plan for Reconciliation*

NEW YORK   AUGUST 20, 1962

. . . .

74. IT IS TO BE hoped that the existing stalemate resulting from the breakdown of the Adoula-Tshombé talks, due to the refusal of Mr. Tshombé to sign the final communiqué can be ended. Any steps in this direction would be very welcome, as, for example, the acceptance by Mr. Tshombé of the prime minister's offer of two posts in his cabinet for the representatives of Conakat or of his offer of a vice-presidency for Mr. Tshombé himself. Obviously the settlement of the problem by means of conciliation, mutual understanding, and negotiation must be sought by every possible means. In this regard, I have felt it my duty to say that the delays and evasive tactics which have been so artfully employed by Mr. Tshombé are dangerous and cannot be indefinitely tolerated either by the United Nations or by the Central Congolese Government, whose general effectiveness and performance are seriously impaired by the continuing existence of the problem of Katangese secession. It is my hope that, with the firm support and assistance of all Member states, it will be possible in the near future to see some real progress toward a solution, which means of course, the end of the secessionist effort of Katanga. Should progress toward that solution not come quickly, I am inclined to believe that the United Nations, both because of a virtually inevitable deterioration in the Congo and its own financial limitations, may soon be confronted with the necessity of deciding whether to withdraw its military force from the Congo or to go to the other extreme of specifically authorizing ONUC to seek, by all necessary measures, to end Katangese efforts at secession.

75. Since in press and corridor recently there has been much comment and speculation about certain "proposals" which I am said to have in mind, some clarifying words from me on this subject would seem appropriate.

Security Council Official Records, Seventeenth Year, Supplement for July, August and September 1962, document S/5053/Add.11.

76. The crux of the Congo trouble being the Katanga problem, it has been my purpose to exert every effort to ensure, by means other than military force, the unity of the Congo by bringing to an end through agreed constitutional arrangements the attempted secession of Katanga. I have for some time had under consideration a number of possible next steps, short of resort to force, which ONUC might usefully take in the event of failure of the Adoula-Tshombé talks to make progress toward reconciliation of the differences between the Central Congolese Government and Katanga. I had in mind particularly means of inducing Mr. Tshombé to abandon his secessionist ambitions and to take some earnest strides in the direction of national unity.

77. Pursuant to my appeal of July 31, I have discussed these next steps with several delegations, particularly those of states which have given major support to ONUC or which are in a position to bring some influence to bear on Mr. Tshombé.

78. In addition, the area of agreement among Congolese concerning national reconciliation has begun, at least, to be defined in recent months and it is, therefore, possible to suggest a general basis for reconciliation.

79. I am instructing my representative in Leopoldville, Mr. Robert Gardiner, to present a program of measures to Mr. Adoula, the prime minister, and, with his agreement, to Mr. Tshombé, the provincial president of Katanga. These measures have my full support. The main elements of the program are set forth in the following paragraphs.

80. A constitution for a federal system of government in the Congo is now in preparation and all provincial governments and interested political groups have been invited to submit their views. The United Nations, on request of the Government of the Congo, is assisting this process by making available international experts in federal constitutional law. It is my hope that work on a draft constitution will be completed in thirty days.

81. A new law is needed to establish definitive arrangements for the division of revenues between the Central Government and the provincial governments, as well as regulations and procedures for the utilization of foreign exchange. The Central Government should submit such new law to Parliament only after consultations with provincial governments. Until that process is completed, the Central Government and the provincial authorities of Katanga should agree: (*a*) to share on a fifty-fifty basis revenues from all taxes or duties on exports and imports and all royalties from mining concessions; (*b*) to pay to the Monetary Council or institu-

tion designated by it, which is acceptable to the parties concerned, all foreign exchange earned by any part of the Congo. The Monetary Council should control the utilization of all foreign exchange and make available for the essential needs of Katanga at least 50 per cent of the foreign exchange generated in that province.

82. The Central Government should request assistance from the International Monetary Fund in working out a national plan of currency unification, and put such a plan into effect in the shortest possible time.

83. Rapid integration and unification of the entire Congolese army is essential. A three-member commission of representatives from the Central Government, Katanga Province, and the United Nations, should prepare within thirty days a plan to bring this about. Two months thereafter should be adequate to put the plan into effect.

84. Only the Central Government should maintain government offices or representation abroad.

85. As an essential aspect of national reconciliation, the Central Government should be reconstituted to provide representation for all political and provincial groups. It is noted that Mr. Adoula, the prime minister, has already made certain specific offers in this regard.

86. Reconciliation should be served by a general amnesty for political prisoners. In addition, all Congolese authorities, national, state, and local, should cooperate fully with the United Nations in its task of carrying out United Nations resolutions.

87. The proposed steps toward national reconciliation are fully in accord with the statement made on July 29 by Mr. Adoula. They likewise should be acceptable to Katanga and all other provinces of the Congo, judging from recent statements of Congolese leaders. Mr. Tshombé, therefore, should be able to indicate his acceptance promptly. The United Nations, of course, stands ready to give all possible assistance in their implementation. I urge Member governments to support these approaches by urging Congolese of all sectors and views to accept them forthwith.

88. While consultations on these approaches are going on I would hope that no actions will be taken to distract from this new effort to achieve agreement. At the same time certain actions are required by the Central Government, by the provincial authorities of Katanga and by neighbouring states, both to begin putting the proposals into effect, and to prevent any distracting incidents from any quarter. All Member states of the United Nations should take the necessary measures to assure that

there are no unauthorized movements to the Congo of mercenaries, arms, war material, or any kind of equipment capable of military use.

89. I believe that the Katanga authorities must consider these proposals and respond to them affirmatively within a quite brief period so that concrete steps can begin, according to a time-table which Mr. Gardiner is authorized to propose. If, however, after this period Katangese agreement is not forthcoming, I will emphatically renew an appeal to all governments of Member states of the United Nations to take immediate measures to ensure that their relations with the Congo will be in conformity with laws and regulations of the Government of the Congo.

90. Further, failing such agreement, as I indicated in my statement of July 31: "I have in mind economic pressure upon the Katangese authorities of a kind that will bring home to them the realities of their situation and the fact that Katanga is not a sovereign state and is not recognized by any government in the world as such . . . this could justifiably go to the extent of barring all trade and financial relations." In pursuance of this, a firm request would be made by me to all Member governments to apply such a ban especially to Katangese copper and cobalt.

91. I hope that drastic measures will not prove necessary, although they may be fully justified. A number of governments have responded to my appeal of July 31 with promises of support in varying degree. In the light of my consultations in recent days, I believe the time has come to move ahead resolutely to a solution of the problem of Katanga secession. I therefore intend to pursue the course of action I have indicated.

---

6. *Statement to the Press*

NEW YORK   SEPTEMBER 5, 1962

I FIND ENCOURAGING the favorable responses which Prime Minister Adoula and Provincial President Tshombé have given to the proposals which I had submitted to them as reported in document S/5053/Add.11, and which subsequently have come to be known as "the plan."

UN Press Release SG/1315.

Since both parties have now accepted the plan, I am asking the Officer-in-Charge of the United Nations operation in the Congo, Mr. Robert K.A. Gardiner, to communicate to both parties my gratification over their actions and my request that steps be taken immediately to implement all of the provisions of the plan.

The acceptances are a necessary and important step forward, but they are no more than that. Their true significance will be revealed only as the specific provisions of the plan are put into effect. The immediate implications of the acceptances, if they are earnestly meant, are clearly the following:

1. The Central Government and the Katangese authorities have now formally agreed to reconcile their differences peacefully, on the basis of the plan, and there should therefore be no further resort to force by anyone in Katanga. Indeed, there would seem to be on this basis no further need for troop movements in Katanga on either side.

2. All pretensions to the secession of Katanga from the Republic of the Congo must be regarded as abandoned.

3. The parties will undertake, without delay, the implementation of the provisions of the plan. The United Nations, of course, will afford all possible assistance toward this end.

4. The implementation measures should be guided scrupulously by the provisions of the plan itself and fairly applied.

I have presented this plan to the parties because of my conviction that it would provide a reasonable basis for ending conflict and insecurity in the Congo. The parties, therefore, may be assured that I will afford them all possible assistance and extend every effort to ensure its implementation. In this regard, I note with satisfaction the expressions of support for the plan by a number of countries, and I assume that this backing may be counted upon until the plan is fully executed.

FROM TRANSCRIPTS OF PRESS CONFERENCES

JUNE—AUGUST

DURING THE PERIOD from June 5 through August 2, U Thant held five news conferences—two in New York, the others in London, Oslo, and Helsinki. Ostensibly all were routine meetings not called to deal with any particular question. As a group, however, they provided an excellent example of how useful this device can be in affording the Secretary-General a channel for transmitting his views to the public—as well as to Member states—on issues which are not officially before any United Nations organ, and for clarifying and elaborating on opinions he had previously expressed in other contexts.

In replying to questions at a luncheon of the United Nations Correspondents Association on April 24, 1962, U Thant had said he could do no more to halt nuclear test explosions than to appeal to the parties concerned to heed resolutions of the General Assembly on this subject. He did go further, however, in press conferences on June 5 and July 11. The change followed an announcement that the United States would conduct thermonuclear tests at high altitude on July 9. In his June 5 statement, the Acting Secretary-General said the proposed tests belong "to a different category and, I feel, a more undesirable one." He expressed concern especially because outer space had been recognized as the common property of all countries. Further, he called the tests "a manifestation of a very dangerous psychosis which is in evidence today." On July 11, two days after the United States test explosion, he recalled his previous statement and said, "I repeat my protest again today." He expressed the belief that "the Soviet Union will follow suit and poison the atmosphere still further." His prediction proved to be correct. The Soviet Union exploded a 30-megaton device during the first days of August.

Thant also dealt with another question which was to arise from time to time in the future—how to handle communications from divided countries whose legal status was in dispute. The normal procedure was for such communications to be circulated as official United Nations documents only when a Member state so requested. The Acting Secretary-General made an exception in May 1962 on a memorandum from the Democratic Republic of Germany (East Germany) on the nonproliferation of nuclear weapons and transmitted it to the United Nations Disarmament Commission. His action brought a protest from the Federal Republic of Germany (West Germany). In the June 5 press conference, Thant explained his position in detail (see p. 170). He noted that the General Assembly resolution (1664 (XVI)) soliciting comment on nuclear nonproliferation, was the first one ever adopted by the Assembly to use the word "country" rather than the usual "state" or "Member state." He added: "I therefore felt, and I still feel that, because of the importance of the subject matter and because of the wording used in this particular resolution, I should transmit all communications on this subject from any quarter, irrespective of the fact that these communications come from Member states or from non-member states." He said he had sought the views of his legal counsel before acting and added "While on this subject, I wish to say that, if I had received a communication from Peking in time on this subject, I would have acted in the same manner in which I did act."

1. From Transcript of Press Conference

NEW YORK   JUNE 5, 1962

THE ACTING SECRETARY-GENERAL: It is some six weeks since we last met. Many things have happened in the interval. The General Assembly is due to resume its sixteenth session on Thursday. I thought, therefore, we should get together once again at the present time.

Before throwing open the floor for questions, I would like to refer to one or two major issues. The first is the Congo, where the talks between Prime Minister Adoula and Mr. Tshombé, which had been interrupted in April under somewhat dramatic circumstances, were resumed in Leopoldville on May 22.

ONUC officials deliberately avoided any role in the talks during their first stages, but now, at the request of the parties themselves, Mr. Gardiner[1] and Mr. Rolz-Bennett[2] are sitting in at each of the sessions in order to be available for any assistance that may be requested. Before the resumption of the second round of talks, Mr. Gardiner held exploratory discussions, first with Prime Minister Adoula in Leopoldville and then with Mr. Tshombé in Elisabethville. Having thus ascertained the positions of the two leaders, Mr. Gardiner formulated a number of informal suggestions with a view to facilitating and expediting the reconciliation of their differences.

The two leaders and their aides have been meeting regularly, usually, in fact, twice daily, morning and afternoon, their discussions centering on

UN Note to Correspondents No. 2603.

[1] Robert K.A. Gardiner, officer-in-charge of ONUC.
[2] José Rolz-Bennett, chief UN civilian officer at Elisabethville.

working papers prepared by ONUC in consultation with the parties. There is no need to talk about the progress made to date, as this is already known to you through the short joint communiqués which, in accordance with an agreed procedure, are issued at the end of each meeting. It is noteworthy that the two parties have already agreed on integrating the Katangese gendarmerie with the Congolese National Army, with United Nations assistance.

It is still too early, of course, to assess the ultimate results to be expected from the Leo talks, but the earnest manner in which the meetings are being held, the improved atmosphere, and the degree of accord already registered are at least encouraging signs . . . .

. . . . QUESTION: May I ask two questions: First, there has been some confusion as to whether you recognize East Germany. Would you be good enough to clarify your position on East Germany; and, second, how do you feel about the American high-altitude, nuclear testing in the Pacific?

THE ACTING SECRETARY-GENERAL: There has been a lot of misunderstanding of my action regarding the transmission of a communication—an unsolicited communication—from a country on the subject of "the conditions under which countries not possessing nuclear weapons might be willing to enter into specific undertakings to refrain from manufacturing or otherwise acquiring such weapons and to refuse to receive in the future nuclear weapons in their territories on behalf of any other country".

It is, I think, worth recalling that, since the inception of the United Nations, more than 1,665 resolutions have been adopted. In none of these resolutions—I repeat: in none of these resolutions—was the word "country" ever used. The word used was "state" or "Member state." Only in this particular resolution, resolution 1664 (XVI), for the first time in the history of the United Nations was the word "country" used. Therefore, if you know a little of the background of the presentation of this particular resolution, you will have some food for thought.

I therefore felt, and I still feel, that, because of the importance of the subject matter and because of the wording used in this particular resolution, I should transmit all communications on this subject from any quarter, irrespective of the fact that these communications came from Member states and from non-Member states.

Then, of course, the controversy centered around the definition of the term "country." It would be fruitless to go into a juridical and legalistic discussion of the concepts "country" and "state." But my interpretation of the term "country," as distinct from "state," is that a state is a territory politically organized and a country is a territory not necessarily organized politically.

Therefore, when I received a communication on this subject from the Democratic Republic of Germany, or East Germany, or the Soviet-occupied zone of Germany—or whatever name you may give that particular territory—I felt that it was a subject which was so important that the Disarmament Commission might find it useful to study this particular document. I sought the views of my legal counsel, who agreed with me that this particular document should be forwarded to the Disarmament Commission.

Of course, in the subsequent exchange of letters between me and the permanent observer of the Federal Republic of Germany, I clarified my position. This transmission of a communication from that particular area does not in any way imply recognition, does not in any way imply any attitude on my part toward that particular territory. I acted as I did because of the importance of the subject matter and because of the wording used in this particular resolution. The exchange of letters to which I have just referred was simply meant as a clarification of my position. I made this clear in my reply to the permanent observer of the Federal Republic of Germany.

While on this subject, I wish to say that, if I had received a communication from Peking in time on this subject, I would have acted in the same manner in which I did act.

Regarding the second question, relating to the projected high-altitude tests: On a previous occasion, I made known my position on the general subject of nuclear tests. On that occasion, I made it clear that I was in complete agreement with the General Assembly resolutions of the sixteenth session on the banning of nuclear tests. The projected nuclear and thermonuclear tests at high altitudes belong, of course, to a different category and, I feel, a more undesirable one. In the first place, these tests, when announced, were objected to very vigorously by many eminent scientists all over the world, and scientists with no axe to grind. Secondly, it is common knowledge that outer space is no country's territory. It is the common property of all countries. And I feel that these projected high-altitude tests are a manifestation of a very dangerous psychosis which is in evidence today.

QUESTION: Are you satisfied with the way things are shaping up with regard to the New Guinea conflict and the way the countries concerned are responding to your continuous appeals?

THE ACTING SECRETARY-GENERAL: It is common knowledge that Mr. Ellsworth Bunker had been conducting private and informal discussions with the two parties concerned since the third week of March and when these discussions were suspended Mr. Bunker came to New York and discussed with me a formula which he proposed to present to the two governments as a basis for further discussions. I was in complete agreement with the formula proposed by Mr. Bunker and I encouraged him to go ahead with his plans. Thus the Bunker proposals were presented to the two governments in April. The Government of Indonesia promptly announced that it was ready to resume negotiations on the basis of the Bunker proposals. The Government of the Netherlands suggested a few modifications. Among these suggested modifications is the one pertaining to paragraph 4 of the Bunker proposals.

These suggestions of the Netherlands government were transmitted to the Indonesian government by Mr. Bunker and the Indonesian government again agreed to resume negotiations on these revised proposals. While Mr. Bunker was awaiting a definitive reply from the Netherlands, we had news of hostilities in West New Guinea. At that time, of course, it will be remembered, I appealed to both governments to resume negotiations on the basis of the Bunker proposals, and then the Netherlands government agreed to resume negotiations on these proposals.

That is the position. There was some misunderstanding regarding my noncompliance with the request of the Netherlands government to send observers to the area. It will be recalled that the Government of the Netherlands made similar requests to my predecessor, Mr. Dag Hammarskjöld, on several occasions, and Mr. Dag Hammarskjöld did not comply with these requests. I also did not comply with these requests because my paramount consideration at that time was, and at the present time is, to bring the two parties together at the conference table. If I had to decide to send observers to the area because of the changing situation and new developments, I could not send civilian observers. I would have to send military observers and I did not feel competent to send military observers to any area without the authorization of the Security Council.

Therefore, since my whole purpose was to bring the two parties together at a round-table conference in the presence of a third party and settle their differences peacefully, I had to reject the request of the Netherlands, as my predecessor had done on more than one occasion in the last one and a half years. Now I should think that the two parties would get together, in the presence of Mr. Bunker, to thrash out the formula in more detail. If this formula is acceptable to both, formal negotiations will take place, under my auspices and in my presence, in the United Nations. That is the arrangement.

. . . . QUESTION: First, may I ask you what is the number of mercenaries in the Congo? Second, may I draw your attention to paragraph 329 of the Ruanda-Urundi report? There is a mention there of the practical possibility of replacing the Belgians either through the United Nations or bilaterally. Is the replacement to which there is reference to be decided by the Secretary-General or the General Assembly or the Security Council, and what are the possibilities?

THE ACTING SECRETARY-GENERAL: Regarding your first question, we have been receiving reports that more mercenaries are coming into Katanga. Of course, it is difficult to substantiate these rumors, and we have no means of knowing the exact number of foreign mercenaries now in Katanga.

Regarding the second question, on Ruanda-Urundi, the report of the Commission will be officially made available to all delegations and the press tomorrow, and, of course, it is for the General Assembly to decide on the future course of action on the basis of that recommendation. I do not think that the Security Council should be involved in this particular item.

. . . . QUESTION: May I come back for a moment to New Guinea. You mentioned the question of paragraph 4 of the Bunker plan. What kind of guarantees could the United Nations give for an impartial plebiscite in New Guinea, and could it give such guarantees without a special mandate of the General Assembly?

THE ACTING SECRETARY-GENERAL: At this stage the United Nations is not involved yet. After the two parties come to an agreement on a formula, formal negotiations, as I indicated earlier, will take place in my presence at the United Nations, and when those formal negotiations are completed satisfactorily then I have to seek the decision of the General Assembly. Of course, I cannot implement any agreed formulation without the mandate of the General Assembly. I have a feeling that, if everything goes well, this item will be inscribed on the agenda of the seventeenth session, and the General Assembly should adopt a resolution to take note of these agreements and to give directives to the Secretary-General on how to implement these provisions.

QUESTION: Can you comment on the situation in Laos? I know that one of the ambassadors of the great powers visited you recently, and when he came down after the conference with you, we asked him whether he had discussed the question of Laos, because it is persistently rumored that this great power might put the question of Laos before the United Nations. Was that broached to you by that power or any other Member of the United Nations?

THE ACTING SECRETARY-GENERAL: My answer is no; and regarding the Laotian situation, there is already a machinery in existence for dealing with the situation. Not only is that machinery in existence: the machinery is in operation; and, of course, although the situation is far from satisfactory, there are some encouraging signs regarding the situation in Laos. Both President Kennedy and Premier Khrushchev agreed at the Vienna Summit Conference last year that Laos must be neutral. Of course, this position is in strict conformity with the Geneva Armistice Agreements of 1954. It will be recalled that the Geneva agreements of 1954 stipulated the whole of Indo-China to be neutral. Of course, what was then called Indo-China is now called Laos, Cambodia, North Vietnam, and South Vietnam. Only Cambodia is neutral, as the Geneva agreements of 1954 intended the whole area to be.

Another encouraging sign today is that both the United States of America and the Soviet Union have agreed to seek a diplomatic, and not a military, solution of the Laotian problem; and both the United States of America and the Soviet Union agree that Prince Souvanna Phouma is the only man who can wield more or less effective control over the country of Laos. I think these are encouraging signs.

.... QUESTION: In the light of your observation that it is known to the United Nations that mercenaries are returning to Katanga, I wonder if you consider that a violation of any armistice agreement, and what does the United Nations propose to do about it?

THE ACTING SECRETARY-GENERAL: As I have indicated earlier, we have unconfirmed reports of the infiltration of foreign mercenaries into Katanga; and, of course, under the Security Council mandate, I have been authorized to use a requisite measure of force, if necessary, to arrest these mercenaries. Therefore, the question of the employment of force must be considered. But as you all know, the United Nations at present is in a rather peculiar position: many Member states who have undertaken to bear the expense of the Congo operation do not favor any fresh United Nations military initiative in the Congo; and many Member states who do not pay anything to the United Nations for the Congo operation have been advocating a more vigorous policy. Hence, as I have said, the United Nations is in a rather peculiar position, and as I have indicated on an earlier occasion, if the current talks break down, I propose to present my views on the next steps to the Congo Advisory Committee for advice; and, if necessary, I may have to seek the views of my principal advisors; and perhaps a fresh Security Council mandate may be necessary.

West Irian. The Bunker proposals referred to by the Acting Secretary-General provided for a two-stage transfer of West Irian (West New Guinea) from the Netherlands to Indonesia. The first stage was to be a transfer to a United Nations Temporary Executive Authority. The plan also called for a plebiscite before 1969 to determine the eventual disposition of the territory. The latter provision was dealt with in paragraph 4 of the plan which was mentioned by Thant (p. 173).

Congo. In his reply to the final question on the Congo problem, Thant remarked that "many Member states who have undertaken to bear the expenses of the Congo operation do not favor any fresh United Nations military initiatives in the Congo, and many Member states who do not pay anything to the United Nations for the Congo question have been advocating a more vigorous policy." The United Kingdom was chief spokesman for the first group (along with Belgium) and the Soviet Union was leader of the latter.

2. From Transcript of Press Conference

LONDON   JULY 7, 1962

. . . . THE ACTING SECRETARY-GENERAL: Regarding the United Nations operations in the Congo, there seem to have been some misunderstanding and misconceptions in certain quarters regarding the use of force. If you go into the Security Council resolutions, you will notice that the United Nations has a very limited function to perform in the Congo. First of all,

UN Note to Correspondents No. 2616, July 12, 1962.

the United Nations forces in the Congo were authorized by the Security Council to prevent civil war. That is the first function. Secondly, the United Nations forces were asked to maintain law and order, to maintain peace and to prevent chaos. Thirdly, the United Nations forces in the Congo were authorized to arrest, detain and deport foreign mercenaries with a requisite measure of force if necessary. That is the actual wording used in the relevant Security Council resolution; so the United Nations forces in the Congo were authorized to use a requisite amount of force if necessary in arresting, detaining, and deporting foreign mercenaries in the Congo. The United Nations forces in the Congo have never been authorized to initiate any military action. I think it is clear from all the relevant Security Council resolutions, of course, that in a situation when the United Nations is attacked I have authorized our people there to retaliate as an exercise of the right of self-defense, but it is not my intention, it has never been my intention, it will never be my intention to use any military initiative. I have no such mandate. So the question of the use of force does not arise.

QUESTION: Do we interpret that to mean that you have no jurisdiction to prevent the secession of Katanga?

THE ACTING SECRETARY-GENERAL: The Security Council resolutions do not stipulate that the United Nations should impose any political solution on any part of the Congo, so the United Nations very rightly feels that the question of the Constitution, or the question of secession, or the question of the autonomy of the particular region is not the proper function of the United Nations on which to pass judgment or to make any statement. Of course when the United Nations organs, particularly the Security Council, considered the question of the Congo, one pertinent provision of a resolution stressed the need for the unity and territorial integrity of the Congo. The United Nations forces have been authorized to maintain the unity and territorial integrity of the Congo, but the Security Council resolutions do not authorize me to prevent secession or to impose any political solution on any part of the Congo.

. . . . QUESTION: I wonder if you could tell us about the latest progress in your efforts with the Dutch and the Indonesians?

THE ACTING SECRETARY-GENERAL: This is one problem about which we all should be very happy. Since December of last year I have been in touch with the Government of the Netherlands and the Government of Indonesia in the hope of settling their dispute by peaceful means. In response to my appeal both governments nominated their permanent representatives in New York to contact me, separately of course, and I have been able to sound them out about their line of thinking and their operations. In March I deputized an American diplomat, Mr. Ellsworth Bunker, to get the two together in informal and secret talks. Mr. Bunker met them together and negotiations took place in a place close to Washington. Late in March the negotiations were interrupted for a variety of reasons and last month I appealed both to President Sukarno and to the prime minister of the Netherlands to resume negotiations on the basis of the Bunker proposals. As you all know, Mr. Bunker on my behalf presented his own proposals to the two governments as a basis for discussion. The government of Indonesia announced publicly that it accepted the Bunker proposals in principle. The government of the Netherlands announced publicly that it was prepared to resume negotiations on the basis of the Bunker proposals. The two formulations seemed to be a little different, but my interpretation was that there was no material difference between the two attitudes. President Sukarno wanted me to clarify the Netherlands position. After contact with the Netherlands government I was in a position to communicate the Netherlands attitude to the government of Indonesia. The Netherlands government also feels that it can accept the Bunker proposals in principle, so President Sukarno was satisfied with the public statement of the Netherlands government and the latest information is that the two governments are sending their delegates to the United States early next week for a resumption of the negotiations. The present arrangement is that the two delegations will resume their talks under the auspices of Mr. Bunker to consider the formula and if they come to an agreement on this, further negotiations will take place under my auspices in New York, where detailed discussions will be held. I am pretty optimistic about the outcome of these talks.

.... QUESTION: Could we have your comments on the suggestion made that the Food and Agriculture Organization of the United Nations should be located in Berlin?

THE ACTING SECRETARY-GENERAL: A lot of attention has been given in the last few weeks to the possibility and desirability of moving some branches of the United Nations, or some offices of the UN family to Berlin. My view on this suggestion is that the United Nations should consider the propriety of moving some of its offices to Berlin provided that the Big Four—that is to say, the United States, the United Kingdom, the Soviet Union, and France—which are primarily concerned with a solution of the Berlin problem come to some sort of an agreement on the future of Berlin. Of course the United Nations cannot take any action without the consent of the four big powers. So when they come to an agreement on any formulation, and if they feel that some branches of the United Nations should be shifted to Berlin, then my personal feeling is that the United Nations should respond to this request.

. . . .

---

3. From Transcript of Press Conference

OSLO   JULY 11, 1962

THE ACTING SECRETARY-GENERAL: Ladies and Gentlemen of the Fourth Estate,

I am very happy indeed to be here in Oslo and particularly to meet with you and present some of my views to you and exchange certain views with you on the important problems facing the United Nations today.

I am not sure which aspects of the United Nations activities you are more interested in, but I want to state a fact which is worth remembering. In the United Nations family, that is the United Nations Headquarters as well as our sister agencies, there are 18,000 men and women employed. Out of these 18,000 men and women only 1,500 are directly concerned with the discharge of the political activities. The remaining 16,500 are solely concerned with the discharge of nonpolitical activities of the United Nations. So it is obvious that the political activities are but just a fragment of the UN activities. The United Nations is concerned in a very large measure with the nonpolitical activities like the economic activities, social activities, trusteeship activities, activities in the field of World Health Organization, International Labour Organisation, United Nations Educational, Scientific and Cultural Organization, and so on.

But the political activities of the United Nations have been receiving more attention than the nonpolitical activities, because understandably the political developments are more newsworthy and more sensational, and they attract public attention much more strongly than the social and

UN Note to Correspondents No. 2624, July 23, 1962.

economic activities undertaken by the United Nations organization. Of course, as far as the discharge of the political functions is concerned the United Nations apparatus is weak and, if I may say so, inadequate. But one should realize that in the discharge of the nonpolitical activities, particularly in the economic field and the trusteeship field, the United Nations has been able to do a very significant and positive job. That is one aspect of the UN activities which I would like to bring to the attention of the members of the press.

Another fact which I have in mind is the new phenomena which we are facing at the moment. Since the end of World War II the rich countries are getting richer and the poor countries are getting poorer in terms of their national income. I think this division of the world into rich countries and poor countries is much more serious and ultimately much more explosive than the division of the world on ideological grounds. So with this in mind the United Nations General Assembly at its fifteenth session—that was in 1960—passed a resolution requesting the Member states, particularly the rich Member states, to contribute at least 1 per cent of their global national product to international aid. And at its sixteenth session again—that was last year—the General Assembly passed a resolution launching the Development Decade, as you are no doubt aware.

The primary purpose of that resolution was to see that the underdeveloped countries gain an additional national income of 5 per cent every year for the next ten years. And the General Assembly also feels rather strongly that the developed countries of the world today are in a position to render this aid, to narrow the bridge between the rich countries and the poor countries, in any case to arrest the widening gulf between the rich countries and the poor countries.

There seems to be a consensus of opinion that if this trend is allowed to go on, if this gulf is allowed to get wider and wider, it will increase tensions and they might, as I have said, eventually be more explosive than any other divisions in the world today. So this launching of the Development Decade, in my view, is one of the most important and significant activities of the United Nations in its whole career of seventeen years.

Well, to touch on some of the political issues before the United Nations I'll take a few more minutes of your time. As you know, the problem of the Congo is the most important problem facing the United Nations today. When we consider the problem of the Congo we have to bear certain facts in mind. First of all there has been a definite improvement in the situation in the Congo. If you compare the present situation and the situation prevailing last year or the year before last you will find certain differences. First of all, two years ago there was no parliament functioning. Now there is a parliament functioning. A year and a half ago there was not even a central government. Now there is a central government, recognized by almost every Member state of the United Nations. A year ago there was scarcely law and order in every province. Now, relatively speaking, there is law and order in the Congo except in Katanga.

So it must be admitted that the situation in the Congo *has* improved, but not to the extent that the UN activities in the Congo have fulfilled the mandates of the General Assembly and Security Council resolutions. The Security Council has authorized me to do certain things in the Congo. First of all, the United Nations forces in the Congo have been instructed to maintain law and order. Secondly, our forces have been instructed to prevent civil war. And thirdly, our forces have been instructed to maintain the unity and territorial integrity of the Congo which is, I think, a very important provision of the Security Council resolution—to maintain the unity and territorial integrity of the Congo. And another important mandate of the Security Council is for the UN forces to arrest and detain and deport foreign mercenaries with a requisite measure of force, if necessary. So the UN troops have been authorized to use a requisite measure of force, if necessary, in arresting and detaining and deporting foreign mercenaries.

It is clear from this mandate that the United Nations troops in the Congo are not expected to take any military initiatives. It has never been the intention of the Security Council, nor is it my intention to launch any military initiatives or operations in any part of the Congo. But of course, the United Nations troops in the Congo have been authorized to retaliate, if attacked, by way of exercise of self-defense.

The developments last December, it may be recalled, were the result of Tshombé's gendarmerie blocking the streets of Elisabethville, thus obstructing the UN forces from discharging their obligations in the context of the relevant Security Council resolutions. When the UN forces were authorized to arrest foreign mercenaries with the requisite measure of force, if necessary, they must have the freedom of movement, they must have the right of access to any place where they suspect foreign mercenaries are being harbored. The first requisite for the successful discharge of this obligation is to have freedom of movement.

When Mr. Tshombé's gendarmerie in Elisabethville put up road blocks in the town of Elisabethville, our forces had to remove them by force.

They were attacked by the Katangese gendarmerie and the UN forces had to hit back as an exercise of the right of self-defense. Thus hostilities flared up. These developments were very much misunderstood in certain countries. It was construed by sections of the press and the public in some western European countries that the United Nations had launched military operations against the Katangese people. It was certainly not the case. The United Nations troops have no mandate whatsoever to launch any military operation. The functions of the United Nations troops in the Congo are clearly defined in the relevant resolutions of the Security Council.

Of course the question of the Congo can be simplified in a very few words. The problem of the Congo is the problem of Katanga. And the problem of Katanga is the problem of finances. And the problem of finances in turn is the problem of Union Minière. If only Union Minière seriously means to contribute to the peaceful solution of the problem I think the problem of the Congo will be solved. The case is very simple, if I may put it that way. The Union Minière, and for that matter, Tanganyika Concessions, have been operating in Katanga for a number of years under Belgian administration. There have been practices, traditional practices, adopted by the Union Minière and the Central Government in Leopoldville even at a time of Belgian administration. Certain revenues have to go to the Central Government, certain revenues have to go to the provincial government. There has been an orderly distribution of revenues for a number of years. But since July 1960 when Belgium gave independence to the Congo difficulties cropped up, because the traditional practice regarding the distribution of revenues could not be enforced.

Union Minière alone gave $39 million to Elisabethville last year. Out of the revenue of $65 million received by the Katangese régime in Elisabethville in 1961, $39 million came exclusively from Union Minière. Not a single penny went to the Central Government, as had been the practice before, for a number of years.

So this is the main problem of the Congo. All that the United Nations wants to do in the Congo is to maintain law and order and to maintain the unity and territorial integrity of the Congo including the maintenance of the practices which prevailed in the country before the transfer of power.

So far, of course, I have been encouraging the leaders, both the prime minister, Mr. Adoula, and Mr. Tshombé, to come to a peaceful settlement of their problems. I have tried my best to bring the two leaders together and my representatives both in Leopoldville and in Elisabethville have been instructed to create a climate favorable for the conduct of these negotiations.

As you know, two meetings took place, and the last meeting was adjourned only a few days ago without achieving any positive results. I am still trying to bring the two together. But if our efforts fail, I have certain steps in mind for the United Nations to take. And I have discussed these ideas with the representatives of the key delegations in New York, and I am discussing the same ideas with the leaders of the governments of the countries I have visited and I propose to visit. And perhaps it may be necessary for me some time toward the end of July or the beginning of August to call a Security Council meeting where I have to present the latest situation in the Congo so that the Security Council may be in a position to review the whole situation in the context of the latest developments and give me a fresh mandate if necessary or clarify the previous mandate.

I have been advised that the floor should be open to questions. I will be very glad to answer questions which you may like to put.

. . . . QUESTION: Sir, do you believe the situation in Berlin could be improved by the stationing of UN troops or by some other kind of UN presence?

THE ACTING SECRETARY-GENERAL: Regarding Berlin my own thinking is: if the four big powers primarily concerned with the problem of Berlin come to any agreement in any form, the United Nations should respond to such an agreement, either in the form of some kind of UN presence or in the form of the shifting of parts of the UN offices to Berlin or in whatever form they may agree to, because, as you all know, the big four powers are directly involved with the solution of the Berlin problem, and I think if they come to any agreement in any form, the United Nations should respond to this agreement.

QUESTION: Sir, in your briefing on the Congo problem you mentioned that you had discussed with key delgations and the countries you visited certain proposals you had in mind. Would you be more specific on your proposals? And the second question I would ask you is if in your opinion a controlled arms embargo for the Middle East would be desirable to reduce tensions between the Arab states and Israel?

THE ACTING SECRETARY-GENERAL: Regarding the first question: Since the Congo problem is directly concerned with the Security Council I had informal and private discussions with the representatives of the big powers which are represented in the Security Council. And of course I discussed with leaders of the British government in London during my brief visit there last week, and I propose to discuss these ideas with the government leaders in France where I will be next week, and of course I have discussed with the representatives of the United States and the Soviet Union too. Besides these big powers in the Security Council I have also discussed with the foreign minister of Belgium, Mr. Spaak. I do not think it will be in the public interest for me to reveal these ideas at this moment.

Regarding the second question on arms embargo for the Middle East I think it is primarily the concern of the relevant organ of the United Nations to decide. It is not for the Acting Secretary-General to express one view or the other on this subject. Of course if the relevant organ of the United Nations decides one way or the other it is my duty to implement such a decision.

QUESTION: Sir, what is your view on the reports of the military build-up in the Fukien province of Red China and the reports from nationalist China that the national Chinese government want to invade the mainland.

THE ACTING SECRETARY-GENERAL: On these matters I do not know anything beyond the press reports. So there is no means of assessing the truth of these reports and so I do not think I am competent to pass any judgment on these reported developments.

QUESTION: Mr. Secretary-General, what is your view on the European economic community?

THE ACTING SECRETARY-GENERAL: Well, to be frank I am not very familiar with the full implications of this projected European economic community in the context of the United Nations Development Decade. It needs further very close study. But of one thing I am sure. If the projected European economic community is inward-looking, parochial, and bellicose, it is not desirable. If the projected European economic community is outward-looking, imaginative, tolerant, and full of vision vis-à-vis the economic condition of the world at large, then it is very desirable. This is my assessment.

QUESTION: Sir, may I return to a question directly related to your work and that is the financial problem of the United Nations. The bonds issue has helped you over the crisis for the time being, but I do not know if that can solve the problem on a long-term basis. How do you expect the financial problems of the United Nations to be solved satisfactorily on a long-term basis?

THE ACTING SECRETARY-GENERAL: When we speak of the financial problems of the United Nations I think we should make a distinction between the normal expenses involved and the abnormal expenses. Regarding the normal expenses of the UN operations the United Nations is financially very solvent. Almost every Member state complied with the obligations under the United Nations Charter and there has been very little arrears outstanding. If I remember right regarding last year's assessment the United Nations has collected about 95 per cent of the dues. That is as far as the normal expenses are involved.

Regarding the peacekeeping operations like the Congo and the Middle East of course the United Nations is heavily in debt. If I remember right, the latest figures regarding collections is 73 per cent for the Middle East operations and 65 per cent for the Congo operations have been collected. Of course under the mandate of the General Assembly resolution of the sixteenth session, I have appealed to the Member states to purchase bonds and I want to take this opportunity of expressing my profound thanks to the people and government of Norway for their very active part in sponsoring the relevant resolution in the sixteenth session of the General Assembly and for their outstanding contribution toward the implementation of this resolution by coming out as the first Member state to buy UN bonds.

Of course, so far, about forty Member states have pledged or actually purchased bonds in the amount of approximately $66 million. And Washington may perhaps come out with its decision some time at the end of this month or perhaps beginning of next month. The Senate Committee has endorsed President Kennedy's proposals, and the matter is now before the House Committee. If the House Committee follows suit and endorses President Kennedy's proposal Washington will buy bonds in the amount of $25 million plus whatever amount that may be pledged by other Member states or other sources. That means, in effect, as of the moment Washington will buy, if the House Committee approves of President Kennedy's proposals, $25 million plus $66 million, that is approximately $91 or $92 million. So that will mean, in effect, the United Nations will have approximately $155 million and in anticipation of certain prospective purchases perhaps we may have $160 million, as against the anticipated $200 million.

So if we get this amount, of course the United Nations will be in a position to carry on the UN operations in the Congo at the present level for some time. If the General Assembly decides to maintain the present level of indebtedness the United Nations will be able to carry on much longer. If the General Assembly decides to redeem the present debts, of course the United Nations will be able only to proceed with its activities for a much shorter time. This is the matter for me to report back to the General Assembly at its next session, and regarding the political and military situation in the Congo, as I indicated earlier, I have to report to the Security Council in good time.

. . . . QUESTION: Sir, can you tell us your personal opinion about the last high altitude test?

THE ACTING SECRETARY-GENERAL: Oh, United States nuclear tests? Yes. I think on a previous occasion I made my views known to the public through a press conference. In the context of the General Assembly resolutions on the banning of nuclear tests—and of course I am in full agreement with these resolutions—I feel that the United States, or for that matter any other power, should not explode high altitude nuclear devices. The General Assembly resolutions mention nuclear tests; but the tests conducted the day before yesterday belong to a different category and they are more undesirable from my point of view for several reasons.

Of course, nuclear tests in general are undesirable in the context of the General Assembly resolutions, but these high altitude tests are more undesirable. In the first place, outer space has been agreed to by all Member states of the United Nations to be used exclusively for peaceful purposes. And secondly, many eminent scientists all over the world have protested against these high altitude tests. Of course there is a division of opinion among the scientists themselves. I am not a scientist but my feeling is: science in this particular field is still in its infancy. I think many things are still in the dark. Many scientists will confess that they are not aware of the full implications of these tests. So if I am to cite an analogy, these tests seem to me like a child playing with a naked razor blade without being conscious of the full implications of what he is doing. And another point is, after these United States tests I am almost sure the Soviet Union will follow suit and poison the atmosphere still further. So on a previous occasion I had expressed my views in the context of the General Assembly resolutions and I repeat my protest again today.

. . . .

4. *From Transcript of Press Conference*

HELSINKI　　　JULY 20, 1962

. . . . QUESTION: Mr. Secretary-General, will you stand as a candidate next year for the office of Secretary-General?

THE ACTING SECRETARY-GENERAL: So far, I have not made up my mind to offer myself for the next full term. Of course, I have to decide one way or the other during the forthcoming session of the General Assembly. As you all know, my present term expires on April 10, 1963 and, in fairness to the world organization, I must make my position clear a few months before the expiry of my term. My decision will depend on a few factors, if I may say so. For instance, I want to be pretty sure that I shall have the necessary means at my disposal to carry out the duties entrusted to me by the various organs of the United Nations if I am to carry on with my present task.

. . . . QUESTION: In a speech which you made about a couple of years ago, you expressed your view that ideological ties were something which could be passed over. Has your belief grown weaker or stronger during the time that has since passed?

THE ACTING SECRETARY-GENERAL: That is one of the lessons of history which I have always cherished. That lesson, as I have stated on a previous occasion, is that no country has permanent friends or permanent enemies, but only permanent interests. What one regards as one's friend today may be one's enemy tomorrow, and, in the same way, what one may regard as one's enemy today may well turn out to be a friend.

If one reads the history of mankind thoroughly and closely and deeply, one comes to the conclusion that no country in the world had permanent friends or permanent enemies, but only permanent interests. I feel rather strongly that the tensions in the world today, tensions born out of political ideologies, tensions born out of deep convictions in certain political ideologies, are not a permanent feature of human society.

UN Note to Correspondents No. 2627, July 26, 1962.

I may recall, for instance, the wars of the Crusades fought in Europe hundreds of years ago. In those times the Christians thought and believed that the Muslims were heretics, and that all Muslims must be killed. In the same manner, the Muslims also believed very strongly that the Christians were heretics and that all Christians must be put to the sword. Therefore, out of this psychological climate, built up for many years, the wars of the Crusades were fought, resulting in the deaths of thousands and thousands of both Christians and Muslims.

When tempers calmed down, it was realized that Christians and Muslims can live peacefully side by side, without coming into conflict with one another, and now, Christians and Muslims and, for that matter, Buddhists and Jews and Hindus are living peacefully, side by side, without conflict. I believe very strongly that these intense ideological conflicts, these conflicts born out of very strong convictions, are not a permanent feature of our society.

QUESTION: How do you visualize the role of the United Nations in the future? Will it be a world government or an arbiter of international disputes?

THE ACTING SECRETARY-GENERAL: Regarding the concept of the role of the United Nations in the world today, there are two schools of thought. One school maintains that the United Nations should be merely a debating forum or a conference machinery, that the United Nations should debate and discuss the problems which come up before the forum and do nothing more. On the other hand, there is another school of thought which maintains that the United Nations must develop into a really effective instrument for international conciliation, a really effective instrument to maintain peace and to prevent war. So, there are at present two schools of thought.

My personal feeling is that the vast majority of the Member states of the United Nations belong to the second school. They favor the concept of a growing United Nations; they favor the concept of a United Nations performing the functions of a real conciliator of international disputes, a real preventer of wars. I feel that only a very small minority of Member states subscribe to the view that the United Nations must be concerned only with debates and discussions, and nothing more. Of course, I agree that debates are a very civilized form of international conflict. They are necessary, but I also believe that the United Nations must be concerned with more activities than mere discussions and debates. That is my personal concept of the future of the United Nations, and I understand that the Government of Finland also subscribes to this view.

. . . .

---

5. *From Transcript of Press Conference*

NEW YORK　　　AUGUST 2, 1962

. . . . THE ACTING SECRETARY-GENERAL: On the invitation of the Soviet government, I propose to leave for Moscow on the 24th of this month. As in the case of previous visits, I shall take the opportunity of exchanging views with Mr. Khrushchev and other leaders of the Soviet Union on several issues facing the United Nations today. I have no particular item in mind for the moment, and of course I do not think it would be in the public interest for me to reveal now the specific items I propose to raise with the Soviet leaders.

QUESTION: Concerning this tentative new agreement between the Netherlands and Indonesia, do you have in mind any safeguards to ensure that the people of New Guinea will be more fortunate in expressing their views and exercising their right of self-determination than the people of Kashmir have been?

THE ACTING SECRETARY-GENERAL: Regarding the question of West New Guinea, the basic principle is that, whatever the two governments agree, will be agreeable to me. That is the basic principle, the basic purpose of my negotiations with the two governments. Of course, as you know, informal preliminary agreements were reached between the two governments' representatives last week under the auspices of Mr. Ellsworth Bunker who deputized for me in these informal negotiations. Of course Mr. Bunker was in constant contact with me throughout these negotiations. The two parties have come to a preliminary agreement on the modalities in the transfer of authority over West New Guinea and the implementation of the right of the Papuan people to self-determination.

UN Note to Correspondents No. 2635.

The present arrangement is that these preliminary agreements have to be confirmed by the two governments, and then formal and official negotiations will take place under my auspices some time in the middle of August. As I stated a couple of days ago, I am optimistic about the final outcome of these negotiations and I also feel that it will be very desirable for the General Assembly to endorse such an agreement and also to authorize me to implement the provisions of that agreement, without any financial involvement to this Organization. The present arrangement is that the Netherlands and Indonesia will table a joint resolution during the first couple of days of the seventeenth session of the General Assembly, and it has also been agreed that I should appoint a special representative for the territory immediately after the adoption of that resolution.

. . . . QUESTION: In Helsinki you said that before deciding to offer yourself for a full term you wanted to be sure that the necessary means were at your disposal for carrying out the duties entrusted to you. I would like to ask what these means are that you are talking about, and secondly do you have this assurance and, if not, when will you be able to decide that you will offer yourself for a full term?

. . . .

THE ACTING SECRETARY-GENERAL: All means, including financial. Of course I want to be pretty sure that the large majority of the Member states of the United Nations really want to contribute toward the development of the United Nations as a really effective instrument for international conciliation and a really potent force for peace. I want to be sure of this, and I also want to be sure whether I shall be able to play my little part in trying to bridge the gulf between the two giants. One of my primary objectives in accepting this present post was to try to create conditions whereby the big power blocs could come to a greater understanding regarding each other's points of view because I have a feeling, a very strong feeling, that in the second half of the twentieth century, the primary responsibility of leaders of thought and leaders of men all over the world should be directed toward the achievement of two objectives. Number one is to narrow the widening gulf between the rich and the poor countries, and number two is to create better understanding between the different ideological groups.

I attach very great significance to these two objectives, because as you all know, since the end of World War II the rich countries are getting richer and the poor countries are getting poorer, and this trend has been going on uninterruptedly. I think this division of the world into the rich and the poor is much more real and much more serious, and ultimately much more explosive, than the division of the world on ideological grounds.

Secondly, of course, I think it is the function of the leaders of men today to try to create better understanding between the East and the West. If I may be more candid, let me say this: to many Americans communism is an evil as absolute as nazism or murder, and anyone who questions this dogma is regarded as being afflicted with this contagion. In the same way, many Russians believe that capitalism is an absolute evil, like a hideous crime. My own belief is that both these extreme concepts are wrong. It is the duty of leaders of thought all over the world today, in the shadow of the nuclear bomb, to bridge this widening gulf and bring about conditions for a better understanding between these two giants.

QUESTION: Do you think that the newly proposed constitution for the Congo will result in the reunification of the Congo, and how long do you think United Nations Members should wait for this development before they apply sanctions to Katanga? Do you think you could call upon them for such sanctions yourself, or would the Security Council have to do it and are there votes in the Security Council to do that? How many permanent members, for example, would vote against a measure like that?

THE ACTING SECRETARY-GENERAL: About the drafting of the new Constitution for the Congo, as you all know, a parliamentary committee of the Congo has been working on a draft resolution for some time. This committee comprises all shades of political opinion in the Congo, including a member of the Conakat Party of Mr. Tshombé. The prime minister's office has also drafted a constitution based on the draft of that parliamentary committee.

Prime Minister Adoula has asked me to make available to him three or four constitutional experts to examine the draft, to go over it, to give finishing touches to it, so that he may be in a position to present the revised draft constitution to Parliament when it convenes in September.

One of the conditions of his request is that the constitutional experts, which the United Nations has to provide to him in the form of technical assistance, should be familiar with the workings of a federal type of constitution. He also indicated that he would be glad to have among these experts one from Africa. So I have suggested to him three countries from which these experts should be drawn. They are Nigeria, Switzerland, and Canada. I asked for his comments on my views.

Yesterday morning he came back with the suggestion that a fourth expert, preferably from India, should be included. So I am in contact with the governments of these four countries with a view to getting the services of competent constitutional lawyers for the Congo.

The present arrangement is that they will be in Leopoldville about the middle of August. I feel that they will be able to discharge their responsibilities in the course of three or four weeks, so that the final draft recommended by them will be placed before Parliament when it convenes in September.

Of course, I want to make this very clear: that whatever advice they offer to the government and to the Parliament will not necessarily reflect the views of the Secretary-General or the United Nations, as in the case of other technicians offered to that country or, for that matter, to any other country.

I also want to bring to your attention the procedures to be followed in revising the Constitution of the Congo. Of course, in the United States, also, if you want to revise the Constitution, or modify or amend the Constitution, you have to go through certain processes. The same processes apply to the case of the Congo.

First of all, Parliament must accept the amendment to the Constitution. That is the first stage. Then this amended Constitution, ratified by Parliament, must be endorsed by every provincial parliament in the Congo. This amended constitution must be ratified by all the six provincial parliaments in the Congo. If one provincial parliament rejects it, the revised Constitution is rejected. That is the situation.

. . . . QUESTION: Mr. Secretary-General, when you were in Helsinki you mentioned the transfer of power agreement between Belgium and the Congo in reference to payment of revenues. Would you say that under that agreement the onus of responsibility was placed upon such companies as the Union Minière and Tanganyika Concessions to continue to pay their revenues directly to the Leopoldville government? If so, has not the whole method of payment of revenue been in violation of this agreement?

THE ACTING SECRETARY-GENERAL: Yes. I think this is the whole crux of the problem.

As I have made clear on more than one occasion, the problem of the Congo is not as complicated as it has been made out to be in certain parts of the world. I think it is plain if we try to get at the root of the matter.

The problem is this: very big mining companies have been in operation in the Congo, particularly in Katanga, for nearly fifty years. There has been a system of distribution of revenues followed by these mining companies. A major part of the revenues went to the Central Government, and of course some part of the revenues went to the provincial government. This practice had been in operation since the inception of these mining companies in Katanga. Nobody denies this.

Then, two years ago, when the transfer of power took place, Belgium and the Central Government of the Congo agreed that the same practice should be carried on uninterrupted. That means, in effect, the mining companies operating in Katanga are required to follow the same practice as they had been following for the last fifty years before independence. That is simple enough.

But now what is the situation? In the last two years these mining companies did not pay a single cent to the Central Government, and they have been paying all their revenues to the provincial government in contravention of the agreement arrived at between Belgium and the Central Government of the Congo at the time of the transfer of power in July 1960.

Therefore, the position is this: The Central Government of the Congo requested the United Nations to do certain things. Of course, you know what things are authorized by the Security Council and the General Assembly. But in plain language, the Central Government of the Congo requested the United Nations to restore the conditions which were prevailing at the time of the transfer of power, to return to the *status quo*. It is as simple as that.

To cite a concrete analogy—of course, without any intention of offending anybody—supposing in Alaska there are fantastic gold mines in operation for fifty years—fabulous gold mines which have been exploited in Alaska—and these gold mining companies in Alaska have been paying their revenues to Washington for fifty years. Then suddenly two years ago the Governor of Alaska declared, "All revenues must come to me, not to Washington." Then he enlisted the assistance of certain foreign mercenaries from nearby countries. Perhaps he paid them as much as $1,000 per head per month. Then he threatened Washington, "Don't interfere in my internal affairs. Alasks is independent. I am President. Mr. 'B' is the Foreign Minister." So the government in Washington, the federal government, requests the United Nations to come to its assistance and asks the United Nations to restore the conditions which have been prevailing for fifty years. And the United Nations comes to the assistance of Washington. It is as plain as that analogy, however farfetched it may seem.

But there is a section of opinion, of course, in this country, as well as in a few other countries, that: the Governor of Alaska has certain political views which are identical to their own. The people of Alaska are more disciplined than the people of Massachusetts or Ohio. The armed forces in Alaska are better trained—they have more stability—while the government in Washington is nonaligned, neutral. Such views are dangerous.

The thinking of such people is not based on the facts, on justice, on fair play, on equity. It is based on certain considerations which are not at all relevant to the issues at stake.

This is the position.

QUESTION: Mr. Secretary-General, it is said that some Union Minière officials fear that, if they should now decide to pay revenues to the Central Government, Mr. Tshombé and his mercenaries would retaliate against the mining properties in Katanga. Is the United Nations prepared to guarantee any security to protect these mining interests?

THE ACTING SECRETARY-GENERAL: Yes. I have been in contact with the important governments directly concerned with the mining corporations operating in Katanga, and I have given them certain assurances.

Of course, as I have indicated earlier, these governments have been in daily consultation for the last five days. They have assured me that they will come up with their own formula in the course of the next one or two days.

. . . .

THE WEST IRIAN AGREEMENT

AUGUST—OCTOBER

ALTHOUGH U THANT'S initial intervention in the West Irian (West New Guinea) controversy in December 1961 had been limited, it was to become within a few months a major effort at mediation. He disclosed at a press conference on March 27, 1962, that he had been in "close consultation" with Dutch and Indonesian representatives "in secret and informal talks." He also reported that he was being represented by U. S. diplomat Ellsworth Bunker, who had been meeting with the two parties outside New York. In another meeting with the press, on April 24, he threw more light on the secret negotiations. He disclosed that the Bunker talks had been taking place "near Washington" (actually at Camp David in Maryland) and that Bunker had presented his own formula for a settlement. At the time he had made his statement the talks were in suspension and Bunker was devoting his efforts to getting them resumed.

By June the details of the Bunker plan had become known and Thant himself had endorsed it. It called for a phased transfer of the West Irian territory from the Netherlands to Indonesia, with the United Nations taking over administration of the territory for the first stage and an eventual plebiscite before 1969 to permit the people to decide their own future. At a news conference in London on July 7, Thant reported that the negotiations were about to be resumed and that once the parties agreed in principle, detailed discussions would be held in New York under his own auspices. "I am pretty optimistic about the outcome of these talks," he said.

At another press conference in New York on August 2, Thant said the two parties "have come to a preliminary agreement on the modalities in the transfer of authority over West New Guinea and the implementation of the right of the Papuan people to self-determination." He said the parties had agreed to embody the agreement in a joint resolution to be laid before the General Assembly in September for approval. The final agreement was reached August 15. It was approved by the Assembly on September 21 by 89 votes to none, with 14 abstentions (resolution 1752 [XVII]).

The settlement was significant for several reasons. One was that it represented one of the first major initiatives of the Acting Secretary-General in the field of peacekeeping. Another was that the agreement for the first time placed a territory under the direct administration of the United Nations. A third was that the operation was financed voluntarily by the Netherlands and Indonesian governments.

It was hailed as an important success for both Thant and the United Nations, but it had one embarrassing aspect. Once Indonesia took over the administration of the territory, it decided that it would not conduct a supervised plebiscite. Thant had more than once expressed confidence that Indonesia would carry out its undertakings in the letter and spirit of the agreement and of the United Nations Charter. (See p. 340.)

---

1. Statement at Ceremony for Signing an Agreement between Indonesia and the Netherlands

NEW YORK   AUGUST 15, 1962

ON THIS EVENTFUL OCCASION, when the agreement between the Republic of Indonesia and the Kingdom of the Netherlands in regard to the future of West New Guinea (West Irian) is about to be signed, I would like first of all to congratulate the two governments on their willingness to settle this question by peaceful negotiation, and also on their spirit of "give and take" which has made possible the conclusion of this agreement.

I am sure I am right in saying that, as a result, there will be not only an easing of tension in the area, but also an increased feeling of mutual trust and confidence between the two governments. It is a good augury that, with the signing of this agreement, diplomatic relations are to be resumed between the two countries, and I am sure that their future relations will be marked by the friendliness, understanding, and cordiality that have prevailed during these negotiations.

I would also like to take this opportunity to place on record, publicly, my gratitude to Ambassador Ellsworth Bunker who has acted on my behalf during the preliminary negotiations between the two governments and whose patience, integrity, and diplomatic skill have contributed so greatly to the successful conclusion of this agreement.

There are several unique features about this agreement. One is that, if the General Assembly endorses it, the United Nations would have temporary executive authority (established by and under the jurisdiction of the Secretary-General) over a vast territory for the first time in its history. Another is that the entire expenses to be incurred under the terms of this

UN Press Release SG/1291.

agreement are to be shared by the two governments and will not impose a burden on any of the other member governments. Considerable executive responsibilities are placed on the Secretary-General and Secretariat of the United Nations, some of which have necessarily to be undertaken, in the interests of peace and security, in anticipation of the approval of the General Assembly. It will be my endeavor and that of my colleagues to fulfill these tasks to the best of our capacity.

If these responsibilities are to be discharged to the satisfaction of all concerned, I shall need the willing cooperation of both governments, especially during the period of transition. I hope that my task will be facilitated by the scrupulous adherence on the part of both governments to the letter and spirit of this agreement. Without it my task would become immensely difficult, and I earnestly appeal to both governments to make their cooperation available to me in the fullest measure.

Before closing, I would like to congratulate once again the representatives of the two governments on the imminent signature of this historic agreement which, in line with the principles of the Charter, has settled peacefully a long-standing problem, with benefit to all concerned.

2. *Statement in the General Assembly*

NEW YORK   SEPTEMBER 21, 1962

BY ADOPTING the resolution sponsored by Indonesia and the Netherlands, the General Assembly has brought into force the agreement between these two states concerning West New Guinea—that is, West Irian. At the same time the Assembly has placed on the Secretary-General a very heavy responsibility indeed. I accept this responsibility and shall endeavour, to the best of my ability, to carry out the tasks entrusted to me under the Agreement.

I feel that this agreement sets an epoch-making precedent. Under it, for the first time in its history, the United Nations will have temporary executive authority—established by and under the jurisdiction of the Secretary-General—over a vast territory.

General Assembly Official Records, Seventeenth Session, 1127th plenary meeting.

The agreement is unique in another respect: although the United Nations has a vital role to play in implementing the agreement, the general membership of the Organization will not be required to meet additional financial burdens, as the entire cost of the United Nations operation will be borne by Indonesia and the Netherlands in equal proportions.

This novel settlement may well be a step in the gradual evolution of the United Nations as an increasingly effective instrument for carrying out policies agreed upon between Member governments for the peaceful resolution of their differences, in line with the Charter. On this basis, and at the request of the two governments, I have had to authorize certain steps in connection with the implementation of the agreement, in anticipation of its approval by the Assembly.

The agreement itself was made possible because of the spirit of accommodation between the two governments and their willingness to settle this long-standing dispute which had poisoned the relations between them. I am glad that, with the settlement of this dispute, diplomatic relations are to be resumed, and I hope that the future relations between the two governments will be marked by the same spirit of friendship, understanding and cordiality that made the agreement itself possible.

Some kind words have been said about my role in bringing about this agreement. I am grateful for these expressions of appreciation. I should, however, like to point out that a major burden of responsibility was borne, ably and willingly, by Mr. Ellsworth Bunker, who acted on my behalf during the preliminary negotiations. I have already paid public tribute to his patience, integrity, and diplomatic skill, which contributed so significantly to the successful conclusion of this agreement.

The representative of the Netherlands has just drawn special attention to the various articles of the agreement which provide the people of the territory with the opportunity to exercise freedom of choice. I am confident that the Government of Indonesia will carry out these undertakings, not only in the letter and spirit of the agreement itself, but also in the spirit of the Charter.

I have already referred to the heavy responsibility which is now placed on the shoulders of the Secretary-General. I know I can count on the cooperation of my devoted colleagues in the Secretariat who have shown in the past that they can always rise to the occasion. We shall all count upon the full cooperation of both governments, without which, of course, our task cannot be satisfactorily and successfully carried out.

I should like to inform the Assembly that I am arranging for copies of all instruments and documents in connection with this agreement and the resolution of the General Assembly thereon which has just been adopted to be transmitted to the Security Council for its information.

---

3. Message on the Transfer of Authority in West Irian

NEW YORK   SEPTEMBER 28, 1962

ON THE ASSUMPTION by the United Nations of its responsibility for the temporary administration of the territory of West New Guinea (West Irian), I should like to offer my sincere good wishes for the future of the territory. It is my hope that during its presence in the territory, the United Nations will receive the wholehearted cooperation of all. The United Nations Temporary Executive Authority will, to the best of its ability, endeavor to ensure the welfare of the inhabitants as provided in the agreement and solemnly underwritten by the Governments of the Netherlands and Indonesia.

The Administrator appointed by the Secretary-General will have the main responsibility of carrying out the tasks entrusted to the Secretary-General under the agreement. In the performance of his duties, he will be assisted by a group of international civil servants to carry on with the civil administration. There will be present small detachments of security forces under the United Nations command, including the contingent from Pakistan, whose function will essentially be to help the administrator in the maintenance of law and order in the territory.

I hope all of you will extend to the administrator and to his colleagues every help that they will need in carrying out the terms of the agreement. With the goodwill of all parties concerned I am sure the United Nations will be able to fulfill its role in carrying out the agreement in line with the Charter. I am confident that the spirit of understanding and accommodation shown during the period of the negotiation will continue to prevail and that the territory will make rapid progress in the years to come, and enjoy its full measure of prosperity.

UN Press Release SG/1330.

4. *Statement for Radio Netherlands*

NEW YORK   OCTOBER 1, 1962

THIS FIRST OF OCTOBER, when the United Nations Temporary Executive Authority in West New Guinea, or West Irian, comes into existence, signifies an important date for all of us. It is, in the first place, the culmination of difficult and protracted negotiations between Indonesia and the Netherlands which have led to full agreement with regard to the future of the territory. I am most pleased to see peaceful change and pacific settlement of disputes, as envisaged in the Charter, applied to this problem which had embittered relations between the two countries for a considerable time. Another purpose of the United Nations Charter, developing friendly relations among nations, will be fulfilled when, as a result of the settlement of this dispute, diplomatic relations between the two countries are resumed.

While the settlement of this dispute, on whatever terms, would already have been a notable achievement for the United Nations, the present agreement contains a number of novel features whose importance can hardly be overestimated. Under the agreement, a United Nations temporary executive authority will be established by, and under the jurisdiction of, the Secretary-General. The operation of this authority will, I am sure, be an object of study for many years to come by scholars in the legal and political fields. I might mention one interesting feature. There will be two transfers of authority. First the Netherlands administration will be transferred to the United Nations executive authority and this authority in turn, some time after May 1, 1963, will hand over full administrative responsibility to Indonesia. The period of United Nations authority is again divided in two phases, each symbolized by a different display of flags, and though these periods are relatively short, they indicate an orderly and phased transfer from one position to another.

There is another feature of this agreement which deserves attention: the consideration that has been given to the rights and interests of the

UN Note to Correspondents No. 2673.

inhabitants of the territory and the United Nations concern for the implementation of the relevant provisions.

It has been said, and not without justification, that the settlement of international disputes, if they are allowed to continue for a considerable time, becomes progressively more difficult and eventually impossible. This refers, of course, to a settlement as envisaged in the United Nations Charter. The present dispute was coming close to falling into this category. Thanks to the devoted efforts of the representatives of the two countries, and I should not omit to mention my representative, Ambassador Bunker, a solution was found at the eleventh hour, a solution that does honor to all concerned.

The first of October is therefore a significant day, not only in the life of the two countries most directly concerned, or the peoples of the territory, but also for the international community which, last week, with expressions of great satisfaction, approved the modalities of the settlement.

Introduction to the Seventeenth Annual Report

NEW YORK   AUGUST 24, 1962

CONTINUING THE PRACTICE initiated by Trygve Lie and followed by Dag Hammarskjöld, U Thant issued the introduction to his first annual report as a separate document summarizing his views on major problems of the year. It was a sort of state-of-the-world message and during his later years it was timed for release about the time the General Assembly opened its annual sessions.

In the introduction, dated August 24, 1962, Thant noted that the Congo problem continued to weigh heavily upon the Organization and that the situation at the time of writing was particularly crucial. He expressed the belief, however, that both the Congo situation and the United Nations financial difficulties would soon take a favorable turn. On the positive side, he cited the agreement between the Netherlands and Indonesia ending their long-standing conflict over West Irian or West New Guinea, as the Dutch called it.

The introduction provided the opportunity for him to voice his own concept of the United Nations and to express his views on the so-called "crisis of confidence" the Organization was going through. If any doubt remained as to whether he would follow in the footsteps of Lie and Hammarskjöld in trying to strengthen and expand the influence of the United Nations, he dispelled it at the very beginning of the introduction. He praised Hammarskjöld for his "unique contribution" to the development of the Organization as a dynamic force for peace, and asserted, "In my view, too, the responsibilities of the Organization in these changing times call for a dynamic rather than a static approach."

He called attention to the concern in some countries over the power shift in the United Nations resulting from the membership explosion, and to demands for weighted voting and to a growing trend to bypass the United Nations. While strongly opposing any departure from the principle of one-state, one-vote, he said he was not concerned over the tendency to settle major issues outside the Organization. Such a practice, Thant said, was not necessarily undesirable and he would welcome it so long as peace was made more secure. He stated that it was never intended that all problems should be settled within the United Nations and that many problems, taken out of the United Nations for discussion, finally came back to the Organization for ultimate settlement. The Acting Secretary-General concluded that the "crisis of confidence, if indeed there is such a crisis, is a passing phase." "I have faith," he said, "that the United Nations will survive this 'crisis' and emerge stronger than ever before as a force for peace."

THE YEAR covered by the present report has been a critical period in the life of the Organization. Amidst its efforts to resolve the continuing and urgent problem of the Congo, the United Nations suffered the tragic loss of Dag Hammarskjöld, its dedicated Secretary-General, and other members of his staff who accompanied him on his last journey to this troubled land. I have elsewhere paid tribute to his great personal qualities, to his unique contribution to the development of the United Nations in its formative years, and to his vision of the United Nations as a dynamic force for peace. In my view too the responsibilities of the Organization in these changing times call for a dynamic rather than a static approach.

Since the late Secretary-General signed, on August 17, 1961, the introduction to his last report on the work of the Organization, the Congo crisis has continued to weigh heavily on the United Nations. The rounding up of mercenaries in Katanga and the serious incidents which followed in September 1961 culminated in the tragic death of the Secretary-General. The cease-fire signed in October was not long or ever fully honoured by the Katangese and the Security Council spelled out in November its authorization to the Secretary-General to use force in order to complete the removal of the mercenaries. At the end of that month, Katangese outrages against United Nations personnel, civilian and military, and an overt attempt by roadblocks to immobilize the ONUC force in Elisabethville, brought about a situation there so explosive that even the uneasy peace that had prevailed since September could no longer be preserved. Hostilities broke out in December 1961 through failure of the Katangese to fulfil a promise to remove a strong roadblock. Later that month, after hostilities had come to an end by mutual agreement, a meeting was arranged between Prime Minister Adoula and Mr. Tshombé at Kitona, in an effort to reconcile their differences. Agreement was, in fact, reached but Mr. Tshombé held it to be, so far as he was concerned, conditional on acceptance by the Katangese legislature and it was honoured only in its less important aspects. During the first months of 1962 the United Nations continued its effort to bring about a peaceful and mutually acceptable end to the Katangese secession. Prime Minister Ad-

General Assembly Official Records, Seventeenth Session, Supplement No. 1A (A/5201/ Add. 1).

oula and Mr. Tshombé were brought together again for talks, this time in Leopoldville, and although large areas of agreement seemed to be reached, the talks collapsed in June of this year. It has become increasingly clear that the Katangese provincial authorities and the forces supporting them have felt that time is on their side, and must accordingly be gained at all costs; they make gestures of reconciliation leading to no practical results, whenever the pressure builds up, while at the same time seeking to further the aims of secession.

The core of the Congo problem is that of the secession of Katanga; the problem of the Katanga secession is primarily a problem of finance; the problem of finance, in turn, is the problem of the major mining companies. This is not an oversimplification of the facts. The end of the secession of Katanga would not mean a solution to all the problems of the young Congolese republic. Far from that. But as long as this secession is not ended, neither can the Congo move forward on the way to recovery, nor can the United Nations effectively fulfil its mandate of effective and massive technical assistance to the Republic.

The present situation in the Congo, which is particularly crucial—as I stated in the appeal sent to all Member states on July 31, 1962—in view of the lives, effort, and money already expended and currently being expended by the United Nations and the financial crisis into which this unprecedented drain on its resources has brought the Organization, must improve before long. Even as this is being written, a new effort toward reconciliation is being made with, it appears, new promise. Progress in the Congo is as essential for the good name of the Organization as for the Organization's continued usefulness in similar circumstances that may arise in the future.

II

Throughout the past year the financial difficulties confronting the Organization became increasingly serious as a result of the continuing need to incur large expenditures for ONUC and UNEF while a number of Member states failed to pay their assessments for the maintenance of these peacekeeping forces.

In an effort to ease the cash problem, and maintain the Organization's solvency pending a long-term solution for its financial requirements, the General Assembly at its sixteenth session adopted two exceptional measures. The first of these was the request to the International Court of

Justice for an advisory opinion on the question of whether the expenditures for maintaining ONUC and UNEF constitute "expenses of the Organization" within the meaning of Article 17, paragraph 2, of the United Nations Charter and therefore represent binding legal obligations on Member states to pay their assessments for these operations. The second measure was the authorization granted to the Secretary-General to issue during 1962 and 1963 up to $200 million of United Nations bonds bearing interest at 2 per cent per annum, with the principal repayable over a twenty-five year period.

On July 20, 1962, the International Court of Justice, by a nine to five majority, gave an affirmative answer to the question posed to it by the General Assembly. As of August 1, 1962, forty-six governments, including four non-Member states, had announced their intention to purchase United Nations bonds having a total value of more than $72 million. Actual bond sales had been made at that date to eighteen governments in the amount of $27,308,257.

If, as a result of the Court's opinion, Members in arrears in the payment of their ONUC and UNEF assessments make payments of the amounts due, and substantial pledges and purchases of United Nations bonds are forthcoming from other Members who have not yet been able to announce their intention to purchase United Nations bonds, the long-range financial prospects for the Organization would be more encouraging than has been the case since the beginning of the large peacekeeping operations several years ago.

For the immediate future, however, the financial difficulties confronting the Organization must be expected to continue, since no provision has been made for assessing Members for the costs of ONUC and UNEF beyond June 30, 1962, and some delay must be realistically anticipated before the Members in arrears pay their full assessments. Nonetheless I sincerely hope and believe that Member governments, who are all agreed on the indispensable role of the Organization in the world of today, will take appropriate action to solve its financial problems, which may otherwise severely limit its usefulness for the future.

III

In the course of the year, positive action was taken toward international cooperation in the peaceful exploration and use of outer space. Earlier difficulties were overcome, and in March 1962 the enlarged Committee on the Peaceful Uses of Outer Space met under encouraging signs, and later on, in May and June, the Scientific and Technical and the Legal Sub-Committees held their first session in Geneva.

The willingness of the two leading powers to cooperate in outer space exploration was expressed in a heartening exchange of messages between the President of the United States and the chairman of the Council of Ministers of the USSR, holding out prospects of a cooperative approach to the immense task of probing cosmic space and using the knowledge so gained for the benefit of all mankind.

The Scientific and Technical Sub-Committee agreed upon a series of recommendations concerning the exchange of information, the encouragement of international programs, and the organization of international equatorial sounding rocket facilities which offer a basis for practical and useful action.

In the Legal Sub-Committee no agreement was reached on the proposals submitted. However the discussions were regarded by delegations as a useful exchange of views on a number of important legal questions. It is my firm hope that a cooperative approach between the leading powers may be evolved without delay in this field, so as to ensure that the exploration of outer space will not be a source of discord and danger, but an area of understanding and increased confidence.

To provide a focal point for international cooperation in this field, a public registry of information furnished by states on orbital launchings has been established within the Secretariat, as well as an Outer Space Affairs Section, including scientific advisers, to assist the Committee in receiving and disseminating voluntary information supplied by Member states. Within the United Nations family, the World Meteorological Organization, the International Telecommunication Union and the United Nations Educational, Scientific and Cultural Organization are engaged in far-ranging studies on specific space problems, and the first reports prepared by the specialized agencies will be laid before the Assembly at its seventeenth session.

IV

While the progress in outer space has thus been somewhat encouraging, the same cannot be said in regard to the important problem of disarmament. The eighteen-nation Disarmament Committee had the advantage that for the first time eight non-aligned states were participating in it. I feel that their participation is a significant event. For one thing, it is a recognition of the fact that disarmament is a subject in which all nations, big and small, are concerned, and not just the great military powers. Further, the nonaligned states have been an important element exercising a moderating and catalytic influence in helping to bridge the gap between extreme positions of either side. It is regrettable that one of the members of the Committee, a great power, did not take part in its work. In spite of their meeting for three months between March and June of this year, and again from the middle of July, and in spite of orderly and business-like discussions in depth of the complex problem of disarmament, which helped to clarify the approaches of the parties, little progress has been made. At the same time, it is encouraging that both sides have, for the first time, submitted detailed draft treaty plans and that, in spite of the lack of progress, the parties are determined to continue their negotiation.

I feel that, in this field as elsewhere, certain steps have to be taken first. It is my conviction that to facilitate progress in the field of general disarmament, the first step has to be a cessation of nuclear testing. This question therefore deserves priority and I hope that the suggestions of the nonaligned countries, such as that contained in their joint memorandum, and in other ideas they have put forward, will provide a practical basis for a solution of this problem. I also sincerely hope that the nuclear powers will realize that the whole world is hoping and praying that an agreed first step may be taken soon.

V

On August 15, 1962, an agreement was signed between the representatives of the Governments of Indonesia and the Netherlands in regard to West New Guinea (West Irian). This agreement represented the culmination of nearly five months of negotiations which were initially held under the auspices of Ambassador Ellsworth Bunker, who acted as my representative, and were transferred to United Nations Headquarters when most of the points under negotiation had been discussed and preliminary agreement had been reached on them.

The agreement remains to be ratified by both governments and also needs to be approved by the General Assembly as a priority item in its seventeenth session. I believe that there will be no difficulty in this regard. I also feel that implementation of the agreement will not only lead to an easing of tension in the area, but also to a greater sense of trust and confidence between the two countries, which are to resume diplomatic relations.

One of the unique features of this agreement is that for the first time the United Nations will have temporary executive authority (established by and under the jurisdiction of the Secretary-General) over a vast territory. At a later stage, the United Nations will assist and participate in arrangements by Indonesia for the act of self-determination by the people of the territory. It is also noteworthy that the entire expenses that may be incurred under the terms of the agreement are to be shared by the two governments and will not impose a financial burden on the United Nations.

VI

The Charter recalls the determination of the United Nations "to promote social progress and better standards of life in larger freedom." This should serve as a timely reminder to all of us to rededicate ourselves to the task of making the Charter of the United Nations a living hope for all humanity; to eradicate poverty as a prime cause of conflict; and to strive energetically and purposefully toward the general welfare of mankind, as a basis for a just and enduring peace.

Never before in history have there been greater opportunities to meet this challenge. Never before has man held within his grasp the means with which to eliminate progressively want and disease and to build a lasting foundation for a world free from privation and fear. The technological and scientific achievements of the past decade stagger the imagination and stand out as a tribute to man's creative genius. No doubt we are on the threshold of even greater achievements. Yet much of the creative power of man unfortunately continues to be applied in large measure to the deplorable purpose of increasing his destructive potential, thus accentuating existing differences and conflicts. The dangers inherent in the continuation of the armaments race and nuclear tests are only too apparent. If this Organization is to make the principles enshrined in the Preamble of the Charter a living reality, there must be no pause in the determined, sincere, and continuing campaign to reduce world tensions and hostility. The people of the world who continue to live in such a tense and surcharged atmosphere, replete with the ever present threat of total destruction, are entitled to look forward to the dawn of a new era in which every man, woman, and child in every country can be expected to live above want and in dignity, at peace with themselves and with the rest of mankind.

The emergence in recent years of scores of territories from colonial rule to independence and the clear prospect that the remaining colonial areas will shortly take their rightful places among the family of nations lend urgency to demands upon the international community to provide them with material and technical assistance, if these new nations are to achieve the monumental tasks of making their newly won independence meaningful through as rapid development of their economic and social potential as possible.

While much has been accomplished in the past two decades to mobilize resources on an international as well as on a bilateral basis to assist in lifting the living standards of two-thirds of the human race living in poverty and want, it is abundantly clear that the rate of development has fallen far short of meeting the needs and hopes of emerging peoples, and the risk cannot be ignored that their disappointment may well overflow to the extent of endangering an orderly pace of development. I have said and would like to repeat that the present division of the world into rich and poor countries is, in my opinion, much more real and much more serious, and ultimately much more explosive, than the division of the world on ideological grounds.

In a timely decision the General Assembly designated the present decade as the United Nations Development Decade, a global effort to mobilize, in cooperation with the specialized agencies, the accumulated experiences and resources of mankind in a full-scale and sustained attack on poverty, disease, hunger, and illiteracy. These evils are not only affronts to human dignity; each intensifying the other, they menace the stability of governments, aggravate tensions, threaten international peace.

In launching the United Nations Development Decade, the General Assembly has dramatized the importance and urgency of the work to be accomplished for reversing the trend toward wider differences in levels of living between rich and poor countries. Whether or not the latter will be able to achieve self-sustained growth over the next few years depends primarily on their own efforts and on an increase in international cooperation and assistance for which the Organization is at present neither the only instrument nor the most important channel. Member states have made it clear, however, that they wish the Organization to play a central role and to be a focal point for the formulation and evaluation of measures and policies which may affect or influence the pace and direction of the development process in national or regional contexts.

In addition to making recommendations to governments, the General Assembly and the Economic and Social Council have taken steps to ensure increased action through United Nations organs. Less conspicuous than the thrashing out of the political issues with which the United Nations is seized, but hardly less far reaching in the long term, are the intensification of the work on industrial development and the emphasis laid on projections, planning, and programming for balanced economic and social development. The resolve of the Economic and Social Council to convene a United Nations Conference on Trade and Development is a major move toward stimulating thought and practical action of worldwide scope in a crucial area. The progress already made in the preparations for the United Nations Conference on the Application of Science and Technology for the Benefit of the Less Developed Areas is a further harbinger of the growing capacity of the United Nations system to inspire, and help in bringing about, the achievement of the objectives of the Development Decade.

With the bolder approach of the Council and of its Commission on International Commodity Trade to the preoccupying questions of commodity prices and trade expansion, the decision of the Council to establish a Committee on Housing, Building and Planning, the setting up in the Secretariat of an Economic Planning and Projections Centre and of a Centre for Industrial Development evidence the determination of our governing bodies to assert the over-all responsibilities of the Organization and to improve its ability to contribute effectively to progress toward the objectives of the Development Decade.

With the increased contribution that the regional commissions and their secretariats are making to the global effort by assuming spearhead functions on the strength of their knowledge and experience of local conditions, with the growing interplay of operational work and research activity, and with the closer cooperation among agencies of the United Nations family exemplified by such projects as the joint UN/FAO World Food Program, the Organization should be able to play, in the worldwide strategy for fostering economic and social development, a role not less important than that devolving upon it for peacekeeping operations. As in the case of peacekeeping operations, its response to the challenge is conditioned by the ability to mobilize the services of experienced and dedicated personnel, and by the sustained availability of adequate financial resources, including provision for a controlled expansion of the staff resources necessary for carrying out the tasks laid on the Secretariat in a growing body of unanimously adopted resolutions.

In this mobilization for speedier progress in economic and social development, the major effort has to be made by the countries themselves. In addition, two facts merit special attention.

The first is that the United Nations and its related agencies can go forward in their greater responsibilities from positions of considerable strength. Not only do they command a wealth of knowledge and experience, as also the services of a number of dedicated and talented people; they also have the full confidence of the developing countries they wish to serve.

In this connection, the increased resources of the Expanded Programme of Technical Assistance and its reorientation toward higher priority objectives and improved procedures are worthy of note. The Special Fund, for its part, is demonstrating dramatically the fundamental soundness of its approach and the rich potentialities of its assistance to large scale, high impact preinvestment projects. At the same time, the modest but steady growth of the operational and executive personnel programme has revealed the suitability of this type of assistance for an increasing number of situations.

The United Nations family of organizations is thus both eager and technically and organizationally qualified to assume the larger responsibilities placed upon it by the United Nations and requested of it by the developing nations. This is the first fact to be recognized in facing the challenge of the United Nations Development Decade.

The second fact, highly relevant to the first, is at this moment not quite so encouraging. It arises from the reality that bringing about the indispensable rate of advance in the low-income countries is going to cost much money. Many if not most of the low-income countries are making serious, in some cases even heroic, efforts to extract from their own very limited available resources the substantial amounts they must invest in their development. At the same time, a greater measure of assistance is required of the wealthier countries. The sum total of their contributions must be increased progressively during the United Nations Development Decade, and a growing proportion of that assistance could with undoubted advantage to each and to all be channelled through the United Nations.

Will the required resources be forthcoming for a coherent, constructive program that can lift the developing countries to the place of self-sustaining growth as partners in a dynamic world economy? The task is one for all people of all nations, and it is sufficient to unite the world. It will not be accomplished without vigorous leadership and without the enthusiastic participation of the thousands of millions of ordinary men and women in the advanced and the low-income countries alike and together. In this task, the United Nations can, given the means, play a unique and indispensable role.

VII

In recent years the membership of the Organization has increased by more than double its original number and has made considerable progress toward true universality. A cursory examination of the growing number of items inscribed in the agenda of recent sessions provides convincing evidence of the wide scope of the subjects, from urgent items affecting the welfare of the international community to minute details of "housekeeping." In these circumstances it is not surprising that the conduct of business in the General Assembly and its Main Committees has in recent years become increasingly complicated and, in some instances, excessively prolonged. In his letter of April 26, 1962, the President of the General Assembly during its sixteenth session transmitted to me for circulation to all delegations of Member states a memorandum containing certain suggestions concerning changes which might be made in the work of the General Assembly in the interest of greater speed and efficiency. In commending the President's timely suggestions to the consideration of the General Assembly, I wish to enlarge upon a few of the points dealing with the broader aspects of the work of the General Assembly, namely the problems arising from resumed sessions and the creation of subsidiary organs having overlapping terms of reference. The General Assembly of the United Nations was conceived as a body which, among other things, would provide leading statesmen of the Member states with an opportunity to come into close contact with each other and to lend not only greater authority to the Assembly's work, but, what is even more important, to help shape the decisions of individual Member governments on major issues. All too frequently, this purpose has been defeated in the general debate for reasons set forth by the president.

As regards his remarks concerning the grouping of items dealing with different aspects of the same problem, it is useful to bear in mind that it is not only the substance of the debate to which consideration must be given by each delegation, but also to the conclusions and recommendations which may have to be formulated. Were similar questions to be considered collectively, as suggested, it might avoid in turn the duplication of discussion as also the proliferation of special and other committees with overlapping responsibilities. This is true of the political as well as the economic field. To mention just one example, in the field of non-self-governing territories, some four committees and special committees are dealing with matters that might usefully be combined, thus relieving the concerned delegations of otherwise added burdens and at the same time reducing costs and staff requirements. It may perhaps be possible to concentrate all the work in this field under the special committee which was set up pursuant to resolution 1654 (XVI).

I wish particularly to commend the proposal that the date for the beginning of the regular session of the General Assembly be advanced to the first Tuesday in September, thus adding two weeks to the duration of the Assembly's session. Such an extension might contribute materially to avoiding resumed or special sessions by giving added time for the conclusion of the Assembly's business during the regular session.

If I have touched upon an aspect of the work of the General Assembly, which is master of its own procedures, I have done so for two reasons. One of them is the personal reason that I have some experience of the floor. Secondly, I feel that the General Assembly should indeed be the parliament of mankind, in these days of rapid change, with the ever-present threat of nuclear global war. The present procedures might have suited an Assembly with fewer members and confronted by less momentous issues. They do not suit the present, when the membership is already approaching 110, and the agenda items, too, may exceed a hundred. A streamlining of procedures has thus become progressively more urgent and necessary, so that the voice of the Assembly may be heard with respect, and in time, all over the world.

VIII

I have so far dealt with specific problems and issues which have been engaging my personal attention. Before closing I would like to deal with a more general problem—that of the so-called "crisis of confidence" in the United Nations. The same historic process which has liberated so many countries and regions in the world from colonialism and which has enabled the Organization to make steady progress toward universality of membership has also upset the original balance of forces within the United Nations. As a result there are suggestions that the principle of one vote per member will perhaps have to be reconsidered. I would like to state unequivocally my position on this proposal. On this, as on any other proposal, I am bound by the Charter provisions as they stand. In the Preamble itself the United Nations expresses its determination "to reaffirm faith . . . in the equal rights . . . of nations large and small." Article 2, paragraph 1, states more explicitly: "The Organization is based on the principle of the sovereign equality of all its Members." At the same time, and as a natural corollary, there is a reciprocal responsibility on the part of all sovereign states to recognize and respect the sovereign rights of other states. I believe that if the United Nations is to survive as a dynamic force for peace and security, these provisions have to be honoured in the letter and the spirit of the Charter.

I have heard it said that if the Charter provision on this subject is not revised then there will be an increasing tendency to settle major issues outside the United Nations. This prospect does not discourage me for a variety of reasons. In the first place, I do not believe that it was ever the intention that all problems should be solved within the United Nations, nor was the United Nations conceived as the sole means of conducting international diplomacy. Clearly it is a relatively novel method of diplomacy, continuously available in the service of peace in addition to the normal bilateral and multilateral channels. To the extent that problems which pose a potential threat to the peace and security of the world may be solved by discussions among the powers mainly concerned, whether within or outside the United Nations, the peace of the world is made more secure and I welcome it. Oftentimes it may happen that when such a settlement has been negotiated outside of the United Nations, the terms of the agreement may be brought forward for formal ratification by a principal organ of the United Nations in order to give it added authority and solemnity. Lastly, I have observed that many problems which are, hopefully, taken out of the United Nations' context finally come back to the United Nations for debate, negotiation, compromise, and ultimate settlement. This is particularly true of global issues in which the small powers are as much interested as the major powers.

For these reasons I believe that the "crisis of confidence," if indeed there is such a crisis, is a passing phase. I have faith that the United Nations will survive this "crisis" and emerge stronger than before as a force for peace. In restating my faith in the United Nations I am moved by one more consideration, and that is the increasing tendency to involve the United Nations in the process of combating want and poverty and disease and in helping the advancement of the developing countries. Earlier in this introduction I have dealt at length with the United Nations Development Decade. Here I would like to say only this: that the constructive work of the United Nations "for the promotion of the economic and social advancement of all peoples" is the solid basis on which the political effectiveness of the United Nations must rest. The steady and unobtrusive work of the United Nations and its family of agencies to further economic and social progress may not make headlines, but it is more lasting in its contribution to the prosperity, and the peace, of the world.

U THANT
Acting Secretary-General

August 24, 1962

Statement Broadcast by Radio Moscow

MOSCOW   AUGUST 30, 1962

TODAY I AM CONCLUDING my five-day visit to the Soviet Union, and my heart is filled with thankfulness for the people and the government of this great country under Chairman Khrushchev for having made this visit possible.

I am no stranger to this country, since I had visited it in 1955, though in a different capacity. In Moscow, in Yalta, and in Kiev I saw very striking changes. Innumerable new buildings have arisen in seven years; streets are cleaner and the people look happier. There was even a festive air in some of the places I visited. As usual, warmth and friendliness were in evidence all around.

The leaders of the Soviet Union with whom I had the opportunity to exchange views on some of the major problems facing the world today, impress me with their desire for peace and their keenness to do away with the vestiges of the last war. But fear and suspicion which for so long have characterized international relations are still in evidence here as in the West.

Let me be candid. When the Soviet foreign policy did concern itself with what was happening in the rest of the world—for instance in the Congo—it did so out of fear and suspicion: fear of losing potential friends and suspicion of what it regarded as "imperialist."

And I beg to be excused for saying that the Russian people do not fully understand the true character of the Congo problem. This lack of understanding is probably due to the absence of presentation of the other side of the coin, and I am sure that if only they have the means of knowing all the facets of the problem they will certainly revise their opinion of the nature of the United Nations' involvement in the Congo and decide to shoulder their share of the heavy responsibilities now being undertaken by the world organization in seeking a peaceful solution of the Congo problem.

I am saying all this with a heavy heart, because diplomacy demands honeyed words. I am not a believer in honeyed words, since they will not

UN Press Release SG/1307.

help the great and courageous people of the Soviet Union to arrive at a balanced appraisal of the situation.

I am particularly grateful to the president of the presidium of the supreme soviet of the USSR, Mr. Leonid Ilyich Brezhnev, for having graciously granted me an audience; to Chairman Khrushchev, who received me as a member of his family and who gave me an illuminating exposition of the Soviet approach to major problems; to Mr. Kosygin, first deputy premier; to Mr. Gromyko, foreign minister, and to other Soviet leaders for the opportunity provided to me for a most friendly and useful exchange of views.

I shall certainly cherish the happiest memories of my present visit to this great country for years to come, and I very sincerely wish the people of the Soviet Union peace and prosperity, and friendship with all peoples which they desire.

I also want to take this opportunity of offering my grateful thanks to the people and government of the Ukrainian SSR for the very warm hospitality accorded to me during my brief stay in Kiev.

"Progress toward Peace"
From Address at the University of Warsaw
WARSAW, POLAND   AUGUST 31, 1962

. . . .

I DO NOT BELIEVE that it is possible to reach general and complete disarmament overnight, because the arms race is merely an external manifestation of a deep-rooted feeling of mistrust and lack of confidence. This mistrust has built up over the years and will not die a sudden death.

Progress toward its removal is one of the major tasks, not only of statesmen but also of men and women of good will all over the world. In this task of making progress toward better understanding of each other, I feel again that the non-aligned countries can play a valuable role.

In particular I feel that one of the first steps in making progress in this direction is the cessation of nuclear testing. Equally important is the prevention of the spread of nuclear weapons.

It is a sad commentary on the situation of the world today that the means for the extermination of the human species is now in the hands of the three or four great powers. In due course, it will pass into the hands of many governments, large and small.

There was a time when only the United States had nuclear weapons. This was followed by a time when only the United States and the Soviet Union had such weapons. Later the United States, the Soviet Union and Britain possessed them. And now France has joined the nuclear club. It seems likely that one or two other countries may shortly manufacture these terrible weapons.

It is also obvious that during the next few years the manufacture of engines of mass destruction will become cheaper and easier. There is no end to this process until many states will be in a position to inflict incalculable destruction on the rest of mankind.

As I have stated on a previous occasion, if all sovereign states were governed by rulers possessed of even the rudiments of sanity, they would be restrained from committing such colossal crimes. But experience has

UN Press Release SG/1299.

shown that, from time to time, power in one country or another falls into the hands of rulers whose sanity is clouded by the pursuit of individual or national glorification.

There is still another hazard to mankind that stems from the sheer number of people who handle these weapons of mass destruction. I have no doubt that the designers and manufacturers of nuclear weapons have attempted to install in them certain mechanical safeguards against accidental firing or explosion.

There are, however, no final or foolproof safeguards against the possibility of human or mechanical failure. The danger of war by accident is therefore ever present. This is one aspect of the problem on which there can be no two opinons.

No one in his senses can maintain that testing of nuclear weapons can contribute to human happiness. We must bend all our energies to put a stop to these tests. Time is already running short, and every day's delay entails untold risks. The greatest risk lies in doing nothing, in wasting time in hair-splitting and meanwhile in piling up nuclear and thermonuclear weapons. The hydrogen bomb is a greater evil than any evil it is intended to meet.

One fact clearly emerges out of the negotiations and discussions both inside and outside the United Nations. This fact is that action can be taken on major issues only if the United States and the Soviet Union are in agreement.

Disarmament, the cessation of nuclear weapons tests, and the prevention of the spread of nuclear weapons are problems which call for an immediate solution. Only a spirit of trust and understanding by both sides can lead to a satisfactory solution of these pressing problems and thereby meet the greatest challenge of our time.

Address on United Nations Staff Day

NEW YORK   SEPTEMBER 14, 1962

ONE OF THE MAJOR worries in the United Nations Secretariat during U Thant's first months as Acting Secretary-General was the possible consequences of wider geographical distribution. Thant was well aware of this and he seized upon the occasion of Staff Day to reassure those who feared the geographical adjustments might cost them their jobs. While endorsing the plans, which had been initiated before he took office, he told the staff the changes would be made as vacancies arose and new posts were created and that he would not permit the changes to affect the legitimate interests of the existing career staff. He also broke a piece of bad news: because of the UN financial crisis pay increases would have to wait.

I AM VERY HAPPY to be with you on this occasion and to have this opportunity to say a few words to you. I know that it is many years since the Secretariat had occasion to celebrate Staff Day on such a big scale as is planned for this year. I hope that in the years to come Staff Day may be an annual function. I believe that it is a good idea for us to get together like this once a year, and to rededicate ourselves to the high principles of the Charter as well as the great traditions of the Organization.

Today I would like to begin by thanking all my colleagues in the Secretariat for the wonderful support and cooperation they have given me from the time that I took charge as Acting Secretary-General. On that occasion I referred to the many problems facing the Organization and said: "If I am to discharge these responsibilities, surmount these difficulties, and resolve these problems, I shall need, in the first instance, the wholehearted support, friendly understanding, and unstinting cooperation of all my colleagues."

I want to take this opportunity to acknowledge publicly my deep debt of gratitude to all my colleagues for the excellent team spirit they have shown. During the ten months that I have been in charge, the work of the Organization has become no easier. The Congo continues to be a drain on

Unnumbered mimeographed document.

our reservoir of experienced men and women. We have undertaken new responsibilities, for example, in West New Guinea. I know that many of my colleagues have had to work long hours and bear heavy burdens, and they have done so cheerfully. For all this I am truly grateful.

Friends, as you are all aware, the United Nations is supposed to be undergoing a "crisis." I have referred at some length to this problem in my introduction to the annual report, which many of you might have had a chance to read. If we are to survive this "crisis" I shall need the continued understanding and esprit de corps of all staff members. We have to show the world that we, coming as we do from different countries with different ideologies and traditions, are united in the service of the United Nations.

Working as we do here, we have a great opportunity to learn that in this complex world of today there is no point in thinking in terms of black and white. It is no longer true to say that there are two sides to every question: there are many sides. We thus have a unique opportunity to cut through clichés and to see how right-minded persons can have widely divergent views on the merits of specific proposals for solving the problems of our complex existence. We have to learn to understand each other and to develop a spirit of "one world." We have to develop such a spirit because, thanks to the technological revolution, especially in the field of transport and communication, we have indeed only "one world" today. I would therefore hope that my colleagues in the Secretariat would look upon their service in the United Nations as an opportunity for not only propagating the spirit of "one world," but for setting an example of "one worldliness" to the rest of the world. In this way the Secretariat can help the Organization to survive the so-called "crisis", and to emerge stronger than before in its ability to serve the cause of peace.

There is, however, one crisis which is real—and that is the financial crisis. I have recently had occasion to meet with the staff committee representatives and I have listened to their problems and grievances with sympathy. I wish I could do more to redress those grievances, but there is the problem of matching resources with needs. In view of the present financial situation of the United Nations I feel that in some cases the redress of even the most genuine grievances may have to wait. I would appeal to you to be patient meanwhile.

One other problem which I know has been agitating you all is the question of "geographical distribution." Here again I would like to say this—that I believe that this problem should be solved if the United

Nations is to be more effective in the future. At the same time, I would assure you that in doing so I would certainly not allow the legitimate interests of the existing career staff to be adversely affected. We all know that the Secretariat is effective only to the extent that it commands the confidence of all Member states. Such confidence requires that no Member state should nurse a grievance that it is not adequately represented in the Secretariat for lack of effort on the part of the Secretary-General. However, I do not believe that this problem can be solved overnight, but only over a period of time as vacancies arise and new posts are created. I would also need to have the willing cooperation of the underrepresented countries themselves if we are to solve this problem speedily and to our mutual satisfaction.

Before closing I would like to wish all of you the best of everything and hope that the festive program that has been planned for today will be an enjoyable one. I myself look forward very much to participating in these festivities.

DURING LATE AUGUST and early September 1962, U Thant held his first private talks, as Acting Secretary-General of the United Nations, with Nikita Khrushchev and John F. Kennedy. He also visited the capitals of Brazil, the Soviet Ukraine, Poland, Czechoslovakia, and Austria. His talks in Moscow and Washington were especially important because of the critical problems in which the two super powers were involved. The main ones were the Congo and the developing Cuban missile crisis. His visit to Moscow represented a restoration of normal relations between top-level Soviet officials and the office of Secretary-General, which had been virtually nonexistent during the previous two years since the Kremlin broke with Dag Hammarskjöld over the conduct of the Congo operations. Thant had also had his differences with the Soviet Union over the Congo, but he was able to maintain contact. One of the things he discussed with Khrushchev, he confirmed later, was his plan of national reconciliation in the Congo. It was during this visit that he made a most unusual statement in a broadcast to the Soviet people. He asserted, in his usual frank way, that "the Russian people do not fully understand the true character of the Congo problem." This, he said, was probably due to the fact that they had heard only one side of the problem. There were no public repercussions, but privately some Soviet officials let it be known that they were annoyed.

Among other subjects discussed by Thant in Moscow and Washington were the critical UN financial situation, disarmament, and Berlin. He said he did not exclude a possible meeting between Khrushchev and Kennedy on Berlin, but declined to say whether he was acting as a go-between in trying to set up such a meeting. He said he was in favor of summit meetings but that he would not reveal "what transpired between me and the heads of government." One of the surprising results of his talks with the super powers was his conclusion that the Cuban situation was "psychological rather than military" and that it was not likely to generate a serious crisis.

The main source of information on these visits was his press conference on September 17, 1962, after his return to Headquarters. One of the things he was asked about was his speech at the University of Warsaw on August 31, in which he expressed concern over the arms race. Among other things, he said time was running short for a ban on nuclear testing and that the key was agreement between the United States and the Soviet Union. He told UN correspondents he was a firm believer in the importance of personal relationships in diplomacy and that "it would be helpful if the leaders of governments, particularly the leaders of important countries, were to meet from time to time to exchange views." Thant was to press for such summit meetings many times in the future.

MR. PIERRE J. HUSS (President, United Nations Correspondents Association): Mr. Secretary-General, permit me to welcome you back, before we start, from your continental journey to capitals and suburbs and Black Sea resorts. I hope your strenuous trip has been a reward in itself. I may, at the same time, express the wish, in the name of the United Nations correspondents, that when we meet after the Assembly we shall also have cause to celebrate the success, from your standpoint, of this Assembly session.

THE ACTING SECRETARY-GENERAL: Thank you very much, Mr. Huss. I shall make a very brief introductory statement before giving the floor to the correspondents present here. I thank you for your very kind words.

Since we last met early in August, I visited a few Member states at the invitation of the respective governments. The countries that I visited were Brazil, the Soviet Union, the Ukrainian SSR, Poland, Czechoslovakia, Austria and, of course, the United States of America. In fact, my last week's visit to Washington was my first official visit to the capital of the United States in my present capacity.

I exchanged views with the government leaders on some of the major problems facing the world today, and particularly problems before the United Nations. I came back with one indelible impression, that all governments which I met want the United Nations to perform as its founders wished it to perform. There is a consensus among them that the United Nations should develop into a really effective instrument for the promotion of peace and the prevention of war. They differ only in the organizational and procedural aspects of the functioning of this Organization. These aspects, of course, will be the subject of further attention of the Member states.

Since we last met, many important things have taken place involving in some way the United Nations. The Netherlands and Indonesia have come to an agreement after a prolonged dispute regarding the modalities of the transfer of administration of West New Guinea to Indonesia and the implementation of the right of self-determination of the people of West New Guinea.

In the Congo, the constitutional experts, sent under the auspices of the United Nations, are actively involved in the drafting of a new constitution, at the request of the Central Government of the Congo, designed to

UN Note to Correspondents No. 2662.

meet the aspirations of all sections of opinion in that country. As you all are no doubt aware, I have presented my proposals to the Central Government of the Congo and Mr. Tshombé, with a view to implementing, without further delay, the relevant Security Council resolutions. The results of these proposals are still awaited.

I shall not take more of your time with further observations; the floor is now open to questions.

QUESTION: The last time we met, you spelled out some of the conditions which you had in mind before deciding to accept candidacy for the post of Secretary-General. Since then you have travelled to these capitals, and I wonder whether you are now prepared to tell us if you have made a decision, and what it is.

THE ACTING SECRETARY-GENERAL: Actually, I have nothing much to add to the statements I made on one or two previous occasions. I have not decided one way or the other regarding my availability for the next term. Of course, as I have indicated earlier, my decision will be governed primarily by a few considerations, including the prospects of an early settlement of the Congo problem, the prospects of the stability of this world Organization as a potent force for peace, and the prospects of my playing a humble part in bringing about a more favorable atmosphere for the easing of tensions, and, if I may say so, the prospects of my ability to bridge somewhat the gulf between the two giants.

My decision, of course, will depend on these factors, among others. And, as I have indicated earlier, I must announce my decision—to be fair to this world Organization, to the service of which I am very much devoted—in the course of this session of the General Assembly. I believe that the picture will be clearer some time in the next month or so, and only then will I be in a position to decide one way or the other.

Of course, I want to add this: before I come to any decision—whatever I decide—I want to be satisfied that my decision will not impair or minimize the effectiveness of this Organization in its operations.

QUESTION: In Warsaw, you spoke on the question of the atomic peril, atomic testing, and the nuclear race, and, at the conclusion of your speech at the University, you stated that time is already running short and that every day of delay entails untold risks. In that same speech, you also referred to what you have just stated: that much depends on the two giants. I was wondering whether you feel it would be worthwhile and useful for the two giants, upon whom hangs the fate of mankind, to meet at a very early date and take up these very perilous problems.

THE ACTING SECRETARY-GENERAL: As you all know, I am a confirmed believer in the importance of the human factor, in the importance of personal relationships in diplomacy, in international relations. I believe that it would be helpful if the leaders of governments, particularly the leaders of important countries, were to meet from time to time to exchange views. Of course, in my speech at Warsaw University, and elsewhere, I made this point very clear, and I feel that, in the shadow of the hydrogen bomb, we—and, when I say "we," I mean particularly the people from small countries—must bend all our energies to bringing about conditions for the easing of tension, for the elimination of the fear and suspicion which has been in existence for so long. I think that I reflect the conscience of the whole world when I say that. The people are becoming more and more impatient with the slowness of the progress in disarmament negotiations, and particularly on the question of a test ban, which, as you all know, did not make any headway in Geneva and is coming up again as an item before the seventeenth session of the General Assembly. I am inscribing the disarmament item on the agenda of the seventeenth session under rule 15 of the rules of procedure.

QUESTION: Mr. Secretary-General, I would like to ask a question about Cuba. The Government of Cuba says it is in danger of invasion by the United States and reports armed attacks from vessels coming from United States ports. The United States government says that the Soviet presence in Cuba threatens its security and that it will intensify its surveillance. The Government of the Union of Soviet Socialist Republics says it is aiding Cuba with arms and indicates it will fight if Cuba is invaded. Inasmuch as all three of these concerned countries speak of a break of the peace, do you in this situation have any suggestions to make to them or do you visualize any initiatives which the General Assembly, the Security Council, or yourself can take to safeguard the peace of the world in this area?

THE ACTING SECRETARY-GENERAL: This is of course very delicate ground to tread on, but my own belief is that the United States will not attack Cuba and that Cuba will not attack the United States. I am convinced of it. But in this connection I want to make a very brief observation. Most Americans have been restless for some time in the past two years at the presence of what they regard as hostile elements just ninety miles from their coast.

To go back a little to the history of the postwar period, you will recall that at every session of the Communist Party Congress in Eastern European countries, some sort of a European Monroe Doctrine was adopted and reiterated. You will no doubt recall that most of the Russians also have been telling the world that elements they regard as hostile have been just across their frontier for seventeen years. Of course it is far from my intention to equate these two positions. I am just stating the facts as I see them. As I indicated earlier, I do not think for a moment that the United States intends to invade the Soviet Union or for that matter that the Soviet Union intends to invade the countries where the United States forces are based.

I do not believe for a moment that it is the intention of the big powers to launch aggression. I think the matter is more psychological than military, and in this respect I think much can be done by wielders of mass media like you—journalists, editors, and those who wield very great influence through television and radio—not only in this country but in the Soviet Union and elsewhere, to present the true facts objectively and fairly. I do not think personally that the developments which you are referring to will generate a very big crisis.

QUESTION: Mr. Secretary-General, in talking with Soviet Chairman Khrushchev and President Kennedy, could you say whether you got the impression that either or both would be willing to sit down and try to talk out a peaceful solution of the Berlin question before the end of the year?

THE ACTING SECRETARY-GENERAL: Of course, the question of Berlin came up in the course of my discussions with the leaders of these big powers, but there was no indication on the part of these leaders that they would want to discuss this question in the immediate future in the United Nations. I do not, of course, exclude the possibility of their meeting at a later stage. It is difficult for me to envisage the exact timing: whether it will be before the end of the year or after the end of the year.

QUESTION: You said that you had presented the Central Government of the Congo and Moïse Tshombé with a plan and asked for its implementation without further delay toward the unification of the Congo. You are still awaiting the results. How much longer will you wait?

THE ACTING SECRETARY-GENERAL: I have indicated both to the prime minister of the Congolese government and to Mr. Tshombé that I expect their replies in the course of the next four or five weeks. That was in the middle of last month. Of course, no definite target has been set for the receipt of their replies. As you all know, Prime Minister Adoula has replied to me in the affirmative that he and his government accept the terms of this plan. Mr. Tshombé, as you all know, has also reacted, if I may say so, in his traditional manner which, of course, is not very clear to me. I am still expecting a reaction from him and I hope to be able to hear from him in the course of the next couple of weeks.

QUESTION: Recently, Thailand and Cambodia have issued statements that the United Nations might be asked to watch their frontier and look into their differences. Have you been approached on this matter? And do you feel that the United Nations can help reduce the present tension in that area?

THE ACTING SECRETARY-GENERAL: On this question I have been in contact with both governments. I am still in the process of negotiations. I hope to be able to contribute to the success of these deliberations. The success of these negotiations and discussions depends on several factors, including the availability of the right person to represent me in that area, as desired by the two governments.

. . . . QUESTION: You said a short while ago that in a month or so you may be able to see more clearly the conditions which will be contingent on your decision regarding your availability. What events do you expect to take place within a month or so that may determine your course of action?

THE ACTING SECRETARY-GENERAL: As I have just stated, among the factors which are going to govern my decision will be the prospects of an early settlement of the Congo problem, the prospects of a really effective development of the United Nations as a force for peace, and the prospects of the financial stability of this Organization, as well as the prospects of my being able to play some sort of a humble role as a conciliator of difficulties.

. . . . QUESTION: Yesterday, there were reports from President Kennedy's headquarters in Newport that he is more or less expecting a visit later this year from Mr. Khrushchev, and this more or less followed a visit from you. Did you carry out any liaison work between the two chiefs of government on this?

THE ACTING SECRETARY-GENERAL: As you know, I am in favor of these "summits," and, beyond this, I do not think that I should reveal what transpired between me and the heads of government.

QUESTION: In your appraisals of the world situation, you have frequently used the expression "the two giants." I wonder whether, in your line of thought, recent developments in Europe, especially regarding Europe's unity, would have brought some changes in that way of conceding the world situation in your mind.

THE ACTING SECRETARY-GENERAL: After the experience of my visits to some European countries, I still cling to my old theory and I still think in terms of the two giants, because these two countries are really giants. In this context, I think some of you are already aware of my line of thinking. I believe very strongly in the Hegelian concept of thesis, antithesis, and synthesis, and I also believe that unmistakable forces are at work toward a synthesis. I am convinced that this world is heading for a synthesis. If we may recall a little of history, I am sure you will agree with me that religious tolerance two hundred or so years ago was regarded as a sin, and not only as a sin, but as a colossal crime. But it is no longer regarded as such in the twentieth century.

Now, of course, political tolerance or tolerance of political ideologies or beliefs is still regarded, if not as a sin, as some sort of crime. I believe strongly that this attitude is also a passing phase. I believe in the march of humanity toward a synthesis.

In saying this I also want to make one thing clear. I am a firm believer in parliamentary democracy; I believe very strongly that parliamentary democracy is the only type of society which is congenial to the growth of human freedom, human happiness, and human genius. I believe in human dignity, I believe in fundamental freedoms like freedom of expression, freedom of thought, freedom of belief, freedom of conscience, freedom of association and the freedom to choose your own lawmakers. I believe in these freedoms, but this belief, this conviction, does not shut me off from the knowledge that there are hundreds of millions of people who believe otherwise. I am absolutely aware of this fact.

To give a religious analogy, I am a Buddhist; I believe that Buddhism as a religion is superior to other religions, but this conviction does not blind me to the fact that there are hundreds of millions of people who believe otherwise. I understand this, and because of this understanding I believe in peaceful coexistence. Whether we like it or not, I believe communism is going to stay; I believe capitalism is going to stay; I believe parliamentary democracy is going to stay. As Buddhism, Christianity, Islam, Hinduism, and all other religions are existing peacefully in amity, I believe a day will come when these different societies, communist societies, capitalist societies, socialist societies, or any other type of societies are going to exist peacefully. I believe in these things.

QUESTION: What is the position with regard to the implementation of the agreement regarding West New Guinea and what can you add to what is already stated in point 10 of the supplementary agenda items? When will this matter come up in the General Assembly?

THE ACTING SECRETARY-GENERAL: The arrangement is that the two governments, the Government of the Netherlands and the Government of Indonesia, will sponsor a joint draft resolution in the early stages of the General Assembly, most probably on September 20.

QUESTION: In view of your remarks on the Cuban situation, as it is known in the United States, do you envisage any role for the United Nations or for you personally in reducing the tension?

THE ACTING SECRETARY-GENERAL: On such matters I think the best thing will be for one of the parties directly involved to indicate an intention or desire to get the United Nations involved, one way or the other, at this stage.

. . . . QUESTION: Mr. Secretary-General, in your trips to the various parts of the world, did you find the same degree of support for the principle of coexistence in all the capitals?

THE ACTING SECRETARY-GENERAL: It is really difficult to define the degree of support, because it is something intangible. But my feeling is that every government of every Member state of the United Nations expressed its desire to see the United Nations develop into a really effective instrument for peace. The difference, as I have indicated, is on the organizational and procedural aspects of the functions of this Organization. . . .

Statement at the Unveiling of a Plaque in Memory
of Dag Hammarskjöld and
Those Who Died with Him

NEW YORK   SEPTEMBER 17, 1962

DURING HIS TEN YEARS in office, U Thant paid many tributes to his predecessor, Dag Hammarskjöld. One such occasion was at the unveiling of a plaque outside the meditation room at United Nations Headquarters on the first anniversary of the death of Hammarskjöld and the colleagues who died with him in the plane crash at Ndola, Northern Rhodesia. He called their deaths a "vagary of fate" and said that he was confident Hammarskjöld saw no extraordinary risk in his journey. It was a risk, he said, being taken by many thousands of men and women involved in UN peacekeeping operations around the world. Many of them are entitled to the accolade "hero of peace," he said, and "Dag Hammarskjöld was definitely one." At one of his press conferences (March 27, 1962) Thant was asked what, if any, steps he planned to take to insure that the United Nations would not again find itself without an administrative head if he should be killed while travelling. He replied "I do not know how to devise ways and means of averting the prospective disaster or catastrophe which you have in mind."

WE ARE GATHERED here this morning in a ceremony whose purpose it is to pay solemn tribute to cherished colleagues lost just one year ago in the train of duty. But this occasion serves also to enrich the present for each of us by recalling the strength, courage, wisdom, and devotion to the international ideal of those who were so abruptly taken from us. The great require no eulogy. It is thus with Dag Hammarskjöld, whose inspired works in more than eight years of dedicated service to this Organization live after him and recall his imposing stature more eloquently than any words I might pronounce.

The other day I received a letter informing me that a year ago, at the time of the crash, some African students wrote some moving laments about the death of Mr. Hammarskjöld. These were students from various

UN Press Release SG/1319.

parts of Africa who were attending the Africa Literacy and Writing School in Kitwe, Northern Rhodesia, which is about forty miles west of the scene of the tragedy at Ndola. Since these expressions came straight from the hearts of young Africans, I take the liberty of reading one of them to you, which was written by David Rockson of Ghana:

The world leader is dead, yet he speaks;
He speaks to the world in accents soft and clear.
What is he saying to Africa?
Yes, what is he saying to the world?
The message is: "peace on earth".
The message is: "unity among the nations".
Citizen, if thou art constrained to mourn
   Dag Hammarskjöld,
Pray God to make you a peacemaker, too.

It is particularly appropriate, I think, that we meet on this occasion in the outer area of the United Nations Meditation Room. For that room was of deep and very special concern to Dag Hammarskjöld. He devoted very much of time and thought and planning to its conception and to its arrangement. He wished it to be universal in its invitation—to appeal to all who come into this house to find in that room an atmosphere uniquely conducive to quiet reflection, to introspection, to an inward look away from the tumult and cynicism of the world around us. He wished that room to have a symbolism all its own, expressed in the massive solidity and strength of the center stone of Swedish ore and the reach toward eternity of Bo Beskow's impressive al fresco. You are invited to visit and make use of this room.

Dag Hammarskjöld, with his profound knowledge and perception of man—of man's history and ways—would be the first to recognize that it is the way of fate to make the commonplace suddenly and dramatically momentous. It was in such a vagary of fate that my late predecessor and his companions lost their lives a year ago. For Dag Hammarskjöld, Secretary-General of the United Nations, the trip of a year ago to the Congo and the incidental mission to Ndola were natural and unexceptional acts undertaken purely and without question in the line of duty. The September journey was not his first to the shattered Congo, where he had gone with the same spirit as previously to other troubled areas. As was well known to his close collaborators on the thirty-eighth floor of this building, Mr. Hammarskjöld accepted the invitation of the prime minister of the Republic of the Congo last September to visit that country on the eve of the opening of the sixteenth session of the General Assembly primarily because he saw in it an opportunity to reduce if not remove the Congo as a critical and bitter issue before that Assembly. The main, though unpublicized objective sought was to induce Mr. Tshombé to go to Leopoldville, or elsewhere in the Congo, for talks with Prime Minister Adoula toward the ending of the Katanga secession through reconciliation of the differences between the Central Government and that province. I have no doubt that, had Mr. Hammarskjöld lived, he would have achieved that objective, which was, indeed, later twice achieved, although with disappointing results to date. The United Nations effort in the Congo persists, however, and will, in time, I am confident, fully succeed.

As to the fateful flight to Ndola, we know, from one of Mr. Hammarskjöld's last messages, that it was only when he reached Accra, en route to Leopoldville, that he learned, from a "tendentious" press report, as he put it, that the latest United Nations effort to eliminate mercenaries in Katanga had encountered stubborn resistance and that serious fighting had broken out in Elisabethville between United Nations troops and mercenary-led elements of the Katangese gendarmerie. This unexpected news must certainly have come to him as a severe shock. In the light of these circumstances, it was then both natural and necessary for him, as Secretary-General, to do all that he could do to bring the fighting to an end and to stop any further bloodletting. This, clearly, was why Mr. Hammarskjöld and his companions took the ill-fated trip to Ndola. When they embarked upon it, they had sound reason to anticipate that it would be successful in inducing Mr. Tshombé to enter into reconciliation talks, no less than achieving the cease-fire.

I am confident that Dag Hammarskjöld saw no extraordinary risk in his journey to Ndola, which was, in fact, attended by much more than normal precautions. One may be even more positive that he would not have hesitated a moment had any such risk been apparent.

There are, to be sure, certain unavoidable risks in any United Nations field operation: the hazards of chartered flights to unfamiliar airfields, of vehicular accidents, of health in harsh climates, of sniper's bullets. United Nations personnel are often subject to such hazards in missions far and wide. If, however, the United Nations is to project its peacekeeping actions into the areas of active conflict, as it must if its peacemaking function is to be really worthwhile, such risks to its personnel cannot be entirely avoided.

It is fitting here, I believe, to commend highly those many—indeed, many thousands—of men and women, civilian and military, from within and without the United Nations Secretariat, who have served and now serve the Organization in its peacekeeping operations in various parts of the world, from the Congo to New Guinea, not infrequently at considerable personal sacrifice, under conditions of genuine hardship and at times of danger. The casualties suffered by United Nations personnel in the field have been substantial enough to establish that peacemaking can be costly also in lives.

In the United Nations peace operations such as Palestine, Kashmir, Suez, and the Congo, there have been those who are, indeed, entitled to the accolade "hero of peace." Dag Hammarskjöld was definitely one. By odd coincidence, another was his fellow countryman, Count Folke Bernadotte, who on this very date in 1948, gave his life in Jerusalem while serving the United Nations in the quest for peace in a war-ridden Palestine.

We honor also today Count Bernadotte's memory and his sacrifice, and the memory of all those others who have given their lives in the peace actions of this great Organization.

The Meditation Room, on whose outer wall the plaque rests, was poetically described by Dag Hammarskjöld in these prophetic words: "This is a room devoted to peace and those who are giving their lives for peace. It is a room of quiet where only thoughts should speak."

The plaque about to be uncovered from now on will serve as a reminder for all those who pass by it, for all the generations of the future, of the deep gratitude, the sense of tragic loss, and the profound sorrow over colleagues prematurely gone, which we who live today carry in our hearts for those sixteen who are no longer with us.

Will you please join me in standing as the plaque is unveiled.

The inscription on the plaque, which is done in bronze, reads as follows: "In memory of Dag Hammarskjöld, Secretary-General of the United Nations 1953 to 1961, and those who with him lost their lives at Ndola in September 1961 in quest of peace in the Congo."

May *they* rest in peace. May *we* secure it.

THE CUBAN MISSILE CRISIS

THE CUBAN MISSILE CRISIS of October 1962 was preceded by more than three years of steadily worsening relations between the United States and the government of Premier Fidel Castro. The erosion began within a few months after the revolutionary leader came to power on January 1, 1959. The problem started with Havana's increasing ties with Moscow and Peking and with the progressive nationalization of United States businesses on the one hand and with the suspension of the U.S. agreement to buy Cuban sugar on the other. The situation was aggravated further by U.S. support of Cuban political refugees, many of whom were actively engaged in counterrevolutionary activities aimed at overthrowing the Castro government.

The United States-Cuban dispute first came before the United Nations on July 18, 1960. In a complaint to the Security Council the Cuban minister for foreign affairs, Raúl Roa, accused the United States of "harboring war criminals, aiding counterrevolutionary forces, violating Cuban air space and carrying on a campaign of economic strangulation." These were serious charges, but the Council debate was brief. The United States and the Latin American countries took the position that this was a hemispheric problem and should, therefore, be dealt with by the American states themselves. The Council accepted this view by adopting a resolution, sponsored by Argentina and Ecuador, citing Article 52 of the Charter, noting that the dispute already was being considered by the Organization of American States (OAS) and adjourning further consideration of the question until a report was received from the OAS. There were 9 votes to none, with the Soviet Union and Poland abstaining.

Article 52 states, *inter alia:* "The Security Council shall encourage the development of pacific settlement of local disputes through . . . regional arrangements." A precedent had already been set in 1954 when the United States persuaded the Council to leave the Guatemalan question to the OAS. Cuba was not happy with the Council's decision and a few weeks later asked the General Assembly to take up the question. Although the issue was placed on the agenda, it was not debated immediately. So on December 31, Cuba asked once more for an urgent meeting of the Security Council, charging that the United States intended to commit direct aggression against Cuban territory. During the debate on January 4 and 5, the Cuban foreign minister accused the United States of setting up training camps for Cuban exiles in Guatemala, Honduras, and Florida in preparation for an invasion of Cuba. Members of the Council, however, could agree neither on the existence of a threat nor on the terms of a resolution. No vote was taken. Meanwhile, President Dwight D. Eisenhower broke off diplomatic relations with Cuba.

These events were clearly a prelude to the Bay of Pigs fiasco—the invasion of Cuba by 1,500 Cuban refugees later admitted to having been armed with United

States weapons and trained with United States assistance. The invasion took place on April 17, 1961, two days after debate on Cuba's earlier complaint had begun in the Assembly's First Committee. On April 21 the Assembly adopted a resolution, sponsored by seven Latin American countries, which referred to the Security Council resolution of July 19, 1960, and urged Member states to use all peaceful means to remove existing tension. The Cuban-United States dispute was again inscribed on the agenda of the Assembly in September 1961 and considered by the Assembly during February 1962, but no resolution was adopted.

This is where matters stood when U Thant took office. A series of developments early in 1962 intensified the dispute and contributed to the critical situation which brought the world close to war a few months later. One of these was the adoption of the harsh Final Act of the eighth meeting of the consultation of ministers of foreign affairs of the American republics held at Punta del Este, Uruguay, from January 22 to 31. The Kennedy administration had played a leading role in organizing the Punta del Este meeting and in pressing for measures to isolate the Castro government. Among other things the Punta del Este session declared that communism was incompatible with the principles of the inter-American system, excluded Cuba from the Inter-American Defense Board, provided for the immediate suspension of trade with Cuba in arms and other implements of war, and directed the OAS to study the feasibility of extending the trade suspension to other items. Equally important was a letter dated February 19, 1962, in which the Soviet Union informed the General Assembly that Cuba would not have to stand alone but that it could rely on the aid and support of the Soviet Union.

The Cuban government charged that the Punta del Este resolutions were at variance with the United Nations Charter and that the exclusion of Cuba from the OAS because of its social system violated the principles of nonintervention. On February 22, Cuba asked for an immediate meeting of the Security Council to consider the question. By 4 votes to none, with 7 abstentions, the Council failed to adopt the proposed agenda. Cuba again, on March 8, requested a Council meeting, this time to consider asking the International Court of Justice to give an advisory opinion on the legality of the Punte del Este resolutions. Cuba's main challenge was based on the contention that the OAS, as a regional agency under the United Nations Charter, did not have the right to take enforcement action without authorization by the Security Council. The Council rejected the Cuban proposals.

Up to this time the Acting Secretary-General had watched with interest, but had taken no public position on the Cuban question. On March 27, 1962, he was asked at a press conference about the tendency to refer disputes to regional organizations rather than deal with them in the United Nations. He replied that he found himself in complete agreement with President John F. Kennedy, who maintained that "reliance on regional organizations in no way conflicts with reliance on the United Nations" and added, "I do not see any reason why the two are incompatible." Thant had not taken any initiative up to that time to head off the growing threat to peace. Perhaps the main reason was that the United States itself did not see any cause for concern even though it had been determined from aerial photographs that the Soviet Union had established surface-to-air missile sites in Cuba. On September 13, President Kennedy told a news conference the Soviet installations were not a serious threat, but he pointedly warned that if Cuba were to "become an offensive military base of significant capacity for the Soviet Union, then this country will do whatever must be done to protect its own security and that of its allies." Discovery of the Soviet missile installations came at about the time Thant was visiting both Moscow and Washington.

At a press conference on September 17, barely a month before the missile crisis came to a peak, Thant minimized the importance of the dispute and indicated he saw no immediate United Nations role. On the basis of his talks with leaders of the two superpowers, he expressed the opinion that the problem was "more psychological than military" and that he did not think developments would "generate a very big crisis." When asked specifically whether he envisaged any UN role he replied, "On such matters I think the best thing will be for one of the parties directly involved to indicate an intention or desire to get the United Nations involved. . . ."

The missile crisis burst upon the world on the night of October 22, 1962, when President Kennedy stunned the public by asserting that the Soviet Union, despite its statements to the contrary, was building offensive missile sites in Cuba for medium- and intermediate-range ballistic missiles capable of striking most major cities in the western hemisphere. He called for a naval and air quarantine on shipments of all "offensive" military equipment to Cuba, increased aerial surveillance of Cuba, reinforcement of the American naval base at Guantanamo and at the same time an urgent meeting of the Security Council to consider the problem.

There was no doubt now that the United States-Cuban dispute, which had been sidestepped and minimized time after time, must be met head on if catastrophe was to be averted. Thant did not wait for the outcome of the Security Council debate but, at the urging of "a large number of Member governments," dispatched an urgent appeal to Chairman Khrushchev and President Kennedy to "refrain from any action which may aggravate the situation and bring with it the risk of war." He proposed specifically that they agree to a voluntary suspension for a period of two or three weeks of all arms shipments to Cuba and of the quarantine measures involving the search of ships bound for Cuba. The story of the Thant initiative and the response is told in the texts reproduced below. Many, including Thant himself, believed this was the single most important initiative taken by him. Although it is generally agreed that both Kennedy and Khrushchev desired to avoid a confrontation and that they were eager to find a peaceful settlement, it is equally true that Thant's intervention offered a convenient out and made it easier for them to back down without losing face. More than once the office of the Secretary-General has proved useful in this respect.

Thant's role was overshadowed to some degree by the dramatic nature of the near confrontation, but it did not pass without some public recognition by the United States and the Soviet Union. In a joint letter, dated January 7, 1963, U. S. Ambassador Adlai E. Stevenson and Soviet Deputy Foreign Minister Vassily V. Kuznetsov expressed their appreciation of his efforts and declared that the degree of understanding reached between them and the progress in the implementation of this understanding made it unnecessary "for this item to occupy further the attention of the Security Council at this time."

Thant's success in dealing with Castro was less notable. This was partly due to the fact that the United States and the Soviet Union had carried on their talks about United Nations inspection of the Cuban missile sites without consulting him. When Soviet officials spoke of inspection, Thant apparently had assumed that they had consulted Castro. So when Castro expressed a willingness to receive the Secretary-General, it was believed that the main purpose of the visit would be to set up inspection machinery. In a letter to Khrushchev dated October 28, Thant said he hoped to reach a satisfactory understanding with Kuznetsov, "as well as with Premier Castro" on the modalities of verification by United Nations observers "to which you have so readily agreed." Two days later Thant flew to Havana with a group of aides whom he had hoped to leave behind "to continue our common effort toward the peaceful solution of the problem." Thant left Cuba the following day with his aides and their baggage including typewriters and other equipment intended to form the nucleus of a UN presence. Castro had made it plain that he would accept no UN inspection.

Although the Secretary-General was keenly disappointed, he tried to put the mission in its best light when he arrived back in New York. There was agreement, he said, that the United Nations should continue to take part in the peaceful solution of the problem. He said he was reliably informed that the dismantling of the Soviet missiles was in progress and that their shipment back to the Soviet Union was at hand. He did not mention inspection, however. It remained for Castro himself to put this question in perspective in a letter to Thant on November 16 in which he said "we have given you—and we have also given it publicly and repeatedly—our refusal to allow unilateral inspection by any body, national or international, on Cuban territory."

---

1. Statement in the Security Council

NEW YORK   OCTOBER 24, 1962

TODAY THE UNITED NATIONS faces a moment of grave responsibility. What is at stake is not just the interests of the parties directly involved, nor just the interests of all Member states, but the very fate of mankind. If today the United Nations should prove itself ineffective, it may have proved itself so for all time.

Security Council Official Records, Seventeenth Year, 1024th meeting.

In the circumstances, not only as Acting Secretary-General of the United Nations but as a human being, I would be failing in my duty if I did not express my profound hope and conviction that moderation, self-restraint and good sense will prevail over all other considerations.

In this situation where the very existence of mankind is in the balance, I derive some consolation from the fact that there is some common ground in the draft resolutions introduced in the Council. Irrespective of the fate of those draft resolutions, that common ground remains. It calls for urgent negotiations between the parties directly involved, though, as I said earlier, the rest of the world is also an interested party. In this context, I cannot help expressing the view that some of the measures proposed or already taken, which the Council is called upon to approve, are very unusual and, I might say, even extraordinary except in wartime.

At the request of the permanent representatives of a large number of Member governments who have discussed the matter among themselves and with me, I have sent, through the permanent representatives of the two governments, the following identically worded message to the president of the United States of America and the chairman of the Council of Ministers of the USSR:

I have been asked by the permanent representatives of a large number of Member governments of the United Nations to address an urgent appeal to you in the present critical situation. These representatives feel that in the interest of international peace and security, all concerned should refrain from any action which may aggravate the situation and bring with it the risk of war.

In their view it is important that time should be given to enable the parties concerned to get together with a view to resolving the present crisis peacefully and normalizing the situation in the Caribbean. This involves on the one hand the voluntary suspension of all arms shipments to Cuba, and also the voluntary suspension of the quarantine measures involving the searching of ships bound for Cuba. I believe that such voluntary suspension for a period of two to three weeks will greatly ease the situation and give time to the parties concerned to meet and discuss with a view to finding a peaceful solution of the problem. In this context, I shall gladly make myself available to all parties for whatever services I may be able to perform.

I urgently appeal to your Excellency to give immediate consideration to this message.

I have sent an identical message to the president of the United States of America/chairman of the Council of Ministers of the USSR.

I should like also to take this occasion to address an urgent appeal to the president and prime minister of the Revolutionary Government of Cuba. Yesterday Ambassador García Incháustegui of Cuba recalled the words of his president, words which were uttered from the rostrum of the General Assembly just over two weeks ago, and I quote: "If the United States could give assurances, by word and deed, that it would not commit acts of aggression against our country, we solemnly declare that there would be no need for our weapons and our armies" . . .[1]

Here again I feel that on the basis of discussion some common ground may be found through which a way may be traced out of the present impasse. I believe it would also contribute greatly to the same end if the construction and development of major military facilities and installations in Cuba could be suspended during the period of negotiations.

I now make a most solemn appeal to the parties concerned to enter into negotiations immediately, even this night, if possible, irrespective of any other procedures which may be available or which could be invoked. I realize that if my appeal is heeded, the first subject to be discussed will be the modalities, and that all parties concerned will have to agree to comply with those responsibilities which fall on them before any agreement as a whole can become effective. I hope, however, that the need for such discussion will not deter the parties concerned from undertaking these discussions. In my view it would be shortsighted for the parties concerned to seek assurances on the end result before the negotiations had even begun.

I have stated in my message to both the president of the United States of America and the chairman of the Council of Ministers of the USSR that I shall gladly make myself available to all parties for whatever services I may be able to perform. I repeat that pledge now.

During the seventeen years that have passed since the end of the Second World War, there has never been a more dangerous or closer confrontation of the major powers. At a time when the danger to world peace was less immediate, or so it appears by comparison, my distinguished predecessor said: "The principles of the Charter are, by far, greater than the Organization in which they are embodied, and the aims which they are to safeguard are holier than the policies of any single nation or people."

He went on to say: ". . . the discretion and impartiality . . . imposed on the Secretary-General by the character of his immediate task may not degenerate into a policy of expediency . . . A Secretary-General cannot

---

[1] General Assembly Official Records, Seventeenth Session, 1145th plenary meeting, paragraph 58.

serve on any other assumption than that—within the necessary limits of human frailty and honest differences of opinion—all Member nations honour their pledge to observe all Articles of the Charter." (See volume III of this series, p. 309.)

It is after considerable deliberation that I have decided to send the two messages to which I have referred earlier, and likewise I have decided to make this brief intervention tonight before the Security Council including the appeal to the president and prime minister of Cuba.

I hope that at this moment, not only in the Council Chamber but in the world outside, good sense and understanding will be placed above the anger of the moment or the pride of nations. The path of negotiation and compromise is the only course by which the peace of the world can be secured at this critical moment.

---

2. Exchange of Messages with Chairman Khrushchev

OCTOBER 25 and 26, 1962

(a) Message to Chairman Khrushchev

In continuation of my message of yesterday and my statement before the Security Council, I would like to bring to Your Excellency's attention my grave concern that Soviet ships already on their way to Cuba might challenge the quarantine imposed by the United States and produce a confrontation at sea between Soviet ships and United States vessels, which could lead to an aggravation of the situation. What concerns me most is that such a confrontation and consequent aggravation of the situation would destroy any possibility of the discussions I have suggested as a prelude to negotiations on a peaceful settlement. In the circumstances I earnestly hope that Your Excellency may find it possible to instruct the Soviet ships already on their way to Cuba to stay away from the interception area for a limited time only, in order to permit discus-

UN Press Release SG/1357.

sions of the modalities of a possible agreement which could settle the problem peacefully in line with the Charter of the United Nations.

I am confident that, if such instructions could be issued by Your Excellency, the United States authorities will take action to ensure that a direct confrontation between their ships and Soviet ships is avoided during the same period in order to minimize the risk of any untoward incident taking place.

If I could be informed of the action taken by your government on the basis of this appeal, I could inform President Kennedy that I have assurances from your side of your cooperation in avoiding all risk of an untoward incident.

I am at the same time addressing the enclosed appeal to President Kennedy.

U THANT
Acting Secretary-General

(b) Message from Chairman Khrushchev (Unofficial translation from Russian)

Dear U Thant,

I have received and studied your telegram of October 25. I understand your anxiety for the preservation of peace, and I appreciate highly your efforts to avert military conflict.

Indeed, if any conflict should arise on the approaches to Cuba—and this may become unavoidable as a result of the piratical measures taken by the United States—this would beyond question seriously complicate the endeavors to initiate contacts in order to put an end, on a basis of negotiation, to the critical situation that has now been thrust on the world by the aggressive actions of the United States.

We therefore accept your proposal, and have ordered the masters of Soviet vessels bound for Cuba but not yet within the area of the American warships' piratical activities to stay out of the interception area, as you recommend.

But we have given this order in the hope that the other side will understand that such a situation, in which we keep vessels immobilized on the high seas, must be a purely temporary one; the period cannot under any circumstances be of long duration.

I thank you for your efforts and wish you success in your noble task.

Your efforts to ensure world peace will always meet with understanding and support on our part.

The Soviet government has consistently striven, and is striving, to strengthen the United Nations—that international Organization which constitutes a forum for all countries of the world, regardless of their socio-political structure, in order that disputes arising may be settled not through war but through negotiations.

N. KHRUSHCHEV

---

3. Exchange of Messages with President Kennedy

OCTOBER 25, 1962

(a) Message to President Kennedy

I have today sent a further message to Chairman Khrushchev expressing my grave concern that Soviet ships already on their way to Cuba might challenge the quarantine imposed by your government and produce a confrontation at sea between Soviet ships and United States vessels, which could lead to an aggravation of the situation. I have also stated that what concerns me most is the fact that such a confrontation and consequent aggravation of the situation would destroy any possibility of the discussions that I have suggested as a prelude to negotiations on a peaceful settlement. I have accordingly expressed to him my earnest hope that Soviet ships already on their way to Cuba might be instructed to stay away from the interception area for a limited time only, in order to permit discussions of the modalities of a possible agreement which could settle the problem peacefully in line with the Charter of the United Nations.

In continuation of my message of yesterday and my speech before the Security Council, I would now like to appeal to Your Excellency that instructions may be issued to United States vessels in the Caribbean to do everything possible to avoid direct confrontation with Soviet ships in the

UN Press Release SG/1358.

next few days in order to minimize the risk of any untoward incident. If I could be informed of the action taken by your government on the basis of this appeal, I could inform Chairman Khrushchev that I have assurances from your side of your cooperation in avoiding all risk of an untoward incident. I would express the further hope that such cooperation could be the prelude to a quick agreement in principle on the basis of which the quarantine measures themselves could be called off as soon as possible.

U Thant
Acting Secretary-General

(b) Message from President Kennedy

Excellency:

I have the honor to transmit a reply from the President of the United States to your message to him of October 25:

I have your further message of today and I continue to understand and welcome your efforts for a satisfactory solution. I appreciate and share your concern that great caution be exercised pending the inauguration of discussions.

If the Soviet government accepts and abides by your request "that Soviet ships already on their way to Cuba . . . stay away from the interception area" for the limited time required for preliminary discussion, you may be assured that this government will accept and abide by your request that our vessels in the Caribbean "do everything possible to avoid direct confrontation with Soviet ships in the next few days in order to minimize the risk of any untoward incident." I must inform you, however, that this is a matter of great urgency in view of the fact that certain Soviet ships are still proceeding toward Cuba and the interception area.

I share your hope that Chairman Khrushchev will also heed your appeal and that we can then proceed urgently to meet the requirements that these offensive military systems in Cuba be withdrawn, in order to end their threat to peace. I must point out to you that present work on these systems is still continuing.

Accept, Excellency, the renewed assurances of my highest consideration.

Sincerely yours,
Adlai E. Stevenson

4. *Exchange of Messages with Prime Minister Castro*

OCTOBER 26 and 27, 1962

(a) Message to Prime Minister Castro

I hope that Ambassador García-Incháustegui has conveyed to Your Excellency the appeal that I addressed to you and to President Dorticós through him in the course of the statement I made before the Security Council on October 24. I then recalled the following words of President Dorticos, uttered from the rostrum of the General Assembly on October 8: "Were the United States able to give us proof, by word and deed, that it would not carry out aggression against our country, then, we declare solemnly before you here and now, our weapons would be unnecessary and our army redundant."

I added that I believed it would also contribute greatly to finding a way out of the present impasse "if the construction and development of major military facilities and installations in Cuba could be suspended during the period of negotiations."

As Ambassador García may have reported to you I have received fairly encouraging responses to my appeal for negotiations and a peaceful solution of the problem from the president of the United States and from the chairman of the Council of Ministers of the USSR. Your Excellency can make a significant contribution to the peace of the world at this present critical juncture by directing that the construction and development of major military facilities and installations in Cuba, and especially installations designed to launch medium range and intermediate range ballistic missiles, be suspended during the period of negotiations which are now under way.

UN Press Release SG/1359.

It would encourage me greatly to have an affirmative reply to this appeal very urgently.

U THANT
Acting Secretary-General

(b) Letter from Prime Minister Castro
(Translation from Spanish)

Your Excellency,

On the instructions of the Revolutionary Government of Cuba I have the honor to transmit to you the following message:

Your Excellency,

I have received your message dated October 26, and express my appreciation of your noble concern.

Cuba is prepared to discuss as fully as may be necessary, its differences with the United States and to do everything in its power, in cooperation with the United Nations, to resolve the present crisis. However, it flatly rejects the violation of the sovereignty of our country involved in the naval blockage, an act of force and war committed by the United States against Cuba. In addition, it flatly rejects the presumption of the United States to determine what actions we are entitled to take within our country, what kind of arms we consider appropriate for our defense, what relations we are to have with the USSR, and what international policy steps we are entitled to take, within the rules and laws governing relations between the peoples of the world and the principles governing the United Nations, in order to guarantee our own security and sovereignty.

Cuba is victimizing no one; it has violated no international law; on the contrary, it is the victim of the aggressive acts of the United States, such as the naval blockade, and its rights have been outraged.

The Revolutionary Government of Cuba would be prepared to accept the compromises that you request as efforts in favor of peace, provided that at the same time, while negotiations are in progress, the United States government desists from threats and aggressive actions against Cuba, including the naval blockade of our country.

At the same time I express to you our willingness to consider attentively any new suggestion you may put forward; furthermore, should you consider it useful to the cause of peace, our government would be glad to receive you in our country, as Secretary-General of the United Nations, with a view to direct discussions on the present crisis, prompted by our common purpose of freeing mankind from the dangers of war.

Unreserved respect for the sovereignty of Cuba is the essential prerequisite if Cuba is to contribute with the greatest sincerity and goodwill, grudging no step toward the solution of the present problem, and joining forces with all those peoples who are struggling to save peace at this dramatic moment in the life of mankind; Cuba can do whatever is asked of it, except undertake to be a victim and to renounce the rights which belong to every sovereign state.

I reiterate the assurances of my highest consideration.

Major Fidel Castro Ruz

Prime Minister of the Revolutionary Government of Cuba.

Accept, Your Excellency, the assurances of my highest consideration.

> DR. MARIO GARCÍA INCHÁUSTEGUI
> Ambassador
> Permanent Representative of Cuba
> to the United Nations

5. *Letter to Prime Minister Castro*

OCTOBER 28, 1962

I HAVE RECEIVED with much gratitude and deep appreciation your kind letter of October 27. I am particularly pleased to note that the Revolutionary Government of Cuba is prepared to accept the suggestion that I made as an effort in favor of peace, provided that, at the same time, while negotiations are in progress, the United States government "desists from threats and aggressive acts against Cuba including the naval blockade of your country".

I am also glad to note your willingness to consider any new suggestion that may be put forward. I am deeply sensible to the honor that your government has done me in inviting me, as Secretary-General of the United Nations, to visit Cuba with a view to having direct discussions on the present crisis, prompted by our common concern to free mankind from the dangers of war.

I have much pleasure in accepting your invitation. I hope to be able to leave early next week. I hope to bring a few aides with me and to leave some of them behind to continue our common effort toward the peaceful solution of the problem.

UN Press Release SG/1360.

I also note and appreciate your feeling that the unreserved respect for the sovereignty of Cuba is an essential prerequisite to any solution of the problem.

I would very much hope that it might be possible for me to discuss with you all important aspects of the problem. It would be my hope that as a result of these discussions, a solution would be reached by which the principle of respect for the sovereignty of Cuba would be assured, and it may also be possible for action to be taken which would reassure other countries which have felt themselves threatened by recent developments in Cuba.

U THANT
Acting Secretary-General

6. *Letter to Chairman Khrushchev*

OCTOBER 28, 1962

I WISH TO EXPRESS my deep gratitude to Your Excellency for sending me a copy of your message to President Kennedy dated October 28, in reply to President Kennedy's letter to Your Excellency of October 27.

I note the constructive proposals you have made in order to remove tension in the Caribbean area. I believe that when these proposals are implemented the situation in the Caribbean area will be normalized.

I would like to inform Your Excellency that I have accepted an invitation extended to me by Prime Minister Fidel Castro on behalf of the Revolutionary Government of Cuba to visit his country. I feel that at the present time such a visit could contribute to the peaceful solution of the problem. As I stated in my letter to Premier Castro, the result of my discussions with him could lead to a solution "by which the principle of respect for the sovereignty of Cuba would be assured, and it may also be possible for action to be taken which would reassure those countries which have felt themselves threatened by recent developments in Cuba."

UN Press Release SG/1363.

I am particularly gratified to note that you have already instructed your officers to take the necessary measures to stop the building of missile bases, to dismantle them, and to return the missiles to the Soviet Union, and that you are ready to come to an agreement that representatives of the United Nations may verify the dismantling of these bases.

I am also happy to note that the Soviet government has sent to New York the first deputy minister for foreign affairs of the USSR, Mr. Kuznetsov, with a view to assisting me in my efforts. Mr. Kuznetsov is an old and valued friend, and I look forward very much to exchanging views with him as soon as he arrives. I shall discuss with Mr. Kuznetsov, as well as with Premier Castro, the modalities of verification by United Nations Observers to which you have so readily agreed, and I hope that I shall be able to reach a satisfactory understanding with them.

I am convinced that, with the spirit of cooperation and concern for peace that you have shown, the outcome of these discussions will be successful and satisfactory to all the parties concerned.

U THANT
Acting Secretary-General

7. Statement at Airport on Return from Havana

OCTOBER 31, 1962

I RETURN FROM Havana after fruitful discussions with the leaders of Cuba. These discussions were conducted strictly in the context of my correspondence with Premier Fidel Castro, resulting from the proceedings of the Security Council meetings. There was agreement that the United Nations should continue to participate in the peaceful settlement of the problem.

UN Press Release SG/1368/Rev. 1.

During my stay in Havana, I was reliably informed that the dismantling of the missiles and their installations was already in progress and that this process should be completed by Friday. Thereafter, there would come their shipment and return to the Soviet Union, arrangements for which are understood to be in hand.

One last word. At my request, the Cuban government has agreed to return, on humanitarian grounds, the body of Major Anderson to the United States.

---

8. *Exchange of Letters with Adlai E. Stevenson, Permanent Representative of the United States to the United Nations, and V. Kuznetsov, First Deputy Foreign Minister of the USSR.*

(a) Letter from the Representatives of the United States and the USSR, January 7

On behalf of the governments of the United States of America and the Soviet Union we desire to express to you our appreciation for your efforts in assisting our governments to avert the serious threat to the peace which recently arose in the Caribbean area.

While it has not been possible for our governments to resolve all the problems that have arisen in connection with this affair, they believe that, in view of the degree of understanding reached between them on the settlement of the crisis and the extent of progress in the implementation of this understanding, it is not necessary for this item to occupy further the attention of the Security Council at this time.

The government of the United States of America and of the Soviet Union express the hope that the actions taken to avert the threat of war in connection with this crisis will lead toward the adjustment of other differ-

Security Council Official Records, Eighteenth Year, Supplement for January, February and March 1963, documents S/5227 and S/5229.

ences between them and the general easing of tensions that could cause a further threat of war.

(b) Text of Letters to the Representatives of the United States and the USSR (identical except for the opening sentences), January 8

I have received the letter of January 7 signed by you and the First Deputy Foreign Minister of the Union of Soviet Socialist Republics in which you have informed me that "while it has not been possible for our governments to resolve all the problems that have arisen in connection with this affair, they believe that, in view of the degree of understanding reached between them on the settlement of the crisis and the extent of progress in the implementation of this understanding, it is not necessary for this item to occupy further the attention of the Security Council at this time."

The letter has been issued as a Security Council document. I am also drawing the attention of the president of the Security Council to this letter, in order that he may inform the other members of the Council.

I share the hope expressed by your governments that "the actions taken to avert the threat of war in connection with this crisis will lead toward the adjustment of other differences between them and the general easing of tensions that could cause a further threat of war." I am also confident that all governments concerned will refrain from any action which might aggravate the situation in the Caribbean area in any way.

I also take this opportunity to thank you and your government for the appreciation expressed in the letter in regard to such assistance as I may have been able to render.

U THANT
Secretary-General
of the United Nations

Statement in the General Assembly Accepting a Full Term as Secretary-General

NEW YORK   NOVEMBER 30, 1962

ONE OF THE widely discussed questions at United Nations Headquarters during the summer of 1962 was whether U Thant would offer himself for a full term as Secretary-General or retire when he had served out the remainder of Dag Hammarskjöld's term. It was a decision that had to be made in the fall of 1962 so that the General Assembly could act upon it. On July 20 Thant told a press conference in Helsinki that he had not yet made up his mind. He said for one thing that he wanted to be "pretty sure that I shall have the necessary means at my disposal to carry out the duties entrusted to me by the various organs of the United Nations." At a press conference in New York on August 2, he was asked to explain what "means" he was talking about and to say when he would make his decision. His reply to the first question was that he had in mind financial means among others and that he wanted to be "pretty sure that the large majority of the states Members of the United Nations really want to contribute toward the development of the United Nations as a really effective instrument for international reconciliation and a really potent force for peace." He said he also wanted to be sure that he would be able to play his "little part in trying to bridge the gulf between the two giants." The latter was always one of his primary objectives and one which neither of his predecessors had been able to do during the final days of their service. On September 17, he said he still had not reached a decision regarding his availability for a full term. The governing factors, he said, were still the prospects for an early settlement of the Congo problem and "the prospects for my playing a humble part in bringing about a more favorable atmosphere for the easing of tensions."

From the beginning there never was any question but that he could have the job for a full term if he wanted it. On November 30, 1962, the Security Council recommended unanimously that he be made Secretary-General instead of Acting Secretary-General and that his term run for five years including the thirteen months he had already served. The General Assembly approved the recommendation, also by a unanimous vote. His salary was raised from $20,000 a year to $27,500 and his annual allowance from $20,000 to $22,500. The existing provision of a furnished residence for the Secretary-General was continued.

In his acceptance speech in the Assembly on November 30, he made no reference to any understanding on his future role. He said, however, that "if I now accept this extended term, it is because I do believe that I may be able to play a role, however humble, in the easing of tensions and in bridging the gulf between the major powers." It was on this note that he cast aside the title of Acting

Secretary-General and the shadow of uncertainty which had hovered over his first months in office. One of the conditions mentioned by him in his August 2 press conference was not referred to in his acceptance speech. This was his desire for assurances that the financial means would be provided to enable the Organization to meet its obligations. The financial crisis continued to be one of his major problems.

EXACTLY FIFTY-SIX WEEKS ago today I assumed what was to me an unfamiliar role, as Acting Secretary-General of the United Nations. Today the General Assembly has done me the further honour of appointing me to serve the normal term of five years as Secretary-General of the United Nations, beginning with my assumption of the office as Acting Secretary-General on November 3, 1961. I am grateful to you Mr. President, for your very gracious words, to the president and members of the Security Council for their unanimous recommendation, and to the General Assembly for my unanimous appointment as Secretary-General. I deeply appreciate and value this mark of your confidence in me, which I shall endeavour, to my utmost, to justify and deserve.

On this occasion, I would recall the words of my distinguished predecessor on his reelection to a second term. He said: "Nobody, I think, can accept the position of the Secretary-General of the United Nations, knowing what it means, except from a sense of duty."[1] He had had over four years experience in that office when he made the statement. My experience has been shorter, but I believe that I do know what that office means, and I accept my extended mandate with humility and out of a sense of duty.

I also take this occasion to reaffirm my oath of office, and I solemnly swear to exercise in all loyalty, discretion, and conscience the functions entrusted to me as Secretary-General of the United Nations, to discharge these functions and regulate my conduct with the interests of the United Nations only in view, and not to seek or accept instructions in regard to the performance of my duties from any government or any other authority external to the Organization.

At the same time, I enter upon this fresh period of service to the international community with a due sense of responsibility. When I was questioned on this subject at a press conference on September 17, 1962, just

General Assembly Official Records, Seventeenth Session, 1182nd plenary meeting.

[1] See volume III of this series, p. 663.

before the present session of the General Assembly began, I stated that my decision to accept the position of Secretary-General for a longer term would: ". . . be governed primarily by a few considerations, including the prospects of an early settlement of the Congo problem, the prospects of the stability of this world Organization as a potent force for peace, and the prospects of my playing a humble part in bringing about a more favorable atmosphere for the easing of tension, and, if I may say so, the prospects of my ability to bridge somewhat the gulf between the two giants" (see p. 224).

If I now accept this extended term, it is because I do believe that I may be able to play a role, however humble, in the easing of tensions and in bridging the gulf between the major powers. In this task, I shall count upon the assistance of my colleagues in the Secretariat, who have, as always, shown a truly admirable team spirit, marked by ungrudging effort, willing cooperation, unflagging devotion to duty, and dedication to the high purposes of the Charter. Without their assistance I could not have achieved much during the last year, and I wish to take this opportunity to pay tribute to them. I shall call on them for advice and assistance, as I have done in the past year, individually, collectively, or otherwise, as the occasion may demand.

I referred a moment ago to the problem of the Congo, a problem which has been with us for over two years and to which I referred in my acceptance speech of last year (see p. 23). The problem remains unsolved in spite of the best efforts of all concerned. As a consequence, the financial problem of the Organization also remains unsolved. Both these problems must, however, be solved, and soon, if the usefulness of the Organization for the future is not to be seriously affected. And today I appeal anew to all Member governments, who have come to value the usefulness of this Organization, to assist in solving these long-standing issues.

On the credit side, I may perhaps recall that the Organization was able to settle one source of tension in South and South East Asia, namely, the problem of West New Guinea (West Irian). The implementation of the tripartite agreement between the governments of the Netherlands and Indonesia and the United Nations, which was approved earlier in the current session of the General Assembly, has worked smoothly, and I am sure that we will be able to carry this unique operation to a successful conclusion, with the cooperation and scrupulous observance of the terms of the agreement by the governments concerned. Again, in the Cuban crisis which seemed so serious some five weeks ago, I believe we are now over the most dangerous phase, even though complete agreement on all outstanding aspects has not yet been registered.

I now look at the years ahead. I would hope that these years would be marked by an improvement in the international climate, and by better understanding of the difficult problems which the world faces today. These problems can be solved only by good will and mutual understanding, and by a spirit of give and take. When the future of mankind itself is at stake, no country or interest group can afford to take a rigid stand, or claim that its position is the only right one, and that others must take it or leave it. No difficult problem can be solved to the complete satisfaction of all sides. We live in an imperfect world, and have to accept imperfect solutions, which become more acceptable as we learn to live with them and as time passes by. In solving these complex problems, I myself and the Secretariat, of which I am proud to be the chief administrative officer, are at the service not only of all Member governments but of the peoples of the United Nations.

"East-West Relations and the United Nations"
Address at Johns Hopkins University

BALTIMORE, MARYLAND   DECEMBER 2, 1962

ON DECEMBER 2, 1962, two days after U Thant had expressed the hope of being useful in bridging the gap between the two super powers (p. 253), he delivered a major address at Johns Hopkins University on the subject of "East-West Relations and the United Nations." An analysis of the existing relationships, he said, "may disclose fruitful avenues which may be explored in the future in order to improve East-West relations on which, if I may say so, the future of peace and of mankind depends so much."

IN TAKING THIS SUBJECT as my theme this afternoon I have been moved by the consideration that the changing character of relationship between the United States and the Soviet Union has had a major impact, not only upon the contemporary world, but also on the work of the United Nations. I believe that it is timely, and it may be useful, to trace the relationship between these two major powers over the last few decades and then to examine various aspects of the present relationship. Such an analysis may disclose fruitful avenues which may be explored in the future in order to improve East-West relations on which, if I may say so, the future of peace and of mankind depends so much.

When we look at recent diplomatic history, especially during the period after the Second World War, the shift of alignments between nations has taken place, as we can see, with startling speed. Soviet-American relations are no exception to this generalization. One may recall that the United States maintained its policy of nonrecognition of the Soviet régime for well nigh sixteen years until, in 1933, President Franklin D. Roosevelt changed this policy. In the period between World War I and World War II, despite the vision, almost utopian, of global collective security which was held by President Wilson, the United States stayed outside the

United Nations Review, January 1963.

League of Nations. This circumstance, however, did not prevent the United States from being an active proponent of international peace, as evidenced by the conclusion of the Kellogg-Briand Pact for the Renunciation of War (1928), and of the naval treaties of Washington (1921) and London (1930). The Soviet Union entered the League of Nations only in 1934, mainly as a consequence of the rise of the nazis in Germany, and remained a supporter of the League until a few months before the outbreak of the Second World War.

It was, however, only with the beginning of the Second World War that the United States and the Soviet Union gradually established a relationship which could be described as cordial. This development was, however, the result of the recognition of a common danger, caused by the presence of a common foe, namely the Axis powers. Although President Roosevelt may have had certain long-range views on the value of improved relations with the Soviet Union, irrespective of the circumstances of the Second World War, the impression is unmistakable that their wartime friendship contained an element of a "marriage of convenience," which was forced on both parties by the circumstances.

In the 1930s, as in other periods of history, the alignments of nations were based on considerations of national interest and security. The inherent weaknesses of the League of Nations, as shown during this period in more than one crisis, encouraged nations to form alliances outside the League, which in turn made the League less effective. This process culminated in the inability of the League to prevent the Second World War. Once the war had started, the United States found itself moving away from its traditional isolationism, even before the Japanese attack on Pearl Harbor forced it to become a major participant in the Second World War. Being immune from the ravages of war on its own territory, the tremendous industrial and agricultural potential of the United States enabled it to become, not only the arsenal, but also the granary of the Allies.

The Greatest Hope

This experience of forced involvement in world affairs, coupled with the preeminent position of the United States as the world's greatest industrial power, made it inevitable that the United States should finally abandon its traditional policy of isolationism. The United States was thus instrumental in the signing of the Atlantic Charter in 1941, and was in the vanguard of the movement for the establishment of a postwar international organization. Thus the United States gave up the concept of a "Fortress America" and gradually came to recognize the fact of mutual interdependence of nations. The conferences of Moscow (1943), Dumbarton Oaks (1944), and Yalta (1945) were significant milestones in bringing to birth the United Nations as the greatest hope for war-weary humanity.

Thus the United Nations was born at a time when the two great powers were working in close cooperation, and the Charter of the United Nations was framed on the assumption that this cooperation would continue. It was on this basis that the members of the United Nations conferred on the Security Council "primary responsibility for the maintenance of international peace and security," and agreed "that in carrying out its duties under this responsibility the Security Council acts on their behalf" (Article 24). Further, the members of the United Nations agreed "to accept and carry out the decisions of the Security Council in accordance with the present Charter" (Article 25). The Security Council was to be "so organized as to be able to function continuously" (Article 28). It was also provided that decisions of the Security Council on all matters other than procedural matters shall be made "by an affirmative vote of seven members, including the concurring votes of the permanent members" (Article 27), thus introducing the well-known principle of the veto, which may be described positively as the principle of unanimity among the big powers.

The Security Council was then envisaged as the most important among the principal organs of the United Nations, vested with primary responsibility for the maintenance of international peace and security. This tremendous responsibility could have been discharged by the Security Council only if the harmony between the two major powers could have been continued. We all know that before long the differences between the USSR and the United States became very sharp, beginning with the controversy over the presence of Soviet troops in Iran (1946), and reaching a climax with the Korean war (1950). This was the beginning of the era of the cold war. Future historians may undertake learned analyses of this period with a view to allocating responsibility, and even blame, for the emergence of the cold war. I wish here merely to note the fact of bipolarity, which before long characterized the work of the United Nations, and which continues to this day to affect the effectiveness of the United Nations, and in particular the Security Council.

The advent of the cold war and the fact of bipolarity in international relations generate political tensions not only in the United Nations, but all over the world. Even so, the situation today is less grim than it was before the Second World War. In the thirties there was one aggressive nation wishing to dominate the world by force—Hitler's Nazi Germany. Today there are two great powers, neither wanting war, but each so apprehensive of the other that they are convinced they must possess greater military might. Hence the frantic nuclear arms race. A clash between the two would mean the destruction of mankind. This explains why a growing number of nations wish to be nonaligned, to fight for neither side, to keep the two giants apart, to lessen the tension between them and to reduce the danger of nuclear accidents. In this way, the period of two-power predominance within the United Nations gave way to a tripolar situation.

While this process of tripolarization was going on in international relations, another significant change was in evidence in the relationship between the two big powers. In the late forties and early fifties the political system—and theories, such as inevitability of war—prevailing in the Soviet Union were increasingly regarded elsewhere as a definite threat to political and economic systems in other parts of the world. In my view the system created and maintained by Stalin was manifestly ruthless and obsolescent even before his departure. Mr. Khrushchev, who is now in control of the reins of government, belongs to a different category of leaders, with a coherent philosophy of the world based on the thesis, not of the inevitability of war, but of the imperative of competitive coexistence. We may or may not agree with his philosophy or with his aims, but we have very good reasons to believe that he does not want war.

The West does not seem to appreciate the full significance of this obvious change of political climate in the Soviet Union. Throughout the fifties most Western leaders saw the world as a battlefield between two antagonistic systems militantly expressing the principles of good and evil. Hence compromise was betrayal: evil could be held at bay only by iron-clad alliances, held together by mutual fear and backed by the constant threat of nuclear war. While this attitude could be criticized as a modern version of Hobbesian pessimism, it nevertheless provided a stable and fixed frame of reference in which decisions could be taken.

This concept of iron-clad alliances and this view of the world purely in terms of black and white was, in essence, the Western response to Stalinism. However, this attitude persisted even when the character of Soviet challenge was already changing. This view of the world scene was perhaps partly responsible for many newly independent countries pursuing a policy of nonalignment. President Kennedy proved himself to be a leader of vision and imagination when, early last year, he proposed a neutral Laos in return for a cease-fire. Thus the President wisely admitted that the attempt to create a series of pro-Western governments in Asia had failed. He accepted the view that the best the West could hope for in Asia—and for that matter Africa—is governments which fear outside interference and subversion as much as they hate colonialism; and that the function of Western policy should be the creation of a framework within which they can exercise their own freedom of choice.

Emergence of a Dominant Group

I now revert to my review of the last decade. The Korean armistice of 1953, the Geneva conference on Indo-China of 1954, and the Bandung conference of 1955 brought a new element into the picture, although the last two conferences took place outside the auspices of the United Nations. In 1955, sixteen new nations were admitted to the United Nations in a package deal, including some Asian and Arab countries. The new nations of Asia, while rejoicing in their liberation from colonial rule, took it upon themselves—as already noted—to constitute a third or middle element, anxious to conciliate, to the extent possible, the rivalry between Washington and Moscow. The process was further continued with the admission of three African countries and one Asian country in 1956, one African and one Asian country in 1957, another Asian country in 1958 and seventeen new countries (of which sixteen were from Africa) in 1960. In 1961 there were four new admissions, of which three were from Africa, and in the current session we have had six new members, of which four were from Africa. As a result, the United Nations has expanded from a membership of fifty-one at its inception to 110 today, and the Afro-Asian countries have emerged as one of the dominant groups within the United Nations.

With the rapid growth of Afro-Asian membership we have entered on a new era in which it is no longer true to say that there is a tripolar situation, but rather a multipolar situation. As is obvious to anyone who works day after day in the United Nations, it is misleading to think of the Afro-Asian members of the United Nations as a solid bloc: there is any number of alignments within the Afro-Asian group. And, while on certain questions—as, for example, colonialism—they maintain a basic accord, on other issues they act quite independently of each other, and, in fact, have on occasion shown considerable rivalry when contesting for seats on the major organs. Thus the simple formula of East-West confrontation, which was replaced by the East-Neutral-West situation, has been superseded by a complex and fluid pattern of international relations.

One result of the increased membership of the General Assembly, and the emergence of the numerically strong Afro-Asian element in it, has been to give the General Assembly added strength, as the only universal organ among the principal organs of the United Nations, in which all members can participate with equal rights, coupled with the fact that the Security Council cannot act effectively on any issue on which the major powers cannot reach prior agreement. The General Assembly has thus become the battleground of the cold war. Both the major powers are anxious to secure the support of the General Assembly for their respective stands on major world issues, and have shown a willingness to accommodate themselves to the views of the uncommitted countries to the extent that their basic positions permit them a little elbowroom. This fact explains to some extent the dissatisfaction with the United Nations, especially on the part of those countries which were used to having much their own way in the past and now find it necessary to woo the uncommitted countries in an effort to muster the necessary majorities in the Assembly.

Some Cooperation Evident

Some East-West cooperation has become evident lately in the technological and scientific fields and also in the matter of cultural and other exchanges between the Soviet Union and the United States. Perhaps the most significant development in this regard is cooperation in the field of outer space, but even this is conditioned by the political climate and is subject to the climatic vicissitudes of the cold war.

In difficult areas such as disarmament there is very little doubt in my own mind that the introduction of a third element has been very useful. While there was some agreement between the two major powers on broad principles, as reflected in the Zorin-McCloy statement of last year on general and comprehensive disarmament, further progress has been delayed and may hopefully be reached only in the Geneva discussions. The unanimous report of the expert committee on the economic consequences of disarmament has helped to dispel certain misconceptions and apprehensions in regard to economic obstacles in making progress toward a disarmed world. On the question of nuclear tests, too, considerable progress has been made since March last, when the Geneva conference began; and it is to be hoped that the impasse which now exists in regard to underground tests may be resolved by discussions at the scientific level directed toward reaching agreement on mutually acceptable procedures of verification.

I may say a few words at this point on a subject which has occupied a considerable amount of my time and attention and which was a cause of much concern and even anxiety during the last six weeks. I refer here to the situation in Cuba. It became apparent in late October that there was danger of a direct confrontation between the two major powers, and that every possible step should be taken to avert this confrontation. I gave expression to this feeling in the Security Council, by an odd coincidence on United Nations Day, and I addressed an appeal both on that day and on the next to the heads of the two governments, to which I received an encouraging and positive response from both quarters. Most of you may have been familiar with the subsequent developments which have been reported so fully, and sometimes so inaccurately, by the mass media everywhere. In spite of periods when there seemed to be little progress, the negotiations advanced steadily to a point at which it is now possible to report agreement on certain fundamentals between the two major powers. There may be many who may wish for a more complete and comprehensive solution of the Cuban crisis, but in this imperfect world, we have, at least for the moment, to accept less than perfect solutions.

Looking to the future, I hope that the spirit of compromise which marked the discussions between the Soviet Union and the United States in the case of Cuba may help the solution of some of the outstanding cold-war issues of the world today, both general and local. I have already referred to the question of disarmament and nuclear testing. There are various other issues like Berlin on which it may become imperative to reach solutions on the basis of compromise and the principle of give-and-take on both sides. In all these situations the United Nations is available to the major powers, as it is to all its members, as a channel of friendly contact and informal discussion, and not merely a forum for public debate.

I have already referred to the United Nations as the battleground of the cold war, which is mainly due to the fact that it is the greatest public forum in the world today. In this forum it is possible over the years to debate great issues, and to enlarge the area of agreement and narrow the differences, so that over the years the solution of the most intractable problems may become feasible. For example, no one will question that the work of the United Nations has been in no small measure responsible for the astonishingly rapid emergence of so many African countries as sovereign states and full members of the international community. I would hope that the General Assembly may become even more effective as a public assembly by providing opportunities for friendly personal contacts between the leaders of the world, as also for rational debate on difficult issues, so that the United Nations truly serves the purpose set out in the Charter "to be a centre for harmonizing the actions of nations."

I may refer briefly in this context to the increasing use of the United Nations as an organ for pragmatic executive action on behalf of the world community. The United Nations has undertaken, as in the case of West New Guinea (West Irian), quasi-governmental tasks, in addition to its traditional peacekeeping role in the Middle East, and, more recently, in the Congo.

In this context I would like also to refer to the broad spectrum of instruments for international cooperation which are available in the United Nations in nonpolitical fields and especially in the economic, social, and humanitarian fields. The designation of the current decade as the United Nations Development Decade is a concrete recognition of the role of the United Nations and its family of agencies in the promotion of economic and social development, the importance of which has been stressed even in the Charter. I cannot help feeling that too much attention has been given in the past to the military, ideological, and political factors which tend to divide the world into various groups and interest blocs. The time has come for us to direct our attention more to the economic and social structure of society, and particularly to the disparity in the wealth of nations, which is one of the root causes of political tension. It is possible, within the United Nations, to stress the common responsibility of nations, rich and poor, in the economic and social fields, and to organize north-south as well as east-west cooperation for the promotion of human welfare.

In this field, the resources available so far to the United Nations have been small, almost marginal, in relation to the resources which have been expended by governments on a bilateral basis. I believe, however, that the United Nations and its family of agencies provide a unique opportunity for organizing a global attack on the common problems of mankind. In this way the United Nations can also help prevent the world from becoming frozen into antagonistic interest blocs. In this context, the tendency toward close economic integration of highly organized and developed societies is a factor which causes considerable apprehension among the less developed countries, and it is necessary that special steps be taken to allay this apprehension.

International Understanding

In the important task of breaking down ideological barriers, I believe that nongovernmental cooperation can also be of very great significance. Professional organizations on a global basis, meetings of scientists and technologists from all over the world, youth exchange programs and so forth, may help greatly in the promotion of international understanding. The General Assembly adopted two years ago a resolution on measures designed to promote among youth the ideals of peace, mutual respect, and understanding among peoples. It is necessary to promote these ideals, not only among youth, but also, if I may say so, among adults. I believe that the exchange of visits by celebrities in the field of culture, art and sport, by political leaders, by eminent intellectuals and poets, all these may help to create mutual respect and greater understanding.

In the promotion of international understanding, newspapers and journals, radio and television, and other media of mass communication can be of great help. International communication has now been speeded up to an extent which was inconceivable a generation ago. I cannot, however, say that the mass media have played as valuable a part as they are capable of playing in promoting better international understanding. It is important that their reporting should never lack objectivity or a proper regard for facts even where national emotions have been aroused.

Today the issues involved are so complex, and there are so many diverse interests, that it is a truism to say that every question has many sides. I believe that the mass media are capable of making a special effort to develop more open, receptive and unbiased minds among their readers and audience.

One of the great tasks of education all over the world is to educate the young for peace because, on the question of peace, no man of goodwill can be neutral. We have not only the task of eradicating ignorance and illiteracy in the less-developed countries, but also of correcting the distorted image of foreign countries which prevails so often in advanced countries, if we are to create a basis for durable peace among nations. I would hope that it is not too difficult for the advanced countries, despite their different ideologies, to stress their common aspirations, their similar cultural values, and their identical interest in survival.

At this point I wish to address myself particularly to American educationists and leaders of thought. The United States is the one society in which the philosophy of material progress is a spectacular success. Democracy is not inhibited, as it is in Europe, by either the threat of social upheaval from below or the memory of a conservative past. But two world wars and an intervening depression have greatly affected American confidence in the continuity of progress. Political and social changes elsewhere worry most Americans. The revolt of the colonial people, who are in fact the ultimate heirs of 1776, and their desire to fashion their own way of life seem to be frightening and incomprehensible to the descendants of those who started it all at Lexington and Concord.

It is little use trying to meet this new situation with conventional responses. The attempt to pin the blame on scapegoats and subversives may have been emotionally comforting, but it has probably weakened the confidence of the American people. Nor is more and bigger defence spending the real answer. As we are already witnessing, nuclear power has reduced the traditional influence of military strength on national security. It provides such a devastating armory that the price of a victory could be greater than the sum of all the defeats in past history. The point of diplomacy, therefore, is to avoid a war of such dimensions, and this means that many solutions are now accepted which in previous generations would have been the occasion for war. The less the influence of military factors, the more the strength of the other potent forces that make history.

What has happened is that the revolutionary concept of a meaningful future is, in our lifetime, seizing the minds of the masses. The real challenge to the United States is how to promote this trend toward a better future for all humanity. I believe that this promotion should conceivably be to ensure the proper use of the fruits of wealth, so as to ease the contrast between its own abundance and the poverty of mankind elsewhere.

To illustrate my point, let me cite one glaring instance. In Asia, Africa, and Latin America, living standards have largely remained stationary, or have even declined. Throughout the last decade, the fall in the price of raw materials, while priming the affluent societies of the West, has not only cancelled out the sum total of Western aid, but in many cases has led to an absolute drop in national income. One great lesson of this phenomenon is that the world will not live in harmony so long as two-thirds of its inhabitants find difficulty in living at all.

I further believe that the age is past when governments can claim that each nation by itself provides its own shield of security. The unprecedented scientific and technical progress of recent years has made this concept somewhat outmoded. If we are to survive in this nuclear and space age, we must move forward, however slowly, away from the concept of the absolute freedom of action of the sovereign state, toward the community of ideas and identity of interests that cut across national, cultural, and ideological boundaries.

The United Nations, to me, does not represent a vague ideal of universal peace and brotherhood which has its appeal only to starry-eyed idealists and moralists. Far from it. It is hardheaded, enlightened self-interest, the stake that all humanity has in peace and progress and, most important of all, survival, that dictates the need for the United Nations as a practical, institutional embodiment of the needs of nations on a shrinking planet, as a potent and dynamic instrument at the service of all nations, east and west, north as well as south.

The ideas that I have expressed today are not new. The thesis that all nations share an abiding interest in peace, progress, and prosperity, and that relations between nations should accordingly be based on faith and justice is an old and time-honored concept. To illustrate this point, I cannot do better than to recall President Washington's farewell address when he said:

Observe good faith and justice toward all nations. Cultivate peace and harmony with all . . . nothing is more essential than that permanent, inveterate antipathies against particular nations and passionate attachments for others should be excluded, and that in place of them just and amicable feelings toward all should be cultivated. The nation which indulges toward another an habitual hatred or an habitual fondness is in some degree a slave.

THE FINANCIAL SITUATION

IN THE INTRODUCTION TO his first annual report, dated August 24, 1962, U Thant noted that the financial difficulties of the United Nations had become increasingly serious during the year. He mentioned two developments which might ease the difficulties: the purchase of additional United Nations bonds by Member states and the payment of assessments by Members in arrears on ONUC and UNEF. At its sixteenth session the General Assembly had asked the International Court of Justice for an advisory opinion on the question of whether assessments for peacekeeping operations constituted "expenses of the Organization" within the meaning of Article 17, paragraph 2, of the Charter and therefore represented binding obligations. On July 20, 1962, the Court gave an affirmative answer by 9 votes to 5. The five dissenters were Judges Jules Basdevant of France, José Luis Bustamante y Rivero of Peru, V. M. Koretsky of the Soviet Union, Lucio M. Moreno Quintana of Argentina, and Bohdan Winiarski of Poland. The Secretary-General appeared before the Fifth Committee on December 3 to urge that it uphold the views of the Court. To do otherwise, he said, would be "a blow at the authority and standing of both the Court and the Assembly." The Fifth Committee and the General Assembly itself, on December 19, did adopt a resolution accepting the Court's opinion. The vote in the Assembly was 76 votes to 17, with 8 abstentions. The action, however, failed to induce states in arrears to pay their assessments for ONUC and UNEF.

In another appearance before the Fifth Committee on October 4, Thant called attention to "an overwhelming desire" on the part of Member states for United Nations expansion in certain major fields despite the Organization's financial difficulties. In view of new and expanded programs in the economic and social field and in other areas, such as outer space, increased expenditures were inescapable, he said. In formulating his 1963 budget, he said, his keynote had been "controlled expansion." This he defined as full and effective use of existing staff and resources, and a reasonable approach in the scheduling of studies, reports, and conferences, and in the establishing of work programs generally.

1. *From Statement in the Fifth Committee*

NEW YORK   OCTOBER 4, 1962

. . . . I AM DEEPLY impressed by the spirit of optimism which prevails and which Member states continue to show in the future role of this Organization. This spirit is amply reflected in the new and challenging work programs proposed by the principal organs and endorsed by the General Assembly itself.

It is quite apparent from the many resolutions adopted by the General Assembly at its sixteenth session that there is an overwhelming desire on the part of the majority of Member states for expansion in certain of the major fields of activity of this Organization. A significant step in this direction was taken when the General Assembly decided by resolution 1710 (XVI) to designate the next ten years as the United Nations Development Decade thus beginning a new experiment in human cooperation. The Economic and Social Council had before it my report on this subject at its thirty-fourth session this year, and the General Assembly will consider the report, together with the observations stemming from the discussions of the Council, at its present session. The Council has also endorsed new and expanded programs in the fields of industrialization, natural resources, economic projections and programing, and balanced economic and social development. New and expanding work programs are also in evidence in the area of political and Security Council affairs. Extensive meetings have been held at Geneva on the question of disarmament, both nuclear and conventional, a matter of vital interest to the entire world. Furthermore, as a result of General Assembly resolution 1721 (XVI), new and important tasks have been entrusted to the Committee on the Peaceful Uses of Outer Space. There has been a marked increase in the United Nations responsibilities for the servicing of special commissions and committees established by the General Assembly, both in regard to the ren-

General Assembly Official Records, Seventeenth Session, Annexes, agenda item 62, document A/C.5/925.

dering of assistance and support to the newly independent nations, and the carrying out of the mandates of the Assembly concerning non-self-governing territories.

All of these new activities, to which the most urgent priority is attached, have placed a heavier burden upon the substantive staff of the Secretariat. They have also, and this is sometimes forgotten, added considerably to the level of general expenses and to the workload of the servicing departments to meet in particular the formidable related conference program and the growing responsibilities in the field of public information. They have taxed existing resources to the point where it has become extremely difficult to plan and implement work properly, to the inevitable detriment of its quality and effectiveness. The task of meeting this heavier and expanding workload has not been made easier by our conscious efforts to expedite a recruitment program designed to improve geographical distribution of staff while at the same time endeavouring to obtain the services of certain categories of specialized personnel in an increasingly competitive outside market.

In formulating the budget estimates for 1963, therefore, I have kept these developments in mind. It is my considered opinion that under these circumstances one cannot reasonably and logically maintain a policy of stabilization. I was led inevitably, therefore, to consider a new and more realistic approach in so far as the estimates for 1963 are concerned. The policy I have advocated for 1963, is, I believe, certainly more realistic; it may not however be so new, since to some extent although on a broader basis it reflects the views of the General Assembly and this committee as expressed in resolution 1449 (XIV) concerning the need to establish priorities within work programs. I have adopted as my keynote the phrase "controlled expansion". . . .

There is, I think, a natural tendency for one to concentrate on the "expansion" aspect and to gloss over the more important word "controlled." In my interpretation, a policy of "controlled expansion" can be implemented only if two important conditions are met. The first condition is a responsibility which rests with the Secretary-General and which requires him to assess accurately from year to year what staff expansion, if any, is necessary to meet the new tasks and services called for by Member states, taking into account the full and effective utilization of existing resources. The second condition, however, is a responsibility which falls upon the Member states themselves and which it is hoped would manifest itself in the decisions they jointly take in the principal organs and in the

General Assembly. It calls for the exercising of certain disciplines in the establishment of the work program, in the more precise determination of the order of priority according to which these work programs are to be implemented, and a reasonable approach to the setting of deadlines for the completion of studies and reports and the scheduling of necessary related conferences. It is only through this approach that programs of work can be rationalized and matched with available resources, and a policy of controlled expansion successfully pursued by a combination of these two conditions.

. . . .

2. Statement in the Fifth Committee

NEW YORK   DECEMBER 3, 1962

ON THE SUBJECT which is going to be discussed in this committee this afternoon, the committee will no doubt recall that, by its resolution 1731 (XVI) of December 20, 1961, the General Assembly requested an advisory opinion of the International Court of Justice on the question whether certain expenditures authorized by the Assembly in connection with United Nations operations in the Congo and in the Middle East are "expenses of the Organization" within the meaning of Article 17, paragraph 2, of the Charter. The Fifth Committee is also aware that, by a majority opinion, the Court answered this question in the affirmative in its opinion of July 20, 1962. The time has now come for this committee to consider that opinion.

At the very outset, I must express my hope that the Fifth Committee, in its advice to the Assembly, will follow the time-honoured tradition whereby each principal organ of the United Nations respects and upholds the views, resolutions, and decisions of other principal organs in their respective fields of competence. Not to do so in the present case would be not only a departure from the tradition relating to all the past precedents concerning advisory opinions of the Court, but also a blow at the author-

General Assembly Official Records, Seventeenth Session, Annexes, agenda item 64, document A/C.5/952.

ity and standing of both the Court and the Assembly in a matter vital to the future of the United Nations.

It has no doubt been noted by all the members of this committee that the Court, at the very outset of its opinion, distinguished between the question whether certain expenditures are "expenses of the Organization" and the question of how those expenditures are to be apportioned. It was to the first of these questions that the Court returned an affirmative answer. On the second question the Court's opinion makes it clear that the Assembly is not bound to apportion the expenses of peacekeeping operations in the same manner as it apportions the regular budget, and that the Assembly may adopt whatever scale of assessment for such operations as appears just and fair to it in the circumstances. The committee, I am sure, will wish to keep this distinction in mind while considering this matter. It follows that the question of apportionment may be more appropriately considered at a later stage.

I believe that the financial problem of the Organization, which in substance is the question now before this committee, is a vital one. A financially bankrupt United Nations would be an ineffective United Nations, if, indeed, it could survive on such a basis. The financial issue is thus one which, if I may say so, transcends political controversy. In their various ways, I believe all states represented in the United Nations have found that the Organization is useful, and indeed indispensable, in the modern world. It is on this basis that I trust that the committee will deal with this item.

In the introduction to my annual report I expressed my sincere hope and belief that Member governments, who are all agreed on the indispensable role of the Organization in the world today, would take appropriate action to solve its financial problems. Furthermore, in my statement before the General Assembly on the occasion of my election, I referred to the fact that, before the present session of the Assembly opened, I indicated that my acceptance of a further term of office would depend, in part, on the prospects of the stability of this world Organization as a potent force for peace and I appealed to the governments of Member states, which have come to value the usefulness of this Organization, to assist in solving the financial problems if the usefulness of the Organization for the future is not to be seriously affected. I renew those appeals today in the belief that the decisions of this Committee will help resolve the financial difficulties of the Organization, and represent a vote of confidence in its future.

THE SITUATION IN THE CONGO

DECEMBER 1962—JANUARY 1963

WHEN U THANT was elected Secretary-General for a full five-year term on November 30, 1962, the situation in the Congo was somewhat better than it had been in the fall of 1961, but it was far from satisfactory. Although discussions were in progress on the Plan of National Reconciliation, the Katangese authorities continued to drag their feet on important issues such as ending their foreign representation abroad, agreeing to share foreign exchange with the central government and assuring freedom of movement for United Nations forces. On December 10 the United Nations officer-in-charge, Robert K. Gardiner, informed the provincial president, Moïse Tshombé, of the Secretary-General's disappointment and notified him that phases III and IV of the plan would be applied. Phase III provided that the central government would ask all interested states to place an embargo on the importation of copper and cobalt, two of Katanga's major sources of income. Phase IV provided that, if such measures failed, governments would consult on further steps to force acceptance of the plan.

The Secretary-General appealed to Belgium, one of the original supporters of the plan, to exert every possible influence to encourage the cooperation of Katangese authorities. He also urged the governments of Portugal, South Africa, and the United Kingdom to prohibit the shipment of Katangese copper ore through territories under their jurisdiction. Prime Minister Cyrille Adoula addressed similar requests to seventeen interested governments.

At the time these measures were being taken, the military situation in South Katanga deteriorated once more. During the closing months of the year, the Katangese gendarmerie launched an intense campaign of harassment against ONUC troops producing a situation similar to that existing at the end of 1961. At this time Tshombé was threatening to initiate a "scorched-earth" policy while almost at the same moment talking about implementing the Plan of National Reconciliation. On January 12 he suddenly left Elisabethville for Kolwezi. Two days later Thant received a message from Tshombé and his ministers from Kolwezi announcing their readiness to end the secession of Katanga, to grant UN troops full freedom of movement and to carry out the Secretary-General's Plan. Kolwezi was the last important mining center still occupied by the gendarmerie at this time. Tshombé agreed on January 16 to the peaceful entry of UN forces into Kolwezi. This was done without bloodshed on January 21. Thus, in twenty-four days of activity ONUC had gained control of all important centers in Katanga, and the Katangese gendarmerie had ceased to exist as a fighting force. The ONUC casualties during this period numbered ten killed and twenty-seven wounded.

Nevertheless, Thant's handling of the situation was challenged by the President of Ghana, Kwame Nkrumah, who accused him of "vacillation and lack of resolution" especially in permitting Tshombé to travel to Kolwezi and back to Elisabethville instead of placing him under arrest. The Secretary-General, in the two long letters reproduced below, defended his action and explained in detail his reasons.

---

1. Remarks to the Advisory Committee on the Congo

NEW YORK   DECEMBER 13, 1962

SINCE OUR LAST MEETING on November 6 I have talked with all members of the committee, individually or in small groups, about developments in the Congo; there has been circulated an extensive report to the Security Council on the plan and we have circulated to you in recent days certain letters; others are being handed to you here today. By these various means you have been kept informed and given just about all the information we have.

There was a good deal of press coverage, including speculations, before the local papers closed down because of the strike, about various new "plans," such as the so-called "Spaak plan" and the "McGhee plan".

There is, in fact, only *one* plan, and that is the Plan of National Reconciliation which I have sponsored and which you received a long time ago. It was also reproduced in full in the report to the Security Council.

Mr. Spaak and Mr. McGhee, as you know, had no new plans, but they did advance some ideas about procedures and implementation, but these did not prove feasible.

We are therefore going ahead with the plan *in toto* and we are now in the stage of calling upon states to give effect to the pressures envisaged in phases I through IV of that plan. This you will see from the letters which have been distributed to you.

Now as regards the letters, you will note that they take different forms, according to the party addressed. One letter, which has been distributed

UN Press Release SG/1393.

to you, is the letter of warning which Mr. Gardiner has already sent to Mr. Tshombé. As yet there has been no response from and no public comment on this letter by Mr. Tshombé.

The letters calling upon certain states to take actions of one kind or another spring directly from the plan. There are, of course, other actions involving pressure which the Congolese government itself can take and that government will, I am sure, take them in due course. On our part, as you know, there are nonmilitary steps outside of the plan as well as under it, such as I outlined to you in our October meeting, which ONUC can take and will proceed to take one by one.

In other words, we are now in a phase in which all of the pressures available to us will be exerted on the basis of careful selection and planning and with every effort made to avoid armed conflict. If, however, Mr. Tshombé should elect to order his gendarmerie to attack us, we will defend ourselves fully and hit back to the full extent of our capacity. The United Nations troops are alerted and are being prepared for any such eventuality.

Members of the committee will be interested to learn that Mr. Tshombé now has access to what goes on in this room. In a letter of December 7, which Mr. Tshombé addressed to Mr. Mathu concerning the fighting at Kongolo, he quotes a passage from the confidential summary of the 70th meeting of this committee on October 12, circulated to members of the Security Council for their confidential information. Typically, however, Mr. Tshombé missed the point of the passage.

The Katangese gendarmerie at Kongolo, who had been surrounded by the ANC for a long time, have left the town. With the concurrence of Mr. Adoula, a detachment of ONUC is being placed in the town and a Nigerian unit is now en route to Kongolo for this purpose.

The aerial activities by Katangese planes in North Katanga seem to have ceased. Because of the loss of the Ethiopian jet fighters and the Indian Canberras, the ONUC fighter plane force is now very weak, consisting at present of only three Swedish jet fighters. However, four additional Swedish jet fighters, thanks to the very great sense of cooperation and understanding of the Swedish government, are being added to the Force; the Ethiopian fighter crews will be soon returning to take over F-86 aircraft which the United Nations is obtaining. We have just been informed that the Philippine government will provide six jet fighters with crews.

About midday, I received a message from Mr. Gardiner, transmitting the text of a letter dated December 12 from Mr. Tshombé to me. The text of this letter may now be distributed to you. On first look, as you will see, it would appear to be an encouraging development. You will readily understand, however, that in view of our past experiences with Mr. Tshombé, we are not jumping to any hasty conclusions. We are studying it very carefully and have asked Mr. Gardiner to get Prime Minister Adoula's reaction to it. It could be that this new development is not unrelated to the new steps.

This I believe will serve to bring you fully up to date. I now welcome any comments the members may wish to make.

---

2. Statement with Regard to Recent Events in the Elisabethville Area

NEW YORK   DECEMBER 31, 1962

I WAS INFORMED by the officer-in-charge of the United Nations Operation in the Congo at Leopoldville, Mr. Robert K. Gardiner, and by the commander of the United Nations Force, Lieutenant-General Kebbede Guebre, yesterday, December 30, 1962, that the ONUC operation which had begun on the afternoon of December 28 to remove all of the roadblocks of the Katangese gendarmerie in the Elisabethville area had been completed. Thus, all firing and fighting had ceased on that date. From these numerous roadblock positions the gendarmerie, on December 22, 1962, resuming again on December 24 and continuing through the morning of December 28, had been firing intermittently, and at times heavily, upon United Nations troops in the Elisabethville area. On the night of December 27 to 28, heavy mortar fire was added to the previous small arms fire, indicating the participation of mercenaries. Throughout this period the United Nations troops, with remarkable restraint in the face of

Security Council Official Records, Eighteenth Year, Supplement for January, February and March 1963, document S/5053/Add. 14, annex XXXI.

the unprovoked and continuing firing upon them, and in spite of casualties of two killed and ten wounded, strictly observed the orders of their commander not to return the fire. The Katangese gendarmerie, incidentally, is the regular Katangese army and not, as sometimes misstated in the press, police. They are said to number about 18,000, they are heavily armed and are often led in battle by some of the 500 or more white mercenaries still on the Katanga payrolls, thanks to mining revenues.

It has been reported that in the early hours of the morning of December 28, 1962, Mr. Tshombé sought to prevent his troops from firing, but, either because his officers and troops would not obey him or for some other reason, he did not succeed in doing so. Later in the day, although he again agreed to bring about a cessation of firing and also agreed that the gendarmerie roadblocks and strong points from which the fire was coming should be removed, he refused to sign a statement to that effect. Consequently, since the firing persisted, in midafternoon on December 28 the United Nations troops, in self-defense, were ordered at last to protect their security and their freedom of movement by clearing away the roadblocks and strong points. This has been accomplished now in an action of two days' duration in which there have been only light fighting and light casualties. That is to say that by normal military standards they would be considered light, but they must be regarded as heavy for a United Nations force whose function is peaceful and which is armed for defense only. The United Nations casualties during the period December 27 to 30 were seven dead and twenty-nine wounded. We have no figures on Katangese casualties but they also are thought to be light, since the gendarmerie and their mercenary officers usually fled in the face of impending combat, leaving their weapons and sometimes their vehicles as well.

The gendarmerie forces have been cleared away from the perimeter of Elisabethville to a considerable distance and they will not be permitted to return or to reestablish their positions. In the light of the unhappy experience of September 1961 involving the wanton bombing of ONUC personnel by Katangese Fouga jets piloted by mercenaries, and of the recent extensive bombing and strafing activities in North Katanga by the greatly enlarged Katanga air force, protective sorties by ONUC aircraft were ordered on December 29 and 30 against the Katangese military aircraft based at the Kolwezi military airfield, with a view to ensuring that neither the aircraft nor the airfield could be used for offensive strikes against the United Nations troops. The Swedish jet fighters rendered most effective support in this respect in an indispensable defensive action, and thus contributed significantly to the success of the valiant Ethiopian, Indian, Irish, and Tunisian troops engaged in the Elisabethville-Kipushi operation, of the Ghanaian and Swedish troops in the Kaminaville area, and of the Congolese contingent safeguarding Kamina base. In this context, I am bound to deny categorically any reports that ONUC fighter planes undertook bombing raids. They employed only cannons and rockets. Indeed, they have no bombs. Nor did they carry out any sorties against any targets in the Elisabethville area. Their sorties were directed only at the Kolwezi-Kengere military airfield. The airfield in Kolwezi town was avoided.

Some may say loosely that there was a "third round" in Katanga. That was not the case. There would have been no fighting at all if the Katangese gendarmerie had not made it unavoidable by indulging in senseless firing for several days. In view of the results of the ONUC operation, there may be some who would be inclined to refer to a United Nations "military victory." I would not like this to be said. The United Nations is seeking no victory and no surrender in Katanga, for the United Nations is not waging war against anyone in that province. We are there—as we are in the rest of the Congo—only because in mid-July 1960 the newly independent Central Government appealed to us to come to its aid in helping it to secure the withdrawal from its territory of all non-Congolese military personnel and to maintain law and order within a Congo whose territorial integrity and political independence needed protection. In this connection, resolutions of United Nations organs also called for vigorous United Nations action to safeguard the unity, territorial integrity, and political independence of the Congo, and entrusted to the United Nations Operation in the Congo the double mandate of eliminating mercenaries from Katanga and preventing the occurrence of civil war. The United Nations Operation in the Congo, including—we must now particularly emphasize—Katanga, firmly seeks to discharge all of these responsibilities. But it has no other purpose there and will move in no other direction. We operate always in the hope that these objectives can be attained without resort to force. We have never taken the initiative in the use of force in Katanga or elsewhere in the Congo, and we do not intend to do so. We do not use the force we have for political ends and we do not intend to intervene in the political affairs of the Congo, of the province of Katanga or of any other province.

On the other hand, it must be clearly said that we support the Central Government as the only legitimate government of the Congo, and we do not and will not, therefore, recognize any claim to secession or to independence on the part of the province of Katanga, or deal with Mr. Tshombé or any other official of Katanga in any capacity other than that of provincials.

Mr. Tshombé left Elisabethville, apparently on December 28, 1962, by some means and route unknown to me, but entirely of his own volition. It seems that his colleagues in the top echelon of Katangese officialdom, such as Mr. Munongo, Mr. Kimba, and Mr. Kibwe, also left. But in general the local officials remained and the city is being run as usual by them.

On December 28, after four days of intermittent firing which had then become heavy in Elisabethville, I sent a message to Mr. Gardiner in Leopoldville suggesting that he might go to Elisabethville to have a very frank and serious talk with Mr. Tshombé. I advised Mr. Gardiner that he might assure Mr. Tshombé that the United Nations in the Congo has no designs on him or on his future position or career in or out of Katanga province. Then he should seek to convince Mr. Tshombé that the United Nations Operation in the Congo is determined to move without further delay toward the full implementation of its mandate under the Security Council's resolutions. Mr. Gardiner was to inform Mr. Tshombé that the gendarmerie roadblocks and strong points in the Elisabethville area would have to be removed, and that ONUC personnel must have full freedom of movement throughout Katanga, which would necessarily mean freeing the Jadotville road and establishing ONUC presence in Jadotville, Kolwezi, and Kipushi. Mr. Gardiner also was to seek agreement of the provincial president on a plan to be devised by Mr. Gardiner for the complete and immediate elimination of mercenaries from Katanga and for bringing Katangese aerial offensive activity to a speedy end. Unhappily, Mr. Tshombé left Elisabethville surreptitiously, before Mr. Gardiner could get there to see him. I understand that he has been in Salisbury, Rhodesia, seeing Sir Roy Welensky and holding a press conference.

Mr. Tshombé and his ministers were not under any restraint by the United Nations and were not being molested by the United Nations in any way at the time of their voluntary departure from Elisabethville. In fact, Mr. Tshombé's ministers, apparently in anticipation of the gendarmerie attack, which I suppose they knew to be coming, seem to have left the town some days in advance of their president, or at least they were not at all in evidence there last week. Should they return to the city, which is a matter for their own decision, they would not be interfered with by the United Nations, unless they should undertake to incite the population to commit hostile acts against United Nations personnel. The United Nations is not interfering with the government, administration, or economy of Katanga, either on a municipal or a provincial level. I have no idea whether Mr. Tshombé will actually return to Elisabethville.

In Elisabethville, quiet has prevailed, since fighting in the city itself was largely avoided; the population, African and European alike, has remained calm, the local police and other officials have been cooperative and normal conditions have virtually returned. In Kipushi, the United Nations troops were cheered by the local population as they entered the town. There has been no hint of a "scorched-earth" policy in those localities.

This military action, just brought to a clear and possibly decisive conclusion, has underscored the persistent efforts which have been under way for more than a year now to achieve, through talks at Kitona and Leopoldville and more lately through the Plan of National Reconciliation, a peaceful solution of the problem of Katanga. Now that the fighting has stopped, attention may again be focused on the course of peaceful action to be pursued. It is my intention to persevere in the effort to secure the implementation of the Plan of National Reconciliation. When I presented it last August, I considered that plan to be a thoroughly reasonable basis for the accommodation of the differences between the Central Government and Katanga province, and I still regard it as sound and reasonable. It was accepted by both parties. I would now hope, therefore, for a speedy implementation of its provisions. By speedy, I mean in a short period of perhaps a fortnight, before other measures might have to be weighed. The time has passed for long delays, protracted discussions, and talk of negotiations, which have in the past only served Mr. Tshombé's interests. Only acts can count now.

As an immediate step, I would hope to see, at the earliest possible date, the arrival in Leopoldville of the long overdue representative of the Union Minière du Haut-Katanga to discuss with Mr. Adoula and with the Monetary Council the arrangements for paying to the Central Government, through its Monetary Council, all of the Union Minière foreign exchange and tax revenues, as foreseen in Mr. Tshombé's offer in his letter to me dated December 12, 1962 [annex XX]. I had understood that this Union Minière representative was to have come to Leopoldville long ago, and I really do not understand why he has not appeared there.

Similarly, since the United Nations has some time ago guaranteed his transportation and protection, and since Mr. Adoula has approved his coming for technical discussions, I would hope that there would be no further delay in the arrival in Leopoldville of the representative of the Bank of Katanga whose participation in the technical aspects of the talks on revenue arrangements is indispensable.

As to Mr. Tshombé, who, after all, has on more than one occasion signified his acceptance of my Plan, it is clearly to be expected of him that he should at once send the senior officers of the Katanga gendarmerie to Leopoldville to take the oath of allegiance to the President of the Republic of the Congo, thus registering the integration of the gendarmerie into the national army. These officers would be protected both by the Central Government's amnesty proclamation and by the United Nations, which would also guarantee their transport. He should also, as I have just indicated, authorize a representative of the Bank of Katanga to go to Leopoldville forthwith. He must assure full liberty of movement for all ONUC personnel throughout Katanga; and he must cooperate with the United Nations in devising a plan for the immediate elimination of all mercenaries from Katanga. Finally, he must accept the customs and immigration officers of the Central Government in the performance of their functions in Katanga as elsewhere in the Congo.

As to Mr. Adoula, I would expect that he and his government should support and press for early action in Parliament on the Constitution called for in the plan which, as I understand, would be subject in Parliament to amendments desired by any of the provinces, including Katanga, or by others. I am confident that Mr. Adoula is fully aware of the very great importance attaching to this aspect of the plan. I also assume that Mr. Adoula and his government will take all necessary steps to ensure that the amnesty recently proclaimed by President Kasavubu will be applied fairly and effectively. I have been gratified by Mr. Adoula's readiness to meet and converse with the representative of the Union Minière and to hold discussions on revenue matters in Leopoldville with all other interested parties, including a representative of the Bank of Katanga.

I would reiterate my previous call to both parties, which they have both agreed to heed, to halt all troop movements in Katanga province while the efforts for a final settlement are under way.

I also call attention to the several letters addressed to certain governments some time ago seeking support of the plan. I expect early replies to those letters and I hope that they will generally be positive. I trust that it will be unnecessary to send reminders.

Having said all this, and repeating that the United Nations hopes for and continues to seek a settlement without further recourse to armed force, I wish to make it entirely clear that the United Nations Force in the Congo, pending the settlement, will not relax its vigilance nor cease to increase its readiness to meet my contingency. It definitely will not again tolerate attacks upon it without responding quickly and sharply.

I am seeking, and I believe there is now within sight, an early end to the critical divisions between the Central Government and the province of Katanga. In a unified Congo, Katanga province, its people and its leaders will play the influential role clearly belonging to a section of the country so bountifully endowed with natural resources. I am sure this reflects the wishes of the Members of the United Nations and of the overwhelming majority of the Congolese people, including very many Katangese. I am convinced that we must witness an early beginning in the reduction of United Nations military strength in the Congo and an increasing concentration on United Nations technical assistance to the people of that country. I call upon the leaders of the Congo with great earnestness and urgency to assist me in a speedy achievement of these ends.

A detailed report covering the matters touched upon in this statement will be submitted to the Security Council before long.

---

3. *Letter to Kwame Nkrumah, President of Ghana*

NEW YORK   JANUARY 12, 1963

I ACKNOWLEDGE receipt of your Excellency's recent message which was delivered to me by your permanent representative to the United Nations in a covering note of January 11, 1963.

I read the very serious allegations in your letter with deep concern, but I am sure that you would not have made them were it not for either

UN Press Release SG/1416.

misinformation or misunderstanding on your part about what the United Nations is doing in Katanga, or a combination of the two. I assure you that the misapprehensions implicit in these allegations are entirely unfounded.

First of all, as regards Mr. Tshombé, the policy I have followed in the conduct of the United Nations Operation in the Congo is to adhere strictly to the mandates defined for the operation by the resolutions of United Nations organs, and to avoid all actions of an arbitrary nature which could not be soundly based in terms of our authority. I have never heard it questioned by anyone, including the Central Government, that Mr. Tshombé is the legitimate president of the province of Katanga. It is on this basis and on this basis alone that the United Nations has dealt with him from the beginning. The United Nations has never at any time dealt with Mr. Tshombé "in his capacity as so-called president of the illegal state of Katanga," as you state it, because the United Nations has never at any time or in any way recognized the secession of Katanga. To the contrary, as your Excellency surely knows, the United Nations has consistently and persistently done all that it can to bring an end to the secessionist ambitions of Mr. Tshombé and others in Katanga, and in this the troops of the Ghana contingent in ONUC and one of your own countrymen, Mr. Robert Gardiner, have given invaluable assistance.

As regards the decision to permit Mr. Tshombé's return to Elisabethville and his freedom of movement, there was in my view no other course that could be legally taken by the United Nations. I note your reference to the Security Council resolution of February 21, 1961. Mr. Tshombé, as head of the provincial government, has been in and out of Elisabethville constantly since the United Nations first went there in early August 1960. He was, to the best of my knowledge, legally chosen for the position and has a firm legal claim to it. There has been and there is no basis on which the United Nations could restrict his movements or intervene with his right to perform his official duties except for the reasons that have been stated by me publicly, namely if he or any other Katangese official should overtly incite to violence against ONUC or should advocate a scorched-earth policy. Should he do this we will certainly take him in hand. We are not, however, in Katanga or elsewhere in the Congo, intervening in internal political affairs; we are not putting officials in office or taking them out of office; we are not supporting or opposing any official and we have no intention of doing so, for that would be entirely beyond our mandate and would have the United Nations Operation pursuing a political course which, in my view, would prove ruinous to it.

Moreover, the Central Government, at the time Mr. Tshombé was permitted to return to Elisabethville and to his responsibilities, had not and has not yet taken any action against Mr. Tshombé. There is no warrant for his arrest, there are not formal charges against him, there is no legal process concerning him and there has been no attempt to have him removed from office. In this connection I must point out that ONUC does not try ever to substitute itself for the legitimate government of the Congo, which is the Central Government, at Leopoldville.

I must take exception to your Excellency's statement about the "vacillation and lack of resolution in the Secretariat handling of the Congo situation." Here again an allegation is made which is without foundation. The Secretariat, which I head and for whose acts I assume full responsibility, has been exerting every effort in the most diligent way to carry out the mandates given to the United Nations operation by the various resolutions. The policy has rightfully been to exert first every possible effort to achieve a peaceful resolution of the problem of Katanga, and I need not detail for you the long and varied efforts we have exerted toward this end, including the Kitona talks, the Leopoldville talks and most recently the Plan of National Reconciliation. The employment of force has been always an action of last resort, but as the record of ONUC will amply attest, we have not hesitated to employ it when it becomes necessary. Indeed, the most striking examples of this have been in the recent successful actions at Elisabethville, Kipushi, Jadotville, and Kaminaville. In the latter action, in fact, the troops of the Ghana contingent participated most valiantly. In the conduct of the operation in the Congo we have adhered also to another and highly practical principle, namely that of thorough preparation of both political and military levels before any move is undertaken. It may well be that you have mistaken this for "vacillation" but I assure you that we would not be as far advanced in the Congo as we are today had not this principle been adhered to. To move on any other basis would be to court a setback and this we always seek to avoid. Incidentally, only this morning, the Ethiopian troops were given a friendly welcome by the people as they entered the important Katangese railroad city of Sakania.

It will be of interest to your Excellency, I am sure, to know that on January 11, just prior to the receipt of your letter, I was visited by the representatives of all African Members of the United Nations here who gave me unqualified endorsement of the policies we are following in the Congo.

Since we had learned of the substance of your letter from press releases out of Accra prior to its receipt by me, I am sure that you will not mind my intention to release my reply to you.

I may assure your Excellency of my confidence that through perseverance and steadfastness in the policy we have been pursuing, the Congo difficulties with which the United Nations is concerned will before long be resolved. In this unrelenting effort I very much hope for your Excellency's continuing understanding and support.

---

4. Statement on Meeting of Katanga Cabinet

NEW YORK   JANUARY 15, 1963

LATE IN THE AFTERNOON of January 14, I received a note from the permanent representative of Belgium to the United Nations, to which was annexed a message, without addressee, emanating from "M. Tshombé and his Ministers meeting in council at Kolwezi." The message was signed on January 14 at 0900 hours.

I welcome the message, which indicates a readiness to end secession, to give freedom of movement to United Nations personnel throughout Katanga and to undertake the full implementation of the Plan of National Reconciliation.

I most earnestly hope that this statement will be promptly and fully implemented and thus bring to an end the conflict and destruction which have been needlessly experienced in Katanga. The United Nations will certainly give its full assistance and support to the implementation of the promise implicit in Mr. Tshombé's statement.

UN Press Release SG/1417.

5. *Letter to President Nkrumah*

NEW YORK   JANUARY 20, 1963

I ACKNOWLEDGE receipt of your Excellency's latest message which was delivered to me by your permanent representative to the United Nations by his covering letter of January 16, 1963. I note that with reference to my reply to your earlier message, it is your view that if there is any misinformation or misunderstanding about the issues you have raised it is in the United Nations Secretariat. I have no desire and see no need to enter into a dialogue that could become prolonged, but I feel that I owe it to you to inform you on what I consider to be the actual facts concerning those issues and this I shall try to do in the following paragraphs.

Reference is made to a warrant for Mr. Tshombé's arrest. By this, I take it, is meant the *"mandats d'amener"* (which can be translated as "orders to appear" and are not in fact warrants of arrest) which were issued in the names of Mr. Tshombé and other Katangese ministers in September 1961. We are aware of no other such documents. We learned subsequently that in September 1961 the *mandats* were on file in the Elisabethville office of ONUC. The Elisabethville office of ONUC at that time was in the charge of Dr. Conor Cruise O'Brien, who is now your government's employ as Vice Chancellor of the University of Ghana, and therefore he could inform you on the details of this matter. Dr. O'Brien, though he has later, as an author, given much attention to these documents, did not at the time report that they were in his possession, or, so far as I can ascertain, seek instructions, or indicate any action he proposed to take about them.

In any case, it would seem clear that these *"mandats d'amener"* have long since lost whatever practical meaning they may have had. Since their issuance in September 1961, Mr. Tshombé has met with Prime Minister Adoula at Kitona in December of that year, and at Leopoldville for many weeks between March 1962 and June 1962, without any suggestion from

UN Press Release SG/1420, January 21, 1963.

Congolese authorities that any legal action against him was pending. Moreover, in August 1962 both Prime Minister Adoula and Mr. Tshombé publicly accepted the Plan of National Reconciliation put forward by me, and ever since then the only contention advanced by the Congolese government was that Mr. Tshombé was not living up to his promise through failure to implement the provisions of the Plan—a contention that I have affirmed. Furthermore, President Kasavubu, in November 1962, issued a declaration of amnesty, as called for in the Plan of National Reconciliation, and that declaration was publicly reaffirmed by both President Kasavubu and Prime Minister Adoula on January 15, 1963. Finally, as late as January 14 and 16, 1963, Prime Minister Adoula and Mr. Tshombé exchanged letters reaffirming their will to achieve national reconciliation. In view of all these circumstances, the subpoenas of September 1961 clearly have no application. The key point in this regard, of course, is that the United Nations cannot fairly be held responsible for what has happened because it did not take an action which it was not called upon and really had no authority to take. It is not without significance that the Government of the Congo itself has never criticized the United Nations on this particular score. I may add in this connection that in September 1961 ONUC had instructions, as it has now, to restrain and detain, in self-defense and in the maintenance of law and order, any Katangese official who may overtly incite hostility and violence against the operation and its personnel.

As to the investigation into the tragic death of Mr. Patrice Lumumba, which was conducted as a result of the Security Council resolution of February 21, 1961, and any question of action by the Secretariat on this matter, the Investigation Commission's report speaks for itself and it is clearly for the Government of the Congo to decide upon any further measures to be taken.

The proposed new federal constitution for the Congo was not put forward by the Secretariat at all. To the contrary, that document was elaborated by the Central Government of the Congo itself with the aid of four eminent international experts who were recruited by the United Nations as a form of technical assistance at the request of the Central Government. They neither sought nor took any guidance from the United Nations in carrying out their task. The United Nations Secretariat itself has played no part at all in the drafting of the proposed new constitution. There is no basis whatsoever, therefore, for asserting that the United Nations is "forcing a federal constitution upon the Congo."

The "U Thant Plan" or "Plan of National Reconciliation" to which reference is made was merely a proposal submitted by me to Mr. Adoula and Mr. Tshombé, which they were entirely free to accept or reject. It was stipulated only that the plan was not subject to negotiation. Both parties promptly accepted the plan.

The statement is made that Mr. Tshombé is being treated in an "entirely different" way from that in which the United Nations authorities deal with the other privincial administrations in the Congo. Mr. Tshombé is being dealt with only as a provincial president and in exactly the same manner as other provincial presidents. It is also suggested that the United Nations should have no further dealings with Mr. Tshombé in his capacity as provincial president or in any other capacity. Mr. Tshombé as of now is accepted by the Central Government as the provincial president of South Katanga, and this, necessarily, has a decisive bearing on the attitude of ONUC.

I take this occasion to repeat my assurance to you that there has been neither "vacillation" nor "lack of resolution" in the policies and action of ONUC. There has been, however, and on this I have been insistent, scrupulous regard for the mandates of the Security Council resolutions and persistent effort to seek peaceful solutions. In this regard, I recall with gratification the statement titled "Ghana Supports United Nations Action in Katanga," issued as Ghana Press Release No. 171 on December 14, 1961, in which it is said that "The Government of Ghana wishes to place on record its strong support for United Nations action in Katanga and its opposition to the attempt by any power or powers to bring pressure on the Secretary-General to deviate from the Mandate entrusted to him by the Security Council."

May I say finally that I note with satisfaction that we are in complete agreement in expressing the hope that Mr. Tshombé will "join hands with the Central Government of the Congo and use whatever powers [he] may have to strengthen the unity of the Congo," as Your Excellency has very aptly stated in your letter of December 21, 1962, to Mr. Tshombé, which was communicated to me by your permanent representative on December 28.

6. Message to Robert K. A. Gardiner, Officer-in-Charge of the United Nations Operation in the Congo, and Lt. Gen. Kebbede Guebre, Commander-in-Chief of the United Nations Force in the Congo

NEW YORK   JANUARY 22, 1963

THE NEWS about ONUC's entry into Kolwezi and Baudoinville is most heartening, especially since the move into Kolwezi was entirely peaceful and unattended by any of the threatened destruction.

It follows that freedom of movement for ONUC personnel throughout Katanga as elsewhere in the Congo is now fully and firmly established. The achievement of this objective, which was indispensable to the fulfill-ment of ONUC's mandates, has been possible only by the close collabo-ration and teamwork of the civilian and military branches of ONUC, and between ONUC and United Nations Headquarters.

There has been rare devotion to duty by the staff. The patience, re-straint, courage, and military skill of the ONUC Force deserves commen-dation in highest terms. The officers and men of the Force have served with great distinction and have given invaluable assistance to the United Nations effort to ensure unity, peace and progress in the Congo.

Please accept my warmest congratulations on the way you both have been discharging your onerous responsibilities and convey these same sentiments to all of the ONUC staff members, officers, and other ranks under your respective leadership, and especially to Generals Prem Chand and Noronha and to those commanding officers of all contingents in the field for the invaluable services they have rendered to the United Nations.

UN Press Release SG/1422.

RELATIONS BETWEEN CAMBODIA AND THAILAND

OCTOBER AND DECEMBER

THE UNITED NATIONS first became involved in Cambodia-Thailand border difficulties near the end of 1958 after Thailand occupied the temple of Preah Vihear, which Cambodia considered to be part of its territory. At the request of the two governments, Dag Hammarskjöld designated Johan Bech-Friis as his special representative. Bech-Friis visited Cambodia and Thailand in January and February 1959, and during his visit the two governments decided to reestablish normal diplomatic relations. The International Court of Justice ruled by 9 votes to 3 on June 15, 1962 that the temple was situated on Cambodian territory and that Thailand should withdraw any forces stationed there. Tension between the countries continued, however, and on October 19 U Thant informed the Security Council that he was sending a personal representative to the area at the request of the two parties. He named Nils G. Gussing for the mission. Gussing, like Bech-Friis, was a Swede. He arrived in the area on October 26. On December 18 the Secretary-General informed the Security Council that Gussing had been appointed for a period of one year beginning January 1, 1963. The mission was finally withdrawn at the end of 1964. This was another example of the exercise of executive authority by the Secretary-General without a mandate from the Security Council or the General Assembly. He merely reported to the Council on his decision and on subsequent developments.

---

1. Letter to Members of the Security Council

NEW YORK   OCTOBER 19, 1962

I HAVE THE HONOUR to inform you that the governments of Cambodia and Thailand have had an exchange of communications with me in which accusations of aggression, incursion, and piracy were made by one party

Security Council Official Records, Seventeenth Year, Supplement for October, November and December 1962, document S/5220, annex.

and denied by the other. As a result of further discussions, the two governments have requested me to appoint a personal representative to inquire into the difficulties that have arisen between them. As I believed that this would represent a constructive measure entirely within the scope of the Charter, I have given an affirmative response to this request, and after receiving agreement from the two governments, I have appointed Mr. Nils G. Gussing, a national of Sweden, as personal representative of the Secretary-General. He is scheduled to proceed to the area early next week.

In view of the nature of the action I have taken, I thought it appropriate to inform the members of the Security Council.

2. Letter to the President of the Security Council

NEW YORK   DECEMBER 18, 1962

IN MY LETTER to the members of the Security Council of October 19, 1962 I submitted information on the requests made to me by the governments of Cambodia and Thailand to send a special representative to the area to inquire into the difficulties that had arisen between these two countries.

Mr. Nils Göran Gussing, whose appointment was agreed to by the two governments, arrived in the area on October 26, 1962, and has had discussions with the prime ministers, the ministers for foreign affairs and other high officials of both countries. He has also conducted a number of investigations in the border areas, on both sides of the international frontier.

I am gratified to report that I have been given to understand both by the special representative and by the representatives of the two governments that, although serious problems remain to be solved, the activities of the United Nations representative have coincided with a lessening of tension between the two countries, to which the tone and the contents of the press and the radio broadcasts bear witness.

Security Council Official Records, Seventeenth Year, Supplement for October, November and December 1962, document S/5220.

Lately I have held further discussions with the permanent representatives of Cambodia and Thailand to the United Nations, as a result of which agreement was reached on the desirability of appointing a special representative of the Secretary-General in the area for a period of one year, beginning January 1, 1963. His terms of reference would, in general, require him to place himself at the disposal of the parties to assist them in solving all problems that have arisen or may arise between them. The most immediate among these would be the reactivation of the agreement concerning press and radio attacks, concluded between the parties in New York on December 15, 1960, and the lifting of restrictions on nationals of the two countries who are now forbidden to land on the airports of the other country while in transit. It is hoped that in due time consideration may be given to the question of the resumption of diplomatic relations.

As a measure of their goodwill both governments have signified to me their willingness to share on an equal basis all costs involved in the mission of the special representative—who will be assisted by a small staff—so that no budgetary provision on the part of the United Nations will be required.

In view of the nature of the action envisaged, I thought it appropriate to make this report to the members of the Security Council.

❧ 1963 ❧

THE SITUATION IN THE CONGO

FEBRUARY AND MARCH

ON FEBRUARY 4, 1963, U Thant reported to the Security Council that the situation in the Congo had improved to such an extent that an early withdrawal of United Nations forces was in sight. Although an immediate disengagement was not anticipated, he said, a phasing-out schedule was being formulated, and the reduction of United Nations troops would be gradual but steady. The Secretary-General noted criticism and "public misunderstanding" of the United Nations operations in the Congo, but maintained that United Nations objectives were well on the way toward full achievement. He said ONUC's record was one in which the Organization "may take pride." At a press conference in Geneva on May 3, 1963, Thant said: "My own personal feeling is that the primary function of the United Nations in the Congo has been fulfilled." He said the withdrawal of United Nations forces was proceeding at an accelerated rate and that the troop level had been reduced from 19,500 to 13,500 since mid-1962. He predicted it would be down to 7,500 before the end of 1963.

1. Report to the Security Council

NEW YORK   FEBRUARY 4, 1963

1. IN THE COURSE of the past year, the officer-in-charge of the United Nations operation in the Congo has submitted to me, and I have in turn had circulated to the Security Council, a series of fifteen reports on developments relating to the application of the Security Council resolutions of

Security Council Official Records, Eighteenth Year, Supplement for January, February and March 1963, document S/5240.

February 21 and November 24, 1961. It will be recalled that in the first of these resolutions it was urged in particular that measures should be taken to prevent civil war in the Congo and to ensure the evacuation of foreign military and paramilitary personnel and political advisers not under the United Nations command, as well as of mercenaries. In the second resolution, which was adopted after armed attacks had been made on United Nations troops by Katangese forces led by foreign mercenaries, the Security Council deprecated secessionist activities against the Republic of the Congo (Leopoldville) and demanded that such activities in Katanga should cease.

2. The latest report of the officer-in-charge of the United Nations Operation in the Congo [S/5053/Add.15] on developments relating to the application of the Security Council resolutions of February 21 and November 24, 1961, affords encouraging information, in the sense that it indicates that an important phase of the operation has been completed. I feel it appropriate and timely, therefore, for me to report to the Security Council at this stage in order to present an accounting of the extent to which the mandates given to ONUC by the Security Council resolutions have been fulfilled and of the aspects of those mandates that remain to be implemented, and to suggest what a look ahead may indicate as to the tasks to be fulfilled and the resources that will be required for that purpose.

3. At the beginning of 1962, there was hope, following Mr. Tshombé's declaration at Kitona, that the problem of the secession of Katanga might be speedily settled. That hope was quickly dispelled, however, when Mr. Tshombé in effect disavowed his promises as soon as he returned to Katanga. A subsequent six months of dilatory "negotiating" by Mr. Tshombé, half of that time being spent in talks with Prime Minister Adoula in Leopoldville, served only to waste time and to raise questions of bad faith. During the entire year from December 1961 to December 1962, the Katangese provincial authorities were evasive on the question of the expulsion of foreign mercenaries and on the issue of freedom of movement for ONUC personnel. Indeed, because of its determination to make all possible efforts toward peaceful reconciliation, ONUC, seeking throughout 1962 to avoid doing anything that might impede those efforts, exercised considerable restraint in pressing the issues of freedom of movement and elimination of mercenaries. During that year, however, Mr. Tshombé and other Katangese provincial authorities repeatedly avowed

that no more mercenaries were engaged in Katanga. We now know positively that this was not the case.

4. It was imperative that the problem of the attempted secession of Katanga, which not only caused impoverishment and instability in the rest of the Congo, but also threatened the peace of the African continent and imposed on the United Nations itself serious political and financial difficulties, should be finally settled. I myself, therefore, following consultations with a number of governments, proposed in August 1962 the Plan of National Reconciliation. This plan was promptly accepted by Prime Minister Adoula and Mr. Tshombé. It was only a proposal which the parties were entirely free to accept or reject.

5. The failure of the Katangese provincial authorities, after more than three months, to take any practical steps to implement this plan, and their continued lack of cooperation with other activities of the United Nations, led me in December 1962 to advance certain measures designed to bring economic pressure to bear on the Katangan provincial authorities and thereby to bring the Katangese problem to an early and peaceful solution. The Government of Belgium was thus asked to exert every possible influence on the Union Minière du Haut-Katanga, a Belgian corporation, which is part of a powerful international financial complex, to induce it to desist from paying to Katanga province the revenues and taxes due to the Government of the Congo. States which had jurisdiction over territories through which Katangese copper was exported, namely Portugal, the Republic of South Africa and the United Kingdom, were requested to take measures to prohibit the shipment of such copper until the question of the payment of Union Minière revenues was settled [S/5053/Add.14, annexes XIV and XV]. Other interested governments were requested by the Central Government of the Congo, with my support, not to permit the import of copper and cobalt from Katanga into their territories [ibid., annex XVI]. Developments in Katanga since these letters were written have overtaken the requests contained in them. I do, however, express my special appreciation to those governments which had already intimated to me their readiness to cooperate with the United Nations in the implementation of my appeals.

6. On December 12, 1962, Mr. Tshombé offered to permit the Union Minière to transfer to the Monetary Council of the Republic of the Congo all foreign exchange generated by Katangese exports, provided that after deduction of the needs of the Union Minière, 50 per cent of such exchange would be returned to Katanga [ibid., annex XX]. Despite this

gesture, for which I expressed by appreciation [ibid., annex XXI], there was a long delay on the part of the Katanga provincial authorities in arranging for representatives of the Bank of Katanga and of the Union Minière to proceed to Leopoldville for discussions on this matter.

7. Instead of further acts of cooperation by the Katangese provincial authorities, there ensued provocative military action by the Katangese gendarmerie and its mercenary elements, which Mr. Tshombé was unwilling or unable to control. After United Nations troops had been fired at for six days without retaliation, I was obliged, with great reluctance, to authorize the ONUC military actions that began on December 28 last. The successive stages of those actions, culminating in the peaceful entry of ONUC forces into Kolwezi on January 21, 1963, have been detailed in the last report of the officer-in-charge [S/5053/Add.15].

8. Full freedom of movement for ONUC personnel throughout Katanga has thus been fully and firmly established. ONUC could never hope to discharge the mandates given to it with regard to law and order, prevention of civil war and the elimination of mercenaries, without freedom of movement. It was with this in mind that freedom of movement for ONUC was provided for in the plan.

9. It is a matter of very great regret to me that the recent military actions were attended by some loss of life and by some damage to property. Because of the skill and restraint with which these actions were conducted, the casualties and damage were remarkably light. I wish to pay tribute to the courage, skill, devotion to duty, and forebearance shown by all those—in both the civilian and military branches of ONUC—who were connected with these events. This tribute applies equally to those many members of the Secretariat at United Nations Headquarters and in other United Nations offices throughout the world who have been assisting the Congo operation as an extra work load. Nor do I forget the countries and governments providing contingents to the Force. The actions were highly successful. But I would like to emphasize that the United Nations claims no victory in such situations; nor does it speak of enemies. It is only too happy that the military action forced upon it last December is over; and it is thankful that this came about with comparatively little fighting. For a peace force, even a little fighting is too much and only a few casualties are too many.

10. It was my concern at all times during these events to offer every opportunity to Mr. Tshombé and his provincial ministers to give practical evidence of their readiness to accept and put into effect the Plan of Na-

tional Reconciliation and thus avoid further needless bloodshed. I also found it necessary to warn Mr. Tshombé very seriously against carrying out the threats of massive destruction which he announced to the press from time to time.

11. Despite the unncessary fighting which had occurred since December 28, 1962, it was still my conviction that the only practical course to the reconstruction of a united Congo would be through national reconciliation. Therefore, when on January 14, 1963 I received the message of Mr. Tshombé and his ministers [S/5053/Add.15, annex V] indicating that they were ready to proclaim the end of the attempted secession of Katanga, to grant freedom of movement to United Nations troops, and to cooperate with the United Nations, I immediately welcomed the statement [ibid., annex VI] and commended it to the attention of the president and of the prime minister of the Congo. It was, indeed, with the Congolese authorities that the final decision rested, since only they could confirm the promise of amnesty which was the one condition which Mr. Tshombé and his ministers attached to their voluntary declaration of a change in course. The replies of Prime Minister Adoula and President Kasavubu [ibid., annexes VII and VIII] confirming that the amnesty proclamation of November 26, 1962 remained valid despite the changed circumstances became available the following day. Their messages, moderate in tone and emphasizing peaceful reconciliation and cooperation in reconstruction, were statesmanlike and encouraging.

12. The unopposed entry of United Nations troops into Kolwezi on January 21, 1963, and the subsequent return of Mr. Tshombé and his provincial ministers to Elisabethville after their reiterated assurances of their determination to carry out the Plan of National Reconciliation were significant and hopeful notes. The arrival of Mr. Iléo as minister resident of the Central Government in Elisabethville on January 23 symbolizes the restoration of the Central Government's authority in South Katanga. This, taken together with the numerous other concrete measures toward reintegration reported in the officer-in-charge's last report, indicated that the authority of the Central Government was being rapidly restored throughout Katanga. As this report is being written, Mr. Tshombé has communicated the list of names of senior officers of the Katangese gendarmerie, who, under the provisions of the plan, are to be transported by the United Nations to Leopoldville to take the oath of allegiance to President Kasavubu, thus signalling the integration of the Katangese gendarmerie into the Congolese National Army (ANC).

13. In the light of these events, it is now possible to reach some conclusions about the fulfilment of the mandates laid down by Security Council resolutions on the Congo. This is a record of achievement under extraordinarily difficult conditions and one in which the United Nations may take pride. There is also so much still to be done that it may be rightly said that we are just at the beginning of a new phase of the operation, in which a radical change in emphasis and direction will take place.

14. The policies and purposes of the United Nations with respect to the Republic of the Congo, as set out by the Security Council in its resolutions—especially that of November 24, 1961—are the following:

(a) to maintain the territorial integrity and the political independence of the Republic of the Congo;

(b) to assist the Central Government of the Congo in the restoration and maintenance of law and order;

(c) to prevent the occurrence of civil war in the Congo;

(d) to secure the immediate withdrawal and evacuation from the Congo of all foreign military, paramilitary, and advisory personnel not under the United Nations command, and all mercenaries; and

(e) to render technical assistance.

These are the mandates governing the actions of the United Nations operation in the Congo.

15. It may be noted that in the prevention of civil war, the resolution of February 21, 1961, provides for "the use of force, if necessary, in the last resort," while the resolution of November 24, 1961, authorizes "the use of a requisite measure of force, if necessary . . ." in the apprehension of mercenaries. In these respects, as in the use of its arms in simple self-defense, ONUC has acted with utmost prudence and restraint. The Force, although heterogeneous in its composition, is well disciplined, well officered, and reliable. It is a thoroughly professional body.

16. The extent to which the above-mentioned mandates have been carried out, under the limitations on action decreed by the Security Council resolutions, may now be briefly reviewed.

(a) Maintenance of Territorial Integrity and Political Independence

17. The most serious threat to the territorial integrity of the Republic of the Congo has been the secessionist activity carried on since July 11, 1960, by the provincial authorities of Katanga. The integrity of the Congo was in a symbolic sense restored by the entry, with the consent of Mr.

Tshombé, of United Nations troops into Katanga in August 1960. Despite unceasing efforts by the United Nations Force to prevent civil war and to create secure conditions in which the Katanga provincial authorities might enter into discussions with the Central Government for a peaceful reintegration of Katanga into the Republic, the Katanga provincial authorities persisted in their secessionist intrigues and activities. The recklessness of these activities was underscored by the unprovoked attacks of mercenary-led elements of the Katangese gendarmerie on United Nations troops in Elisabethville in September and December 1961 and in December 1962.

18. It is significant that since its free and peaceful entry into Katanga province in early August 1960, the United Nations Force there has enjoyed, almost without exception, good and friendly relations with the African people of Katanga. In recent months this has been increasingly true also of the non-African populations in Albertville, Elisabethville, Kipushi, Jadotville, Baudouinville, and Kolwezi. Moreover, armed clashes between ONUC troops and the gendarmerie have occurred in general only when elements of the gendarmerie have been led by European mercenary officers. Despite frequent statements by Mr. Tshombé that he accepted reintegration, no real progress in that direction was achieved until after the recent military operations in Katanga.

19. In view of the subsequent public renunciation of secession by Mr. Tshombé and his ministers at Kolwezi; their declaration that they would henceforth cooperate with the United Nations in the full implementation of the Plan of National Reconciliation; the complete freedom of movement achieved by ONUC throughout Katanga; the neutralizing and disarming of the Katanga gendarmerie; the elimination of the Katanga air force; the flight of the mercenaries; and the new situation as regards the revenues of Union Minière du Haut-Katanga, it may be reasonably concluded that the attempted secession of Katanga is at an end. Given an absence of alertness or a too-rapid withdrawal of the ONUC troops, it is conceivable that it could be revived. There are interests and elements in the Katanga scene which would always favour and flirt with it. There could be a regrouping and rearming of the gendarmerie or parts of it as a new secessionist force. But Katanga's secession has never had the firm support of the mass of the people and it now appears that with most of them its demise has passed virtually unnoticed. Indeed, most of the people of North Katanga have at all times strongly opposed secession and given their full support to the Central Government.

20. There have been other separatist attempts in the Congo, of course, but none of these has had the same importance or financial support as the Katanga pretensions, and they are now more or less quiescent. Happily, there appears to be no direct threat to the independence of the Congo from external sources. Thus it can be asserted that, as to territorial integrity and political independence, the mandate of the United Nations operation has been largely fulfilled, except for the caretaker role that it must still play.

(b) Assistance in the Restoration and Maintenance of Law and Order

21. It was the inability of the national security forces of the Congo, because of their mutiny one week after independence, to carry out their task of maintaining law and order that led indirectly to the decision by the Security Council to launch the United Nations Operation in the Congo. There was a breakdown of administration and of economic life; there were political disputes verging on civil war, and intertribal differences which often took a violent form. For a considerable period, the results of ONUC's efforts could at best be palliative, seeking desperately in some areas only to prevent a complete breakdown of law and order. When the new Central Government came into power in August 1961, ONUC was able to coordinate its efforts in a much more effective way with those of the Congolese authorities, and from that time on the situation has shown in general a steady improvement. In the former Equateur province, for example, it has not been found necessary to post United Nations troops for a considerable period. In Leopoldville, for quite a long time, and more recently in such areas as Stanleyville, Bukavu, and Albertville, conditions have become much more settled and secure, and this is reflected in some resumption of economic activity and a return of many foreign nationals.

22. In Katanga, the continuing pursuit of secessionist policies by the provincial authorities has maintained conditions in a constant disturbed state of turmoil until very recently. It now appears, however, that law and order have been firmly restored in the main centres of Katanga, and it is expected that the ONUC presence will have the same effect in rural areas where fighting has occurred between ANC troops and Katangese gendarmes. In any case, during the transitional period of the reintegration of Katanga into the rest of the republic, the problem of keeping law and order in Katanga will be a delicate one. This is recognized by the Central Government which has tentatively agreed to place its own security forces

in South Katanga under United Nations command and has accepted, at least in principle, that the introduction of its armed units into South Katanga should be spread out over a period of time. The transitional period during which the full authority of the Central Government is to be installed in Katanga unavoidably embodies many problems, some of which impose no little strain on the relations between the Central Government and ONUC. As regards the introduction of the ANC into South Katanga, the issues are essentially those of pace and method. The United Nations operation, in the interest of order, security, and public tranquility, prefers a gradual introduction, based on an orderly plan, and insists for the time being on a single command, to avoid confusion and conflict.

23. Unfortunately, it appears that intertribal differences in the former provinces of Kasai seem to have been accentuated by the division of that province into smaller provinces more or less along tribal lines. Serious clashes continue to occur between ANC troops and Jeunesse elements in the province of South Kasai, as well as between tribal elements. An intensified presence of United Nations troops in this area seems to be called for very soon.

24. The officer-in-charge and the commander of the United Nations Force have been asked to consult with Congolese authorities about the extent and approximate length of time of the continuing need of the Congolese government for United Nations military assistance in the maintenance of law and order. It is perhaps an easy and safe guess to make that some United Nations armed troops will be required and will still be in the Congo a year from now. Circumstances, however, could change that picture. The reduction from present strength can and will be very substantial, but for some time to come much will still remain to be done by ONUC under its mandate to help preserve law and order.

(c) Prevention of the Occurrence of Civil War in the Congo

25. The resolution conferring on ONUC the mandate to prevent the occurrence of civil war was adopted on February 21, 1961, at a time when there were two sets of competing governmental authorities, one in Leopoldville and one in Stanleyville, each claiming to be the legitimate government of the Republic of the Congo and each with elements of the ANC under its control. In addition, there were two other administrations, in South Kasai and Katanga, seeking to secede from the government and the territory of the Congo.

26. This desperate situation was improved as a result of the formation in August 1961 of a Government of National Unity acceptable to all parties concerned, other than the secessionist authorities of Katanga province.

27. Clashes occurred subsequently between elements of the ANC and the Katanga gendarmerie, the latter supported by mercenaries. While endeavouring to limit these hostilities, in particular by pressing for a peaceful solution, ONUC obviously could not, consistently with decisions of the Security Council calling for the maintenance of the territorial integrity of the Congo and for an immediate end to the secessionist activities in Katanga, regard and deal with such hostilities as "civil war" actions under the terms of its mandate. Now, however, these hostilities, which ONUC had always, but not always successfully, sought to halt have finally come to an end following the decision of the Katangese provincial authorities to terminate their secessionist activities and the seeming distaste of both mercenaries and gendarmerie for any more fighting.

28. It may therefore be considered that ONUC's mandate relating to civil war has been fulfilled in a major degree, although an alert and effective watch over the situation will be indispensable for some time.

(d) Removal of Military, Paramilitary and Advisory Personnel and Mercenaries

29. This aspect of ONUC's mandate was brought into effect by the Security Council resolution of February 21, 1961, at a time when the intervention of such personnel in Congolese affairs and, in particular, the military support given by these hired gunmen to the secessionist efforts of the Katangese provincial authorities, were flagrant and intolerable. A number of mercenaries were apprehended and expelled from the Congo in April 1961 and a further number of political and military advisers of the Katangese authorities were expelled in the succeeding months. However, the cooperation of the Katangese provincial authorities in this matter was altogether ineffective and unreliable, and on August 28, 1961 ONUC undertook action of its own to round up foreign military personnel in Katanga. A considerable number of personnel, particularly those loaned by the Belgian government to the Katangese provincial authorities, left Katanga in the next few days, but many mercenaries succeeded in escaping and a renewed attempt to proceed with this operation led to the hostilities which began on September 13, 1961. Mercenary elements

played a leading role in those hostilities and also in those of December 1961. Following this latter clash, Mr. Tshombé agreed to the evacuation of mercenaries but remained evasive on this point throughout the year 1962. Consequently, there were an estimated four hundred mercenaries still in the Katangese gendarmerie at the beginning of the operations of December 1962-January 1963. The successful conclusion of these operations has resulted, it appears, in the flight of most if not all remaining mercenaries from Katanga via Angola, with the exception of a small number now in United Nations custody.

30. It may therefore be concluded that for all practical purposes the mandate relating to mercenaries has been fulfilled. It is, however, open to question whether there may not still be among the technicians who serve the Katangese provincial authorities, or among the non-Congolese residents of South Katanga, a number of persons who overstepped the limits of legitimate activity and acted as political and possibly military advisers or as mercenaries. The possibility of a number of expulsions on this ground cannot, therefore, be excluded.

(e) Civilian Operations and Technical Assistance

31. The breakdown of law and order and the mass exodus of foreign technicians after the mutiny threatened a collapse in public administration, public services, and in the economy which gave to the technical assistance operations of the United Nations in the Congo a scope and magnitude surpassing by far that ever before considered. ONUC civilian operations involving an impressive collaboration between the United Nations and the specialized agencies, for much of the time under emergency conditions, helped to provide essential public services which the organizations financed in large measure. Since the reestablishment of a constitutional government, the emphasis has been increasingly on advisory rather than operative staff. Moreover, the assistance given is limited by the funds available, which consist of the voluntary contributions of governments.

32. There will continue to be a need for assistance on a massive scale during the ensuing period of reconstruction, following which the program of technical assistance to the country could eventually assume a more normal character.

33. Mr. Cyrille Adoula, prime minister of the Congo republic, wrote to me on December 20, 1962 [annex I], requesting assistance in a number of

ways seeking the modernization and training of the Congolese armed forces. I have responded favourably to this appeal and consultations between the prime minister and the officer-in-charge on the procedures to be followed are now under way in Leopoldville.

34. I have opened consultations with the Government of the Congo on the question of the channelling of future aid to the Congo. There will be, of course, a continuation of multilateral or United Nations aid. The question is the extent to which it may now have become advisable and desirable also to envisage an increase in bilateral aid. Although heretofore the United Nations has been inclined to seek to have all aid to the Congo channelled or at least cleared through its offices, it is apparent that the United Nations alone will not have the resources to meet the vast needs of the Congo. The attitude of the Central Government will, of course, be decisive in determining how the aid should be given, and although that attitude is being sought, it has not yet been ascertained. Obviously, it will be essential to try by some means to avoid subjecting the Congo to the dangers of a politically motivated competition between states as to the provision of assistance.

35. A decisive phase in the United Nations Congo experience has been concluded. That is the phase of active military involvement by United Nations troops. This does not, however, automatically indicate an immediate military disengagement in the Congo by the United Nations. To do that could result in quickly undoing almost everything that has been achieved by the United Nations operation in more than two and one-half painful and costly years. It may be that a smaller United Nations armed force in the Congo will be needed for some time, as the military and police resources of the Central Government are still inadequate to cope with endemic problems of tribal warfare and maintenance of law and order. However, there will be a progressive reduction in the strength of the United Nations Force, and an early disengagement cannot be ruled out. A phasing-out schedule is now in process of formulation, in consultation with the officer-in-charge and the commander of the Force, taking into account tasks to be performed, contingent withdrawals and rotation schedules. The first stage of the phasing-out will be reached about the end of February and thereafter the process will be gradual but steady. This reduction process, naturally, will be promptly reflected in a substantial reduction in the costs of the operation. This, in turn, will lighten—although it will not eliminate—the severe financial strain which the United Nations has been experiencing largely because of its heavy expenditures in the Congo.

36. It is perhaps still too early to draw any final conclusions from the United Nations Operation in the Congo. The lines of certain lessons that may be learned from this extensive and intensive experience begin to become apparent, however.

37. Merely to maintain a huge operation, involving political and military as well as economic activities, within the territory of a sovereign, independent state is a task of very great complexity and delicacy. There are unavoidable problems in the daily relations with the national government. There are at Headquarters the inevitable problems that spring from the differing attitudes of Member governments toward the issue and approaches to it. There are external as well as internal influences at work. To keep the operation going and on an even keel demands very much, both from United Nations Headquarters and in the field, in the way of patience, endurance, forbearance, tact, and firmness. The key to success, no doubt, is to have a clear definition of the basic principles on which the operation is to rest and to adhere strictly to them. In the case of the Congo operation, these principles were defined clearly enough by the Security Council resolutions, although inevitably there were differences of views among the Members as to how the principles should be interpreted and applied. There has been, for example, the principle of noninterference in the internal political affairs of the Congo. This principle has been observed and the United Nations has scrupulously avoided any support for or opposition to any Congolese official or candidate, whether in the national or provincial governments. The United Nations has avoided any intervention in the internal politics of the country, beyond the opposition to secession in general required by the Security Council resolutions and the constitutional suggestions embodied in the Plan for National Reconciliation, which, after all, was only a proposal which each party was free to accept or reject.

38. The United Nations Operation in the Congo has also adhered to the principle of avoiding the use of force for political purposes, although it is true that the very presence and activity of the United Nations Force in the Congo has been an important factor in giving effective weight to United Nations opposition to secession, whether in Katanga, Kasai, or elsewhere in the country. It is in the Congo, of course, for this and other purposes, at the specific request of the government of the country. But the United Nations has never used the arms at its disposal to further the political aims of any group or individual in the country or to interfere with its political processes. Even with regard to secession, civil war, and the elimination of mercenaries, the employment of the Force has been in

the most limited manner, with limited objectives, without the Force itself taking any military initiatives, and only then as a last resort.

39. There are some who have been critical of the policy governing the United Nations Operation in the Congo, either because on the one hand it has used the Force under its command too sparingly and too cautiously, or on the other because of the mere presence of the Force, let alone its use. I am convinced of the wisdom of the course originally ordered by the Security Council resolutions. Quite apart from the profound and possibly shattering implications which would flow from a United Nations policy decision to employ force to regulate the internal political affairs of a country, even at the request of or with the acquiescence of its government, to have done so in the Congo would have had a most adverse impact on both Congolese and international public opinion, besides inevitably creating some unmeritorious and troublesome martyrs. It seems to me, on the basis of the Congo experience, that the only sound way to inject an international armed force into a situation of that kind is to ensure that it is for clearly defined and restricted purposes, is fully under control of the Organization and always maintains its primary posture of arms for defence.

40. Quite possibly no activity ever engaged in by the United Nations has suffered so much as the Congo operation from public misunderstanding of its purposes and activities. Much of this misunderstanding, of course, has been due to the deliberate campaign of the well-financed Katanga propaganda machine, which in some countries has been not inconsiderably aided and abetted by organized special interests with ulterior motives, such as hostility to the United Nations or interests, financial or other, in Katanga. The United Nations, through its public information services, has striven valiantly to counteract this propaganda, but has enjoyed only partial success. It is by no means clear how the United Nations, which must always seek to adhere to fact and truth, can fend off the insidious attacks of unscrupulous propaganda. This vital problem will require very careful attention in connection with any future operation of a kind similar to that undertaken in the Congo.

41. Finally, the experience of the Congo operation demonstrates the great practical utility of an advisory committee arrangement in the conduct of such a highly complex and politically sensitive activity. The Advisory Committee on the Congo has been invaluable to me, as it was to my predecessor, in providing an indispensable means of testing proposed lines of action, exchanging viewpoints, and obtaining sound guidance.

. . . .

2. Remarks to the Advisory Committee on the Congo

NEW YORK   MARCH 20, 1963

I HAVE CALLED this meeting to inform you and to consult with you about the arrangements that have been proposed to me by Prime Minister Adoula with regard to the modernization and training of the Congolese armed forces—the ANC.

As you know, the ANC, from the very beginning of United Nations involvement in the Congo, has posed certain serious problems for both the Congolese government and the United Nations. Indeed, the condition of the ANC has been a vital factor in the course of Congo events since the first week of the country's independence.

In the early stage of the United Nations Operation in the Congo, efforts were made to assist the Congolese government, on its initiative, in the training and reorganization of the ANC, so that it could take its place as an effective and reliable arm of the government in the maintenance of law and order, and so that it could be organized in such a way as not to be a crippling burden upon the finances of the Congo.

General Kettani of Morocco, who was the first deputy force commander of the United Nations Force in the Congo, was entrusted with the initial United Nations step in this direction, and he was followed in this function by General Iyassou of Ethiopia. For various reasons, these early attempts of the United Nations were never very effective.

The general political situation in the Congo, until August 1961, when the present government came into power, was reflected in the condition of the ANC, which was to all intents and purposes split into three rival factions. Even after August 1961, the continued secessionist stand of Katanga and the difficulties in Orientale province made it extremely difficult to institute an orderly and effective program of ANC training and reorganization.

UN Press Release SG/1149.

When Mr. Adoula visited United Nations Headquarters in February 1962, the reorganization and retraining of the ANC was one of the most important of the subjects which he and I discussed. At that time, Mr. Adoula outlined for my benefit the delicate and difficult nature of the question, from the point of view of supplying proper cadres of officers, of reducing the size of the force and of altering its state of mind, especially in relation to the civilian population. He wished the United Nations to give what assistance it could to his government in facing these problems.

I acted accordingly, and several countries responded favorably to my request to them to supply French-speaking officers for the training of the ANC and particularly in relation to the establishment of an officers training school. We found it very difficult to recruit French-speaking officers for this purpose, but succeeded in some degree, although they were never called upon.

I have been in correspondence with the prime minister since December 20, 1962, on the practical measures to be taken to train and modernize the ANC. This assumes added significance, now that there is a hopeful prospect of the integration of all soldiers in the Congo into the national army.

I would not have called this meeting, if simply a question of bilateral assistance by various governments to the Government of the Congo were involved. There is more to it than this, however, for there are obvious implications with regard to selection where the United Nations is involved.

You will note from his letters that the prime minister is anxious for this scheme to go forward with the collaboration and coordination of the United Nations. That is, the United Nations is asked to provide something in the nature of an "umbrella" for the program. You will note also that I have asked, and the prime minister has agreed, that the composition of that "umbrella," that is, of the coordinating group, be broadened. The details of the functioning of this coordination remain to be discussed and worked out with Mr. Adoula.

In view of these facts, I wish to have the advice of the Committee before proceeding with the practical implementation of the program.

As it stands now, as you will note from the correspondence, the prime minister has proposed that the necessary assistance be sought from the countries he has specified. He has had assurances, I gather, that these countries will provide the assistance requested. The Government of the Congo alone, therefore, has made the selection of the countries from whom assistance is sought. This is the prerogative of the government of a sovereign independent state. The financial responsibility for the costs of that assistance, you will note, rests entirely with each assisting country.

For my part, I have asked that the composition of the group to undertake on behalf of the United Nations the coordination of the program of assistance should be broader than the group of nations actually giving the assistance. The prime minister accepts this broadening.

In order to get the program under way—and there is obvious urgency in providing this assistance to the ANC—it would next be necessary for me to send letters to the countries from whom the prime minister seeks assistance, indicating the nature of the prime minister's request, the composition and function of the coordinating group, the financial responsibility, and other necessary details. It will be appreciated that there is a close relationship between the training of the ANC and the phasing out of the United Nations Force in the Congo.

ALTHOUGH THE Soviet Union agreed with U Thant's assessment of the military situation in the Congo, it was not at all happy with the political situation. In a letter to the Secretary-General dated March 2, 1963, Soviet Ambassador Nikolai T. Fedorenko accused the Western powers of interfering in the internal affairs of the Congo and of attempting to keep "their protégé," Moïse Tshombé, in power as president of Katanga province. He urged that the Congolese National Army be given a free hand to move into Katanga province, declaring that this would make it pointless for United Nations forces to remain either in Katanga or in other parts of the Congo. He challenged Thant's conclusion that some United Nations forces must remain in the Congo for the maintenance of law and order and would still be in the Congo a year from now. Fedorenko said in part: "The removal of the United Nations forces from the Congo without delay will enable the Congolese government to extend its authority throughout the territory of the country, and this will be in conformity with the national interests of the Congolese people and in accord with the resolutions of the United Nations concerning the restoration of the unity and territorial integrity of the republic of the Congo." The Soviet position found little support, however, even in the Congolese government. Fedorenko closed his letter with these friendly words to Thant: "The Soviet government has appreciated and continues to appreciate the efforts which you have personally made in your capacity as Secretary-General to protect the sovereignty of the republic of the Congo and to thwart the unceasing efforts to destroy its territorial integrity and independence."

CONGOLESE ARMED FORCES

On December 20, 1962, Prime Minister Adoula of the Congo wrote U Thant requesting United Nations assistance in the modernization and training of the Congolese armed forces. The Secretary-General naturally was interested since improvement in the Armée nationale congolaise was a prerequisite to withdrawal of UN forces. Adoula made it clear that the responsibility for training the Congolese belonged to the Central Government, but he wanted the United Nations to assist in recruiting certain personnel and in coordinating the program. He asked particularly that the United Nations help obtain French-speaking advisers and that it urge the Belgian government to continue to provide equipment and instructors. Thant replied on December 27 that the United Nations was ready to comply fully with the requests.

Complications developed, however, when the Congolese government informed the officer-in-charge of ONUC, in a letter dated February 26, 1963, that it had requested technicians and advisers from Belgium, Canada, Israel, Italy, and Norway. The officer-in-charge replied that the composition of the mission should be broadened to give it a more representative character. He suggested that three African states—Ethiopia, Nigeria and Tunisia—should be included. The Secretary-General reported to the Congo Advisory Committee on March 20 that Adoula had agreed to the UN suggestion. Some members of the Advisory Committee continued to withhold approval of the plan, nevertheless, on the ground that the procedure under which certain European countries were to provide the Congo with military assistance was in conflict with United Nations resolutions. Adoula insisted that, as a sovereign nation, the Congo had the right to seek military assistance from whatever sources seemed desirable. The principal resolution in question was one adopted by the General Assembly, on September 20, 1960, at its fourth emergency session. Paragraph 6 of this resolution, referred to in the documents below, called upon all countries to refrain from providing military assistance in the Congo except upon request by the Secretary-General.

In a statement to the Congo Advisory Committee on April 23, Thant said there was no doubt but that Adoula had the right to request military aid from any and all countries, but that it was also within the discretion of the United Nations to decide whether it would provide an "umbrella" for the modernization program. He noted that the selection of particular countries to carry out this program would have inevitable political implications.

The crucial point was whether the Central Government should seek aid from Belgium and Israel. Belgium, as the former administering power and a backer of Katanga, was suspect by many, particularly among the African nations. Israel, of course, was considered by the Arab states as an enemy. On May 12, Adoula informed the Secretary-General that he intended to appeal for bilateral assistance from any countries that would be willing to provide such help, though that should in no way be regarded as ruling out United Nations assistance. The result, as Thant later noted with regret, was that the program proceeded without UN participation. Help came mainly from Belgium, Israel, and Italy.

1. From Statement to the Advisory Committee on the Congo

NEW YORK   APRIL 23, 1963

. . . . WE MEET NOW to resume discussion of the question of the retraining and modernization of the Congolese armed forces, and in particular the role of the United Nations in this program. As you know, I postponed this meeting for one week in order to allow time for more informal discussions on this important subject, and especially so that the members of the committee would have the opportunity for informal exchanges of views with Mr. Bomboko.

I believe that these informal discussions at least have served to clear up some misunderstandings. It was my hope, of course, that they would find a solution to this problem, which is an urgent one both for the Congolese government and people and for the United Nations, which still has continuing responsibilities in the Congo.

You have received the letter of April 16 addressed to me by Prime Minister Adoula, which seeks concurrence on an interpretation of the relevant provision of the resolution of the General Assembly—paragraph 6 of resolution 1474 (ES-IV) of the fourth emergency session, adopted in September 1960—as not imposing, in the present and very much changed circumstances, a limitation of his government's freedom to seek the assistance it may need where it may deem it advisable.

The real practical sense of this interpretation, of course, would be in its application to states providing the assistance requested. Even under the resolution, the Government of the Congo is free to approach any government for assistance.

UN Press Release SG/1472.

The restrictive burden of the resolution really falls on the states thus approached, for the resolution requires such requests to be made to them only through the United Nations, "during the temporary period of military assistance"—that is to say, so long as the United Nations Force is in the Congo. Granting Mr. Adoula's request presumably would make it easier for states to respond.

Based on my talks with Mr. Bomboko in the past few days, I can say that it is correct to interpret the prime minister's letter as not insisting upon a United Nations "umbrella" or coordinating machinery, for the modernization and training program. Nor would the Secretary-General be called upon to make the requests for assistance.

In other words, if the Congo government decided to go ahead, as its sovereign right entitles it to do, with the training program as previously outlined, the United Nations would not be held responsible for that training program or for any implications of it.

It emerges from the informal discussions that no one questions the right of the Government of the Congo to perform all the functions and have all the prerogatives of a sovereign state, and no one wishes to limit those prerogatives. On the other hand, if the United Nations is called upon to play a coordinating function in a program of this importance, or to make the requests, it clearly is within the discretion of the United Nations to decide whether such a role is suitable or not, more especially in the light both of the spirit and of the letter of the Security Council and General Assembly resolutions governing its presence in the Congo.

It is also true, of course, that the problem of the resolution does, in fact, have the effect of limiting the freedom of choice of the Congolese government by imposing a restraint on states willing and able to provide the aid.

It must be borne in mind that it is essential that the Congolese armed forces be modernized and trained without delay, more especially in view of the likelihood of the departure from the Congo of the United Nations Force by the end of 1963. Indeed, these two events have a practical interrelation.

We have also to consider the inevitable political implications flowing from the selection of particular countries to carry out this program. As I understand it, the Government of the Congo is anxious that, while ONUC is still in the Congo, all significant aid to the Government of the Congo should be requested through United Nations channels.

The problem, therefore, is to devise, if possible, a formula by which the needs of the Congolese government, as stated by Prime Minister Adoula, can be reconciled both with the terms, or the intent, of the resolution governing the United Nations presence in the Congo and with the views of the members of this committee.

I would now like to hear the views of the members on the question before us. In so doing, I seek the advice of the committee on how I am to answer Prime Minister Adoula's letter, taking into account the urgency of the problem and the necessity of making some practical progress.

At the outset, it will be useful, I think, to ask Mr. Bomboko to summarize his interpretation of the Prime Minister's letter and of the situation as it now stands, as he sees it.

2. *Letter to Prime Minister Adoula*

NEW YORK   APRIL 29, 1963

I HAVE THE HONOUR to acknowledge receipt of your letter of April 16, 1963 [section VI] raising in particular the question of the application of paragraph 6 of the General Assembly's resolution of September 20, 1960 [1474 (ES-IV)] to your government's freedom of action with regard to seeking assistance in the training and reorganization of the Congolese armed forces.

I have given most careful and thorough consideration to the points of view set forth in your letter and have undertaken extensive consultation on it with the members of the Advisory Committee on the Congo. As a result, I am able to inform you that there is full accord here on the need and the urgency of a program for the training and reorganization of the Armée nationale congolaise (ANC) and there is strong hope that means will be found to institute such a program. The position also is emphasized by everyone that the sovereign rights and authority of your government are fully recognized and there is no wish or intent to restrict them in any way. It may be pointed out, moreover, that it is not questioned that the phrase in paragraph 6 of the resolution reading "during the temporary period of military assistance through the United Nations" means that

Security Council Official Records, Eighteenth Year, Supplement for April, May and June 1963, document S/5240/Add.2, annex VII, May 21, 1963.

paragraph 6 has application only so long as the United Nations Force is required to remain in the Congo. I may add that there is general concurrence in your assertion that the resolution in question was adopted at a time when political circumstances in the Congo were very different from those now prevailing. I would wish to add, however, that the view has been expressed by many here that only the General Assembly itself may give an authoritative interpretation of the resolution in question.

Mr. Justin Bomboko and your representative at the United Nations will have informed you fully of the discussions that have taken place here on this subject and of the views expressed and the positions taken by the several delegations comprising the Advisory Committee on the Congo. You are aware, therefore, of the variations in viewpoints that have been manifested, including the alternative suggestions that have been offered.

As to the references that have been made to the agreement between the Secretary-General and the President of the Republic of the Congo, I would like to observe that this agreement does not in my view—and, of course, could not—derogate from the resolutions adopted by the General Assembly and the Security Council. In fact, this very point was made explicitly by the Secretary-General in his letter of April 26, 1961,[1] which was stated to be part of the definitive agreement and was published together with the text of the initialled agreement in the annexes to the above-mentioned document.

You will understand, I am sure, that in the light of all the circumstances I have to inform you with regret that I do not find it possible to reply to your letter in such way as to give you the satisfaction you seek with regard to the interpretation of the resolution. I continue to hope, however, that a way will be found to make it possible for the ANC to receive the assistance it so urgently needs, and I assure you that I shall do all that I can toward helping you obtain the necessary assistance.

U THANT
Secretary-General of
the United Nations

---

[1] Security Council Official Records, Eighteenth Year, Supplement for April, May, and June 1961, document S/4807, annex II.

FROM TRANSCRIPTS OF PRESS CONFERENCES

FEBRUARY-MAY

U THANT devoted much thought to the strengths and weaknesses of the United Nations, to directions in which it was developing and to its potentials. On numerous occasions, he dealt with the role of the small nation and with his belief that the United Nations must stick to a policy of "one country, one vote." In a press conference in Kingston, Jamaica, on February 19, he reiterated this view and declared that the voice of the smaller countries would have "greater weight and greater authority" if the General Assembly continued to grow in influence as it had been doing in recent years because of the use of the veto by the permanent members of the Security Council. He summed up his assessment of the United Nations as being more than a "moral force" but less than a big power in the sense that it has at its command no battalions or massive weapons. The United Nations, he said, would be "as strong or as weak as its Member states wish it to be."

From Transcript of Press Conference

KINGSTON, JAMAICA   FEBRUARY 19, 1963

.... QUESTION: You were quoted recently making a comparison between the Russian troops in Cuba and United States forces in South Vietnam. You said they were something similar. Will you elaborate on that?

THE SECRETARY-GENERAL: At my last press conference in New York the question was posed soliciting my comments on the presence of Russians on Cuban soil. I took that occasion to make a brief observation to the effect that it is extremely delicate for one in my position to make any general observations on such a situation. I also remarked that in the same way as there had been adverse comments on the presence of Russian

UN Note to Correspondents No. 2736, March 6, 1963.

personnel on Cuban soil, there have been adverse comments regarding the presence of American troops in South Vietnam. So these are situations we have to face in the context of the cold war without going into the merits and demerits of such phenomena. Of course, it was not my intention to equate the two situations. I was just stating the fact that these phenomena create tensions, create misunderstanding, create adverse comments and, of course, the only means of tackling the situation is to ease tensions, to bring about better international understanding, to bridge the gulf between the two power blocks, and that is what I have been trying to do.

QUESTION: Mr. Secretary-General, now that the military operations in the Congo are at an end, what are the next steps likely to be taken to get the country back on its feet?

THE SECRETARY-GENERAL: Yes. The military phase of the United Nations operations in the Congo is almost over, as you know, and the United Nations has been concentrating on massive nonmilitary aid in the way of technical assistance and civilian operations in the Congo. I think to stabilize the situation in the Congo what is necessary is an unparalleled economic aid program and training programs, and of course, to some extent, the United Nations military presence will be necessary for some time to restore law and order in turbulent areas of the country to function as more or less a police force for some time to come. It is difficult to anticipate how long the United Nations military presence will be necessary in that country, but as I have indicated at an earlier press conference in New York, a phasing-out process will start at the end of this month. The United Nations military will be phased out gradually and it is anticipated that by the end of March the United Nations force will number approximately 13,000 instead of the present 19,500 which is, I am sure you will agree with me, quite a substantial reduction.

.... QUESTION: Mr. Secretary-General, the small nations of the world are greatly outnumbered by the large nations. Some of us have a long history and some have a short history, like Jamaica. What do you see as the contribution these small countries can make through the United Nations to peace in the world?

THE SECRETARY-GENERAL: Well, under the provisions of the Charter it will be recalled that every Member of the United Nations enjoys the same rights and privileges, irrespective of the size of that country or the size of the population. The principle of "one country, one vote" has been in existence in the United Nations. I think it is perfectly in line with the established democratic principles in every democratic country, whether a man is rich or poor, he can exercise the right to vote. He has the same rights as any other individual in any human society. The same principle applies to Members of the United Nations. Yes, I agree with you that the emergence of new states and the entry of these new states into the United Nations create certain problems, but I am convinced that these small countries are going to play a significant role in the maintenance of international law and order and in the solution of the problems which the United Nations has been faced with for a number of years. As you will recall, under the Charter of the United Nations the Security Council is the principal organ charged with the responsibility of maintaining law and order, but because of the disagreement between the big powers, and because of the Charter provisions of the well-known veto system, for the Security Council to take such action it needs the votes of seven Members, including the votes of five permanent Members. If one of the five permanent Members, that is, the United States, the Soviet Union, the United Kingdom, France, and China—if any one of these five permanent Members cast a negative vote—then the resolution is not carried. That means, in effect, for the passage of a resolution the unamimous vote of the five permanent Members is absolutely essential, but our experience has shown in the past seventeen years or so, since the inception of the United Nations, that no major decision could take place without the agreement of the big powers. That is a fact. If any decision is to be made on a major problem, if there is no agreement between the United States and the Soviet Union, then the Security Council is more or less impotent. That is why more and more resort has been made to the General Assembly in the last seven years on any issue on which the Security Council could not take any specific action. The action has shifted to the General Assembly. That has been the trend in the last seven years. So the General Assembly, comprising all the 110 Members of the United Nations is getting more and more authority, which normally was the prerogative of the Security Council. As the General Assembly is getting more and more influential, if I may say so, the voice of the smaller countries will get greater weight and greater authority.

QUESTION: Did you favor scrapping the Security Council?

THE SECRETARY-GENERAL: No, no, I don't favor the scrapping of the Security Council. We are all striving at bringing about better understanding between the big powers.

. . . . QUESTION: It has been said in some quarters that the United Nations has no real powers to enforce certain sanctions which may be imposed or recommended by a resolution. Would you care to comment on this for us, whether you think that the United Nations would require more authority to impose sanctions such as have been imposed on South Africa in relation to Southwest Africa?

THE SECRETARY-GENERAL: As a matter of fact, the United Nations will be as strong or as weak as its Member states wish it to be. If the Member states want a strong United Nations, I am sure it will be strong. If the Member states want the United Nations to be weak, it is inevitable that the Organization will remain weak. But, at the moment, my assessment of the United Nations is: it is not just a moral force, and at the same time it is not a big power in the sense that it has at its command battalions and massive weapons. I think at this particular stage the United Nations is somewhere in between. It is, in a way, the cumulative result of massive public opinion which cannot be ignored by any country, big or small, and I also believe that the United Nations is growing from strength to strength but, as I have stated earlier, it depends on the wish of the Member states.

. . . . QUESTION: May I take you on to another delicate subject? I understand that the Revolutionary Government of Cuba has requested still another special aid program through the United Nations agencies. Can you confirm whether this is the case? What is your opinion and reaction?

THE SECRETARY-GENERAL: Before I left New York there was some comment in the American press regarding this Special Fund program for Cuba. I think most of the comment has been based on misunderstanding of the processes involved. As you know, the Special Fund operates distinct from the rest of the United Nations Secretariat. There is a governing board which considers all requests for Special Fund aid. It is called the Governing Council. It was constituted at the time the Special Fund was formed. Mr. Paul Hoffman, a very prominent American, is the managing director of the Special Fund program operations. Since the start of the Special Fund program for the last four years, the Governing Council of the Special Fund decided to launch 288 programs in various countries all over the world. Of course, Special Fund programs operate differently from the technical assistance program. As you know, they deal primarily with preinvestment fields like surveys for irrigation and mining. Of course, the request has to come from a Member state. Since the inception of the Special Fund program, I was informed that 288 programs have been launched in all parts of the world. This Cuban project which is in the news right now is the two hundred and eighty-ninth program. The Governing Council of the Special Fund decided to comply with the request of the Cuban government for that particular project as early as May 1961, nearly two years ago, but the decision was not implemented due to many factors including political considerations prevailing for the last one and a half years, as you are no doubt aware. The practice prevailing in the Special Fund operation has been that all the Special Fund projects have been treated as nonpolitical. For instance, in Formosa some Special Fund projects were in operation. When a Special Fund project was launched in Formosa, the Russians did not object because this program was considered purely nonpolitical, for the good of the people, for the amelioration of the plight of the poor people in that particular country. In the same way, when Special Fund projects were launched in Israel, the Arabs never objected because these operations were considered strictly nonpolitical, so in this particular instance of Cuba also, the Governing Council, which consists of eighteen members, including the United States and the Soviet Union—it was decided as early as May 1961—to comply with the request of the Cuban government but it was deferred, as you know. Now, the managing director of the Special Fund feels that it has been too long deferred, more than one and a half years, so he decided to go ahead with the decision of the Governing Council, just to make certain surveys in Cuba regarding farm projects. It may be of interest to some people that Special Fund operations have nothing to do with the Secretary-General. Mr. Hoffman informed me before I left New York that not a single cent of United States money will be involved in the preliminary survey which will be undertaken by the Special Fund very soon. Well, thank you very much, ladies and gentlemen, for this opportunity, and I am sure you have asked most of the questions which you have in mind. . . .

2. From Transcript of Press Conference

NEW YORK   APRIL 11, 1963

.... THE SECRETARY-GENERAL: First of all, I want to take this opportunity of making a brief comment on what I consider to be an historic document. It is with a deep sense of gratification that I read the encyclical "Peace on Earth" issued today by His Holiness Pope John XXIII. No doubt because of the universal significance of peace, the message has been addressed not only to the members of the Catholic Church but to all men on earth. I can well understand the profound emotion which Pope John XXIII has said he felt when signing this document of far-reaching significance, for in addressing his thoughts to the peace of the world in this nuclear era he was indeed appealing for man's survival and for the application of human knowledge, not to death but to life, and for the dignity of man in a community of understanding.

The encyclical, among others, calls for a strengthening of the United Nations, thus focussing attention on the fact that peace is an international responsibility. At the same time, it calls for such specific measures as a reduction of arms stockpile, a ban on nuclear weapons, a general agreement on progressive disarmament and an effective method of control which is a primary responsibility of the big nations. To the voice expressed in favor of these measures by the overwhelming majority of nations and peoples of the world has now been added this heartening and noble call by His Holiness Pope John XXIII.

The contents of the encyclical are certainly in harmony with the purposes and objectives of the United Nations. They come as a timely reminder that the faith of mankind still hinges precariously in the deadly balance of nuclear devastation and will contribute very significantly to intensify the efforts of all those who are confident that the human race has enough wisdom to preserve its own species, a species with a record of splendid achievements in the realms of art, science, literature, and religion.

UN Note to Correspondents No. 2755.

Let me take this opportunity of offering my respectful homage to His Holiness for his great wisdom, vision and courage in his ceaseless endeavors for the cause of peace and human survival.

Ladies and gentlemen, the floor is yours.

QUESTION: Mr. Secretary-General, we are happy to be with you again, and, of course, we appreciate the fact, and we hope it is an exemplary one, that you have summoned us only to give us important news. Your comments on the Pope's encyclical certainly is and will be important news. May I ask the first question?

Could you tell us what stage has been reached as of now in your endeavors to solve the question of a United Nations patronage of the organization of the Congolese National Army, if that is possible?

THE SECRETARY-GENERAL: You know that I recognize the right of the Congolese Central Government to get the Congolese National Army trained in any manner it wishes, but that matter has been deferred from month to month since I first discussed this with Prime Minister Adoula, when he came here in February 1962. I have established contacts with him regularly, but because of certain factors this could not take effect earlier. Last December, Prime Minister Adoula wrote to me that he wanted to go through with his original plan of training the ANC, and he asked me if I would be agreeable to provide some sort of United Nations umbrella, or some sort of United Nations coordinating function for this program. Strictly in compliance with the Security Council and General Assembly resolutions, I replied to him that I would comply with his request.

Later on, I got a formal request from the acting prime minister, when Mr. Adoula was away, specifying certain countries which the Central Government of the Congo proposed to invite for the provision of instructors in certain specific fields of ANC training. This poses a problem, not in terms of the resolutions, because in the terms of the Security Council and General Assembly resolutions my duty is to comply with the request of the Central Government and to get in touch with the countries mentioned in the request, with my endorsement, to provide the necessary instructors for the specific purposes. That would be strictly in line with the Security Council and General Assembly resolutions, but, as you are no doubt aware, there are definite political implications if I were to comply with the request without due consideration being given to the political aspects of the request. So I convened a meeting of the Congo Advisory Committee and sought their views.

Of course, at the first meeting no member of the advisory committee could comment categorically in the absence of instructions from their respective governments. Then the second meeting was scheduled, and before it took place, I talked to some members of the advisory committee to get their private views. Last week, I got a request from Prime Minister Adoula asking me to postpone the meeting of the Congo Advisory Committee until next Tuesday, when he proposed to send his foreign minister, Mr. Bomboko, to participate in the discussions. In due deference to his wish, the Congo Advisory Committee meeting which took place last Monday did not take up this question, and now, as I explained at the beginning of this conference, it will be considered next Tuesday at 3:30 p.m.

But the position is this. Under the terms of General Assembly resolution 1474 (ES-IV), adopted in September 1960, when the situation in the Congo was very different from what it is now—I think I need to stress this fact: when that particular resolution was adopted in September 1960, there was no government in the Congo; actually there were four sets of governments in the Congo. Because of that confused situation, my predecessor, Mr. Hammarskjöld, inscribed that item on the agenda of the General Assembly. The General Assembly considered the situation in detail and adopted resolution 1474 (ES-IV).

The relevant substantive paragraph says:

Without prejudice to the sovereign rights of the Republic of the Congo, [the General Assembly] calls upon all states to refrain from the direct and indirect provision of arms or other materials of war and military personnel and other assistance for military purposes in the Congo during the temporary period of military assistance through the United Nations, except upon the request of the United Nations through the Secretary-General for carrying out the purposes of this resolution . . . [and of other resolutions].

That means, legally speaking, that all requests from the Central Government to any Member state for the provision of military assistance or even military instructors must be channeled through the United Nations. Member states can comply with such a request only on receipt of my endorsement or my request to them. That is the situation.

On the other hand, as I have just said, there are delicate political implications. Therefore, we have to find a compromise between these two situations. I am hopeful that at the next meeting of the Congo Advisory Committee, in which the foreign minister of the Congolese central government will participate, we shall come up with a constructive decision.

QUESTION: Mr. Secretary-General, I wonder if you would be willing to comment on two specific aspects of the Pope's encyclical. Where he and you just now speak of all the people of the world and he spoke of the world Organization for all the people of the world, does not this raise the issue of universality? The other aspect is disarmament. Is there anything that you would care to say about the deadlock in the present disarmament negotiations in Geneva?

THE SECRETARY-GENERAL: When His Holiness made a reference to the desirability of the United Nations developing into a really effective force for peace, I found myself in complete agreement with his approach. Of course, unfortunately, the United Nations does not yet reflect all humanity or represent all countries and all shades of views, but I think we are moving in the right direction.

Regarding your second question on the disarmament deadlock in Geneva, my feeling is that we should not give up hope. Although there has been a difference of view on the substantive question of a nuclear test ban, there is an obvious desire on all sides to come to an early agreement on this crucial issue facing mankind today. I believe in the maxim "if there is a will, there is a way," and I am rather optimistic about the outcome after the Easter recess.

QUESTION: Mr. Secretary-General, would you comment on the efforts of the Western powers to set up a nuclear NATO force; particularly, do you feel this is in keeping with the principles set forth in the encyclical which you have so strongly endorsed?

THE SECRETARY-GENERAL: We have to recognize that these developments, or these phenomena, are facts of life today. I do not think it would be very fruitful to go into the merits or demerits of these phenomena, but all I want to say at this moment is that one finger on the trigger is much better than many fingers on the triggers—at least much safer. . . .

. . . . QUESTION: At your last press conference, you expressed concern about the situation in Southeast Asia. You have taken certain steps to look into that situation. Have you anything further to say on that question today? I should also like to know if you have looked into the situation in Laos, to see if there is anything that the United Nations can do to prevent another crisis there.

THE SECRETARY-GENERAL: Of course, the United Nations is not directly involved in the general situation in Southeast Asia, although we are keeping a very close watch on developments there.

With regard to Laos, the present situation is, if I may say so, the legacy of the past—the unfortunate past—characterized by massive military aid on one side and clandestine military aid on the other, resulting in a more or less chaotic state. In view of the geography, with two countries bordering Laos which are not members of the United Nations, I do not see how the United Nations can be usefully and effectively involved in finding a solution to the Laotian problem. The neutrality of Laos has been guaranteed by an agreement signed by fourteen countries, and I feel that it is now time for those fourteen countries to get together and try to find a solution.

. . . . QUESTION: The other day, in opening the committee on apartheid, you made some remarks to which the South African minister has objected and about which he has attacked you in a rather personal manner. Would you care to comment on the South African minister's views?

THE SECRETARY-GENERAL: I do not think it will serve any useful purpose if I comment.

QUESTION: Do you think it would be helpful if the Secretary-General were cut in on the so-called hot-teletype-line which is supposed to wind up in Moscow and Washington, so that there would be another machine in the Secretary-General's office with outlets in Moscow and Washington?

THE SECRETARY-GENERAL: I welcome, of course, this hot-line agreement; it is a development in the right direction. Regarding the necessity or advisability of installing a direct line to the United Nations, I have not given sufficient thought to it, but if the two heads of governments, President Kennedy and Chairman Khruschev, feel that it is necessary, I will also welcome it.

. . . . QUESTION: Returning for a moment to your concern with the Congo, I am not sure if I am correctly interpreting you when I think that what you are saying is that you liked the Adoula proposal in principle, but you have been having troubles with it when it came to specifying countries; you ended your remarks that you were hoping for a compromise solution next Tuesday. I wonder if you could tell us what kind of a compromise you could see in this matter?

THE SECRETARY-GENERAL: A compromise which does not necessarily conflict with the spirit of the General Assembly resolution and, at the same time, does not impair the political susceptibilities of many Member states.

QUESTION: With the transition of West Irian from the United Nations Technical Assistance Authority to Indonesia two weeks away, do all reports from that area indicate that it will go smoothly?

THE SECRETARY-GENERAL: Yes, the record of UNTEA in West Irian, or West New Guinea, has been a matter for gratification to us all. The operation has been running very smoothly. The transfer of administration will take place on May 1 at 12:30 p.m. I have sent my chef de cabinet, Mr. Narasimhan, to represent me at the ceremonies. Of course, the actual handing over will be undertaken by the administrator, Dr. Abdoh. I think the United Nations operation in that particular region is a matter for pride for us all. . . .

3. *From Transcript of Press Conference*

GENEVA   MAY 3, 1963

THE SECRETARY-GENERAL: Ladies and gentlemen, I am very glad indeed to meet with you once again after a lapse of almost a year. Many things have happened since then.

Regarding the Congo, the unity and territorial integrity of the country has been restored, as required by the Security Council resolutions. The Central Government now holds sway over the whole country. One problem still remains to be solved—that is the problem of retraining and modernization of the Congolese armed forces and, in particular, the role of the United Nations in that program.

This historic city of Geneva has been the scene of the disarmament conference for many months, and naturally you may wish to hear my views on the progress, or lack of progress, of the disarmament negotiations.

As you are no doubt aware, I consider the problem of disarmament the greatest problem facing mankind today. The general public, and even many men in positions of authority, have not realized what would be

UN Note to Correspondents No. 2765.

involved in a war with hydrogen bombs. The very existence of the hydrogen bomb has made the continued existence of the human species doubtful. Therefore, it is fitting that the disarmament conference has been dealing with the question of a nuclear test ban as one of top priority.

Opinion is divided regarding the progress of the negotiations here. Many observers are already striking a pessimistic note, while others are still hopeful of a successful outcome. I belong to the second category. The Eighteen-Nation Committee on Disarmament now meeting here represents something new in the long process of negotiation. This new development must be viewed from the broad perspective of years in which there was not even a positive exchange of views on the various aspects of disarmament.

For many years disarmament negotiations and debates were characterized by disputes over the question of priorities, the question of partial measures or package deals, the composition of disarmament committees, and so on. The establishment of the Eighteen-Nation Committee on Disarmament by the sixteenth session of the General Assembly in 1961 marked a historic turning point in disarmament negotiations, and I am convinced that the inclusion of eight nonaligned nations in the committee and the growing strength of general public opinion regarding the immediate and imperative need for a test ban treaty are factors which merit an optimistic note. Above all there is the fact that two present heads of super-powers—President Kennedy of the United States of America and Chairman Khrushchev of the Soviet Union—are dedicated to the cause of peace, and they represent a new force in international relationships, although each of them has to contend with a difficult domestic opinion which is highly critical of their accommodating attitudes.

Ladies and gentlemen have you any questions?

. . . . QUESTION (interpretation from French): Will United Nations troops in the Congo be entirely withdrawn this year or in 1964 at the latest? Can the Leopoldville government engage specialists of its own choosing as instructors for the Congolese Army, whatever their nationality, or must it still take the views of the United Nations organization into account?

THE SECRETARY-GENERAL: Regarding the first question, the United Nations is in the Congo as a result of several resolutions adopted by the Security Council and the General Assembly. The United Nations has been entrusted to perform certain functions within the framework of those resolutions. If those competent organs of the United Nations feel that all the necessary functions have been performed, I am sure they will decide to disengage from the Congo. My own personal feeling is that the primary function of the United Nations in the Congo has been fulfilled. The unity and territorial integrity of the Congo have been achieved since January last, so there has been a restoration of law and order. But when we speak of law and order in a country like the Congo we have to speak in relative terms. There is no such thing as complete peace or complete law and order. There may sometimes be a case of murder or of assault, but these things happen in Geneva, Manhattan, or anywhere else. Therefore, when we speak of peace or the restoration of law and order in the Congo we have to speak in relative terms. My personal feeling is that, mainly because of the financial situation of the whole Organization, the process of disengagement from the Congo will be speedier than was anticipated last year. To give you an instance, the United Nations had 19,500 men serving in the Congo last year. At the moment the United Nations has only 13,500 men, that is, a reduction of about 6,000 men. Our present intention is to reduce the United Nations forces still further. Perhaps during the second half of this year the strength of the United Nations Force in the Congo will be approximately 7,500.

QUESTION: Could you tell us something about your plan to send observers into Yemen for supervising the evacuation of United Arab Republic and Jordan troops?

THE SECRETARY-GENERAL: I submitted a report on this question to the Security Council just before I left New York; actually the report was submitted on April 29. I set out in detail the processes entailed in the prospective United Nations involvement in Yemen. As you all know, general agreement has been reached between the three powers concerned—the United Arab Republic, Saudi Arabia, and Yemen. As a result of that agreement I have asked General von Horn to visit the area, survey the requirements, and submit a report to me as soon as possible. General von Horn is now in Saudi Arabia; tomorrow he will be in Yemen, and most probably he will be submitting a report next week. On the basis of his report I have to take certain action. Of course, before taking any action it may be necessary for certain steps to be taken. Perhaps the Security Council may be involved for the purpose of coming to a decision. It is, of course, still not very clear, but it all depends on the nature of the United Nations operation based on General von Horn's report.

. . . . QUESTION: Will the force being sent to Yemen be intended to be an effective police force or more in the nature of a United Nations presence?

THE SECRETARY-GENERAL: It will depend primarily on the recommendations of General von Horn and perhaps on the attitude of the Security Council.

QUESTION (interpretation from French): Where do we stand with the implementation of the U Thant plan in the Congo, its financial implications and the modification of the Loi fondamentale with regard to a federalist structure?

THE SECRETARY-GENERAL: The so-called U Thant plan, or the plan of conciliation, has been accepted in principle both by Prime Minister Adoula and by Mr. Tshombé. Of course the process of implementation will take some time. The restoration of the unity and territorial integrity of the Congo was accepted only three and a half months ago, and I think it is a little too early to say when all the terms of the reconciliation plan will be implemented, but I am very hopeful that both sides will honor their pledges. . . .

THE YEMEN QUESTION

APRIL AND JUNE

THE YEMEN QUESTION first came before the United Nations late in 1962 when U Thant submitted to the Credentials Committee at the seventeenth session of the General Assembly a memorandum stating that credentials had been received from more than one delegation of Yemen. This reflected the internal power struggle that was in progress at the time in that country. Actually, the Secretary-General had received three sets of credentials. The first was dated September 9 and was signed by the Imam of Yemen. The second, dated December 7, also was for the Kingdom of Yemen, but was signed by the Minister for Foreign Affairs. The third was dated December 8 and was signed by Brigadier Al-Sallal, who claimed to have been chosen president on September 26. Fighting was going on between the loyal forces of the Imam and what they called the "self-proclaimed régime" of the Yemen Arab Republic. On December 20, the Assembly decided by 73 votes to 4, with 23 abstentions, to approve the recommendation of the Credentials Committee that the delegation of the Yemen Arab Republic be accepted.

The matter might have ended there had not other Arab countries become involved in the civil conflict, Saudi Arabia on the side of the Imam and the United Arab Republic on the side of the new republican government. On April 29, 1963, Thant reported to the Security Council that he had been consulting regularly since the Fall of 1962 with the representatives of the Arab Republic of Yemen, Saudi Arabia, and the United Arab Republic with a view to helping find a peaceful solution. He disclosed further that he had dispatched Under-Secretary Ralph J. Bunche to Yemen and the UAR in late February and early March on a fact-finding mission. Diplomat Ellsworth Bunker was on a similar mission at the same time, under the auspices of the United States government, and the results of his talks had been reported to Thant.

These initiatives were undertaken with the consent of the three countries concerned but without any directive or authorization by the Security Council. By the time Thant made his first report to the Council on April 29, he had received separate communications from the three countries confirming their acceptance of identical terms of disengagement and agreeing to have impartial observers check on the implementation of the disengagement. He informed the Council that he had dispatched Major General Carl von Horn, chief of staff of the United Nations Truce Supervision Organization in Palestine, to work out the modalities including the size of the force needed. On May 27 he reported that not more than two hundred men would be required and, in another report on June 7, that the cost would be borne by Saudi Arabia and the United Arab Republic.

It was at this stage that the Soviet Union requested a meeting of the Security Council. The Soviet representative said the reports submitted by the Secretary-General contained proposals on which only the Security Council could make decisions under the Charter. Although Thant had not asked for Council authorization, he had foreseen the possible need for such action. In a press conference on May 3, he had said that the Council perhaps might be involved in reaching a final decision, but that this would depend "on the nature of the United Nations operation based on General von Horn's report." When the Council met on June 10, Thant did not object to Council action but merely stressed the urgency of the situation. On June 11 he again addressed the Council, declaring that it was not the question of establishing the observation mission that was at issue, but "the question of what and how much should go into the resolution about that matter." At the conclusion of the two-day debate, the Council adopted a resolution "noting with satisfaction" the initiatives taken by the Secretary-General and formally requesting him to establish the mission as defined by him. The vote was 10 to none, with the Soviet Union abstaining.

The United Nations Observation Mission in Yemen began its operations on July 4, 1963, with the United Nations Emergency Force in the Middle East supplying administrative and logistical support. While the Yemen operation was not a major peacekeeping operation in comparison with the ones in the Suez Canal area and in the Congo, it was a significant extension of the peacemaking potential of the office of Secretary-General since all arrangements for the disengagement of the foreign troops, for the establishment and administration of the United Nations Mission and even for its financing were handled by Thant.

1. Report to the Security Council

NEW YORK   APRIL 29, 1963

SINCE THE FALL of 1962 I have been consulting regularly with the representatives to the United Nations of the Governments of the Arab Republic of Yemen, Saudi Arabia, and the United Arab Republic about certain aspects of the situation in Yemen of external origin, with a view to making my office available to the parties for such assistance as might be desired toward ensuring against any developments in that situation which might threaten the peace of the area. I have encountered from the begin-

Security Council Official Records, Eighteenth Year, Supplement for April, May and June 1963, document S/5298.

ning a sympathetic and cooperative attitude on the part of all three representatives and their governments.

2. It was in this context that, after clearance with the respective governments, I asked Mr. Ralph J. Bunche to go to Yemen and the United Arab Republic in late February and early March on a fact-finding mission primarily devoted to talking with the presidents of Yemen and the United Arab Republic, in that order, with the purpose of ascertaining their views on the situation and what steps might be taken to ease tension and restore conditions to normal. It was left open whether Mr. Bunche would eventually go also to Saudi Arabia, but developments made this unnecessary. Mr. Bunche carried out this mission and reported fully to me on his talks, which I found encouraging. Subsequently, I was informed that the United States government, on its own initiative, sent Mr. Ellsworth Bunker to Saudi Arabia on a somewhat similar but unconnected mission. Mr. Bunker later visited Saudi Arabia on two other occasions and also had extensive talks in Cairo with President Nasser. Mr. Bunker kept me informed on the results of his missions. These talks in the end proved fruitful and from them emerged the agreed terms of disengagement. Mr. Bunker's efforts are much appreciated.

3. As a result of these activities, it is now possible for me to inform the Security Council that I have received from each of the three governments concerned, in separate communications, formal confirmation of their acceptance of identical terms of disengagement in Yemen. The will of all three of the interested parties to ease the situation has been the decisive factor, of course, and they are to be commended for their constructive attitude.

4. In substance these terms are the following: the Government of Saudi Arabia, on its part, will terminate all support and aid to the royalists of Yemen and will prohibit the use of Saudi Arabian territory by royalist leaders for the purpose of carrying on the struggle in Yemen. Simultaneously, with the suspension of aid from Saudi Arabia to the royalists, the United Arab Republic undertakes to begin withdrawal from Yemen of the troops sent on request of the new government, this withdrawal to be phased and to take place as soon as possible, during which the forces would withdraw from field activities to their bases pending their departure. The United Arab Republic has also agreed not to take punitive action against the royalists of Yemen for any resistance mounted by them prior to the beginning of their disengagement. There would likewise be an end to any actions on Saudi Arabian territory by United Arab Republic

forces. A demilitarized zone to a distance of twenty kilometers on each side of the demarcated Saudi Arabia–Yemen border is to be established from which military forces and equipment are to be excluded. In this zone, on both sides, impartial observers are to be stationed to check on the observance of the terms of disengagement and who would also have the responsibility of traveling beyond the demilitarized zone, as necessary, in order to certify the suspension of activities in support of the royalists from Saudi Arabian territory and the outward movement of the United Arab Republic forces and equipment from the airports and seaports of Yemen. The United Arab Republic and Saudi Arabia have further undertaken to cooperate with the representative of the United Nations Secretary-General or some other mutually acceptable intermediary in reaching agreement on the modalities and verification of disengagement.

5. In view of the provisions in these terms for a demilitarized zone and impartial observers, and with the consent of the parties, I have asked Major General Carl Carlson von Horn, chief of staff of the United Nations Truce Supervision Organization in Jerusalem, to proceed without delay to the three countries concerned for the purpose of consulting with the appropriate authorities on details relating to the nature and functioning of United Nations observers in implementation of the terms of disengagement and to report to me with his recommendations as to the size of the set-up that might be required to discharge this reponsibility. My preliminary view is that the requirements of men and equipment will be modest and will be needed for three or four months, at the most. I have been thinking in terms of not more than fifty observers, with suitable transportation, aerial and ground, for patrol purposes. A few helicopters, possibly three or four, and a similar number of small aircraft such as "Otters," together with the required jeeps and lorries, should suffice.

6. As to the financing of any such activity by the United Nations, I have it in mind to proceed under the provisions of General Assembly resolution 1862 (XVII).

7. I intend to make a further report to the Security Council with particular reference to the question of United Nations observers after General von Horn has reported to me on his discussions on this subject with the parties concerned.

2. From Statement in the Security Council

NEW YORK   JUNE 10, 1963

I HAVE ALREADY communicated to this Council, in my four reports relating to developments affecting the Yemen situation, my conception of the measures involving United Nations action which might be taken in fulfilment of the terms of disengagement accepted by the parties. These measures, in the form of a United Nations observation function, have been carefully studied, and though the physical conditions in the area are rugged, they are considered feasible within the scope indicated.

As I have already reported to the Council, there are at this time no financial implications for the United Nations involved in the proposed observation operation, in view of the fact that the governments of Saudi Arabia and the United Arab Republic have agreed to defray the expense of the operation over a period of two months.

In addition to this, I think that I need only say that General von Horn is alerted and is ready to proceed to the area with elements of an advance party on twenty-four hours' notice. Reports reaching me recently underscore the growing urgency of the need for the United Nations observation operation.

. . . .

Security Council Official Records, Eighteenth Year, 1037th meeting.

3. *Statement in the Security Council*

NEW YORK   JUNE 11, 1963

IF I SPEAK to you again so soon, it is because of my concern that the United Nations observation assistance called for under the terms of disengagement in Yemen, as agreed upon by the parties, should be provided with the least possible delay. I am naturally hopeful that the informal consultations that have been going on in an effort to achieve general agreement on the wording of the resolution relating to the Yemen observation mission will prove fruitful. I am compelled to say that I feel strongly that it would not be in the interest of peace in the Near East, and certainly not in the interest of this Organization, if it should for any reason fail to provide the observation assistance requested by the parties, or delay much longer in doing so.

From my informal talks with members of this Council, I am of the firm impression that everyone agrees that the observation function called for should be provided. This, in my view, is a key point, along with two other key points—namely, that the parties concerned are themselves agreed on the need for United Nations observation, and have asked for it; that the parties also are prepared to bear the cost of the operation for a period of two months, and possibly for a total period of four months, should that prove necessary.

It is not, then, as I see it, the question of the establishment of the proposed observation mission that is really at issue now in the Council, since everyone agrees that this operation is necessary. Rather, it is the question of what and how much should go into a resolution about that matter.

I am prepared to commence the operation immediately. The Council is already aware that it will be a modest mission, not exceeding two hundred people, including some carefully selected and experienced military officer observers and a small number of other ranks. Its duration should

Security Council Official Records, Eighteenth Year, 1038th meeting.

not exceed four months, and it could be concluded in two. In the event that more than two months should be required, I would certainly report this fact to the Council in advance.

Finally, I should like to warn that there is growing evidence that the agreement on the terms of disengagement may be jeopardized if the United Nations observation personnel are not on the spot. I earnestly hope, therefore, that the Council will find it possible to achieve prompt agreement on this matter.

"The United Nations as a Force for Peace"
A Message to the People of Sweden

NEW YORK   MAY 1, 1963

U THANT had planned to visit Sweden to deliver an address on April 30, but was forced to cancel his trip because of "unanticipated" developments which he did not explain. It was generally known, however, that he was in the midst of private negotiations which were to lead to the sending of a United Nations observer mission to Yemen. He had reported to the Security Council on April 29 that he had been consulting regularly with representatives of Yemen, Saudi Arabia, and the United Arab Republic on the problem since late in 1962 and that discussions still were in progress. In his message to the Swedish people, he enumerated UN peacekeeping operations and examples of "quiet diplomacy" with only a bare mention of Yemen. He listed it as one of several potentially dangerous spots on which the United Nations might keep a watchful eye and lend its support to efforts of the parties concerned to reach peaceful settlements.

IT IS A MATTER of regret to me that the responsibilities of my office, which quite often make unanticipated demands upon my time and movements, have kept me from going to Sweden at this time, as planned. But I take this opportunity to convey to all of the people of Sweden the substance of the remarks which I intended to make. They relate to peace, which must be the most vital concern of peoples everywhere, whatever their political leanings. Peace, in my view, knows no party lines.

In our time there are new and compelling reasons why we should seek peace, and the conditions which make it possible, with more determination than ever before.

One could simplify the functions of the United Nations in this search by saying that it was an association of sovereign states devoted principally to remedying and liquidating the grievances and injustices of the past, to adjusting and solving the tensions and dangers of the present and to laying the foundations for a more stable and happy future. It is with

UN Press Release SG/1477.

the second of these main streams of activity that I propose to deal in this message, for if we do not devise means of tackling and making safe the violent antagonisms which sometimes arise in the world in such a way that they do not spread and infect the community of nations, then all our efforts to improve on the past or to plan for the future will be in vain.

These activities are also of particular interest to you here in Sweden who have contributed so much to these pioneering efforts. In saying this I am not only thinking of my predecessor and your great compatriot, Dag Hammarskjöld, who unquestionably did more than any man to develop the machinery of the United Nations so that it could with increasing effectiveness meet its awesome responsibilities for world peace, and who, in his tireless and fearless pursuit of his duty, met his tragic death. I am not only thinking of Count Folke Bernadotte, who gave his life as United Nations mediator in Palestine in one of the earliest efforts of the United Nations to keep the peace. I am also referring to the officers and men who have served the United Nations bravely and loyally in the Middle East and in the Congo, and to the many Swedes who have served and are serving as international civil servants in one capacity or another throughout the world. It would be difficult to think of any other country showing greater practical support for the United Nations than Sweden—a support expressed not only in the loyalty of its government to the ideals of the United Nations but also in the service of its citizens.

The United Nations has responded in a practical way to a variety of crises in its eighteen years of existence, and has, in the process, developed practices and precedents which have greatly enlarged its capacity to deal with emergencies. I mentioned the great contribution of my predecessor to this evolution. Another very important factor has certainly been the necessity, recognized by all concerned, of dealing with certain dangerous situations effectively without involving them in the stresses and strains of East-West struggle. A third factor has been the increasing reliance of the smaller nations upon the United Nations, the increasing influence of their moderating voice in the United Nations, and their loyal support of its efforts to keep the peace. These efforts have also entailed an increased responsibility and workload for the Secretary-General and his staff and a growing recognition, in most quarters, of the value of the Secretariat as an objective international civil service. This too is a most significant institutional development.

One of the most encouraging of the pragmatic developments that I have mentioned has been the increasing use of the military personnel of

Member states for the maintenance of the peace in various parts of the world under United Nations auspices and the adaptation of the military art to the task of maintaining the peace.

Methods of using military personnel productively on a far smaller scale than is envisaged in the Charter have been evolving since the early years of the United Nations. These relatively modest enterprises have all been directed to the control of explosive situations before they get out of hand and spread. In Greece in 1947 and 1948 the military attachés of the members of the United Nations Commission proved themselves invaluable as an observer group in checking on infiltration into Greece from her northern neighbors. In Kashmir, an observer group of military officers was formally set up by the Security Council and is still operating.

The first truce agreements in the Palestine war in July 1948 were enforced on the ground by some seven hundred United Nations military observers working under the United Nations mediator and his chief of staff. This team later developed into the United Nations Truce Supervision Organization after the conclusion of the armistice agreements between Israel and her Arab neighbors in 1949. This organization played, and is still playing, a vital role in keeping the peace in the Middle East and in regulating frontier incidents in such a way that they do not develop into much more serious conflicts.

A far larger scale and more unusual international peacekeeping organism was evoked by the critical situation which arose in October 1956 following the armed intervention in the Suez Canal area of the forces of Israel, France, and the United Kingdom—the creation of a United Nations police and peacekeeping force, the United Nations Emergency Force in the Middle East, which allowed for a peaceful withdrawal from Egyptian soil of the armed forces of France, the United Kingdom, and Israel, and the clearance of the vital waterway—the Suez Canal. The Force still watches over the peace on the once troubled frontier between Israel and the United Arab Republic. It presents one major problem—it is so useful and necessary that it is hard to envisage a date when it can be withdrawn from the area.

The Lebanon crisis of 1958 evoked another kind of United Nations military organization, a corps of six hundred observers to watch over the borders of Lebanon for foreign infiltration, but it was in July 1960 that the United Nations was confronted with its most complex and pressing peacekeeping task to date. So much has been written about the Congo and the United Nations involvement there in the past two and a half years that I shall do no more here than to mention the general proportions of this problem, which have a tendency to be obscured by a wealth of dramatic and controversial detail. On the appeal for help by the new Government of the Congo, the United Nations, literally at a few hours' notice, undertook to be the guarantor of law and order, and the watchman against external interference from many sources. It also became the counsellor of a newly independent state which had had little preparation for independence, on all the problems that beset a country the size of Western Europe, which occupies a vital, strategic, and economic place in the world, and which, by its very potential wealth and possibilities, is a target for a bewildering variety of foreign interests.

There is still a long and difficult road ahead both for the government and people of the Congo and for the United Nations which is assisting them, but given the fearsome complexity of the problem and the crosscurrents and conflicts of interests at all levels, from the global level to the tribal level, which afflict the Republic of the Congo, it is remarkable that this pioneering effort by the community of nations has not only saved one of its members, the Congo, in its time of trial, but has turned a situation of great potential danger to Africa and to the world into a most promising experiment in world responsibility. Sweden has done more than its share in the support of this historic effort.

Another operation, also involving an unprecedented role for the United Nations, has meanwhile passed off peacefully and successfully and, as is the rule with successful peacekeeping operations, has attracted virtually no publicity whatsoever. It has in fact been successfully and formally concluded on this very day. I refer to the transfer of West Irian from Dutch administration, through an interim period of United Nations administration safeguarded by a United Nations force, to the administration of Indonesia, the entire operation taking place with the mutual agreement of the parties concerned. This is the first time in history that an international organization has assumed direct administrative authority for a territory in the process of historic transition.

In certain situations the United Nations and the Office of the Secretary-General can provide a useful middle ground on which the parties may meet without any loss of face or prestige, and accommodate their differences in a civilized and dignified manner. I like to think that the United Nations played a useful role of this kind in the resolution of the Cuban crisis last October, a crisis which for a few days seemed to bring the world very near to the nuclear disaster which all men dread. There are situations of a less portentous nature in which also the course of mediation and moderation can be of assistance to the parties. I refer, for example, to the differences between Somalia and Ethiopia and between Thailand and Cambodia. There are times when the world community, through the United Nations, may usefully keep a watchful eye on a potentially dangerous situation and lend its support to the efforts of those concerned to solve outstanding differences in a peaceful and constructive way. Such a situation existed prior to the independence of Rwanda and Burundi, and it is a source of gratification to find that the difficulties foreseen have, for the moment at least, apparently evaporated. Such situations exist today in Yemen and in Southeast Asia.

In such situations the technique of quiet diplomacy—a technique in which my predecessor excelled—can make the difference between a disastrous breakdown of understanding and communication and a constructive advance toward a resolution of differences.

I have voiced a guarded optimism on the potential of the United Nations as a force for peace and of the achievements which are already to its credit. It would be unrealistic if I did not also mention the practical basis upon which alone such activities can continue. Your country has, I have said, made great contributions to the efforts of the United Nations, both in men and in resources. There is, nonetheless, at the present time a very serious financial crisis facing the United Nations due to the failure of some members to pay their contributions toward the peacekeeping operations of the Organization. The International Court of Justice has recommended that the expenses of the peacekeeping operations of the United Nations should be part of the normal assessment of the Member states. I hope very much that the time will soon come when all Members of the United Nations will find it possible and, indeed, desirable to respect this opinion of the World Court.

I have said nothing of the great basic problems of disarmament or of the special preoccupations of the great powers. I hope that the United Nations operations I have mentioned may, in their modest way, be a pointer in the right direction and an encouragement in the constructive future use of the military art. They are the first gropings, imperfect admittedly, toward the kind of international authority which is one of the inescapable conditions of agreed disarmament.

I said last year at Uppsala that the United Nations must ultimately develop in the same way as sovereign states have done, and that, if it is to have a future, it must eventually assume some of the attributes of a state.

It must have the right, the power and the means to keep the peace. We are only in the beginning and the process will surely take several generations. But the peacekeeping operations already conducted by the United Nations provide the hope that we are on the road to these essential developments.

Message on the Occasion of the Transfer of Administration of West Irian to Indonesia

NEW YORK   MAY 1, 1963

THE TERMINATION of the United Nations administration of West Irian ended an eight-month episode in which the United Nations for the first time ruled a territory. U Thant called it "a unique experience, which has once again proved the capacity of the United Nations to undertake a variety of functions, provided it receives adequate support from the states Members of the Organization."

ON THE OCCASION of the transfer of administration of West Irian (West New Guinea) from the United Nations to the Government of the Republic of Indonesia, in accordance with the Agreement of August 15, 1962, as noted by the General Assembly by resolution 1752 (XVII), I should like to recall that for some eight months the United Nations has carried out its responsibility in the territory, initially through the United Nations observers, following the cessation of hostilities, and since October 1, 1962, through the United Nations temporary executive authority.

During this period, the United Nations has made the necessary preparation for a gradual transfer of full administrative control to the Republic of Indonesia. For us in the United Nations this has been a unique experience, which has one again proved the capacity of the United Nations to undertake a variety of functions, provided it receives adequate support from the states Members of the Organization.

Throughout the period of UNTEA administration, I have been impressed and gratified by the spirit of accommodation shown by the Governments of the Republic of Indonesia and the Kingdom of the Netherlands. They have displayed a realistic approach to the many problems that we have encountered during the UNTEA period. In recent weeks, the two governments have reestablished diplomatic relations, and this is a happy sequel to the solution of the West Irian (West New Guinea) question.

UN Press Releases SG/1473 and Add. 1, April 29 and May 2, 1963.

In its undertaking in this territory, the United Nations has been served with distinction by the administrator, Dr. Djalal Abdoh, and under his leadership by a group of international civil servants representing thirty-two nationalities. I would like to take this opportunity to pay a tribute to them for their dedication and loyalty, and also to express my personal gratitude to them. They have been ably assisted during the earlier period of UNTEA by officials of the former Netherlands administration, in the latter period by officials recruited from personnel provided by the Government of Indonesia and by local officials during the whole period of UNTEA. All these officials have given UNTEA unstinted support in order to enable the United Nations to fulfill its role.

While there have been a few incidents in the earlier part of the administration, by and large the situation in the territory has remained peaceful and calm. I wish to take this opportunity to thank the inhabitants of the territory for this display of confidence in the United Nations. The Security Force under the able command of General Said-Uddin Khan has contributed much to inspire this feeling of confidence.

In their own respective fields of competence, the specialized agencies have given the UNTEA assistance and advice when called upon to do so. To these agencies I want to convey my sincere thanks for their cooperation.

I would also like to announce that, in consultation with the Government of Indonesia, I have decided in principle to designate a few United Nations experts, serving at Headquarters and elsewhere, to perform the functions envisaged in article XVI of the Agreement. These experts will visit Irian Barat (West New Guinea) as often as may be necessary and spend such time as may be required to enable them to report fully to me.

Their duties will, prior to the arrival of the United Nations representative to be designated under article XVII, be limited to advising on and assisting in preparations for carrying out the provisions for self-determination, except insofar as the Government of Indonesia and I may agree upon their performing other expert functions.

It gives me much pleasure to announce that, in consultation with the governments concerned, I have decided to establish a United Nations Development Fund for Irian Barat (West New Guinea) as a "Fund in Trust," and open to contributions from Member states of the United Nations and the specialized agencies. The fund will be used to finance preinvestment and investment projects in Irian Barat, acceptable to the Government of Indonesia, and in cooperation with the United Nations technical assistance to Indonesia. It is my hope that many governments will contribute liberally to this fund.

Before I conclude, I want to convey to the people of the territory my sincere good wishes for their future prosperity and happiness. I am confident that the Republic of Indonesia will scrupulously observe the terms of the agreement concluded on August 15, 1962, and will ensure the exercise by the population of the territory of their right to express their wishes as to their future. The United Nations stands ready to give the Government of Indonesia all assistance in the implementation of this and the remaining parts of the agreement.

ARTICLE XVI of the agreement provided that at the time of the transfer of authority from the United Nations to Indonesia, the Secretary-General would designate a number of United Nations experts to remain in West Irian to advise and assist in preparations for self-determination as provided in the agreement. Article XVII provided for the appointment by the Secretary-General of a representative to assist in the self-determination arrangements as chief of the experts mentioned in Article XVI.

THE FINANCIAL SITUATION

On May 14, 1963, the General Assembly convened its fourth special session to seek a way out of the Organization's worsening financial situation. The Assembly had dealt with the problem at its regular sessions in 1961 and 1962, but this was the first time that a session had been held to consider the financial situation exclusively. U Thant appeared before the Fifth Committee on May 15, to stress the need for urgent action. At the conclusion of six weeks of debate, the Assembly adopted a number of resolutions but failed to agree on a formula for liquidating the United Nations deficit or for the financing of future peacekeeping operations. It appealed for voluntary contributions to reduce the deficit and extended until December 31, 1963, the time limit for the sale of United Nations bonds. It also voted to continue the Working Group on the Examination of the Administrative and Budgetary Procedures of the United Nations, known as the Working Group of 21, which had been trying unsuccessfully to find a solution to the financial woes of the Organization. When Thant made his next appearance before the Fifth Committee on October 16, 1963, he reported with regret that "this problem is still with us" and "the general situation remains serious."

1. Statement in the Fifth Committee at the Fourth Special Session

NEW YORK   MAY 15, 1963

My main purpose in being here today is to convey through you, to the members of the Fifth Committee, my earnest hope for a constructive and fruitful outcome of the deliberations on which you are about to embark. Despite the various measures that have been taken, the unhappy fact remains that the Organization continues in a state of serious financial difficulty. I shall not burden you here and now with detailed figures of unpaid obligations and growing deficits. You will find these set forth, I

UN Press Release SG/1502. The summary record is given in General Assembly Official Records, Fourth Special Session, Fifth Committee, 594th meeting.

trust with sufficient clarity and completeness, in the report issued yesterday on the United Nations financial position and prospects. Needless to say, I, together with the controller and the deputy controller, will be ready at all times to furnish such amplifications or explanations as may be called for.

I would, however, like to assure you that during the four months that have elapsed since the seventeenth session, the Secretariat, for its part, has not been inactive. First, much time and attention have been devoted to the collection of contributions in arrears and, although this situation is still far from satisfactory, the fact that about forty governments have, during these four months, paid arrears totaling some $16 million, is not without encouragement.

Second, similar efforts have been made, and will continue to be made to promote the sale of United Nations bonds up to the authorized limit of $200 million. As of now, we are short of this target by approximately $50 million; but if the Assembly sees fit to accept my recommendation for an extension of the period within which subscriptions can be made, to December 31, 1963, I am hopeful that we may make further progress toward our goal.

Third, with a view to minimizing the financial burden on Member states, I have chosen to follow a policy of strict austerity so far as 1964 regular budgetary expenditures are concerned. The preparation of the initial 1964 budget estimates has proceeded on that basis.

And, lastly, as I hope will be evident from the report that was issued on May 8, 1963 (A/5416), every effort is being and will be exerted to reduce the costs of the Congo operations as rapidly as possible. Although it is not possible to predict the future course of events in the Congo, it can be safely estimated that ONUC expenditures will drop from the level of $10 million a month that has prevailed until recently, to approximately $5.5 million a month, over the last part of 1963. Nor, in the light of recent trends and developments, is it unreasonable to anticipate a complete military disengagement by the end of this year.

The major accomplishment, however, in the past few months, has been the thoroughgoing examination of the administrative and budgetary procedures of the United Nations, with reference, particularly, to the financing of peacekeeping operations, that has been undertaken, on the Assembly's behalf, by the Working Group of 21, under the distinguished chairmanship of Ambassador Adebo.[1] It is a matter of regret, of course,

---

[1] Chief S. O. Adebo, permanent representative of Nigeria.

that in spite of the sincere efforts at compromise and accommodation, the group was unable to reach agreed recommendations. Nevertheless, I would venture to suggest that its deliberations reflected an encouragingly wide consensus on certain guiding principles and that its report will constitute a useful point of departure for the further consideration of longer-term methods and arrangements.

I sincerely hope that the search for more permanent solutions will not be relaxed, although it is open to debate perhaps, whether the moment is ripe for any real breakthrough. In any event, I consider it imperative, as I have stated in my report on the financial position, that the General Assembly takes action at this special session to assure that the Organization will have the necessary cash resources to defray its continuing operations in the Middle East and in the Congo, either by assessing the costs of these continuing operations among Members, or by such other methods as the Assembly may devise.

If this is accomplished, and the other measures currently under way resolutely pursued, there is good hope, I believe, that the Organization will be on its way to financial solvency.

Members, I am sure, are well aware that the Organization's financial problem has been one of my major and continuing preoccupations. I have stated on many occasions before this Committee, and in other public forums, that this problem is, in every sense, a vital one—perhaps *the* most vital one before the United Nations. If I may repeat what I said here last December. . . "a financially bankrupt United Nations would be an ineffective United Nations, if indeed it could survive on such a basis. The financial issue is thus one, which, if I may say so, transcends political controversy." That is what I said last December. I added on that occasion my belief that in their various ways all states represented in the United Nations had found that the Organization is useful and, indeed, indispensable, in the modern world. I very much hope, therefore, that it will be on this basis and with this overriding consideration uppermost in mind, that the Fifth Committee and the special session will deal with the question before it.

2. From Statement in the Fifth Committee

NEW YORK   OCTOBER 16, 1963

I THANK YOU for giving me this opportunity of meeting with the members of the Fifth Committee and presenting the budget estimates for the financial year 1964.

When I had the honour of addressing this committee in October last year I felt that, before offering comments on the estimates which I had proposed for 1963, it was necessary to give priority to a matter of cardinal importance, namely, the financial position and prospects of this Organization. Regrettably, this problem is still with us and, while here and there we may find grounds for optimism, the general situation remains serious, as I have described in the introduction to my annual report on the work of the Organization, and the United Nations is likely for some time to come to continue to operate under a serious financial deficit, while the cash position outlook is causing considerable anxiety.

In a report to this committee last May I indicated that the Organization's deficit in respect of the regular budget, UNEF and ONUC, which totalled $74 million at the beginning of the year, was estimated at $101 million as at June 30 and might increase to $140 million by the end of the year. The deficit at June 30 was, in fact, $114 million.

At its special session in the summer of this year, the General Assembly approved new assessments for UNEF and ONUC for the second half of 1963, and decided to extend to the end of this year the period during which United Nations bonds could be sold. These factors had not been taken into account in my May projection of the year-end financial position and it now appears that at the end of 1963 the Organization will have unpaid obligations totalling $162 million. Net cash resources at that time may be estimated at $50 million. On this basis the deficit will be some $112 million.

General Assembly Official Records, Eighteenth Session, Annexes, agenda item 58, document A/C.5/988.

Although, as a result of the Assembly's actions in June, this projection of the cash position at the end of the year is more optimistic than my forecast of last May, it is likely that not more than 10 to 15 percent of any new assessments in respect of the regular budget, UNEF and ONUC for 1964 will be paid during the first three months of next year, nor more than 25 to 30 percent during the first six months of 1964. This situation is far from reassuring. I therefore trust that governments of Member states will find it possible to meet the request of the General Assembly to pay the arrears in assessments which now total more than $100 million, and to respond to my appeal to buy the balance of some $50 million of United Nations bonds that remain unsold.

It is, of course, open to the Secretary-General, and indeed I conceive it to be his duty, to take certain steps aimed at improving the finances of the Organization. Where the regular budget is concerned, it is certainly his duty to exercise at all times the utmost economy consistent with efficiency. But it is obviously not possible, without seriously impairing normal activities of the Organization, to find in mere reductions of the regular budget a remedy for an overall financial situation which is so difficult. The ultimate decision whether the Organization shall flourish or languish from lack of financial resources must rest with Member states themselves.
. . . .

Nevertheless, I have endeavored, in the face of so serious a situation, to hold expenses to an absolute minimum without hampering the execution of essential programs. To meet this objective, I have taken a rigidly conservative line, as the budget document itself attests: whatever additions it contains by comparison with the 1963 appropriations are unavoidable increments or flow from decisions taken by the General Assembly or other principal organs of the United Nations.

Yet it will not escape any one of us that, however necessary such conservative action may be—for, after all, we have been operating for several years under serious deficits—it is not a policy which could in other circumstances commend itself to the Members of the United Nations. The Members have demonstrated beyond the possibility of doubt that they wish our Organization to grow; they have demonstrated that in resolutions of the Assembly, the Councils, the commissions, and the committees. These resolutions do no more than reflect the desire of peoples everywhere to see the work of the United Nations expand in volume and intensity and come closer to their daily lives. It is therefore a task of manifest difficulty, in the face of growing demands from all parts of the world—above all, from the developing countries—for the Secretary-General to impose the strict policy of consolidation and containment which a precarious financial situation may seem to dictate.

Yet for 1964 I have proposed such a policy. In large part, this has been possible because the total resources, particularly the staffing resources, authorized for 1963 have not yet been put to full use. But, as I have already reported to you, this situation is undergoing a change, and there is a progressive improvement in the rate of recruitment to established posts. We are beginning to overcome some of the difficulties that have confronted us: the need, for example, to recruit increasing numbers of specialists in specific and technical fields, while also observing the requirements of geographical distribution. It appears therefore that this policy of containment will be of short duration, for it is surely axiomatic that with so many complex problems facing the world the United Nations must be ready to undertake new and expanding work programs in the major fields in which it plays so prominent a role. It would, by that token, be unrealistic not to provide for a certain rate of growth in the activities of the Organization, together with a corresponding increase in the budgetary provision for coming years.

Clearly, however, this increase in the future level of the budget must be controlled and maintained within reasonable limits. Let me very briefly reiterate the measures for achieving this end which I outlined to this Committee last year; they are cooperative measures in which the Member states and the Secretariat must play an equal part. First and foremost, we must make sure that all existing resources are used to maximum effect. For this purpose, the Secretariat must seek the cooperation of Member states and the principal organs in order to ensure that their work programs and related conference schedules are rationalized; that the work is governed by a clear order of priorities and phased over a reasonable period of time; that the manpower available to the Secretary-General is fully utilized and that the end results are not only consonant with the efforts exerted by the Secretariat and the Member states but also with the level of expenditure incurred. These measures, which I have sketched in briefest outline, I consider to be indispensable if the Secretariat is to achieve and maintain the highest standards of quality in its basic research, studies, and reports. . . .

"Education in Our Changing Times"
From Address at Mount Holyoke College

SOUTH HADLEY, MASSACHUSETTS   JUNE 2, 1963

U THANT talked and wrote often about the cold war and its effects on the international well-being. In this commencement address, he appealed to the younger generation to seek a better understanding of alien ideologies and, in so doing, to remove the fear and mistrust upon which the cold war was based. He said ideological fanaticism was a greater threat to the human race than the religious fanaticism of past centuries. The Secretary-General noted that both capitalist and communist doctrines had undergone subtle changes, but that "each side is convinced that it alone represents the true philosophy of peace and that the other side is a warmonger." It was this atmosphere of mutual suspicion, he suggested, which complicated efforts to build an effective world authority.

.... AN EFFECTIVE WORLD authority, like any other governmental system, must be based on power. It cannot grow out of a paper constitution or a Charter or the formation of international agencies in specific fields, though all these in themselves may make useful contributions. As nation-states grew out of the unifying power of the stronger feudal lords, so must a society of nations grow out of the needs of its largest and most powerful constituent members.

It is impossible to conceive in our day of a world authority that could physically overawe the giant states of the United States of America and the Soviet Union. All that seems possible is to employ the strength of the two giants to back a system of preventing war between other countries. But how is war to be prevented in disputes between the two giants themselves? It seems to me that one of the first steps to be taken is to attempt to do away with the cold war which has been such a marked feature of international relations since the end of the Second World War.

We in the United Nations are all too familiar with the cold war. The curious thing about the cold war is that it is not a battle for more terri-

United Nations Review, June 1963.

tory, or even for more political power. As it is waged in the United Nations, it is a battle for the votes of the uncommitted and for the minds of the unconverted. History is full of examples of religious intolerance, but the ideological fanaticism that we see today seems to me sometimes to be even more implacable, and certainly more deadly and dangerous to the human race, than the religious fanaticism which marked the history of past centuries and occasioned such extreme instances of man's inhumanity to man.

One remarkable feature of the cold war is that each side is so completely convinced of its own rightness. The doctrines of capitalism and communism have, in fact, undergone some subtle changes since the major exponents of these theories expounded their dogmas. There is no doubt that some of the theories of communism, for example, were influenced by the conditions of extreme laissez-faire of private enterprise, the ruthless exploitation of labor, including the labor of women and children, and the accumulation of wealth and power in the hands of a few, that marked the rise of capitalism in the eighteenth and nineteenth centuries. While communist dogma may still speak of capitalism as though it has remained unchanged over the last century, in fact capitalism has undergone a change. Even in the capitalist countries, society has awakened to the dangers of unrestricted private enterprise, and the societies practicing the most advanced theories of private enterprise have found it necessary to adopt, at the same time, stringent laws to avoid the danger of extreme concentration of economic power in the form of monopolies. Far from labor's being exploited, united labor has learned its own strength. Small men and women everywhere have in a way become capitalists, with a stake in the development of their own societies. Social welfare legislation has made sure not only that child labor is outlawed, but that children are given opportunities for education and for choosing their own careers.

On the other hand, while some capitalists may not wish to concede this point, I believe that communism too has undergone many changes. For example, there are many communists in the world today who do not believe in the inevitability of war between the two rival systems of society. In the Soviet Union the leaders talk in terms of competitive coexistence. I can well understand why they should wish to compete with the capitalist societies to provide better standards of living for their own people, since they believe in the inherent superiority of their system, and this would be the surest way of demonstrating it.

While thus the practice of capitalism and of communism has perhaps come a little closer than the extreme antithesis assumed by dogmatists in the past, there is still the ideological fanaticism to which I referred and which complicates our existence. Each side is convinced that it alone represents the true philosophy of peace and that the other side is a war-monger. Both sides mistrust the intentions of the other and are also very much afraid that one side might achieve some technological break-through in the field of missilery or nuclear warfare, or even defense systems against nuclear attack, which gives it an advantage over the other. If this atmosphere of mistrust and fear continues and if, meanwhile, the stockpiling of nuclear arms and the development of more deadly engines of destruction should continue unchecked, surely the danger of total anni-hilation of mankind to which I referred earlier is becoming "nearer, clearer, deadlier than before."

It is in this context that I feel that I should address myself today mainly to the younger generation. Those of you who are leaving this institution of learning today will in due course be responsible as citizens, as mothers and as enlightened members of the public in shaping not only the policies of your country but—what is even more important—the minds of the young. Your first task, I think, should be to try to understand each other better and to remove in this process the fear and mistrust that character-ize the attitudes of the major protagonists of the cold war. . . .

Statement on the Occasion of the Death of Pope John XXIII

NEW YORK   JUNE 3, 1963

ALTHOUGH U THANT himself was a devout Buddhist, he maintained a most un-usual relationship with both Pope John XXIII and Pope Paul VI. He exchanged messages with the Vatican on numerous occasions. He welcomed especially the efforts of the two Roman Catholic leaders toward peace. In opening a press conference in New York on April 11, 1963, the Secretary-General praised Pope John's encyclical "Peace on Earth" as an historic document whose contents "are certainly in harmony with the purposes and objectives of the United Nations" (p. 318). Less than two months later, on June 3, Thant was to have the sad duty of commenting on the death of the pontiff whom he described "as the very em-bodiment of mankind's own aspirations."

Thant first met Pope Paul on July 11 when he was granted an audience. Thant said in a press conference in Rome later the same day that they "exchanged views on some of the items directly concerned with the United Nations and with the Catholic Church." Among these was the persecution of the Buddhist majority in South Vietnam by the Catholic government of President Ngo Dinh Diem.

A MOST NOBLE LIFE has come to an end and a spirit of the highest human qualities is no longer with us. The death of His Holiness Pope John XXIII is deeply felt by men everywhere who saw in him a symbol of universal-ity, peace, and harmony. Athough he was the head of the Roman Catho-lic Church, Pope John XXIII in his recent and memorable encyclical "Pacem in Terris" spoke for all men and to all men in restating his belief in the dignity of the individual, in fundamental human rights, in justice, and in an effective international order. His was truly an ecumenical mes-sage of farsighted significance.

History offers few examples where the affection and respect of mankind have been so overwhelmingly centered on one single human being as in the case of His Holiness Pope John XXIII. That this respect and affection should have developed in such a short period of time and should have

UN Press Release SG/1514.

transcended both national and religious boundaries is even more rare.

In identifying himself so unreservedly with the cause of peace and international understanding, Pope John XXIII became the very embodiment of mankind's own aspirations in this uncertain period of history. It is therefore fitting that the Pope's last moments on this earth should have been accompanied by what the Vatican has aptly called a "plebiscite of prayer."

The thinking and actions of Pope John XXIII were unfailingly guided by a full measure of confidence in the potentialities of mankind. Let this confidence be a source of inspiration to us all so that we too may usefully serve the cause of peace and understanding among men.

"A United Nations Stand-by Peace Force" From Address before the Harvard Alumni Association

CAMBRIDGE, MASSACHUSETTS   JUNE 13, 1963

LIKE TRYGVE LIE and the late United States Secretary of State, George C. Marshall, U Thant chose a Harvard University commencement exercise as the setting for an important address. Marshall launched the Marshall Plan at a Harvard commencement in 1947 and a year later Lie called for the creation of "a small guard force" by the United Nations as distinct from a big power striking force envisaged in Article 43 of the Charter. Thant, in an address to the Harvard Alumni Association on commencement day, June 13, 1963, proposed the establishment of a United Nations stand-by peace force. Looking back on almost twenty years of United Nations experience, Thant concluded it was not practical to have a permanent United Nations force either of the type projected in Article 43 or of the type proposed by Lie. As an alternative, he said it would be better if Members of the United Nations, in their national planning, would earmark suitable units which could be made available at short notice for United Nations service. Such a standby peace force, he said, would not only be less costly than a permanent United Nations force, but would avoid the problem of having a standing army with nothing to do. Thant noted that since 1946 "there has been a tacit transition from the concept of collective security, as set out in Chapter VII of the United Nations Charter, to a more realistic idea of peacekeeping." There has also been, he said, "a change in emphasis from the use, in practice, of the military forces of the smaller powers. . . ." He stressed, however, that while the standby peace forces he proposed have very little in common with the forces foreseen in Chapter VII "their existence is not in conflict with Chapter VII."

Thant's proposal in reality was a projection of a study concluded in 1958 by Dag Hammarskjöld, who had also rejected the concept of a standing United Nations force. Hammarskjöld suggested that interested Member states should be in readiness to make units available to the United Nations on request and that the Secretariat should maintain contact with such governments on their state of readiness for participation in United Nations peacekeeping operations. Thant specifically called upon Members in their national military planning "to make provision for suitable units which could be made available at short notice for United Nations service and thereby decrease the degree of improvisation necessary in an emergency." He noted that the Scandinavian countries had already earmarked military components for standby training and called upon other states to follow their lead. Like Hammarskjöld, however, he preferred to leave the formalization of a standby force on an ad hoc basis to be put into action as the occasion demanded.

. . . . I AM GOING TO TALK today about one particular aspect of our problems, namely, peacekeeping and the use of international peace forces by the United Nations. Due partly to the lack of unanimity among the great powers ever since 1946, and partly to the radical change in the nature of war resulting from the development of atomic and hydrogen weapons, there has been a gradual change in thinking on questions of international security in the United Nations.

There has been a tacit transition from the concept of collective security, as set out in Chapter VII of the United Nations Charter, to a more realistic idea of peacekeeping. The idea that conventional military methods—or, to put it bluntly, war—can be used by or on behalf of the United Nations to counter aggression and secure the peace, seems now to be rather impractical.

There has also been a change in emphasis from the use of the military forces of the great powers, as contemplated in the Charter, to the use, in practice, of the military resources of the smaller powers, which has the advantage of not entangling United Nations actions in the antagonisms of the cold war.

Although there has been one collective action under the aegis of the United Nations—Korea—and although in 1951 the Collective Measures Committee, set up by the General Assembly under the Uniting-for-peace resolution, actually published in its report a list of units earmarked by Member states for service with the United Nations in actions to counter aggression, actual developments have in practice been in a rather different direction.

The nature of these developments is sometimes confused, wittingly or unwittingly, by an attempt to relate them to the use of force to counter aggression by the Security Council provided for in Chapter VII of the Charter. In fact, the peacekeeping forces I am about to describe are of a very different kind and have little in common with the forces foreseen in Chapter VII, but their existence is not in conflict with Chapter VII. They are essentially *peace* and not fighting forces and they operate only with the consent of the parties directly concerned.

In this context, it is worth noting that *all* of the permanent members of

UN Press Release SG/1520, June 12, 1963.

the Security Council have, at one time or another in the past fifteen years, voted in support of the creation of one or other of these forces, and that none of them has in any case gone further than to abstain from voting on them.

Since 1950, the United Nations has been called on to deal with a number of critical situations of varying urgency. The most urgent of these have been what are sometimes called "brush-fire wars," meaning, I take it, small conflagrations which, unless controlled, may all too easily ignite very much larger ones.

If we briefly look through the United Nations experience with this kind of operation, we can see that from small and informal beginnings a useful body of precedent and practice has grown up over the years of using military personnel of Member states on peacekeeping operations. In Greece in 1947, the United Nations Special Committee on the Balkans found that professional military officers were invaluable as an observer group in assessing the highly complicated and fluctuating situation. The Security Council itself set up an observer group of military officers in India and Pakistan to watch over the Kashmir question. This observer group, which was set up in 1948, is still operating.

A much larger use of military observers by the United Nations was made when, in July 1948, the first truce agreements in the Palestine war were supervised on the ground by some seven hundred United Nations military observers working under the United Nations mediator and the chief of staff. This team developed into the United Nations Truce Supervision Organization after the armistice agreements between Israel and her Arab neighbors were concluded in the period from February to July 1949.

This organization of officers from many countries still plays a vital role in keeping the peace in the Middle East and in reporting on and dealing with incidents which, though small in themselves, might all too easily become the cause of far larger disturbances if not dealt with. Its indefatigable members in their white jeeps are now a familiar and welcome part of the Middle Eastern landscape.

A peacekeeping organization of a different nature made its appearance as a result of the Suez crisis of October 1956. Confronted with a situation of the utmost urgency in which two of the permanent members of the Security Council were directly involved, the General Assembly voted for the urgent creation of a United Nations force. This was essentially *not* a force designed actively to fight against aggression.

It went to Egypt with the express consent of the Egyptian government and after the other parties concerned had agreed to a cease-fire. It was designed not to fight but rather to allow those involved to disengage without further disturbance. It allowed for the peaceful resolution of one of the most dangerous crises which had faced the world since the Second World War. It also, incidentally, allowed for the clearance by the United Nations of the Suez Canal, which had been blocked during the previous military action.

The United Nations Emergency Force in the Middle East has for six years watched over the borders of Israel with the United Arab Republic in the Gaza Strip and through the Sinai Desert. It also watches over the access to the Gulf of Aqaba and to the Israeli port of Elath. What was once a most troubled and terrorized frontier has become peaceful and prosperous on both sides, and the very presence of the United Nations Force is both an insurance against a resumption of trouble and a good excuse not to engage in it. It presents us with one serious problem. To maintain an army of over five thousand men costs money, but at present the parties concerned have no wish to see it removed.

In 1958 another very tense situation, with quite different origins, occurred in Lebanon. After the success of UNEF, there were suggestions in many quarters that another United Nations force should be collected and dispatched to that country. Here, however, the problem, though aggravated by external factors, was essentially a domestic one.

The Security Council therefore set up a three-man observer group and left the Secretary-General considerable latitude as to the methods to be employed to make this group effective in watching over the possibilities of infiltration from outside. A highly mobile group of six hundred officers was quickly organized to keep watch from ground and air, while the crisis itself was resolved by negotiation and discussion. By the end of 1958, it was possible to withdraw the United Nations observer group from the Lebanon altogether.

The greatest and most complex challenge to the United Nations in the peacekeeping field arose a few days after the Congo gained its independence from Belgium on June 30, 1960. The general proportions of this problem are sometimes obscured by a wealth of dramatic detail and are worth restating. Harassed by mutiny, lawlessness, and the collapse of public order and services from within, and afflicted by foreign military intervention as well as by ominous threats and other forms of interference from without, the new Government of the Congo appealed to the United Nations for help.

The Security Council committed the United Nations to respond to this appeal and thus made the Organization not only the guarantor of law and order and the protector of the Congo against external interference from any source, but also the adviser and helper of a newly independent state which had had virtually no preparation for its independence.

By filling, in the space of a few hours, the very dangerous vacuum which existed in the Congo in July 1960, the urgent danger of a confrontation of the great powers in the heart of Africa was avoided and the territorial integrity of the Congo preserved. The new leaders of the Congo have been given at least a short breathing-spell in which to find their feet. Despite its shortcomings, which must be judged in the light of the fearsome complexity of the problem, the United Nations operation in the Congo is, in my opinion, a most promising and encouraging experiment in international responsibility and action.

The blue helmets of the United Nations Force are known throughout the Congo as the symbol of security. Its soldiers have given protection at one time or another in the last three years to almost every Congolese public figure and almost every group, both African and non-African, when danger and violence threatened them. It is worth noting that, now that the withdrawal of the United Nations Force in the Congo is in sight, the deepest regret, and even alarm, is expressed by the very groups who used to be its most hostile critics and detractors.

In the Force, soldiers from other African countries work side by side in this vast tropical country with those from farther away. Their loyalty to the United Nations, their team spirit and comradeship have been an inspiration to all those who value the peacekeeping role of the United Nations.

I will end my catalogue with two more operations, one of which has already been successfully concluded, and which also involved an unprecedented role for the United Nations. I would like to refer first to the transfer of West Irian from Dutch rule, through a temporary period of United Nations executive authority, backed by a United Nations Security Force, to the administration of Indonesia. This entire operation has taken place with the agreement of the parties concerned, and in consultation with them.

The second is the dispatch to Yemen of an observer team as a basis for the disengagement of the United Arab Republic and Saudi Arabia from the affairs of Yemen. This operation will be paid for by the two parties concerned, and has been undertaken at their request and that of the Government of Yemen.

Although these are peace forces, service in them is hard and can be dangerous. In the Middle East, the United Nations has registered casualties not only from accidents and disease, but from mines. Both there and in West Irian, as also in Yemen, the terrain and the climate are inhospitable. In the Congo, we have had, unfortunately, serious casualties from unwanted fighting as well as from other causes, and I very much hope that we shall have no more.

I have only mentioned here the peacekeeping activities which have involved the use, in one way or another, of military personnel. If I were to mention the many other tense situations in which the United Nations, and my office in particular, have been used as a meeting-ground and as an instrument for mediation and peaceful settlement, the list would be much longer.

To sum up, we have now had experience of three major peacekeeping forces and a variety of military observer and truce supervisory operations. Each of the three forces has been different in composition, nature, and task, but they have shared certain common characteristics.

All three were improvised and called into the field at very short notice; all three were severely limited in their right to use force; all three were designed solely for the maintenance of peace and not for fighting in the military sense; all three were recruited from the smaller powers and with special reference to their acceptability in the area in which they were to serve; all three operated with the express consent and cooperation of the states or territories where they were stationed, as well as of any other parties directly concerned in the situation; and all three were under the direction and control of the Secretary-General acting on behalf of the organs of the United Nations.

These facts may now seem commonplace; it is a measure of the progress that has been made that even ten years ago they would have seemed very unusual.

By the standards of an efficient national military establishment, these forces have considerable disadvantages. Obviously, a force put together only after the emergency with which it is to deal is in full swing, will inevitably have some shortcomings. There is difficulty in recruiting at very short notice exactly the right kind of units for the work in hand, and in operating a force whose units and officers meet each other for the first time in the midst of a delicate operation. There are differences not only of language and tradition but of training, equipment, and staff procedures. There are differences in pay and emoluments which, if not handled carefully, can cause considerable problems of discipline and morale. Staff-work and command are especially difficult where every decision has important political implications.

Although these contingents from Member states are under the operational control of the United Nations, disciplinary powers are still vested in the national authorities and this could be, although in fact it never has been, the cause of very serious difficulties for the United Nations Force commander and for the Secretary-General.

The fact that the military establishments of the permanent members of the Security Council cannot be used cuts us off from the most obvious sources of equipment and personnel. The improvised nature of these operations also gives rise to various problems of logistics.

In our experience, these difficulties, which are inherent in the pioneering nature of these operations, have been offset by the enthusiastic cooperation of Member states and by the spirit and comprehension of the officers and men of the contingents which have made up the United Nations forces. It is an encouraging thought that in the military establishments of some thirty or more countries in the world there are now large numbers of officers and men who have served the United Nations with distinction in one or other of these operations and have added thereby a new dimension to their experience.

The improvised approach also makes it possible on each occasion to make up the United Nations force from the countries which are, politically and in other ways, most suitable for the operation in hand, and at least the United Nations is not afflicted with the age-old problem of having on its hands a standing army with nothing to do.

In my opinion, a permanent United Nations force is not a practical proposition at the present time. I know that many serious people in many countries are enthusiastic about the idea, and I welcome their enthusiasm and the thought they are putting into the evolution of the institution which will eventually and surely emerge. Many difficulties still stand in the way of its evolution.

Personally, I have no doubt that the world should eventually have an international police force which will be accepted as an integral and essential part of life in the same way as national police forces are accepted. Meanwhile, we must be sure that developments are in the right direction and that we can also meet critical situations as and when they occur.

There are a number of reasons why it seems to me that the establishment of a permanent United Nations force would be premature at the present time. I doubt whether many governments in the world would yet be prepared to accept the political implications of such an institution and, in the light of our current experience with financial problems, I am sure that they would have very serious difficulties in accepting the financial implications.

I believe that we need a number of parallel developments before we can evolve such an institution. We have to go further along the road of codification and acceptance of a workable body of international law. We have to develop a more sophisticated public opinion in the world, which can accept the transition from predominantly national thinking to international thinking.

We shall have to develop a deeper faith in international institutions as such, and a greater confidence in the possibility of a United Nations civil service whose international loyalty and objectivity are generally accepted and above suspicion. We shall have to improve the method of financing international organization. Until these conditions are met, a permanent United Nations force may not be a practical proposition.

But we have already shown that, when the situation demands it, it is possible to use the soldiers of many countries for objectives which are not national ones and that the soldiers respond magnificently to this new challenge. We have also seen that, when the situation is serious enough, governments are prepared to waive certain of the attributes of national sovereignty in the interest of keeping the peace through the United Nations. We have demonstrated that a loyalty to international service can exist side by side with legitimate national pride.

And, perhaps most important of all, we have shown that there *can* be a practical alternative to the deadly ultimate struggle and that it is an alternative which brings out the good and generous qualities in men rather than their destructive and selfish qualities.

Although it is perhaps too early, for the reasons I have already given, to consider the establishment of a permanent United Nations force, I believe there are a number of measures which could be taken even now to improve on our present capacity for meeting dangerous situations. It would be extremely desirable, for example, if countries would, in their national military planning, make provision for suitable units which could be made available at short notice for United Nations service and thereby decrease the degree of improvisation necessary in an emergency.

I take this opportunity publicly to welcome and express my appreciation for the efforts of the Scandinavian countries in this direction. Denmark, Norway, and Sweden have for some time now engaged in joint planning of a stand-by force comprising various essential components to be put at the disposal of the United Nations when necessary. It would be a very welcome development if other countries would consider following the lead of the Scandinavian countries in this matter.

At present, the activities of the United Nations are overshadowed by a very serious financial crisis, a crisis which stems directly from the costs of the special peacekeeping operations in the Middle East and the Congo and from the failure of some Members to pay their assessments for those operations. Although the sums of money involved are small in comparison to the sums spent by many countries on military budgets, they do, nonetheless, present a very serious financial and political challenge to the stability of the United Nations.

The United Nations is the sum of all its Members and, to develop in the right direction, it must maintain this global character. On the other hand, I am convinced that the Organization must maintain and develop its active role in keeping the peace. I therefore view with the gravest concern the prolongation of the financial crisis of the United Nations with its very serious political overtones, and I trust that we may see a solution of the problem before too long.

I am concerned at this financial crisis more particularly because I see, in the long run, no acceptable alternative method of keeping peace in the world to the steady and sound development of the peacekeeping functions of the United Nations. It is no longer possible to think rationally in terms of countering aggression or keeping the peace by the use of the ultimate weapons.

However improvised and fumbling the United Nations approach may be, we have to develop it to deal with the sudden antagonisms and dangers of our world, until we can evolve more permanent institutions. There has been already a great advance in the world toward cooperation, mutual responsibility, and common interest. I have described some of the pioneering cooperative efforts made by the United Nations to keep the peace.

I believe that these efforts constitute vital steps toward a more mature, more acceptable, and more balanced world order. We must have the confidence and the means to sustain them and the determination to develop out of them a reliable and workable system for the future.

I am a firm believer in the organic development of institutions. I also firmly believe that, if the United Nations is to justify the hopes of its founders and of the peoples of the world, it must develop into an active and effective agency for peace and international conciliation by responding to the challenges which face it. May we have the courage, the faith, and the wisdom to make it so.

From Transcript of Press Conference

NEW YORK   JUNE 28, 1963

IN HIS PRESS CONFERENCE of June 28, 1963, U Thant noted what he called "unmistakable trends toward new alignments in the world set-up." He expressed the belief that before the end of the 1970s there would be four big powers instead of the two which had dominated the world since the Second World War. The two new ones, he said, would be China and a united Europe. He made these additional elaborations in response to questions: he did not believe major countries such as mainland China and Germany would still be outside the United Nations in the 1970s; Britain would continue to perform "very important functions" in the world structure either independently or as a component of a unified Europe; African countries had reasserted their desire for African unity at the Addis Ababa Summit Conference, but their role in the next decade was "difficult to anticipate." These new trends, he said, were something for world leaders to think about in their future planning.

. . . . QUESTION: Concerning the peacekeeping operations in Yemen, are they proceeding at a satisfactory pace and do you anticipate any future difficulties over that financing when the two months mentioned will be up?

THE SECRETARY-GENERAL: At present the UN operations in Yemen have been going on smoothly. As you all know, an advance party led by General von Horn is already there. They established headquarters with effect from June 13 and they have even been doing certain reconnaissance and observation duties. The main body of the reconnaissance party, comprising Yugoslavs, are en route. They are expected to be in Yemen perhaps in the next couple of days. And as you all know, the Canadians are also joining the reconnaissance team about the same time. As anticipated, the total strength of the Yemen observation team will be approximately two hundred, as I have reported to the Security Council. So for the purpose of calculation of the term "two months," I feel that it will be appro-

UN Note to Correspondents No. 2773.

priate to calculate the commencement of the term with effect from the date when the main reconnaissance party establishes headquarters inside Yemen.

QUESTION: Mr. Secretary-General, are you concerned about the possibility of a limited arrangement to be concluded in Moscow next month in the British-United States-Russian talks, possibly including some new international commission outside the framework of the United Nations?

THE SECRETARY-GENERAL: From all available accounts, I regret to have to say that I am not very hopeful about the outcome of the projected three-power conference in Moscow next month. In the context of the present attitudes, I very much doubt that a test-ban treaty will be concluded this year, although of course the public announcements by atomic powers that they will not explode an atomic or hydrogen bomb, provided others do not explode one, is a very encouraging development. My feeling is that the big powers have, in a way, missed the bus in the Geneva negotiations.

QUESTION: Mr. Secretary-General, it is generally recognized that communist China will soon explode nuclear weapons, thus bringing it into the nuclear club. Is there anything that can be done to anticipate this crisis, as it will be then among the nuclear powers?

THE SECRETARY-GENERAL: Yes, it will be very difficult, if not impossible, to prevent China from exploding an atomic bomb, possibly this year, and probably next year. On this, I want to make a very brief observation. If my reading of modern history is correct, there are certain unmistakable trends toward new alignments in the world set-up. As you will recall, there have been fluctuations and vicissitudes in the fortunes of the big powers. For instance, in the 1920s and 1930s Britannia ruled the waves, and in the 1930s Hitler's Germany dominated the world scene. After the Second World War, and particularly in the 1950s, two big powers emerged, the United States of America and the Soviet Union. In the early 1960s, that is, for the last two and a half years, those two powers still retained their preeminent position.

My feeling is that in the 1970s, if there are 1970s, the world will witness four big powers—the United States of America, Europe, Russia, and China. I am convinced that it will be the path of wisdom for world leaders to take these considerations into account in their formulation of foreign policies.

QUESTION: In your very important Harvard speech on the United Nations stand-by peace force you stated: "There has been a tacit transition from the concept of collective security, as set out in Chapter VII of the

United Nations Charter, to a more realistic idea of peacekeeping. The idea that conventional military methods—or, to put it bluntly, war—can be used by or on behalf of the United Nations to counter aggression and secure the peace, seems now to be rather impracticable" (p. 354).

Would you say that in fact the concept of a United Nations fighting force composed of great power units, as envisaged in Chapter VII of the United Nations Charter, has been overtaken and outmoded by events, that is, by the development of the ultimate nuclear weapon, and, further, that there is no acceptable alternative method of keeping peace in the world to the steady development of the peacekeeping operations in the direction of an international police force that could hold the line until the United Nations methods of mediation and conciliation had resolved the issue?

THE SECRETARY-GENERAL: Yes, I hold to these views strongly, and you will no doubt agree with me that the original framers of the Charter had made certain assumptions, which did not prove to be true. I think it is utterly impracticable for the United Nations to perform the functions of a peacekeeping organization, if the atomic powers themselves are involved in such an operation. That means, in effect, that the United Nations cannot overawe the nuclear powers. I think that is an accepted fact. What the United Nations can do, and should do, is to prevent brush-fire wars, which, of course, have the potentialities of exploding into wider conflagrations and, thereby, bringing a direct confrontation between the big powers. As the situation exists at the moment, United Nations activities are bound by very severe restrictions and limitations, and the United Nations functions in the performance of peacekeeping activities do not conform to the aspirations of those who framed the Charter. I think we have to take this into consideration.

QUESTION: Mr. Secretary-General, I should like to ask you a question on the Buddhist issue in South Vietnam. As you well know, about 95 per cent of the Vietnamese population is Buddhist and they are discriminated against by a minority of about 3 to 4 percent of Roman Catholics, who now control the entire South Vietnamese government. I understand that Ambassador Malalasekera of Ceylon, who is a former Vice-President of the World Buddhist Federation, has received instructions from his government to bring the matter before the United Nations. Also, you have received a telegram from Norodom Sihanouk of Cambodia on the same matter. Would you care to tell us what you think could be done by the

United Nations since South Vietnam is not a member of the United Nations?

THE SECRETARY-GENERAL: It is true that I received a number of communications from many organizations all over the world, and also communications from more than one Member state, drawing my attention to the alleged religious persecution in the Republic of Vietnam, requesting me to use my good offices to bring about a peaceful settlement of the crisis and to remedy the grievances.

As you know, there are very serious limitations to any exercise of the Secretary-General's initiative in such a situation. I have taken certain steps, very discreetly, to see that this alleged discrimination against the Buddhists is remedied.

I want to stress, once again, my attitude toward such problems. As you all know, I am a very staunch advocate of religious tolerance. Although I am a Buddhist, I have a very high esteem and respect for the very noble ethical aspects of many other religions—of course, apart from the formal and ritualistic aspects of religions. I say this not as the Secretary-General of the United Nations nor as a Buddhist. My feeling is that, if the legitimate grievances of the Buddhists in the Republic of Vietnam are not redressed in time, there are possibilities of repercussions in many other areas of Asia, particularly where, so far, Buddhists and Catholics have been living in complete amity. Of course, nobody would like to see a repetition of such incidents in other areas of the world. Therefore, I want to take this opportunity of appealing to President Diem to exercise tolerance and to settle the matter in the name of peace, justice, and fair play.

QUESTION: Mr. Secretary-General, in your short term of service, the United Nations has undertaken two major peacekeeping operations—in West Irian and Yemen—with the agreement of the parties concerned. Am I right in assuming that one more is anticipated in North Borneo? Would you care to state under what circumstances the Secretary-General requires affirmative action by the Security Council and the General Assembly when he is asked for peacekeeping assistance by the parties concerned and there is no financial commitment by the United Nations?

THE SECRETARY-GENERAL: In the two previous instances, namely, the United Nations involvement in West Irian and the United Nations involvement in Yemen, two different procedures were adopted. In the case of West Irian, the parties directly concerned came to an agreement on certain lines of action, and this agreement was placed before the General

Assembly, which took note of this agreement. I proceeded with the implementation of the agreement on the understanding that the parties directly concerned were to share the expenses equally. So the operation was concluded very smoothly.

In the case of Yemen, as you know, the Security Council was involved, but even in that particular instance the parties directly concerned agreed to share the expenses. So there are no hard and fast rules governing the United Nations involvement in such situations, provided that the parties directly concerned agree to share the expenses and provided that the United Nations has no financial commitments and involvements.

QUESTION: Would you like to comment on the Manila agreement reached by the foreign ministers of Indonesia, the Philippines, and Malaya, and, further, on your role as agreed by the foreign ministers to mediate in the exercise of the rights of self-determination of the British North Borneo people?

THE SECRETARY-GENERAL: Since the beginning of the idea of Malaysia, I have taken an interest in the developments in that particular area, and I sent my chef de cabinet, Mr. Narasimhan, twice to the area to explore the possibilities of a peaceful solution of the problem in the context of the attitudes held by the three governments—the governments of Indonesia, the Philippines, and the Federation of Malaya. Last week, I received a copy of the report and recommendations of the conference of foreign ministers of the Federation of Malaya, the Republic of Indonesia, and the Republic of the Philippines held in Manila between June 7 and June 11. In the report it was stated:

The ministers reaffirmed their countries' adherence to the principle of self-determination for the peoples of non-self-governing territories. In this context, Indonesia and the Philippines stated that they would welcome the formation of Malaysia, provided the support of the people of the Borneo territories is ascertained by an independent and impartial authority—the Secretary-General of the United Nations or his representative. The Federation of Malaya expressed appreciation for this attitude of Indonesia and the Philippines, and undertook to consult the British government and the governments of Borneo territories, with a view to inviting the Secretary-General of the United Nations or his representative to take the necessary steps in order to ascertain the wishes of the people of those territories.

Thus, it is clear that some kind of United Nations role is contemplated by the three governments, but I am still awaiting an official approach, which I am told may be expected only after the meeting at the level of heads of government, which is expected to take place before the end of July.

QUESTION: Mr. Secretary-General, what you said today about the prospects for a test-ban treaty and big-power relations in a way differed sharply from other opinions which you held on the possibilities of a test ban treaty when the outward circumstances did not seem better than today. May I ask you two questions in this regard? What has made you take such a dim view right now? And what role for the United Nations do you consider when these four big powers should emerge, particularly in view of the fact that one of these powers, China, is not represented here and one major part of the other power of Europe, namely Germany, is not a member of the United Nations?

THE SECRETARY-GENERAL: As to your first question, I want to make it clear that I am essentially an optimist regarding the conclusion of a test-ban treaty. What I said a few moments ago was that I am not very hopeful of the conclusion of a test-ban treaty as a result of the projected three-power meeting in Moscow next month. What I want to stress is this: there is no immediate prospect of the conclusion of a test-ban treaty—although, of course, if the political and psychological climate is more congenial to the conduct of negotiations, success will be in sight.

Regarding your second question, as to my anticipation of the emergence of four powers in the seventies, it is, of course, too early now to anticipate the prospective United Nations role in such an eventuality, particularly in view of the exclusion of some of the important powers from United Nations membership at present. But I do not believe that by that time—in the seventies, for instance—that problem will exist.

. . . . QUESTION: If I understood you correctly a few minutes ago, you anticipated that, by 1970, there would be four major powers, and you included Europe as one of them. Is it your assumption that Europe will be united at that time? That is my first question.

Secondly, in the light of the alignments in Africa and the possibilities of unification in Africa, do you care to comment on Africa's status at that time?

THE SECRETARY-GENERAL: Of course, these are concerned with a hypothetical situation. I have no means of knowing or anticipating whether Europe in the 1970s will be united. Perhaps Britain will be a component unit of that Europe in the 1970s, or perhaps it will not.

As for Britain, of course my feelings are well known. Although it may or may not be a great power in the strict military sense, it has an extraordinary maturity, which I very much respect, and it will continue to perform very important functions in the world set-up, particularly after it has been shorn of all colonial ties.

Regarding the position of the African states, we witnessed one very heartening economic development a few weeks ago. I am referring to the African summit conference, which took place in Addis Ababa. As you know, His Imperial Majesty, the Emperor of Ethiopia, invited me to attend the conference as an observer, and I accepted the invitation. I was looking forward to this meeting but, unfortunately, I developed a toothache and, on the advice of my dentist, I had to cancel my projected visit. I can assure you that it was not a diplomatic toothache, and I am sure that our African friends realize this.

One of the encouraging aspects of the African summit conference was the publication of a declaration which, in my view, is historic—as historic as the Bandung Declaration of 1955. The heads of state of the African countries reasserted their desire for African unity and African solidarity and, more important, African interdependence. What struck me particularly was the moderate tone of the declaration, and the positive approach to the problems which they are facing today. Of course, it is difficult to anticipate the role which African countries will play in the next ten years or so.

QUESTION: Going back to your comment a few moments ago about the foreign ministers' meeting in regard to Malaysia, it is not quite clear to me whether, if the United Nations were to conduct a plebiscite or referendum among the Borneo territories that have been proposed as part of Malaysia, it would be necessary for the General Assembly, or possibly the Security Council, to take some action to approve—in other words, to enable the United Nations to conduct such a referendum.

My other question, relating to the same subject, is this. Is it possible that you will send a representative to the heads of government meeting which, you say, will be held sometime during July?

THE SECRETARY-GENERAL: Regarding your first question, if the three governments directly concerned ask me to conduct a plebiscite in the areas, to ascertain the wishes of the people, I am sure that a clear mandate from a competent organ of the United Nations will be necessary.

As to your second question, concerning the possibility and advisability of my sending a personal representative to the projected summit meeting to be held before the end of July, the matter is still under discussion with the governments concerned.

.... QUESTION: Sir, can you give us your evaluation of the response of the various Member states to the floating of the United Nations bonds? And secondly, in view of the declared intention of certain countries not to subscribe to the bonds, or even to pay for the interest on the principal, do you intend to propose any stand-by measures to arrest the financial situation? Do you propose to place before the General Assembly any stand-by measures to deal with the situation? In other words, would you be prepared to ask for an extension of your mandate to continue floating the bonds?

THE SECRETARY-GENERAL: For the moment I do not propose to ask for an extension of the period of the sale of bonds beyond December 1963. Of course I shall have to report to the General Assembly on the financial situation as usual. The budget, as you know, is under preparation. The budget estimates for 1964 are before the advisory committee. I appeared before the advisory committee last week, and explained to the committee the general policy underlying the preparation of the budget, which is one of consolidation and containment, if I may say so. But regarding the possibility or advisability of extending the period of the sale of bonds, I have not given this sufficient thought for the moment. I think it is up to the Members of the General Assembly to take any action they deem fit to take in the forthcoming regular session of the General Assembly.

QUESTION: Mr. Secretary-General, do you contemplate any further changes among your top executive staff, and do you foresee any change in the way you work with them from the way you have described in the past, changes in terms of special advisers or a cabinet concept?

THE SECRETARY-GENERAL: I do not propose to effect any change in either the personnel or the functions of the under-secretaries for the moment. About the method of operation for the procedures of consultation, I made this clear in my speech on November 30, when I was appointed Secretary-General of the United Nations.

QUESTION: Mr. Secretary-General, can the United Nations expect to take effective action in a serious crisis in the future, such as that of the Congo, as long as two of the permanent members of the Security Council refuse to recognize their financial obligations to the Organization?

THE SECRETARY-GENERAL: It is certainly difficult, of course, for the United Nations to launch any major peacekeeping operations on similar lines as the one in the Congo, if two permanent members of the Security Council have different views regarding the allocation of financial responsibility for such operations. But I hope very much that a satisfactory formula can be worked out before too long. . . .

Address on Science and Technology before the Economic and Social Council

GENEVA   JULY 8, 1963

THE UNITED NATIONS CONFERENCE on the Application of Science and Technology for the Benefit of the Less-Developed Areas was held in Geneva, from February 4 through February 20, 1963. This conference, attended by some 1,600 persons, was designed to focus attention on the practical possibilities of speeding up development through the use of modern scientific and technological methods. U Thant was unable to attend the Geneva meeting, but sent a message endorsing its goals and stressing the need to maintain the momentum generated by the discussions. He followed through with an address before the Economic and Social Council on July 8. Since the conference had not been empowered to make recommendations, the Secretary-General decided to make his own after studying the conference proceedings and conferring with key conference officials in New York. His proposals to the Economic and Social Council included action to assist in the establishment of national research facilities in the developing countries, or possibly regional centers, and the allocation of more resources in the advanced countries to science and technology for the benefit of the less-developed areas. He suggested that international organizations devote a larger portion of their budgets to this field.

THE UNITED NATIONS Development Decade could be a phrase conceived in hope, but destined only to lead to a cycle of debates, resolutions, and reports; or, it could be a period of action that improves the lot of the general run of mankind to a greater extent than during any comparable period. I know that all of us want it to be the latter. All representatives of governments here today, and all other persons, wherever they may be, who understand the gravity of the issues that are posed by the widening of the gap between the rich and the poor nations, undoubtedly hope that the will and the means can be found to meet the great challenge which was laid down by the General Assembly in its resolution on the United Nations Development Decade.

UN Press Release SG/1536. The summary record is given in Economic and Social Council Official Records, Thirty-sixth Session, 1271st meeting.

In one section of that resolution 1710 (XVI), the Secretary-General was requested to develop proposals for "the intensification of research and demonstration as well as other efforts to exploit scientific and technological potentialities of high promise for accelerating economic and social development."

Let me illustrate what this could mean, and its relationship to international cooperation. Suppose that the world had a way of producing electric energy, economically and safely, in any village, by means of small generating units utilizing power from the sun or from any other source. When this technological point is reached, a demand would arise for several millions of dollars of capital aid, for the purpose of locating such an energy unit in every village. Additional demands for capital would soon also arise from the impetus that the wider availability of electric power would give to economic development and, especially, to industrialization. Training courses would be urgently required for the persons who would operate and maintain these units once they were installed. Here, we are again reminded that the development of human resources, surely the true aim of technological advance, is also an essential condition for it.

But it is not just a question of being put in a position of needing *more* capital and *more* training. Once the new technological device is ready for adoption, capital can be embodied in more useful forms and training courses can become more useful than before. By the same token, earlier programs of capital and technical aid may become superseded. National development plans, too, may need revision; as also economic projections.

I have purposely chosen an unusually dramatic example. Most technological advances, however, are relatively small—a slight improvement in a plow, a machine that reduces the amount of heavy manual work in a factory, a new cost-saving way of managing an operation or organizing the layout of work. Thus, even while we recognize the cumulative effect of the many smaller improvements in techniques that can undoubtedly be made in every field, we must also be prepared for the revolutionary impact to be expected from some of the larger breakthroughs. If we are to realize the aims of the Development Decade, we have a job to do that will not be easy. Therefore, to strengthen our resolution, let us proclaim in a high, rather than a low key, the inspiring possibilities. Technology can be the most powerful force in the world for raising living standards, and our task is to harness it for that purpose.

You have before you in documents E/3772 and Add. 1 a summary report of the United Nations Conference on the Application of Science and Technology for the Benefit of the Less-Developed Areas. An account of the genesis, preparation, and organization of the conference appears in the main report. One aspect to which I wish to call special attention was the extremely solid and valuable support which was given from the beginning by the entire United Nations family of agencies. The cooperation of our colleagues from ILO, FAO, UNESCO, WHO, ITU, WMO, and IAEA was outstanding, both in arranging for the conference and in contributing to the substance of it, and we return sincere thanks to them.

The body of the main report, largely made up of short summations of the written and oral discussions in the twelve major subject sections of the conference, draws heavily on a report which was submitted to me by the conference secretary-general. A wider range of inquiry would be hard to imagine. Map-making, preferably by photogrammetry, was stressed as being often a needed first step for developing countries. The implications of rising population pressure were debated; thus, the prospect was noted of arable land per head of population falling, by the year 2000, to roughly half an acre, as against 1.18 acres in 1959, and the need was recognized for strenuous efforts to conserve water. Some attention was given to the resources of the seas, especially to fisheries and other food possibilities, and to demineralization to help relieve water shortages. If I may digress at this point, could it not be envisaged that our scientific knowledge would some day reach a point where it would be possible to launch a comprehensive, cooperative project to develop the varied and almost unlimited resources of the seas for the benefit of all mankind?

Some other questions taken up were: the challenge to devise processes and plants for the heavy chemical industry that will reduce the minimum size of economic operations below the level in the advanced countries; and the somewhat contrasting situation in the iron and steel industry, where relatively small plants can already be built and operated economically, requiring in general only the transfer of known technology from the advanced to the developing countries. This list could be very much extended and still not begin to reflect the breadth of the discussions—let alone, of course, their specific content and depth. Indeed, the whole report should be read as merely a brief introduction to the substance of the work of the conference. However, in an eight-volume report, which is expected to be available in printed form by the year's end, an attempt will be made to provide a definitive account of the written and oral proceedings, readably presented and reasonably priced to commend it for wide perusal and use. In addition, the papers that were contributed to the general and the specialized sessions, as well as the reports of the conference secretary-general on the individual sessions and the reports of the rapporteurs, will continue to be available in their original form.

Our objectives are practical ones. The conference was intended to have a practical effect. The participants in the conference having ably discharged their function, it remains not merely to preserve an accurate record of the information they brought, and the views they contributed, but also to follow up. Certain steps have already been taken with the aim of determining what the follow-up action should be. On this question, I have had the benefit of consultations, both at the government level and in the Administrative Committee on Coordination, and my views are summarized in part three of the report which is before you. I solicit your consideration of those views. They are in no sense final, but they do indicate, I feel, the direction in which a start should be made.

Today, I think you would wish me to speak only of the main considerations, which I believe are three. First, it is necessary to build centers of scientific and technological strength in the less-developed countries. Second, it is necessary to focus more resources, in the advanced countries, on science and technology for the benefit of the less-developed countries. Third, it is necessary to make a judicious assessment of priorities.

Under "centers of strength" I include several different things, which are all vital if science and technology are to strike roots in the soil of the less-developed world—roots without which they cannot be expected to grow. Science and technology cannot be exported or "pushed" out from their habitat in the advanced countries; they have to be imported or "pulled" in by the developing countries themselves, when and as the most forward-looking and qualified people of those countries feel the need, and are able to define it.

Every developing nation undoubtedly requires its own scientific and technological "establishment." The heart of an establishment is people. There is no country that does not need at least a minimum number of its own highly trained scientists, to help assure its intellectual independence and dynamism. Moreover, the developing countries need to expand very rapidly the numbers of their middle-level technicians. We thus come back to the problem of finding practical ways to accelerate education and training. UNESCO, of course, has considerable interest where basic science is involved, while the ILO, the United Nations itself and all the agencies of the United Nations family are concerned with various aspects of technology. Apart from training, Member governments should also keep in mind the crucial question of incentives. Middle-level careers, essential for national development, are today too often regarded as unrewarding for the individual.

An establishment will also include institutions and resources. Each developing country needs laboratories and other research facilities. It also requires some organization, such as a national science council or research council, to help guide research and formulate policy. Working closely with the government's national planning body, that organization can ensure that the importance of promoting scientific advance is not overlooked or underestimated when the plan is drawn up, and it can also reduce the risk that the plan may allocate scarce resources, without first taking foreseeable technological changes into account.

Research facilities are as necessary to the developing countries as facilities for training, with which they can often be advantageously combined in a local university. I hope that research facilities in the advanced countries will be placed more and more at the disposal of the developing countries. However, it is also essential to establish more adequate and better oriented as well as more numerous research institutions in the developing countries themselves, as was, for certain purposes, suggested by the United Nations Conference on New Sources of Energy two years ago. These then should be linked up with research institutions in the advanced countries, so that there may be a continuous exchange of knowledge and of scientific staff.

There is urgent need for such research facilities in the developing countries. Some problems can only be properly investigated in the underdeveloped world—for example, problems connected with diseases or with plant life peculiar to the tropics. Other problems can be studied in the advanced countries up to a point, but the final stages of research and the pilot operations should be carried out close to where the results are to be applied, so as to assure successful adaptation. Consequently, and because research institutions can become centers of great strength for the developing countries, I believe that we have here a subject for emphasis in the programs of the United Nations family of organizations in the immediate future. The Special Fund has had useful experience in this field already, and could logically serve as a main support for a broader attack on the problem if it were to be provided with adequate resources.

Not all of these research institutions should necessarily be conceived of as national institutions; some might advantageously be established on a regional, or even an interregional, basis. This is obvious where the problems are common to all humid regions in the tropics, or to all arid regions; but it may apply, too, to some other investigations. Multinational research institutions should make it possible to economize on skilled manpower and financial resources, encourage wider use of the findings, and especially benefit small countries unable to proceed with the research on their own. Such regional and interregional research institutions should, in my view, be linked, in some appropriate way, with the United Nations regional economic commissions, directly or through the three newly created development planning institutes.

The second essential is to focus more resources in the advanced countries on science and technology for the benefit of the less-developed countries. The purposes of the Development Decade require the deep involvement of the energies and assets of the less-developed countries themselves, and also a substantially increased transfer of resources to those countries, by way of additional cooperation from the advanced countries, many of which have already been extremely generous in their cooperation. But, when we count not only the cost of developing the applicable new methods—and preparing the people to receive them—but also the cost of the new equipment with which to carry the new methods into practical effect throughout the underdeveloped areas, the total resources required will certainly be large. In other words, the application of science and technology in the poorer countries will be an expensive operation. No useful purpose would be served by disguising that fact.

It is not a question of money alone. The scientific community will have to become much more deeply involved in the whole development effort, both individually and through its scientific organizations. Many scientists have already left their ivory towers to engage in practical activities, but the institutional means through which they can serve the cause of the development of the less-developed areas have not been perfected, and their actual involvement in such work is still rather marginal. Fortunately, some of the best scientists and technologists are now being associated with the work of the United Nations and its related agencies, as members of advisory committees and panels. This kind of arrangement has proved very useful to us, and I hope it has been mutually profitable. In this context, I would like to acknowledge with gratitude the assistance rendered to me by the United Nations Scientific Advisory Committee, as also the help rendered by the scientific advisory panel in connection with the organization of the conference. However, still more needs to be done along these lines.

Let me revert now to material and financial resources. In a seriously undertaken program of international cooperation for bringing the benefits of science and modern technology to those who do not yet share in those benefits, the rewards will be great, but so also must be the input of resources. Otherwise, as the Council cannot but be aware, the nations whose representatives voted for the resolution on the United Nations Development Decade—as all did—will have sown fine words and reaped a harvest of very meager results.

To say that the United Nations and its related agencies should be enabled to dispose of some part of the necessary additional resources is surely no radical doctrine. As I have mentioned already, it would seem entirely reasonable to seek ways of channelling larger resources in this endeavor through the Special Fund and the expanded program of technical assistance. It would, however, seem to me desirable that a larger portion of the budgets of certain of the international organizations should be devoted to this field and, furthermore, that the budgets themselves should be strengthened, so as to enable these organizations to play their part on an expanded basis more nearly in consonance with the need. As far as the United Nations itself is concerned, it would be proper to enlarge the provision for those of its activities as are most directly related to industrial and other technology. If I am not proposing this immediately, except to the limited extent that it may be possible to make internal adjustments within our present means, it is only because of the overriding financial crisis of the United Nations, of which you are fully aware.

At the same time, I would emphasize that an important part of the role of the United Nations family must be the catalytic role. It will be necessary to keep the possibilities for useful further action under continuing and detailed review—but often try to get others to take that action. The major contribution of resources must be looked for, at present, from bilateral arrangements; this includes private action—by foundations, industries, and so on—as well as public action. One instrument is, of course, the bilateral aid programs as such. Another might be a whole array of going programs not tied to the aid programs in any formal sense. For example, a practice of devoting special attention to the technological problems of the developing countries, or of a particular developing country, might spread among the agricultural colleges and their associated research laboratories and experiment stations in the advanced countries. Much benefit could result from this. The same applies to teachers' colleges, public health organizations, and other centers of technical knowledge and skill, so numerous in the advanced countries.

It may also be that the research and development programs to which some Member governments are devoting large financial resources could be of help. Within them, there may be certain activities that could, without any detriment to the work for which they have been authorized, yield also the answers to certain technical problems confronting the less-developed countries. The concept of an accidental by-product benefit to civilians from defense or space research, sometimes referred to as the spillover effect, is already familiar. Conceivably, if thought were to be given to the matter, there could be some effort consciously to seek concurrent joint-product effects that would help to accelerate development in the less-developed countries. I would hope that some Member governments might wish to examine their research and development program from this new point of view.

To call assessment of priorities the third essential is not to suggest that the technological needs of the less-developed countries are confined to any one sector or area. In fact, technological improvement is coextensive with the development process itself—almost if not quite the essence of it. That is a major reason why it would not seen practicable to establish a new United Nations agency for science and technology. All the agencies have tasks to perform in this field, which they are especially well equipped to perform, and the best assurance of a vigorous, unified, and consistent effort lies in intensifying their individual action, while at the same time perfecting the cooperation among them, and seeing that any gaps are closed, through the mechanism of the Administrative Committee on Coordination. Steps have in fact now been taken to establish a sub-committee on science and technology of the ACC, to which reference is made in the ACC's report to the Council as well as in my own report. But obviously, within each field of activity, resources would be spread too thin if no decisions were taken on priorities and points of concentration.

Our Department of Economic and Social Affairs has started to review its varied work programs at Headquarters and in the regions, from the point of view of the scientific and technological issue. The largest and most important single concentration point for the department, undoubtedly, is the technological work directly related to industrialization and natural resources—water, energy, minerals. Cartography goes with it, and transport must also be added. What is needed might in part be achieved by substantially accelerating the program of building up technological institutes to which I have already referred. We are also now beginning to make some headway, through our center for industrial development and our resources and transport branch, in assembling a body of engineering and industrial economic skills which can be made available on request in such areas as manufacturing, mining, power, roads, railways, and water. We plan to continue to develop, on our staff and within our auxiliary services, such a corps of engineers and related technical experts. For example, it may be possible to regularize the establishment of panels of individuals willing and able to serve from time to time on suitable assignments, and also to enter into agreements with institutions and firms under which they will furnish us with qualified personnel for such assignments at our request.

Other parts of our work have their concentration points, too, for the application of science and technology. In housing construction, new techniques to reduce costs are greatly needed. Community development work has an important part to play in transfer and adaptation at the grass-roots levels, as distinct from the level of the university, laboratory, or experiment station in the developing country itself. The techniques of training in public administration and of development planning may also be mentioned as illustrations.

Finally, in widest perspective and with a view to invigorating the whole follow-up to the conference, I suggest that there might be established an agreed special list of new inventions, adaptations, or cost reductions, each having a potential developmental effect of extraordinary dimensions, directly or through its ultimate repercussions. The automobile was clearly an invention in that class for the Western world. Would a new kind of car or truck, tailored in price, durability, and other specifications to what developing countries can afford, qualify for a place on such a list? Certainly, better roads, more mechanical-mindedness, and many other desirable things might follow almost automatically once such a vehicle came into general use. Would the small energy unit to which I referred earlier be another example? Would economical desalinization plants for areas short of fresh water be another? Would the mass application of certain new teaching aids and techniques, such as a system for using radio and television for greatly accelerating all kinds of education and training, be yet another? In the field of physical or mental health, would there be some particular piece of technical research that should go on even a short list of this kind?

These questions cannot be answered today, but further study of relative needs, on the one hand, and of the feasibility of achieving a breakthrough in the different areas of need, on the other, might yield some answers, with experts from the less-developed countries playing an active part in advising both on needs, in the larger sense, and on technical specifications. The final stages of research and field testing would also, in each case, be carried out in one or more of the less-developed countries, with the help, for example, of a regional or interregional research institution, so as to assure acceptability of the product in the actual location where it was to be used. Thus, transfer and adaptation would be a built-in, integral part of the technical solution itself. It is my belief that, in addition to bilateral governmental and United Nations resources, it will be possible to obtain the support of foundations and similar private institutions to bring designated special priority research tasks to a successful conclusion. For my part, I would certainly be willing to lend my full support to seeking such additional assistance.

May I in conclusion offer certain suggestions to the Council, as regards action it may wish to consider taking at this session for following up the conference on science and technology.

First, it would be useful if the Council's discussion could indicate how much importance the Council itself attaches to scientific and technological work—its place among the services that the United Nations and the related agencies can and should render during the Development Decade.

Second, the Council's guidance would be appreciated with regard to any of the specific program suggestions I have advanced, particularly the research institutions in the less-developed areas and the recruitment of stand-by auxiliaries to perform missions in industrial and other appropriate technical fields.

Third, the Council's help is needed in finding the best ways of securing for the United Nations and the related agencies such additional resources for scientific and technological work as may appear to the Council to be necessary.

Fourth, it has been suggested, in my report and in the report of the ACC, that the Council may wish to establish an advisory committee on science and technology. Suggestions were also included on how, if that were the case, the committee might be constituted and how it might report to the Council, with a view to achieving the closest possible relationship with the work of all the international agencies concerned. Decisions in relation to the need for such an advisory committee appear to be in order.

Should the Council decide to establish an advisory committee in this field, that committee could clearly play an important part. For example, if the concept of a list of especially important research items finds favor, then the drawing up of such a list will have to be taken in hand. Again, if the Council considers that regional and interregional institutions, as well as national ones, need to be established and strengthened in the less developed areas, then it would be logical to draw up a scheme for an effective and reasonably complete network of such institutions for the less developed world as a whole, and a phased plan for bringing them into operation. Arrangements for examining these or other matters, and preparing recommendations on them, could no doubt be worked out by the Council's committee, in conjunction with the United Nations Scientific Advisory Committee and the principal scientific and technological committees of the specialized and related agencies.

The United Nations Conference on the Application of Science and Technology for the Benefit of the Less-Developed Areas has focused attention on the sort of practical approach by which the whole effort of the United Nations Development Decade could be accelerated. Much will depend on decisions to be taken now by the Council.

From Transcript of Press Conference
ROME   JULY 11, 1963

U THANT'S relations with the press remained cordial through his ten years as Secretary-General. He did not hesitate, however, to criticize the news media on occasion or to appeal to the press to correct what he felt to be its shortcomings. One example is found in the transcript of his July 11 press conference in Rome in which he was asked about press reports that the Egyptians were using poison gas against the population of Yemen. Thant noted that his observation mission in Yemen had investigated such reports and had found them without foundation. Noting that the Soviet Union had planes and technicians in the United Arab Republic and that the United States had planes and technicians in Saudi Arabia, he suggested that the mass media may have been engaging in cold war propaganda. He appealed for objectivity and fair play in dealing with news emanating from Yemen. Another example is found in an interview with David Sureck in the *Saturday Evening Post* (p. 432) in which he said news coverage of the United Nations was not adequate. He believed too much stress was placed on sensational and controversial aspects of the news and not enough on what he described as "the modest but effective assistance" which the United Nations family gives to developing nations.

. . . . QUESTION: Mr. Secretary-General, there have been several press reports stating that you have ordered observers from the United Nations in Yemen to investigate charges that the Egyptians have been using poison gas against the population of Yemen. Is this information correct, and in case these charges prove right, what action would the United Nations take against Egypt?

THE SECRETARY-GENERAL: About four weeks ago an American journal carried a story with the allegation that the United Arab Republic planes dropped some poison gas bombs inside Yemen over the royalists. About the same time, the permanent representative of Saudi Arabia to the United Nations saw me and brought to my attention the same charge. I immediately asked General von Horn, who is in charge of the United Nations Yemen Observation Mission, to investigate the charges and re-

UN Note to Correspondents No. 2776, July 15, 1963.

port to me immediately. He did the investigation and he reported to me that he was unable to substantiate these charges. That was about four weeks ago and then, when I got to Geneva last Sunday I got a cabled complaint from the Saudi Arabian permanent delegate to the same effect. I immediately asked my office in New York to ask the United Nations Yemen Observation Mission to investigate the charges again, and I asked my office also to ascertain the full facts from both governments, the United Arab Republic and Saudi Arabia. Up till last night I was in contact with my office and the replies were not yet received. On this I want to make one observation which I hope is relevant to this question. It is common knowledge that there are Soviet planes and Soviet technicians in the United Arab Republic, and also it is common knowledge that there are American planes and American technicians in Saudi Arabia. So, the situation in Yemen is really delicate if we consider this in the context of the cold war.

I would like to take this opportunity of appealing to the press and all the wielders of mass media who are actual moulders of public opinion, to be objective in their reporting and in the coverage of news which is likely to have repercussions in the context of the cold war. Most of you, I am sure, know that certain newspapers and periodicals have certain attitudes toward the United Arab Republic, and certain newspapers and certain periodicals have certain attitudes toward Saudi Arabia, because journalism, like diplomacy, is a case of conditioned reflex—if you know what I mean—their reactions and their assessments and their observations of situations, in a particular area, are generally influenced by their own attitude toward the countries primarily involved in such situations. So, just for the sake of peace and for the sake of justice and fair play, I would appeal to journals and periodicals to try to be as objective as possible in the coverage of news, particularly of news emanating from Yemen.

QUESTION: In case one day you get a report from General von Horn confirming that poisoned gas has been really used, what will you do?

THE SECRETARY-GENERAL: My action has to be based on the actual findings of our man on the spot. It all depends on the results of the investigations. As you know, we have provisions in the Charter and the rules and regulations of the United Nations to resort to a certain course of action on the basis of these findings, but it will not be very helpful, I am afraid, to discuss the potential actions to be taken in such a hypothetical situation.

QUESTION: It was reported that one of the topics of your audience with His Holiness the Pope this morning dealt with the persecution of the Buddhist majority in Saigon some weeks ago, and I just wanted to know if these reports are false or if they are true?

THE SECRETARY-GENERAL: During my audience with His Holiness the Pope, we exchanged views on some of the items directly concerned with the United Nations and the Catholic Church. Of course, I do not think it will be in the public interest for me to reveal the nature of the questions discussed, but this much I can say. From all accounts, the developments in the Republic of Vietnam are disturbing, and on a previous occasion, before I left New York, I made a public appeal to President Diem to exercise tolerance and to redress the legitimate grievances of Buddhists in his country, and to exercise justice and fair play for the sake of peace and amity. Of course, I am very much concerned with the developments in that country, since I have been getting many complaints and requests, not only from private organizations, but also from certain Member states of the United Nations.

QUESTION: Could you tell us your general impressions during your recent trips in Hungary and Bulgaria, above all regarding the possibilities of development in peaceful coexistence between the two blocks, East and West, especially in the light of the Chinese-Russian split?

THE SECRETARY-GENERAL: I am getting more and more convinced that every leader of government in the world today wants genuine peace, and nobody in his senses wants war. That applies both to the East and West, as I discovered from my personal meetings and discussions with leaders of governments everywhere. Regarding the current discussions in Moscow between the Soviet leaders and the Chinese communist leaders, of course, it is difficult, if not impossible to speculate on the outcome, but I just want to make one brief observation on this. China is passing through a phase which the Soviet Union passed through in the 1920s and 1930s. In the early stages of nation-building on their own concept of the economic and social philosophy, we have to be prepared to hear more rigid positions and more drastic measures taken by those countries, which are going through this phase. I think it is a common phenomenon also with newly independent countries. I am convinced that it is just a question of time. In course of time, China will also liberalize its attitudes as the Soviet Union has done.

. . . . QUESTION: The problem of Hungary has been present on the international scene for many years, but it has now come apparently to an end, and this is simply one of the reasons for your recent trip to Budapest. Of course, I understand that it must be one of the duties of the United Nations to have a broader view of the problems, and to put aside some of them which may be of concern to only some states, in order to achieve a broader view of the problems that are of interest to mankind as a whole. Now I want to ask you, Mr. Secretary-General—you who are a strenuous defender of democracy—if you believe that, as the United Nations has put aside the problem of Hungary, so should the free world forget the vicissitudes of a people who strenuously wanted liberty?

THE SECRETARY-GENERAL: The question of Hungary was discussed at the last session of the General Assembly, as you no doubt remember, and the General Assembly adopted a resolution asking me to use my initiative in any manner I wished regarding the problem of Hungary. You will notice that the resolution and the debates leading to its adoption are not very clear regarding my responsibilities. Of course, on one thing I am clear. I am not obligated to report to the General Assembly on my visit to Hungary. The Government of Hungary invited me long before I was appointed Secretary-General of the United Nations. The invitation was renewed to me in my present capacity, so when I visited Hungary in my present capacity I could not, of course, divorce myself completely from the resolution adopted at the last session. I had certain functions to perform in the context of that particular resolution. At the same time, my primary motivation was to ease tension, to bring about better international understanding, and to see for myself how far the Hungarian government has gone toward liberalizing its attitudes and its concepts. I came back with one thing clear in my mind. I noticed definite signs of stability.

Regarding the question of forget and forgive, it is my feeling that the General Assembly has passed many resolutions in the last seventeen years and many of these resolutions, although passed with the endorsement of the vast majority of the Member states, were just ignored by those Member states primarily concerned. So it is not just a case of all the Member states complying with the provisions of the resolutions adopted at the General Assembly. There are many cases, let me repeat, there are many cases where some Member states just ignored the recommendations of the General Assembly in the past seventeen years.

. . . . QUESTION: Are you interesting yourself in the question of Cardinal Mindzenty?

THE SECRETARY-GENERAL: The name of Cardinal Mindzenty did not feature in any of the United Nations General Assembly resolutions, but since I feel that it has some relevance to the easing of tension and the restoration of better international relations, I tried to understand the situation regarding Cardinal Mindzenty, while I was in Budapest. I do not think it will be in the public interest for me now to reveal the nature of my exchange of views with Prime Minister Kádár, but I am hopeful that this problem will be settled in due course.

. . . . QUESTION: I understand a few days ago a decision was taken by you and the government of my country, Sweden, according to which the Swedish troops serving in the Congo will leave the country in a few months' time. Has any similar decision been taken with regard to troops of other Member states serving in the Congo?

THE SECRETARY-GENERAL: As you are no doubt aware, the Security Council has authorized the Secretary-General to perform certain specific functions in regard to the Congo. For instance, the restoration of law and order, prevention of civil war and the expulsion of foreign mercenaries, and maintenance of unity and territorial integrity of the Congo. I feel that after more than three years of United Nations involvement in the Congo, almost all these requirements have been fulfilled. So it is my intention to recommend to the Security Council that the United Nations should be completely disengaged militarily from the Congo before the end of this year. Of course, I am not competent to decide definitely on this line of action. All I propose to do is to submit the report to the Security Council in August with my specific recommendation to disengage militarily from the Congo before the end of this year. Of course, the decision rests with the Security Council. Particularly, because of the financial crisis, I feel very strongly that the United Nations should not carry on with these peacekeeping operations in the Congo beyond 1963, and I feel it is now time for the United Nations to regard the Congolese government like a government of any other independent country, and that the government should be allowed to stand on its own feet. . . .

DISARMAMENT

DISARMAMENT was one of the problems uppermost in the mind of U Thant from the day he took office. He referred to it frequently in speeches, press conferences, and in his annual reports. In August 1963 he finally had something positive to counterbalance his pessimism over the accelerating arms race. He was invited to Moscow to witness the signing of a treaty, by the United States, the United Kingdom, and the Soviet Union, banning the testing of nuclear weapons in the atmosphere, in outer space, and under water. Although the agreement did not actually reduce the world's armaments, it was as Thant said "a significant break-through" in the long deadlock which had produced little or no agreement over the years. Like many others, Thant believed the agreement might at least be a first step toward the reduction of international tension. In the introduction to his annual report, issued on August 20, the Secretary-General said the partial test ban treaty "may be the beginning of a new era of better understanding between nations." He also welcomed the memorandum of understanding of June 20, 1963, establishing a direct communications link between Moscow and Washington, popularly known as the "hot line." On October 17, Thant had another occasion to welcome a United States-Soviet agreement, this time on a resolution to exclude all weapons of mass destruction, including nuclear weapons, from outer space. He saw it as still another sign of relaxing tensions between the superpowers.

1. Statement on the Signing of the Nuclear Test-Ban Treaty

MOSCOW   AUGUST 5, 1963

ON THIS HAPPY OCCASION, I should like, first of all, to thank the governments of the Soviet Union, the United States, and the United Kingdom for having invited me to be present here at this historic ceremony. I regard this gracious gesture more than anything else as an expression by

UN Press Release SG/1557.

the three governments of their deep faith and confidence in the United Nations and all that it stands for.

In the situation that confronts humanity today, with the accelerating arms race and with no significant abatement in mutual suspicions and mistrust, any agreement between the major powers is a significant event. What makes this present occasion a truly historic one is the fact that today for the first time we are witnessing an important and, I have no doubt, significant breakthrough in the protracted and often seemingly frustrating negotiations that have been conducted in the field of disarmament over the years.

This agreement has been made possible by the statesmanship and courage displayed by the leaders of the three powers and equally by the untiring and devoted efforts of their able negotiators, to all of whom I extend my sincere and heartfelt felicitations. It is my earnest hope that, in the same spirit of accommodation and understanding that has characterized the recent negotiations, every effort will be made to reach agreement on the discontinuance of all test explosions of nuclear weapons for all time. This is clearly envisaged by the preamble to the present treaty itself, and is devoutly hoped and prayed for by peoples the world over.

The agreement signed today will not eliminate the risk of war: only general and complete disarmament and the establishment of adequate and effective international machinery for maintaining peace will achieve this. This same thought has no doubt prompted the signatories of the treaty to proclaim in its preamble that their principal aim is the speediest possible achievement of an agreement on general and complete disarmament under strict international control in accordance with the objectives of the United Nations. However, as the three-power communiqué so rightly puts it, the present agreement constitutes an important first step toward the reduction of international tension and the strengthening of peace.

Although the test-ban issue has virtually monopolized the agenda of successive sessions of the General Assembly of the United Nations, other equally important measures aimed at the relaxation of tension have been repeatedly brought up for discussion. I should like to refer briefly to some of them, but the order in which I deal with these measures will not, I hope, be construed in any way as an indication of priorities or their relative importance.

First, there is the question of the wider dissemination of nuclear weapons. Repeatedly, the General Assembly has referred to the danger of the proliferation of nuclear weapons and has called upon all governments to make every effort to achieve a permanent international agreement, subject to inspection and control, on the prevention of the wider dissemination of these weapons of mass destruction. It is significant that while the resolutions of the General Assembly place a special responsibility on the nuclear powers to refrain from relinquishing control of such weapons to others not possessing them, they recognize at the same time that the countries not possessing nuclear weapons have a great interest and an important part to play, which they could do by refraining from manufacturing or otherwise acquiring such weapons and, further, by refusing to receive such weapons in their territories.

The problem of the means of delivering nuclear weapons is an equally important one. There have been proposals for limiting the production of delivery systems and for the destruction of all but an agreed limited number in the early stage of an agreed program of general disarmament. It is my hope that this important issue will receive further consideration by all the concerned parties with a view to reaching a satisfactory solution.

The problem of surprise attack has also figured in the past in debates at the United Nations. Proposals made during recent weeks could lead to the early renewal of the surprise attack talks which have been adjourned since December 1958.

I would also hope that the proposal, initiated in the fall of 1961, for convening a special conference for signing a convention on the prohibition of the use of nuclear and thermonuclear weapons for war purposes, will now receive wider support.

Finally, I should like to mention the problem of denuclearized zones in different geographical areas in the world. Various proposals bearing on this have been made from time to time. Obviously, the initiative must come from the countries in the regions as has been the case in respect of Africa and Latin America. But it is equally clear that the proposals must have the support and the backing of the nuclear powers themselves. I should like to express my earnest hope that such support will be forthcoming.

I have touched upon only some of the more important measures that are directed at further relaxation of existing tensions. I am happy to note that there are indications that the three governments who participated in the recent talks will continue to negotiate in a determined effort to find further ways and means for the maintenance of international peace and security. I should like to close by wishing them all success in their endeavors.

2. Statement on Arrival at New York Airport

NEW YORK   AUGUST 7, 1963

I JUST CAME BACK from Moscow after attending the ceremony of the signing of the partial test-ban treaty. The mood in Moscow was one of hope and optimism. The psychological climate was better than at any other time.

I believe that the agreement on a partial test-ban treaty was a breakthrough. It means the dawn of a new era of improved international relations. The big three are now consulting on the next step to take, which will cover a nuclear testing and general and complete disarmament treaty.

My feeling is that there is progress in sight, very early, particularly in the field of nuclear testing. It is too early to predict the prospects of a nonagression pact now, but a declaration of nonaggression is a definite possibility.

UN Press Release SG/1562.

3. Statement in the General Assembly

NEW YORK   OCTOBER 17, 1963

I HAVE ASKED for the privilege of addressing the General Assembly because of the importance of this occasion and because of its significance for the United Nations. The adoption of this resolution by the General Assembly implies the acceptance by the Organization of the continuing political and moral responsibility for its implementation. The resolution is the result of joint efforts by the two great powers, the United States of

General Assembly Official Records, Eighteenth Session, 1244th plenary meeting.

America and the Union of Soviet Socialist Republics. Today's Assembly action demonstrates that these efforts conform with the interests of all mankind and with the purposes and principles of the United Nations.

The purpose of the resolution is to exclude nuclear and all other weapons of mass destruction from outer space. Its implementation should assist the powers principally concerned, as well as all other Members of the United Nations, to give practical effect to their desires to prevent the spread of nuclear weapons and other weapons of mass destruction and to place the necessary restrictions on the use, for military purposes, of scientific and technological developments.

Agreement on this resolution is significant as another collateral measure which could facilitate the achievement of general and complete disarmament. It takes us an important step further along the road to that goal. In addition, it is significant as registering another area in the relaxation of tension between the great powers and as a positive advance toward stable international peace and world security.

In the existing circumstances when there is an evident easing of the international situation accompanied by the conclusion of concrete agreements, it is necessary to persevere with renewed determination in making progress toward the solution of the central problem of our time: that is, the achievement of general and complete disarmament.

I am sure that I speak for all Members and all peoples in expressing great satisfaction at this favorable development and in voicing the hope that this agreement is a good augury for the future.

EXCHANGE OF MESSAGES WITH
FOREIGN MINISTERS OF INDONESIA,
MALAYA, AND THE PHILIPPINES

As a result of agreements reached with the United Kingdom government, the Federation of Malaya attained full independence within the British commonwealth on August 31, 1957. In May 1961 the prime minister of the new country proposed the formation of an enlarged Federation of Malaysia to consist of the Federation of Malaya, North Borneo, Sarawak and Singapore. Britain, as administering power for North Borneo, Sarawak and Singapore, agreed in principle that the Federation of Malaysia should be established by August 31, 1963. The proposal ran into trouble, however, when both Indonesia and the Philippines objected. The Philippines challenged British sovereignty over North Borneo (Sabah) which had belonged to the Filipino Sultan of Sulu until 1878. President Sukarno of Indonesia denounced the proposed federation as a "neocolonialist concept." He met with President Diosdado Macapagal of the Philippines and Prime Minister Abdul Rahman of Malaya in Manila on July 30, 1963, to seek a compromise. Six days later they sent a cable to U Thant asking him to dispatch a mission to North Borneo and Sarawak to ascertain whether or not the people of those territories wished to join the federation. Thant agreed on August 8 to undertake the mission on the condition that Britain consented. The teams, which would go to the two territories, would be directly responsible to his representative, and the Secretary-General's conclusions would not be subject to ratification by any of the governments concerned, even though they would be permitted to observe the survey.

The terms were accepted. Laurence V. Michelmore, a member of the United Nations Secretariat, was appointed on August 12 to head the eight-man mission. The survey was brief. The mission arrived in the territories on August 16 and departed on September 5. The Secretary-General's conclusions, made public on September 14, stated that a majority of the people of both Sabah and Sarawak were in favor of joining in the proposed Federation of Malaysia. Two days later the federation was proclaimed. The matter was not closed, however. Both Indonesia and the Philippines later expressed reservations on the finding of the United Nations Malaysian Mission. The situation deteriorated during the following months until it reached the point of armed conflict between Malaysian forces and infiltrators from Indonesia. Up to this time it had remained outside the United Nations, except for the survey mission sent by the Secretary-General. It may be worth noting here that at a press conference on June 28 Thant expressed the opinion that "if the three governments directly concerned asked me to conduct a plebiscite in the area, to ascertain the wishes of the people, I am sure that a clear mandate from a competent organ of the United Nations will be necessary."

---

1. Message from the Foreign Ministers of Indonesia, Malaya, and the Philippines

AUGUST 5, 1963

WE HAVE THE HONOR to inform you that the heads of government of the Federation of Malaya, the Republic of Indonesia, and the Republic of the Philippines, meeting in a summit conference in Manila from July 30 to August 5, 1963, in order to implement paragraphs 10 and 11 of the Manila Accord of July 31, 1963, have agreed as follows:

. . . . 4. Pursuant to paragraphs 10 and 11 of the Manila Accord, the United Nations Secretary-General or his representative should ascertain, prior to the establishment of the Federation of Malaysia, the wishes of the people of Sabah (North Borneo) and Sarawak within the context of General Assembly resolution 1541 (XV), principal 9 of the annex, by a fresh approach, which in the opinion of the Secretary-General is necessary to ensure complete compliance with the principle of self-determination within the requirements embodied in principle 9, taking into consideration: (I) The recent elections in Sabah (North Borneo) and Sarawak but nevertheless further examining, verifying and satisfying himself as to whether: (a) Malaysia was a major issue if not the major issue; (b) electoral registers were properly compiled; (c) elections were free and there was no coercion; and (d) votes were properly polled and properly counted; and (II) the wishes of those who, being qualified to vote, would have exercised their right of self-determination in the recent elections had it not been for their detention for political activities, imprisonment for political offenses or absence from Sabah (North Borneo) or Sarawak.

5. The Secretary-General will be requested to send working teams to carry out the task set out in paragraph 4.

6. The Federation of Malaya, having undertaken to consult the British government and the governments of Sabah (North Borneo) and Sarawak under paragraph 11 of the Manila Accord, on behalf of the three heads of government, further undertake to request them to cooperate with the Secretary-General and to extend to him the necessary facilities so as to enable him to carry out his task as set out in paragraph 4.

UN Press Release SG/1559.

7. In the interest of the countries concerned, the three heads of government deem it desirable to send observers to witness the carrying out of the task to be undertaken by the working teams, and the Federation of Malaya will use its best endeavors to obtain the cooperation of the British government and the governments of Sabah (North Borneo) and Sarawak in furtherance of this purpose.

In line with this agreement we have the honor to invite you to take the necessary steps in order to carry out the task envisaged in the above-quoted agreement.

The costs incident to the accomplishment of this task will be borne by the governments of the Federation of Malaya, the Republic of Indonesia, and the Republic of the Philippines.

2. *Reply from the Secretary-General*

NEW YORK   AUGUST 8, 1963

I ACKNOWLEDGE RECEIPT of your communication dated August 5 sent through Mr. Alfred MacKenzie, the resident representative of the United Nations Technical Assistance Board in Manila. I regret the delay in sending this reply, which was due to my absence from Headquarters.

I have noted the terms of reference which I or my representative would be expected to follow. I believe that this task can be carried out by my representative.

I intend to set up two working teams under the over-all supervision of my representative, one of which will work in Sarawak and the other in North Borneo.

I note that the Federation of Malaya has undertaken to consult the Government of the United Kingdom and the governments of North Borneo and Sarawak requesting them to cooperate with the Secretary-General and to extend to him the necessary facilities to enable him to carry out his task.

I have always made it clear that I can undertake this responsibility only with the consent of the Government of the United Kingdom. I am in contact with the permanent representative of the United Kingdom and

UN Press Release SG/1563, August 9, 1963.

shall take the first steps in regard to this mission only after I have received an affirmative answer from him in behalf of his government.

I note that the three heads of government deem it desirable to send observers to witness the carrying-out of the task by the working teams. I wish to make it clear that the working teams working under the supervision of my representative will be responsible directly and exclusively to me.

I note that the costs necessary to the accomplishment of the task will be borne by the three governments. I estimate that the entire mission may consist of some ten officials and the total extra cost, on account of travel, per diem, etc. but not salary, may be of the order of some $30,000. Separate accounts of these expenses will be maintained and reimbursement claimed from the three governments in due course.

When they have completed the task, the working teams will report through my representative to me, and on the basis of this report I shall communicate my final conclusions to the three governments and the government of the United Kingdom. It is my understanding that neither the report of my representative nor my conclusions would be subject in any way to ratification or confirmation by any of the governments concerned.

My representative and his colleagues will of course make every effort to complete the task as quickly as possible. An exact timetable can be worked out and reported to me for approval only after my representative has had the opportunity to discuss the problems involved on the spot with all concerned.

I am sending identical messages to the foreign ministers of the other two governments which met in Manila. In view of the public interest in this question, I am also publishing this reply tomorrow.

3. Announcement to the People of Sarawak by Laurence Michelmore, Representative of the Secretary-General

SARAWAK   AUGUST 19, 1963

THE UNITED NATIONS Malaysia Mission has come to Sarawak in response to the request made to the Secretary-General by the heads of government of the Federation of Malaya, the Republic of Indonesia, and the Republic of the Philippines meeting in a summit conference in Manila from July 30 to August 5, 1963. The Government of the United Kingdom has extended full cooperation and all facilities to the Mission.

The three governments have asked the Secretary-General to ascertain by a fresh approach the wishes of the people of Sabah (North Borneo) and Sarawak concerning the establishment of the proposed Federation of Malaysia within the principles laid down by the General Assembly of the United Nations regarding the circumstances in which the integration between a non-self-governing territory and an already independent state should come about. In conducting its inquiry the mission will take into consideration whether in the recent elections in Sabah (North Borneo) and Sarawak: (a) Malaysia was a major issue if not the major issue; (b) electoral registers were properly compiled; (c) elections were free and there was no coercion; and (d) votes were properly polled and counted.

The mission will also solicit information concerning the wishes of any persons, who being qualified to vote would have exercised their right of self-determination in the recent elections, had it not been for their detention for political activities, imprisonment for political offences, or absence from the territory. The mission will hold hearings in different parts of the territory with a view to as wide a consultation with the population as may be necessary and possible. It would, therefore, welcome information and expressions of opinion from both elected representatives as well as from

UN Press Release SG/1566.

leaders and representatives of groups and persons who may show interest in setting forth their view to the mission. The time and place of the mission's hearings have already been announced and applications for hearings can be made directly to the mission. Local district officials will have information on the mission's program. The mission's work would be facilitated if, whenever possible, the view of those appearing before the mission are submitted in written form as far in advance of the hearing as possible. Because of the practical difficulties of translation into English it will be appreciated if all communications are submitted, as far as possible, in English. In view of the short time available for the mission to conclude its task it may not be possible for all those wishing to be heard to be granted oral hearings. Those unable to meet the mission but who may be anxious to present their views may always do so in the form of a written communication.

The mission is happy to be in Sarawak and wishes to thank the government and people for their kindness and hospitality.

4. *Final Conclusions Regarding Malaysia*

NEW YORK SEPTEMBER 14, 1963

IN RESPONSE to the request made by the governments of the Federation of Malaya, the Republic of Indonesia, and the Republic of the Philippines, on August 5, 1963, I agreed to ascertain, prior to the establishment of the Federation of Malaysia, the wishes of the people of Sabah (North Borneo), and Sarawak. As foreseen in my communication of August 8, 1963, a mission was established, comprising two teams, one for Sarawak and the other for Sabah (North Borneo), working under the supervision of my personal representative. The mission has now completed the inquiry assigned to it and has reported to me.

I wish, first of all, to express my gratitude to the three governments for the confidence they placed in me by requesting that I should undertake the task of ascertaining the wishes of the population of Sarawak and

UN Press Release SG/1583.

North Borneo (Sabah) prior to the establishment of Malaysia. I also wish to express my appreciation to the Government of the United Kingdom and to the authorities of the two territories for having given their agreement to the inquiry and their full cooperation to the Mission.

It was always understood that the ascertainment would be completed within a limited period of time, and my communication of August 8 noted that every effort would be made to complete the task as quickly as possible. I later informed the governments concerned that I would endeavor to report my conclusions to them by September 14. During the course of the inquiry, the date of September 16, 1963, was announced by the Government of the Federation of Malaya with the concurrence of the British government, the Singapore government and the governments of Sabah and Sarawak, for the establishment of the Federation of Malaysia. This has led to misunderstanding and confusion and even resentment among other parties to the Manila agreement, which could have been avoided if the date could have been fixed after my conclusions had been reached and made known.

There was no reference to a referendum or plebiscite in the request which was addressed to me. I was asked to ascertain the wishes of the people "within the context of General Assembly resolution 1541 (XV), principle IX of the annex, by a fresh approach" which in my opinion was necessary "to ensure complete compliance with the principle of self-determination within the requirements embodied in principle IX," taking into consideration certain questions relating to the recent elections. The mission accordingly arranged for consultations with the population through the elected representatives of the people, leaders of political parties, and other groups and organizations, and with all persons who were willing to express their views, and every effort was made to ascertain the wishes of the special groups (political detainees and absentees) mentioned in the Manila joint statement. The mission gathered and studied all available documents, reports, and other material on the governmental institutions, political organization, electoral processes in the two territories, and other matters relevant to its terms of reference.

The governments of the Federation of Malaya, the Republic of Indonesia, and the Republic of the Philippines deemed it desirable to send observers to witness the carrying out of the task, and the Government of the United Kingdom decided that it also wished the same facility. Although I did not consider the arrangements for observers to be part of the Secretary-General's responsibility, I endeavored to help the governments concerned to reach agreement, and I am pleased that an understanding was finally arrived at so that observers of all the governments concerned could be present during at least part of the inquiry. It is a matter for regret that this understanding could not have been reached earlier, so that all observers could have been present in the territories for the entire period of the inquiries and that questions of detail pertaining to the status of the observers unnecessarily delayed even further their arrival. A more congenial atmosphere would have been achieved if the necessary facilities had been granted more promptly by the administering authority. The mission, however, made its records, including tape recordings of all its hearings, available for the use of the observer teams to enable them to inform themselves as fully as possible of what had occurred before their arrival.

The basic assessment which I was asked to make has broader implications than the specific questions enumerated in the request addressed to me by the three governments. As mentioned previously, I was asked to "ascertain, prior to the establishment of the Federation of Malaysia, the wishes of the people of Sabah (North Borneo) and Sarawak within the context of General Assembly resolution 1541 (XV), principle IX of the annex, by a fresh approach, which in the opinion of the Secretary-General is necessary to ensure complete compliance with the principle of self-determination within the requirements embodied in principle IX."

Concerning the integration of a non-self-governing territory with an already independent state, principle IX provides:

Integration should have come about in the following circumstances:
(a) The integrating territory should have attained an advanced stage of self-government with free political institutions, so that its peoples would have the capacity to make a responsible choice through informed and democratic processes;
(b) The integration should be the result of the freely expressed wishes of the territory's peoples acting with full knowledge of the change in their status, their wishes having been expressed through informed and democratic processes, impartially conducted and based on universal adult suffrage. The United Nations could, when it deems it necessary, supervise these processes.

I have given consideration to the circumstances in which the proposals for the Federation of Malaysia have been developed and discussed, and the possibility that people progressing through the stages of self-government may be less able to consider in an entirely free context the implications of such changes in their status than a society which has already experienced full self-government and the determination of its own affairs. I have also been aware that the peoples of the territories are still striving for a more adequate level of educational development.

Having reflected fully on these considerations, and taking into account the framework within which the mission's task was performed, I have come to the conclusion that the majority of the peoples of Sabah (North Borneo) and of Sarawak, have given serious and thoughtful consideration to their future, and to the implications for them of participation in a Federation of Malaysia. I believe that the majority of them have concluded that they wish to bring their dependent status to an end and to realize their independence through freely chosen association with other peoples in their region with whom they feel ties of ethnic association, heritage, language, religion, culture, economic relationship, and ideals and objectives. Not all of these considerations are present in equal weight in all minds, but it is my conclusion that the majority of the peoples of the two territories, having taken them into account, wish to engage, with the peoples of the Federation of Malaya and Singapore, in an enlarged Federation of Malaysia through which they can strive together to realize the fulfillment of their destiny.

With regard to the more specific questions referred to me, my conclusions concerning the recent elections in Sarawak and Sabah (North Borneo), and after the examination and verification reported by the mission, are:

(a) Malaysia has been the subject of widespread and intensive public debate, and was a major issue in the recent elections in the two territories;

(b) electoral registers were properly compiled;

(c) the elections took place in an atmosphere free enough to enable the candidates and political parties to put their case before the electorate, and the people were able to express themselves freely by casting their votes in a polling system which provided the basic safeguards for secret balloting, and measures for the prevention and correction of abuses;

(d) the votes were properly polled and counted;

(e) persons otherwise eligible to vote but who were unable to do so because of detention for political activities, or imprisonment for political offenses, numbered somewhat less than one hundred in Sarawak, and even less in Sabah (North Borneo) at the time of the elections. Testimony given by this group, especially in Sarawak, indicated that they would have opposed the Federation of Malaysia if they had participated in the election. The actual votes of this group would not have been sufficient to have had a material effect on the result. The mission has given much attention to the possible effect which the absence of these persons, some of whom were officials of the anti-Malaysia party, might have had on the campaign. The mission considered the similar question concerning some

164 persons whose activity was restricted to some extent, but who retained the right to vote. Noting that the anti-Malaysia party scored convincing electoral victories in many of the areas to which these persons belonged, I accept the mission's conclusion that a substantial limitation of the campaigning potential of the group opposed to the Federation of Malaysia has not occurred so as seriously and significantly to have affected the result of the election.

(f) the mission made special efforts to obtain reliable information regarding persons who were absent from the territories at the time of the election, particularly as a result of possible political or other intimidation. The evidence available indicated that the number of such persons, otherwise qualified to vote, did not exceed a few hundred, and that their number could not have affected the results of the election. I note that the principal officials of the party in Sarawak opposed to the Federation of Malaysia agree with this assessment, and I accept it.

Bearing in mind the fundamental agreement of the three participating governments in the Manila meetings, and the statement by the Republic of Indonesia and the Republic of the Philippines that they would welcome the formation of Malaysia provided that the support of the people of the territories was ascertained by me and that, in my opinion, complete compliance with the principle of self-determination within the requirements of General Assembly resolution 1541 (XV), principle IX of the annex, was ensured, my conclusion, based on the findings of the mission, is that on both of these counts there is no doubt about the wishes of a sizable majority of the peoples of these territories to join in the Federation of Malaysia.

In reaching my conclusion, I have taken account of the concern expressed with regard to the political factors resulting from the constitutional status of the territories and about influences from outside the area on the promotion of the proposed federation. Giving these considerations their due weight, in relation to the responsibilities and obligations established in Article 73 and General Assembly resolution 1541 (XV) in respect of the territories, I am satisfied that the conclusions set forth above take cognizance of, and are in accordance with, the requirements set forth in the request addressed to me on August 5, 1963, by the foreign ministers of the Republic of Indonesia, the Federation of Malaya, and the Republic of the Philippines.

Before concluding, I would like to pay a tribute to my personal representative, Mr. L. Michelmore, my deputy representative, Mr. G. Janecek, and to all the members of the United Nations Malaysia Mission who accomplished a sensitive and difficult task in a relatively short period, but at the same time in a thorough and wholly adequate manner. In a sense, it was a pity that the work of the mission had to be accomplished within certain deadlines. But I do feel that, while more time might have enabled the mission to obtain more copious documentation and other evidence, it would not have affected the conclusions to any significant extent.

From the beginning of this year I have been observing the rising tension in Southeast Asia on account of the differences of opinion among the countries most directly interested in the Malaysia issue. It was in the hope that some form of United Nations involvement might help to reduce tension that I agreed to respond positively to the request made by the three Manila powers. I would hope that the exercise in which my colleagues and I have been involved in this regard will have this effect, and that the coming into being of Malaysia will not prove to be a continuing source of friction and tension in the area.

The emergence of dependent territories by a process of self-determination to the status of self-government, either as independent sovereign states or as autonomous components of larger units, has always been one of the purposes of the Charter and the objectives of the United Nations.

Whatever the origins of the proposal of Malaysia may have been, it seems to me in the light of actual events, including the present exercise, that we have witnessed in Sarawak and North Borneo the same process leading to self-government. I fervently hope that the people of these territories will achieve progress and prosperity, and find their fulfilment as component states of Malaysia.

Introduction to the Eighteenth Annual Report

NEW YORK   AUGUST 20, 1963

IN THE INTRODUCTION to the eighteenth annual report, U Thant was able to cite a number of successes which he believed had contributed to strengthening the United Nations and to brightening the international outlook generally. These included the negotiated settlement of the Cuban missile controversy, a notable improvement in the Congo situation and the signing of the partial nuclear test ban by the United States, the United Kingdom, and the Soviet Union. The Secretary-General, deeply concerned over the heavy financial drain caused by the Congo operation, expressed the belief that the time had come to pull out the United Nations force and hand over full responsibility for the maintenance of law and order to the Congolese government.

I

THE YEAR UNDER review has been marked by a number of developments which on the whole may be said to have brightened the international outlook and strengthened the United Nations as a result. The Cuban crisis, which erupted rather suddenly in October 1962, provided the United Nations with the opportunity to help avert what appeared to be impending disaster. A large number of Member states not directly involved in the crisis consulted with me on the need for action to ward off a confrontation of the two major nuclear powers which seemed inevitable, and I was encouraged to take the initiative in making certain proposals which had the immediate effect of tending to ease the situation. As a result of the high sense of responsibility and statesmanship demonstrated by the leaders of the powers directly concerned, as well as the assistance which the United Nations was able to give, the danger of a major conflagration was averted. The United Nations also provided, both through the Security Council and the Secretariat, an opportunity for dialogues among

General Assembly Official Records, Eighteenth Session, Supplement No. 1A (A/5501/Add. 1).

the interested parties. By the end of the month the situation had ceased to present the aspects of an imminent crisis, and by the end of the year had reached a point where it ceased to give rise to anxiety.

The turn of the year also marked a sudden change for the better in the Congo. As a result, the terms of the United Nations mandate in the Congo, as far as the military force is concerned, have now largely been fulfilled. External military interference in the Congo has ceased, the territorial integrity of the country has been secured, and law and order have generally been restored and are being maintained, although the situation in one or two areas still gives some cause for concern. There were, however, moments of anxiety in December 1962 and January 1963 when it appeared that major acts of sabotage—some already committed and many more threatened—by the secessionist régime in Katanga might disrupt the economic life not only of Katanga, but also of the Republic of the Congo itself. Fortunately, good sense prevailed in the end and the most serious of the threatened acts of sabotage did not take place. In the subsequent months there has been a steady improvement in the Congo situation, which is reviewed in greater detail below.

The year also saw the successful conclusion of the operation of the United Nations Temporary Executive Authority in West New Guinea (West Irian) and the first occasion for the exercise by the United Nations of executive authority, however temporary, over a vast region. Thanks to the cooperation of the two governments primarily involved, the United Nations team was able, on May 1, 1963, to hand over the administration of the territory to the Republic of Indonesia, as envisaged in the agreement between the governments of Indonesia and the Netherlands on August 15, 1962.

Toward the end of the year under review the United Nations has had to assume new responsibilities. The Yemen operation is now in full swing and is discussed in greater detail below. At the request of the governments of the Federation of Malaya, Indonesia, and the Philippines and with the concurrence of the United Kingdom, I have sent a team of United Nations officials to Sarawak and North Borneo to carry out certain tasks as envisaged by the three governments. Both the Yemen operation and the Malaysia mission have their special difficulties and problems, but they are continued evidence of the usefulness of the world body in reducing tension and facilitating a peaceful solution of issues which might otherwise lead to strained relations among the interested governments for a protracted period.

The year is closing on an optimistic note on account of the signing of the partial nuclear test ban treaty. This has given the whole world a feeling of hope, and I trust that the year to come will justify the current mood of optimism.

There has been much constructive work in the various fields of activity which are briefly mentioned in the succeeding sections of this introduction, and described in the annual report. In the field of outer space there has beeen some progress, though no spectacular results have been achieved. Some progress has also been made in the process of decolonization, although a few chronic problems remain to be solved. The United Nations Conference on Science and Technology was a milestone in the Development Decade, and preparations are now under way for the United Nations Conference on Trade and Development. Both the expanded program of technical assistance and the Special Fund are continuing and stepping up their fruitful activities. However, the financial problem posed mainly by the cost of certain peacekeeping operations remains unsolved; and although the proposals I have in mind for winding up the military phase of the Congo operation may, if accepted, reduce the impact of the problem to some extent, the financial issue is a priority item the solution of which is the primary responsibility of Member governments if the Organization is to continue to be effective in the cause of peace, and of constructive effort for "the promotion of the economic and social advancement of all peoples."

II

The achievement of disarmament continues to be the most important problem of our time. After many years of persistent but fruitful effort, two events took place recently, in the context of the disarmament negotiations, which I believe are of major significance—the signing in Geneva on June 20, 1963 of the memorandum of understanding establishing a direct communications link between Moscow and Washington, and the signing in Moscow on August 5, 1963, of the treaty banning nuclear weapons tests in the atmosphere, in outer space and under water.

In the field of disarmament, as elsewhere, certain preconditions have to be met before substantial progress can be registered. The agreements recently concluded do constitute important first steps, and help to meet these preconditions.

Many countries, and in particular the nonaligned countries, both in the General Assembly and in the Eighteen-Nation Committee on Disarmament, insisted that in the absence of a test ban treaty no real progress could be envisaged in other fields of disarmament and that the cessation of tests should therefore receive the highest priority. The signature of the treaty is a recognition by the major nuclear powers of the validity of this approach.

The test ban treaty, although limited to three environments and marginal to the central problem of disarmament, is an important objective in itself. It will directly serve the humanitarian aim of ending the danger of ever-increasing radioactive fall-out resulting from nuclear explosions. But it will also help restrict the spread of nuclear weapons and impose limitations on the development of new weapons of mass destruction, and thus be a factor in slowing down the arms race. This treaty could also point the way to the conclusion of a comprehensive treaty including a ban on underground tests.

Equally if not more important are the political implications of the test ban treaty. If this treaty is followed by agreement on other measures aimed at lessening international tension and establishing confidence among states, it may be the beginning of a new era of better understanding between nations, and create a more favourable international climate that would facilitate progress toward general and complete disarmament and the goal of stable international peace and security, which remains the primary purpose of the United Nations. It would seem, therefore, all the more urgent that the partial test ban treaty now concluded by the main parties be made universal by the accession of all states.

I believe that the opportunity so eagerly awaited by mankind will not be missed because of considerations of national interest, and that the enduring cause of world peace will prevail over short-range political considerations. I am strengthened in this belief by the improved relations between the Soviet Union and the United States, which have come about in spite of the difficulties of these two great world powers in reconciling new developments and requirements in the field of defence with their diverse interests and those of their respective allies.

The process of negotiating disarmament measures through the long years of mistrust about the intentions of the "other side" has been a formidable and sometimes baffling task. The usefulness and timeliness of the work of the Eighteen-Nation Committee on Disarmament has been amply proved in the short span of its existence. The committee provides an effective forum for harmonizing the responsibilities of the great powers with the interests of other countries and thus of humanity as a whole. In conditions of reduced international tension and of an improved political climate, the role of the committee may become even more significant than heretofore.

It will require the collective effort and wisdom of all members of the international community to ensure that the momentum generated by the recent agreements is maintained until the goal of global security and freedom from fear of war is reached.

III

In the course of the year, the development of cooperation in outer space exploration and use continued in an encouraging manner, especially in the scientific and technical field.

The Scientific and Technical Sub-Committee of the Committee on the Peaceful Uses of Outer Space, at its second session held in Geneva in May 1963, agreed upon a series of new or revised recommendations concerning the exchange of information, encouragement of international programs, education and training, potentially harmful effects of space experiments, and the organization of international sounding rocket facilities. The meeting of the sub-committee provided once more the occasion for the scientists of the two leading space powers to continue their private talks on cooperative space programs.

The World Meteorological Organization, the International Telecommunication Union, and the United Nations Educational, Scientific and Cultural Organization continued to participate actively in the field of peaceful exploration and use of outer space.

No agreement was reached on legal problems relating to outer space but a valuable exchange of views took place in the committee and its legal sub-committee. The discussion revealed areas of agreement as well as disagreement, and also indicated that on some questions there were encouraging indications of rapprochement. It must be borne in mind that the principal legal problems relate to issues of military security, and that in some respects it is difficult to separate the legal questions of peaceful use from problems of disarmament. Yet the effort should continue to be made to formulate more concrete principles of law and procedures that will foster the peaceful use of outer space. This is a task that cannot be left to the slow processes of customary law, but needs to be pursued vigourously by United Nations bodies in view of the rapid development of space technology, and the accelerated rate of space launchings.

IV

During 1963, United Nations activities in the economic and social field have been conducted with constant reference to the United Nations Development Decade. The United Nations Conference on the Application of Science and Technology for the Benefit of the Less-Developed Areas has already been described as a milestone in the decade, and the forthcoming United Nations Conference on Trade and Development should be another of no less importance. The spirit of the decade has enlivened the discussions in the Economic and Social Council and in its subsidiary organs; it has inspired many resolutions and will no doubt stimulate the work required for their implementation; it has sharpened the sense of purpose within the United Nations family, and is spurring their efforts toward a greater concentration of resources on tasks of recognized priority; and it is fostering a closer cooperation among all the organizations and agencies concerned.

The milestones already passed or in sight in the drive to move forward are, however, not enough. We have embarked on a long journey, and on the road ahead we also need guideposts which could indicate to us how to match resources and requirements. When the time comes, in a year or so, to assess the progress made, to project current developments into the second half of the decade, to identify and remedy shortcomings and imbalances, it would certainly be most useful if achievements and advances could be seen against a background of well-defined objectives, at least for those sectors and areas of activity in which intentions can be translated into programs of action. The more projects undertaken at the national level or through international cooperation in any given field can be related to each other in a framework designed to produce a combined and cumulative effect over the period, the greater will be the chances of sustaining and justifying the hopes that the proclamation of the decade has aroused.

The expanded program of technical assistance, which was initiated at a time when the highly developed nations were becoming more conscious of the vital importance of extending technical help to those which were less fortunate, was a prelude to the Development Decade, in which it is now playing a very leading part.

The improved financial situation of the program has been one encouraging sign: for the period 1963–1964, it has become possible to plan for the first time on the basis of an income of slightly over $100 million for the two years together. The increased resources have made it possible to meet, fairly satisfactorily, the rapidly increasing demands arising from the emergence of many independent countries in Africa, although these resources are not enough to allow for badly needed expansion in other regions. However, there is still no assurance that contributions will continue to increase at the rate which is necessary for the continued progress of a growing program.

Speaking generally, there is no doubt that the efficiency of the program has been steadily improving. It seems clear that this is partly due to improved techniques on the part of the participating organizations; it is also very largely due to more careful selection of projects by governments, which, in turn, can be partly accounted for by the spreading practice of national economic planning.

The Special Fund, for its part, has continued to fulfill the General Assembly's intention that it be "a constructive advance in United Nations assistance to the less-developed countries." The pace of its operations accelerated during the period under review. New priority development projects approved for its assistance extended both the scope and the geographic distribution of the fund's activity. The total program approved to date amounts to 327 major projects in 120 developing countries and territories. Toward the program's cost of $672 million, the Special Fund is contributing 42 per cent, and the developing countries the remainder.

These accomplishments reflect not only sound criteria on the part of governments and wise management principles on the part of the Special Fund; they are also the result of effective contributions by the United Nations and its related organizations which serve as executing agencies for the Special Fund. There is, however, one major disappointment, which must be voiced: governmental pledges to enable the fund to finance new projects in 1963 were some 25 per cent below the $100 million target. It is therefore to be hoped that all participating governments will help the fund to obtain the $100 million it urgently requires in 1964. The scale of this major program in the United Nations Development Decade must be raised somewhat more closely to the needs of the low-income countries, more closely to their capacity to absorb its assistance, and more closely to the ability of the Special Fund and the executing agencies to help meet those needs.

The need for more multilateral development assistance is very real. The time for meeting that need is rapidly growing shorter, because the processes of development are inevitably protracted—training is a vast, long, and difficult as well as essential task, social and economic transformations are not easily prepared nor speedily accomplished, and investment on the scale required to achieve the aims of the Development Decade will not be forthcoming unless preinvestment work is completed in time.

The sums required and which can be effectively used, both for preinvestment and investment, are not nearly so large as many imagine. The resources required from the industrialized countries are within their capacities to provide; there are perhaps only one or two among them which are as yet devoting even one-half of the proposed 1 per cent of their steadily increasing national income for development in the developing countries. However, many of the political leaders of the industrialized countries are aware of the growing danger to their prosperity and world peace represented by the widening gap between their affluent and dynamic economies and the nearly static situation in so many of the developing countries, where progress is slow and inadequate in relation to population increase.

V

The operations of the United Nations involving the use of military personnel are varied in character and objectives. The truce observation missions in the Middle East and Kashmir and the United Nations Emergency Force in the Middle East have continued to perform their essential peacekeeping duties without notable incidents. Three other more recent operations, the United Nations Operation in the Congo, the United Nations Temporary Executive Authority in West Irian and the United Nations Yemen Observation Mission, have attracted considerable attention.

The United Nations commitment in the Congo has now lasted for more than three years. In that time it has proved an exceptionally heavy burden on the resources of the Organization and of its Members, and there have been times when it seemed that hope of positive results was not very bright.

In 1963, however, the situation has improved very considerably and, as I mentioned earlier, the United Nations mandate in the Congo, especially in its military aspects, has been largely fulfilled. While good reasons have been put forward for the continuation of the United Nations military commitment in the Congo, I sincerely believe that the time has come when, for various reasons, it is necessary to envisage the early withdrawal and winding-up of the United Nations Force in the Congo. It can no doubt be argued that some useful tasks could still be performed by the Force, but I am of the opinion that the time has now come when the Congolese government should assume full responsibility throughout the Congo for the maintenance of law and order. I believe that in the past three years the government and the people of the Congo have begun to develop the means by which they can assume this responsibility. The retraining of the police and the army is, of course, a vital factor in this development, and as this progresses, there will be a parallel increase in the ability of the Congolese authorities to maintain law and order throughout the republic.

Originally it was envisaged that the greater part of the assistance to be rendered to the Government of the Congo by the United Nations would be in the field of technical assistance, or what is now called civilian operations. Here, despite the great difficulties of the last three years, the United Nations has, with the help of the specialized agencies, played an indispensable role in the Congo in providing experts for the maintenance of the essential services of the country, while at the same time providing training facilities designed to make it possible for the Congolese themselves to assume these responsibilities quickly. It is extremely important that this part of the United Nations effort should not suddenly be allowed to lapse for financial reasons. If it proved necessary suddenly to pull out these essential experts and close down the program of training in various fields, the government and people of the Congo would suffer a severe setback, and much of the effort of the United Nations in the past three years would have gone to waste.

I therefore hope that governments will continue to support the civilian operations in the Congo by contributions to the Congo Fund, until such time as it can become a normal technical assistance program under the usual auspices.

As in many countries, the future in the Congo is unpredictable and many difficulties and problems certainly lie ahead. I believe that the United Nations operation in that country, allowing for all its shortcomings and despite the violent criticism which has been levelled against it at various times and from various quarters, has provided a bridge from the desperate situation which existed in July 1960 to a solid basis from which the government and peoples of the Congo can now progress toward a prosperous and peaceful future. If this belief is justified, it will mean, quite apart from the benefits that accrue to the Congo, that a great and novel experiment in international cooperation has proved its worth in a very difficult situation. For that success great credit is due to all concerned, and in particular to the governments which have so generously provided assistance in many forms. Much is still required, but it is perhaps a measure of what has been achieved that we are now able to envisage a great reduction in the scope and cost of this operation.

VI

Owing to the loyal cooperation of the governments of the Republic of Indonesia and of the Kingdom of the Netherlands, the United Nations operation in West New Guinea (West Irian) did not encounter any major difficulties and was successfully concluded on May 1, 1963, with the transfer of the administration of the territory from the United Nations Temporary Executive Authority (UNTEA) to the Republic of Indonesia. The United Nations military observer team, the small international staff under the United Nations Administrator and the security force were guided solely by the provisions of the Agreement of August 15, 1962, which the General Assembly took note of in its resolution 1752 (XVII). After the cease-fire arrangements had been successfully implemented, the main responsibility of the international administration from October 1962 on was to ensure that there was no disruption in the public services and economic life on account of the departure of the Netherlands administration, and also to prepare the population for the important political changes which were taking place. Whatever may have been usefully accomplished during this brief period of seven months, the United Nations Temporary Executive Authority owes its success to the unfailing assistance from the government parties to the agreement (which also shared the expenses of the operation), the devotion of all those from many different nationalities who served with UNTEA, and the calm and friendly attitude of the population. On March 13, 1963, I was in a position to announce the decision of the Republic of Indonesia and the Kingdom of the Netherlands to resume normal relations and to exchange diplomatic representatives. This was a happy outcome of the solution of the question of West New Guinea (West Irian). The United Nations stands ready to assist the Government of Indonesia in the implementation of the remaining part of the agreement relating to the act of free choice by the inhabitants of the territory and to help the same government in the economic development of West Irian through a voluntary fund open to contributions from states Members of the United Nations and the specialized agencies.

VII

In the course of 1962, I received communications from Thailand and Cambodia concerning certain difficulties which had arisen between them. At the same time the two governments expressed a desire to find a solution to their dispute through one of the procedures enumerated in Article 33 of the Charter concerning peaceful settlement of disputes by negotiation and they requested me to appoint a personal representative for this purpose. On October 19, 1962, I informed the members of the Security Council of my affirmative response to the above request and my appointment of a personal representative.

According to the terms of reference, my personal representative is at the disposal of the parties to assist in solving all problems that have arisen or may arise between them, and the Governments of Cambodia and Thailand have both agreed to share equally all the costs involved. The two governments also requested me at the end of 1962 to extend the term of my personal representative for a period of one year, beginning January 1, 1963.

From October 26, 1962, my personal representative has remained in the area in continuous contact with the governments and high officials of both countries. A number of investigations have been made at the request of one or the other party, and certain suggestions advanced for their consideration on appropriate steps that could lead to improved relations between them. As long as the two governments consider that my personal representative can help them in dealing with a delicate and often tense situation, I am willing to continue to provide such services, whose value and efficiency will depend very much on the goodwill of the two governments and their sincere desire to normalize their relations.

VIII

The United Nations Yemen Observation Mission was established, after the Security Council had adopted its resolution of June 11, 1963, to facilitate the implementation of the disengagement agreement by the parties concerned in Yemen. The operation is agreed upon and financed by the parties themselves, and its success will depend upon the good faith of the two parties in carrying out the agreement.

In the conditions prevailing in Yemen, the implementation of the disengagement agreement is not an easy matter for either side, and it is as yet too early to make a judgment on the effectiveness of the mission in assisting in bringing about the actual disengagement. It is to be hoped, however, that the efforts of this mission in very difficult conditions, combined with the efforts of the parties themselves, will bring about the disengagement and the restoration of peace in Yemen, which is the desire of all concerned.

It will be clear from the preceding sections on the Congo, West Irian, and Yemen that many Member states have made available to the United Nations military personnel for various very constructive tasks of peacekeeping. I have accordingly designated as my military adviser a senior military officer who was formerly the military adviser for the Congo operation. He and the small but expert military staff working under him in my office have played a truly valuable role in the support and functioning of the operations I have just mentioned.

IX

One of the major developments of recent years has been the attainment of independence by a large number of countries and peoples formerly under colonial rule, whose right to freedom and equality is written into the Charter. Without intending to minimize the efforts of the peoples themselves in securing their freedom and the contribution of the respective administering powers, it may be said that the Organization, through its various organs, has made an important contribution toward this welcome development. The significance of this historic and dynamic process to the international community and to the future course of world events can be gauged from the transformation of the United Nations itself as a result of the increase in its membership from the original 51 to the present 111 Members. The widening of the membership has also brought the Organization nearer to its goal of universality.

In this connection it is relevant to recall the year 1960, when, at its fifteenth session, the General Assembly admitted seventeen newly independent countries—sixteen of them from Africa—to membership in the United Nations bringing the then total membership to one hundred. By that time there was overwhelming recognition of the need for bringing about, by peaceful means and in an orderly manner, the inevitable transformation of the remaining colonial areas from dependence to independence as speedily as possible. This, coupled with the belief of the Member states that the emancipation of all dependent peoples would remove one of the major obstacles to the maintenance of peace, led to the adoption by the General Assembly on December 14, 1960, by resolution 1514 (XV), of the Declaration on the granting of independence to colonial countries and peoples.

The importance of this question to the Organization is evident from the amount of attention devoted to it by the General Assembly. The progress of implementation of the Declaration was extensively discussed in general terms, and also in relation to individual territories, by the General Assembly at its sixteenth and seventeenth sessions as well as by the special committee which the General Assembly established for that purpose. It is a matter for satisfaction that progress toward independence is being made in a number of the territories which the special committee has examined this year, and mention may be made in this connection of Kenya, Northern Rhodesia, Nyasaland, and Zanzibar.

With regard to Portuguese territories and South West Africa, the Member states responsible for their administration have refused to cooperate with the United Nations or to implement its resolutions. In the case of Southern Rhodesia, the United Kingdom has continued to maintain its constitutional position concerning that territory, but has cooperated with the special committee in its study of this question and has discussed the matter with a sub-committee of the special committee in London.

The question of the territories under Portuguese administration has lately been the subject of discussion in the Security Council on the initiative of the African Member states. In its resolution of July 31, 1963, the Security Council has requested me to ensure the implementation of the provisions of that resolution, to furnish such assistance as I may deem necessary and to report to the Security Council by October 31, 1963. The resolutions of the General Assembly on South West Africa (1805 (XVII)) and Southern Rhodesia (1760 (XVII)) had already entrusted to me certain functions in relation to these territories.

X

The situation in the Republic of South Africa continued to be a source of increasing concern during the period under review. The question of the racial policies of the Government of the Republic of South Africa has been before the United Nations, in one form or another, ever since 1946. Successive resolutions of the General Assembly and the Security Council expressing their serious concern at the racial policies of the South African government, which not only are not in conformity with its obligations and responsibilities under the Charter but are also a source of international friction, have been ignored by the Government of the Republic of South Africa. The Security Council has again been seized of this matter recently, and the participation in the meetings of the Council of several foreign ministers of independent African states reflects the urgency and seriousness of the problem. I sincerely hope that, in response to the repeated recommendations and decisions of the United Nations organs, the Government of the Republic of South Africa will abandon its policies of apartheid, and also implement measures aimed at bringing about racial harmony based on equal rights and fundamental freedoms for all the people of South Africa.

XI

In the course of the year under review the financial situation of the Organization has remained serious owing to the continued failure of a number of Member states to pay their assessed contributions to the costs of the United Nations Emergency Force (UNEF) and the United Nations Operation in the Congo (ONUC). Thus at June 30, 1963 arrears for UNEF totalled $27.3 million and for ONUC, $72 million; at the same date the United Nations was operating under a deficit of some $114 million.

The drain on available resources was increased by the fact that for the period July 1, 1962 to June 30, 1963 the General Assembly authorized expenditures for UNEF and ONUC up to a certain maximum, without appropriating the amount involved. The proceeds of the bond issue during this period compensated in some measure, but fell considerably short of covering total expenses during the twelve months involved as well as the accumulated arrears in contributions dating back to 1957 in the case of UNEF and to 1960 in the case of ONUC.

In a report to the General Assembly at its special session in May-June 1963, at which it considered the financial position of the Organization, it was indicated that, if all existing factors continued to operate the deficit might reach a total of $140 million at December 31, 1963 and that cash resources would have been reduced to a dangerously low level.

Certain actions taken by the General Assembly at its special session may be expected to alleviate the situation to some extent. Thus, for the period July 1, 1963 to December 31, 1963, an amount of $9.5 million was appropriated for UNEF and $33 million for ONUC, to be financed by a combination of assessed and voluntary contributions. By a resolution on arrears in assessed contributions for these two operations, the door was opened to more flexible arrangements, within the letter and spirit of the Charter, for bringing payments up to date, including the possibility of payment by installments. The authorized period during which United Nations bonds might be sold was extended from December 31, 1962 to December 31, 1963. Moreover, as plans for the systematic reduction and eventual termination of the military component of ONUC proceed, the main financial burden giving rise to present difficulties will gradually be lifted.

These are bald figures which have to be faced; and while it is to be hoped that the prospects for improvement referred to above will yield some favourable results, the fact remains that the Organization is likely for some time to come to operate under a serious financial deficit and cash position causing constant concern.

I trust that Member states will not fail to bear in mind the vital nature of this problem, which, if allowed to persist without adequate and timely measures for its solution, must inevitably impair the effectiveness of the Organization and jeopardize its very existence. To the same end, the further endeavors to evolve a satisfactory method of financing future peace-keeping operations involving heavy expenditure deserve the attention and support of all concerned.

XII

Toward the end of May 1963 a historic meeting took place in Addis Ababa—the meeting of the heads of thirty-two independent African States. It was a matter of deep regret to me that, although I had been invited to be present at this meeting by the head of state of the host government, it was not possible for me for personal reasons to attend the conference. Besides adopting a number of important resolutions on various questions of general interest as well as problems of special interest to Africa, the conference also approved a charter and decided to establish an organization of African unity. I was deeply impressed by the statesmanship shown by the African leaders at this conference and the reasonable and moderate tone of the resolutions which they approved. In regard to the Organization of African Unity, it is of course well-known that regional organizations are not precluded under the Charter of the United Nations provided that "their activities are consistent with the purpose and principles of the United Nations." The Charter of the Organization of African Unity specifically states that one of its purposes shall be "to promote international cooperation, having due regard for the Charter of the United Nations and the Universal Declaration of Human Rights." I was also impressed by the recognition by the leaders of the independent African states of the basic fact of their interdependence, not only among themselves but as members of the international community.

I said in the introduction to the annual report a year ago that the Organization was facing a so-called "crisis of confidence," which was due to the emergence of so many independent states in Asia and Africa and the consequent change in the original balance of forces within the United Nations. Today, a year later, I feel I can say without being charged with undue optimism that this "crisis" has largely disappeared. I see on the other hand increasing recognition of the usefulness of the United Nations, not only among statesmen, but also among ordinary citizens. I believe that today there is a better awareness of the United Nations, both on the part of those who support it, and of those who criticize it—mainly because of an inadequate understanding of the limitations under which we work; and oftentimes the United Nations is taken to task merely because it mirrors the complex problems and the shortcomings of the world. However, the public pronouncements of leaders in every walk of life and the statements made recently by both spiritual and temporal heads show that much hope is placed in the United Nations as an instrument for the promotion of better understanding and an enduring peace.

One element in the strength of the United Nations is the progress toward universality that the Organization has made so steadily during recent years. I believe that this progress should be maintained and encouraged, and should not be reversed even when situations arise involving deep emotions and strong convictions. I also believe that there should be room in the United Nations for Member governments with widely differing political, economic, and social systems. It is only by providing and maintaining a common meeting-ground for all peace-loving states which accept, and are willing and able to carry out, the Charter obligations, that the Organization can fulfil one of the basic purposes of the Charter: "to be a centre for harmonizing the actions of nations."

Recent developments which have already been reviewed at some length in this introduction support an encouraging view of the future. These developments have been taken in certain quarters, perhaps with somewhat more optimism than is justified, as ushering in a new era. The General Assembly has already recommended several measures, which could now be followed up as a result of the improved political climate following the signature of the partial test-ban treaty, and I referred to most of them in a statement I made on that occasion. There are no doubt other steps which have not, so far, been discussed by the General Assembly, which could also usefully be taken. In this regard, the next twelve months may prove to be an interesting and perhaps even a fruitful period.

There is much discussion nowadays on ways and means to improve the peacekeeping capacity of the United Nations and its effectiveness as a dynamic instrument for safeguarding international peace and security. I welcome such discussion because it reflects an appreciation of what the Organization has already been able to achieve, sometimes under great handicaps. It is, no doubt, true that very often the problems that are left at the door of the United Nations are the difficult ones. This is as it should be; and in view of this circumstance, the United Nations cannot be expected to find without exception a satisfactory solution to every problem. At the same time, looking ahead, it is reasonable to assume that, as the Organization succeeds in solving one difficult problem after another, and resolving differences between Member governments, it is gaining in strength and effectiveness almost imperceptibly. It is my earnest hope that this process will provide us with an ever-widening field of useful service in the cause of peace.

U Thant
Secretary-General

August 20, 1963

EXCHANGE OF COMMUNICATIONS WITH THE PRESIDENT OF THE REPUBLIC OF VIETNAM

ON AUGUST 31, 1963, U Thant made a formal appeal to Ngo Dinh Diem, president of the Republic of Vietnam, to end the alleged mistreatment of Buddhists which had caused widespread concern in many parts of the world, particularly in Africa and Asia. The Secretary-General had disclosed in a press conference June 28 that he had received communications from all over the world on the situation and that he had taken "certain steps, very discreetly, to see that this alleged discrimination against the Buddhists is remedied." At that time he appealed through the press to President Diem to exercise tolerance. Later, in a July 11 press conference in Rome, Thant indicated that this was among questions discussed during an audience with Pope Paul VI. In a letter to the Secretary-General on September 5, Diem declared that the action taken by the Saigon government "has no other objective than to free the Buddhist hierarchy from all outside pressure and to shield the development of Buddhism from any external influence that works against the interests of the Buddhist religion and against the higher interests of the state." The issue came before the General Assembly in September. While the question was under consideration Diem invited the Assembly to send representatives of several states to look at the situation. The invitation was accepted and the Assembly president, Carlos Sosa Rodríguez, announced on October 11 that he had appointed a mission consisting of representatives of Afghanistan, Brazil, Ceylon, Costa Rica, Dahomey, Morocco, and Nepal to make the trip. The mission arrived in Saigon on October 24 and was still engaged in its study on November 1 at the time of the *coup d'état* in which Diem was killed. The Assembly received the mission's report on December 7. Four days later the Assembly decided that further consideration of the item was not necessary. The report contained a full record of the mission's inquiry, including transcripts of testimony, both from private individuals and government officials, but it contained no conclusions or recommendations since the necessity had been eliminated by the *coup*.

1. *Letter to President Ngo Dinh Diem*

NEW YORK   AUGUST 31, 1963

I HAVE THE HONOUR to inform Your Excellency that the Asian and African states Members of the United Nations, through their representatives to this Organization, have come to see me to express their grave concern at the situation that has arisen in the Republic of Vietnam, and have asked me to request Your Excellency's government to take all necessary steps to normalize the situation by ensuring the exercise of fundamental human rights to all sections of the population in the republic.

It is in the light of humanitarian considerations to which we all, as members of the human family, are bound that I have felt it my duty to transmit the above request, adding to it my own personal appeal to Your Excellency, as the head of the Government of Vietnam, to find a solution to the questions which are so deeply affecting the population of your country, in accordance with the principles laid down in the Universal Declaration of Human Rights.

U THANT
Secretary-General of
the United Nations

General Assembly Official Records, Eighteenth Session, Annexes, agenda item 77, document A/5542, September 23, 1963.

2. Letter from President Diem

SAIGON   SEPTEMBER 5, 1963

I HAVE THE HONOUR to acknowledge the receipt of your recent message in which you were kind enough to inform me of the concern shown by the representatives of African and Asian States Members of the United Nations with regard to the situation in Vietnam.

I thank you for the opportunity this gives me to clarify fully the Buddhist question, to which your message refers.

First of all, I can assure you that there has been no suppression of Buddhism in Vietnam since the establishment of the republic. Any allegation to the contrary is nothing but an imperialist invention. The Buddhist question is not a question of suppression, but a phenomenon of the development of Buddhism, a growing-pain of Buddhism, which should be viewed in its historical context, that of an underdeveloped, newly independent country—a country, in other words, which is short of cadres and of financial resources but desirous of rapidly asserting itself. Like the other movements in process of expansion which are linked to the independence movement, the Buddhist movement began to develop all the more quickly because it was held in check during the colonial period. In this unduly rapid development, Buddhism, like other movements, both public and private, is suffering from a shortage of cadres both qualitatively and quantitatively, and this offers the East and the West an opportunity to infiltrate if not to impose their own cadres who try to take over the leadership.

This results in ideological deviations, which in practice are reflected in techniques of political agitation and propaganda and in the organization of riots and *coups d'état* for the benefit of foreign interests. This is the tragedy of Buddhism in Vietnam; it will no doubt be the tragedy of Buddhism in the other countries of Asia.

We hope that, instead of allowing themselves to be poisoned by an international conspiracy of the East or the West against the Republic of Vietnam the fraternal African and Asian countries will benefit from the experience in our country and forestall the crises which they will possibly have to face.

Every government is in duty bound to uphold public order and also to ensure that alien cadres both from the East and the West, with their specific ideologies and policies, do not mar the original purity of Buddhism and the other movements. In other words, the action taken by the Government of the Republic of Vietnam in connection with the Buddhist question has no other objective than to free the Buddhist hierarchy from all outside pressure and to shield the development of Buddhism from any external influence that works against the interests of the Buddhist religion and against the higher interests of the state.

I am also happy to be able to inform you that a solution has already been found to the Buddhist question which bears witness to the merits of the policy pursued by the Vietnameses government. Freed from the evil influence of foreign agitators and adventurers, the Buddhist hierarchy has resumed charge of the Buddhist community and of the pagodas throughout the territory of Vietnam.

I request you to be kind enough to communicate this message to the representatives of the African and Asian states Members of the United Nations.

NGO DINH DIEM
President of the Republic of Vietnam

EXCERPTS FROM TWO INTERVIEWS

ALTHOUGH U Thant held frequent press conferences, he rarely gave exclusive interviews. He did, however, give two such interviews in September 1963, one to Alistair Cooke for the radio program "International Zone" and one to David Sureck for *The Saturday Evening Post*. These are worth noting not only because of their rarity but because they illuminate the Secretary-General's thinking on many questions, on his own role, on the potential and the weaknesses of the United Nations, and on his personal philosophy. Here, for example, he elaborated in some detail on his initiatives in West Irian, Yemen, and Malaysia, which he described as "a new phenomenon in the performance of the United Nations functions, particularly closely relating to the office of the Secretary-General." These operations had two major elements in common: each was undertaken by the Secretary-General at the request of the parties concerned without prior reference to the Security Council or the General Assembly, and each was carried out at the expense of the parties themselves with no cost to the United Nations. The West Irian question eventually was placed before the Assembly for its endorsement after a settlement had been reached (p. 194). So was the Yemen observer mission finally approved by the Security Council after Thant's representative had negotiated an agreement of disengagement and arranged for a United Nations team to observe the withdrawal of Saudi Arabian and United Arab Republic military forces (p. 327).

Asked about charges in the press that he was exceeding his authorized functions, as defined in the Charter, Thant replied that no Member government had complained, although such a possibility could not be excluded, and that he was guided by the views of states, not by a section of the population or a section of the press. In his own view, he said, his interventions in West Irian, Yemen, and Malaysia were within his authority and responsibility since they were not prohibited by the Charter.

1. From Transcript of Alistair Cooke on "International Zone"—A Conversation with U Thant

NEW YORK   SEPTEMBER 1963

ALISTAIR COOKE: Ladies and Gentlemen, I am Alistair Cooke and today we are on the thirty-eighth floor of the United Nations Secretariat building in New York in the office of the Secretary-General. Now, since November 1961 the Secretary-General has been U Thant, and once again we are privileged to sit and talk with him about the state of the world, about the progress of the United Nations, about many things that had not come up when we last talked with him.

Mr. Secretary-General, there seems to be a great deal of misunderstanding abroad about the financial condition of the United Nations. Now would you tell us what caused the crisis in the first place? And what the present financial condition of the United Nations is?

U THANT: Yes, Mr. Cooke, I agree with you that there has been a great deal of misunderstanding regarding the financial difficulties of the United Nations. If I may put it that way, the UN finances can be classified into two categories: The normal expenses, and the abnormal expenses, or in other words, the regular budget and the peacekeeping budget.

ALISTAIR COOKE: Now by peacekeeping, this is for emergency operations like the Gaza Strip, the Congo.

U THANT: Yes, as far as the regular budget is concerned the United Nations is quite solvent. Almost all the Member states paid up their dues and if I remember rightly there is a very, very small amount of arrears outstanding. But the problem arises in regard to the peacekeeping operations for, as you have just said, in the Congo and in the Middle East. Regarding this financing of the peacekeeping operations there are two

Transcript of "International Zone", No. 36, UN Radio and Visual Services, September 1963.

schools of thought in the United Nations. The first school maintains that the General Assembly is quite competent to allocate financial responsibility on Member states toward the peacekeeping expenses, while, of course, a minority of the Member states including two big powers, two permanent members of the Security Council, don't agree with that view. They maintain that the Security Council, which is the principal organ of the United Nations for peacekeeping operations, is the only competent organ to allocate financial responsibility for peacekeeping operations. In my view, Mr. Cooke, the 1964 session of the General Assembly will be historic, in that the Member states have to decide one way or the other.

ALISTAIR COOKE: Now, in the meantime is the United Nations in decent financial shape?

U THANT: No, I am afraid not. And, as you know, the United Nations has spent over $350 million for the Congo alone and for the Middle East operations the United Nations has been spending at the rate of $20 million a year.

ALISTAIR COOKE: Well now, how much is that fund in arrears from noncontributors?

U THANT: If the Member states which have refused to pay for these peacekeeping operations still maintain their position my guess is that the United Nations will be in the red by $140 million at the end of 1963.

ALISTAIR COOKE: Well now, doesn't this situation inhibit the possibility of further peacekeeping operations? If there is a crisis somewhere, won't you think twice, won't the United Nations think twice, the Assembly, everybody, about initiating another operation that's going to cost money that will take you further into the red?

U THANT: Yes, I feel very strongly that if some Members continue to maintain their present position the United Nations will not be able to discharge its obligations under the Charter. As you no doubt will agree with me, there are two schools of thought regarding the functions of the United Nations. One school maintains that the United Nations must be a mere forum for debates and discussions and nothing more. The other school, which is, of course, shared by the vast majority of the Member states maintains that the United Nations must develop into a really effective instrument for maintaining peace and for the creation of a congenial climate for better international relations. Needless to say, I subscribe to the second school.

ALISTAIR COOKE: Something else occurs to me which is a kind of peacekeeping operation, a very early stage, which we used in the League of

Nations and which has been used all the way through the history of the United Nations. What I am thinking of is the observers that were sent for instance to Malaysia and to West Irian, and to Yemen, to look into a dispute. Now, under what conditions do you send observers out?

U THANT: Well, this is a new phenomenon in the performance of the United Nations functions, particularly closely relating to the office of the Secretary-General. Well, as I have just already pointed out, there are three instances in the past year or so. First of all, there was the case of West Irian. In that instance the governments concerned, the Governments of Indonesia and the Netherlands, came to an agreement, of course with my good offices. And they wanted me to comply with the terms of the agreement and I had to send a United Nations temporary executive authority, which is known as UNTEA, to the area. . .

ALISTAIR COOKE: Excuse me, Sir, but is the new thing about this the fact that these disputing governments came to you in the first place and not to a body of the United Nations? . . . is that the new thing?

U THANT: That is a new development.

ALISTAIR COOKE: Well now, isn't this very delicate? There have been charges that possibly you are going beyond your function as is sanctioned by the Charter. What does the Charter say about this?

U THANT: Actually the Secretary-General, being a principal organ of the United Nations, has certain functions to perform and certain responsibilities to undertake. I won't share the view that the Charter does not provide for such performance on the part of the Secretary-General. Actually, the Charter does not prohibit the Secretary-General from the performance of such functions. But in all such cases, in West Irian, in Yemen, in Malaysia, I complied with the request of the relevant governments concerned on the definite understanding that all expenses to be incurred would be shared by the principal parties concerned.

ALISTAIR COOKE: Oh, by the governments, not by the United Nations?

U THANT: Not by the United Nations. There is no financial implication whatsoever for the United Nations. And in all such cases, in West Irian, for instance, I reported to the General Assembly of my action and the General Assembly took note of my action. I propose to do the same thing in regard to Yemen and, of course, for the assessment of public opinion in Sarawak and North Borneo, it belonged to a different category. It didn't involve UN administration, it didn't involve a prolonged period of UN observation, it involved the UN assessment of public opinion in these two countries. . . .

ALISTAIR COOKE: What is the—I know you don't agree with it, obviously—but what is the argument that you have exceeded or may be exceeding your proper initiative?

U THANT: To my knowledge there has not been a single Member state who questioned my actions.

ALISTAIR COOKE: But it is in the press—in the British . . .

U THANT: In the press, in a section of public opinion, for instance.

ALISTAIR COOKE: Yes . . .

U THANT: But in the performance of my duties, of course, I have to be sensitive to the views of the Member states, that is Member governments, not a section of a population, or a section of the press.

ALISTAIR COOKE: Do you see any change in the development of the secretary-generalship that might possibly begin to arouse suspicion or make some Member nations think you are exceeding? This did happen after all with Mr. Hammarskjöld.

U THANT: Yes, of course, one cannot rule out such a prospect. Sooner or later I am afraid I have to run into such criticism, but so far I have not run into any such opposition.

ALISTAIR COOKE: I wonder if the explosion that we all talk about, of Asia, Africa, and the great multiplying of members of African and Asian states—if this is having an effect on the structure of power in the United Nations?

U THANT: Well, the entry of many new states, particularly from Asia and Africa give a certain character, certain new aspect to the functioning of the United Nations—I have no doubt about it. And also, you are no doubt aware, I believe in the universality of its membership, of the membership of the United Nations. I am convinced that the admission of new Members from Asia and Africa is a good trend, it makes for strengthening of the United Nations and I don't share the view that the entry of many African states weakens the structure of the United Nations. In the first instance, I believe in universality and secondly. . .

ALISTAIR COOKE: One man, one vote. . .

U THANT: One man, one vote, and secondly, in my experience, many new states are exercising their functions with maturity and with a level-headed approach to all problems as is indicated by the performance of many African states, not only inside the United Nations but also at that historic summit conference in Addis Ababa in May 1963. And, I may as well make some observations, brief observations, on this aspect of transition from the dependent status to the independent status. As I see the situation, there are two aspects to the problem. It is true, I am sure that some countries gain independence completely unprepared for the new types of responsibilities they are expected to shoulder. The other aspect of the problem is, if independence is too long delayed, unnecessarily deferred, my experience is that extreme forces come to the surface and dominate the scene. Such a situation does not help the cause of peace, or progress, and far from that, these situations actually contribute toward the complication of international relationships. So my feeling is that it is a very good thing for the world community as well as for the cause of peace and progress that more and more independent countries join the United Nations.

ALISTAIR COOKE: Now, we believed in the last days of the League of Nations, before the second war destroyed it, that we were approaching an age where nationalism would mean less and less, but now we find that we are getting more and more nationalistic states with pride, natural pride, in their new nations. Now, doesn't this mean with 111, 112, 120—it is going to be—new nations, that we are going to have a much harder time inside the United Nations getting the general consensus?

U THANT: Yes, in a way, of course, it will complicate the operation of the United Nations in the . . . almost all of its principal organs. But my feeling is this complication will be just a passing phase as in all human developments; and the future is for more stability and the increased contribution of these smaller states for the stability, not only of this world organization but for the peace and progress of mankind. . . .

ALISTAIR COOKE: Mr. Secretary-General, tell me, we've been hearing from many heads of states, and all of them speaking quite cautiously, that the recent partial nuclear test-ban treaty is a first step toward disarmament. Now I wonder what your opinion is and, if you think it is a first step, why?

U THANT: Well, I had the privilege of being invited by the three big powers to be present at the ceremony of the signing of this partial test-ban treaty in Moscow on August 5, 1963. In my view, it is a definite breakthrough in the cold war and it is symbolic of the improved international relations, particularly relations between the East and the West and it seems to me that it is a dawn of a new era. Apart from the psychological and political aspects, it is common knowledge that the conclusion of this partial test-ban treaty will deny these atomic powers from further poisoning the atmosphere, which in itself is a very significant step forward, and the mood in Moscow at the signing ceremony was one of hope and optimism all around. And everybody seemed to have a cautious optimism about the future progress of disarmament negotiations. Of course, there are still several steps to be taken in the light of this initial agreement. I have indicated some areas in Moscow in which the big powers can usefully exchange views. I don't know, of course, how far these ideas will take roots, but everybody seems to be convinced that the signing of the partial test-ban treaty is a forerunner of more agreements, not only in the field of nuclear testing, but also in the field of general and complete disarmament, which is the aspiration of all humanity. And for the conclusion of such a treaty, I want to take this opportunity of paying a tribute to the very valiant and persistent efforts of these nonaligned countries which have contributed more or less in a psychological way toward the successful conclusion of this treaty.

ALISTAIR COOKE: And what is the contribution that you think they have made?

U THANT: Their contribution has been all along for the banning of all nuclear tests. That has been their theme, year after year, in the General Assembly and in the disarmament commission in Geneva also. I think this moral impact, this psychological impact also has yielded some fruits. As I indicated to you on a previous occasion, I think there are two concepts regarding all problems. In the West, the stress is on the development of the intellect. I think the aim of education generally—when I say the West, of course I mean to include the United States, the United Kingdom, Europe, and Russia also—the aim of education generally is to create doctors, scientists, engineers, and to discover outer space, to go to the moon, and Mars and the stars. That is the primary aim of Western education. In the East traditionally, the aim has been the development of the moral and spiritual aspects of man. We are being taught to discover ourselves, to discover what is happening inside us, to try to appreciate the values, for instance, of humility, tolerance, the philosophy of live and let live, and the desire to understand the other man's point of view. These qualities were traditionally developed in the East, at the expense of intellectual development. So my feeling is the pure intellectual development unaccompanied by a corresponding moral and spiritual development is sure to lead humanity from one crisis to another. This intellect must be tempered by the moral and spiritual aspects of life. So, I feel very strongly that for the development of man, all three aspects must be fully integrated. This development must be in all three fields, intellectual, moral, and spiritual, and I have definite indications of this harmonizing trend also. As you are no doubt aware, I am a believer, a strong believer in the Hegelian concept of thesis, antithesis, and synthesis, and I am also confident that there are unmistakable trends toward the synthesis.

2. *From Interview by David Sureck in The Saturday Evening Post*

NEW YORK   SEPTEMBER 21, 1963

QUESTION: What in your view is the single most important cause of world tension?

ANSWER: I do not believe it possible to speak of one single most important cause of tension in the world of today. I am, of course, aware that there are those who speak of the cold war, or more narrowly of the antagonisms between the United States and the Soviet Union as being the single most important factor responsible for the tension that has prevailed in the last years. In my view, existing tensions of a political nature cannot be thus oversimplified; one should rather think in terms of different aspects of political tension not only between the two giants, but broadly between the two blocs which they lead. Indeed, it should be added that both within the Western and the communist blocs there are tensions among some of their members which seem to have been somewhat exacerbated in recent months and this renders the picture even more complex in the political field.

Moreover, I should like to add that, in my opinion, world tensions today cannot be ascribed solely to political and ideological differences. I consider that in the economic field a situation has been developing which is perhaps even more fraught with danger, namely the widening gap between the industrialized nations and the developing countries of Asia, Africa, and Latin America. I consider this widening gap in economic progress and prosperity between the wealthy and the poor nations as more dangerous and ultimately more explosive than political or ideological differences.

United Nations Review, January 1964.

In summing up, I believe we could say that there is no single most important cause for tension in the world in which we live but rather a complex of political, economic, and social causes for world tension. To the United Nations devolves an increasingly important role in the easing of this tension. The role played by the United Nations in the Caribbean crisis is the most recent and perhaps the best example of the usefulness of the world organization when a confrontation of major powers is looming. As to the economic and social causes for world tension, our work is less visible; nonetheless, the United Nations and its family of specialized agencies are engaged in a worldwide struggle against poverty, disease, and illiteracy, by rendering assistance to governments as requested and within the limits of our resources in such fields as agriculture, public health, education, labor, and many others.

QUESTION: What lesson has the world learned from the Cuban crisis? At the time you said: "During the seventeen years that have passed since the end of the Second World War, there has never been a more dangerous or closer confrontation of the major powers."

ANSWER: I reaffirm my view that the Cuban crisis represented the most dangerous and the closest confrontation of the major powers since the Second World War. The main lesson of the Cuban crisis was twofold: (a) that the United Nations is not just a debating society, but can play a crucial role in the solution of important issues; and (b) that some "give and take" on the part of all concerned is required to solve major issues. It was the spirit of willingness to "give and take" on the part of all the parties concerned and the usefulness of the United Nations as a mediator that made it possible in the first instance to avert the confrontation and in due course to ease the crisis itself.

QUESTION: What if there had been no United Nations?

ANSWER: It is difficult to imagine the course of events had there been no United Nations. The somewhat rigid positions taken at the beginning by the major protagonists demonstrated the usefulness of having a machinery which could be utilized to avoid a direct confrontation and to alleviate the very dangerous tension. The debate in the United Nations and the intervention which I felt necessary to undertake are generally recognized as having contributed to reduce the crisis at its critical point.

QUESTION: What do you foresee for the future of East-West relations?

ANSWER: I am optimistic about the future, which does not mean that I believe that the easing of tension in an ultimate climate of understanding and harmony can be achieved either easily or swiftly. However, since the

Caribbean crisis there have been positive and repeated indications of a desire on the part of both the United States and the Soviet Union to find solutions to their major differences, through negotiation and compromise. Such an attitude has found an echo in many of the allied powers belonging to both blocs, although unfortunately not among all of them. Already the world political climate is more relaxed and favorable than it has been in many years. To improve further this climate which is conducive to fruitful negotiations is a responsibility that falls upon every nation in the world and particularly, of course, upon the two major world powers. In this respect, the United Nations can make a positive contribution, as became apparent during the Caribbean crisis.

UN Action in the Congo

QUESTION: What special significance do you attach to the United Nations action in the Congo?

ANSWER: The progress made toward Congolese unity and toward reducing the threat of civil war, will make possible, I hope, a concentration of effort and resources on the civilian side of the operation, with asistance to the country in such vital fields as public administration, education, health, and agriculture. Any large-scale assistance will depend, of course, on the voluntary contributions of countries who may wish to assist in the development of the Congo. There will be a progressive phasing out of the United Nations military force. The United Nations experience in the Congo has demonstrated the ability of the United Nations, on short notice, to provide quickly a substantial armed force, and to use that force in carrying out mandates defined by United Nations organs responsibly, effectively, and with restraint.

. . . .

Widening Economic Gap

QUESTION: The economic gap—already substantial—between industrialized and developing countries is widening. What is needed to bring about a more equitable balance?

ANSWER: You speak of a widening gap, and it is true that, taking all the developed countries together on the one hand and the developing countries on the other, the gap is still widening in terms of per capita income. This is a very serious matter—more serious perhaps in the long run than East-West political tensions. But one has to be careful about such concepts. In the first place, if one considers the spread of education, the improvement of health conditions, and the reduction in mortality in underdeveloped countries, the contrast between developed countries and the underdeveloped world is steadily becoming less sharp. In terms of such important indicators of the standard of living, the gap is closing rather than widening. Secondly, some countries in the underdeveloped world are going ahead very rapidly, more rapidly, in terms of the rate of economic growth, than the majority of industrialized ones. Indeed, we find that the countries which have been making the most progress are those in an intermediate position, the poorer of the industrial countries, such as Italy and Japan, and the wealthier of the underdeveloped ones, such as Brazil and Mexico. The countries which have failed most conspicuously to join the march of progress are those at the bottom of the per capita national income scale, and the seriousness of the matter for mankind as a whole is aggravated by the fact that this group includes some of the most populous countries of the world.

In the United Nations the overriding priority in our economic and social work is to help improve the level of living of the hundreds of millions of people who are now suffering from malnutrition, lack of housing, and other conditions incompatible with human dignity. We believe that all countries have actual and potential human and natural resources through whose fuller development and utilization such improvement can be achieved; and our objective is to enable every country, including those with a rapidly rising population, to achieve a rate of economic growth which would ensure a significant rise in per capita incomes year by year. We believe that decisive steps toward such self-sustaining growth can be taken by nearly all the less-developed countries during the 1960s, a decade which was proclaimed the United Nations Development Decade by the General Assembly in 1961.

I submitted to the United Nations Economic and Social Council proposals for action in the United Nations Development Decade. These proposals aim at intensifying efforts toward more economic and social programing, more training and more saving in underdeveloped countries, through more self-help as well as through increased international cooperation. More international aid is required for the financing of sound development projects in underdeveloped countries; but even more important is the need to enable those countries to earn what they require from abroad by exporting more of their products at more remunerative and stable prices. Further technical cooperation and the transfer of science and technology must be intensified in strategic sectors such as agriculture, natural resources, industry, housing, health, transport, and communications—a key factor being the mobilization of human resources, with special stress on the younger generation.

Office of the Secretary-General

QUESTION: The first United Nations Secretary-General, Trygve Lie, has described your job as "the most impossible job in the world." What did you think about it on the day you were sworn in?

ANSWER: A feeling of humility and an overwhelming sense of responsibility to which were added a dawning hope that the unanimous support which has so generously been accorded to me would make "the most impossible job in the world" a little less impossible.

QUESTION: What has given you the greatest measure of satisfaction?

ANSWER: I can recall two moments of deep satisfaction. The first was when it became apparent that the United Nations, through the office of the Secretary-General, had played a useful role during the most crucial and dangerous days of the Caribbean crisis. The other, when the military phase of the United Nations operation in the Congo was brought to a successful and almost bloodless conclusion with the end of secession in Katanga, so that the Congolese government and people, with the assistance of the United Nations and the bilateral cooperation offered to them by several governments can now devote their energies to the development of their country. It may be added that the compromise solution of the New Guinea crisis, with the United Nations acting as a temporary executive authority for the transfer of administration of that territory, was most gratifying to me. And last but not least, I should say that the gradual easing of the financial crisis, which confronted the United Nations when I took office, has also been a very reassuring development.

International Service

QUESTION: Some people say it is impossible to be free of ideological ties or to be completely neutral. Is this true?

ANSWER: If a man of integrity joins the United Nations Secretariat—and the Charter places emphasis on integrity as one of the requirements for those to be recruited as international civil servants—there can never be any basic contradiction between his convictions and the purposes and principles of the United Nations. If he has some prejudices, a sense of fair play and a devotion to duty can be a salutary antidote to any intolerant approach.

It should be added that the daily work of the Secretariat, whose members are recruited on a wide geographical basis, allows each and every one of us a daily contact with the most diverse cultural and social backgrounds of our colleagues and fellow-workers. In that sense, I believe it can legitimately be said that a United Nations spirit is created among the staff, a spirit characterized by an honest striving for impartiality and objectivity arrived at through a daily awareness and appraisal of different points of view.

QUESTION: Would the United Nations function better if it were out of New York, out of the United States?

ANSWER: The decision to locate the United Nations in the United States was taken with the near unanimous agreement of the founding fathers of the United Nations. In reaching this decision they no doubt had in mind the fact that the League of Nations had been handicapped by the nonparticipation of the United States. The decision to locate it in New York was also taken after due consideration had been given to other cities within the United States. If any fresh decision is to be taken with regard to the location of the United Nations, this would have to be taken by the General Assembly.

QUESTION: A good deal of misunderstanding exists about the purpose of the United Nations. Some Americans claim that the United Nations is part and parcel of a "communist conspiracy" while extremists in the Soviet Union, on the other hand, frequently refer to the United Nations as a "tool of Western imperialism." How does one dispel the confusion about what the United Nations is, and what it is not; what it can do, and what it cannot do?

ANSWER: Much of the misunderstanding about the United Nations arises from the concept, in the minds of most people, of the United Nations as an entity outside of, and different from, its constituent Members. This, of course, is a misconception. The United Nations is an intergovernmental organization made up of 110 Member governments representing various shades of opinion and having various interests. The United Nations is not only the Secretariat or the Secretary-General or any of the other organs—it is primarily these 110 Member governments.

The United Nations thus reflects the differences and divisions in the world today. If it is deemed imperfect in one sense or another by the advocates of one or another line, it is because it mirrors the imperfections of the world around us.

QUESTION: Is there a cultural conflict among representatives coming to the United Nations from diverse parts of the world? As an Asian and a Buddhist, what were your early reactions to New York and the United States? What of United States literature, newspapers, motion pictures?

ANSWER: I believe that the environment of United Nations Headquarters offers unique opportunities for cultural enrichment rather than cultural antagonisms. Each one of us, from whatever part of the world he comes and however diligently he has studied in his home country has always much to learn from his colleagues and the United Nations. In that sense, I consider our Headquarters in New York—as well as the United Nations sub-headquarters at the Palais des Nations in Geneva and the headquarters of the specialized agencies—as universities *sui generis,* where one is always absorbing knowledge and broadening horizons while at the same time contributing to the common pool his own national patrimony of cultural values. As to the second part of the question, I have for many years had an abiding interest in United States writers, particularly those who produced their best work at the close of the nineteenth century and during the first decades of the twentieth century. Ever since I took up my duties on the thirty-eighth floor, however, there has unfortunately been practically no time for me to keep abreast of current literary movements in this country. On the other hand, I do endeavor to follow closely the press of this country and make it a point of reading every day several of your leading newspapers. As to motion pictures I have time only to see an occasional movie.

Sovereign Equality of States

QUESTION: Do you consider it fair that a small Member state—such as Cyprus with half a million population or Togo with less than 2 million—should have the same vote in the United Nations as the United States with its 170 million or the Soviet Union with 200 million?

ANSWER: The Charter is based on the principle of the "equal rights" of "all nations large and small." Article 2(1) of the Charter states: "The Organization is based on the principle of the sovereign equality of all its Members." This is merely a restatement of the democratic principle of the equality of all citizens under a national constitution. This is one of the fundamental principles of the Charter.

QUESTION: Representatives to the United Nations are appointed to their posts; they are not elected. How can the "voiceless millions" make known their wishes on United Nations questions?

ANSWER: The United Nations, as already pointed out, is an intergovernmental organization. In the United Nations the "voiceless millions" are heard through the representatives of their countries. In my judgment they are quite effectively heard, because in the General Assembly all Member governments have an equal voice and an equal opportunity to persuade other Member governments to share their point of view. The regular annual sessions of the General Assembly begin traditionally with a general debate, in the course of which practically every Member government participates and makes known its views on the various major issues of the day. I would say that this general debate does give an opportunity for the "voiceless millions" of the world to make their voice heard in the United Nations.

In addition, the people of dependent territories have the right to present petitions to the United Nations and many of their representatives have been granted hearings throughout the years before the competent bodies of the Organization. There are several cases of persons who first appeared before the United Nations as petitioners and later, upon the attainment of independence by their respective countries, became president, prime minister, or an important member of the government.

QUESTION: What do leaders from the newly independent and developing countries expect from the United Nations? And how does the United Nations family provide assistance without being accused of intervening in a country's domestic affairs?

ANSWER: Above all, the leaders from the newly independent and developing countries expect from the United Nations assistance which is competent, impartial, disinterested, and without strings. United Nations assistance is tough in that it calls for considerable sacrifice and burdensharing on the part of the requesting government. In our experience, however, this is not resented, for the United Nations sticks firmly to the principle that assistance rendered must be based entirely on the request of governments and on reasonable priorities set by them. The United Nations has, of course, no axe to grind in any country and its program of assistance represents a partnership, a form of full and voluntary cooperation. Almost all countries that receive help also contribute help, financial and in the form of experts; and, in the decision-making, all countries have an equal voice.

QUESTION: As a former journalist, do you believe that the world press covers the United Nations adequately and honestly?

ANSWER: It is true that in my early years my ambition was to be a political journalist. I gave it up to enter the service of my country, yet I never divorced myself entirely from journalism and indeed I was the head of the Burmese press and broadcasting services, and was thus able to maintain close contact with press and radio professionals. I have always cultivated such personal contacts in my subsequent positions as permanent representative of Burma to the United Nations, Acting Secretary-General and Secretary-General. I feel very close to working newspapermen and I like to think of myself as sensitive to their needs and their professional problems just as I hope they consider me to be vitally interested in the field of information, be it journalism, radio, or television.

As to the coverage of the United Nations by the world press, I would say that, on the whole, it is not adequate. At times the coverage of political events in which the United Nations is involved suffers from an overemphasis on the sensational and controversial aspects of the news. Conversely, not enough attention is given to the slow but genuine progress the world organization is able to make toward the peaceful solution of a potentially dangerous situation. And as to nonpolitical news emanating from the United Nations and its family of specialized agencies, we feel that it is still regrettably inadequate and fails to give world opinion a day-to-day picture of the modest but effective assistance which the United Nations family is able to give Member states especially those of developing areas of Asia, Africa, and Latin America, in their unremitting struggle against poverty, disease, and illiteracy. I would welcome a determined effort by the world press to increase and intensify its coverage of our economic, social, and educational news.

QUESTION: Despite undersecretaries and advisers, there are certain decisions—momentous ones affecting the delicate balance of war or peace—that can be made only between the Secretary-General and his conscience. How do you and your conscience get along?

ANSWER: It is indeed true that, at times, the Secretary-General is utterly alone when faced with a decision that might affect the outcome of a serious political crisis. In a broader sense, however, he is not ever really alone. Beyond the undersecretaries and advisers on whom he relies, and the representatives of Member governments with whom he exchanges views, there is in the background an invisible presence which to him is very real and comforting: the yearning for peace and brotherhood of untold millions which increasingly expresses itself in the nonmeasurable but unmistakable existence of a world public opinion.

QUESTION: United Nations observers have noted that during periods of extreme anxiety and pressure, you never lose your appearance of tranquillity and inner calm. It has been suggested that perhaps your Buddhist asceticism provides you with a shield against emotional upset? Comment?

ANSWER: It is true that the spiritual and ethical values of Buddhism provide serenity, strength, tolerance, and humility. I believe that similarly the ethical values of any of the world's great faiths—Hinduism, Christianity, Judaism, or Islam, for instance—would likewise strengthen anyone is a position of high responsibility who draws on spiritual values in difficult moments.

QUESTION: What is your political credo?

ANSWER: I believe in democracy and in the institutions that the democratic and representative form of government embodies, based on free elections and the essential freedoms as outlined in the United Nations Declaration of Human Rights. I am aware, however, that there are millions in the world who adhere to other political credos and whose views would be taken into account and respected, as long as they are not in contradiction with the basic principles of the United Nations Charter and the Declaration of Human Rights.

QUESTION: What will some future journalist, writing one hundred years from today, describe as the most significant event of our time?

ANSWER: The signing of the Charter of the United Nations in San Francisco on October 24, 1945.

From Transcript of Press Conference

NEW YORK   SEPTEMBER 12, 1963

TWO WEEKS after U Thant had appealed to Ngo Dinh Diem, president of the Republic of Vietnam, on behalf of the Buddhists, the question was raised again in his September 12 press conference. He took the occasion to voice his first strong criticism of the Government of South Vietnam. He described the situation there as chaotic and as "going from bad to worse." Two major virtues of democracy, he said, were completely absent: the ability to change governments by peaceful constitutional processes and the ability to conduct public affairs by persuasion, not force. Thant disclosed that he had been in constant contact with United States Ambassador Adlai E. Stevenson on the problem, in view of the role of the United States in Vietnam, but he would not say what suggestions, if any, he had made. These interventions were the beginnings of Thant's personal involvement in Vietnam.

. . . . QUESTION: Many weeks ago, you told us of your quiet diplomatic efforts to help to end the persecution of the Buddhists in Vietnam. Now some of the key figures in this terrible drama are coming to New York: the archbishop, brother of the president, has arrived; the sister-in-law is coming. My questions are these. Do you intend to establish personal contact with these people? And, secondly, in what way do you think that the United Nations can most usefully take action to help to resolve the situation?

THE SECRETARY-GENERAL: Regarding the first question, so far I have not received any intimation that some of the leading figures of the Republic of Vietnam are coming to New York or to the United Nations. If I receive any request from any one of them, I will be glad to receive them here.

Regarding your second question, the item has already been inscribed on the draft agenda of the forthcoming session of the General Assembly. Actually fourteen Member states have requested the inscription. Therefore, the possibilities are that the question will be discussed in the forthcoming session. Of course, I have no means of knowing the trend of the

UN Correspondents Note No. 2798.

discussion or the outcome of the debates, but all I want to say at this stage is that I am sure you will agree with me that the situation in the Republic of Vietnam is going from bad to worse.

I cannot think of any other country today where the situation is as chaotic as the situation in that unfortunate country. As you all know, one of the great virtues of democracy is its ability to change governments by peaceful constitutional processes and without resort to force—a feature which is completely absent in the Republic of Vietnam. Another great virtue of democracy is that it uses persuasion and not force in the conduct of its public affairs—again, a feature which is completely absent in the Republic of Vietnam.

QUESTION: In the recent resignation of General von Horn, he mentioned certain differences with Headquarters. I was wondering whether you would care to comment or elaborate on his resignation.

THE SECRETARY-GENERAL: There has been a lot of coverage in the press in the last week or so regarding the resignation of General von Horn. I hope my report on the United Nations Yemen Observation Mission, submitted to the Security Council on September 4 set the record straight. But I just want to add a few more observations on this. The United Nations has to perform its operations in Yemen with one major consideration. It has to operate within the financial resources available for that purpose. As you are aware, the United Arab Republic and Saudi Arabia had agreed to contribute $200,000 each toward the expenses of the operation for two months. So in the conduct of the observation mission in Yemen, the primary consideration is that this must be confined within the four corners of the financial resources available for that particular period.[1] And General von Horn's main complaint, obviously, was that Headquarters had not been able to comply with all his requests—a complaint which has been contested by other observers in Yemen. So on August 20 he submitted his resignation. On August 21, after due consideration, I accepted his resignation. On August 25, from Cairo, General von Horn withdrew his resignation. Since I had given sufficient thought to this matter, it became my painful duty not to be able to accept his withdrawal. Therefore, his resignation stood.

By way of passing, I wish to say that I have a very high esteem for General von Horn, for his past dedicated service in the cause of the United Nations, and also because of the country from which he comes—

---

[1] The fact is, however, that despite the financial situation, all of his requests which were considered reasonable were met.

Sweden, whose people have consistently dedicated their resources in the cause of the United Nations, and shown their faith and trust in this world Organization. I hope his resignation and my acceptance of his resignation will be understood in this light, and there is nothing personal in this whole affair.

.... QUESTION: In view of the special position of the United States in South Vietnam, have you conveyed your views on this problem to President Kennedy and Secretary of State Rusk? And since you are a Buddhist and also a man interested in peace, have you any suggestions as to what the United States can do in order to ease this crisis?

THE SECRETARY-GENERAL: I have been in constant contact with the permanent representative of the United States regarding the situation in the Republic of Vietnam. I cannot say more than that.

.... QUESTION: In previous years, as the session of the General Assembly was about to open, you have given us your ideas on universality of membership in the Assembly and in the United Nations. Now there have been some changes in the world. I wonder if you would give us your comments on the status of your ideas about universality of membership, particularly with reference to the People's Republic of China and the maintenance of Portugal and South Africa within the Organization.

THE SECRETARY-GENERAL: There are two issues involved here. The first issue is concerned with universality, a principle which is implied in the Charter itself and a principle to which I fully subscribe. I still maintain this position. I believe in the desirability of universality of membership in the United Nations.

Regarding the question of Portugal and the Republic of South Africa, I have no views to offer except that if the General Assembly or any other competent organ of the United Nations wishes to take any action, there are definite provisions in the Charter. If I may point them out to you, Articles 5 and 6 are relevant in this context.

QUESTION: I have two questions, Mr. Secretary-General. Do you still expect the over-all deficit of the United Nations at the end of 1963 to be in the neighborhood of $140 million? If the deficit is maintained, is there any danger of your having to give up other peacekeeping operations, just as you are doing in the Congo?

THE SECRETARY-GENERAL: I still estimate that the over-all deficit at the end of this year will be in the neighborhood of $140 million, and I still maintain that without authorization to me by any competent organ of the

United Nations, I cannot undertake to discharge any operations in any part of the world for the purpose of peacekeeping.

QUESTION: Would you have to give up any others besides the Congo?

THE SECRETARY-GENERAL: There are two major United Nations military operations, UNEF and the Congo. As you all know, I am guided primarily by the availability of financial resources. Regarding the Congo, the special session of the General Assembly authorized me to spend certain specific sums for ONUC and UNEF up till December 31, 1963, and I will not have a single cent to spend for these operations beyond December 31, 1963. Of course, it is for the General Assembly or any other competent organ of the United Nations to come to a decision very quickly, particularly regarding the Congo operations. I have suggested to certain Member states and to all the members of the Congo advisory committee that if I am to proceed with the military operations in the Congo beyond 1963, I would need a financial authorization very quickly, in any case not later than the first week of October this year, because I have to readjust the supply pipelines and I have to readjust the logistics. If I am authorized very late in the year—for instance, in November or December—the pipelines have to be restored at tremendous expense.

While on the subject, I want to clarify one point which is not properly understood in certain quarters. As I indicated on May 15 this year in the Fifth Committee, it is not unreasonable to anticipate the complete withdrawal of United Nations military forces from the Congo by the end of 1963, for two reasons. The primary reason is financial. The secondary reason is related to the fulfilment of the Security Council mandates.

Regarding the financial aspect, as I just said a moment ago, I am authorized to spend only up to December 31, 1963. If I am asked to operate beyond the year, there are a few factors which should be taken into consideration. The first factor is the size of the armed forces. In my position, I have to abide by the advice of my military commanders and military adviser. The advice tendered by my military people for the effective discharge of United Nations obligations in the Congo is that the minimum force required in the Congo is six thousand officers and men, and not less. Otherwise, in their view, the United Nations would be so exposed to the risk that the world Organization may be discredited at some time or another. If ONUC is not in a position to discharge its obligations effectively, then it is better for us not to have a token force there.

The second point relates to the functions of ONUC. As you know, certain elements[2] all over the world were very critical of the way in which ONUC discharged its responsibility in the Congo because of the exercise of a requisite measure of force in certain circumstances. These same elements are now coming out with a proposal to maintain United Nations forces for another six months beyond 1963. Of course, it is a difficult situation. When I say that some elements were very critical of ONUC for its exercise of a requisite measure of force in certain circumstances and that these same elements now want the United Nations to stay on, I wonder if they want the United Nations forces in the Congo to perform the functions of Boy Scouts or Sunday school teachers—a proposition, of course, which I cannot accept.

If it is agreed that there must be a certain police force in Manhattan, how can you restrict the activities of the policemen? How can you instruct them never to use force in any circumstances? I cannot understand such an attitude. If the United Nations is to perform its legitimate functions in the Congo for the maintenance of law and order and for the performance of its obligations as instructed by the Security Council, then it must be free to use a requisite measure of force if necessary in certain circumstances. This is a point that I want to stress.

Of course, Prime Minister Adoula made a request, on August 22, that consideration be given to retaining a force of three thousand troops beyond December 1963. As you all know, I yield to no one in my desire to see the Congo peaceful and prosperous, but we also have other considerations—military considerations, financial considerations—which I cannot overlook without a specific mandate from a competent organ of the United Nations.

. . . . QUESTION: Do you expect the United Nations to play any role in the context of the discussions which may take place on the future of the city of Berlin and related matters? I have in mind a suggestion made recently by Foreign Minister Gromyko, in a two-hour meeting in Moscow with Dr. Thomas Dehler, vice-president of the West German Bundestag, that a German peace treaty should sanction the wall around West Berlin and turn it into an enclave between sovereign states, presumably administered by the United Nations as a *corpus separatum*.

THE SECRETARY-GENERAL: The question of Berlin is completely outside the competence of the United Nations. As I have indicated on a previous

[2] When speaking of certain "elements", the Secretary-General was not referring to governments, but to certain sections of the public and the press.

occasion, this is a question which can be settled only with the agreement of the four big powers primarily concerned. So far, to my knowledge, there has been no indication on the part of any of these four big powers of an intention to involve the United Nations in a settlement of this question.

. . . . QUESTION: You have just outlined your basic philosophy on what one might call the active peacekeeping of the United Nations, as in the Congo. My question relates to what might be called, also in this context, passive peacekeeping—observation, as it goes on in Yemen. If at the beginning of November the fighting in Yemen still continues, as reports indicate it may well do, what kind of scar will that leave on the visage of the United Nations as a peace organ?

THE SECRETARY-GENERAL: We have to look at these problems in this light. When I received the request of the two governments—actually three governments—to undertake certain functions based on the agreement of the governments concerned, I felt that I had no alternative, as in the case of Malaysia. In the case of Malaysia also, when three heads of government met in Manila and came to a unanimous agreement, and asked me to undertake certain functions based on that agreement, I felt I had no alternative but to comply with their joint request.

Of course, in the case of Malaysia, as you know, I undertook to discharge these responsibilities on three conditions: firstly, the administering authority of the territories must agree to the operation as indicated by the three heads of government; secondly, the three governments involved must agree to contribute toward the expenses of such an operation; and, thirdly, I made it clear to the three governments that my findings or my conclusions would not be subject to any ratification or confirmation by any government.

On that basis I sent a team to undertake the work requested by the three governments.

In the case of Yemen, also on the basis of the agreement arrived at between the governments of the United Arab Republic and Saudi Arabia, and on the basis of the agreement of the two governments concerned to contribute toward the expenses of the United Nations operations, the United Nations observation team in Yemen has started operations. There was no alternative, to me. Of course, if I refused to comply with their joint request there were certain possibilities, none of which would be conducive to peace. That much I can say. . . .

THE SITUATION IN THE CONGO

AUGUST AND SEPTEMBER

THE WITHDRAWAL of United Nations forces from the Congo continued during the spring and summer of 1963 as political conditions became more and more stable. Although serious problems remained, U Thant said in his annual report issued on August 20 (p. 404): ". . . the time has come when, for various reasons, it is necessary to envisage the early withdrawal and winding-up of the United Nations Force in the Congo." At a press conference on September 12, the Secretary-General disclosed that Prime Minister Adoula had requested that the United Nations leave a force of three thousand men in the Congo beyond the end of 1963. He was not too happy about the prospect. First of all, he noted that his military advisers had told him that a minimum of six thousand would be needed to avoid undue exposure to risk. He also pointed out that he had been authorized to spend money on ONUC only up to December 31, 1963, and that he would need new authorization very quickly to give him time to readjust the supply pipelines and the logistics. Thant was concerned over the fact that "certain elements" of the public and the press, which had been most critical of the exercise of force by United Nations troops were the same elements pressing the United Nations to stay on in the Congo. "I wonder," he said, "if they want the United Nations forces in the Congo to perform the functions of Boy Scouts or Sunday school teachers—a proposition, of course, which I cannot accept." He asserted that if United Nations troops remain in the Congo they must "be free to use a requisite measure of force." Thant reviewed the situation fully in a report to the Security Council dated September 17, 1963, in which he raised the question of keeping some United Nations troops in the Congo after the end of the year. He made no specific recommendations, however. He simply commented that there were cogent reasons in support of Adoula's request and also in favor of early withdrawal of the forces. He reported that as of September 13, the total number of men in the United Nations force was down to 7,975, as compared to the peak strength of 20,000 in June, 1961. On October 18, acting upon the request of the Congolese government, the General Assembly decided to extend the stay of United Nations forces until June 30, 1964.

1. Report to the Security Council

NEW YORK   SEPTEMBER 17, 1963

1. THIS REPORT is devoted primarily to the question of United Nations military disengagement in the Congo (Leopoldville).

Phasing Out

2. The United Nations Force in the Congo now has been deployed over the vast expanse of that country for more than three years. Although at its peak strength, in June 1961, it numbered about twenty thousand officers and men, as of September 13, 1963, it had been reduced to 7,975, by means of the phasing out which has been taking place according to schedule since last February.

3. The United Nations Force in the Congo was established under the Security Council resolution of July 14, 1960. The Security Council resolutions of July 14, July 22, and August 9, 1960, and of February 21 and November 24, 1961, set forth various mandates for the United Nations Operation in the Congo (ONUC), and later on this report will give some indications of how those mandates have been carried out. Although no specific terminal date for the Force has been set by any Security Council resolution, the General Assembly, at its fourth special session on June 27, 1963, adopted resolution 1876 (S-IV) which, in the absence of any subsequent action, establishes, in effect, a terminal date. For that resolution appropriates money and authorizes me to expend money for the Force in the Congo up to December 31, 1963 only, with no indication that any extension of the Force beyond that date was envisaged.

4. In the light of the General Assembly's resolution, I am proceeding with the phasing out schedule for the Force, which has had to be carefully prepared and geared to available transport, and which looks toward the

Security Council Official Records, Eighteenth Year, Supplement for July, August and September 1963, document S/5428.

complete withdrawal from the Congo of United Nations troops by December 31, 1963.

Prime Minister Adoula's Letter

5. There is now an important new factor bearing on the question of military disengagement. In a letter dated August 22, 1963, Prime Minister Adoula, while agreeing with the substantial reduction of the United Nations Force that has been taking place during the past few months, sees a need for the continued presence of a small United Nations Force of about three thousand officers and men through the first half of 1964. He expresses the belief that it is not yet time to envisage the possibility of withdrawing the United Nations troops entirely. That letter is annex I to this report (see section 2 (a) below). The prime minister's appeal, beyond question, calls for very serious consideration, especially when taken in the context of the wording of paragraph 2 of the Security Council resolution of July 14, 1960. But the appeal must also be weighed in relation to the practical considerations. My reply to the prime minister's letter is set forth in annex II (see section 2 (b) below).

The Financial Factor

6. From the standpoint of my ability to act, the financial situation is unavoidably controlling. It has been my view all along that given the required finance, I could continue to maintain the force in the Congo at the needed strength as long as necessary, assuming, of course, that there would be no directive to the contrary from a responsible United Nations organ. But the required finance will be lacking after the end of this year, unless some new action is taken by the General Assembly, as has been the practice in the past, to appropriate funds and authorize their expenditure for the Force for a definite or indefinite period in the next year. Here I would like to warn that if any such new action is contemplated, it must be taken very soon, since, in anticipation of its termination by December 31, supplies for the Force are no longer being fed into its logistics pipeline. Because pipeline supplies are procured on the basis of a six months lead, the current needs of the Force are being met from supplies ordered much earlier. To establish and feed supplies into a new pipeline would take much time and would be very costly.

7. As to finance, I may point out that the total cost to the United Nations as of August 31, 1963 of its involvement in military and civilian assistance in the Congo since the middle of July 1960 amounts to $401,008,771, of which about $43,500,000 is related to the civilian operations (technical assistance) program. It has been possible to finance the military aspect of the ONUC operation since last year only by utilizing for this purpose most of the proceeds from the sale of United Nations bonds, and by permitting the unpaid obligations of the Organization arising from the Congo operation to accumulate by scores of millions of dollars. The substantial reduction in the strength of the Force has, of course, greatly lightened its cost in recent months. Nevertheless, in view of the serious financial condition of the United Nations, brought about by the refusal or failure of many Members to pay the special assessments, the continuance for very much longer of heavy expenses incident to a military force in the Congo might well threaten the Organization with insolvency. This consideration naturally exerts a very strong influence on my thinking about the question of military disengagement.

Essential Size of a Force

8. The appeal made to me in the letter from the prime minister proposes that a force of three thousand men, equipped with means of rapid movement, be maintained in the Congo through the first half of 1964. Quite apart from the question of the urgency of the need for such a force, the prime minister's appeal raises an important question as to the essential size of any force that should be maintained after the end of this year.

9. All of the senior United Nations military advisers, both in the Congo and at Headquarters, have advised me that the minimum strength of a United Nations force in the Congo in the foreseeable future should be not less than six thousand officers and men. Their view has been that a force of less strength would not only have little practical utility in assisting in the maintenance of law and order, but would also be vulnerable through inability to protect itself, its bases, and its lifelines in an emergency. The present Force commander, however, in response to my query, has recently informed me that in view of an improved capability on the part of the National Congolese Army (ANC), and assuming maximum cooperation with it in such spheres as joint patrolling, he would consider that a force of five thousand officers and men could be main-

tained without too great risk, if adequate air support for personnel and vehicle airlift could be ensured.

10. It follows that a force of no more than three thousand would be, to all intents and purposes, only a token force. Even this, some say, could serve a useful purpose. It is no doubt true that the mere fact of the presence of a United Nations force of any size in the country exerts a restraining influence and in general makes a positive impact for good. Morover, it is said that the presence of even a very small number of United Nations troops is a form of insurance, for, if serious troubles again beset the Congo, it would be much easier for the United Nations to extend timely assistance if this could be built on an existing nucleus.

11. The United Nations military advisers agree that the Congolese army and police are still lacking the ability to assume full responsibility for law and order in the country, and that therefore a case can be made for the need of military assistance from outside beyond 1963. There is the continuing problem of lack of discipline in the ANC. Some tribal conflict persists. There is still an inadequate exercise of governmental authority in many areas. It is also the case that a United Nations force in the Congo must rely primarily upon itself for air transport, secure airfields, dependable signals communications, and logistics requirements.

12. It is thought by the military advisers that the requirement for the Force, if it were to be extended beyond the end of this year, would be an infantry brigade of three infantry battalions plus two additional battalions, together with adequate signals, air transport, and logistics units. The total personnel required would thus be between five thousand and six thousand. A force reduced to this extent should be deployed in such manner that its units would be able to support each other.

Cost of a Force

13. It is roughly estimated that the cost of a force of approximately 3,400 officers and men, including the administrative and field staff required for the operation for a period of six months from January 1, 1964, would be about $13,350,000. The cost of a force of 6,000 for the same period would probably be not less than $25 million.

Mandates Given by the Security Council

14. In my report to the Security Council of February 4, 1963, I dealt with the implementation of the mandates given in the Security Council

resolutions of July 14, 1960 and of February 21 and November 24, 1961. My general conclusions at that time were that an important phase of the United Nations Operation in the Congo had been completed, that most of the aims of the operation had been in large measure fulfilled, but that it would be necessary for the United Nations to exercise vigilance, to provide military assistance over a transitional period to assist the Congolese government in maintaining law and order and, within the limits of the funds available, to provide technical assistance on as large a scale as possible during the period of reconstruction. In the intervening months there have been no striking new developments, but a further assessment of the situation is now in order.

15. There can be no doubt that a major turning point has been reached this year in the United Nations Operation in the Congo. From this, certain conclusions may be drawn which apply particularly to the United Nations force there. While it cannot be denied that the Congolese government does not yet have at its disposal national military and police forces fully adequate to the needs of security and order, it can definitely be said that despite all the difficulties great strides forward have been made over the last three years.

16. The mutiny of the Congolese Force publique which, together with the intervention of Belgian troops, first brought on the Congo crisis in July 1960, resulting in the United Nations operation coming into the country in response to the government's urgent appeal, was quickly suppressed and the Belgian troops were withdrawn soon after the United Nations troops were deployed. The danger of secessionist movements in various forms would seem, for the present at any rate, to have been largely eliminated. The demands of the resolution adopted by the Security Council on February 21, 1961, concerning the withdrawal from the Congo of foreign military and paramilitary personnel and mercenaries have also been met, and for the first time in the Congo's more than three years of independence it would appear that no organized and subversive military groups under the leadership of foreign military personnel are active on Congolese territory. There have been recently, however, some disquieting but as yet unconfirmed reports about the threat of new activity.

17. The policies and purposes of the United Nations set out at length in the resolution adopted by the Security Council on November 24, 1961 would also appear to have been substantially implemented. The territorial integrity and political independence of the Republic of the Congo

have been maintained; and there is, at present, no serious threat of civil war.

18. There has been marked progress toward restoration of law and order, but here it must be emphasized that the situation is still far from reassuring. There are sporadic reports from many parts of the country of incidents of abusive treatment, criminal assault, robbery and pillaging, and occasional murder, attributable to unruly elements of the ANC and in Katanga also to ex-Katangese gendarmerie, as well as to activities of the Jeunesse groups (organized youth elements of several political parties). In this regard it must be pointed out that while further progress toward restoration of law and order in the Congo may be registered by June 1964, it would be a reasonable assumption that a good case for a further prolongation of the United Nations Force in the Congo, on the same grounds as now, could also be made at that time. I am assured by many that there has been a substantial improvement in the degree of discipline prevailing in the ANC, but few disagree that the need for the retraining and reorganization of that Army continues to be acute. It is also pertinent to note that the Congo is now united under a single, constitutional, and internationally recognized Central Government, which has been in continuous existence since August 2, 1961.

19. It seems to me to be reasonable not to expect the United Nations to underwrite for any country permanent insurance against internal disorders and disturbances, by indefinitely providing an important part of the internal police power for exclusively internal use, when external threats have ended.

20. Regarding the aspect of international peace, I think that on balance it may be prudently observed that there has been an improvement in the internal conditions of the Congo to a sufficient degree to lead to a major amelioration in the international aspect of the situation, which is to say that the Congo's internal situation no longer poses a serious threat to international peace.

Uncertainties

21. There are, however, some serious uncertainties and imponderables in the Congo situation. The authority and the effective functioning of the services of the Central Government are still not well established in the south of Katanga. The plan to reintegrate the ex-Katangese gendarmerie

into the ANC has been a conspicuous failure, with only some 2,600 registering and possibly 15,000 others in hiding, many of them retaining their arms. A quite recent report confirms that many ex-members of the Katangese gendarmerie are drawing their wages and leaving their civilian jobs in Elisabethville, in such numbers and with such timing as to suggest a response to orders and a directed scheme to return them to organized contingents. Mr. Tshombé's future intentions are unknown. He is still out of the country. Some believe that he is only awaiting the withdrawal of the United Nations troops to make a new move. He and three of his former ministers—Munongo, Kimba, and Kibwe—are believed to be in Rhodesia. Their potential for troublemaking undoubtedly remains high. A good many among the non-African population in Katanga are still not resigned to the permanence of Central Government authority over Katanga. Rumors and fears persist in some quarters about the possibility of a recrudescence of mercenary activity in Katanga. Economic conditions generally are not good. There is anxiety about the possibility that the national election scheduled for the spring of 1964 may be attended by serious tribal clashes.

The National Congolese Army in the South of Katanga

22. As anticipated in my previous report, the introduction of the ANC into the south of Katanga, which by agreement was to be phased, has proved to be a most delicate operation. In the first place, the ANC units concerned were conscious of the hostility and concern of much of the European and Congolese population, and at the same time were apprehensive about their own security in the midst of a gendarmerie which had not yet dispersed and in some cases still bore arms. They faced the provocations of the continued display of secessionist emblems and sentiments. In order to reduce the possibilities of friction, it was arranged with the Congolese authorities that the ANC in the south of Katanga should be placed temporarily under the operational control of ONUC, which for the time being would exercise primary responsibility for maintaining law and order. In practice, the discipline of the ANC was not always sufficiently firm. Following some disturbing incidents involving Congolese troops, it was agreed that they should be temporarily located in camps with guard duties at some vital installations, and they no longer carried arms in cities when off duty. There were, however, a few attempts by

Congolese troops to leave their stations and to go to the support of comrades insulted or molested while on leave in the towns. ONUC troops in such situations were interposed to preserve order.

23. Happily, no serious incident of this kind has occurred since early June, and the ANC has taken appropriate disciplinary steps in connection with the earlier incidents. This phase of the ANC entry into Katanga is hopefully now ended. For a time it involved ONUC, which has been obliged to stress the importance of maintaining peaceful conditions, in some differences of opinion with the Congolese authorities, who, in view of the eventual withdrawal of the whole ONUC Force, are understandably anxious to have their troops established in South Katanga in full strength and without restriction at the earliest possible date. It may be noted that there are now more than three ANC battalions in the south of Katanga with elements at Elisabethville, Jadotville, Kolwezi, Kipushi, Dilolo, Kasenga, Mokambo, and Sakania. As one step toward creating a normal garrison role for Congolese troops in this area, arrangements are being made to have their families brought there.

Transfer of Responsibility

24. ONUC plans soon to transfer primary responsibility for security in southern Katanga into the hands of the Congolese government and to help facilitate friendly contacts between the ANC and the local population. In this connection, I must pay a warm tribute to the ONUC troops who, by their steadiness and impartiality, have earned the respect of the inhabitants, both Congolese and non-African. The arrangements which have been in force since the introduction of the first units of the ANC into southern Katanga in February 1963 were for the period of emergency following the end of the secession of Katanga. Under arrangements now being worked out the ANC will shortly assume full responsibility for law and order in southern Katanga as elsewhere in the Congo, and ONUC troops, while they remain, will stand by to assist the ANC where necessary and to help to meet emergencies should they arise.

Training of the National Congolese Army

25. As noted in my report of last February 4, the Prime Minister of the Republic of the Congo had requested the assistance of the United Nations in the reorganization and training of the ANC, and I had acceded to

the request, which was in accordance with paragraph 2 of the Security Council resolution of July 14, 1960.

26. I subsequently had circulated as a Security Council document further exchanges of letters between the Congolese government and me on that subject [p. 308]. It was clarified that the Congolese government wished me to request Belgium, Canada, Israel, Italy, and Norway to provide personnel for training and organizing the various military services, while the United States of America would provide material only. It was also the wish of the Congolese government that the United Nations should organize the program of assistance, mainly through a coordinating committee composed of members from the participating countries, with the addition of Ethiopia, Nigeria, and Tunisia. Even under those circumstances, however, I could not avoid some misgivings about the United Nations assuming sponsorship over what was essentially a bilateral program of military assistance by a particular group of states. Therefore, I referred the matter to the Advisory Committee on the Congo, which I found shared my doubts. All members were in full accord on the need and urgency of a program for training the ANC, but the view was widely held that such training could most appropriately be given by those states which had provided contingents to the United Nations Force. I concluded, therefore, that it was inadvisable to accede to Mr. Adoula's request, while continuing to hope that a way would be found to make it possible for the ANC to receive the necessary training assistance.

27. Later on, Mr. Adoula informed me that his government intended to appeal for bilateral assistance in the reorganization of its army, while still wishing that the United Nations could be associated with the task. I have no official knowledge of subsequent developments, but I understand that Belgian officers are to organize a training scheme in the Congo, although this seems to be still in a very preliminary and exploratory stage. There would appear to be little basis for optimism about the prospects for significant progress in the training and modernization of the ANC by June 1964.

28. It is a matter of great regret to me that United Nations participation in the ANC training program has not been possible, since stability in the Congo must depend to a great extent on the discipline and effectiveness of its armed forces. Very much remains to be done in this regard. As a matter of record, it may be mentioned that as early as February 1962, I had stressed to Prime Minister Adoula the need for expediting the training of the ANC and my willingness to assist that effort with a plan that

would offer training by officers recruited by the United Nations from African and other countries. Mr. Adoula was in accord with my suggestion and the proposed approach, but the idea was never acted upon by the Congolese government, apparently because of disagreement about it within the government itself.

Training of Police

29. The question of the training of the ANC would have lesser importance if law and order could be protected in various localities by the local police forces. Unfortunately, those forces tend to be badly organized, poorly paid, and highly sensitive to political influence. In Leopoldville itself a police revolt occurred in May.

30. The Nigerian police serving in the Congo, by the example set by their conduct and effectiveness, have had a very helpful impact on the Congolese police. It is very satisfying, therefore, that the Nigerian government has now undertaken to help the Congolese government in the reorganization and modernization of the Congolese police force, which in the long view is also a vital necessity for the country. It appears likely that a Nigerian police unit will continue to serve in the Congo after the end of the year.

Consultations

31. Since receipt of the letter of appeal from Prime Minister Adoula I have consulted on the matter with a good many representatives, including all of the members of the Congo Advisory Committee. These consultations have revealed sharp divisions of opinion ranging from those who wish to see the prime minister's request granted without qualification, to those insisting on the withdrawal of the Force by or before the end of this year.

32. Most of the members of the advisory committee support the prime minister's request, although not all of them unconditionally. Some insist that enough United Nations troops must be maintained to ensure that they can discharge their tasks, or feel that Prime Minister Adoula should give a commitment that his request would not be renewed beyond June 1964. The view was also advanced that the Security Council should first be consulted on the issue of prolongation. Others were noncommittal, indicating a preference to rely upon the judgement of the Secretary-Gen-

eral and his military advisers. There was general recognition of the very great difficulty of obtaining financial support for an extension of a force of any size. It follows that from these consultations no conclusive advice emerged.

Risks

33. There are, beyond doubt, some serious risks involved in an early withdrawal of the Force. There have been risks in the United Nations Operation in the Congo all along and there are some now. I do not try to predict what may happen in the Congo when the United Nations troops are withdrawn, whether that may be at the end of December, next June, or indeed, even later. I hope for the best, and to the extent of the available resources everything possible will be done to protect the huge investment in men, money, and material which the United Nations has made in the Congo, to ensure that the tremendous United Nations effort will not have been futile. I am ever mindful that the greatest cost to the United Nations of its Congo enterprise has been the lives of many dedicated servants of peace, including, now two years ago, the life of Dag Hammarskjöld.

Civilian Operations

34. As in the case of military assistance, lack of finance is also threatening to cripple and, indeed, soon bring to an end the United Nations civilian operations program in the Congo, which by means of the Congo Fund, supported by voluntary contributions, has provided desperately needed technical assistance. It has been my hope that United Nations civilian assistance to the Congo could be continued and substantially increased after military assistance would be no longer required. My policy in that regard is unchanged. But the outlook for a special assistance beyond the limited aid afforded through regular channels is definitely unpromising.

35. In July, I was informed that by the end of that month the hard currency resources of the Congo Fund would be exhausted. I therefore appealed to Member states in late July and early August for further contributions, but the response to the appeal has been meager. Cash contributions have been received in the amounts of $1 million from the United States as an advance on a matching basis, $500,000 from the United Kingdom, and $75,000 from Denmark in payment of a pledge

made before the appeal. Subsequent to the appeal, pledges have also been made by Norway for $35,000 and by Finland for $25,000. If no other contributions are forthcoming, the anticipated cash deficit at year's end is estimated at between $1.6 million and $2 million. In addition, an estimated $4 million is needed to cover 1964 commitments.

Summation

36. Prime Minister Adoula has sent to me an appeal which could be met only if it should be the will of the General Assembly that financial provision be made to cover the costs of maintaining United Nations troops in the Congo beyond the end of 1963. If such a decision is reached in good time, the appropriation for the purpose should be sufficient to support a continuing force in the Congo of from 5,000 to 6,000 officers and men.

37. My sole purpose in this report has been to present the issue in its authentic setting. There are cogent reasons in support of prolonging the stay of the United Nations Force, the strongest of which is, of course, the request of Prime Minister Adoula that this be done. There are also impressive reasons for an early withdrawal of the Force, the most compelling of which is the Organization's already serious financial plight.

38. There can be no doubt that the presence of a United Nations force in the Congo would continue to be helpful to the government and the country, through the first half of 1964—or longer. But it cannot be doubted either that the time must soon come when the Government of the Congo will have to assume full responsibility for security and law and order in the country.

39. It is not excluded, of course, that if, through lack of financial provision, the United Nations cannot meet the prime minister's request to keep the Force in the Congo after the end of this year, certain countries may be willing to make some of their military units available to the Congo under bilateral arrangements. Once the United Nations Force is withdrawn there could be no question of such arrangements being inconsistent with the position of the Security Council.

40. My policy with regard to United Nations involvement in the Congo is unchanged. I have always wished to see the fullest possible effort exerted to meet the pressing needs of the Congo, in both military and civilian spheres. To that end, I have sought to ensure that the United Nations Operation in the Congo is so conducted as to achieve maximum

efficiency and effectiveness in the fulfilment of the general mandates laid down by the Security Council.

---

2. *Exchange of Letters with Prime Minister Adoula*

(a) Letter Dated August 22, 1963, from Prime Minister Adoula to the Secretary-General

The question of maintaining the United Nations Force in the Congo is now a matter of the utmost urgency for us and is of the greatest concern to my government.

In view of the impact which your statements on this subject have produced on world opinion, I felt obliged to express my view, *inter alia,* at the press conferences which I held during my official visits to London on July 22 to 26, and to Dublin, on July 26 to 28, 1963. I feel that the time has come to begin direct discussions in order to harmonize our views, especially since, though our attitudes differ on this problem, our objectives remain the same.

I fully appreciate your concern not to prolong the stationing of United Nations troops in the Congo any longer than is absolutely necessary. Nevertheless, we believe that the time has not yet come to visualize the possibility of terminating their mission.

Our evaluation of the situation takes into account the difficulties of all kinds which the maintenance of the United Nations Force in the Congo creates for the United Nations. That is why we agree with your decision to reduce the United Nations contingent at present stationed in our country.

We should like to see a highly mobile force of three thousand men maintained.

This force will enable us to concentrate on the current organization of our own security forces and to proceed with their progressive deployment throughout the whole country. The takeover from the United Nations troops will thus be carried out in the optimum conditions. We anticipate that this task can be completed by the end of the first half of 1964.

Security Council Official Records, Eighteenth Year, Supplement for July, August, and September 1963, document S/5428, annexes I and II.

I take this opportunity to renew my expression of gratitude for the task carried out by the United Nations in the Congo and for the important part which you personally have played in that connection.

Our position, as stated above, derives from the concern which we feel that this undertaking, which has cost so much effort and sacrifice, should bear fruit and achieve the objectives which the United Nations and the Congo have set themselves.

CYRILLE ADOULA
Prime Minister of
the Congo (Leopoldville)

(b) Letter Dated September 16, 1963, from the Secretary-General to Prime Minister Adoula

I have the honour to acknowledge receipt of your letter of August 22, 1963 on the subject of maintaining in the Congo through the first half of 1964 a United Nations military force of reduced size.

I am sorry for the delay in replying to your letter, but I know that Mr. Dorsinville, our officer-in-charge in Leopoldville, has explained to you that I had not wished to reply until I had undertaken consultations on the subject with a number of representatives of Member states here, and particularly with all of the members of the Congo Advisory Committee.

I have given most careful thought to your request and am setting forth in some detail my views on this and related questions in a report which I am submitting to the Security Council in a few days. I am, of course, incorporating your letter in that report and I thank you for permitting its release for that purpose. It had been distributed privately to all of the members of the Congo Advisory Committee immediately upon its receipt.

To my great regret, I have no choice but to inform you that as of now I lack the means of granting your request. The explanation of this is that the General Assembly, at its fourth special session, adopted on June 27, 1963 a resolution [1876 (S-IV)] which appropriated funds and authorized me to expend money for the United Nations Force in the Congo only until December 31, 1963. Therefore, any extension of the Force beyond the end of this year will require new action by the General Assembly providing financial support for the Force. I have made this clear in all of my consultations and, of course, I am emphasizing it in my report to the

Security Council, where I also warn that any such action in the Assembly must be taken without delay.

I should also mention that it is the view of all of the United Nations military experts and advisers that the minimum size of any United Nations Force to be maintained in the Congo, if it is to have more than token utility, must be not less than five thousand to six thousand officers and men. I feel bound to honour the considered advice on this question given to me by the United Nations military experts.

You will understand from what I have said above, I am sure, that the matter of prolonging the stay of the United Nations Force is not in my hands. You may be assured, however, that the Members of the United Nations will give most serious consideration to your request and will approach it with sympathetic understanding.

I extend to you always my most earnest wishes for the continued well-being of the Congo and for your own good health.

U THANT
Secretary-General of
the United Nations

Statement at the Consecration Ceremony of the Church Center for the United Nations

NEW YORK   SEPTEMBER 22, 1963

THE CHURCH CENTER is situated on United Nations Plaza, directly opposite United Nations Headquarters. It has no direct connection with the United Nations, but is a religious institution under the direction of the National Council of Churches in the United States. It has a nondenominational chapel on the street level, but is mainly an office building in which a number of nongovernmental organizations are tenants. The consecration ceremony provided another opportunity for Thant to express his belief in the close link between the great religions and the aims and principles of the United Nations. He previously had warmly welcomed the efforts of Pope John XXIII on behalf of world peace and had established a cordial relationship with his successor, Pope Paul VI. He told his audience at the Church Center that the new structure would serve as a reminder of the need to strive for the realization of spiritual as well as material values.

THE CHURCH CENTER for the United Nations which is being consecrated today is aimed at serving as a Christian symbol and a focal point of Christian education in international relations. As such, it has considerable significance and its activities will render, no doubt, a most useful purpose.

I see in the establishment of this center, however, an even larger meaning—one which is close to the very roots of the United Nations and is shared by the great number of nongovernmental institutions devoted to the teaching and to the support of the principles of the Charter. The United Nations, in effect, was intended to be not only an organization of governments but in a sense also an association of the peoples of the world. The chain of nongovernmental institutions supporting the United Nations from one confine to the other of the globe and promoting a clearer understanding of the aims, the limitations, and the activities of the United Nations, constitute a most important link between the Organiza-

UN Press Release SG/1587.

tion itself and people everywhere. It is fitting in this context to recall that the opening words of the Charter are not attributed to the governments signatories of the covenant, but are spoken on behalf of the "peoples of the United Nations."

In reading the statement on the purposes of the Church Center, I have noted that it not only intends to establish relationships, among others, with the United Nations and its related organizations, but also stresses the fact that it is an act of faith in the present and future of the United Nations and of the work of the churches for peace. It thus emphasizes, since its very inception, a broad spirit of service, one which goes beyond any narrow or sectarian conception.

I am sure that I can say without fear of contradiction that there are many provisions in the Charter of the United Nations which conform to the tenets of all great religions. One of them can be found in the Preamble where "the peoples of the United Nations" are asked "to practice tolerance and live together in peace with one another as good neighbours."

Experience shows us that dogmatic belief and intolerance go hand in hand. Wherever the one appears, the other is not far off. A peaceful progress in social development, in morality, knowledge, art, science, and philosophy, is possible only in a society where tolerance and freedom of thought prevail.

What above all helps to promote this sense of tolerance in a people is that universal and all-embracing kindness and love which, I believe, is the key to all great religions, and which is the foundation on which all moral and social progress is based.

Your building of sober architecture—the newest addition to the fast-growing family of constructions in the United Nations Plaza—will serve as a timely and constant reminder of the need to strive for the realization of spiritual as well as of material values. The quest for peace, whether in the minds of men or in the relations between states, can be successful only if adequate satisfaction is given to the basic aspirations of mankind for a better life, a life of ethical fulfillment as well as of material well-being. To sacrifice one or the other is to mutilate the essence of man.

Much has been said about the rapid scientific and technological advance and how far behind this progress lags our ability to solve the basic problem of living in peace with our fellow men. This is a generally accepted estimate of a rather obvious situation. But what is not so widely recognized as yet is that the solutions have now to be found through the means and in the context of international cooperation as much as through national efforts.

Your center is being inaugurated at the time when the United Nations General Assembly is meeting at its eighteenth regular session. Leaders of governments of every continent are gathered together once again to examine the state of the world and to deliberate about ways and means of solving international problems.

The eighteenth session has opened in an atmosphere of renewed hope. The partial test-ban treaty signed in Moscow on August 5, while in itself is an agreement of modest proportions, has opened the door to further and more meaningful steps in the direction of peace and disarmament.

I have no doubt that the Church Center has been founded with the aim, among others, of promoting awareness for international cooperation.

I have very great pleasure in welcoming its establishment and look forward to its contribution toward furthering tolerance, understanding, and friendship between peoples everywhere.

THE YEMEN MISSION

SEPTEMBER—NOVEMBER

THE UNITED NATIONS mission to Yemen had barely begun when word leaked out that its commander, Major General Carl von Horn, was engaged in a serious controversy with United Nations Headquarters in New York over his insistence on additional logistical support, particularly transport planes to airlift personnel and supplies. The dispute led to the resignation of von Horn on August 20 and to his subsequent press conference in Beirut in which he attacked the United Nations and asserted that Headquarters officials had "foggy ideas about reality." In his book *Soldiering for Peace,* published in 1966, the Swedish general gave his version of the controversy in detail. The blowup, according to von Horn's account, was precipitated by a message from him advising Headquarters that the United Nations reconnaissance squadron would have to be withdrawn from Yemen unless he received an additional Caribou plane within the next few days. He said the tone of the reply was "dictatorial." "I was told that everything was being done that could be done," he said, "and I was advised, in so many words, to stop bellyaching and get on with my job." He replied with a priority message to U Thant personally "telling him exactly what I thought about the administrative failure that was strangling the mission." According to von Horn's account, Thant advised him to take a tighter hold on administrative procedures and insure that reasonable economy was observed. Thant also told him that his "somewhat offensive remarks" were "entirely unwarranted." The next step was von Horn's resignation. He told Thant he felt he had lost the confidence of the Secretary-General and therefore had no choice but to quit.

The intensity of the backstage drama was not generally known at the time, nor was it fully disclosed in the Secretary-General's report on von Horn's resignation. In accepting the general's resignation, in fact, Thant had asked him to arrange his departure with "propriety" so as to avoid undesirable publicity. The Secretary-General dealt with the matter in a report to the Security Council on the Yemen situation on September 4, 1963, and at a press conference on September 12. He said at the press conference that all of von Horn's requests that were considered reasonable had been met, but that Headquarters had not been able to comply with all of them because the Yemen operation had to be confined within the financial resources available. The matter ended with von Horn withdrawing his resignation and Thant rejecting the withdrawal. "Since I had given sufficient thought to the matter," Thant said (p. 443), "it became my painful duty not to be able to accept his withdrawal."

1. Report to the Security Council

NEW YORK   SEPTEMBER 4, 1963

1. ON JUNE 11, 1963, the Security Council adopted a resolution requesting me to establish an observation mission in Yemen on the basis outlined in my report to the Council of April 29, concerning certain developments relating to Yemen, elaborated on in my further reports of May 27 and June 7. That resolution, in its operative paragraph 3, requests the Secretary-General to report to the Council and is the basis for this report.

2. Upon the adoption of the resolution of June 11, I immediately took steps to establish the United Nations Yemen Observation Mission (UNYOM). On June 13, the advance party of UNYOM, led by Major General Carl Carlson von Horn, who had been appointed by me as commander of the mission, arrived in Yemen. The object of the advance party was to undertake preparations for the mission to be set up and become operational in the shortest possible time, through making the necessary contacts, preliminary surveys, administrative arrangements, and establishing a communications system. The headquarters of the mission was set up in Sana, and a liaison office was placed in Jidda. The United Nations Emergency Force (UNEF) Liaison Office in Cairo assists in maintaining liaison with the appropriate authorities of the United Arab Republic.

3. There is a small civilian staff, based at Sana, consisting of twenty-eight international staff members and twenty locally recruited employees.

4. On the military side, UNYOM has a reconnaissance and an air unit. The reconnaissance unit consists of 114 Yugoslav officers and other ranks who were transferred from the Yugoslav contingent serving with UNEF. It arrived by ship at Hodeida on July 4. The unit was promptly deployed, with platoons being placed in Jizan and Najran, Saudi Arabia,

Security Council Official Records, Eighteenth Year, Supplement for July, August and September 1963, document S/5412.

and in Sa'da, Yemen. The air unit of about fifty officers and other ranks has been provided by the Royal Canadian Air Force, employing Caribou and Otter aircraft and H-19 helicopters. It is based in Sana, Jizan, and Najran. In addition to these two units, there is a small military headquarters staff based in Sana and six military observers stationed in Hodeida and Sana.

5. The operation of the mission is considered as having begun on July 4, 1963.

6. The function of the mission is to check and certify on the observance by the two parties of the terms of the disengagement agreement. This entails ground patrolling in the buffer zone and surrounding areas by the units stationed in Jizan, Najran, and Sa'da, and air patrolling in the mountainous central part of the buffer zone where land patrolling is impossible. The military observers stationed in Sana and Hodeida are primarily responsible for observing and certifying the withdrawal of troops.

7. It is to be noted particularly that by the provisions of the agreement on disengagement, UNYOM's functions are limited to observing, certifying, and reporting. This operation has no peacekeeping role beyond this and therefore it has a more restricted range of activity than the United Nations Truce Supervision Organization in Palestine and the United Nations military observers group in India and Pakistan, not to mention the United Nations Emergency Force and the United Nations Operation in the Congo. It could not, in fact, effectively undertake any broader functions with the personnel, equipment, and funds now available to it. It bears emphasis, also, that the agreement on disengagement involves only Saudi Arabia and the United Arab Republic by the former's intention to end activities in support of the royalists from Saudi Arabian territory and the latter's intention to withdraw its troops from Yemen. UNYOM, therefore, is not concerned with Yemen's internal affairs generally, with actions of the Government of Yemen, or with that government's relations with other governments and bordering territories, nor does UNYOM have any authority to issue orders or directions. The parties themselves are solely responsible for fulfilling the terms of disengagement on which they have agreed.

8. The United Nations Yemen Observation Mission encounters unusual hardships. Physical conditions in Yemen are severe. The terrain is rugged. Local supplies and facilities are meager. Funds are limited. UNYOM personnel and aircraft have been subjected to gunfire and are

frequently in danger. In the circumstances, the members of the mission are due great credit for their courage and devotion to duty, and their persistence, often beyond the call of duty, in performing their assigned tasks.

9. On August 20, I received a cable from General von Horn, firmly submitting, for urgent reasons, his resignation as commander of the mission. After very careful consideration, I accepted the resignation, effective as of August 31, 1963, in the belief that this would be in the best interest of the mission and of General von Horn himself. At my request, the deputy commander of the Yemen observation mission, colonel Branko Pavlović, agreed to serve for the time being as acting commander. Colonel Pavlović had served with distinction in this same capacity during General von Horn's three-week absence from the mission on leave in July.

10. There have been recently some rather irresponsible and reckless accounts of conditions relating to the mission. My purpose is to present a true picture. I had, in fact, some time ago directed Major-General Rikhye, my military adviser, to go to the area to inspect the mission and assist it in solving its problems. On September 2, I received a cable sent jointly by Colonel Pavlović and General Rikhye, informing me that they had just completed an inspection tour of all elements of the Yemen observation mission. They assured me that "despite personal hardships, difficulties in supplying fresh rations and unavoidable lack of amenities, the morale of mission personnel is indeed very high." They added that there is not and has never been any serious shortage of rations, though ration stocks reached a low level at one point owing to a temporary uncertainty as to the best means of transportation. The ration stock position, they asserted, "never reached a critical stage" and the ration scales have always been maintained "in accordance with United Nations standards." They also advised me that the present strength of the mission in personnel is adequate to carry out its tasks if these are limited to observation and report only. They observe, however, that the parties are making increasing demands on UNYOM to undertake tasks, such as investigation of incidents, not covered in the mission's terms of reference. Since efforts to procure the proper type of helicopters have been unsuccessful and the H-19 type have proved unsuitable, there is a need for an additional three aircraft of the Otter type and these are being provided.

11. Although short and specific reports are received regularly from UNYOM on the results of its daily observation and patrolling, from

which it is possible to gain some impression of the daily progress, or lack of it, in the implementation of the disengagement agreement, it is not possible at this stage to obtain from the mission any detailed or conclusive report. When possible, I will, of course, submit such a report to the Council.

12. UNYOM reports that it has no firm figures on the number of United Arab Republic troops actually withdrawn and the number of fresh United Arab Republic troops that have arrived as replacements. Although United Arab Republic sources in Yemen withhold exact information on grounds of security, they state that some thirteen thousand troops from the United Arab Republic have been withdrawn. The figure of fifteen hundred for new arrivals has been cited but has not been verified as accurate. UNYOM observers have noted departures of United Arab Republic troops in substantial numbers, but have also seen replacements arriving, though in apparently lesser numbers.

13. There has likewise been an indicated reduction in the extent of assistance from Saudi Arabian territory to royalist ranks and supporters in Yemen, but such traffic has certainly not come to an end. In fact, UNYOM air and ground patrols report a recent possible increase in vehicular and animal traffic across the border.

14. There have been various complaints presented to UNYOM by both parties. Where appropriate and possible, these complaints have been investigated by UNYOM. In general, they fall into two main categories, as follows:

(a) allegations of offensive action by United Arab Republic forces against royalist positions in Yemen and on Saudi Arabian territory;

(b) activities in support of the royalists emanating from Saudi Arabia.

15. It is to be expected that in a situation of the kind found in Yemen, there would be some spectacular allegations about the conduct of one side or the other. This has happened. UNYOM, where possible, has sought to investigate such allegations.

16. Observations of the mission to date indicate clearly enough that in some important respects the terms of the disengagement agreement have not been fulfilled by either of the parties. Some of the complaints about United Arab Republic air actions have been investigated by military observers, and on occasion UNYOM personnel have witnessed such actions. In recent weeks, United Nations patrols have also observed trucks and camels carrying weapons and ammunition as well as food and other

stores crossing the Saudi Arabian border toward areas held by Yemen royalists.

17. UNYOM, because of its limited size and function, can observe and certify only certain indications of the implementation of the disengagement agreement. It can, within limits, also serve as an intermediary and as endorser of good faith on behalf of the parties concerned, and it is my intention to have the mission perform these roles to the maximum of its capability.

18. In sum, it cannot be said at this stage that encouraging progress has been made toward effective implementation of the disengagement agreement. Both parties have expressed a willingness to cooperate in good faith with the United Nations observation mission and on the whole they have done so, particularly in assisting it to function in the area. But with regard to carrying out the specific provisions of the disengagement agreement, the actual situation depends on the position mutually taken that fulfillment by one side is contingent on fulfillment by the other. UNYOM reports, for example, that on the Saudi Arabian side troops and equipment remain in the buffer zone and that vehicular and animal traffic carrying goods of undetermined nature continues between points on both sides of the border. Within Yemen, United Arab Republic troops remain in the buffer zone, and since royalists continue active, United Arab Republic air and ground actions against them continue. There have been two recent instances of United Arab Republic air and ground actions against targets in Saudi Arabian territory, alleged to be supply dumps for aid to the royalists. UNYOM has been lately advised, however, that such attacks across the border will cease. No plan for phased withdrawal of United Arab Republic troops has been received. The Saudi Arabian government insists that its official aid to the royalists ceased long ago, and claims that the traffic in the buffer zone and across the border is "normal commercial traffic," though it is not denied that there is a flow of aid to the royalists from private sources in Saudi Arabia, without government sanction. As regards continuing illicit traffic in arms and ammunition, as distinguished from the normal trade which has been traditional for centuries, across the border by private sources, the Saudi Arabian government now advises of its willingness to cooperate with UNYOM in checking also that flow and to this end is willing to assign Saudi Arabian liaison officers to United Nations patrols and to set up the necessary number of check posts in Saudi Arabian territory where United Nations observers could be stationed to check on convoys with the assistance of Saudi na-

tional guardsmen. United Arab Republic authorities maintain that since assistance from Saudi Arabian territory continues, enabling the royalists to maintain their offensive capabilities, any step taken by the United Arab Republic in implementation of the agreement leads to an increase in royalist activity. United Arab Republic air action against the royalists within Yemen also continues. Recent UNYOM observations in the Sa'da area would indicate that there has been no decrease in fighting in that locality. In fact, the situation has deteriorated to such an extent there that observation in that area by UNYOM may no longer be feasible.

19. The Security Council adopted its resolution of June 11 on the understanding that the governments of Saudi Arabia and the United Arab Republic had agreed to defray the expenses, over a period of two months in the first instance, of the United Nations Yemen Observation Mission called for in the terms of disengagement. As indicated above, the observation mission became operational with the arrival of the main body of the Yugoslav reconnaissance unit on July 4. The two months period, therefore, expires on September 4. It is now obvious that the task of the mission will not be completed by that date. Indeed, this possibility was foreseen in my report of June 7, in which I pointed out that at the end of the first two months of the mission, an appeal to the parties for additional financial assistance could be made. Accordingly, I have approached both parties through their representatives to the United Nations to defray the expenses of the Yemen operation for a further period of two months, as from September 4. I have received oral assurances from the two representatives that their governments agree to do so.

20. On several occasions I have stressed to both parties the urgent necessity of tightening and speeding up the implementation of the terms of disengagement and I intend to continue efforts to this end, and, if necessary, to intensify them.

2. *From Report to the Security Council*

NEW YORK   OCTOBER 28, 1963

. . . .

26. THE SECURITY COUNCIL, by its resolution of June 11, 1963, requested me to establish in Yemen a United Nations observation operation, on the basis of the fact "that the parties directly concerned with the situation affecting Yemen have confirmed their acceptance of identical terms of disengagement in Yemen . . . ," and the further fact that the Government of Saudi Arabia and the United Arab Republic had agreed to defray the expenses of this operation for two months. On the grounds that the disengagement agreement had not been fulfilled and United Nations observation was therefore still required, these two governments undertook to meet the expenses of UNYOM for a further period as from September 4, 1963, until November 4, 1963.

27. In anticipation of this date, in order to be prepared either to withdraw the mission personnel, vehicles, and equipment, or to maintain it beyond that date should this be desired, I have been conferring over the past fortnight with representatives of the governments of Saudi Arabia, the United Arab Republic, and Yemen. It emerges from these consultations that there is a general appreciation of the helpful assistance rendered by the United Nations mission in Yemen and of the manner in which it has conducted itself. The view is also general among the parties that the continuation beyond November 4 of a United Nations presence in some form, although not necessarily including military components, would be desirable and useful. On the other hand, one of the two governments concerned with financing UNYOM has indicated that it is not prepared, on the basis of the existing situation, to share the cost of UNYOM beyond the November 4 commitment. The position of the Government of Saudi Arabia on this question, as it has been communicated to me, is that any extension of UNYOM beyond November 4 would depend upon concrete evidence that the agreement on disengagement is

Security Council Official Records, Eighteenth Year, Supplement for October, November and December 1963, document S/5447.

to be implemented within a specified period of time, which in effect means a time schedule for the withdrawal of United Arab Republic troops. As of now, therefore, assuming no change in the situation as regards fulfillment of the disengagement agreement, the Government of Saudi Arabia has made it clear that it undertakes no commitment concerning an extension of UNYOM beyond November 4.

28. In the light of this latter circumstance, it has been necessary for me to take the essential preparatory steps looking toward the complete withdrawal of UNYOM by November 4, beyond which date there will be no financial support for it.

29. In the course of my consultations with the parties I have made clear my own dissatisfaction with the mandate of UNYOM as now defined. That mandate, set forth in the disengagement agreement, is so limiting and restrictive as to make it virtually impossible for UNYOM to play a really helpful and constructive role in Yemen. Indeed, given the nature of the situation and of the terrain, it is not possible for UNYOM with its present personnel, or for that matter, with a much expanded establishment, to observe fully, let alone to certify to the satisfaction of both parties, what specifically is being done in the way of disengagement. I frankly see little prospect that the disengagement agreement could be so amended as to correct this deficiency.

30. I have no doubt, however, that a continuing United Nations presence in Yemen, of some kind but not necessarily having military attributes, would be most helpful and might even be indispensable to an early settlement of the Yemen problem, which clearly is primarily political and will require a political solution.

31. It is my intention, therefore, to maintain a civilian United Nations presence in the area, given, of course, the necessary agreement of the parties directly concerned. The terms of reference of such a presence would need to be worked out in consultation with the states concerned. The cost of such a presence would be small and it could, in fact, be initially financed by the existing authorization to the Secretary-General to enter into commitments to meet unforeseen and extraordinary expenses relating to the maintenance of peace and security in the financial year 1963 [General Assembly resolution 1862 (XVII), para. 1(a)].

3. *Report to the Security Council*

NEW YORK   OCTOBER 31, 1963

1. THIS REPORT is supplemental to my report of October 28, 1963 [S/5447].

2. In the afternoon of October 31, the permanent representative of the Government of Saudi Arabia communicated to me a new and urgent message from his government on the subject of the extension of the United Nations Yemen Observation Mission (UNYOM) beyond November 4. This message, in substance, stated that despite the fact that the other party to the disengagement agreement had not carried it out, the Government of Saudi Arabia, being desirous of helping the United Nations complete its mission of peace in the Yemen area, and desirous also of saving human lives, has decided to participate in the financing of UNYOM for a further period of two months as from November 5.

3. In view of the fact that the Government of the United Arab Republic had previously expressed its view that UNYOM should be extended as well as its willingness to continue to share in the expenses of UNYOM for a further period of one or two months, the problem of financing a continuing mission is thus removed.

4. The representative of the Government of Yemen had also indicated that it was the view of his government that the continued presence of UNYOM beyond November 4 would be desirable and helpful.

5. In the light of these circumstances, and particularly of the new development incident to the latest message from the Government of Saudi Arabia, I have ordered the cancellation of the preparations that were under way for the withdrawal of UNYOM by November 4. Therefore, UNYOM, in approximately its present form and size, will continue from that date for a further period of two months and its expenses will be borne in equal shares by the Governments of Saudi Arabia and the United Arab Republic.

Security Council Official Records, Eighteenth Year, Supplement for July, August and September 1963, document S/5447/Add. 1.

4. *Report to the Security Council*

NEW YORK   NOVEMBER 11, 1963

1. THIS REPORT is a further supplement to my previous reports [S/5447 and Add. 1], and is submitted for the purpose of information and clarification.

2. In document S/5447/Add.1, I informed the Security Council that the United Nations Yemen Observation Mission (UNYOM) would be continued from November 4 for a further period of two months, in pursuance of the wishes of the two parties to the disengagement agreement as indicated by their willingness to continue to share the cost of UNYOM for that additional period.

3. In my report to the Council on May 27, 1963, in which I communicated my intention to establish the mission in Yemen, I estimated that the observation function in Yemen would not be required for more than four months.

4. The continuation of UNYOM for another two months after November 4, goes beyond that original estimate. Therefore, although believing that no meeting of the Council on the subject was required, I have consulted the Council members informally in order to ascertain that in the light of the circumstances as reported there would be no objection to the extension. There was none.

Security Council Official Records, Eighteenth Year, Supplement for July, August and September 1963, document S/5447/Add. 2.

Note Verbale to Governments Offering Standby
Military Units to the United Nations

NEW YORK   OCTOBER 1, 1963

THREE AND a half months after U Thant delivered his Harvard speech advocating the creation of a stand-by peace force by the United Nations, (see p. 354) he acknowledged that several countries had offered to make available military units to be called upon to serve in peacekeeping operations of the Organization. The offers came mainly from the Scandinavian countries, which had already made generous contributions to the United Nations operations in the Middle East, the Congo, and other places, and from some other countries including the Netherlands and Canada. Thant noted in the following communication to the governments concerned that the creation of a stand-by force had not been authorized by competent United Nations organs, but he accepted the offers nevertheless with the understanding that the United Nations would bear no financial responsibility until and unless the units were requested.

COMMUNICATIONS concerning offers of "standby" military units which could be made available to the United Nations on request have been addressed recently to the Secretary-General by the governments of Denmark, Finland, the Netherlands, Norway, and Sweden. Informal approaches on the same subject have been made by some other governments. The units in question would be for use in United Nations peacekeeping operations and would be kept in readiness for assignment to United Nations duties.

The Secretary-General, in welcoming and accepting these offers, has emphasized the conditions implicit in them, namely that the troops thus designated would be available to the United Nations whenever they might be called for by the Organization to meet a peacekeeping need, and that unless and until the troops should be called for, the offer to make them available would have no financial consequences for the United Nations.

UN Press Release SG/1588.

The Secretary-General has also pointed out that generally the peace-keeping operations of the United Nations in which military personnel are employed are undertaken on the basis of specific authorization by one of the competent United Nations organs. The exact composition of the military body required by the specific operation, as regards particularly such factors as nationality and language, is necessarily and largely influenced by the *locus* and the nature of the situation giving rise to the need for the peacekeeping operation. There is, of course, no authorization for the creation of a standing or stand-by United Nations force as such.

TWO MEMORIAL ADDRESSES

On OCTOBER 21, 1963, U Thant took part in a memorial tribute to Mrs. Eleanor Roosevelt at Philharmonic Hall in Lincoln Center. She had died in 1962, but on this occasion the Secretary-General was lending his prestige to the launching of a drive on behalf of the Eleanor Roosevelt Memorial Foundation. Less than a month later, on November 26, he spoke in the United Nations General Assembly in tribute to the late United States President, John F. Kennedy, who was assassinated on November 22.

---

1. Address at Memorial Tribute to Eleanor Roosevelt at Philharmonic Hall, Lincoln Center

NEW YORK   OCTOBER 21, 1963

IT IS ALREADY nearly one year since Mrs. Eleanor Roosevelt died, but she remains, and will always remain, a very vivid memory in the minds of those of us who were fortunate enough to know her and to work with her, and even, I believe, of those who only knew of her. Mrs. Roosevelt required no special effort or treatment to make a strong impact during her lifetime or to be long remembered after her death—her personality, her ideals, and her work were one combined force, and it is an unforgettable one. The Eleanor Roosevelt Memorial Foundation will be a most appropriate monument to her if it can carry on even a part of the great humanitarian work to which Mrs. Roosevelt devoted her life and her phenomenal energy.

Mrs. Roosevelt was a dominant figure in the early years of the United Nations, for she came nearer than anyone else ever has to being an actual embodiment of the commonly held ideals and aims of the peoples of the world. In the United Nations she was the center of activities devoted to

UN Press Release SG/1607.

the fundamental decencies, and in her work in this area she rose above the typical day-to-day petty rivalries and political squabbles. Her personality, courage, generosity, and dedication placed her in a class by herself and gave her a unique position of universal confidence and respect. She was thus able to pursue highly idealistic aims with the greatest energy without fear either of being misunderstood or of being thought unrealistic or starry-eyed. She was in fact, in her own inimitable way, a very practical and down-to-earth person. She was also, as I said at the time of her death, truly the first lady of the world.

It is, perhaps, misleading to try to single out her specific work in the United Nations from the mainstream of her amazing range of activity, for the whole of it was based on a broad and affectionate humanitarianism. But this humanitarianism and her deep concern for the underprivileged found an historic focus in the United Nations—especially in the work of the Human Rights Commission, and in the proclamation of the Universal Declaration of Human Rights. She could not only communicate with the oppressed and the exploited the world over, she could identify with them. When she spoke of rights and liberties, she evoked no mere theory but a practice and a way of life.

Mrs. Roosevelt's patient and untiring work as chairman of the Commission on Human Rights and its drafting committee was a major factor in giving shape and substance to the Universal Declaration of Human Rights. It was she who, as one of the nine members of the original commission, proposed, as chairman of its first session at Hunter College in the Bronx in April 1946, that the bill of rights should be drafted in the form of a declaration or manifesto to be followed by conventions that would be legally binding on states. This has been the basis ever since of the United Nations approach to human rights. It was her persistence and tact which guided the immensely complicated work of drafting the declaration in 1947 and 1948, and her energy and enthusiasm which sustained others in this great labor. As delegate of the United States on the Third Committee of the General Assembly, she was the guiding spirit of the eighty-five meetings which led finally to the text which was unanimously accepted by the Assembly in 1948.

Though the impact of this historic document may well take generations to achieve its full force, its importance in the development of human institutions and in the place of the individual in history is already great and is increasing. Mrs. Roosevelt's signal contribution to this achievement was the formal counterpart of her tireless practical activity for the defenseless, the underprivileged, or the unfortunate throughout the world as well as in her own country, and gives an historic frame to that activity.

She was one of those rare individuals whose courage, vision, and goodwill—and indeed outright goodness—can light up a whole period of history and give comfort and hope to humanity even in times of the greatest anxiety and despair. She was a living, active symbol of generosity, selflessness, and of a profound faith in mankind's essential goodness and promise. May the Eleanor Roosevelt Memorial Foundation continue in the great work to which she dedicated all her strength. If it carries on in the spirit of Eleanor Roosevelt, it will, I am sure, flourish.

In a world in which human rights are still delayed and denied, it is well for us to recall that Eleanor Roosevelt nourished the dream and the hope that the Declaration of Human Rights might one day become the Magna Carta of all mankind.

---

2. *Statement in the General Assembly in Tribute to John F. Kennedy*

NEW YORK   NOVEMBER 26, 1963

TODAY WE are gathered in this Assembly of 111 Member governments to pay solemn tribute to the memory of a martyr. I feel bound to participate in this occasion not only on my own behalf, but also on behalf of the entire Secretariat.

On September 20, 1963, Mr. John F. Kennedy, President of the United States of America, addressed the General Assembly of the United Nations. He said, *inter alia:* ". . . we meet today in an atmosphere of rising hope, and at a moment of comparative calm. My presence here today is not a sign of crisis but of confidence. . . . I have come to salute the United Nations and to show the support of the American people for your daily deliberations."[1]

General Assembly Official Records, Eighteenth Session, 1264th plenary meeting.
[1] General Assembly Official Records, Eighteenth Session, 1209th plenary meeting, para. 37.

Exactly nine weeks later, President Kennedy fell a victim to an assassin's bullet, and all of us at the United Nations felt that we had lost a friend—not only a friend of the Organization, not only a friend of peace—but a friend of man.

I recall, with equal vividness, a time some two years ago when the United Nations was plunged in gloom because of the sudden death of its Secretary-General. At that time President Kennedy made a special appearance before the General Assembly of the United Nations, and in the course of his address he said: "So let us here resolve that Dag Hammarskjöld did not live—or die—in vain. Let us call a truce to terror. Let us invoke the blessings of peace. And, as we build an international capacity to keep peace, let us join in dismantling the national capacity to wage war."[2]

Although we all know that man is born under sentence of death with but an indefinite reprieve, death is a tragedy whenever it comes. It is human to feel sorrow at the passing away of anyone dear to us, even when death comes as a merciful release from chronic suffering and pain. But when a young and dynamic leader of a great country, with his brilliant promise only half-fulfilled, is felled in the prime of life by an utterly incomprehensible and senseless act, the loss is not only a loss to the bereaved family, whose head he was, nor even the country over whose destiny he presided with rare ability and distinction as head of state. It is a loss suffered by the entire world, by all humanity, for the late president embodied a rare and quite remarkable combination of intellect and courage, of vigor and compassion, of devotion to the arts and sciences, which was focused on serving his basic concern for the well-being of all mankind.

It is a strange irony that President Kennedy, like President Lincoln—I note that some have already begun to speak of Kennedy as a younger Lincoln, dedicated as both were to the paths of peace and reconciliation—should have come to a violent end at the hands of an assassin. I have the feeling that President Kennedy was sincerely seeking to carry forward to fulfillment the monumental task which began in this country a hundred years ago.

Throughout his public career President Kennedy sought to reduce tension, to uphold the law and to discourage violence, whether in word or deed. On June 10, 1963, he observed: "And if we cannot end now our differences, at least we can help make the world safe for diversity. For, in

---

[2] *Ibid.*, Sixteenth Session, 1013th meeting, para. 41.

the final analysis, our most basic common link is that we all inhabit this planet. We all breathe the same air. We all cherish our children's future. And we are all mortal."

President Kennedy was mortal like the rest of us. Not so his place in history, where he will live as a great leader who sought peace at home and abroad and who gave his life as a true martyr in the service of his country and of all mankind.

Let us all, here and now, draw inspiration from his example, and let us resolve that he did not live, or die, in vain. Let us call a truce to terror. Let us invoke the blessings of peace.

"The Guilty Generation"
From Address at Dinner of American Association for the United Nations
NEW YORK   NOVEMBER 11, 1963

. . . . IT WILL generally be agreed that, in recent years the main source of conflict is ideological. In the economic field it may be described as the conflict between capitalism and communism. It has also been depicted— and here there is room for argument—as the conflict between democracy and totalitarianism. It is this ideological conflict which has been christened the cold war, and which has plagued international relations in the period following the Second World War.

I do not believe that some day the whole world will turn out to be either capitalist or communist. I am not aware of a single compelling factor which would inevitably turn the United States into a communist society nor do I see any prospect of Russia some day turning capitalist. Many perceptive economic analysts have noted that neither capitalism nor communism has remained unadulterated over the years and both systems have shown a capacity for adapting themselves to changed circumstances. Furthermore, there are many countries in the world today, especially developing countries, which have found it necessary to follow a course which represents a compromise between the two systems, which may be called a mixed economy or a socialistic pattern of society. In such cases they have taken over elements from both systems and assimilated them in an effort to retain the value of private initiative without sacrificing social and economic justice.

At the present time, we have also to deal with another source of conflict which is also a direct consequence of the Second World War. One of the basic aims of the Charter of the United Nations was to promote the development of non-self-governing territories to the status of nationhood. The decade following the Second World War saw most of the countries of Asia gain their independence from colonial rule, so that today there are only a few vestiges of colonialism still left in Asia. It is only in the last five years that we have seen a most remarkable progress in Africa in the same

UN Press Release SG/1614.

direction. The conflict in Africa today is mainly centered around those colonial territories where enough progress is not being made toward self-government. How long it will take to complete the process of decolonization in Africa is anybody's guess. I hope that, for the good of the world, the process is not delayed unduly. As I have said on another occasion it is the experience of history that when freedom is delayed too long, extreme forces rise to the surface and dominate the scene, and in the long run pose a threat to the orderly development and peaceful progress of the countries involved.

There is one more source of conflict to which I may refer at this stage. In the nineteenth century millions of human beings whose skin was not white accepted, somewhat philosophically, the "white man's burden." Today there is no such acceptance of this outmoded doctrine. In this country itself we have witnessed during recent years a remarkable assertion of the rights of all citizens, irrespective of their color, to take part fully in the political life, and to share equally in the economic and social progress, of the country. There are many other countries, no doubt, where there may be a problem of minorities who feel that their legitimate rights are not fully recognized. In all these countries the struggle continues, and I am sure it will continue until the legitimate grievances of the minorities are redressed and they have the assurance of fair treatment. There is, however, only one country which has officially continued to differentiate between man and man on the basis of the color of his skin and of his racial origin, and this discrimination has been enshrined as a cardinal principle of state policy. The prospect is far from rosy and I cannot regard with equanimity the future in this part of the world.

The postwar world has witnessed yet another revolt—the revolt of the have-nots. Just as black- and brown-skinned humanity accepted over the centuries the "white man's burden" they were also willing to accept poverty as a fact of life. The last fifteen years have been marked by a categorical rejection of this concept. While the ideological conflict has resulted in a division of the world into East and West, the gap between rich and poor countries has led to a kind of North-South division of the world. The rapid growth of population and the lack of economic and technological progress in the developing countries have led to a situation where inevitably the gap between the rich and poor countries has steadily continued to widen. I regard this as a most dangerous situation.

Economic aid alone is no solution to this problem because such aid, although very desirable, is no substitute for fair and stable prices and expanding markets which the developing countries need in order to get themselves over the hump of industrialization. Many economists have pointed out that the financial assistance given in the form of economic aid in the last decade, large as it has been, had hardly made up for the loss sustained by the developing countries on account of falling commodity prices. This explains the increasing interest of the developing countries in the work of the United Nations in the economic field. They look to the world Organization for global plans and a world machinery for expanding world trade and extending the right kind of aid. They also look for assistance to enable them to make up rapidly for the stagnation and shortages that have in many cases marked the long era of colonial rule, and to build bridges over the gulfs inevitably created in the dissolution of colonialism.

If my brief reading of human history as represented in the above analysis is correct, we have in the world of today three or four causes of conflict and tension, which are either legacies of past conflicts, or which closely parallel those that have characterized ancient history and the history of the Middle Ages. First and most dangerous of all, we have the ideological conflict between East and West. Then we have the North-South conflict between the rich and poor, the have and have-not countries. We also have the struggle against colonialism and the struggle for equality, especially for racial equality. Religious conflicts have not entirely disappeared and can still be a source of friction here and there. The most serious of these, as I have stated above, is, of course, the ideological conflict in its various manifestations.

A solution to these problems and these conflicts cannot be expected overnight. It has to be sought with patience and diligence at the conference table and elsewhere, using the force of argument instead of the argument of force. This is the main task of the United Nations which under the Charter is designed "to be a center for harmonizing the actions of nations in the attainment of . . . common ends."

We may ask at this point what are these common ends. Surely the most important of these common ends is the survival of humanity itself! In an eloquent message on the occasion of United Nations Day 1963 the president of India, who is also renowned as a philosopher, stated: "Humanity is not a mere organization but a living organism united from within by those spiritual values which are inseparable from man's dignity and freedom. . . . There is one God, hidden in all things, all pervading, the inner soul of all things. We tear asunder this invisible bond and break the body of humanity if we use violence against one another." Whatever our divisions and differences, we have this common interest in survival; and in the world of the hydrogen bomb there is no alternative to the peaceful solution of our differences. In modern war, there is only one victor, and his name is Death.

Similarly, we have a common stake in human progress and prosperity. I have had occasion to observe elsewhere that the technological progress of man has been so rapid that, properly applied, it can produce enough of the world's goods to go around for all, so that all may live free from want and hunger. The goal of the Charter of the United Nations, "to promote social progress and better standards of life in larger freedom" is within reach of us, provided we have the will to share our abundance. It is no longer necessary to think in terms of narrow national interest, and in fact it is shortsighted to pursue an instinctively insular approach to international economic problems. Prosperity like peace is indivisible, while poverty has to be stamped out like the plague that it is.

In regard to ideological, religious, and racial conflicts, the Charter calls on us "to practise tolerance and live together in peace with one another as good neighbours." Almost a month from today we will be celebrating the fifteenth anniversary of the Universal Declaration of Human Rights, which I called the other day the Magna Carta of mankind. In the United Nations we have been trying hard to appeal to the conscience of man to fight racial discrimination and religious intolerance.

Even this very session of the General Assembly has adopted a declaration on the subject of racial discrimination and is engaged in a similar effort on the subject of religious intolerance. If I may say so, too much importance cannot be given to these activities because they go back to a fundamental fact. Intolerance, the inability or unwillingness to see the other man's point of view, and the refusal to live and let live—these are the basic causes of misunderstandings between human beings as much as between nations. As the UNESCO Charter reminds us, it is in the minds of men that the defenses of peace have to be constructed, since it is in the minds of men that wars begin.

Forty-five years ago today, the First World War came to an end with the signing of the Armistice. The League of Nations was then established, to ensure that mankind would not suffer the calamity of another bloodbath. The political philosophy of the League as embodied in the Covenant is expressed in the basic idea that "international anarchy" is the root cause of war. The founders of the League believed that the world needed a system fulfilling the same function for competing and conflicting ambitions beyond national frontiers, as governments provided for similar situations within national frontiers. This involved the establishment of a legal framework to settle disputes between nations, either by a judicial or arbitral process, and the prevention of a resort to violence in breach of the law by the employment of overwhelming collective force. The League system, to be effective, needed the power to compel compliance with the law. Without this power it could not persuade; but given the power the use of force could have become unnecessary and persuasion would have proved practicable. Unfortunately, the League had neither the will nor the means to organize such overwhelming collective force. It was also handicapped by the absence of the United States and developed into essentially a European club, although a few non-European states were also admitted as members. Thus the League failed to prevent the steady erosion of international morality that we saw in the 1930s, and which culminated in the Second World War. The terrible weapons developed during and since that war have given us the conviction that, if we are not able to prevent a third world war, we shall go down in history—if history should survive—as the guilty generation, the generation which did nothing to prevent the annihilation of mankind itself.

I hope I have said enough tonight to make you feel that the enlightened and courageous support of the international idea that you have given for the last forty years has been worth while. Today there is no alternative to international action for the solution of global problems and conflicts, just as there is no alternative to the methods of peaceful persuasion and conciliation. On the other hand, it is demonstrable that all human beings have a common stake in progress and prosperity, as they have in peace and survival. I hope that on this occasion you will rededicate yourselves to the ideal of international cooperation, so that we may truly be able to say to our children and our grandchildren that we in our generation did our best "to save succeeding generations from the scourge of war."

Letter to the President of the Security Council Concerning the Mission of the Special Representative to Cambodia and Thailand

NEW YORK   DECEMBER 9, 1963

In my letter of December 18, 1962, I informed the Security Council of the agreement which was reached with the governments of Cambodia and Thailand for the appointment of a special representative of the Secretary-General in their area for a period of one year, commencing January 1, 1963. In pursuance of that agreement I appointed Mr. Nils Göran Gussing to serve in that capacity.

Though the two governments agree that Mr. Gussing's presence and availability has been a useful factor, it must nevertheless be stated that the objectives mentioned in the fourth paragraph of my letter have not been fully realized. I have, therefore, recently inquired of the two governments whether, and if so in which form, they would desire this mission to continue. Both governments have now informed me that it is their wish that the special representative of the Secretary-General should continue his activities under the same terms of reference for the calendar year 1964. They have agreed, however, that a small increase in the existing staff of the special representative should be provided, to enable Mr. Gussing to travel more frequently between the respective capitals.

I have felt that, under the circumstances, I should agree to the request of the two governments who have again signified to me their willingness to share, on an equal basis, all costs involved on account of the mission of the special representative so that no budgetary provision on the part of the United Nations will be required.

In view of the nature of the action envisaged, I thought it appropriate to make this report to the members of the Security Council.

U THANT
Secretary-General of
the United Nations

Security Council Official Records, Eighteenth Year, Supplement for October, November and December 1963, document S/5479.

Letter to the Representatives of Australia, Austria, Canada, Denmark, Finland, Ireland, Italy, Japan, the Netherlands, New Zealand, Norway, Sweden, the United Kingdom, the United States, and the Federal Republic of Germany

NEW YORK   DECEMBER 10, 1963

ALTHOUGH the Republic of the Congo (Leopoldville) has received a greater volume of technical assistance from the United Nations than any other country, it is equally true that in the Congo that assistance has staved off disaster. The problems that have threatened the social and economic structure of the country have been kept within manageable proportions through such assistance. There has been an increasing degree of improvement in the rehabilitation of essential services in the country.

However, the needs of the Congo for outside assistance continue to be great, and they extend over every aspect of the economic, social, and administrative life of the country. Replacements by trained Congolese personnel of some of the internationally recruited experts now working in the United Nations assistance programs will take place in the course of 1964, but the number of such replacements will be too small to make a real impact on the program's cost. In fact, the needs of the country for qualified personnel are not less in magnitude than in preceding years.

In reviewing the government's request for assistance in 1964 on the basis of the views expressed by the cooperating specialized agencies and of the level of immediately available resources, I have come to the conclusion that the volume of activities for which the United Nations should take responsibility in 1964 should be limited to the priority projects which are already in existence and could not exceed, in so far as foreign exchange requirements are concerned, a total of $13.1 million. More than half of this total (i.e., $7.1 million) is already underwritten or can be

Security Council Official Records, Nineteenth Year, Supplement for April, May and June 1964, document S/5784, annex VI, June 29, 1964.

hopefully underwritten by financial arrangements falling outside the Congo Fund, as shown by the attached statement.

These already confirmed or foreseen provisions leave unfinanced, however, very essential basic services in the fields of health, education, and judicature for which the only apparent source of funds in 1964 will have to be the Congo Fund. After taking account of the important bilateral contributions being made by the Government of Belgium in each of these fields, there remains an unfulfilled need (in freely usable foreign exchange) of $6.0 million. Of this amount $5.0 million will be used to ensure the continued employment in 1964 of the following categories of internationally recruited personnel: 178 doctors, 800 secondary school teachers, and 52 magistrates, and $1.0 million to cover the costs of experts already engaged in other projects.

Another aspect of the program is the financing of local administrative services for all United Nations and specialized agency, advisory, training, and operational assistance. The Congo government has asked that the United Nations system continue such services until such time as the government itself will be in a position to supply the bulk of the servicing required. It is anticipated that the cost of continuing the service establishment can be met by a combination of resources. I am assured that the Technical Assistance Board field budget will provide $200,000 in foreign exchange, and the lump-sum "overhead cost" subsidy resulting from the funds-in-trust administration by the United Nations of special project (or program) agreements to be financed from funds contributed by the United States of America will provide a further $500,000, also in foreign exchange. It is expected that any remaining foreign exchange requirements as well as the total local currency needs will be met by the Government of the Congo.

I have established a minimum foreign exchange target for Congo Fund contributions of $6.0 million. I am happy to state that in addition to the sums it has already deposited or is about to deposit with the United Nations the Congo government is prepared to make a contribution in foreign exchange toward any cash deficit in the Congo Fund in 1964. I am informed, however, that at this time it does not appear that the government would be able to contribute more than $200,000 per month beginning January 1964 without making an undue sacrifice of other essential needs of the country's economy.

Thus a sum of $3.6 million remains to be obtained from voluntary donors if a total collapse of the health, education, and judiciary systems of the country is to be averted. It is the intention of the Congo government to find alternative methods through its own resources and with the assistance of other interested governments, for the maintenance of these essential services in 1965 and subsequent years. But January 1965 is the earliest date at which such a transfer of financial responsibility can be envisaged.

I therefore address to you this most urgent appeal in the hope that your government will generously contribute to the Congo Fund in order that the United Nations may continue to assist the Republic of the Congo in the coming year in overcoming some of its present difficulties. I should be extremely grateful to you if a favorable response to this appeal could reach my hands before December 31, 1963.

❧ 1964 ❧

"Looking Ahead"
Address at Columbia University
NEW YORK   JANUARY 7, 1964

ON JANUARY 7, 1964, U Thant delivered a major address at Columbia University as one of twenty-four Dag Hammarskjöld Memorial Lectures given in various centers of learning around the world by outstanding leaders. The series was later published under the title, *The Quest for Peace.* It was in this address that Thant called for a third war on all fronts "to make the world safe for diversity." He said that although this war had to be waged in peacetime, it should be waged with as much concentration of total national effort as the two world wars fought to make the world safe for democracy. The concept of peaceful coexistence, he said, has been widely criticized by those who do not see the need to make the world safe for diversity, but, he asked, what is the alternative when human beings come in all sizes, shapes, and in a variety of colors, with an equal diversity in religious beliefs and political ideologies. Thant said the simplest definition of peaceful coexistence is found in the United Nations Charter which calls on all human beings to live together in peace with one another as good neighbors. "If all human beings and all nations large and small were to be moved by this spirit we could indeed make the world safe for diversity and for posterity," he concluded.

I DEEM IT A PRIVILEGE to be able to participate in the Dag Hammarskjöld Memorial Lecture Series. When my distinguished predecessor was killed on September 17, 1961, there was a genuine feeling of sadness and a keen sense of tragedy, which we experienced again when President Kennedy was snatched away from our midst. The contribution that Dag Hammarskjöld made to the development of the United Nations and to the whole concept of international cooperative action to solve major problems will surely go down in history as something unique, since it came at a time when the Organization itself was in its formative stage.

I remember participating as the representative of Burma in the 1,010th plenary meeting of the General Assembly on the afternoon of Wednes-

Press Release SG/1642. Published in *The Quest for Peace: The Dag Hammarskjöld Memorial Lectures,* edited by Andrew W. Cordier and Wilder Foote (New York: Columbia University Press, 1965).

day, September 20, 1961, along with so many of my distinguished colleagues. Tributes were paid to the great personal qualities of the man, his
wide culture, his penetrating intelligence, his amazing grasp of the most
complicated international issues, his intellectual integrity, his courage of
conviction, his tenacity of purpose, his indefatigable industry, and his
tireless stamina. Surely, this was a unique combination of qualities in one
human being, who dedicated the best years of his life to the cause of the
United Nations and the pursuit of peace!

I admired his principles even more than his remarkable personal qualities. To him, the provisions of the Charter were so important—almost
sacred—that he was willing to forgo any temporary advantage that could
be gained by following the easier path of expediency. To him, too, the
institution, the United Nations Organization and its collective interest,
was far more important than the separate interests of the individual
Member states. With his great gift for innovation and improvisation, he
discovered new ways to help keep the peace—witness the practical application of the principle of an emergency force in one situation, of an
observer group in another, and a United Nations presence in a third
context.

Dag Hammarskjöld had a dynamic concept of the Organization. To
him the United Nations was not merely a forum for debate, although he
realized that this was a very important function of the Organization. It
was more important, in his view, that it should be a center for harmonizing the actions of nations in the attainment of common ends. While realizing that many important decisions, whether they related to the halting
of the nuclear arms race or the implementation of general and complete
disarmament, could be settled only by agreement among the major powers, he emphasized at the same time the stake of the nonmilitary powers,
in fact of all mankind, in the survival of the human race. He viewed the
United Nations, therefore, as providing the occasion and the opportunity
for the nonmajor powers to affirm their interest in peace and survival. He
also regarded the Organization, not as a substitute for normal diplomacy,
but rather as an additional and perhaps novel instrument which was
available to Member governments and which could be used by them in
situations where conventional methods of diplomacy might be precluded
for a variety of reasons.

I believe that I was the first on the occasion of that 1,010th meeting of
the General Assembly to give expression to a thought which, no doubt,
had crossed the minds of many of my friends. I said: "Who could be more
deserving of a Nobel Peace Prize than Mr. Dag Hammarskjöld, who fell

in the unrelenting fight for peace, even though the award would be post-humous?" Not long afterward, we all had the satisfaction of learning that the Nobel prize committee had in fact decided to award the peace prize for 1961 to the late Secretary-General.

I shall now turn to the theme I have chosen. I should perhaps begin by explaining the title of my address. I would like to take advantage of this occasion, which comes at the beginning of a new year, to look ahead in the light of the past and to see what the major problems are which we face and what the prospects are for solving them. I would thus hope to have an opportunity to give a conspectus of the situation facing the world Organization in the nineteenth year of its existence.

Twenty-five years ago, when the League of Nations was also nineteen years old, it was already tottering and on its last legs. On the other hand, I believe I will not be accused of partiality if I say that, despite its short-comings, the United Nations has a substantial record of solid achieve-ment during its nineteen years of existence, and I hope I will not be charged with overoptimism if I predict that its most fruitful years are still ahead of it. The great advantages that the United Nations has over the League are its greater universality of membership and the fact that it gives as much importance to economic and social development, the pro-tection and promotion of human rights, and the equal rights of nations, large and small, as to its over-all objective of saving succeeding genera-tions from war. If we are to justify the faith of humanity in our interna-tional Organization and to live up to the promises of the Charter, we can do so only by living up to the principles of the Charter.

I believe therefore that 1964 is a crucial year in the history of the United Nations. This is the time when the Organization has to face up to its responsibilities and solve the problems which hinder its effectiveness. Among the most important of these is the financial problem. The Organi-zation is in debt to the tune of some $134 million. True, its creditors are for the most part Member governments, but I believe it is imperative for the Organization to be financially solvent. I also believe that a bankrupt Organization is bound to be an ineffective one. I am advised that the outlook for 1964 is discouraging, not only because of the serious financial position, but also because of the implications of Article 19 of the Charter. On the other side of the ledger it is noteworthy that a terminal date has been set by the General Assembly for the military operations in the Con-go, which are due to be wound up by the middle of the year. In regard to the United Nations Emergency Force in the Middle East we have undertaken a recent review as a result of which we have been able to reduce the expenditure a little. Most of the other peacekeeping operations we have undertaken are on the basis that the Member governments mainly concerned reimburse the Organization for the expenses involved.

But the basic problem remains, and that is the question of solvency of the Organization. I believe that it is time for all countries, whatever their stand on the merits of particular peacekeeping operations may have been in the past, to make a special effort in 1964 to put the Organization back on its financial feet. If this can be done perhaps we may be able to ensure, with respect to future peacekeeping operations—large or small—that the Organization might be called upon to undertake, that a situation does not arise in which, in the pursuit of peace, the Organization bankrupts itself. I realize that the difference of views among Member governments stems not only from their varying evaluation of specific peacekeeping operations but also from their interpretation of the provisions of the Charter. Even so, I believe that if there is a will to solve this problem a way out may be found without prejudice to the questions of principle involved.

Unless the financial picture improves I am afraid that the effectiveness of the Organization in its various fields of activity, whether they be political or economic, social or humanitarian, or whether they relate to development or decolonization, to disarmament or détente, will be impaired. The present world outlook is, I believe, propitious for settling some of the problems which have plagued international relations in the years following World War II. I cannot help thinking that this congenial atmosphere is also favorable for settling this basic issue of the solvency of the Organization.

I propose to refer later, and in somewhat greater detail to the efforts being made by the major powers to reduce defense expenditures. At this point I would simply like to mention that, including the regular budget of the United Nations, the peacekeeping operations, and the contributions to all the voluntary programs, the total cost of the United Nations to the international community in 1964 will be around $330 million. With these funds the United Nations undertakes a variety of tasks in the field of diplomacy, in the peaceful settlement of controversial and potentially dangerous issues, in furthering the progress of dependent territories to political independence and sovereignty, in promoting economic and social development of the developing countries, in advancing international trade, and in safeguarding human rights. If we think in terms of the defense expenditures of the major military powers alone, all the costs involved in discharging these manifold responsibilities of the United Nations, including its voluntary programs and peacekeeping operations, are approximately one quarter of one percent. If Member governments could be persuaded to see the problem in this perspective and with this sense of proportion, I am sure that they would not feel it a strain to make a special effort to solve the problem of the financial solvency of the Organization.

I would now like to undertake a conspectus of the work of the Organization, as I promised earlier. In its political work the United Nations deals with certain global problems such as nuclear and conventional disarmament as well as certain regional and local problems. I may perhaps begin by dealing with some of the regional and local problems with which the United Nations is directly concerned at the present time.

I mentioned earlier that the military phase of the Congo is to come to an end in the middle of 1964, but that the United Nations Emergency Force is to continue with a little reduction in expenditure. Through the good offices of the United Nations Truce Supervision Organization we were recently able to arrange for the exchange of some prisoners between Syria and Israel. But the over-all outlook in the Middle East today is threatening, and I am very much afraid that there will be more than one occasion in 1964 when Middle Eastern problems will engage the attention of the United Nations. In Yemen we have reduced the military contingent to a handful of observers assisted by a small air arm. The character of the United Nations representation in Yemen has also changed, with the emphasis on the political rather than the military aspects. I hope that, by the time the extended term of the United Nations Mission in Yemen is due to come to an end, the situation may have stabilized sufficiently for us to be able to leave with the assurance that stability may continue.

Another important part of the political work of the United Nations is in the field of decolonization. Both the General Assembly and the Security Council have recently adopted resolutions on the subject of territories under Portuguese administration. I sincerely hope that a just and lasting solution may be found for this problem in 1964. Elsewhere in Africa, especially in Central Africa, it appears that the process of decolonization will continue and that we may have the opportunity to welcome at least two more countries from this part of Africa in the United Nations at the nineteenth session of the General Assembly.

On December 10, 1963, we celebrated the fifteenth anniversary of the Universal Declaration of Human Rights. One of the achievements of the eighteenth session of the General Assembly was the adoption of the Declaration on the Elimination of All Forms of Racial Discrimination. I am encouraged to find that everywhere there is increasing preoccupation with the abolition of discrimination, so that one of the main purposes of the Charter, namely, to promote and encourage respect for human rights and for fundamental freedoms for all without distinction as to race, sex, language, or religion, may become a reality.

History has recorded many examples at different times of man's inhumanity to man, but today we see an awakening of the human conscience to the evils of discrimination. I realize that, even so, traditions die hard, and that the process of elimination of discrimination may take time. There is, however, one country where discrimination is one of the principles of state policy. This policy has been unequivocally condemned by both the General Assembly and the Security Council. I hope that the day is not far off when the impact of public opinion in the rest of the world begins to be felt in that country so that here too there may be an awakening of conscience and a change of direction.

The Charter also emphasizes the importance of employing international machinery for the promotion of economic and social advancement. In recognition of this responsibility of the world community, the sixteenth session of the General Assembly decided to designate the current decade as the United Nations Development Decade. Unfortunately, the resources available to the United Nations have never been wholly adequate to discharge its responsibilities in this field, and as a result it has concentrated on preinvestment and technical assistance. While the World Bank and its affiliates have been able to give some capital assistance for economic development, the bulk of such assistance has been on a bilateral basis between the donor and the recipient countries.

Recently there has been a growing recognition of the many advantages of multilateral assistance for promoting economic development. I believe that this is a welcome trend and I hope that this will have the effect of augmenting and raising to more adequate levels the resources available to the United Nations. At the same time I feel that even if the United Nations is not able, in the immediate future, to offer capital aid to the developing countries it can, and should, make its assistance in the preinvestment field more effective. During the last two years and more I have had the opportunity of observing at first-hand the multiplicity of sources from which technical assistance is provided. To some extent I realize that this proliferation is inevitable; however, I believe that the time has come when we should streamline our own Organization and make it easier for the developing countries to receive aid from us. I also believe that this streamlining could be coupled with better coordination, not only at United Nations Headquarters, but also in relation to the specialized agencies, which have such a distinguished record of achievement in this field. I consider that this need not affect present interagency relationships and that we should be able to preserve the best elements of existing programs in a new setup. Most important of all, I believe that it would enable us to be better prepared for the day when, whether as a result of progress toward disarmament or otherwise, really substantial resources become available to the United Nations, enabling it to offer capital aid to the developing countries.

Before leaving the field of economic development I would like to make one more observation. In the first half of 1964 the United Nations will be convening a major conference in the economic field, namely the United Nations Conference on Trade and Development. While it is true that aid is an important element in promoting the economic development of the developing countries, trade is an even more important factor. The problems of the developing countries in regard to their terms of trade are well known and I do not wish to expatiate on these problems on this occasion. I hope that following the trade conference we will be able to set up some machinery which might be able effectively to harmonize the interests of the advanced and developing countries in regard to international trade. Here is a field where generosity, imagination, and mutual understanding will surely lead to increased prosperity for all.

I said at the beginning that the times are propitious for a settlement of some of the major issues which the world has been facing from the very end of World War II. Surveying the international scene a couple of years after the end of the war, a wit observed that peace had broken out everywhere. The outlook is even more spotty today. For one thing, there is an atmosphere of détente following the conclusion of the test ban treaty in Moscow in August last, an occasion in which I was privileged to participate. I then made a statement in which I detailed some of the measures which had been recommended by the United Nations and which had as their object the relaxation of tensions. In some quarters this statement was misinterpreted as being partial to one or another point of view. This, of course, was not and could not have been my intention and I was only going by the fact that the Assembly had recommended certain measures. I referred then to the question of wider dissemination of nuclear weapons and the dangers of proliferation. I pointed out that the Assembly had called upon all governments to make every effort to achieve a permanent international agreement, subject to inspection and control, on the prevention of the wider dissemination of these weapons of mass destruction. I referred to the problem of the means of delivering nuclear weapons and the proposals for limiting the production of delivery systems and for the destruction of all but an agreed limited number in the early stage of an agreed program of general disarmament. I also mentioned the problem of surprise attack, the proposals for convening a general conference for signing a convention on the prohibition of the use of nuclear and thermonuclear weapons for military purposes, and, finally, a proposal to establish denuclearized zones in different geographical areas of the world. I believe that all these proposals deserve serious consideration and that any progress made in reaching general agreement in regard to any of these proposals will lead to an improvement of the international climate.

The eighteenth session of the General Assembly met in a mood of hope, and the conciliatory statements made by President Kennedy and Foreign Minister Gromyko in the very early stages of the session raised our hopes. In actual fact, however, the only concrete accomplishment of the eighteenth session in the field of disarmament was the agreement of the major nuclear powers, as embodied in a resolution of the General Assembly, not to use space vehicles for purposes of nuclear warfare. Thus there is no sign that a golden age of better understanding has dawned.

However, there are some silver linings among the clouds. Before the close of 1963 two very significant and encouraging developments took place without much fanfare and therefore without generating strong public comments. President Johnson announced, within three weeks of his assumption of office, that military operations at thirty-three military bases—twenty-six of them in the United States—would be halted or curtailed and that more cuts were coming. In a speech made on November 18, 1963, Defense Secretary Mr. McNamara made the important announcement that he believed the Soviet Union had cut its armed forces by 2,250,000 men between 1955 and 1962, thus indicating Washington's desire to reduce arms expenditure. President Johnson's dramatic decision was made about the same time as Chairman Khrushchev announced his government's decision to cut Soviet military spending by $600 million in 1964. More recently a reduction of $1 billion in the over-all defense expenditure of the United States for 1964 has been announced.

These decisions were not the result of negotiations at the conference table, but unilateral decisions. They were obviously reached by the two super-powers with the realization that their previous assumptions regarding the other's military might and intentions were not based on full information. I have no doubt that their actions were also motivated by a sincere response to humanity's yearning for peace and greater understanding. Although the United States and the Soviet Union have not subscribed to the policy of unilateralism, they seem to have come to the conclusion that no progress toward ending the arms race will be made unless and until they slow down themselves. I want to take this opportunity of congratulating the two governments for their courage and vision in arriving at these decisions. It is worth recalling the basic fact that an overassessment of the other's military power is as dangerous as an underestimate. The former risks economic ruin and generates an atmosphere of fear and even panic. The latter invites military adventurism.

The year 1964 starts with the auspicious prospects of arms reduction and cutback of armed forces. The real challenge faced by the developed countries is how to promote economic growth and public welfare without the stimulus of arms production, and then to ensure the proper use of that growth and expansion to ease the contrast between their abundance and the poverty of the rest of mankind.

It is the experience of history that, if we do not press forward when there is a favorable atmosphere, there is a relapse and we are apt to drift helplessly from crisis to crisis, until eventually we find that we are pretty close to open war. This is certainly true of the First and Second World Wars. In this context may I recall the words of the late President Kennedy. In an address that he delivered at the University of Maine on October 19, 1963, he said:

Historians report that in 1914, with most of the world already plunged in war, Prince von Bulow, the former German Chancellor, said to the then Chancellor Bethmann-Hollweg: "How did it all happen?" and Bethmann-Holweg replied: "Ah, if only one knew."

If this planet is ever ravaged by nuclear war—if 300 million Americans, Russians, and Europeans are wiped out by a 60-minute nuclear exchange—if the survivors of that devastation can then endure the fire, poison, chaos, and catastrophe—I do not want one of those survivors to ask another "How did it all happen?" and to receive the incredible reply: "Ah, if only one knew."

If today we are not able to make more rapid progress toward lasting peace it is not for lack of diagnosis of the causes of war. The greatest danger facing the world today is the nuclear arms race. This race has to be halted, and reversed, if humanity is to survive. Two world wars were fought to make the world safe for democracy. Today we have to wage a third war on all fronts. This war has to be waged in peacetime, but it has to be waged as energetically and with as much concentration of total national effort as in times of war. The war we have to wage today has only one goal, and that is to make the world safe for diversity.

The concept of peaceful coexistence has been criticized by many who do not see the need to make the world safe for diversity. I wonder if they have ever paused to ask themselves the question: What is the alternative to coexistence? The world is inhabited by over three billion human beings, and yet the fingerprint experts tell us that no two human beings have identical fingerprints. Human beings come in all sizes and shapes and in a variety of colors. This rich diversity is matched by an equal diversity in regard to religious beliefs and political ideologies. We are thrown together on this planet and we have to live together. That is why the Charter imposes the imperative on all human beings to practice tolerance and to live together in peace with one another as good neighbors. To my mind this is the simplest definition of peaceful coexistence.

Looking ahead, I hope that in the coming years we may all be imbued with this spirit of tolerance. If all human beings and all nations large and small were to be moved by this spirit we could indeed make the world safe for diversity, and for posterity.

From Transcript of Press Conference

NEW YORK   JANUARY 21, 1964

IN HIS FIRST PRESS CONFERENCE of 1964, U Thant disclosed that he was deeply concerned about the possibility of a conflict in Cyprus. He said this was very much in his mind when he said in a speech at Columbia University on January 7 that the situation in the Middle East was "threatening." He noted that one of his aides had been in Cyprus and another one in London in connection with the Cyprus problem. He also threw a bit more light on his concept of his own role. Asked about the possibility that the Security Council and the General Assembly might be too quick to hand over problems to the Secretary-General, he replied that he was conscious of his own limitations and the limitations of his office and that he weighed each problem to determine whether it fell within his competence. If he felt it did not, he said, he made it a rule to refer the matter to the competent United Nations organ.

. . . . QUESTION: Mr. Secretary-General, in your speech at Columbia University, you indicated a belief that 1964 would be a crucial year for the United Nations. Many of us have wondered on what basis you made that statement, since the Assembly was an Assembly of harmony and concord, so to speak, and the situation for 1964 does appear not as explosive as 1963 did. I was just wondering on what basis you made that statement.

THE SECRETARY-GENERAL: As I indicated in that speech, the financial problem of this Organization was uppermost in my mind when I said that the year 1964 would be a crucial year in the life of the Organization. I am sure you will agree with me that the financial problem facing the United Nations today is the greatest problem for this year. I was not necessarily thinking of political or economic or social problems facing this Organization.

QUESTION: In the light of the impending recognition of the People's Republic of China by General de Gaulle, could you please give us some of your assessment and opinion regarding the repercussions of such rec-

UN Note to Correspondents No. 2884.

ognition on the prospects of the reestablishment of the legitimate right of the People's Republic of China in the United Nations?

THE SECRETARY-GENERAL: It is very difficult—and certainly very delicate— to assess the foreign policies or attitudes of Member states. It is particularly so when someone in my position has to assess the attitude of a big power such as France, whose foreign policies and motivations are almost undergoing a revolution, if I may say so. I am sure you will understand my reluctance to pass any comment on the prospective decision of the Government of France on this matter.

All I want to say, at this moment, is that it is difficult to know the true facts about China. News from China or news about China generates such intense emotions everywhere that it is difficult, if not impossible, to discuss this subject rationally and objectively in many parts of the world. I think our attitudes are primarily the result of mass media, as I have stated on previous occasions. Our attitudes toward China—or, for that matter, toward any other subject—are the result of what newspapers we read, what radio stations we listen to, and also, I think, what part of the world we live in. For instance, an average citizen in the United Kingdom will have a different attitude toward China from that which is held by an average citizen in this country.

Without attempting to pass judgement on China—or, for that matter, the prospective French attitude toward China—I just want to invite your attention to a remarkable book on China, one which is, to my knowledge, a most comprehensive, informative and objective book, which was published a few months ago. It is called *The Other Side of the River,* by Edgar Snow, who, to my knowledge, is a great authority on China.

. . . . QUESTION: President Sukarno recently said that Indonesia would abide by the decision of the United Nations and agree to the formation of Malaysia if the world Organization made a second survey on public opinion in the Borneo territory provided the wishes of local leaders now in prison would also be heard and they wanted to join the Malaysia Federation. Would you please give us your reaction to this suggestion and also comment on the recent Manila meeting of President Sukarno and President Macapagal of the Philippines.

THE SECRETARY-GENERAL: I have been in constant contacts with the permanent representative of Indonesia and, for that matter, with the permanent representative of Malaysia, and both Governments have been very kind in keeping me posted with developments. My attitude toward this problem is one of caution and I have been exerting my utmost to create conditions congenial for further steps.

To give you an instance, only last week, exactly on January 15, I appealed to both governments—of course, on a purely personal basis—to exercise the utmost restraint and to maintain calm on the frontiers between Indonesia and Malaysia during the whole month of Ramadan. As you are no doubt aware, Ramadan is very sacred to all Moslems. It is well known as a period of love, a period of forgive and forget, and a period of tolerance. Since both Indonesia and Malaysia are primarily Moslem countries, I took that opportunity to appeal to both governments to exercise restraint and to maintain calm in the area, with a view to creating a congenial atmosphere for further useful steps.

QUESTION: Mr. Secretary-General, the United States secretary of state, Dean Rusk, following you to the rostrum of Columbia University, recently argued that rigid application of the veto in the Security Council, on the one hand, and mechanical reliance on votes in the Assembly, on the other, would both work against the United Nations' future effectiveness. He took a stand against the idea of weighted voting, but he suggested that some solution between these two extremes should be found and that discussions on this problem be held.

My question is twofold. First, have such discussions or explorations been initiated, to your knowledge? Second, not in your capacity as Secretary-General, but as a diplomat with an intimate knowledge of the United Nations, could you put forth some suggestions for a solution—provided you agree with Mr. Rusk's analysis?

THE SECRETARY-GENERAL: I am aware of the current private discussions which are going on between certain capitals on the character and functioning of the future peacekeeping operations of the United Nations, and also on the procedures to be followed regarding the allocation of financial responsibility among Member states toward these peacekeeping operations.

Of course, it is too early now to predict or anticipate the outcome of these discussions. However, I am confident that some kind of suitable and equitable solution will be found before the next session of the General Assembly.

As you are no doubt aware, there are two concepts regarding the functioning of the competent organs of this organization in respect to the peacekeeping operations, as well as the allocation of financial responsibility among Member states. There is one school of thought which maintains that the one who pays the piper must call the tune; in other words, those countries which contribute most toward the peacekeeping operations should have a greater voice in policy. And, of course, there is another school of thought which is subscribed to by a vast majority of Member states and which maintains that the present system, the traditional system, of one country, one vote, should be retained.

Of course, I have no means of knowing what the outcome of the present discussions will be, but I know that if the major powers reach an agreement on the functioning of the United Nations organs in respect of the peacekeeping operations, that agreement must also necessarily get the approval of the competent organs of the United Nations.

QUESTION: There seems to be great pressure on the Republic of Cyprus for the partitioning of that young State. Already the United Nations has some beachhead, however small, in that unhappy development. I should like to ask whether you think that the United Nations can prevent the tragedy of partition, especially the kind that would be imposed on the young State by the pressures of enormous military States.

THE SECRETARY-GENERAL: As you know, I have submitted two reports to the Security Council on this subject. Since then, my personal representative, General Gyani, has gone to Cyprus. My deputy chef de cabinet, Mr. Rolz-Bennett, has been in London and in Cyprus, and he is expected to be back in New York this afternoon. Pending his arrival and report to me, I think I had better reserve judgement.

I can assure you that I shall do my best to help in restoring calm in Cyprus. If I feel at some stage that the Security Council should be involved, I shall of course get instructions from the Council regarding the future line of operations.

It is too early now to anticipate what the future holds in store for Cyprus.

. . . . QUESTION: You recently referred to the situation in the Middle East as "threatening." Could you explain a little further?

THE SECRETARY-GENERAL: When I spoke at Columbia University, I expressed my concern about the prospective developments in the Middle East. I was concerned at that time regarding the future developments in Arab-Israel relations and also in Cyprus. Cyprus is very much in the area, and it was also very much in my mind when I said that. But after the conclusion of the Arab Summit Conference in Cairo, from newspaper reports, I am not so sure whether my deep concern was warranted. Of course, I have not received anything official, but I feel that the situation in that area may not be as explosive as I thought it would be when I spoke at Columbia University.

. . . . QUESTION: There seems to be a tendency to turn the toughest problems, the insoluble ones, over to you, not only in the Assembly but in the Security Council. This has been a good formula thus far. But do you not see the possibility that, if used too often, it may become a factor for evil, or, rather, nothing good? Is it not possible that both the Assembly and the Security Council might through such a procedure be encouraged to give up too easily? Also, if the formula were misused, might it not constitute only a delaying action?

THE SECRETARY-GENERAL: Yes, I am conscious of my own limitations and the limitations of my office—and these views are, of course, generally expressed from time to time by many of my colleagues. But, as far as the discharge of my responsibilities is concerned, I make it a rule, first of all, to consider whether it is within my competence to discharge the tasks expected of me. If I feel that it is not within my competence, I invariably refer the matter to the competent organ of the United Nations. . . .

"Africa and the World Community"
Address to the Algerian National Assembly
ALGIERS   FEBRUARY 4, 1964

ALTHOUGH U THANT had been deeply involved in Asian-African affairs before he became Secretary-General and afterwards, particularly in the Congo operation, it was not until February 1964 that he made his first official visit to the African continent. As he noted in his address before the Algerian National Assembly, it was a moving experience for him. He spoke with deep emotion on the subject of racial discrimination, which he described as a "disease" and a "sickening anomaly," and warned that unless it was curbed or eliminated it would "grow into a destructive monster." He asserted that those who cultivate racial discrimination "are cultivating trouble and they can only reap disaster." A fortnight later the Secretary-General, already back at United Nations Headquarters, sent a message to the Economic Commission for Africa expressing the belief that African states were aware of the need for economic integration and that the formulation of an over-all African economic approach had already begun to develop.

THIS, MY FIRST VISIT to Africa as Secretary-General, is a great and moving experience for me. The emergence of Africa as a community of sovereign independent nations is an event without precedent in history. The peoples of other continents have emerged slowly from the dark times of domination—often in conflict and confusion—and have sometimes taken generations to assume their rightful place in the family of nations. In Africa, no less than thirty-two nations have gained their independence since the Second World War, and of these all but one have gained it since 1956.

This amazing development, which no one would have believed possible even twenty years ago and which is as yet incomplete, has not come about without struggle, without sacrifice and without, from time to time, a certain degree of confusion. But when we look at other similar occasions in history, we see that this, by comparison, has been a remarkably peaceful

UN Press Release SG/SM/3/Rev. 1.

process. For this relatively very peaceful evolution both Africans and the former colonial powers can take credit.

The United Nations, too, has played its part. It focused world attention on colonialism, on the plight and the aspirations of the colonial peoples. Colonies came to be accepted as a proper subject of international concern. The work of the United Nations on behalf of non-self-governing territories, its availability as a forum where all sides may present their case, and its power in educating public opinion to accept new historical trends and situations, have allowed it to play the role of midwife in this rebirth of Africa and to accelerate and ease a process which might otherwise have been slower and far more painful.

Nor do the responsibilities of the United Nations cease when independence has been attained. It affords a company of equals, in which there is engendered for the new and weak state a sense of security and confidence. It provides a forum where new nations can easily get to know the rest of the world, where they may gain experience, perspective, and the habit of working with other nations, even with those with whom they disagree. It offers a place where they can assist in the solution of world problems and make their voices heard on questions of global importance as well as on those which affect their own continent and region. It can also give assistance of many kinds in solving the problems of economic, social, and institutional development which beset so many countries. It may even be called in to help in national emergencies until the government concerned feels strong enough to stand again on its own feet.

The United Nations has contributed in major measure to the acceptance and application by the international community of the precept that, in the interest of all, the developed peoples have the obligation to provide technical and other assistance to those seeking and struggling to develop. This begins to give a new dimension to international morality.

Africa is in a special position in relation to the United Nations programs which tend to bring to the developing countries the benefit of modern technology. The African continent may very well be one of the greatest reservoirs of minerals, oil, natural gas, and hydroelectric power in the world. Coming last in the race for development, Africa should not be made to suffer from any handicap for what is after all an historical accident. The United Nations has a special duty to assist the African nations to assess their natural reserves even if the prevailing conditions of the world market *at present* do not allow for their immediate development for the benefit of Africa itself and the world as a whole. In more ways than one Africa is the keeper of many underdeveloped resources, human and material. Whenever possible these resources must be developed forthwith for the benefit of Africa and the rest of mankind. When not economically feasible, Africa should be rewarded in one way or another for acting as the natural trustee of a great share of the world's natural resources.

I am happy to recall that the share of Africa in the United Nations Technical Assistance Program has grown from 17.9 percent in 1960 to 32.8 percent in 1963–64. In the field of preinvestment activities as financed by the United Nations Special Fund which is directly related to the development of human and natural resources the share of Africa has gone from 8.8 percent in 1959 to 32.5 percent in 1963, the last program approved in January reaching 39.3 percent.

Such are the contributions which the United Nations can make, or is making, to the well-being of emergent Africa. In return, the new states can give, and have already given, to the Organization a new vitality, a new realism, a broader horizon and perspective, a fresh view and a sense of the future, all of which are invaluable to a great and dynamic institution. Many African states have already also made a most significant practical contribution to the work of the United Nations in providing the largest proportion of contingents to the United Nations Operation in the Congo, which is by far the largest and most complex peacekeeping operation ever undertaken by the United Nations.

A large part of mankind, and especially is this true of that smaller part comprising the fortunate, tends to be conservative and to view change and historic development of any kind with extreme apprehension. Such apprehension has often been expressed in the last ten years, especially in relation to the possible effects of the vast increase in the membership of the United Nations upon the future ability of the organs of the Organization to reach responsible decisions.

So far, at least, this apprehension has proved unjustified and it is, therefore, less and less frequently expressed. Instead, the United Nations is well on the way to becoming what it was always supposed to become—an Organization in which are represented all of the peoples of the world, and, what is far more remarkable, an organization which represents their best common interests. Certainly the old groupings, the balances and concentrations of power, have changed or are changing. The basis of international action is now more broadly based than ever before. In my view, this is an eminently desirable development which should give greater, rather than less, stability to the world order and to man's efforts to construct a solid basis for peace and prosperity on our planet. Most of the developed countries have been through a similar process of broadening the basis of popular participation in power, culminating in the achievement of varying forms and degrees of working democracy. In the United Nations it is our duty to prove that such a development is as desirable and rewarding on the international plane as it has long proved to be on the national plane. I believe that the new countries in the United Nations, which are predominantly the countries of Africa, are playing a leading role in this important demonstration.

Emergence from colonial status is naturally and inescapably a difficult process. There are many obstacles, political, economic, administrative, institutional, and psychological to be overcome before a normal state of equilibrium and activity can be reached. I know this well from my own country's experience. I should like to take this opportunity, therefore, to pay tribute to the independent peoples of Africa and their leaders for the great sense of responsibility and, if I may say so, common sense, with which they have taken up their new destinies and their new duties.

As in every region of the world, the aims and aspirations of the different countries of Africa do not coincide, and may often conflict, with each other. Diversity of tradition, character, and resources are, as in most continents, a natural feature of the African scene and give it much of its great interest and vitality. Accepting this fact of life on this continent, African leaders have at least begun to recognize also the overriding importance of the common interests of the African countries—the fact that together they can achieve far more than any one country on its own, no matter what their differences. I believe the sheer weight of logic and events on this continent will compel this recognition to an ever-increasing extent.

The concept of African unity, so stirringly evoked and formulated at the Addis Ababa Conference last year, is a noble and historic one. It will often be difficult to live up to this great idea in the days to come, but I believe that the realism, the idealism, and the pragmatic sense of African leaders will win out over smaller divisive interests.

The desire to fashion its own future in its own way is the lifeblood of a patriotic independent people. It was, and is, the mainspring of the struggle for independence. But to have the maturity to realize that independence is safer, and more free to express itself, within a larger voluntary system of interdependence is already a tremendous political and economic step forward. It is, in fact, what the Charter demands of the whole community of nations, although in the United Nations we are still struggling hard to attain meaningful recognition of this valid and essential principle.

The peoples and leaders of Africa have here the opportunity of organizing a system in which national spirit, action, and policy can be brought into harmony within a larger unity for the general good of all peoples. There have already been promising signs in the past year—I think, for example, of the resolution, within the framework of African unity and with the assistance of leaders of other African countries, of the differences between Algeria and Morocco. I recall also African solidarity in responding last fall to the appeal of the Government of the Republic of the Congo (Leopoldville) for continuing United Nations military assistance until the end of June 1964. I hope and believe that, as the strength and prestige of the Organization for African Unity is built up, other results of importance to the whole world may follow—the denuclearization of Africa, for example. If this concept of unity can be fostered and developed in practice, the nations of Africa will indeed be showing the world real leadership in the evolution of political thought and institutions.

The peoples of Africa have, in the past, especially been the victims of an odious human aberration, an experience which is also, perhaps, an important factor in their present solidarity—I refer to racial discrimination. This is a long and dismal story, too well known to be gone into now in its tragic detail. It is to the credit of our times that racial discrimination is now widely recognized in the international community as a consummate and intolerable evil. In saying this I do not for a moment underestimate the deep scars which this perversity of men leaves upon its victims. Nor do I wish to pretend that the evil is anywhere near to being eradicated. I know too well that it still exists in its most virulent form, and even seeks to expand, in one section of this great continent, and elsewhere in the world as well. It is one of our most difficult and important tasks in the United Nations to find a way of ending this sickening anomaly and meanwhile to curb the disastrous results which it inevitably brings to all concerned.

But I mention this bitter subject here for a different reason. The proponents of racial discrimination have historically been the most emotionally backward and the most spiritually bankrupt members of the human race. Their sickness really arises from a sense of fear and insecurity rather than from a superior pride. They are people, after all, who are not prepared to face life on an equal basis with their fellow men. I believe that any useful approach to this problem can only be taken with this fact in mind. I understand all too well the emotional, even the furious, reaction which radical discrimination, supported by physical force, may engender in its victims. The disease, however, must be treated as a most dangerous form of sickness rather than as a reason for retaliation and violence—that is, with restraint, with the greatest care, and with the firm belief that racists are human beings, albeit mentally ill, who must be rescued and cured from an affliction that they sometimes do not even recognize. The ailment must be diagnosed, its course noted, its virulence isolated, prescribed for and all possible cures tried. Otherwise hate will breed hate and violence will breed violence in a disastrous and vicious circle.

It is easy for me to speak without passion on this subject since I myself am not personally a victim either of the disease or of its consequences. I can only assure the sufferers—on this continent and elsewhere—of my most anxious concern to remedy the present state of affairs. I can only pledge all my best and most urgent efforts to finding a cure, the nature of which I do not yet even know, and to do so before the catastrophe of violent racial conflict erupts in parts of this continent. I hope that the group of distinguished experts whom I have recently appointed to study the problem in pursuance of a Security Council resolution, may be able at least to give some guidance in the right direction. I have no novel or sensational course of action to propose.

As Secretary-General of the United Nations I must also look further than the immediate—and appalling—situation. There is the clear prospect that racial conflict, if we cannot curb and, finally, eliminate it, will grow into a destructive monster compared to which the religious or ideological conflicts of the past and present will seem like small family quarrels. Such a conflict will eat away the possibilities for good of all that mankind has hitherto achieved and reduce men to the lowest and most bestial level of intolerance and hatred. This, for the sake of all our children, whatever their race and color, must not be permitted to happen.

Thinking of the possible consequences and of all the past injustices—almost entirely, I regret to say, attributable to the prejudices, attitudes, and mistaken ideas of non-Africans—I do not feel embarassed to appeal to all Africans to view this problem as a world problem to be solved at all costs, and peacefully if possible. I do not feel hesitant in appealing, even to the victims of prejudice, for restraint and understanding in dealing with it, for nothing less will do, if we are to make a new world which will fulfill the promise of all our generous ideas and of our immense possibilities.

I likewise make bold to caution those who have suffered from racial prejudice not themselves to fall a prey to this wicked virus when the tables are turned in the power structure. Racial prejudice is fatally erosive in any society, whatever the color of those exercising it and of those against whom it is exercised.

I do not mean to suggest for a moment that firmness, indomitable resolution and a determined will to victory are not essential in this struggle. I only ask that every action, every attitude, every expression of opinion or sentiment be weighed carefully both with the ultimate end and with the terrible risks in view. I say this with the interest of both Africans and non-Africans in mind. I mentioned earlier a way in which Africa may already be showing, by political maturity, a new path to the other peoples of this earth. The racial question is an infinitely greater and more fundamental challenge which has a special meaning for Africans. Here also an African example and an African lead, however much of an effort of magnanimity and self-control it may demand, could also gloriously show the way to others.

Having said that, however, let no one in Africa or elsewhere harbor for a moment any illusion that any practice of racial discrimination has any future anywhere on this continent or can long survive here. Discrimination against an African anywhere on this continent is an insult to every African on it in whatever country. Indeed, it is an insult to men of good will everywhere. Those who would cultivate racial discrimination must bear this in mind. They are cultivating trouble and they can only reap disaster.

However bitter the problems of the present, we must, to measure our actions and our ends, look to the future, and now, for once in history, I believe we can afford to do so. Indeed, if we do not, we may well be lost again. What does the future hold for us? We look for a future where national independence and the exercise of fundamental freedoms can be enjoyed by all peoples, without fear of some new domination. We look for a future in which the fulfillment of national goals blends itself with an ever stronger international order. We look for a future in which tolerance, understanding, and mutual assistance will make, at least, a reality of the concept of human brotherhood. If we can achieve that reality and free ourselves from the shackles of hatred, fear, and prejudice, as well as from want and disease, we may hope for a new and great resurgence of creative activity—a vast spiritual and intellectual reawakening of mankind.

I have not mentioned in this speech the great practical and material problems which so many countries, including the newly independent ones, face. We have yet to carry the war on poverty and disease into a decisive phase, and the problems that face us are so vast that our efforts in the United Nations and elsewhere seem pitifully small. If ever human problems demanded unity, cooperation, and harmony among nations, it is these problems, and they provide a compelling and ever-present motive for our determination to combine our efforts in peace rather than divide and waste them in war.

To help nations to pursue their aspirations in harmony and to make their interdependence an advantage rather than a hindrance, the United Nations, however imperfect it may be, is at the disposal of all its Members. It cannot act decisively in any of the areas I have mentioned without the support and understanding of its Members. With that support it can command possibilities far greater than the individual possibilities of nations and can provide the framework in which men can give freely of their best without fear.

We are far from this great aim as yet, but here in Africa I believe the hope is there, and with it the possibility of achievement.

THE SITUATION IN CYPRUS

FEBRUARY AND MARCH

WHEN THE REPUBLIC OF CYPRUS attained its independence on August 16, 1960, its problems were already familiar to United Nations diplomats. The question of Cyprus first appeared on the agenda of the General Assembly in 1954 when Greece sought application of the principle of self-determination for the Mediterranian island then under British administration. It was unable to get action either in that session or in subsequent attempts in 1956, 1957, and 1958, although the Assembly did express confidence on two occasions that the parties concerned would continue their efforts to find a peaceful and just solution. The basic problem was to find a formula under which the Greek and Turkish communities on Cyprus could coexist. A constitution designed to maintain a balance between the interests and rights of the two communities was finally agreed upon in London on February 19, 1959, after discussions in Zurich between the foreign ministers of Greece and Turkey. The situation remained relatively calm until near the end of 1963, when it suddenly began to deteriorate. Fighting broke out between Greek Cypriot and Turkish Cypriot groups, triggered mainly by a series of constitutional amendments proposed to the Turkish community by President Makarios.

The United Nations began its active involvement on December 26, 1963, when Cyprus called for an urgent meeting of the Security Council to consider charges that Turkey had committed aggression and intervened in the internal affairs of Cyprus by violating the island's air space and territorial waters. Turkey denied the charges and the Council adjourned the debate without taking any action.

From then on the United Nations involvement grew quickly. First, Thant informed the Security Council that the governments of Cyprus, Greece, Turkey, and Britain had requested him to appoint a personal representative to observe the situation. This request was reported on January 13, 1964, and three days later the Secretary-General announced that he had appointed Lieutenant-General P. S. Gyani of India as his representative. Meanwhile, on February 15, Britain requested an early meeting of the Security Council to deal with the problem. Cyprus on the same day asked for an urgent meeting of the Council. The question was debated from February 17 to March 4, when a resolution was adopted launching the United Nations on one of its major peacekeeping operations, which was to remain throughout Thant's ten years in office. Under the sweeping March 4 resolution, Thant was given the responsibility for determining the size of the Cyprus peace force, obtaining the troops from Member states, choosing a commander, directing the force and raising the money to finance it. He was also authorized to appoint a mediator and to direct his work. The sponsors of the resolution acknowledged that Thant himself had worked out the terms of the proposal through lengthy private negotiations. Although the resolution was approved unanimously, some countries expressed misgivings about the powers given the Secretary-General. Czechoslovakia, France, and the Soviet Union abstained in a preliminary vote on the key paragraph authorizing the creation of the Cyprus peace force. Although the force, under terms of the resolution, was to remain in existence for a fixed term of three months, the three abstaining countries expressed the belief that the Council was delegating too much authority to a single individual and thereby surrendering its own responsibilities.

The United Nations Force in Cyprus (UNFICYP) became operational on March 27, with Lieutenant-General Gyani as its commander. By June 1964, it included 6,238 military personnel from Austria, Canada, Denmark, Finland, Ireland, Sweden, and the United Kingdom and 173 civilian police from Australia, Austria, Denmark, New Zealand, and Sweden making a total of 6,411. This placed it on a par with UNEF in size, but of course left it far behind ONUC. Thant proposed to name his deputy chef de cabinet, José Rolz-Bennett, as mediator but withdrew his name after Turkey objected. He later named Sakari S. Tuomioja of Finland to the post. He also sent Galo Plaza, former president of Ecuador, to Cyprus as his personal representative to act as an observer independently of the mediator.

Thant's major problem from the beginning was raising the necessary money to finance the Cyprus operation. Under the March 4 resolution part of the cost was to be borne by the parties to the controversy—Cyprus, Greece, Turkey, and the United Kingdom—part by the states contributing military contingents and the remainder by voluntary contributions. This was the first time that the Security Council or the General Assembly had given the Secretary-General the responsibility for finding money to finance wholly a major peacekeeping operation. In the cases of UNEF and ONUC, the Assembly had voted special assessments on Member states leaving it up to the Secretary-General either to collect them or—as it turned out—to get along without the money from those who refused to pay. Thant was to complain often that the reliance on voluntary contributions was not satisfactory and that other means must be found for future peacekeeping operations.

---

1. Appeal to the President of Cyprus and the Foreign Ministers of Greece and Turkey

NEW YORK   FEBRUARY 15, 1964

I FEEL IMPELLED to let Your Excellency know how gravely concerned I am about the apparently deteriorating situation regarding Cyprus, being

Security Council Official Records, Nineteenth Year, Supplement for January, February and March 1964, document S/5554.

fully aware as I am of the difficulties and dangers inherent in that situation. As Secretary-General, I consider it to be my duty to address a most urgent appeal to the governments of Cyprus, Greece, and Turkey to refrain from any acts which might lead to a worsening of the situation and further bloodshed, and I would earnestly request the three governments to use their maximum influence to ensure that there will be no further violence.

It is manifest that sound solutions cannot be found in an atmosphere of violence and bloodshed. I therefore appeal to all concerned, including the members of the two communities in Cyprus and their leaders, to show the greatest possible understanding and restraint, particularly at this time when the Security Council is being convened to seek a solution to the difficulties confronting Cyprus.

---

2. *Statement in the Security Council*

NEW YORK   FEBRUARY 25, 1964

I DEEM IT advisable to make a brief statement at this juncture of the debate on the Cyprus question to provide some clarification, particularly with regard to my own role. Since the last meeting of the Security Council, and, indeed, even before that meeting, I have had discussions with the parties principally involved for the purpose of exchanging views in an effort to clarify and define the major issues. Throughout these discussions, my main preoccupation, of course, has been to determine to what extent common ground might be found among the parties. The members of the Council have been kept informed of what has transpired in the discussions through my private briefing talks with each of the Council members. Indeed, I have very little to add now to what I have already reported to you individually.

As you know, I have engaged in these informal discussions because it was clearly the wish of all the parties that I should do so, and especially because, in view of the seriousness and urgency of the Cyprus situation, it is my desire to do everything possible to help resolve this dangerous crisis. It was in the same light that I responded favourably to the request of the

Security Council Official Records, Nineteenth Year, 1097th meeting.

Government of Cyprus, which was supported by the governments of Greece, Turkey, and the United Kingdom, and proceeded to the appointment of General Gyani as my personal representative to observe the progress of the peacemaking operation in the island. The presence of General P. S. Gyani in Cyprus has been most useful to keep me informed about the situation there and in addition, I believe, has contributed to alleviating tensions in the island. Members of the Council are also aware of the telegram which I sent to the president of Cyprus and to the ministers for foreign affairs of Greece and Turkey on February 15, 1964, requesting their governments to use their maximum influence to ensure that there will be no further violence and appealing to all concerned, including the members of the two communities in Cyprus and their leaders, to show the greatest possible understanding and restraint. The replies to my appeal have been most encouraging, and I am greatly indebted to the governments concerned for their positive response.

The discussions have been devoted primarily to expositions by the parties of their views of the problem and how it might be dealt with. It has been my purpose not to offer solutions but, as I said earlier, to seek common ground. I think it may be safely said that from the discussions the exact positions of the parties have emerged more clearly. The atmosphere throughout the discussions has been good, and I am convinced that there is an earnest desire on the part of all concerned to seek a peaceful solution, although, as may be expected, the positions on certain key issues have been firmly taken and maintained. There has been, I believe, progress on some issues, while certain basic differences persist.

I need only add that the discussions which I have held on the problem of Cyprus have been undertaken within the context of the United Nations Charter and bearing in mind at all times the authority of the Security Council. Needless to say, without the concurrence of the Security Council the question of the Secretary-General sending a peacekeeping force to Cyprus will not arise.

In concluding, may I express the hope that a reasonable and practical way out of what now appears to be an impasse will be found by this Council. I shall, of course, continue to be available and to do whatever may be appropriate in the circumstances to assist toward reaching a solution.

3. *Statement in the Security Council*

NEW YORK   MARCH 4, 1964

SINCE THE draft resolution under consideration by this Council, particularly in its operative paragraphs, 4, 6, 7 and 8 would call upon the Secretary-General to undertake certain responsibilities, I thought that it would be quite appropriate and no doubt helpful to the Council if I should briefly indicate my own thinking about the nature and exercise of these responsibilities.

As I observed in my previous statement the creation of a United Nations peacekeeping force for Cyprus could only come about by positive action of this Council. This action, as the draft resolution specifies, obviously must be predicated upon the consent of the Government of Cyprus, on whose territory the force would be deployed. The draft resolution, in its operative paragraph 4, asks the Secretary-General to establish the composition and size of the force in consultation with the governments of Cyprus, Greece, Turkey, and the United Kingdom. In this regard, it would be my intention, in accordance with well-established practice concerning previous United Nations peacekeeping forces, to keep the Security Council, which would authorize its establishment, promptly and fully informed about the organization and operation of the force, including its composition, size, and command. On the basis of preliminary soundings that I have taken, without, of course, having made any commitments, I may inform the Council that although the problem of composition is delicate and difficult because of the indicated limitations on the range of choice, I very much hope that a force such as is envisaged by this draft resolution, and of adequate size, can be achieved.

I might point out also that in recruiting troops for this force, I would emphasize on the basis of operative paragraph 6 that the force, unlike the peacekeeping forces in Gaza and the Congo, would have a fixed and firm duration of three months. The force thus could be extended beyond three months only by a new action by this Council. I would also draw attention to the provision in paragraph 6 for meeting the cost of the force which is not to be charged against United Nations revenues. In this context I would particularly like to call attention to the last sentence of operative paragraph 6 which states that: "The Secretary-General may also accept voluntary contributions for that purpose," and strongly express the hope that substantial contributions of this nature will be forthcoming since it is already apparent that some appropriate states might more readily provide contingents were it not for the extra financial burden upon them called for by the cost provision of the draft resolution.

I am, of course, also giving thought to the question of the mediator which the draft resolution would call upon me to designate in agreement with the four governments, and I would expect to be prepared to act quickly on this, in accordance with operative paragraph 7 of the draft resolution, once the resolution is adopted.

In sum, although the responsibilities for the Secretary-General foreseen by the draft resolution are serious, they do not differ substantially from past experience and I have no hesitation in undertaking them. I could rely heavily, of course, on the cooperation of the Government of Cyprus and of the other governments mentioned in the draft resolution, for their wholehearted cooperation and assistance are vital to the effective implementation of the resolution.

May I also place on record my gratification at the most skillful manner in which the representatives of Bolivia, Brazil, Ivory Coast, Morocco, and Norway conducted discussions with a view to arriving at a resolution on the matter before this Council.

---

4. Appeal for Voluntary Contributions toward the Financing of the United Nations Peacekeeping Force in Cyprus

NEW YORK   MARCH 7, 1964

THE FOLLOWING is the text of a letter sent today by the Secretary-General to all Member states:

UN Press Release SG/SM/27.

I have the honor to draw the attention of your government to the Security Council resolution of March 4, 1964, on the question of Cyprus. In paragraph 4 of this resolution, the Security Council recommends the creation, with the consent of the Government of Cyprus, of a United Nations peacekeeping force in Cyprus. The formal consent of the Government of Cyprus has since been given and the Council has been informed. In paragraph 6, the resolution goes on to recommend that the stationing of the force be for a period of three months and that all costs pertaining to it be met, in a manner to be agreed upon by them, by the governments providing the contingents and by the Government of Cyprus. In the concluding sentence of paragraph 6, the Secretary-General has also been authorized to accept voluntary contributions for that purpose.

I have had preliminary cost estimates made on the basis of certain assumptions regarding the size and composition of the force, which at this stage are unavoidably very tentative. It has already become clear to me that some of the governments providing contingents may not be able themselves to meet all of the costs involved in the provision of such contingents, and that a large measure of financial responsibility may have to be met from the voluntary contributions contemplated in the Security Council resolution. At present, and on the basis of the assumptions mentioned earlier, it appears that the costs which may have to be met in cash by the United Nations through voluntary contributions may be roughly of the order of some $2 million a month or a total of $6 million for the period of three months specified in paragraph 6 of the resolution.

I shall be grateful if your government could make a voluntary contribution to enable me to meet these costs. Since the acceptance of contingents offered on the basis of the United Nations bearing a part of the whole cost involved from certain countries is conditional on my being able to meet these costs from voluntary contributions, I appeal to your government to make its response as prompt and generous as possible.

5. *Text of Identical Cables to the President of Cyprus and the Foreign Ministers of Greece and Turkey*

NEW YORK   MARCH 9, 1964

I AM VERY CONCERNED once more at the news that a fresh wave of armed clashes involving loss in lives seems to be gripping several areas in Cyprus, with a consequent increase in tension throughout the island. This is all the more regrettable at a time when all efforts are being made to establish the United Nations peacekeeping force recommended by the Security Council. As Your Excellency will recall, I addressed an appeal to all the parties principally concerned, on February 15, 1964, to refrain from any acts which might lead to a worsening of the situation and further bloodshed and to show the greatest possible understanding and restraint, and I was heartened by the positive nature of the responses which I received.

I deem it again my duty to address a most earnest appeal to all the parties involved in the tragic events in Cyprus to exercise all their influence toward halting this senseless violence and bloodshed, which, far from facilitating a solution to the problems facing the island, can only lead to even more tragic, widespread, and deplorable consequences. In particular I feel compelled to renew my earlier appeal to the government and to the people of Cyprus to show the utmost restraint and understanding. While the duty of maintaining law and order rests with the Government of Cyprus, the leaders and members of the Greek and Turkish Cypriot communities bear also a heavy responsibility in bringing to an end the violence which continues to erupt in various places in the island. I therefore wish especially to call upon the leaders and members of the two communities to stop the fighting and to realize that it is essential for

Security Council Official Records, Nineteenth Year, Supplement for January, February, and March 1964, document S/5593, annex I.

them, and for all other parties concerned, to create an atmosphere of peace and quiet which is the first prerequisite for working out a solution for the future in the interests of the happiness and well-being of all the inhabitants of Cyprus.

6. Report to the Security Council on the Organization of the United Nations Peacekeeping Force in Cyprus

NEW YORK   MARCH 12, 1964

1. IMMEDIATELY after the adoption by the Security Council on March 4, 1964, of the resolution concerning Cyprus [S/5575], I took steps to establish the United Nations peacekeeping force in Cyprus (UNFICYP), as provided for in paragraph 4 of the resolution. In my report of March 6, 1964 [S/5579], I informed the Security Council that I had appointed Lieutenant-General P. S. Gyani as commander of the Force, and that he would take up his appointment and assume command immediately after the establishment of the Force. I also informed the Council that I had approached several governments about the provision of contingents for the Force and that, in accordance with the resolution, I was in consultation with the governments of Cyprus, Greece, Turkey, and the United Kingdom of Great Britain and Northern Ireland as to the composition and size of the Force.

2. I have had since that time very full and separate discussions with the representatives of Austria, Brazil, Canada, Finland, Ireland, Sweden, and the United Kingdom and have requested their governments to provide contingents for UNFICYP. I have informed the above-mentioned governments, as well as the governments of Cyprus, Greece, and Turkey, that it would be my intention to establish the Force at an initial strength of

Security Council Official Records, Nineteenth Year, Supplement for January, February, and March 1964, document S/5593.

about 7,000. This initial strength would be reviewed in the light of the circumstances, and having in mind the task entrusted to the Force by the Security Council.

3. On March 9, 1964, the United Kingdom government informed me that it was prepared to match contributions of all other countries up to a total international force strength of 7,000, which would mean in effect a British contingent of about 3,500 troops. In the event of the United Nations Force being increased beyond 7,000, and of any increased contribution being requested from the United Kingdom, that government would have to reconsider the matter, without any commitment at present.

4. The Canadian government, prior to any decision as to its participation in the Force, has submitted a number of questions for clarification which are being discussed with the Canadian representative. The questions raised by the Canadian government include matters pertaining to the organization, status, directives, liaison, and duties of the Force.

5. The Swedish government informed me on March 6, 1964, that it was prepared, in principle, to endeavour to organize, on a voluntary basis, a Swedish contingent of the size of one battalion to form part of the proposed Force, for a period of three months. The prerequisite for Swedish participation was that Sweden would not be the only "neutral nation to contribute troops to such a force." Furthermore, before a final position could be taken by the Swedish government, clarifications were needed on certain questions such as the duration of the undertaking, the size of the Force and its composition, its status, tasks, and powers, as well as its financing. The Swedish government also informed me that its decision in principle to participate in the Force would be based on the unanimously adopted resolution of the Security Council.

6. The Government of Finland has also requested clarification of certain points before taking any final decision as to its participation, including the financing of the Force. The Government of Ireland, as well, has raised a number of aspects on which clarification is requested. The Government of Brazil has found it virtually impossible at this time to respond favourably to my request for the provision of a contingent to the Force, but I have made a new appeal. The Government of Austria has the matter still under consideration.

7. My discussions about contingents with the governments indicated clearly that the provision of the resolution concerning responsibility for meeting the costs of the Force presented an obstacle, at least for some states, to making contingents available.

8. While discussions have continued with a view to clarifying the points raised by the various governments, and taking into account that the financing of the peacekeeping operation constituted one of the key factors in the establishment of the Force, I addressed a letter to all states Members of the United Nations on March 7, 1964, drawing their attention to paragraph 6 of the resolution adopted by the Security Council, which states, *inter alia,* that I may accept voluntary contributions toward meeting the costs pertaining to the Force and requesting their governments to make voluntary contributions to enable me to meet these costs. On the basis of certain assumptions regarding the size and composition of the Force, which at this stage are unavoidably very tentative, it appears that the costs which may have to be met in cash by the United Nations through voluntary contributions may be roughly of the order of some $2 million a month, or a total of $6 million for the period of three months specified in paragraph 6 of the resolution.

9. There have been in the last twenty-four hours certain positive indications which lead me to believe that cash contributions will be forthcoming of the magnitude required to meet the costs of the Force. Assurances have now been received from the United States and the United Kingdom of substantial voluntary contributions, and other countries have also given positive indications of their willingness to make contributions for this purpose.

10. Despite delays resulting from the foregoing circumstances, which were not unanticipated, I am confident that contingents will be provided and the Force will be established in the very near future. Indeed, I hope to be able to report to the Council some positive developments in this regard within the next day or so, since my negotiations for contingents are now coming to a head. Plans are well advanced for the speedy transportation of the contingents to Cyprus immediately they become available. Also, my advance party in Cyprus has reported encouragingly about logistical and other arrangements for the Force.

11. I wish also to inform the Council that in the light of a fresh wave of armed clashes involving loss of lives in several areas in Cyprus, I felt it was my duty to address a message to the president of Cyprus and to the foreign ministers of Greece and Turkey on March 9, 1964, appealing to all the parties involved in the tragic events in Cyprus to exercise all their influence toward halting violence and bloodshed, which, far from facilitating a solution to the problems facing the island, can only lead to even more tragic, widespread, and deplorable consequences. Replies have been

received from the president of Cyprus and from the foreign ministers of Greece and Turkey.

12. The Security Council, in the resolution adopted at its 1102nd meeting on March 4, 1964 [S/5575], recommended that the Secretary-General should designate, in agreement with the Government of Cyprus and the governments of Greece, Turkey, and the United Kingdom, a mediator "for the purpose of promoting a peaceful solution and an agreed settlement of the problem confronting Cyprus." In pursuance of the resolution, and very promptly after its adoption, I have undertaken consultations with the governments of Cyprus, Greece, Turkey, and the United Kingdom concerning possible nominees for the post of mediator. In these informal discussions, my thinking has been that it would be desirable to have as mediator someone already having familiarity with the problem of Cyprus and the United Nations approach to it, and whose ability and objectivity were known and unquestioned, and who, preferably, would also be already known to the parties.

13. Thus, after most careful consideration, I have proposed my deputy chef de cabinet, Mr. José Rolz-Bennett, for the position of mediator. Mr. Rolz-Bennett, to my mind, possesses in eminent degree the necessary maturity, experience, and other qualifications for this post. He, as my representative, was present briefly in London at the time of the conference on Cyprus in January 1964 and met with all the parties attending the conference, including the foreign ministers of Cyprus, Greece, Turkey, and the United Kingdom. From London he proceeded to Cyprus, where he met with President Makarios and Vice-President Küçük. He has continued to work closely with me on this question.

14. Mr. Rolz-Bennett was my personal representative in September 1962 in the then territory of West New Guinea (West Irian) to make preliminary arrangements for the transfer of the administration to the United Nations temporary executive authority for the territory, and later served there as temporary administrator. From January to June 1962 Mr. Rolz-Bennett served in the United Nations Operation in the Congo (ONUC) as its representative in Katanga province, Congo (Leopoldville). Prior to joining the Secretariat in 1958 Mr. Rolz-Bennett served as the permanent representative of Guatemala to the United Nations with the rank of ambassador. He has served on United Nations visiting missions and has represented his country at many international conferences. In addition, Mr. Rolz-Bennett has a distinguished academic record. He was dean of the faculties of humanities and professor of the school of law at the San Carlos University from 1945 to 1955, and honorary professor of

law both at the San Carlos University and at the University of Costa Rica.

15. It is my understanding, from newspaper and radio reports, that the candidacy of Mr. Rolz-Bennett, whose name I have put forward only in private consultations, is not favored by one of the parties concerned, although I have had no official word to this effect. The reaction of three of the parties has been favorable. The question of the appointment of the Cyprus mediator, therefore, remains open for the present. It is, in my view, vital that an agreement be reached on a mediator without much more delay.

---

7. Report to the Security Council

NEW YORK   MARCH 12, 1964

SUBSEQUENT to the issuance of my report [S/5593], I was informed by the Turkish government that, while they thought very highly of the qualities of Mr. Rolz-Bennett as a learned diplomat of great integrity, they would appreciate it if I would endeavor to suggest for the job of mediator another statesman of wide international experience and stature who might also be familiar with the problems of the area concerned.

Security Council Official Records, Nineteenth Year, Supplement for January, February, and March 1964, document S/5593/Add. 1.

---

8. Letter to the Representative of Turkey

NEW YORK   MARCH 13, 1964

I HAVE THE HONOUR to refer to your communication dated March 13, 1964 [S/5596] in which Your Excellency informs me that, unless certain

Security Council Official Records, Nineteenth Year, Supplement for January, February, and March 1964, document S/5600.

requests made to the president of Cyprus are complied with, the Government of the Turkish Republic "by virtue of the right conferred upon it in Article IV of the Treaty of Guarantee, has decided to take appropriate action." This action is specifically to send a force to the island of Cyprus to operate there "until the United Nations peacekeeping force which is envisaged under paragraph 4 of the Security Council resolution of March 4, 1964" can effectively perform the functions entrusted to it. Your Excellency has further requested me to take the necessary steps for the urgent dispatch of the United Nations peacekeeping force.

This decision of the Turkish government is fraught with such grave possibilities that I am hereby addressing to your government the most pressing appeal to reconsider most urgently the decision announced in your message to me. In making this appeal I would point out that in the twenty-four hours since I submitted my report of March 12 to the Security Council on the organization and operation of the United Nations peacekeeping force in Cyprus [S/5593 and Add. 1], considerable progress has been made toward the organization and stationing of the Force. In particular I would draw your attention to the renewed assurance given by the Government of Canada that Canada will participate in the United Nations peacekeeping force. The known state of readiness of the Canadian contingent would allow for its speedy introduction into Cyprus. I would further inform you that in the last few hours I have received notification from the Government of Sweden that it is now taking all measures to assemble a Swedish battalion for Cyprus, and I have also had encouraging news from the governments of Finland and Ireland. You will know already of the pledges of voluntary financial contributions received from the United Kingdom, the United States of America, and some other governments which assure financial support for the United Nations peacekeeping force.

It is in the light of the above-mentioned facts that I am appealing to the Turkish government to refrain from any action which would worsen the tragic situation in Cyprus and which may, in addition, pose the gravest risks to international peace and security. I know that the situation in Cyprus is of most vital interest to the Turkish government and people and I would not make this urgent appeal if I was not convinced, as Secretary-General of the United Nations, that the best hope of emerging from this dangerous crisis is to allow the time necessary for the implementation of the Security Council resolution of March 4, 1964 [S/5575], however much patience this course may require from the parties concerned, and for all parties to refrain, in the meanwhile, from adding to this explosive situation new elements which could only make the problem more insoluble and increase the danger.

U THANT
Secretary-General of
the United Nations

---

9. Statement in the Security Council

NEW YORK   MARCH 13, 1964

IT MAY BE RECALLED that in my report to the Council yesterday, March 12, I expressed my confidence that the United Nations peacekeeping force in Cyprus would be soon established and indicated that I hoped shortly to be able to report some positive developments. It is with considerable gratification that I am able to inform the Council that the Force now is actually being constituted. Since late yesterday I have received firm and official assurances from three of the governments I have approached about providing contingents that those contingents will be available. These governments are Canada, Ireland, and Sweden. With regard to each of these governments certain conditions and prerequisites were defined which either have been met or in my view can be coped with. I may add that there are other promising prospects for troops. In these circumstances, therefore, I am now able to state to the Council that the Force will be established without further delay and that elements of it will soon be deployed in Cyprus. Indeed, a small party of Canadian officers will be en route for Cyprus tonight.

This morning, I received a communication through the permanent representative of Turkey to the United Nations which has since been issued as a Security Council document. I immediately requested the permanent representative to convey to his government my serious concern and my

Security Council Official Records, Nineteenth Year, 1103rd meeting.

urgent appeal to exercise the utmost restraint. A formal reply to his communication has also been sent.

The Council is also aware of the pledges of voluntary financial contribution which I have already received from several governments, which assure the requisite financial support for the United Nations peacekeeping force in Cyprus. I am most grateful to all these governments for their ready and generous response.

---

10. Report to the Security Council

NEW YORK   MARCH 17, 1964

FURTHER TO MY REPORT to the Council of March 12, 1964, on the organization and operation of the United Nations peacekeeping force in Cyprus [S/5593 and Add. 1], I am able to report additional steps with regard to the organization of that Force.

Sizable elements of the Canadian contingent have arrived in Cyprus, and it is indicated that a Swedish advance party and an Irish planning party will proceed to the island shortly. It may be mentioned also that arrangements for the take-over of those British troops already on Cyprus which are to comprise the British contingent are expected to be concluded with the United Kingdom government before long.

On this basis, I am able to say that the United Nations Force in Cyprus is in being. Troops of the Canadian contingent have been taken under the command of the acting commander of the Force, Major-General C. F. Paiva Chaves. The Force will become established operationally when sufficient troops are available to it in Cyprus to make it possible for it to discharge its functions effectively. At that time it will be my intention to inform the Security Council immediately, and that will fix the date from which the three-month period of the duration of the Force, as defined in the Security Council resolution of March 4, 1964, will begin.

It goes without saying, of course, that all troops from all contingents provided to the United Nations Force in Cyprus, including those that have arrived thus far, will be from the moment of their arrival in Cyprus and at all times thereafter, exclusively under United Nations command.

Security Council Official Records, Nineteenth Year, Supplement for January, February, and March 1964, document S/5593/Add. 2.

11. *Statement on the Appointment of the Cyprus Mediator*

GENEVA   MARCH 25, 1964

HAVING RECEIVED the agreement of the governments of Cyprus, Greece, Turkey, and the United Kingdom, I have designated today Mr. Sakari S. Tuomioja as mediator in Cyprus. Mr. Tuomioja, who is at present ambassador of Finland in Sweden, will travel to New York next weekend for consultations with me and will proceed thereafter to his assignment. It is expected that Mr. Tuomioja will proceed to Cyprus by the middle of next week. I want to take this opportunity of expressing my sincere thanks to the Government of Finland, which has kindly consented to grant Mr. Tuomioja leave of absence during the period of his assignment as mediator. During my present visit to the European office of the United Nations in Geneva, I had occasion to meet with General Gyani, the commander designate of the United Nations peacekeeping force in Cyprus (UNFICYP), and to review with him several matters concerning the Force.

General Gyani departed from Geneva yesterday and has arrived in Nicosia today. It is expected that he will assume command of the Force within the next few days. The period of three months prescribed by the resolution of the Security Council will begin as of the date when General Gyani assumes command and the Force has become operational. Mr. Pier Spinelli, whom I had appointed as my personal representative in Cyprus during General Gyani's leave, returned yesterday to Geneva. He has reported to me concerning the situation in Cyprus and I have benefited from his views and observations. General Carlos Paiva Chaves (Brazil), commander of the United Nations Emergency Force (UNEF), is about to return to Gaza after having replaced with distinction General Gyani as commander designate of UNFICYP during the latter's absence. My original purpose is coming to Geneva was to open officially the United Nations Conference on Trade and Development, on which the

UN Press Release SG/A/8.

hopes and future well-being of so many peoples depend. During my brief stay in Geneva I was impressed by the seriousness with which partici- pants are approaching their difficult but historic task, and this reaffirms my belief that the emphasis I gave in my opening remarks on the need for this to be an "action conference" will not have been an exaggeration, and that a new trade policy for development will emerge. I also had occasion to have informal discussions with some members of the disarmament conference which is currently in session.

12. Report to the Security Council

NEW YORK   MARCH 26, 1964

1. IN MY REPORT to the Security Council of March 17, 1964 [S/5593/ Add. 2], I indicated my intention to inform the Council immediately when the United Nations peacekeeping force in Cyprus (UNFICYP) was to become established operationally. I also advised the Council that the date on which the Force was established operationally would fix the date from which the three-month period of the duration of the Force, as de- fined in the Security Council resolution of March 4, 1964 [S/5575], would begin.

2. I now wish to inform the Council that Lieutenant-General P.S. Gy- ani, the commander of the Force, will assume command over it at 05.00 hours on March 27, at which time the Force will become operational under the Security Council resolution.

3. As of the date of its establishment operationally, the Force will consist of the Canadian and British contingents and of advance parties that will have arrived by then. An advance team of the Finnish contin- gent is scheduled to arrive in Nicosia on the evening of March 26; an advance party of the Swedish contingent is due to arrive on March 27; and a reconnaissance team of the Irish contingent is also due to arrive on March 27. The main bodies of the Swedish, Finnish, and Irish contin- gents are expected to arrive in Cyprus within about two weeks.

4. I take this opportunity to express my warn appreciation to the gov-

Security Council Official Records, Nineteenth Year, Supplement for January, February, and March, document S/5593/Add. 3.

ernments which have supplied contingents for UNFICYP, and also to those governments which have made voluntary financial contributions. I would also like at this time, when the United Nations is assuming responsibility for peacekeeping activities in Cyprus to express my appreciation and good wishes to the British military units which have been carrying out this very difficult task since last December, some of whom now become a part of the United Nations Force.

5. With the operational establishment of the United Nations Force, a new phase of the Cyprus situation begins. It has been encouraging to note that the situation in the island, although marred by a few shooting incidents, has, on the whole, become somewhat quieter lately. I very much hope that this improvement may be taken as an indication of the intention of the two main communities in Cyprus to exercise restraint, to cooperate with the United Nations in its efforts to restore peace and normal conditions, and to refrain from all activities which may cause a deterioration of the situation. I may also state at this time that I look forward to the cooperation of all parties, and especially of the government of Cyprus, in the very difficult task which lies ahead for the United Nations Force. The Force will need this cooperation from the government, from the two communities and from all the authorities, including the police and other security forces, if it is to discharge its responsibilities effectively. In this regard, I am instructing the commander that he, and members of the Force as authorized by him, are free to have such contacts as they may deem desirable in order to ensure the proper performance of the functions of the Force as defined in the Security Council resolution of March 4, 1964.

6. The effectiveness of the Force will depend also upon an understanding attitude on the part of all concerned to the resolutions of the Security Council, and to the nature of the United Nations Force itself. It is necessary now only to emphasize that the Force in Cyprus is a United Nations Force, which operates exclusively under the mandate given to it by the Security Council and, within that mandate, under instructions given by the Secretary-General. I would once again point out that the Force is an impartial, objective body which has no responsibility for political solutions and, indeed, which will not try to influence them one way or another. With cooperation and with a positive attitude from all parties, it is my hope that this United Nations Force may make a large contribution to the restoration of law and order and to the return to normal conditions in the island of Cyprus.

Report to the Security Council on Military
Disengagement in the Congo

NEW YORK   MARCH 16, 1964

1. DURING THE FIRST week of March 1964, reports reached the Secretary-General from fully reliable sources that some 400 former members of the Katanga gendarmerie who were then employed by mining companies in the Kolwezi and Jadotville areas of the Congo (Leopoldville), were leaving their jobs and were proceeding to Angola. The men were asserted to be acting in response to a mobilization order and were said to be directed in their movements by two persons known to have been active as mercenaries during the period of Katanga's attempted secession. When it was pointed out to the ex-gendarmes by their employers that they were under contract, they are reported to have replied that they had no claim against the companies whose employ they were leaving.

2. A later report put the estimated number of the former Katangese gendarmes who had left the Kolwezi and Jadotville areas at some 600. The same report also stated that according to information received from trustworthy sources, there were at the beginning of March of this year about 1,800 former Katangese gendarmes receiving training in Angola around Teixeira de Sousa; that with the gendarmes in Angola were about twenty mercenaries; and that more mercenaries had been recently recruited in Europe on behalf of Mr. Moïse Tshombé and instructed to proceed to Vila Luso, where a mercenary camp had already been set up.

3. The foregoing information seems to bear out reports received earlier concerning the activities in Angola of ex-Katangese gendarmes commanded by mercenaries. Certain documents on this subject, submitted to the Fourth Committee at its 1493rd meeting on November 27, 1963, by Mr. Holden Roberto, were circulated by decision of the committee to the Members of the General Assembly. These documents in sections II and III indicated that, in January 1963, 130 mercenaries and 200 Katangese

Security Council Official Records, Nineteenth Year, Supplement for January, February, and March 1964, document S/5428/Add. 2.

gendarmes had left Kolwezi for Dilolo whence they subsequently crossed into Angola. One hundred of the mercenaries were then repatriated, leaving 30 in Angola, together with the 200 ex-gendarmes. It was also indicated that these men in Angola had been organized into military units and were engaged in military training and related activities. They were said to remain under the command of Mr. Tshombé and his emissaries.

4. In view of the length of the frontier between Angola and the Republic of the Congo (2,100 kilometres, including 650 kilometres between Angola and Katanga) and in view of the severe nature of the terrain, it has not been practicable for the Congolese authorities or for the United Nations Operation in the Congo (ONUC) to try to establish an effective border control in this area.

5. In view of the serious implications of this information and on receipt of the reports mentioned in paragraph 1 above, the Secretary-General on March 4, 1964 addressed the following letter to the Permanent Representative of Portugal to the United Nations:

As you know, there have for some months, been reports from a variety of sources concerning the presence in Angola, near the Congolese border of what was formerly the Province of Katanga, of elements of the former Katangese gendarmerie, and in particular of a nucleus of its European mercenary officers. A further report from an entirely responsible source has now been received to the effect that some four hundred former members of the gendarmerie who were employed in the mines at Jadotville have, within a very recent week, left their local employment and crossed the border into Angola, apparently as the result of some form of mobilization order. This report lends colour to previous reports that some kind of regrouping of former members of the Katangese gendarmerie was taking place in territory adjacent to the former Province of Katanga.

With the imminent withdrawal of the United Nations Force from the Congo, such reports, indicative as they are of a possible future attempt to challenge the authority of the Central Government of the Congo from external bases, and thereby to lead to another round of violence and disruption in the Congo, are particularly disturbing. I would be grateful, therefore, if you would request your government to provide me with any information which it may have at its disposal, which might throw light on the reports I have mentioned.

U THANT
Secretary-General of
the United Nations

Statement at the First Meeting of the United Nations Conference on Trade and Development

GENEVA   MARCH 23, 1964

THE UNITED NATIONS Conference on Trade and Development held its first meeting in Geneva on March 23, 1964, after almost two years of planning and preparation. The decision to convene the conference was taken by the Economic and Social Council in August 1962 and subsequently approved by the General Assembly. U Thant addressed the opening session. The conference was attended by representatives of 120 countries and lasted twelve weeks. One of the principal recommendations of the Geneva meeting was the establishment of a United Nations Conference on Trade and Development as an organ of the General Assembly. The Assembly approved the recommendation on December 30, 1964, and directed that the new body meet at intervals of not more than three years. The Assembly also decided to establish a fifty-five-member trade and development board to carry out the functions of the conference between sessions of the latter.

THE PREAMBLE of the United Nations Charter affirms the determination of the peoples of the United Nations "to promote social progress and better standards of life in larger freedom and for these ends . . . to employ international machinery for the promotion of the economic and social advancement of all peoples. . . ."

It is in pursuance of these lofty principles that the idea of calling a United Nations conference on trade and development was conceived.

Indeed, a unique atmosphere of agreement prevails the world over regarding the convening of this conference. Not a single voice has been raised against it in the community of nations, be they large or small, big trading centres or small trading partners. This conference is a notable event in the history of international cooperation and will, I hope, mark a turning point in the work of the United Nations in the economic field.

Why was this conference called? What brought you here, determined to labour without respite for the twelve weeks which lie ahead of you?

Proceedings of the United Nations Conference on Trade and Development, Vol. II, pp. 69–71.

A long chain of events has contributed over many years to the growing conviction that the United Nations must make a determined effort to deal jointly with the problems of trade and problems of development or run the risk of frustrating the efforts of the Organization to maintain world peace. The problem of maintaining peace is as complex as life itself, and it is perhaps our generation that has the best opportunity to realize that international relations are not determined solely by diplomatic intercourse and supporting military might, but are also influenced by people in the fields and in the factories where human beings earn their daily bread.

There appears to be a universal understanding of the urgent reasons for calling this conference. Indeed, without such understanding, the conference might well become a mere exercise in political futility or an abstract seminar of leading statesmen and learned economists from all corners of the world. It is, I am convinced, destined to be neither the one nor the other. As the decisions of the General Assembly and of the Economic and Social Council show, as the labours of your preparatory committee amply prove, as the report of the Secretary-General of the conference points out, the conference was conceived as an instrument of action. It is expected to lay the foundation for and pave the way toward a new trade policy for development and to define the necessary instrumentality for its implementation.

At this point one may ask what are the fundamental premises that underlie our conference?

There are two parallel processes at work in the world that have assumed great importance since the war. One is primarily political, the other primarily economic. They generate tremendous social tensions which can either be directed toward new ways of life and the betterment of standards of living, or express themselves in a series of convulsions.

The postwar years have witnessed the rapid political emancipation of the colonial and semicolonial peoples. In the aftermath of the Second World War, most of the Asian peoples have appeared on the world scene in their own right. In the present decade we have witnessed the emergence of Africa. More recently it would seem that important processes have started to gain momentum among the nations of Latin America. These great historical phenomena are so fully reflected in the United Nations today that it is not necessary to dwell upon them in any great detail.

The political trends to which I have already referred may be observed in the large part of the world usually described in the United Nations as developing areas. But these areas are in fact not developing, or are not developing fast enough; they are suffering from various degrees of acute and persistent underdevelopment; they are not only lagging more and more behind the industrial societies, but in certain cases in absolute terms their living standards are deteriorating, especially taking into account their population growth. Here we are witnessing the dilemma of our times; the fact that political emancipation is not accompanied by a concomitant and desirable rate of economic progress. In spite of the fact that the United Nations designated the nineteen-sixties as the Development Decade, by the end of which a minimum annual target of 5 per cent of growth should be reached, it appears that this modest target cannot be attained without a new approach to aid and trade.

For many decades international trade was associated with the dynamic development of the countries, now highly advanced, that comprise Western Europe and North America. At the same time the traditional, usually precapitalistic, system continued to prevail in the large part of the world that had either not yet started or had not advanced on the road to industrialization. In the time-honoured division of labour, namely, exchange of primary goods for manufactures, the moderate advancement of many underdeveloped areas was secured without affecting the antiquated social and economic systems of their societies. The majority of their people lived under conditions of stagnation, which was to some extent sanctified by their traditional way of life, and which in those days was perhaps tacitly accepted. The postwar period witnessed the fundamental reorientation of the people of the underdeveloped world. Today, there is hardly an underdeveloped area on earth where the people are not aware of the existence of the opulent societies, and also of certain fast-industrializing countries which were only recently at the preindustrial stage; and thus the conditions prevailing in their own countries are no longer acceptable to the people of the underdeveloped countries. This growth of a new social consciousness has necessitated a new approach to the international economy; it has created a dramatic need for rapid economic development of the less-developed areas, for the improvement of agriculture and for the acceleration of the process of industrialization. It has also become obvious that a new international division of labour is required. Further, the emergence of the socialist countries, already advanced on the road to industrialization, as gradually expanding trading nations, has created strong reasons for their fuller integration into the international economy.

The two processes to which I have referred have occurred at the very time when the continuing imbalance between the developing and the developed countries, both in regard to income and trade, has reached an acute, even critical stage. Parallel to this, the scientific and technological revolution taking place in the industrial countries, both East and West, has brought about an unprecedented increase in productivity and national income.

The contrast between the developed and the underdeveloped parts of the world and the awareness of this contrast on the part of the peoples of Asia, Africa, and Latin America, paralleled by growing political awakening together with continued economic bondage and poverty—these are the premises which in my view constitute the real background of this conference.

The people of the world seem today to be aware, perhaps for the first time, that the material resources of the world are adequate for the eradication of poverty, ignorance, and disease, if our technology and science could be fully harnessed to this task, and if all means of world-wide cooperation could be applied on an unprecedented scale.

Indeed, since the establishment of the United Nations great progress has been achieved in this regard. Multilateral and bilateral assistance programs have been established on a scale hitherto unknown. Large-scale transfers of capital and of technical knowledge and skill to the developing countries have been initiated. However, these important manifestations of the sense of responsibility of the international community are, as has been proved, to a marked extent nullified by adverse trends in the terms of trade. This frustrating phenomenon emphasizes the need to control market forces which have until now been permitted to counter government policies. Indeed, there seems to be no reason why we should not begin to approach the international economy in the same spirit as domestic economies. After years of argument, the United Nations, in several resolutions, has requested governments to attach high priority to integrated economic and social planning, and indeed the techniques of development planning have made great strides since the war. Accordingly, national planning includes the trade sector. Why should then the problem of international trade not be approached in the same way by the international community? There must be something wrong with economic policies on the national and international level if they permit the unchecked continuance of the trend toward the growing disparity between rich lands and poor.

The chairman of the Economic and Financial Committee of the last General Assembly, in his closing address, posed a question which I believe echoes the feelings of peoples in the developing countries all over the world. He said: "At the time the developed countries were industrializing, the trading system favoured their development, and it does so even more today. Why can it not function in favour of those who were freed from colonial and semicolonial bonds since World War II? Why does the trading system always favour the same group of countries?" And he continued "Indeed, the essence of international economic cooperation since time immemorial has been trade, and trade should become the main and consciously planned instrument of economic development of less-developed countries, rather than continue to function as an instrument to enrich the already rich."

The pervading presence of these questions and the fundamental need to reverse the trends in trade can be felt in this conference hall. These questions are bound to influence your thinking day in and day out during your labours. It is the dilemma of our times; it is the reason why this conference was convened. Man is very close to conquering what we call the blind forces of nature. How long shall we permit blind economic forces to control human relations on the untenable thesis that the social sciences may not be capable of advancement similar to the progress achieved by the physical sciences?

As I have already said, this conference is designed for action. In this conference hall are assembled leading statesmen and learned economists from big and small countries, rich and poor alike. Political goodwill and economic "know-how" are amply represented here. To apply them requires a spirit of dedication and sacrifice, wisdom, and vision. You can succeed only through a sincere cooperative effort undertaken in the awareness of your common obligation to humanity. You can hardly do less than provide mankind, both in the underdeveloped and in the developed countries, with a framework of principles and active policy to make trade a real vehicle of progress toward economic development and thus to help to secure universal prosperity and peace for this and for succeeding generations.

THE LEAGUE OF NATIONS AND THE
UNITED NATIONS

---

1. *"The League of Nations and the United Nations"*
Address at the University of California

BERKELEY, CALIFORNIA   APRIL 2, 1964

U THANT spoke often about the nature of the United Nations, its strengths and weaknesses, its capabilities and its limitations. One of his most penetrating and comprehensive analyses was presented in two important speeches on successive days, April 2 and 3, at the University of California and at the University of Denver. He noted the changes that had taken place in the United Nations during its first nineteen years and in the role of the Secretary-General, and predicted a gradual and continued evolution as the need arose. Despite the changes, he said, there was a large discrepancy between what was expected of the United Nations, on the one hand, and its resources and authority, on the other. The solution envisaged by Thant was a United Nations with power or, as he sometimes said, "some form of world authority" to replace the concept of absolute freedom of action of sovereign states.

NEXT YEAR the United Nations will celebrate the twentieth anniversary of its birth in San Francisco. It will have then been in existence for almost exactly the same number of years as the effective life of the League of Nations, its forerunner. Some comparison of the experience and development of the two organizations is therefore timely.

The word "failure" is often applied to the League of Nations, and the history, especially of its early and successful years, is not much studied now, or even mentioned. And yet in the closing years of the Second World War the victorious allies hastened to organize and build a new international organization which was, in fact, an improved and

UN Monthly Chronicle, May 1964.

strengthened version of the old League. It was not the League, or the ideas behind it, that failed. Rather its members, in the critical years of the 1930s, failed to use and support it, and to rally under its banner against aggression and other dangers. It was thus that they finally had to face these dangers separately and in disarray in the terrible first years of the Second World War.

President Woodrow Wilson laid the first draft of the Covenant of the League before the Paris conference in 1919 with the words "A living thing is born." Despite disaster and unfulfilled promise, these words have proved to be prophetic, as we can see when we look at the world today as represented in the United Nations. For this first great attempt to move toward a "worldwide political and social order in which the common interests of humanity could be seen and served across the barriers of national tradition, racial differences and geographical separation" (as the League's historian, Mr. Frank Walters, has described it) was an historical event of the very highest importance. The League embodied a concept which has fundamentally altered, in our own century, the entire conduct of international relations and even the general convictions which form the basis of public opinion.

Let us look for a moment at the meaning of this change. Before the League of Nations came into being, it was almost universally held that every state was the sole and sovereign judge of its own acts and was immune from criticism or even questioning by other states. The idea— now generally accepted—that the community of nations had a moral or legal right to discuss and judge the international conduct of its members was not embodied in any treaty or institution until the Covenant. From that time also dates the idea, now almost universally accepted, that aggressive war is a crime against humanity and that it is the interest, the duty, and the right of every state to join in preventing it. That these ideas now seem commonplace is a measure of the vision of the authors of the Covenant of the League.

The Covenant was based on other ideas no less important or fundamental—a new respect for the rights of small nations, the recognition of the need for cooperation in social and economic affairs, the habit of public debate on even the gravest diplomatic issues, the formation of an international civil service. It is the lasting achievement of the League that such ideas are an essential part of the political thinking of our world. Thus the League, as the embodiment of certain ideals and ideas, is very much alive and with us today.

In its time the Covenant of the League was a tremendous step forward, a radical change in the concept of international order. It was a response to the bitter, futile, and appalling experience of the First World War, and in retrospect it may be thought the step was too far-reaching to provide a firm foothold when new and terrible dangers threatened. When its basic ideas were reborn in the closing years of the Second World War, however, they were supported by a far greater public understanding and by an even more compelling necessity for success.

The world has changed so rapidly in the last twenty years that it is hard to remember what it was like in the 1920s and 1930s. Thus we tend to forget how much, in the context of the interwar world, the League actually did or attempted, or how important were the new models of international organization and action which it devised and developed. Despite its fluctuating fortunes, the central purpose of the League remained constant—to be the constitutional embodiment of man's aspirations for peace and a rationally organized world. We, in our time, owe an immense debt to those who, in far harder times, kept this idea alive and did as much as they could to build upon it.

I have already mentioned their achievement in the realm of political ideas. In the practical sphere also, their efforts made it possible for the United Nations, when it came into being in 1945, to build on firm and already existing foundations. Quite apart from the central political structure, many of the new organizations continued and developed from the old with unbroken continuity. The International Labour Organisation was maintained and the Permanent Court at The Hague reestablished as the International Court of Justice. The Economic and Social Council was modelled on plans made by the Bruce committee in the last days of peace in 1939. The WHO and FAO and UNESCO grew out of the corresponding parts of the League Secretariat, while the mandates system of the League was taken over by the United Nations trusteeship system. The League treaty series was maintained without interruption by the United Nations, and many other activities such as the control of narcotic drugs and work for refugees passed from the old organization to the new one.

The Pledge to Cooperate

The basis of both the League of Nations and the United Nations is the pledge by sovereign states to cooperate, a pledge which involves some measure of sacrifice of sovereignty in the common interest. Both organizations were designed as an intermediate base between the international relations of traditional diplomacy, which had become obsolescent with the disasters of the First World War, and were proved inadequate, and even dangerous, with the Second World War, and the theoretical, ultimate aim of a world legislature, if not a world government. Both organizations therefore show the weaknesses of a transitional state—great aims with small means, great responsibilities with little authority, great expectations clouded by deep suspicions, and hopes for the future constantly blurred by fears and prejudices from the past.

National sovereignty is, understandably, a jealously guarded possession. The harmonizing of national sovereignty with the wider interest, in a way that is acceptable to the governments and peoples concerned, is the main task, and necessity, of international organization. The League's experience made this necessity clear, and we can already see a considerable advance since 1919. Certain European organizations in particular, such as the Coal and Steel Community and the Common Market, have gone far in the direction of pooling resources, coordinating policy, and limiting national sovereignty in certain economic fields.

The Charter shows some formal advances over the Covenant in the matter of sovereignty. For example, it forbids the use of force by a state in a manner inconsistent with the purposes of the Organization and obligates the Members to supply armed forces and other assistance to the Security Council and to apply measures called for by the Council.

In the United Nations there have also been practical indications of a changing attitude toward the sanctity of national sovereignty. The acceptance of a United Nations peacekeeping force on the territory of a sovereign state is one such instance, and the provision of contingents of national armies to serve under United Nations command is another. These are small beginnings, but important ones. There is also, I hope, an increasing recognition of the impartiality and objectivity of the United Nations Secretariat. Despite these changes, the United Nations still has only to a very limited extent a separate existence, and possibilities of action, independent of the will of Member governments and the policies of Member states. In a given situation it can advance no further than the parties concerned permit. As my distinguished predecessor pointed out, its capacity to act is, in fact, still to a large extent restricted by fundamental national reactions.

The Vitality of the United Nations

There were major differences in the origins and environment of the League and the United Nations. The League was directly linked with the outcome of the First World War and was thus, from the first, dominated by the European situation. The Covenant of the League was an integral part of the Treaty of Versailles. The League was therefore an aspect of the postwar settlement, with all the advantages and disadvantages of such a position. The United Nations Charter, on the other hand, was drafted before the end of the Second World War and was expressly *not* a part of the postwar settlement. In a sense the League was thus tied from the first to the *status quo* with strong overtones from the past. The United Nations Charter, on the other hand, starting with a statement of purposes and principles for the guidance of the Organization and its members, looks firmly to the future. It is this difference perhaps more than any other that has given the United Nations its vitality.

The Covenant was a remarkable document for its time. Its articles on the reduction in armaments, on aggression, on the judicial settlement of disputes and resort to the Permanent Court of International Justice, on sanctions and on the use of armed force to protect the covenants of the League, were great political innovations in the world of 1919 and have been taken up and developed in the corresponding articles of the United Nations Charter. Unfortunately, in the critical 1930s the leadership, the confidence, and the courage to apply them effectively were lacking, and with disastrous results. The soundness of the principles underlying them was reinforced rather than invalidated by this failure.

In other respects the League's Covenant lacked the dynamism of the Charter. Thus the Covenant lacked a clear statement of such an important objective as development toward self-government or independence, and emphasis on the necessity of economic and social development and human rights as an essential complement to political and juridical, and even military, arrangements to establish a firm basis for peace. The United Nations Charter has provided, in practice, a more flexible instrument than the League Covenant, over a wider field. The abandonment of the over-all rule of unanimity which prevailed in the League Council and Assembly is one symptom of this flexibility. The Security Council has a far wider discretion than the League Council had in determining what constitutes an act of aggression; while the system of specialized agencies makes possible much wider and more functional operation in the economic and social field.

The world of the League was in some ways a far less articulate world than we have today. A large proportion of the world's population was then still in colonial status and played little or no part in the world's affairs. This fact gave a basic lack of representative balance to the

League's position as a world organization, which was aggravated by other factors relating to membership. Despite the primary role of President Wilson in its creation, the United States, by one of history's major ironies, was never a member of the League. The USSR only became a member in 1934, at which time both Germany and Japan had given notice of their withdrawal, to be followed two years later by Italy. Thus the major effort to maintain peace and security in a critical time through the League devolved upon France and Great Britain and had an essentially European basis, which deprived it of much of the moral authority of a truly global organization.

In this regard, the history of the United Nations presents a striking contrast in its steady progress toward universality. Existing in a time of rapid historic change, its membership has more than doubled since its inception, and the majority of its 113 Members now come from Africa and Asia. It is thus more broadly based and less dominated by the greater powers, although the great powers, of course, play an immensely important role in its activities.

Role of the Smaller Nations

It derives added strength and balance from the activities and efforts of the smaller nations, which protect it to some extent from the buffetings of great power rivalries. Unlike the League, from which fourteen countries withdrew during its active history, leaving it with a membership of 53 in 1939, no country has ever withdrawn from the United Nations, however adverse its position in the United Nations might appear to be at any given time.

In its predominantly European setting the successive breaches of the Covenant in the 1930s by Mussolini's Italy, and later, Hitler's Germany, paralyzed the League and rendered it ineffective, while the rise of economic nationalism after the depression of 1929 overwhelmed the promise of its earlier efforts in the economic field. Undoubtedly the mood of the 1930s turned against the system of the League Covenant. It was a bewildering mood, and they were confused and dismal times, when it seemed as if mankind had obsessively condemned itself to learn all over again the clear lessons of the First World War. The League Covenant became the victim of ultranationalist propaganda from all sides. This propaganda, actively pursued by many people in positions of power and responsibility, frustrated the League's efforts, grudged its successes and rejoiced in its failures. Confidence in its promise was undermined, and the system went down to a tragic and inglorious defeat. Only after five years of world war did the victorious nations rally themselves to repeat, with a conviction born of horror, the noble experiment.

In practice it could be said that the League tended to be legalistic in the face of crisis, while the United Nations has been pragmatic. Since the Covenant condemned "resort to war," the Japanese action in Manchuria in the early 1930s was justified as a "police action." The world has learned, in the cruelest way, the danger of such euphemisms. The Charter, of course, expressly forbids the threat as well as the use of force. The successful peacekeeping operations of the United Nations have been essentially improvised responses to particularly urgent problems. None of these operations was clearly foreshadowed in the Charter. The world has become a much smaller and more closely interrelated place in the last thirty years, and trouble can now spread and escalate much faster and with infinitely greater devastation. The relatively greater speed and informality in action of the United Nations in meeting danger, as compared to the League, reflects this fact as much as it does the heightened determination of nations to avoid a third and even more terrible war.

The Idea of Peacekeeping

There were also inherent reasons for this change of attitude and pace in the changing environment in which the United Nations has worked for its first nineteen years. Due partly to the lack of unanimity among the great powers and partly to the radical change in the nature of war resulting from the development of nuclear and thermonuclear weapons, there has been a gradual change in general attitudes on questions of international security in the United Nations.

There has tended to be a tacit transition from the concept of collective security, as set out in Chapter VII of the United Nations Charter, to a more realistic idea of peacekeeping in a changing world. There has also been a change in emphasis, for the time being at least, from the use of the military forces of the great powers, as contemplated in the Charter, to the use in practice of the military resources of the smaller powers, which has the advantage of not entangling United Nations action in the conflicts of the cold war.

Already the concept of absolute sovereignty of a state is unreal, for no country can now exist in isolation. The Charter of the United Nations has taken away the sovereign right to go to war, or even to threaten the use of force in any international dispute. The International Court provides a tribunal for the judicial settlement of legal questions between nations. Many states have given the International Court a wide compulsory jurisdiction.

In the political field, even when there has been open conflict between states, and armed force has been used or threatened, there has been an increasing tendency for the principles of the Charter of the United Nations, rather than military power, to prevail, and on a number of occasions since 1945, the Charter has been a factor in actually preventing or in halting war. The principles of the Charter are clearly acceptable to most of mankind. The acceptance of their practical application, however, involving as it does concepts of national sovereignty long held sacred, is a longer and more difficult task—a task in which the League of Nations failed. If the United Nations has, so far, had more success and has made practical progress in applying the principles of the Charter, it is largely because public thinking on international issues has made great advances and because the dangers to be avoided are greater than ever.

We are now moving away quickly from the world of compartmentalized self-sufficiency into a world where human solidarity daily becomes more essential. Already in humanitarian questions this solidarity is real, as we can see from international responses to natural and other disasters. It is becoming more real in the economic field, and it is clearly a necessity, though not yet a practical reality, in the political field. Here the governments of the world, associated in the United Nations, must realize the ideals which were already accepted in 1919 in the Covenant of the League and were reaffirmed in 1945 in the Charter of the United Nations.

We can thus see how far the world has actually come since 1919 in making the ideas and ideals of the Covenant of the League of Nations into acceptable reality. If we are to make the next step toward world authority and then onward to a world government, it will be by the growth in authority and prestige of the institutions and agencies of the United Nations, and by the development of the provisions of the Charter and the Statute of the International Court. If we can make these documents accepted as binding law, as every government in the United Nations is pledged to accept, then we are on the right path to world authority.

2. *"The Strengthening of the United Nations"* Address at the University of Denver

DENVER, COLORADO   APRIL 3, 1964

YESTERDAY IN California I talked of the League of Nations and compared its twenty years' experience with the development of the United Nations in its first nineteen years. The periods of time themselves are significant. In its nineteenth year the League was facing betrayal, ridicule, and defeat on many sides. With its moral authority and effectiveness irreparably damaged, its remaining members stood at bay before the forces of totalitarianism, and the disaster of total war was soon to follow. Only the great principles and purposes on which it was founded remained untarnished, to be revived in the United Nations with greater strength and validity than ever after five years of war.

The United Nations in its nineteenth year faces a very different prospect. Its membership is steadily progressing toward universality. It has already weathered many storms and faced up, with fair success, to several major international crises. Though very far from adequate as a world organization for the maintenance of peace, it has steadily developed new methods and new strength in response to challenges, and the governments and peoples of the world seem increasingly disposed to put their confidence and support behind it. Indeed, I sometimes think that public opinion is inclined to put almost too much responsibility on the United Nations without considering carefully how tenuous still are its authority and capacity to act, and how meager and improvised are its material resources. Nonetheless the trend is a positive one, and the demonstrable necessity for an effective world organization is now recognized and accepted by the vast majority of mankind. There are, I know, still a few diehard groups and individuals who proclaim their preference for a return to the rugged individualism of the Stone Age, but I believe that the loudness of their voices is out of all proportion to their real importance.

UN Monthly Chronicle, May 1964.

The United Nations has had the advantage of the experience of the League, even of the League's failure to avert war. The Second World War proved in terrible fashion, if further proof were needed, that war is an unqualified disaster, that nations, whether they like it or not, are increasingly interdependent and that some global mechanism is essential if such disasters are not to recur. Developments in armaments, communications, and political and ideological groupings since the Second World War have only served to reinforce this lesson. Our world is today smaller and more interdependent than ever, while our capacity to annihilate each other is far greater than ever.

Those facts of life are so self-evident that we may well now be coming to a point where we can make new strides, not only in practical methods of keeping the peace and of preparing a better future for mankind, but also in the whole concept of political organization for that purpose. I mentioned yesterday what a tremendous step forward was represented in its own time by the League Covenant, with its acceptance of international responsibility, its rejection of war, and its assertion of the rights of all nations both great and small. Our thinking on international organization ever since has been colored by these ideas and by the failure to put them into practice which allowed the Second World War to happen. Since the avoidance of another major war was the principal preoccupation of the authors of both the League Covenant and the United Nations Charter, both documents are focused on war as the central danger.

But now the nature of war itself has changed radically, as well as mankind's attitude toward it. The instruments of war that we now possess make war itself absolute folly from a practical point of view, at a time when civilized men have already come to the conclusion that war is also morally unacceptable. In fact it is beginning to seem almost possible that war on a grand scale may cease, at last, to be a constant feature of history.

New Concepts

If this is so, it will soon be time to turn to new concepts of international order. We have a parallel for this in the development of national states. There was a time in the quite recent past when civil war was an accepted and regular feature of national life, and there are, unfortunately, a few countries where this is still true. When civil war was a prevalent evil, the apparatus of the state was geared to the need to prevent the growth of disruptive forces in the state, and often its development was impeded by this necessity. When this ceased to be necessary, the emphasis on dealing with violent disruption was replaced by an emphasis on the maintenance of justice, law, and order, and political institutions were adjusted and developed to take advantage of this happier state of affairs, in which democracy and freedom could flourish.

Perhaps in the international order also we may soon come to the point where we can afford to transfer our efforts from the prevention of war to the building up of a system of justice, law, and order for all nations and all peoples. I do not wish in any way to minimize the still-existent and appalling danger of war, and our primary aim is still to avoid it, but our long-term aim must be for a reliable system of justice, law, and order, in which the energies, talents, and resources of mankind can bring in their full return. It is in this context that I shall speak today of the strengthening of the United Nations.

The United Nations has grown in many ways in its first nineteen years. Starting with a membership of 51, it now has 113 Members, and there are more to come. This trend toward universality is unquestionably beneficial—indeed it is essential—to an organization one of whose primary functions is to reflect the state of the world as it is and to harmonize the policies of nations. This main difference between the United Nations and the regional pacts such as NATO or the Warsaw Pact, is sometimes overlooked by the United Nations' critics. The United Nations exists to reflect the diversity of the world as it is and to try to bring order, reason and the motivation of common interest into that diversity. If it reflected only one side or the other of the world's problems, it would no longer be able to perform its true function.

The expanding membership of the United Nations has, I know, caused anxiety in some quarters, especially in the older Member states. It has been said that the advent of many new countries would upset the voting balance in the Assembly and would cause irresponsible decisions to be taken. I do not think that anything has happened so far to justify these fears. On the contrary the new nations have brought new and refreshing perspectives to old controversies and issues. They have shown an independence and common sense which compares very favorably, for example, with the long, arid, and vituperative debates of the worst years of the cold war. They have maintained their own views, interests, and differences without upsetting the balance between the great powers by block voting on important issues. In fact they have greatly contributed to a more balanced and realistic atmosphere by staying outside of the East-West ideological struggle. They have loyally supported the United Nations in its peacekeeping operations in sensitive parts of the world, and they have often produced useful and constructive initiatives in finding solutions to great political problems.

The increasing membership of the United Nations has also raised from time to time the old criticism of the one-nation-one-vote system. This criticism overlooks two basic facts—first, that the world consists of sovereign nations of all sizes from very large to very small, and secondly that the United Nations as a truly representative world Organization can only be based on the principle of the sovereign equality of its members whatever their size. From a purely practical point of view also, it is difficult to envisage a workable alternative to the one-vote-per-country system, whatever its apparent inequities, unless the world were to return to the old idea of might is right. A system of weighted voting based on population or resources or wealth would produce results which might be especially unwelcome to those who are critical of the present system. It is well to remember that today Asia and Africa, which contain two-thirds of the human race, command only half of the votes in the Assembly. If another system of representation, based, say, on population, were adopted, a far greater imbalance in the Assembly between the continental groupings would result. As it is, the main groupings of nations each contain both great and small states and a rough balance is thus achieved. The world is perhaps an untidy place, but it is hard to imagine another system by which the voting in the United Nations could be more equitably arranged.

Pragmatic Approach

Yesterday, in comparing the United Nations with its predecessor, the League of Nations, I said that the United Nations' performance had been characterized by a pragmatic approach to problems. This has been especially true in its so-called peacekeeping operations in the Middle East, in the Congo, in Kashmir, and West Irian and, now, in Cyprus, to name the main ones. In these situations, each markedly different from the other, the Security Council, or in the case of the Suez crisis of 1956 the General Assembly, have responded by creating instruments of pacification in order to police or keep under impartial scrutiny an overheated and potentially violent conflict until the temperature could be reduced sufficiently for a solution to be sought. These have not been doctrinaire attempts to apply the letter of the Charter. The tendency has been to follow, rather, the spirit of the Charter, and to devise instruments and modalities, often based on the military personnel of the medium-sized and smaller nations, to provide that minimum of authority and military presence needed to prevent violence or chaos, which could easily spread to other areas or invite outside interference and to provide the time and the opportunity for counsels of peace and restraint to prevail.

These peacekeeping operations are improvised and are of the minimum strength required. They require the consent and cooperation not only of contributing states but of the country or countries in which they are due to operate. Despite their relative weakness in terms of military power and authority, they have proved remarkably effective in the Middle East, both in the fifteen years that the Truce Supervision Organization has been operating, and with the Emergency Force in Gaza after the Suez crisis, as well as in Kashmir, in West Irian, and in the Congo. It is too early yet to assess the United Nations Cyprus operation, one of the most delicate tasks ever assigned to the Organization. I hope very much that it too, despite the formidable complications involved in that tortured island, will prove once again that the moral authority, common interest, and combined will of the community of nations to forestall disorder and prevent war can, through the United Nations, prevail over violence, rivalry, and conflict.

Unprecedented Changes

In its first nineteen years, the United Nations has seen great and unprecedented changes in the world. It has seen a change in the nature of war, a fundamental regrouping of alliances, and a shift in the centers of military, political, and economic power. It has seen the emergence from colonialism to independence of vast areas and huge populations. It has seen developments in communications and technology which have made the world a much smaller place, in the sense of nations being not only more interdependent, but also far more influenced by their increased knowledge and awareness of each other. This era of change has laid great new burdens on the United Nations in its capacity as the agent of peaceful change and development.

It is not only in the political field that the need for new efforts by the world Organization has become apparent. The ever-widening gap between standards of living in the developed and underdeveloped nations presents immense dangers for the future stability and prosperity of the world. Flagrant disregard for human rights, as, for example, in policies based on racial discrimination, can produce frictions and fissures which spread far beyond the borders of one state. The new speed of communication in our world has radically changed the time scale, so that we can no longer afford to be slow in responding to dangers, in remedying injustices or in improving economic and social conditions. Nor in these conditions are the old standards and customs always applicable. Even the Charter, drafted only twenty years ago, has to be, and is, interpreted in new and dynamic ways. The interpretation, for example, of Article 2 (7) on domestic jurisdiction has inevitably broadened in a world where what used to be exclusively domestic and national questions can now have important and sometimes violent effects far beyond the borders of the state in which they originate.

This changing world has put, as I said, all sorts of new burdens and responsibilities on the United Nations. These new problems come to the United Nations because they are of urgent common concern, and because, in many cases, efforts to deal with them by other means have proved futile. No one, and certainly not the Secretary-General, has sought them out and taken them on in order to extend the power and authority of the Organization. Rather, the United Nations is constantly being asked to deal with new problems and new responsibilities which the authors of the Charter only dimly foresaw, or, in some cases, did not foresee at all. Thus, when we talk of strengthening the United Nations, it is not from a point of view of seeking new power or greater glory, of empire building by attempting to extend the influence and authority of the Organization. We speak of strengthening the United Nations, because this is an urgent necessity if the Organization and its members are not to be crushed by the great and actual responsibilities and challenges which our times have put upon them. What becomes more apparent with each successive international crisis, whether in the Congo, Cuba, Cyprus, or the growing economic imbalance of the world, to name only a few, is the very large discrepancy between the aims and responsibilities of the United Nations and what the peoples of the world, through the General Assembly and the Security Council, call upon it to do about them, on the one hand, and the meagerness of the Organization's resources, its authority, and its support both material and political, on the other. In this existing situation the strengthening of the United Nations is not just a theoretical idealistic aim—it is a vital, practical necessity.

I will take, as one major example, the peacekeeping operations of the Organization, which currently exist in the Middle East, in the Congo, in Kashmir, and in Cyprus and may at any moment be required urgently in several other areas. Having little by way of precedent and no standing establishment to lean on, these operations must necessarily be organized by improvisation. They are, notoriously, financed on a shoestring and on a system so insecure that it cannot fail to affect adversely their efficiency and expeditiousness, quite apart from its effect on the general solvency and public reputation of the United Nations. It is well to read the public reports and comments on the United Nations Operation in the Congo against this background and to remember that in the Congo a force which is now less than five thousand strong, and, at its largest, was only about twenty thousand, was given by the Security Council the task of assisting a new government to restore law and order out of chaos in a country the size of the whole of Western Europe. Again in Cyprus there have been great difficulties, which I hope have now been overcome, in establishing an international force on that island, although failure to do so could well have meant war in the eastern Mediterranean.

The United Nations is criticized, and sometimes rightly, for its inadequacy, and sometimes for its lack of expedition, in such situations. But it is important, if such criticisms are to be useful, that they should go to the root of the matter and not be sidetracked by old prejudices or futile name-calling.

When the United Nations is called upon to mount a peacekeeping operation two main problems arise, the question of providing the force and of financing it. The provisions of the Charter for a military force to be made available to the Security Council under Chapter VII do not, for a series of historical and political reasons, prove applicable to the kind of peacekeeping force which is now required. Chapter VII of the Charter envisages collective action by the United Nations against aggression. It also assumes the unanimity of the great powers who are the permanent members of the Security Council and it was drafted outside the context of nuclear and thermonuclear weapons of mass destruction and the theory of the deterrent. The nuclear balance established between the great powers is to some extent an insurance, if an uneasy one, against the kind of aggression which the authors of the Charter had in mind in drafting

Chapter VII. Meanwhile a different series of problems of keeping the peace has arisen, namely the necessity of dealing with smaller conflicts in such a way that they can be contained and isolated from East-West rivalry through United Nations peacekeeping efforts. I may observe in passing that the first time military contingents from one of the permanent members has been used in a United Nations peacekeeping force is the inclusion at the present time of British contingents in the United Nations Force in Cyprus.

While we may welcome the decreasing necessity for the old concept of collective security in the face of large-scale aggression, the new concept of United Nations peacekeeping forces organized not to fight, but to keep the peace, and organized not, as envisaged in Chapter VII of the Charter, on the military establishments of the great powers, but predominantly composed from the armies of medium and small nations, does pose considerable practical problems. The Members of the United Nations have hitherto most loyally responded to the call of the United Nations for assistance in critical situations, and in the Middle East, the Congo, West Irian, and now Cyprus, have made military forces available at considerable sacrifice and often in situations which involve very considerable risks to the officers and men concerned. The United Nations is dependent upon their help and cooperation since it has no standing peacekeeping forces of its own, and until now, no standing arrangements for putting such forces into the field either.

An Exercise in Diplomacy

The problems of improvising such forces are both political and practical. First, nations must be found who are willing to provide forces; next the forces provided must be acceptable to the countries principally concerned in the situation to be dealt with; thirdly, the contributing nations must be reasonably satisfied as to the functions which their military contingents are to be called upon to perform. To meet these requirements requires an exercise in diplomacy and negotiation which is never easy, and is especially difficult when there is an urgent situation such as the current situation in Cyprus, in which previous efforts at peacekeeping have encountered the greatest possible difficulty.

When these problems have been settled, the problems of military planning, logistics, and the welding of the national contingents in a coherent international force remain. By their very nature these operations are improvised, and improvisation in such intricate matters can never be as satisfactory as a well-worked-out, long-term military plan. In this context it is worth noting that the permanent members of the Security Council are precisely the countries whose military establishments are sufficiently large and well-equipped to carry out far-flung military operations, but with the exception of logistical support it has not hitherto been found possible to make use of the military establishments of the permanent members of the Security Council, with the one exception in Cyprus that I have mentioned.

A great deal of attention is now being given to these problems by governments as well as by groups and individuals interested in international affairs and in the practical problems of keeping the peace. These discussions and studies are extremely valuable, not only in working out new methods of improving the peacekeeping performance of the United Nations, but also in airing the problem and in educating public opinion as to its nature and importance. Considerable progress has already been made. The existence and success of international forces under the United Nations is in itself a sign not only of an increasing recognition of the necessity for avoiding the spread of conflict and violence by the efforts of the international community, but also of the development of the thinking of governments on these matters. Certain governments have given special attention to this problem and are in the process of making arrangements by which contingents of their national armies may be made available on a stand-by basis for United Nations service. This is an excellent initiative which will, I hope, be followed by other governments, as it will at least facilitate a certain degree of preparation, training, and planning for future eventualities.

It is often suggested that the time has come for a permanent international peacekeeping force to be established under the United Nations. Obviously this would be a great step forward, but I do not believe that the time has yet come for such a radical advance. Quite apart from the financial problem, of which I shall say more in a moment, there are other fundamental steps which must be made in the whole concept and system of international organization before the governments could readily accept this innovation. To provide the United Nations with its own permanent international force would give it some of the trappings of a world government, which at present it very definitely is not. The very existence of such a force would imply, if the force is to be used effectively, a very considerable surrender of sovereignty by nations, which in its turn would require the acceptance by public opinion of new and radical political principles. Very considerable progress in disarmament would also be a necessary prerequisite. The direction of such a force, its basis in international law, its composition, the rules for its use and the evolution of an accepted body of international law upon the basis on which it would operate are all delicate processes which cannot and should not be hurried, although they should be the object of the most serious attention by governments and by institutions and individuals, for, clearly, some such development must be the ultimate aim. Another necessary condition would be a far wider acceptance than now exists of the impartiality and objectivity of international servants both civilian and military, for without this recognition the force would lack an essential element of moral authority and status. I have no doubt that all these things will come in time. If they do not, our future is dark indeed. Such developments will be an essential part of the working system of world justice, law, and order of which I spoke at the beginning. Meanwhile we must strive to strengthen the system we have and to develop the means which are currently at our disposal to deal with present dangers.

The Financial Crisis

There is certainly a very pressing need at this time to solve the financial crisis surrounding the peacekeeping operations of the United Nations, and this is a matter which must be faced very soon by the General Assembly. Departing from the precedents of the United Nations Emergency Force in the Middle East and the Congo operation, which are assessed on the whole membership of the Organization and which have precipitated the present very grave financial crisis, ad hoc methods of financing have been adopted for United Nations operations in West Irian, Yemen, Cyprus, and certain other operations. Under these arrangements the parties principally concerned have paid for the operations, while the cost of the Cyprus operation is not to be a net charge on the Organization and is to some extent being financed by voluntary contributions. While the response of the governments concerned to appeals for these operations have been most praiseworthy, the ad hoc system cannot be relied on should a major crisis arise in the near future which required urgently from the United Nations a relatively large peacekeeping operation. Therefore, even if the current financial crisis can be solved, it will be necessary urgently to consider the whole question of financing for future peacekeeping operations.

I mentioned earlier the immense changes which have occurred in the world in the last nineteen years and their effect on the United Nations. Recently a considerable demand has arisen that these changes should be reflected in the structure of the United Nations and particularly in the expansion of the membership of the Security Council and the Economic and Social Council and in the structure of the General Committee of the General Assembly. It has been pointed out that although the membership of the United Nations has more than doubled, the composition of these organs still reflects the situation which prevailed in 1945. This matter was actively discussed at the last session of the General Assembly, especially with reference to possible amendments in the United Nations Charter which are now before the Members of the Organization for their consideration and ratification.

With the fluctuations and changes of the past nineteen years the relationship of the various organs of the United Nations to each other has also developed and changed. The Security Council, which for some years seemed in danger of paralysis from the stresses and strains of the East-West struggle, has reemerged recently to resume the key role in dealing with matters affecting peace and security which was allotted to it by the Charter, and the relationship between the Council and the General Assembly would now seem again to be nearer to the original concept of the authors of the Charter, although with a major development of the role of the middle and smaller nations in promoting solutions to critical situations.

Role of the Secretary-General

The role of the Secretariat, and of its chief administrative officer, the Secretary-General, has also developed in response to the challenges which the Organization has been called upon to meet. The office of the Secretary-General, in particular, has been found to be a useful place for the mediation and conciliation of disputes and for informal diplomacy and exchanges of views, while at times the Secretary-General has been called upon to assume executive functions, especially in relation to peacekeeping operations, which have necessarily put upon him responsibilities far greater than those envisaged in the Charter. At the same time it should be made very clear that the Secretary-General is very much a servant of the Organization and can act only within the mandates given to him in a particular situation by the Security Council or the General Assembly and in close and continuous consultation with the Members of the Organization and with the governments particularly concerned in a given problem.

Should this cease to be the case, the position of the Secretary-General would very rapidly become so exposed as to be untenable.

The evolution of an institution as complex and as large as the United Nations, an institution composed of 113 sovereign states with almost limitless responsibilities and possibilities for the present and future good of mankind, will not come about by sudden structural changes or new and sweeping innovations. The strength and effectiveness of such an organization must grow gradually in response to the need for it, and in the process there will, more often than not, be much to criticize and much that in retrospect could have been done better. In this process the active support of governments, as well as their scrutiny and criticism, is the essential factor, and it is encouraging that we can see already the development of the thinking of many governments about the United Nations as an institution and of their own role in it and attitude toward it.

To put the problem in the simplest terms, we are searching for a solution to the autarchic relations between sovereign states which have so often led to war in the past, and an alternative to the settling of disputes between states by trials of military strength. Some form of regulatory international machinery, of government in the true sense of the word, is required. We have to fashion, from the elements now at hand, some form of world authority, however rudimentary, to mitigate the anarchy implicit in the concept of absolute freedom of action of sovereign states.

Such an authority cannot merely consist in a paper constitution and must be based on a certain degree of power. At present, actual power in the world is concentrated in a very few of the largest Member states, who seem to be reaching a tacit understanding that their interest in world peace outweighs any of their other interests. This, if an uneasy basis for world peace, is at least a pragmatic one and a distinct advance over the situation in former times. It provides at least a temporary respite until disarmament begins to become a reality. It also provides at the present time the real framework and balance within which the United Nations has to work and has proved that it can work most effectively, as the agent of reason, mediation, and conciliation.

It is to be hoped that eventually the power of the great states, now precariously held in balance by nuclear armament, will be shifted to supporting, in all ways, the United Nations, which will only then become a true world authority. Until that time the Organization must contrive, with all the support it can muster, to develop its potential in the spirit of the unity of human society and to search continually for a really effective system under which mankind can live together in peace.

THE SITUATION IN CYPRUS

APRIL—JUNE

WITH THE exception of an outbreak of fighting in the Kyrenia mountains on April 26, 1964, the situation in Cyprus had quieted down since the arrival of United Nations forces late in March. U Thant reported to the Security Council on April 29 that "quiet prevails." In another report on June 15 he said there had been "no fighting of consequence for quite some time." He recommended, however, that the force be extended for an additional three months. Withdrawal of the UN troops, he said, might lead to a resumption of fighting. On June 20, the Council voted unanimously to extend the force until September 26.

1. From Report to the Security Council

NEW YORK   APRIL 29, 1964

1. THE UNITED NATIONS peacekeeping force in Cyprus (UNFICYP), on the date of issuance of this report, will have been operational for about one month, that is to say, for one third of the time foreseen in the Security Council resolution of March 4, 1964. This initial period has been devoted to the deployment of the Force, to intensive efforts to prevent a recurrence of fighting, and to contributing to the maintenance and restoration of law and order in accordance with the mandate given to the Force by the Security Council. The commander of the Force and his staff, during this period, have had the opportunity to become intimately acquainted with the nature and complexity of their tasks and the situation in Cyprus, and to establish contacts with all the parties concerned on the island. In this period, at least until last weekend, there had been a relative improvement in the situation in Cyprus, in the sense that except for some sporadic fighting in the Kyrenia range area no major military clash has occurred and situations which might lead to such major clashes were being con-

Security Council Official Records, Nineteenth Year, Supplement for April, May and June 1964, document S/5671.

tained. For such developments the United Nations operation in Cyprus may claim no small credit. The outbreak on April 26, 1964 of serious fighting in the area of the Pentadaktylos range (Kyrenia mountains) is, of course, a setback.

2. Ultimate responsibility for a return to normal conditions in Cyprus must, obviously, rest primarily with the authorities and people of Cyprus themselves, since normality can come about only as a result of a determination by the two communities, so many of whose members on both sides are now armed and active as a sort of loosely organized militia, to lay down their arms and seek to live again in peace. The relationship and the tension between the two main groups of the population continue to be a cause for gravest anxiety. Since the United Nations Force became operational in Cyprus, there have been a number of isolated incidents of shooting in which innocent civilians have been the victims, incidents which have been utterly senseless and are disturbing in their indication of an attitude of irresponsibility and callousness toward human life on the part of those doing the shooting. UNFICYP received reports of a large number of persons missing before the United Nations operation began, and since then further reports have been received that cases are still occurring of persons missing, whose whereabouts are unknown.

3. The United Nations cannot be indifferent to savage acts of this kind and I appeal in strongest terms to all concerned to take immediate steps to bring an end to them.

4. The Force, on its part, has the duty to take all possible steps available to it which might facilitate the resumption of normal life in Cyprus. It must seek always to prevent a recurrence of fighting, while also taking reasonable initiatives designed to lead to a return to conditions in Cyprus under which an ordinary man may move about freely and carry on with his day's work without fear or hindrance. Only slight progress has been made so far toward implementing this third aspect of UNFICYP's mandate. But much careful thought has been given to this aspect of the task and the conclusion has been reached that there are initiatives which can be taken by the operation holding out at least a hope for success, and that these must be undertaken without delay by means of intensive discussion and negotiation with the parties concerned. Toward this end, the mission in Cyprus needs urgently to be strengthened by the addition of a top-level political officer. . . . This need has been underscored by General Gyani, who for too long now has been carrying, with devotion and distinction, the dual load of commanding the Force and conducting negotiations on a

variety of essentially nonmilitary matters. Nothing in this sphere, of course, has been done or will be done which would in any way impinge upon the efforts of the mediator to find solutions to the basic problems. I wish to reiterate my full confidence in both General Gyani and Ambassador Tuomioja as mediator. As commander of the Force, General Gyani, with great ability and complete impartiality, has sought to make the Force effective in the discharge of its mandates from the Security Council.

5. General Gyani, in pursuance of my instructions and, indeed, in accordance with his own views, has consistently sought to achieve the desired and defined objectives of the Force in Cyprus by peaceful means, that is without resort to armed force, the arms of the Force being carried only for clear purposes of self-defense. Despite concerted effort by General Gyani and the Force, and my own earlier appeals, fighting persists in Cyprus, with lives of Cypriots—Greek and Turk alike—being needlessly and pointlessly sacrificed. I wish here to emphasize my view that the United Nations Force was dispatched to Cyprus to try to save lives by preventing a recurrence of fighting. It would be incongruous, even a little insane, for that Force to set about killing Cypriots, whether Greek or Turkish, to prevent them from killing each other. Yet, that is exactly the dilemma which is almost confronting General Gyani in Cyprus today.

6. On the other hand, the Force cannot stand idly by and see an undeclared war deliberately pursued, or see innocent civilians of all ages ruthlessly struck down by snipers' bullets. In view of the Security Council's objective of ending fighting, the action at St. Hilarion of the past few days is especially serious since it clearly was a planned and organized military effort.

7. Both sides have given to General Gyani their versions of the present fighting situation and their reasons for it. Greek Cypriot authorities assert that the action was urgently necessary because armed Turkish Cypriots occupying positions in the hills of the sector were harassing Greek villages by firing against them, endangering lives of the inhabitants and preventing them from cultivating their fields and grazing their animals, and also because of the building by the Turkish Cypriots of an airstrip at the bottom of the range, and the blocking by them of the Kyrenia Road, the only access to Kyrenia. The Turkish Cypriots, on the other hand, justify their holding on to this area militarily because to the south of the range there are three main Turkish villages and in the north one, which,

they assert, would be endangered and harassed if Greek Cypriots controlled the range.

8. Moreover, General Gyani had no notice or knowledge of the action in advance, and therefore he could take no steps to prevent it. He immediately took up this question with the Cypriot authorities, pointing out the implications of a military action of this kind for the future status and effectiveness of UNFICYP. Ever since the fighting began, General Gyani has been exerting every effort to stop the fighting and toward this end has been seeing top officials on both sides. On April 28, 1964, he received assurances of peaceful intent from both the President and Vice-President of Cyprus. The two statements in connection with these matters issued by General Gyani in Nicosia on April 28, are appended as annex II. As of April 29, the fighting has stopped and quiet prevails. There was no interposition of UNFICYP in this situation because the fighting broke out unexpectedly and an interposition under heavy fire would be neither feasible nor helpful. The effort of the commander, therefore, has concentrated on bringing an end to the active fighting, which now seems to have been achieved.

9. The United Nations Force, in view of its mandate to use its best efforts to prevent a recurrence of war, must do all that it possibly can to stop fighting. It has been seeking to do this by all means short of bullets, and it should be solidly backed in this endeavor by all Members of the United Nations. In this it has my fullest support. In this context, I also call attention to paragraph 1 of the Security Council resolution of March 4, 1964.

10. The Force was deployed in Cyprus because the Government of Cyprus, the governments of Greece, Turkey, and the United Kingdom, and all of the members of the Security Council had reached the conclusion that there had been too much fighting, bloodshed, and destruction in Cyprus and it should now come to an end. There was no assessment of blame for what had happened and none is made now. But there must be an end to fighting and it will surely become necessary to determine responsibility if it continues.

11. It is the parties themselves who alone can remedy the critical situation of Cyprus. The authorities of the Government of Cyprus and the leaders of the Turkish community must, with a high sense of responsibility, act urgently to bring completely to an end the fighting in Cyprus, if that island country is to avoid utter disaster. This can mean only that high officials of the government and the Turkish Cypriot leaders will

voluntarily and immediately renounce recourse to force as the way to solution of the problems of Cyprus. That is the critical and decisive need at this juncture. Because it is so, I feel bound to appeal most strongly to President Makarios and Vice-President Küçük to announce publicly, without delay, that, in accordance with the letter and spirit of the Security Council resolution of March 4, 1964, and in view of the operational presence of the United Nations Force in Cyprus, there is no reason for further fighting in Cyprus and therefore they renounce it, calling upon their respective adherents throughout the island to heed their call. Then UNFICYP could begin to function effectively, for it could underwrite security for all, for both Turk and Greek Cypriot alike, and help to restore normal conditions of life for all Cypriots.

12. The mere presence of the United Nations peacekeeping force in the island and its day-to-day efforts at the military level to prevent or stop armed clashes and to help in the maintenance of law and order are not alone enough to effect the kind of improvement in the over-all situation which can really bring about a basic relaxation of tension and a fundamental betterment of deplorable conditions of fear, insecurity, and distress in which very many of the inhabitants of Cyprus now live. Such an improvement is also vital if the efforts of the mediator to promote a peaceful solution of the problem are to bear fruit. On the other hand, in the prevailing climate of mistrust and hostility, the communities concerned in the Cyprus problem are themselves often inhibited from taking the kinds of initiative which might lead to a substantial reduction of tension and conflict, and when proposals are put forth they are likely to be rejected—less on their merit than on the fact of their origin in one group or the other.

13. Taking such factors as the above into account, and in particular having in mind the urgent necessity of making progress in order to avoid having the operation in Cyprus stand still and eventually bog down, I have formulated, with the assistance of the Force commander based upon his experience of the past four weeks, a program of steps and objectives toward the implementation of which, I believe, the United Nations peacekeeping operation should now concentrate its efforts. This program, about which, as a matter of course, the several parties and governments concerned have been informed, will require the cooperation of all those involved as well as their good faith and their confidence in the United Nations peacekeeping operation, if it is to be effective in producing the improvements which all desire. I believe, however, that the Security

Council resolution demands no less than earnest cooperation from all concerned, in the interest of the people of Cyprus and of the maintenance of international peace and security. The program which I have in mind, and which is annexed hereto, is by no means exhaustive, but it can serve as a yardstick against which the governments and peoples concerned, and the members of the Security Council, may measure the progress that is being made toward the objective outlined in the Security Council resolution of March 4, and reaffirmed on March 13, 1964.

14. In situations as complex as that now prevailing in Cyprus, the worst enemies are suspicion, fear, and lack of confidence, breeding, as they so often do, hatred and violence. I believe that it may be useful, therefore, for the Secretary-General of the United Nations to make public at this particular time a program of reasonable objectives which all parties should readily find it possible to support. I earnestly hope that on the basis of the practical goals set forth in this program, Cyprus, with the assistance of UNFICYP, may be able to move significantly toward peace and normality.

. . . .

---

2. Address to the Canadian Parliament

OTTAWA   MAY 26, 1964

THE UNITED NATIONS operation in Cyprus had been under way just two months when Thant addressed the Canadian Parliament in Ottawa. He was seriously concerned by widespread demands for strong action by United Nations forces to disarm irregular troops and impose peace by military force rather than by common consent of the warring Turkish and Greek communities on the island. As in the case of the United Nations Congo operation, Thant believed that most of the advice and criticism he was being subjected to was a result of a fundamental misunderstanding of the nature and purposes of the Cyprus force. Partly because the time seemed right and partly because of Canada's active role in the Cyprus operation, Thant chose the Ottawa speech as the vehicle for a detailed explanation of the objectives. This, he said, was not an enforcement action against aggression but "a preventive and protective police action." He said one essential for such an operation was the cooperation and understanding of a majority of the people. "However incensed we may be at brutal killings and the senseless taking

UN Press Release SG/SM/76.

of hostages . . . we are not conducting a punitive expedition; we are trying to he the people of an embattled and embittered island to live in peace and prosperity again."

FROM THE EARLIEST years of the United Nations, Canada has been one of the most stalwart supporters both of the general activities and of the peacekeeping operations of the Organization. The first of the peacekeeping forces, the United Nations Emergency Force in the Middle East, was largely a result of the efforts of your prime minister, Mr. Lester Pearson, who was then foreign minister, and this remarkably successful operation, which was initiated by him in the General Assembly, has shown the way and set out the guiding lines for all subsequent United Nations operations of this kind.

Besides their gallant service in Korea, officers and men of the Canadian Armed Forces have been a vital part of the United Nations Emergency Force in the Middle East, of the forces in the Congo, and now in Cyprus, and have, in addition, played an important role in the observer operations in the Middle East, in Kashmir, and in Yemen. In the Middle East, the Canadian reconnaissance squadron helps to keep the peace on a long and vital stretch of the desert frontier between Israel and the United Arab Republic, and units of the Canadian Army also run the supply and maintenance depot of the Force. The first commander of UNEF was a Canadian, Lieutenant-General Burns, who served the United Nations with great distinction. In the Congo, where the United Nations military force will be withdrawn fully by June 30 of this year, the Royal Canadian Signals have provided the communications which are the nerve system of the United Nations Force which, for the last four years, has been stationed all over that vast country. Officers of the Canadian Army and the Royal Canadian Air Force have held many key staff positions in the Headquarters, and the present United Nations chief of staff in the Congo is a Canadian officer who has served the United Nations with great courage and ability. A Canadian air unit formed part of the United Nations security force in West Irian (West New Guinea) and provided valuable assistance in an operation which relied heavily on air communications. In Yemen, the Royal Canadian Air Force is the communications link which not only provides all internal transportation between the various posts of the mission but is also the sole means of communication and transport between the mission and the outside world. In Cyprus, the Canadian contingent, the Royal 22nd Regiment and the Royal Canadian Dragoons, was the first to arrive in the island after the adoption of the Security Council resolution of March 4, and to join with the British troops already in the island to take up, under the United Nations command, the immensely difficult task which the Security Council has given us. The Canadian contingent is now responsible for the vital sector of the island north of Nicosia to the port of Kyrenia.

It is clear from this very fine record of Canadian participation in every stage of the development and operation of United Nations peacekeeping that successive Canadian governments have shown the greatest understanding and support of these pioneer efforts. This is why Canada has been one of the foremost exponents of the principle and practice of stand-by units for United Nations use. I could have no better opportunity than this occasion to pay my very warm tribute to the Canadian government and people for the leading role they have taken in these United Nations activities, which are of immense importance to the whole world and to our future. I would add that I know very well that such activities often present great difficulties for governments. It is not easy for any government to lend its soldiers to an international organization and to put them under control of that organization. The nature of the tasks that the United Nations is given often adds to this difficulty, for these are by no means conventional military tasks, but rather a new form of military activity requiring the greatest restraint, fortitude, and understanding both from the soldiers themselves and often from the people in their home countries as well. Their role may often give rise to questions which create anxiety for their families and political difficulties for the government which has made them available. In this context, may I express my special appreciation of the understanding and active support which the Government of Canada, and particularly the minister for external affairs, Mr. Paul Martin, have given to the United Nations in the Cyprus operation.

Such problems require that the support and understanding of the government be matched by the responsibility and restraint of the Secretary-General, the United Nations Force commander and others who exercise authority over United Nations forces. I hope that my presence here and my words on this occasion may strengthen this relationship, upon which so much depends.

In the light of what I have just said it seems appropriate that I should talk today about this aspect of the United Nations work and about some of the problems which now face us. The situation in Cyprus is of great concern at this time and provides an example of a problem of unique difficulty, with which the United Nations has been asked to deal because it has defied all attempts at solution outside the framework of the United Nations. It is a problem in which human lives are being lost almost daily. It is a problem in which the world has a vital interest, since the effects of a total breakdown in Cyprus will be felt far beyond the shores of the island and could all too easily lead to a far wider and more lethal conflict. It is, finally, a problem on which there is general agreement on one point only among the parties concerned, namely, the imperative necessity of a peaceful solution.

I will not discuss here the historical details of the conflict in Cyprus. It is a complicated story and one which the United Nations mediator, Ambassador Tuomioja, is at the present time seeking to unravel with a view to finding a solution with the cooperation of all the parties concerned. Meanwhile, the main task of the United Nations is, through its peace-keeping force in the island, to try to prevent a recurrence of fighting, to restore and maintain law and order, to promote a return to normal conditions and to provide an atmosphere in which a negotiated solution may be feasible. The United Nations Force, consisting presently of some seven thousand men from seven countries, has now been operating in Cyprus for nearly two months. It must be admitted without any discredit to the Force, which is performing magnificently, that at present it is still far from achieving all of its aims, although it has already done much to control and regulate incidents and to prevent the spread of violence or the recurrence of large-scale fighting, and it continues to carry out its duties with increasing self-confidence and effectiveness.

The Cyprus operation differs from previous United Nations peacekeeping operations in one highly significant way. Although the United Nations is present in Cyprus in the context of the potential threat to international peace and security which the consequences of strife in the island present, it is also specifically required to deal with intercommunal strife. This means that in Cyprus the United Nations is for the first time dealing directly with forces inside a state and with conflicts between sectors of the population of that state. In the Middle East, the United Nations Emergency Force polices the frontier between Israel and the United Arab Republic, but has no responsibilities vis-à-vis the population on either side of the frontier. In the Congo, the main aim of the United Nations Force has been to protect the territorial integrity of the Congo and to assist the government in the maintenance of law and order and the protection of human lives and property. As the situation in the Congo developed, its mandate was strengthened by the Security Council with regard to the situations in which ultimately force could be used. In Cyprus the United Nations has to come to grips with the disruptions of day-to-day life due to the conflict between the Greek and Turkish Cypriot communities, and it must do this in such a way as not to prejudice the final solution of the conflict between them. This is a task of great difficulty and complexity, which inevitably makes large demands on the courage, patience, and ingenuity of the United Nations Force.

There has been, of course, much comment and criticism of the performance of the United Nations Force in Cyprus. It is, after all, not only a question of the outcome of Cyprus—the functioning of a United Nations Force is also of the greatest interest and importance for the future and is rightly a subject of public discussion all over the world. It does seem to me, however, that some of the criticisms of the Cyprus operation are based on a fundamental misunderstanding of its nature and purposes, which is another reason for taking this opportunity to speak of this problem.

We in the United Nations in the past weeks have received a good deal of advice and admonition on the conduct of the Force in Cyprus. Much of it, coming from sources some of which in the past were not always in favor of strong action by United Nations peacekeeping forces, advocates stern measures and the use of force in Cyprus to quell disorders, to disarm irregulars, and to impose peace upon the island, not by common consent but by military force. To some extent, this is understandable enough, for the spectacle of disorder and civilian suffering in Cyprus is deeply disturbing, and all possible efforts must be made to put an end to it. The United Nations Force has undoubtedly had the effect of limiting the bloodshed and misery—in fact, a much greater effect than to date it has been given credit for—but this is not enough, and better results must, and I believe will, be achieved. The problem is *how* to achieve them without creating worse problems and disasters for the future, and it is here that there seems to be some misunderstanding.

There appears to be a latent assumption in some quarters that the Cyprus Force is a military expedition on traditional lines and should be conducted as such. Leaving aside the question of the adequacy or suitability of the existing United Nations means for the suggested ends, this is a proposition that must be flatly rejected, for it stems from a concept of action which is not, and cannot be, the basis of a peacekeeping operation authorized by the Security Council of the United Nations in the sovereign territory of an independent Member state. This is not a collective action against aggression undertaken under Chapter VII of the Charter. It is something far more intricate and, if I may say so, something of the greatest value, if it can succeed, as a precedent for the future. It is, in brief, an attempt on the international level to prepare the ground for the permanent, freely agreed solution of a desperate and dangerous situation by restoring peace and normality. The nature of this operation is far nearer to a preventive and protective police action; it is not a repressive military action.

What are the prerequisites of a successful preventive police action? One essential is the cooperation, understanding, and renunciation of violence by the overwhelming majority of the people concerned. No police force in the world could function without such cooperation, and this is a condition we have to get, and are taking steps to get, in Cyprus. A police force does not fight the population it serves or seek a military victory; its business is the protection of persons, the keeping of the peace by enlisting the support of the largest possible number, by persuasion and by establishing mutual trust and confidence. Only in extreme situations may it consider the use of quasimilitary methods as an emergency measure.

We are—and let us be proud of it—trying to move forward from the age of military force to a saner, more creative period of peace, order and justice. However incensed we may be at brutal killings and the senseless taking of hostages—and if I may say so, we are deeply incensed—we are not conducting a punitive expedition; we are trying to help the people of an embattled and embittered island to live in peace and prosperity again. We are not guided by martial criteria, however glamorous and momentarily decisive they may seem, but by the deep desire to solve a human problem by civilized means. It may take a little longer—perhaps very much longer—but I have no doubt that, in terms both of the present and of the future, the effort is worth it and the results will be enduring.

What is more, I believe that the soldiers of the United Nations Force, whatever their dangers and discomforts, understand and believe in what they are trying to do, as do the governments that sent them. For my part, I am acutely aware that their situation is a very difficult and, at times, a dangerous one. I, the commander of the Force, General Gyani, and my special representative, Mr. Galo Plaza, will continue to do everything within our power both to enable them to carry out their tasks effectively and to ensure that they are not exposed to unnecessary risks and tribulations. I assure you of my very deep concern for both the security and the dignity of the United Nations personnel in Cyprus, military and civilian alike. It follows that I find no place in a United Nations peacekeeping operation for either weakness or bravado. In this endeavor we shall need the understanding and the support of the people at home, as well as of the soldiers in the field. I take this opportunity to salute them and their civilian colleagues in Cyprus for their courage and patience, for their discipline and their humanity. I believe that their example will be not the least of the factors that will lead to an improvement in Cyprus.

I hope that the leaders and peoples concerned will also make an effort to understand the United Nations operation in this light. The old people and the children, who perhaps suffer most from the disorders in Cyprus, do not need to be exhorted to be peaceful. There are many others, however, to whom I would appeal. The leaders of armed bands on both sides, whatever their official status, serve no interest, except perhaps their own self-esteem, by random shooting, abductions, terrorism, harassment, and martial demonstrations. The world is long past being impressed by such performances. I have noticed with regret that the local newspapers and information media of both communities in Cyprus also do little to lessen the hatred or to calm the fears of their readers and listeners. Rather, they tend to fan the flames of violence and suspicion by sensational reporting and propaganda, and thus aggravate the very conflicts and disasters which have brought death and suffering to so many of the people of Cyprus. There are great issues at stake in Cyprus for Greece and Turkey, and their preoccupation with the situation is understandable and understood. The press and public opinion of these countries inevitably exercise a strong, if indirect, influence on events in Cyprus, and, here again, too often the voices that should be urging moderation and humanity tend to be, wittingly or unwittingly, the instigators of suspicion and hatred. The leaders, in Cyprus and outside it, have given assurances of their earnest desire to find a peaceful solution and to cooperate with the United Nations. I hope they will also increasingly exercise a restraining influence on violence and extremism.

In the Cyprus situation there has been a tendency for both sides to engage in highly vituperative exchanges of accusations and threats, often issued in the heat of some particular incident. A vicious circle of accusation and counteraccusation, of incident and reprisal, has been created which, far from easing the tension, tends to increase it and to harden the positions and build up the resentments of both parties. This is a process which only the leaders concerned can arrest and reverse, and I most earnestly urge them to do so. The United Nations Force is doing, and will do, its utmost to ensure that moderation on both sides brings benefits to all and disadvantages to none.

I make these comments because there is so very much at stake in Cyprus. It is often said, in this as in other crises, that the prestige of the United Nations is at stake. No doubt it is, but our concentration must always be on doing our very best to resolve the conflict. If we do that steadfastly, the prestige issue is likely to take care of itself. I believe that the United Nations is strong enough, and solidly enough founded in the principles of the Charter and in the loyalty and support of its Members, to stand the strains put upon it. What concerns me is that at stake are the lives, happiness, and prosperity of the people of Cyprus—the young and the old, the farmers, the shepherds, and the townsmen who now go about in fear of their lives, or too often cannot go about at all. At stake too, are the peaceful relations of two great and historic countries—Greece and Turkey—and with them peace in the eastern Mediterranean and the dread possibilities of war in that highly sensitive area. And in the ultimate analysis, at stake is the ability of the world community to organize itself so that we can put war behind us once and for all, and can put peace, order, and justice in its place.

These are the real issues which we face in Cyprus. We face them together with an agreed objective, and that in itself is a great source of hope. But for all its moral authority and good intentions the United Nations, like any peaceful agent of order and justice, cannot be effective without some cooperation, some give and take, some effort to move forward, on the part of the peoples primarily concerned. We cannot and will not force them to a solution of their problems, but we appeal to them to help us to help them before it is too late.

Before concluding, I should like to turn to some more general aspects of the problem of peacekeeping. The basic dilemma which we have to face is a large but simple one. On the one hand, governments and peoples generally accept the need for the United Nations and its central role as the keeper of the peace. Thus the Organization is entrusted, especially in times of crises, with great problems of incalculable importance and danger. On the other hand, we have not yet come to a stage where the necessary political and material support is regularly forthcoming, which would enable the United Nations to meet these problems with the authority and the efficiency with which, for example, an effective national government meets its responsibilities on the national level. This fundamental dilemma not only puts a considerable strain upon the United Nations itself, but, on occasion, involves it in serious and understandable criticism or even hostility. It can also put a severe strain upon governments such as your own, which are determined to live up to their undertakings under the Charter and to support, by deeds as well as words, the United Nations in its endeavors to keep the peace.

It is obviously most desirable that this dilemma should be faced with a view to making the United Nations more effective and more able to serve its Members and the peace of the world at large. At the same time it would be naive to suppose that the obstacles to such progress can be easily or quickly surmounted. There is no short cut. Political, economic, constitutional, and even psychological conditions and concepts of long standing are not changed overnight, nor is it desirable that they should be. There must be, therefore, a sound and gradual development of thought and action at the national and the international level, if, on this matter of peacekeeping, we are to profit from the lessons of the past and plan and act for a more stable and happier future.

Your prime minister recently delivered a very thoughtful and constructive lecture in the Dag Hammarskjöld memorial series,[1] on the subject of increasing the strength and capacity of the United Nations to respond to the demands made of it. In that lecture he emphasized the necessity for preparation and planning in advance of United Nations peacekeeping operations, since the ideal solution of a permanent United Nations force is clearly not politically feasible at the present time. Canada was one of the first countries to earmark troops for United Nations service, and Mr. Pearson has made some most constructive suggestions for the further development and coordination of such stand-by forces, including consultations among the governments who have already earmarked such forces. I believe that consultations and cooperation among interested governments can be of much value in contributing to the improvement of the peacekeeping effectiveness of the United Nations.

Quite apart from such practical consultations, a wide public discussion of this question is most desirable. Such a discussion should range over the

---

[1] See *The Quest for Peace: The Dag Hammarskjöld Memorial Lectures,* edited by Andrew W. Cordier and Wilder Foote (New York, Columbia University Press, 1965), pp. 99-117.

whole complex of problems, political, financial, constitutional, juridical, and psychological, which have to be solved in evolving a dependable world agency for keeping the peace. The kind of problems which are widely, and sometimes hotly, debated today in relation to Cyprus—the extent of the authority of an international force, its relation to the authorities of the state concerned, its right to use force, the lengths to which it can go to restore order and maintain peace—are problems which will constantly arise in the future.

These problems have a fundamental bearing on concepts of sovereignty and on principles of law, as well as on military and civilian organization and method.

They need to be weighed and developed in the broad perspective of world affairs in the future, as well as in the narrow context of Cyprus.

I am gratified that Canada, which has on other occasions given a lead in peacekeeping matters, is here once again looking ahead.

To address this joint session has been a great occasion and a great honor for me. In our different positions, we have, I believe, fundamentally the same aim—the creation of a world where justice, peace, and order can flourish and be enjoyed by all. Together we must develop the means toward this end. Without the confidence and support of its Member governments in good times as well as in bad, the United Nations can never live up to the great ideals and aims of its Charter. For that reason we must continually make the effort to examine problems openly and frankly from all viewpoints. With this end particularly in mind, I am most grateful to have had the opportunity of sharing my thoughts with you today.

---

3. *From Report to the Security Council*

NEW YORK   JUNE 15, 1964

---

124. .... AT PRESENT, due largely, it would appear, to the presence of the Force, there is no fighting in Cyprus, quiet prevails, and there has been no fighting of consequence for quite some time. The extension of the Force may continue to prevent a recurrence of fighting, as the Force is called

Security Council Official Records, Nineteenth Year, Supplement for April, May, and June 1964, document S/5764, paras. 124-128.

upon to do by the Council's resolution of March 4, although, naturally, there can be no certainty about this. It is more than likely, however, that the withdrawal of the Force at this time would lead to an early resumption of fighting, which might well develop into heavy conflict.

125. If the Security Council decides to extend the Force, I regret to have to report that it will be necessary to obtain a new commander for it. General P. S. Gyani, the commander of the Force, informed me before undertaking this assignment that for compelling personal reasons it would not be possible for him to continue in this capacity beyond the original three months' tour of duty, that is, only until June 27. In response to an inquiry from me as to whether his circumstances have changed in such a way as to permit him to consider service beyond June 27, he has recently reiterated the necessity of his being relieved then. In expressing his regrets, he informed me that his situation has not changed and that he must leave the command by the end of this month. General Gyani has rendered highly distinguished service to the United Nations in the exercise of his command in Cyprus. He has demonstrated great competence both in the military and diplomatic spheres. I am deeply grateful for the substantial contribution he has made. In view of the eventuality of having to appoint a new commander of the Force if the Security Council should extend it beyond June 27, I have made an exploratory approach to General Kodendera Subayya Thimayya of India, former chief of staff of the Indian army, who is now retired. General Thimayya has indicated to me that he would be available, should I call upon him, and it is my intention to appoint him commander of the Force under paragraph 4 of the Council's resolution of March 4, if the Force is in fact extended.

126. The approximate amount of voluntary contributions pledged toward meeting the expenses of the Force in its initial period is approximately $5.5 million. The provisional estimate of the United Nations financial obligations for the operation of UNFICYP for the three-month period ending June 27 totals $5,430,000. If the Force should be extended for a second period of three months, it is estimated that the additional costs will approximate $7.3 million. This increased amount for the second period is due primarily to the anticipated claims of certain governments providing contingents to the Force for what is described as "one-time costs" in respect to equipment and supplies taken to Cyprus and also to the fact that not all units have been in Cyprus for the entire period of the first three months. Should the Force be extended, it will remain to be

determined whether this increased amount could be raised through voluntary contributions. I have no assurance of this at present.

127. I feel bound to point out that, although I well understand the reasons for it and realize that there is little or no possibility of change, the method of financing the Force in Cyprus as defined in the Security Council resolution of March 4, is most unsatisfactory. Since funds are available only through voluntary contributions, there is a large degree of uncertainty about what will be actually available, and therefore the planning and advance arrangements essential to an efficient and economical operation are sorely hampered.

128. Parallel with the operations of the Force, efforts at promoting a peaceful solution by mediation and an agreed settlement of the Cyprus problem, as envisaged in paragraph 7 of the resolution of March 4, 1964, have been maintained continuously since I designated Mr. Sakari Tuomioja as the mediator on March 25. In accordance with the terms of reference set out in the resolution, the mediator has throughout the period been in consultation with the representatives of the Cyprus communities and with the governments of Cyprus, Greece, Turkey, and the United Kingdom, seeking to find a sufficient measure of common ground on which to encourage the parties to develop the basis for a long-term solution of the problem. Given the circumstances which have prevailed in Cyprus, including the very wide differences between the political viewpoints and objectives of the leaders of the communities, the task of the mediator could not have been expected to be an easy one, nor likely to lead to positive results in a relatively short time. The mediator's experience has confirmed this and he will continue his patient endeavors with the parties concerned, while reporting periodically to me as envisaged by the resolution of March 4. It will be recalled that, unlike the mandate of the Force, the mediator's mandate does not prescribe any fixed period.

Letter to the Permanent Representative of South Africa

NEW YORK   MARCH 27, 1964

U THANT clashed with the Government of South Africa on numerous occasions over that government's policies of *apartheid,* over specific incidents connected with these policies and over the question of Southwest Africa, later known as Namibia. As in the case of his controversy with Belgium over the Congo problem, Thant applied the rule that one of his functions was to reflect the views of United Nations organs, as expressed in resolutions. He considered that he was on sound ground, therefore, when he sent a letter to South Africa's permanent representative, Ambassador Matthys I. Botha, on March 27, 1964, urging the South African government to spare the lives of three black men facing execution for acts arising from their opposition to apartheid. In his appeal, he cited resolutions adopted by the General Assembly and the Security Council, and recommendations of the Special Committee on the Policies of Apartheid of the Government of the Republic of South Africa. Botha replied that the South African government felt "compelled to give expression to unqualified disapproval" of the Secretary-General's intervention. He called upon Thant to "respect the principle of nonintervention in the judicial processes of an independent state."

MY ATTENTION has been drawn to the death sentences recently passed on three leaders of the African National Congress in Port Elizabeth and to several trials in the country under legislation which provides for death sentences. A number of leaders of the African National Congress and other political organizations are accused in these cases.

I may recall that on October 11, 1963, the General Assembly adopted, by 106 votes to 1, resolution 1881 (XVIII) requesting the Government of the Republic of South Africa "to abandon the arbitrary trial now in progress and forthwith to grant unconditional release to all political prisoners and to all persons imprisoned, interned, or subjected to other restrictions for having opposed the policy of *apartheid*".

On December 4, 1963, the Security Council unanimously adopted resolution S/5471 [182 (1963)], taking note of the General Assembly resolu-

UN Press Release SG/SM/48, March 30, 1964.

tion, and again calling upon the South African government "to liberate all persons imprisoned, interned, or subjected to other restrictions for having opposed the policy of *apartheid*".

On March 23 the Special Committee on the Policies of *Apartheid* of the Government of the Republic of South Africa submitted an urgent report to the General Assembly and the Security Council drawing their attention to the "grave new developments in the Republic of South Africa, namely, that some political prisoners opposed to apartheid have just received death sentences; others are threatened with the same penalty; and all of them risk being hanged."

In the light of the resolutions of the General Assembly and the Security Council, and the recommendations of the special committee, I wish to request you to convey my urgent and earnest appeal to your government to spare the lives of those facing execution or death sentences for acts arising from their opposition to the government's racial policies, so as to prevent an aggravation of the situation and to facilitate peaceful efforts to resolve the situation.

FROM TRANSCRIPTS OF PRESS CONFERENCES

APRIL AND MAY

UNTIL THE spring of 1964, U Thant had carefully avoided expressing substantive opinions on the situation in Southeast Asia except for his statement at a news conference on September 12, 1963 on the absence of democratic processes in the Republic of Vietnam. His first major comment on the nature of the Vietnam conflict and the possible way out was made at a press conference in Paris on April 29, 1964. The views he expressed then, in the light of future developments, showed a deep understanding of the situation. Unfortunately, his words were not heeded. The Secretary-General expressed his conviction that military methods would not solve the problem. "As I see the problem in Southeast Asia," he said, "it is not essentially military, it is political; and therefore political and diplomatic means alone, in my view, can solve it." He elaborated on his views at a press conference in Ottawa on May 26. Citing the Geneva Agreement of 1954 as an example of the sort of political solution he had in mind, he said he was not sure the terms accepted in 1954 could again be put to the test ten years later. "The right solution at the right time could yield the right results," he asserted, "but the right solution at the wrong time could well prove to be futile." As he was in later years, Thant was skeptical about the feasibility of a United Nations role in Southeast Asia, both because of the limitations of its authority and its resources. In this same press conference, the Secretary-General also spoke out vigorously against suggestions that nuclear weapons be used against the Vietcong.

Anybody who proposed this, he said, was "out of his mind." Apart from any lack of assurance that nuclear weapons would achieve effective results, he said, the use of such weapons was sure to generate widespread resentment and bitter criticism. Further, Thant expressed the belief that any employment of nuclear weapons against Asians was likely to raise once again a racial factor just as it did after atomic bombs were dropped over the Japanese cities of Hiroshima and Nagasaki in 1945.

1. *From Transcript of Press Conference*

NEW YORK   APRIL 21, 1964

THE SECRETARY-GENERAL: I am happy to meet with you all once again. Since my last meeting with you at luncheon last month, the Security Council has adopted two resolutions on Cyprus, and my colleagues and I have been busy doing our best to give effect to the Security Council's directives. I know that you have been following with keen interest the developments in regard to the Cyprus situation from day to day. While this continues to be a major concern of the United Nations, I am hopeful of achieving a peaceful solution if the parties concerned can show a spirit of give and take which is an essential prerequisite for the solution of all problems.

Yesterday we released the report of the expert group on South Africa. I take this opportunity to congratulate the experts for having completed their task so conscientiously and thoroughly. I am particularly glad that the experts were able to reach complete unanimity in regard to the recommendations in their report. I would like to commend this report to the earnest attention of all Member governments, and especially those who are mainly concerned with finding a satisfactory solution to the difficult problem which the experts had to study.

I also want to take this opportunity of expressing my heartfelt gratification at the identical moves yesterday of the United States and the Soviet Union to cut back the production of fissionable materials, that is to say uranium 235 and plutonium. I understand that the United Kingdom has also decided today to take similar steps. It is common knowledge that all these three countries have much more than enough of these materials for any weapons needs and, therefore, these steps in themselves will not reduce the respective capacity of the countries to wage a nuclear war. However, these actions can lead to further agreements that will cut off the production of atomic weapons themselves.

UN Note to Correspondents No. 2922.

What is more significant than the actual decisions, is the obvious manifestation of mutual confidence shown by the three governments, and, thus, the international atmosphere is further improved. The present decision of the three governments is a natural follow-up of the partial nuclear test ban treaty signed in Moscow in August last year and the unanimous adoption of a United Nations resolution at the last session of the General Assembly banning the orbiting of nuclear weapons. . . .

QUESTION: From messages that have recently come in in the last few days from both the representatives of Turkey and of Greece, it appears that tensions between these two countries over Cyprus are growing. Could you give us any information that your mediator may have on this aspect of the Cyprus affair?

THE SECRETARY-GENERAL: As you know, the United Nations mediator is concerned primarily with long-term solutions, while the UNFICYP, the United Nations Force in Cyprus, is concerned with the day-to-day activities as outlined in the Security Council resolution of March 4. I have asked Mr. Tuomioja to meet me in Paris on the 29th of this month, while I am there. As you know, he was in Ankara last week, and he will be visiting Athens toward the end of this week, and before I meet him and before I hear his report after the on-the-spot discussions with the leaders concerned, I do not think I should anticipate the nature of his report.

On the problem of Cyprus I have one more observation to make. It will be recalled that at your luncheon last month I stated that there are certain situations in which the United Nations can be effectively involved and there are certain other situations in which the United Nations, because of its stage of development, among other reasons, cannot be effectively involved. I also stated on that occasion that the problem of Cyprus is somewhere in between these two categories. I also do not agree with the concept according to which, whenever a peacekeeping operation is entrusted to the United Nations, people expect this Organization to solve all the problems involved. To give an example, you can expect a ten-year-old boy to lift a weight of, say, ten pounds, but you cannot expect him to lift a weight of one hundred pounds. I think the same applies to the United Nations: there are certain situations in which the United Nations can do effective work but there are certain other situations in which it cannot do effective work.

Of course, I am not implying that I am pessimistic about the outcome of the United Nations activities in Cyprus. It is admitted on all hands that since the United Nations involvement in that unfortunate island the climate has improved to a great degree, although from time to time, of course, we hear of incidents here and there. But I have full confidence in the Force commander, General Gyani, and in the mediator, Mr. Tuomioja. Perhaps after my meeting with the mediator in Paris I may have something more to say regarding this problem.

. . . . QUESTION: Mr. Secretary-General, you recently made two speeches, one at the University of California and one at the University of Denver. In the last paragraph of the last one, you suggested that the great powers might invest enough of their authority in the United Nations to make it a truly effective Organization. What would be the first step in this direction that you might suggest?

THE SECRETARY-GENERAL: It seems to me that the first step in this direction is the education of the public. I think that the people everywhere should be fully informed and knowledgeable, about the aims and objectives of the United Nations and the activities of this Organization. I believe that this is an essential prerequisite for the Member states to have a very positive attitude toward the concept of the United Nations developing into a really effective instrument for the maintenance of peace as it was envisaged in the Charter itself. So long as public opinion remains uninformed or apathetic, I think that the move toward the development of this Organization as a really effective instrument will be very slow. That is one reason why, at every available opportunity, I put across these ideas, particularly to the man in the street.

. . . . QUESTION: Mr. Secretary-General, do you think that the nineteenth session of the General Assembly might be postponed to a later date than usual?

THE SECRETARY-GENERAL: As you all know some of the sponsors of the projected second conference of nonaligned countries have decided to request me to take the necessary steps to postpone the nineteenth session of the General Assembly to a suitable date on the following grounds, among others:

First, the projected second nonaligned conference is scheduled to take place in October of this year.

Secondly, the heads of state and heads of government of approximately half the membership of the United Nations are expected to participate in that conference.

Thirdly, these heads of state and heads of government will naturally be accompanied by their foreign ministers and in many cases by their permanent representatives to the United Nations.

Fourthly, I understand that almost all the substantive items to be taken up at this conference are items before the General Assembly. Therefore, as a result of informal discussions with some of the sponsors I understand that they are going to request me to take the necessary steps to poll all Members under the rules regarding the desirability of postponing the General Assembly to a later date than September. I also understand that this request is coming before the end of this week. As soon as I receive this official request, of course, it is my duty to poll the attitude of the Member states. My understanding is that there is a general consensus among Member states regarding the need for the postponement of the General Assembly. If my understanding is correct, the General Assembly will meet on Tuesday, November 10, of this year.

. . . . QUESTION: The statements made recently by the chairman of the United States Foreign Relations Committee, Senator William Fulbright, asking for an agonizing reappraisal of United States foreign policy seem to have made a profound impression around the world, especially among the uncommitted countries. I wonder whether you would care to comment on them as the United Nations Secretary-General and also as a former chief representative of a neutralist country to the United Nations.

THE SECRETARY-GENERAL: Since I first met Senator Fulbright in Washington in June 1955, I have formed a very high opinion of him. I have always regarded him since that time as one of the truly perceptive foreign affairs analysts of our time. In this context, therefore, his speech on the floor of the Senate last month was of very great interest to me.

I am in agreement with his basic plea to start thinking about "unthinkable thoughts," which I believe should be the guiding principle for all of us, not only Americans, but also Asians, Africans, Latin Americans, Russians, and Chinese. It seems to me that is a very wise dictum.

Of course, a thorough reappraisal of our attitudes toward war and peace is imperative. Problems affecting the future of humanity itself need a thorough reappraisal. When I say problems affecting war and peace, I am thinking of various aspects: problems affecting, for instance, suspicion versus confidence or trust, hysteria versus calm, rigidity versus flexibility. In this context, I would class Senator Fulbright's speech on March 25 in the same category as the historic speech of President Kennedy at American University.

Of course, when I say that I agree with the basic philosophy behind Senator Fulbright's approach to the problems, it does not necessarily mean that I am in full agreement with all his observations and conclusions on specific issues. But I would commend this speech to the attention of all people all over the world.

QUESTION: I wonder what the United Nations plans for the Congo after the end of June when the United Nations forces leave? To what extent will technical assistance be continued?

THE SECRETARY-GENERAL: It is my intention to render all possible technical assistance to the Congo after the withdrawal of ONUC from that country at the end of June this year. But the size of technical assistance depends, as you know, on the availability of financial resources. In other words, the size and character of the United Nations technical assistance programs or civilian operations in the Congo will depend primarily on the availability of funds from the Member states. I am not happy to have to admit that so far the response to my request for more contributions toward the civilian operations in the Congo has not been very encouraging.

. . . .

---

2. From Transcript of Press Conference

PARIS   APRIL 29, 1964

. . . .

IN REPLY to a series of questions on Cyprus, the Secretary-General said:

As you are certainly aware, the question of Cyprus is a question which had been dealt with outside the United Nations for a long time. Then, at last, as the situation deteriorated, the question was put before the Security Council of the United Nations.

The Security Council adopted a resolution on March 4 this year to define some objectives and outline some procedures authorizing me to undertake certain functions.

If I were to define the functions of the United Nations in Cyprus I would say that there are two separate and distinct functions. The first function relates to military operations placed under the authority of the commander of the United Nations Force. The second function relates to

UN Press Releases SG/T/17 and Add. 1.

a long-term political solution, which belongs to the mediator. I think it is very necessary to distinguish and separate these two functions.

The United Nations Force placed under the command of General Gyani is concerned with the day-to-day activities with reference to paragraph 5 of the resolution adopted by the Security Council, for instance, maintenance of law and order. The United Nations Force has to keep open the lines of communication and so on. But it is important to remember that the United Nations Peacekeeping Force has no authority to exercise force to realize its aims. There is a difference between the functions of the United Nations Force in Cyprus and the United Nations Force in the Congo.

I think it is worthwhile to remind you of these distinctions. As regards the United Nations Force in the Congo, the Security Council adopted a series of resolutions, and among these resolutions were those which asked the United Nations Force in the Congo to use a requisite measure of force when necessary to realize certain objectives. These were the instructions of the Security Council. In the case of Cyprus, the United Nations Force has not been authorized by the Security Council to exercise force except in cases, of course, of self-defense. I think it is very essential to remember this difference.

Let me come back to the first question regarding the function of the mediator. I asked Ambassador Tuomioja to come to Paris to report to me on the Cyprus situation. I am sure all of you are aware, he arrived in Paris yesterday and I had two meetings with him, and, of course, it is very difficult for me at this stage to give any assessment of the situation. His task is very delicate and very complicated, even very sophisticated, if I may say so. The resolution of the Security Council does not specify the period for which he was appointed. Perhaps he will not be in a position to make the necessary recommendations to the Security Council within three months. There are indications that he may have to ask me and that, for my part, I may have to ask the Security Council to extend his assignment even beyond three months.

I don't think it would be in the public interest to reveal his thoughts or what my conclusions might be. This is why I very much regret that it is not possible at this point to say what his recommendation is likely to be.

Regarding the question involving the prospective application of the right of self-determination in Cyprus, it is very difficult for me now to anticipate what the recommendations of the mediator would be and what would be the decisions of the Security Council on the recommendation of the mediator.

Coming back to the other question, it is true that I proposed to both the governments of Turkey and Greece to place their contingents in Cyprus under the supreme authority of the United Nations Force commander. The Government of Greece agreed to place its contingent under this authority. As regards the Government of Turkey, we are still in the process of negotiation and I am not in a position now to say what the final attitude of the Turkish government will be, but I am hopeful that the Turkish government will cooperate with the United Nations to realize our aim, which is to find a pacific solution to the conflict . . . I have no official confirmation of the news which was published in the press to the effect that the Turkish government envisaged the sending of an expedition to Cyprus. I have no means of knowing, but all I can say is that the prompt compliance by the Government of Canada with my request for the provision of forces to serve in Cyprus prevented the development of very ugly situations there, and that this response of the Government of Canada to my appeal was highly appreciated not only in the United Nations but all over the world. I want to take this opportunity of expressing my sincere thanks to the Government of Canada and the governments of other countries which sent contingents in answer to the appeal of the United Nations for the peacekeeping operations in Cyprus.

In reply to questions regarding France's arrears in contributions to the United Nations, the Secretary-General replied:

There are some Member states of the United Nations who are in arrears regarding the payment of their contribution, particularly regarding the operation in the Congo. Among these countries is France. Of course the argument of France regarding this problem is well known to you and I have no need to repeat it. The reasons are constitutional, legal and not at all political. I personally brought up this question in the course of my discussions with some of the leaders of the French government during my stay in Paris, and I propose to take up this question again at a convenient time, asking the leaders of France to be kind enough to reexamine this question. It will not be in the public interest for me to tell you what I think of the situation at this stage. I am convinced that the government and the people of France profoundly believe in the ideas and ideals of the United Nations Charter and I am convinced that the government and the people of France have confidence in the United Nations. Therefore, the financial problem regarding French payment, in my view, does not constitute a very serious one.

. . . . To questions concerning Asia, principally Vietnam and Kashmir, the Secretary-General answered:

Regarding the first question, I am sure you will agree with me that it will not be appropriate on my part, as Secretary-General of the United Nations, to try to evaluate the foreign policies of Member states and particularly that of a great country such as France; so I do not want to discuss the implications of the policy of the French government in Southeast Asia. I would like, however, to make a brief comment on this subject. Military methods have failed to solve the problem. They did not solve it in 1954 and I do not see any reason why they would succeed ten years later. As I see the problem in Southeast Asia, it is not essentially military, it is political; and, therefore, political and diplomatic means alone, in my view, can solve it. Regarding the second question—Kashmir—as you know, the Security Council has adopted certain resolutions, and of course, the ideal situation would be that all interested parties should comply with the recommendations adopted by the Security Council.

3. From Transcript of Press Conference

OTTAWA   MAY 26, 1964

. . . . QUESTION: Is there any possibility of the use of a United Nations peacekeeping force in Southeast Asia, particularly South Vietnam?

THE SECRETARY-GENERAL: The matter is under discussion by the Security Council right now. On the question of United Nations involvement or noninvolvement in Southeast Asia, it is a little too early for me to say. I have to be guided, of course, by the decision of the Security Council; but personally speaking, as I have said on previous occasions, the problem of Southeast Asia is primarily political and not military. I feel that political solutions will be more advisable than military solutions. Of course, as I

UN Note to Correspondents No. 2932.

have said, the Security Council is still seized of this matter, and perhaps it may come to a decision in the course of this week.

QUESTION: What do you mean by political solutions, Mr. Secretary-General?

THE SECRETARY-GENERAL: What I mean by political solution is as contemplated, for instance, in the Geneva Agreement of 1954. At that time, of course in a different capacity, I happened to express my view on the provisions of the Geneva Agreement of 1954. I felt at that time that the agreement arrived at in the Geneva conference was very well-meaning and ought to be tried; but as you know, some of the countries primarily involved in the situation in Southeast Asia were not signatories to that agreement, for well-known reasons. But I do not know whether the intention of many governments ten years ago can now be put to the test again. In such situations the time factor is very important. The right solution at the right time could yield the right results, but the right solution at the wrong time could well prove to be futile. That is another danger. Beyond that I do not want to commit myself, since the Security Council is seized of this matter.

. . . . QUESTION: Have you any comment on the suggestion that atomic bombs should be used in South Vietnam?

THE SECRETARY-GENERAL: As you are no doubt aware, I am against the use of atomic weapons for destructive purposes anywhere, under any circumstances. Anybody who proposes the use of atomic weapons for destructive purposes is, in my view, out of his mind.

Let me elaborate on this. First of all, there is the question of radioactivity, which is as deadly as the first physical impact of the bomb. This is recognized by all knowledgeable scientists. Second, the Vietcong, or whoever may be the target of such projected attacks, are not going from one place to another in set, well-defined routes. They are not like ants. They may operate anywhere they like. So I do not see that any effective results will be achieved by such atomic blasts. Third, such action is sure to generate widespread resentment and bitter criticism, particularly from quarters which so far have not been very vocal, and have not been very outspoken regarding the situation in Southeast Asia. Lastly, and this in my view is a very important element, there is, if I may say so, a racial factor in such a projected operation. In 1945, when atomic bombs were dropped over Hiroshima and Nagasaki in Japan, there was a widespread feeling in many parts of Asia that these deadly atomic bombs were dropped on Japanese cities because the Japanese were nonwhites, and it was also argued at that time that the atomic bombs would never have been dropped over cities in Nazi Germany at that time. As you know, Nazi Germany was also at war with the Allies. So there is also a racial element in these things which I would commend to the attention of those who are thinking of launching such atomic blasts.

QUESTION: Do you think it would be helpful to put the truce mission in Indo-China under the wing of the United Nations?

THE SECRETARY-GENERAL: I made it clear a moment ago that I have to comply with any decision of the Security Council in this respect. If the Security Council decides one way or the other it is my duty, of course, to comply with its decision.

QUESTION: Arising out of that answer, you say you are the servant of the Security Council. I can quite appreciate this, but do you feel that as Secretary-General there are occasions when you might lead the Security Council or some organ of the United Nations into certain areas of decision, shall I say, which you feel might be the right thing for the United Nations to do; in other words, that you should take leadership?

THE SECRETARY-GENERAL: That is a very pertinent question, but the situation is this. The United Nations is for the moment at a certain stage of development and has very definite limitations in resources, in authority, and in effectiveness. There are certain situations in which the United Nations can be involved effectively, for instance in the Middle East, in the Congo, and West Irian. In such situations the United Nations can take effective action.

At the same time there are certain situations in which the United Nations cannot be involved effectively because of the inherent limitations in its authority and in its resources, both manpower and financial. So, if the United Nations is asked to perform certain functions which are beyond its capacity, then I do not think I should recommend to the Security Council, or for that matter any other competent organ of the United Nations, the undertaking of certain tasks which in my view are beyond the capacity of the United Nations. As I have stated on earlier occasions, the United Nations may be likened to a young child, still growing, but it must be admitted that it is still young. You cannot ask a ten-year-old child to shoulder a load of, say, two hundred pounds for the simple reason that it will be simply impossible for that child to carry such a load. But if you ask him to carry a load of ten pounds he will readily, and I am sure successfully, do this. In the same way, there are certain situations in which the United Nations can do a very efficient job and there are certain other situations in which the United Nations, at this present level of development, cannot do an effective one. I feel that the situation in Southeast Asia is such that I have my own doubts regarding the competency of the United Nations to undertake the task which is being advocated by some Member nations.

QUESTION: Do you think the time has come when the United Nations should recognize and seat the two Chinas?

THE SECRETARY-GENERAL: The question of the admission or representation of China is sure to come up in the next session of the General Assembly. Regarding this question, as you are no doubt aware, there are two schools of thought. One school maintains that the question is one of the admission of China—the admission of a new Member state. This position has been held by the majority of the Member states. On the other hand, there is another school of thought which maintains that the question is one of representation and not admission. They argue that China is already a Member of the United Nations, China being a founding Member of the United Nations. The question is, who should represent China? This is a concept held by some of the Members who, of course, form the minority. So, on this, I am not competent to take a public position. Of course, I have to abide by the decision of the General Assembly when it meets in the fall.

QUESTION: From where you sit, how is the world looking these days?

THE SECRETARY-GENERAL: This is what some people in the United States would call the $64 question. My general feeling is that the political climate of the world or the psychological climate of the world has improved appreciably in the last few years. There is an evident desire on the part of the big powers to come to some sort of an understanding with each other. There is a general feeling everywhere that tensions must be eased and all possible endeavors must be made to try to understand the viewpoint of the other. I think these are very good indications.

QUESTION: Have you any fears that the smaller nations which are behind in their financial obligations to the United Nations may use the recent firm refusal of Soviet Russia to pay her obligations, particularly those for peacekeeping operations, as an excuse for not paying their obligations and, following that, have you any fears that the current critical financial situation of the United Nations imperils the efficiency and continuance in the future of the Organization?

THE SECRETARY-GENERAL: Yes, there is such a prospect, unfortunately. But the question of the financial contributions, the question of the application of Article 19, for instance, is still the subject of private discussion, particularly among the big powers. It is a little too early now to predict what the outcome of these discussions and behind-the-scenes negotiations will be. And I myself, in my capacity of Secretary-General of the United Nations, have been in constant contact with the Member states concerned, and I have a feeling that some sort of a formula, acceptable to all Member states, could be forthcoming before the meeting of the next session of the General Assembly.

. . . .

From Statement at the Unveiling of
the Hepworth Sculpture

NEW YORK   JUNE 11, 1964

. . . . DAG HAMMARSKJÖLD is very much in our minds today. This great sculpture is a reminder of him, of his outstanding achievements as Secretary-General and of his extraordinary talents and unique personality. It would, I know, have given him the keenest pleasure to have been with us on this unusual occasion, and to have seen the fulfillment of a wish that he had now and then expressed himself while strolling around this very circle. The embellishment of this Headquarters was one of his favorite concerns, and one that he particularly enjoyed. He wanted the building and its surroundings to live up aesthetically to the importance and nobility of the aims and ideals of the Organization. He felt that the United Nations should as far as possible be a place where the best of contemporary creative art could be seen and he constantly looked for ways and means of achieving this. He saw a challenge to improvement in this entrance circle and sought for ways of giving it life and elevation. He would, I think, have been very happy at the way in which this has now been realized.

Personally, though I am strictly a layman on such matters, I am very glad that this vigorous and striking work of art which takes its place here is in a contemporary idiom. I was, indeed, much moved by Miss Hepworth's own account of its meaning and its relationship to Dag Hammarskjöld and to the United Nations. She has, in her own words, conveyed to us a very hopeful and inspiring idea, as well as creating this permanent and beautiful memorial and symbol.

This United Nations Headquarters is relatively new, but already it has a history of its own to which each year adds its associations and events. Thus, layer by layer, a tradition is built up. It is fitting also that the Headquarters should acquire new features as time goes on—works of art which both enhance the beauty of the place and have a meaning and a significance in the context of what we do, and try to do, here. This is, after

UN Press Release SG/SM/84.

all, by its very nature, a historic place and one of the centers of mankind's struggle to master himself and to create a better world. It should reflect mankind's aspirations in every direction, artistic as well as political, economic, and social. It should show a positive tendency in all that it does, and what could be more positive or more inspiring than the evidence of man's creative genius? We have before us today a magnificent example of that creative genius, and it will inspire us both by the hope it holds for the future and by its association with a man who played a great part in shaping and developing the United Nations.

As I look at this majestic abstraction, it conveys to me an impression of vitality, of unity, and of durability which are of particular significance to the United Nations. It is a symbol of the strength which this Organization, in the interest of the world's future, must have in increasing measure. It stands, appropriately, at the portals of our main building.

We speak in many tongues in this place; we have many differences and many disagreements, but also we often agree, although this seems, for some perverse reason, to be less exciting. We have different backgrounds and outlooks and we often see things differently. I do not doubt that these differences will be reflected in the reactions of the viewers of this sculpture. But here in the United Nations we also have a basic aim in common, which is to preserve the peace and to enhance human happiness and dignity throughout the world in accordance with our Charter. I believe that we have far more in common, and far greater common interests, than would often appear from the reports on our activities. One of the things we have in common is the great artistic and cultural heritage of mankind and the world of the creative arts. In the presence of a masterly work of art, whether it be music or sculpture, painting or literature, our daily differences recede and seem far less important. A great work of art is timeless, without nationality or race or religion—apart from the pleasure and inspiration it gives, it serves to remind us of what man at his best, unhampered by prejudice or petty strife, can be and can give. Thus, each one who enters this building, from whatever part of the world he may come, will see this sculpture differently, will put into his view of it some part of his own background and take out from it some of its universal quality and meaning. We are fortunate indeed to have such a work of art before us today. It gives to our abode a new quality, a new dimension. . . .

From Report on the Withdrawal of the United Nations Force from the Congo

NEW YORK   JUNE 29, 1964

THE UNITED NATIONS finally ended its military operations in the Congo on June 30, 1964, almost exactly four years after the Security Council authorized United Nations intervention to prevent the secession of Katanga province. U Thant formally notified the Council of the completion of the withdrawal in a report dated June 29, in which he repeated earlier conclusions that the United Nations objectives had in a large measure been fulfilled. These included the preservation of the territorial integrity of the Congo, the elimination of foreign military personnel and mercenaries, and the prevention of a civil war. The question of maintaining law and order, he said, was the responsibility of the Congolese government and even though disorders continued, the United Nations withdrawal had been carried out with the full consent of the Congolese authorities. With more than twenty thousand United Nations troops in the Congo at the peak of the operation, this was by far the largest peacekeeping undertaking ever embarked upon by the United Nations. During the four years the operation cost the Organization $381,505,000 not including expenditures for civilian assistance. ONUC casualties totalled 235. Dag Hammarskjöld lost his life in search of peace in the Congo. Despite the heavy costs and the financial burden placed upon the Organization, Thant was convinced that the United Nations, as well as the Congo, had gained by the experience. For one thing, he said, it proved the ability of the Organization to meet grave emergency situations and to set up a large-scale military force within a short time. Despite criticism from some quarters, Thant felt that, on the whole, the record of United Nations forces in the Congo was distinguished.

. . . .

132. THE WITHDRAWAL of the United Nations Force from the Congo, now completed, marks the end of only the military phase of the massive assistance operation which the United Nations has been conducting in the Congo during the past four years. It is important to stress this point, since the civilian operations, technical assistance and special fund activi-

Security Council Official Records, Nineteenth Year, Supplement for April, May and June 1964, document S/5784.

ties will continue in the Congo to the extent that financial and other resources are available, subject to the needs and wishes of the Government of the Congo. Indeed, it may even be hoped that it will prove possible to expand them somewhat after June 30, 1964. There will continue to be an office of the special representative of the Secretary-General in Leopoldville, with the special representative also being technical assistance resident representative and representative of the special fund. There will be assistance field offices maintained in a number of other communities in the Congo. Moreover, the resolutions of the Security Council concerning the Congo continue to be applicable, since they have no terminal date.

133. With regard specifically to the United Nations Force in the Congo, which has been the largest and costliest of all the United Nations peacekeeping activities, there are certain observations flowing from the experience of this Force which it seems to me particularly important to make at this stage.

134. The creation of the United Nations Force in the Congo in July 1960 was a remarkable and dramatic manifestation of world solidarity at that time. Whatever its shortcomings, and whatever the political contentions about it, that Force has proved and extended the ability of the United Nations to meet grave emergency situations. In response to the urgent appeal from the Congolese government jointly signed by President Kasavubu and Prime Minister Lumumba, the largest operation in the history of the United Nations was set up, or more accurately, improvised, in an incredibly short time, in order to come speedily to the aid and support of a young and struggling nation. In the circumstances in which that appeal was made, the United Nations would have suffered a severe loss of confidence throughout the world had it failed to respond. This was a crucial situation in which rapid historic change had produced problems of such complexity and danger that all Member states agreed that the United Nations, despite its limited authority and resources, offered the only possible hope of keeping the peace and gaining time for a solution to be found. When ONUC began its activities, the Congo was in a desperate situation, its army disrupted by the mutiny, its essential services on the verge of total disintegration, most of its population in a state of panic or despair, its territory threatened with amputation by the attempted secession of its richest province, and much of its area controlled by foreign troops.

135. During the subsequent four years, thousands of members of the United Nations Force—because of the rotations, a total of more than 93,000—and hundreds of civilians have devoted their best efforts and energies to helping the Congolese rebuild and develop their nation. Many of them, including my predecessor, Mr. Dag Hammarskjöld, have given their very lives toward this end. As a result of these efforts, the Congo situation is now incomparably improved, despite the recent disturbances. Four years have been gained in which the Government and the people of the Congo have had the opportunity to come to grips with their vast problems and to be assisted in meeting some of the worst of them. Four years have been gained in which Congolese public administrators, doctors, professional people, experts of all kinds, and technicians could at least begin their training and begin to gain experience under the guidance and with the expert help of personnel of the United Nations and its specialized agencies. These long-term efforts are now commencing to bear fruit, and they give cause for hope for the future of the Congo.

136. The United Nations Force in the Congo has afforded the United Nations its broadest experience with an operation of this kind. The conduct of this Force, its leadership and discipline, and its restraint, often under severe provocation, have been notably fine. In many places, units of this Force have been in daily contact with the civilian population and have almost always enjoyed good relations with the people. In fact, the Force never at any time or place encountered hostility from the Congolese people. There have been, naturally, some acts of a criminal nature by individuals in the Force, and there were, on occasion, some unfortunate excesses by individual soldiers, mainly under the emotional stress of sniper fire and harassment. Such instances, although relatively few, have been magnified and exploited by those seeking for one reason or another to discredit the United Nations. Over all, it may be said that the record of the United Nations Force in the Congo, in all respects, has been distinguished. It has done its difficult job remarkably well. All of those who served in the Force, the countries that provided the contingents or afforded supporting services and money, and all of the civilian staff serving the Congo operation in the field and at Headquarters, are due great credit and appreciation for the valuable service they have rendered. The Congo Advisory Committee has given indispensable assistance and is due much gratitude.

137. The United Nations Force in the Congo was international in the sense that it was composed of units of troops from a number of different

countries which had been placed under United Nations command. But these troops were never fully merged and consolidated, since the national contingents always maintained their separate identity and uniforms, except for United Nations headgear and insignia, used their own arms, and each national contingent had its own commanding officer. The authority of the commander of the Force did not extend to the discipline of its members, that being left to the commanders of each national contingent. Weaknesses of this nature, in fact, have been common to all of the United Nations peacekeeping forces. There was a typical problem also in the very great variations among the contingents in pay and allowances based on national law and practice. This inevitably has implications for the morale and effectiveness of a force.

138. Maintaining a United Nations Force in a country, especially over an extended period, involves many difficulties in the relations with the government of the country. Despite this fact, throughout the four years of the presence of the United Nations Force in the Congo, the relations with the Congolese government, and with those authorities in charge during that bleak period when there was no government at all, have been generally good and have weathered the relatively few major crises. There have been disagreements, at times serious, about policy. There have been difficulties on the part of governmental officials in comprehending the mandates and functions of a United Nations Force. There have been instances when the United Nations has had to take a firm stand against a wish or even a caprice of the government. But these inevitable experiences have never seriously impaired the efforts of the Force or the effectiveness of other aspects of the United Nations Operation in the Congo. At the present time the relations with the Government of the Congo are good.

139. It was inevitable that over so long a period as four years, in a situation as complex and politically controversial as the Congo, certain impressions, assumptions, and even myths, would have developed, as they have, some of which certainly have had political overtones and no doubt political motivations as well. But they are decisively countered by certain well-documented and firmly established facts. The United Nations intervention in the Congo was directly in response to an urgent appeal from the government of a newly independent country. The United Nations Operation in the Congo at all times has scrupulously avoided intervention in the internal affairs of that country; it has not taken sides in political or constitutional differences; it has not sought to usurp any governmental

authority or ever to act like a government. The United Nations Force in the Congo, from beginning to end, was under strict instructions to use its arms for defensive purposes only, and its record of restraint in this regard had been highly commendable. Other than its successful efforts to eliminate the mercenaries in South Katanga, in pursuance of the Security Council mandate, the Force took no military initiatives involving the use of force; it launched no offensive. The Force, as every United Nations Force must be, was exclusively under United Nations command at all times. The Force, in pursuance of the mandate given it by the Security Council,[1] undertook to assist the Central Government in the restoration and maintenance of law and order, but never permitted itself to become an arm of the government or to be at its beck and call for political purposes. Violation of these two fundamental principles quite likely would have resulted in the disintegration of the Force through the withdrawal of some or all of its contingents. The presence of the United Nations Force has been the decisive factor in preserving the territorial integrity of the country; it has been solely responsible for the cessation of the activities of the mercenaries in Katanga; and it has been a major factor in preventing widespread civil war in the Congo.

140. The United Nations has learned very much from its experience in the Congo thus far; in the circumstances, much of that experience could only be unhappy. Fundamentally, what it has learned there is that the Congolese, in education, training, and experience, and even in their understanding of the concept of nationhood, were unprepared to assume the responsibilities of independence; that fatal division and conflict were built into the political structure of the Congo at the very beginning of its independence; and that the inevitable consequence of these two conditions, acutely complicated by foreign interests and interference, was the collapse and chaos which soon occurred in the Congo, with the United Nations then becoming the country's sole prop and hope.

141. The present situation in the Congo, greatly improved though it is as compared with July 1960, admittedly makes the Congo's immediate future look none too promising. Great and serious problems persist, which can be dealt with only by wise, imaginative, strong, and courageous leadership, effective government, and some measure of understanding support from the people. Failure to overcome present dangers would

---

[1] Security Council Official Records, Sixteenth Year, Supplement for October, November and December 1961, document S/5002.

no doubt bring disintegration and ruin. The Congolese government, in meeting these problems, will still have the assistance of by far the largest of all United Nations technical assistance operations. It may be taken for granted also that developments in the Congo will continue to be of very great concern to the United Nations and to me as Secretary-General.

142. Mr. Moïse Tshombé, who voluntarily left the Congo for Europe a year ago this month, has now returned to his country with the consent of its government, and he is understood to be carrying on talks in Leopold-ville. In this regard, two facts may be recalled. First, the primary reason for Mr. Hammarskjöld's last trip to the Congo in September 1961 was to attempt to bring about talks between Mr. Adoula and Mr. Tshombé, preferably in Leopoldville. Secondly, until the day that Mr. Tshombé left his position as president of the Province of Katanga and departed his country of his own accord, Mr. Tshombé had been given the same protec-tion by the United Nations Force which had been extended in the past to Mr. Patrice Lumumba, Mr. Antoine Gizenga, and others, as long as they sought it. Indeed, on the occasion of Mr. Tshombé's last visit to Leopold-ville in March and April 1962, he came there upon United Nations urg-ing, and under United Nations protection and guarantee of his security. Mr. Albert Kalonji, former president of the Province of South Kasai, who similarly went into voluntary exile in Europe, has also returned to Leo-poldville, and there have been unconfirmed reports that Mr. Gizenga, the former deputy prime minister, may soon be free to leave the island on which the government has kept him for a long time.

143. I make no prediction about the future course of events in the Congo. I wish for the best, even though there have been some recent events which have not been very encouraging. On the other hand, on the economic side, particularly, there have been some brighter signs. It would seem to me that hope for the Congo in the future must depend upon fulfillment of two major and indispensable conditions: (*a*) the retraining and reorganization of the Congolese National Army, including the train-ing of a substantial officer corps; and (*b*) the achievement of national reconciliation among the contending political leaders and factions of the country.

144. In view of the uncertainties affecting the future of the Congo, the question is often asked why the stay of the United Nations Force there is not extended beyond the end of June 1964. The explanation, of course, is to be found in the first place in the fact that there has been no request from the Government of the Congo for an extension of the Force beyond

June 30. Such a request would be an indispensable condition for any action on extension in the United Nations. Had such a request been made, however, action on it could have been taken only by convening a special session of the General Assembly for that purpose, since it was by action of the General Assembly in resolution 1885 (XVIII) of October 21, 1963, that the Secretary-General was authorized to make expenditures for the Force to June 30, 1964, and not beyond.

145. In any event and quite apart from the financial difficulty, I believe that a further extension of the stay of the Force in the Congo would provide no solution to the remaining problems of the Congo. The current difficulties in that country reflect conflicts of an internal political nature with their main origins found in the absence of a genuine and sufficiently widespread sense of national identity among the various ethnic groups composing the population of the Congo. There is little assistance that a United Nations Force could render in that kind of situation, since the solution of conflict depends entirely on the willingness and readiness of the Congolese political leaders, and the traditional chiefs and their respective followers, to merge their factional interests in a true effort toward national conciliation. Moreover, as I indicated in my report of September 17, 1963, (pp. 449–61) the time has come when the Government of the Congo will have to assume full responsibility for security, law, and order in its country as well as for its territorial integrity. The United Nations cannot permanently protect the Congo, or any other country, from the internal tensions and disturbances created by its own organic growth toward unity and nationhood. This is an undertaking which henceforth must be carried out only by the government and the people of the Congo. I believe that this is understood by and is, indeed, the position of the Government of the Congo, since, as I have indicated, that government has not requested a further extension of the United Nations Force in the Congo. It is a position to which all nations should give their understanding, respect, and support in the interest of stability, progress, and peace in the Congo.

. . . .

From Transcript of Press Conference

NEW YORK　　　JULY 8, 1964

IN A PRESS CONFERENCE in New York on July 8, 1964, U Thant suggested that the parties to the 1954 Geneva Agreement on Indo-China convene a new conference in Geneva to seek an end to the fighting. He said he felt that a return to the Geneva conference table, "though perhaps belated, may produce some useful results." He reiterated his view that the United Nations could not play a useful role in a solution but might become involved in seeing that an agreement was observed if the parties to the conference reached such an agreement and asked the United Nations to assist. He noted, however, that some of the parties were not in the United Nations—the People's Republic of China, North Vietnam, and South Vietnam—and said they were "not accountable to this organization." In response to another question, the Secretary-General stated that he had been in touch from time to time with Adlai E. Stevenson, permanent representative of the United States, and that they had had "many occasions to exchange views on the situation in Southeast Asia." As we now know, these contacts during the next few months became a channel for an important peace effort that was to prove a bitter disappointment both to Stevenson and Thant.

. . . . THE SECRETARY-GENERAL: Yesterday I received a memorandum from the permanent representative of the Soviet Union on "Certain measures to strengthen the effectiveness of the United Nations in the maintenance of international peace and security." The main purpose of this memorandum, in my view, is to stimulate thinking on various aspects of Chapter VII of the Charter of the United Nations, particularly the application of Article 42, which deals with the use of force by the United Nations. It is a very interesting document, and its main purport is the well-known Soviet thesis that the Security Council alone is competent to deal with peacekeeping operations and that the Security Council alone is competent to take decisions on various aspects of the United Nations peacekeeping operations. Of course, this position has been contested by several Member states, and it is not for me to express any opinion at this

UN Note to Correspondents No. 2951.

stage. But I am sure of one thing: that the Soviet memorandum, as well as the tentative proposals of certain Western powers on the same subject, are very helpful for all Member states for arriving at a suitable formula, and they are a very good augury for the future negotiations.

It may be of interest to you to know that I have given a lot of thought to this subject. I propose to deal with this, among other things, in my introduction to the annual report, which normally is due to be submitted in August but which, because of the postponement of the General Assembly, I propose to submit only in October.

QUESTION: Mr. Secretary-General, there is only one hot war now in the world and it is in Southeast Asia. Every week, every day, hundreds of people are dying and this massacre of human beings has been continuing for years. Some observers believe that right after November there will be a chance for settlement through a kind of neutralization—which does not necessarily mean a complete and immediate withdrawal of American troops from the area—with a larger role for a United Nations peacekeeping force. I wonder whether you share this view and if you think that the time is ripe for you, for the Secretary-General who is respected by both sides, to do something, for example to call for a temporary cease-fire.

THE SECRETARY-GENERAL: Whenever I read of the death of an American or the death of a Vietnamese my heart bleeds. To me it makes no difference whether the man killed is an American or a Vietnamese. That is why for the last ten years, as I have stated on previous occasions, I have felt rather strongly—and I still feel—that military methods will not bring about peace in South Vietnam.

As you know, I was—in a different capacity—a participant in the Bandung Conference as well as in the Belgrade Conference, where the question of Southeast Asia was discussed in detail, and in June 1955 I also had occasion to discuss this question, among others, in Washington with Mr. John Foster Dulles.

There is increasing evidence that military methods will not bring about a peaceful solution of the problem. From all available accounts over 150 Americans and over 10,000 Vietnamese have lost their lives; over 10,000 villages have been destroyed or demolished or evacuated. I have all along felt that the only sensible alternative is the political and diplomatic method of negotiation which, even at this late hour, may offer some chance of a solution. I still feel that a return to the Geneva Conference table, though perhaps belated, may produce some useful results. Of course, if there is an agreement by the parties primarily concerned, the

United Nations can be involved at that stage to see that the agreement is observed. But I do not see how the United Nations can be involved in the present crisis in South Vietnam particularly in view of the fact that more than one of the parties concerned are not Members of the United Nations and are not accountable to this Organization. Of course, this is not the only reason.

..... QUESTION: Do you consider the emergence of Moïse Tshombé in the Congo as a blow to United Nations policy?

THE SECRETARY-GENERAL: No, I do not think so. As you know, the United Nations has been militarily disengaged from the Congo with effect from the 30th of last month, and it is for the people of the Congo to decide who their government should be, just as for any other independent Member state. Of course, there is a very interesting maxim to the effect that a country gets the government it deserves.

QUESTION: During your visit to the African summit meeting, I understand that many heads of government wish to see you and discuss a number of things with you. Are you going to see them separately, or are you just going to attend the conference?

THE SECRETARY-GENERAL: So far I do not know what arrangements have been made for my participation, if necessary, in the projected African summit meetings, but I will be very glad to contribute to the best of my ability, perhaps behind the scenes, toward the success of this summit conference. There are, of course, indications that I will be asked to meet all the heads of state and heads of government of Africa, individually or collectively.

QUESTION: To clarify the question first asked of you, do I understand that even if the parties concerned, and I am purposely asking the question this way, agree to negotiations on Southeast Asia, the nonmembership of certain parties would either preclude or handicap a possible settlement?

THE SECRETARY-GENERAL: When I said that the only alternative to the present method is the political and diplomatic method of negotiation, although perhaps belated, at the Geneva conference table, I had in mind no involvement of the United Nations at that stage. My thinking is that if there is an agreement at such a conference, then perhaps the United Nations may be usefully and properly involved in seeing that the terms of the agreement are observed.

QUESTION: How do you now see the chances for a settlement in Cyprus, and, in particular, how do you feel about the American initiative in trying to assist the mediator in the Geneva talks at the present time?

THE SECRETARY-GENERAL: There are two aspects to the problem of Cyprus. One is the aspect pertaining to the maintenance of law and order, which involves the day-to-day operations of UNFICYP. The other aspect is related to a long-term solution of the problem of Cyprus. So far as the day-to-day activities of the United Nations are concerned you will no doubt agree with me that UNFICYP has been able to do a magnificent job. As for the search for a long-term solution, this is more or less in the hands of the United Nations mediator, Ambassador Tuomioja.

I think it is worth remembering that the United Nations mediator is a creation of the Security Council with an independent identity. He is free to lay down any program of work or any line of action which, in his opinion, conforms to the mandate of the Security Council. It is not for the Secretary-General, in my view, to give him instructions or to advise him what he should do or what he should not do. So when the Government of the United States discussed with me last week their proposals and their ideas in regard to how to contribute toward the work of the mediator, I informed the United States government that they should contact the United Nations mediator directly, and if the United Nations mediator feels that a certain line of action is necessary and useful, he will no doubt utilize the assistance and cooperation of anybody.

I understand that the United Nations mediator is meeting the representatives of Greece and Turkey, perhaps in the course of the next two or three days, and perhaps he will get the benefit of the views of the United States representative, who, I understand, is already in Geneva. For that matter, the United Nations mediator is also free to seek the advice and cooperation of any Member state.

QUESTION: In your Cyprus report you stated that the arms problem is critical and that it may well be the decisive factor in determining the success of the United Nations effort in Cyprus. Could you tell us whether any progress has been made on this problem?

THE SECRETARY-GENERAL: As I have stated in my report to the Security Council, there are indications of an arms build-up in Cyprus by both sides. It is no doubt a very disturbing development, but so far UNFICYP has not been able to establish categorically the actual size of the build-up and the actual character of this build-up. But as soon as I receive definite information on this, it is my intention to keep the Security Council posted on these developments since, in my view, these are very undesirable, particularly in the context of the Security Council resolutions, and especially during the presence of UNFICYP in Cyprus.

I want to take this opportunity of appealing to both Greece and Turkey to cooperate wholeheartedly with UNFICYP and, for that matter. the United Nations, to contribute to the peaceful solution of the problem of Cyprus.

.... QUESTION: Mr. Secretary-General, have you drawn the attention of the United States government recently to your views on Southeast Asia?

THE SECRETARY-GENERAL: Not recently; but from time to time I have been in contact with the permanent representative of the United States here and we have had many occasions to exchange views on the situation in Southeast Asia.

. . . .

Address at the Opening of the African Summit Conference

CAIRO   JULY 17, 1964

I DEEM IT a great honor, and a distinct privilege, to be permitted to participate in this historic conference. I had indeed hoped to attend the first conference of African heads of state and government held in Addis Ababa last year, which was truly an epoch-making event. Unfortunately, I was prevented at the last minute from doing so, and I have ever since looked forward to this occasion, and the opportunity to greet the leaders of the new Africa, and to exchange views with them.

I referred a moment ago to the first African summit conference as epoch-making, not only because it was the first meeting of its kind, but also because it gave birth to the Organization of African Unity. Its charter, as I had occasion to observe last year, is a historic document reaffirming the desire of the African countries for African unity and solidarity and, perhaps even more important, international cooperation.

The Addis Ababa conference and the Organization of African Unity have already had a measurable impact on the world and on the United Nations. In the United Nations, we have recognized for many years the urgent need to assist the African states in their efforts to make political independence meaningful, as well as the strength of pan-Africanism as a means toward the political and economic progress of the continent as a whole. Thus, while the United Nations has attempted to provide maximum assistance within its resources to help national development programs, it has also participated in regional plans and created institutions such as the Economic Commission for Africa to facilitate cooperation among all African states.

The United Nations agencies have already begun to cooperate with the appropriate bodies of the Organization for African Unity, and we look forward to a much closer association in line with the provisions of the United Nations Charter.

I am gratified to note that the Charter of African Unity not only follows the Charter of the United Nations in form, but reaffirms the funda-

UN Press Release SG/SM/112, July 19, 1964.

mental purposes and principles of the United Nations. In its preamble, it contains a reaffirmation of the adherence of African states to the principles of the Charter of the United Nations and the Universal Declaration of Human Rights. In article II, it lays down as one of the purposes of the Organization for African Unity: "To promote international cooperation, having due regard to the Charter of the United Nations and the Universal Declaration of Human Rights." It reaffirms principles such as the sovereign equality of states, noninterference in internal affairs of states and peaceful settlement of disputes which are enshrined in the United Nations Charter.

The adoption of this Charter by a resurgent Africa is a welcome support to the United Nations. The growth of regional organizations, in accordance with the principles of the United Nations Charter, can only strengthen the United Nations. Indeed, the African states resolved at the Addis Ababa conference to reiterate their desire "to strengthen and support the United Nations" and reaffirm their "dedication to the purposes and principles of the United Nations Charter and (their) acceptance of all obligations contained in the Charter." They decided to bring their vital problems to the United Nations bodies for solution.

Africa has always had a special position in relation to those programs of the United Nations which are designed to assist the developing countries in their stupendous task of promoting the economic and social progress of their peoples. I believe that the vast riches of the continent, some of which have already been explored and exploited, are sufficient to provide in time rising standards of living for all Africans.

Meanwhile, we have the task of assisting African countries in developing their human resources as well as locating and assessing their hidden and unutilized reservoirs of minerals, oil, and hydroelectric power. As I said on a different occasion, "in more ways than one Africa is the keeper of many underdeveloped resources, human and material. Whenever possible, these resources must be developed forthwith, for the benefit of Africa and the rest of mankind."

I may perhaps say a few words on two questions in which the African states have shown great concern: colonialism and racial discrimination. The attitude of the United Nations on these matters—laid down in the Charter and elaborated by the historic Declarations on Human Rights, Colonialism and Racial Discrimination—is unequivocal. The United Nations stands for the self-government and independence of all peoples, and the abolition of racial discrimination without reservations. It can never afford to compromise on these basic principles.

The United Nations has been acutely concerned with these problems since its inception. Today, respect for the right of peoples to self-determination and affirmation of racial equality are not only the principles of the Charter but are embodied in the very composition of the United Nations, half of whose members are newly independent states from Asia and Africa. The United Nations may be proud of its contribution, however modest or seemingly hesitant at times, to the progress which has been made. We can feel gratified at the evolution of the attitudes of all but one or two of the colonial powers. The colonial powers and remaining defenders of racial discrimination are increasingly isolated and can less and less count on the acquiescence and patience of other states. This isolation of the colonialists has itself contributed to the fulfillment of the desire of African states to keep the colonial and racial problems out of the cold war. We can only hope that good sense and realism prevail so that resistance to change by a few diehards will not lead to dangerous conflict on this continent.

I must emphasize that universality is an essential, although implicit, goal of the United Nations. The Organization cannot have full authority and cannot achieve maximum effectiveness until all the peoples who subscribe to its purposes and principles are represented in it. The independence of African states was a source of strength for the United Nations. In my view, this goal of universality required an end to colonialism and an end to the denial of fundamental rights to persons on the grounds of race, religion, language, or sex. Thus, the problems that I have referred to are not only problems of which the United Nations is seized, but problems which affect the status of the Organization itself.

The urge of the African states to achieve adequate representation in all the organs of the United Nations has been recognized by the General Assembly as legitimate, and I hope that before long it will be generally accepted. I also hope that the practical difficulties will be solved and that the continent may be assured of its rightful representation in our councils. May I venture to say, in this context, that the essential question is not so much the number of votes or the number of seats but the contribution which is made by the states to the fulfillment of the purposes and principles of the Organization.

It is sometimes claimed that the formation of blocs or groups within the United Nations weakens the Organization and leads states to make bargains rather than to take positions on the merits of the issues. I do not feel that this is necessarily the case. The United Nations can, of course, have only a limited role to play in a world divided into antagonistic blocs. But the trend toward the recognition of the need for nations to live together in peace as good neighbors—whether it is expressed in the terms "peaceful coexistence" or "positive neutrality" or "nonalignment"—is a hopeful sign. The Charter of the Organization of African Unity has laid down the principle of "nonalignment" and it is a source of gratification that this principle is accepted by other states.

The United Nations Charter itself recognizes the positive value of regional arrangements which are consistent with its purposes and principles. Such regional arrangements can make a valuable contribution toward developing the United Nations as a center for harmonizing the actions of nations in the attainment of the common ends. One can cite many examples in the past two decades to show how solidarity or brotherly feelings among peoples of a region—Asian, Arab, African, or Latin American—and the activities of regional organizations have helped to prevent and contain the development of disputes into serious conflict. So long as the primary and over-riding responsibility of the United Nations for international peace and security is fully recognized and respected, the regional arrangements, basing themselves on such sentiments or common interests, can contribute greatly to the fulfillment of the purposes of the Charter. The task ahead is, indeed, to promote the spread of these sentiments to encompass the entire humanity.

I cannot help referring on this occasion to a problem which has been a matter of serious concern to me ever since I assumed my present responsibilities: I refer to the grave financial position of the United Nations. The Organization finds itself in such straits at the present time mainly because, four years ago, it was called upon to undertake a major peacekeeping operation in the very heart of Africa. After four long years that operation was concluded just a few days ago with the fulfillment of the major objectives laid down by the Security Council and the General Assembly. The serious financial difficulty which has ensued in consequence threatens to impair, not only our ability to undertake future large-scale peacekeeping operations, but our very effectiveness as a world body. This is a problem to which I would like to draw your urgent attention as I believe that all Member states would wish to cooperate in finding ways and means by which the Organization could be enabled to tide over the crisis which looms ahead, and in due course to solve the entire problem on a mutually satisfactory basis.

Let me conclude this brief address with one more reference to the Charter of the United Nations. One of the principal objectives of the founders of the world Organization nineteen years ago was "to save succeeding generations from the scourge of war, which twice in our lifetime has brought untold sorrow to mankind." To achieve this objective, among others, the Charter enjoins the Member states "to practice tolerance and live in peace with one another as good neighbours, and to unite our strength to maintain international peace and security."

How are we to practice tolerance? What states of mind are necessary for all of us to live together in peace with one another as good neighbors? How are we to unite our strength to maintain international peace and security? The answers to these questions lie, it seems to me, in our ability to bring out the best in us and to return to the basic moral and ethical principles of all great religions. Let us, therefore, dedicate ourselves anew to a new pledge: to make Muslims better Muslims, Hindus better Hindus, Christians better Christians and Buddhists better Buddhists.

THE SITUATION IN CYPRUS

JULY—SEPTEMBER

DESPITE THE lull in the fighting, tension continued high. U Thant's concern over a reported build-up of military forces by both the Greek and Turkish Cypriots led him to send identical messages on July 16 to Cypriot, Greek, and Turkish leaders to "halt this perilous trend." Six days later the Secretary-General complained to the Government of Cyprus that Cypriot authorities were denying United Nations forces access to certain areas, although freedom of movement was guaranteed under the so-called Status Agreement which governed the relations between the United Nations forces and the Cypriot authorities. On the same day, July 22, Thant appealed to Cypriot Vice-President Fazil Küçük, leader of the Turkish community, to put an end to infiltration of military personnel and weapons into areas controlled by the Cypriot Turkish minority. Such activities, he pointed out, were clearly in contravention of Security Council resolutions.

Fighting between Turkish and Greek Cypriot forces broke out in various parts of the island early in August. In addition, Turkey intervened with air and naval actions in the northwestern region. The Security Council was called to an urgent session on the evening of August 8. During the early morning hours of August 9, the Council president, with the agreement of all Council members, made an appeal to the Government of Turkey "to cease instantly the bombardment and use of military force of any kind against Cyprus" and to the Government of Cyprus "to direct the armed forces under its control to cease firing immediately." Later the same day, the Council adopted, by 9 votes to none, with 2 abstentions (Czechoslovakia and the USSR), a United States resolution which: (1) reaffirmed the president's appeal; (2) called for an immediate cease-fire by all concerned; (3) called upon all concerned to cooperate fully with the United Nations commander; and (4) called on all states to refrain from any action that might exacerbate the situation. On August 10 Soviet Prime Minister Khrushchev sent a message to Thant saying:

> At this moment the United Nations must do everything to put an end to the bloodshed in Cyprus and thus prevent a development of events dangerous to the cause of peace. The Soviet government expresses the hope that you, Mr. Secretary-General, will on your part take, in accordance with the principles of the United Nations Charter, all possible measures for the speediest implementation of the decisions of the Security Council in which ways for peaceful settlement on Cyprus have been outlined.

The message arrived almost simultaneously with an announcement by the Secretary-General that the governments of Turkey and Cyprus had responded positively and without condition to the cease-fire appeal.

The situation was still quiet when the Council voted on September 25 to extend the mandate of the Cyprus force for an additional three months. Thant seized the occasion to express his unhappiness over the Council's continued reliance upon voluntary contributions to finance the Cyprus operation. He called the arrangement "most unsatisfactory" and warned that he would be forced to "withdraw the Force before the end of the three-month period" if voluntary contributions failed to provide the funds required (see p. 632).

1. Telegram to the Vice-President of Cyprus

NEW YORK   JULY 3, 1964

I REFER to your telegram to me of recent date transmitted in the letter of June 26, 1964, from the permanent representative of Turkey and appearing as Security Council document S/5790 of July 1, 1964.

With regard to your numerous messages in the past, it has been the practice here to acknowledge them in the usual way, since I have not considered it to be my proper function to enter into discussion with you about the political issues which comprise the main substance of your messages. It is not my intention nor is there any reason to depart from this practice with regard to your latest message to which I refer. However, I have noted that in this message you have made certain charges, allegations, and insinuations which unmistakably impugn the objectivity, integrity, and good faith of senior members of the United Nations Secretariat in Cyprus and which, therefore, I cannot permit to pass unchallenged. Indeed, I take vigorous exception to them.

I refer specifically to such statements appearing throughout your telegram as the following: "that . . . state of affairs in Cyprus is not reported to you in an unbiased and objective manner"; that my last report to the Security Council (S/5764) "makes the United Nations a tool of the Greek elements of the constitutional Government of Cyprus"; that on the basis of that report I am "unwittingly being made a party to such insidious scheming"; "the apparently biased attitude of some senior United Na-

Security Council Official Records, Nineteenth Year, Supplement for July, August, and September 1964, document S/5797.

tions officials in Cyprus"; "through your senior officials in Cyprus your report reflects so much Greek influence"; "the biased attitude of some United Nations officials in Cyprus well known to us"; "it may be easier and more convenient for United Nations officials in Cyprus to support the strong against the weak"; "false reporting by your representatives"; "the anti-Turkish bias of the report"; "how biased it all is"; "your report appears to have been written either in full ignorance or in total disregard of the contents of my numerous communications to you."

Permit me to say at the very outset that all such statements are groundless and inexcusable. I recognize without question your right to take exception to anything in my report; that you find grounds for disagreeing with parts of it was not unexpected. For I understand fully the difficulty of your position and of that of the Turkish Cypriot community, and I appreciate the reasons for your anxiety. You may be sure that I wish to see everything done that can properly be done under the resolutions of the Security Council to help the Turkish Cypriot community and the whole of Cyprus return to peaceful and normal conditions. But I do not think that purpose will ever be served by distortion, gross exaggeration, or hysteria.

I wish you to know also that I have full confidence in the senior United Nations officials in Cyprus, military and civilian alike. These highly responsible officials, who have given distinguished service to the United Nations in years past, report to me fully, promptly and faithfully, and their reports on the state of affairs in Cyprus are, I am certain, unbiased and objective. I recognize, naturally, that partisan eyes might see this differently, but this does not alter the facts. I assure you that the United Nations operation in Cyprus is being conducted with absolute integrity and serves no special interests of any community, group, or element in Cyprus; most emphatically do I deny that it is anyone's "tool." I am confident that my last report reflected with reasonable accuracy and without the least bias, the complex situations with which it properly dealt. I may assure you that it was written neither in ignorance nor disregard of the communications you have addressed to me. In this regard I need only observe that their refusal to accept partisan viewpoints is no basis for charging United Nations officials with bias.

May I say, finally, that I am confident that the United Nations officials in Cyprus are carrying out the mandates entrusted to them by the resolutions of the Security Council with complete fidelity in the face of countless difficulties which often originate in the highly emotional and inflexible partisan positions encountered in the island. I am also strongly of the belief that the Turkish community of Cyprus has been in no small degree a beneficiary of the United Nations efforts in Cyprus.

In view of the circulation of your letter to the Security Council, which was done at the request of the permanent representative of Turkey to the United Nations, I am giving similar circulation to my reply to you.

U THANT
Secretary-General of
the United Nations

---

2. Text of Identical Telegrams to the President of Cyprus, the Prime Minister of Greece, and the Prime Minister of Turkey

NEW YORK   JULY 16, 1964

THE REPORTED build-up of military personnel and equipment on both sides in Cyprus has received much attention in recent days and is giving rise to growing concern. You will recall that I drew attention to this problem in my report to the Security Council on June 15, 1964 (S/5764). Since that time I have received from various sources information about a continuing build-up on both sides, as well as repeated expressions of anxiety on this score from a number of governments, including several of those which are providing contingents for the United Nations Peacekeeping Force in Cyprus.

In view of this fact and of the almost daily reports showing that the build-up is continuing, I feel impelled to make an urgent and most earnest appeal to the governments primarily concerned to do all within their power to halt this perilous trend and to reverse it before it leads to a major clash in Cyprus, with all the dangers that such a clash entails. I am fully aware of the suspicions and anxieties which have led to this develop-

Security Council Official Records, Nineteenth Year, Supplement for July, August, and September 1964, document S/5828, July 23, 1964.

ment on both sides. My sole intention is to find a means of stabilizing the situation before it leads to disastrous consequences.

The resolution of March 4, 1964, establishing the United Nations peacekeeping force in Cyprus calls upon all Member states, in conformity with their obligations under the Charter of the United Nations, to refrain from any action or threat of action likely to worsen the situation in the sovereign Republic of Cyprus or to endanger international peace. In my view any action by any party tending to increase the tension and the danger of armed clashes in Cyprus at this time falls squarely within the terms of the resolution of the Security Council of March 4, 1964, and I appeal to all the governments concerned to adhere with the utmost care to their obligations under that resolution.

It is hardly necessary for me to elaborate on either the dangers of the arms build-up in Cyprus or on the effect it must inevitably have upon the efforts of the United Nations peacekeeping force and of the mediator, which, it seems to me, afford the most realistic and timely hope of a peaceful solution. The military build-up in Cyprus must, therefore, be halted immediately and a trend which is clearly increasing the tension and the danger in the island must be reversed.

I therefore deem it my duty to appeal strongly to your government to ensure full observance of both the letter and the spirit of the Security Council resolution of March 4, 1964.

---

3. *Exchange of Messages with the Foreign Minister of Sweden*

JULY 16–22, 1964

THE FOLLOWING is the text of a cable, dated July 16, from S. Torsten Nilsson, minister for foreign affairs of Sweden, to the Secretary-General:

To my regret I have to revert to the grave problem created by the increasing military build-up presently taking place in Cyprus. My govern-

UN Press Release SG/SM/125, July 24, 1964.

ment takes a very serious view of this development. If the present lack of cooperation from the parties directly concerned continues, I am obliged, on behalf of my government, to make a formal reservation in regard to further Swedish participation in the United Nations Force in Cyprus. In the prevailing circumstances I would also appreciate to have your views as to the appropriateness of your taking the initiative to call an urgent meeting of the Security Council for the purpose of reviewing the situation in Cyprus.

The following is the text of the reply from the Secretary-General, dated July 22:

The Secretary-General of the United Nations presents his compliments to the permanent representative of Sweden to the United Nations and has the honor to request him to transmit to the minister of foreign affairs of Sweden the following reply to his cable of July 16, 1964.

I have the honor to acknowledge receipt of your cable of July 16, 1964 concerning the problems created by the military build-up which has been taking place in Cyprus. I share your grave concern about this development and I agree with you that, if it continues, the effectiveness both of the United Nations Force in Cyprus and of the mediator may be gravely impaired.

With this in mind, I have addressed on July 16 appeals to the governments and community leaders principally concerned. I have also on July 22 addressed démarches to the President of Cyprus and to Vice-President Küçük concerning more particular questions affecting the arms build-up in relation to the functioning of UNFICYP.

The information at present available to me does not provide an adequate basis for a helpful report to the Security Council. When such information becomes available to me, I shall most certainly submit a Security Council report. Nor do I consider it advisable at present to seek an urgent meeting of the Security Council, since I do not feel that such a meeting just now would serve any useful purpose.

While fully understanding the position of your government in this matter, I note with regret the formal reservation you have made with regard to further Swedish participation in the United Nations Force in Cyprus, and I very much hope that, in the light of the efforts being made, the situation in Cyprus will improve in such a way as to impress you more favorably.

4. *Communication to the Government of Cyprus on Freedom of Movement of the United Nations Peacekeeping Force*

NEW YORK   JULY 22, 1964

THE SECRETARY-GENERAL of the United Nations presents his compliments to the permanent representative of Cyprus to the United Nations and has the honour to request him to transmit the following message to his government:

I regret to have to convey to you my growing concern about certain matters affecting the status and functioning of the United Nations Force in Cyprus under the Security Council resolutions of March 4, 1964, and June 20, 1964, and under the terms of the Status Agreement concluded between the United Nations and the Government of Cyprus on March 31, 1964. I bring these matters to your attention because they relate so vitally to the effectiveness of the United Nations Force in Cyprus and because of my anxiety that failure by the Force to fulfil its mandate could result only in a worsening of the already critical situation there.

The matters in question are the following. In spite of negotiations between the Force commander and the Government of Cyprus, which have now been going on for some weeks, troops of UNFICYP when on duty are still denied entry into the docks at Limassol, while UNFICYP observers continue to be seriously obstructed in their duties when convoys leave the docks at Limassol, an occurrence of increasing frequency in the past few weeks.

There is also an increasing tendency for United Nations patrols to be refused access to specific sensitive areas, although the commander himself has been told that he personally can visit any of these areas which he chooses. There has, in addition, been an increase in the number of instances of United Nations vehicles and convoys being held up at road-

Security Council Official Records, Nineteenth Year, Supplement for July, August, and September 1964, document S/5843, July 29, 1964.

blocks, and, on occasion, searched, in contravention of the Status Agreement.

All of the above activities fall under the heading of the denial to the United Nations Force of freedom of movement, a right specifically given to it in the Status Agreement and a condition of its presence in the island which is absolutely essential to its proper functioning. In addition, such limitations upon the activities of the United Nations Force, which are well-known and publicized throughout the world, can only lend substance to the suspicions and fears which are at the bottom of so much of the trouble and tension of the island, and in this way they have a most dangerous effect in increasing tension and the risk of clashes. I would, therefore, ask you urgently to take the necessary steps to bring an end to practices of this kind, which hinder seriously the functioning of the Force. I am sure that you will understand the basis for my concern.

5. *Communication to the Vice-President of Cyprus*

NEW YORK   JULY 22, 1964

THE SECRETARY-GENERAL of the United Nations presents his compliments to the permanent representative of Cyprus to the United Nations and has the honor to request him to transmit the following message to Dr. F. Küçük, the Vice-President of the Republic of Cyprus:

On July 16, 1964, I addressed to you, to the president and to the governments of Greece and Turkey an appeal concerning the arms build-up in Cyprus and the serious and harmful effects which it is inevitably having upon the situation in general and upon the effectiveness of the United Nations efforts, through the United Nations Force and through the mediator, to reduce tension in the island and to find an acceptable long-term solution.

I now pursue this matter with you further on certain of its aspects, as I am doing also with the Government of Cyprus, because of adverse effects on the status and functioning of the United Nations Force in Cyprus

UN Press Release SG/SM/124.

under the Security Council resolutions of March 4, March 13, and June 20. I refer particularly to reports which continue to reach me of covert infiltration, mostly under cover of darkness, of arms and personnel in areas controlled by members of the Turkish Cypriot community, and especially in the Kokkina-Mansoura area. Some activities of this kind, in fact, have been observed by patrols of the United Nations Force, while others are reported on the strength of evidence which would seem to be incontrovertible.

While fully realizing the extreme difficulties of the situation in which the members of the Turkish community in Cyprus find themselves at the present time, I would ask you most earnestly to do all within your power to put a stop to such activities. You will, of course, appreciate that the United Nations Force cannot ignore activities which are so clearly in contravention of the resolutions of the Security Council as well as of the law of the land. It is for this reason that I am asking you to take all steps available to you to put an end to them.

6. Statement in the Security Council

NEW YORK   AUGUST 10, 1964

THE PRESIDENT of the Security Council, on August 9, pursuant to the wishes of the Council, directed urgent appeals to the Governments of Cyprus and Turkey to end their hostile activities by a cease-fire. It is gratifying and encouraging that both governments have responded positively and without conditions. On the morning of August 10 the President of Cyprus informed the President of the Security Council that "we shall respect the appeal of the Security Council concerning a cease-fire," and addressed a similar cable to me. In a letter to the President of the Security Council received on the afternoon of the same day, the prime minister of Turkey stated that the Government of Turkey "has decided to stop immediately the action of the Turkish aircraft over the Mansoura-Kokkina region. . . ."

Security Council Official Records, Nineteenth Year, Supplement for July, August, and September 1964, S/5879.

These decisions of the two governments now afford an opportunity for definitely ending fighting and relaxing tension in Cyprus, and it will be my purpose to take the fullest possible advantage of this opportunity by exerting every effort toward constructive peacekeeping arrangements in all areas of the island. In consequence, I have instructed the Commander of the Force to cooperate fully with all parties in making the cease-fire thoroughly effective and to take every initiative and to lend all assistance toward this end. I strongly appeal to the Governments of Cyprus, Greece, and Turkey and to the Turkish community of Cyprus to extend full cooperation and support to General Thimayya and to the United Nations Force in Cyprus which he commands, in their peacekeeping efforts.

I have also asked Mr. Galo Plaza, my special representative in Cyprus, to return there promptly, and it is expected that he will do so by the end of the week.

The appeal of the president of the Security Council for a cessation of fighting was reaffirmed by a resolution of the Security Council, which also calls for an immediate cease-fire. That cease-fire is now in effect. This is a development that must be warmly welcomed. We must now look forward rather than backward and we must hope and strive for a durable restoration of peace and normality in Cyprus and the ultimate solution of its critical problems.

In the light of the present situation, I do not believe that any useful purpose would be served by submitting the report on the incidents of fighting which have taken place in Cyprus since August 5 that was suggested by the president of the Security Council at its 1142nd meeting, on August 8. I have consulted the president of the Council about this and have his concurrence in my decision not to submit such a report at this time.

---

7. *Telegram to Chairman Khrushchev*

NEW YORK   AUGUST 10, 1964

I AM GRATEFUL to Your Excellency for your cable of August 9 [S/5880] drawing my attention to the recent events in Cyprus. As you are aware,

Security Council Official Records, Nineteenth Year, Supplement for July, August, and September 1964, document S/5881.

the Security Council yesterday [1143rd meeting] endorsed an appeal made by the president of the Security Council addressed to the governments of Turkey and Cyprus requesting an immediate cease-fire. The president of the Security Council has received a reply [S/5871] today from Archbishop Makarios, president of Cyprus, informing him of his willingness to accept the appeal and informing him also that he had ordered a cease-fire unilaterally beginning the evening of August 8. Similarly, a reply [S/5875] was received today by the president of the Security Council from Mr. Ismet Inönü, prime minister of Turkey, informing him that the Turkish government has decided to stop immediately the action of the Turkish aircraft in the Mansoura-Kokkina region. His communication also contains an explanation of the position of the Government of Turkey.

It is my fervent hope that the parties concerned will comply unreservedly with the terms of the Security Council resolution adopted yesterday [193 (1964)] and take every positive step to restore peace in that area. In my capacity as Secretary-General of the United Nations I will continue to do my best in promoting a peaceful settlement of the problem in conformity with the principles of the Charter of the United Nations.

U THANT
Secretary-General of
the United Nations

8. From Report to the Security Council

NEW YORK   SEPTEMBER 10, 1964

. . . .

212. IT IS WITH deep regret and sorrow that I report to the Council that the United Nations mediator in Cyprus, Mr. Sakari Tuomioja, died in Helsinki on September 9, as the result of the stroke which he suffered on August 16. This is a severe blow to the mediation effort. Mr. Tuomioja had served as mediator with great ability and dedication and now his life has been given in the effort.

Security Council Official Records, Nineteenth Year, Supplement for July, August, and September 1964, document S/5950.

213. Mr. Tuomioja had kept me informed of his activities, plans and thinking on the question, but had not submitted a formal report to me. At the time he was stricken he was about to depart from Geneva for a new round of mediation talks in Athens, Ankara, and Nicosia.

214. Having consulted the four parties principally concerned, as defined in paragraph 7 of the Security Council resolution March 4, 1964, and having found that they all consider it important to designate a new mediator without delay, I am taking the necessary steps toward this end and expect shortly to be in a position to inform the Security Council of that action.

215. The resolution of the Security Council of March 4, 1964 [186 (1964)], in providing for the Force that was to be established in Cyprus, defined the function of that Force only in general terms, namely, to prevent a recurrence of fighting and, as necessary, to contribute to the maintenance and restoration of law and order and a return to normal conditions. Given the political complexity of the Cyprus problem, it was manifestly impossible for the Council to do more than this at that time. I undertook, in these circumstances, to organize the Force and establish it in Cyprus, while recognizing that it would be subject to some limitations. Thus, UNFICYP was given a very heavy responsibility without any precise definition of its general mandate to guide it so that it might know clearly just what it was entitled to do and how far it might go, particularly in the use of force. This inadequacy and lack of clarity in the mandate of the Force has been, obviously, a handicap to its operation. The Force has, of course, been subjected to much pressure from, on the one hand, those who would wish it to go much further than it has gone, particularly in the employment of armed force, and, on the other hand, those who would feel that at times the Force tries to go too far on the territory of a sovereign state.

216. Despite these handicaps, and under most trying and dangerous circumstances in general, the Force in Cyprus has functioned extremely well. It has not, obviously, been able to achieve the full objectives defined in the general mandate of the Security Council. It has not, for example, been able to prevent altogether "a recurrence of fighting," for there have been two serious engagements—at St. Hilarion and in the Tylliria area—since the arrival of the Force in Cyprus. But the presence of the Force in Cyprus was a major factor in bringing the fighting in these two areas to a quick end and in preventing those episodes from escalating. Nor can there be any doubt that had the Force not been deployed in Cyprus over

these six months, there would have been far more fighting on the island than there has been, with resultant heavy casualties and devastation. As to maintenance and restoration of law and order in Cyprus, there has been a considerable improvement in the security situation since the deployment of the Force and its police arm. To mention only one sphere, incidents involving the beating, shooting, and kidnapping of civilians have been greatly reduced. As regards a return to normal conditions, there has also been vast improvement in the situation since the arrival of UNFICYP, although conditions on Cyprus are today, without question, still far from those prevailing on the island prior to the outbreak of communal fighting in December 1963. But there have been significant advances from the dire situation that existed when the Force arrived in Cyprus. This is reflected in such developments as much more freedom of movement, and much less harassment, on the roads; as the harvesting, with good results, thanks to the assistance of the Force; as the lifting of the sieges of a number of Turkish communities; as the restoration of public utility services; and as the increased movement of essentials. Nevertheless, UNFICYP has found on innumerable occasions great resistance, and indeed sometimes adamant refusal, from both the government authorities and the Turkish Cypriot leadership, concerning proposals designed to promote a return to normal life, if such arrangements, in their view, seem in any way to prejudice their political objectives.

217. It must be said, however, that despite all efforts of the United Nations, at Headquarters and in the field, conditions in Cyprus today are far from good; indeed, they are very unsatisfactory when viewed from the perspective of the hopes for Cyprus which motivated the Security Council's resolution of March 4. But if the United Nations mission and Force had not been established on the island and had not been exerting ever since every possible effort on behalf of peace and reason, conditions in that tragic country would be immeasurably worse, with all of the implications which this would have for the peace of the region and of the world.

218. I think it is necessary to point out, with regard to the reference in the Security Council resolution to "a return to normal conditions," that there has been all along and continues to be what I consider to be a misunderstanding on the part of the Turkish community of Cyprus and of the Turkish government as to the function and duty of the United Nations Force in Cyprus. The position of the Turkish side is that by a "return to normal conditions," the Security Council intended a complete restoration of the situation in Cyprus exactly as it was before the fighting

broke out in December, including, of course, the restoration of the constitutional situation. Therefore, in their eyes, UNFICYP should have been employing force, wherever and whenever necessary, to restore, over the opposition of the Cypriot government, the constitutional situation relating to the privileges, rights, and immunities of the Turkish community in Cyprus. Thus, in this view, UNFICYP should not regard the Cypriot government or any acts taken by it as legal; the present Cypriot army, the National Guard, should be considered as illegal and should be treated as such by UNFICYP; the importation of arms by the Cypriot government should be considered illegal under the Cypriot Constitution and should be stopped by UNFICYP in pursuance of the Security Council's resolutions.

219. I have not, of course, accepted these positions and have pointed out to those who hold them that the Security Council did not indicate such intentions in adopting its resolutions on this question.

220. On the other hand, UNFICYP was not established by the Security Council as an arm of the Government of Cyprus, and it has not been permitted to fall into such a course. It respects at all times the sovereignty and the independence of Cyprus and the authority of the government, but it acts independently in the discharge of its mandate, in accordance with the resolutions of the Security Council.

221. The plain fact, therefore, is that the United Nations Force in Cyprus is in the most delicate position that any United Nations mission has ever experienced, for it is not only in the midst of a bitter civil war but it is dangerously interposed between the two sides of that war. In that situation, the United Nations operation has had to exert every effort to maintain objectivity, to serve fairness and justice, and to avoid taking sides while doing all possible to alleviate suffering. Thus, in recent weeks, UNFICYP has been devoting major efforts toward eliminating or lessening the hardship experienced by many Turkish communities in Cyprus because of the economic restrictions which have been imposed by the Government of Cyprus.

222. With regard to this policy, which has become quite vigorous since the fighting of early August was ended by the cease-fire called for by the Security Council, one can understand the evident concern of the Government of Cyprus for the security of the country in view of the recurrent threats emanating from Turkey about Turkish landings on the island, and particularly in view of the tragic experience of the island with the Turkish air raids of early August. But allowing for the security factor, the conclu-

sion seems warranted that the economic restrictions being imposed against the Turkish communities in Cyprus, which in some instances have been so severe as to amount to a veritable siege, indicate that the Government of Cyprus seeks to force a potential solution by economic pressure as a substitute for military action.

223. The policy of economic pressures has definitely caused much hardship to the Turkish population; it has nourished bitterness on the Turkish side; it has hardened the Turkish position; it has greatly increased tension and would no doubt lead to a new eruption of fighting if continued, particularly in the arbitrary and constantly changing manner in which it was being applied.

224. It is, therefore, a cause for no little encouragement that it has been learned, on the eve of this report, that the Government of Cyprus has substantially relaxed these economic restrictions and that supplies are now flowing into the Turkish Cypriot areas in accordance with accords thus far reached.

225. I feel compelled also to express the view that the aerial attacks on Cyprus communities by Turkish aircraft in early August, whatever their supposed tactical significance, were most unfortunate and have made the solution of the Cyprus problem far more difficult. These raids on defenseless people killed and maimed many innocent civilians, destroyed much property, and inevitably led to a stiffening of the positions of the Cypriot government, as might have been anticipated. I trust that they will not be repeated, for whatever reasons.

226. On not very convincing grounds of national security, the Government of Cyprus, despite the assurances given to me by the president of Cyprus in his message of August 6, 1964 (S/5855), has recently sought to impose restrictions on movements of the Force which, in effect, would go very far toward nullifying freedom of movement for UNFICYP. The projected restrictions would be so extensive that they would cripple the effectiveness of the Force and make its continued presence in Cyprus virtually useless. I have, of course, vigorously protested to the Government of Cyprus against these restrictions, and have demanded that they be lifted. But as at the date of the submission of this report, there has been no satisfactory response. The security needs of Cyprus will be fully respected by the Force, but it cannot fulfil the mandates of the Council from a virtually static posture. There is implicit in this problem a question of mutual trust and good faith.

227. A recent crisis, which at present is only in abeyance, relates to the intended rotation of a part of the Turkish contingent stationed in Cyprus. It will be recalled that in the early stage of the deployment of UNFICYP in Cyprus, I had proposed to the governments of Greece and Turkey that their contingents stationed in the island should be placed under United Nations command in Cyprus, although not as contingents in the United Nations Force in Cyprus (see S/5764, para. 116). This proposal was acceptable to Greece but was rejected by Turkey since in effect it would mean the return of the Turkish troops to their barracks. When, quite recently, an impasse developed between Cyprus and Turkey over the projected rotation of part of the Turkish contingent, I appealed to both governments to employ moderation and restraint in this situation, and specifically urged the Government of Turkey to postpone for a few weeks the scheduled rotation of the Turkish troops (see S/5920). The rotation has been deferred and the Turkish government is due commendation for its helpfulness in this critical situation. . . .

---

9. Statement in the Security Council

NEW YORK   SEPTEMBER 25, 1964

WITH REGARD to the resolution which has just been adopted unanimously by the Council, I deem it necessary to make the following comments. Before doing so, however, I should like to say that I am very much aware of the complexity of the Cyprus situation and the difficulties involved in finding a consensus in the Security Council which could be formulated into a resolution.

The Security Council has extended the United Nations peacekeeping force in Cyprus [UNFICYP] for a further period of three months on the basis of its resolution of March 4, 1964. It has also reaffirmed its subsequent resolutions on this matter and the consensus arrived at on August 11, 1964. The functions of the Force, in accordance with the resolution of

Security Council Official Records, Nineteenth Year, 1159th meeting.

March 4, are, in the interest of preserving international peace and security, to use its best efforts to prevent a recurrence of fighting and, as necessary, to contribute to the maintenance and restoration of law and order and a return to normal conditions.

Both I myself and the Force will continue to discharge this mandate which we have received from the Council. In doing so, it is my intention to continue to seek full respect for the freedom of movement for the Force which not only is indispensable to the implementation of the mandate but also is provided for in the agreement concerning the status of the Force signed on March 31, 1964, by the Government of Cyprus and the United Nations. It will also, of course, be my intention to continue to initiate any actions which would prove necessary for the implementation of the mandate to prevent a recurrence of fighting and contribute to the maintenance and restoration of law and order and a return to normal conditions. I shall continue to rely on the cooperation of the Government of Cyprus and all the other parties concerned and I wish, on this occasion, once again to appeal to them to join their efforts with those of UNFICYP in endeavoring to reestablish peace on the island.

As the members of the Council are aware, Archbishop Makarios, president of Cyprus, has sent me a communication, dated September 15, 1964, outlining certain measures designed to ease tension and to promote a return to normal conditions in Cyprus. I am already in touch with the commander of UNFICYP concerning the ways and means by which these measures may be implemented, and I have requested him to review the whole question of measures which may bring about an improvement in the situation in Cyprus. It is also my intention to direct the commander to engage in discussions with the Government of Cyprus, as well as the leaders of the Turkish Cypriot community, concerning the initiatives mentioned in paragraph (c) of President Makarios' statement of September 15, 1964.

In this respect, I wish once again to state that I welcome President Makarios' suggestions as an important step toward reducing tensions in Cyprus and enabling UNFICYP to carry out its mandate effectively.

In my report of August 29, 1964, to the Security Council, and again in my report of September 10, I brought to the Council's attention the situation arising from the intention of the Turkish government to proceed with the normal rotation of one third of its contingent and the refusal of the Government of Cyprus to allow it.

While questions pertaining to the stationing in Cyprus of the Turkish and Greek national contingents do not strictly fall within the mandate conferred upon me and the Force by the Security Council, I indicated to the Council that it was my intention to continue to search for a satisfactory solution of the problem concerning the rotation of the Turkish contingent. These efforts have continued, and I am now in a position to inform the Council that the parties concerned have agreed to the proposal which I submitted to them, whereby the Kyrenia Road, now under the control of Turkish and Turkish Cypriot armed personnel, will be placed under the exclusive control of UNFICYP; no armed personnel or armed posts other than those of the United Nations Force will be allowed on the road; traffic on the road will be free for all civilians. The proposal also provides for the withdrawal of any positions of the Turkish national contingent which would be within one hundred yards of the Kyrenia Road, with the exception of a limited number of houses in Geunyeli which are required by the contingent for offices, accommodations for officers, and for the maintenance and repair of vehicles. The detailed implementation of this arrangement will be entrusted, naturally, to General Thimayya, the commander of UNFICYP.

The Government of Cyprus, without prejudice to its position on the question of the Turkish contingent's presence in Cyprus, will not interfere with the rotation of the contingent. The United Nations Force will observe in the usual manner the movement of the outgoing and incoming elements involved in the rotation.

I wish to express my appreciation to the Government of Turkey for having withheld the intended rotation of its contingent in order to allow time for discussions to take place on the basis of my proposals, and to the Government of Cyprus for its cooperation in finding a satisfactory solution to this very delicate question.

Since my report of September 10, 1964, to the Council on the United Nations operation in Cyprus, two additional pledges, one for $100,000 and the other for $2,500, have been received with respect to the expenses of the Force for the second three-month period, ending September 26, 1964.

In view of the Council's decision to extend the period during which the Force is to be stationed in Cyprus for an additional period of three months, and in view of its decision that all costs pertaining to the Force should be met in accordance with the provisions of operative paragraph 6 of the Council's resolution of March 4, 1964, I shall, of course, continue my efforts to obtain further voluntary contributions to cover the costs of the Force while at the same time endeavouring, with the cooperation of the governments providing contingents, goods, and services to the Force, to ensure that the costs chargeable to the special account for UNFICYP are held to the absolute minimum required for its effective operation.

I must, nevertheless, reiterate the view I expressed in my report to the Council of June 15, 1964, that this method of financing the Force is most unsatisfactory, and to repeat my statement in that report that I have no assurance that the funds required to extend the stationing of the Force in Cyprus by a further three-month period can be raised through voluntary contributions.

Although the Council has directed that the Force be extended, it has maintained the financing of the Force on the basis of voluntary contributions. Moreover, express opposition has been stated in the Council to the use for this purpose of any other United Nations finances.

If, therefore, after the endeavours I have referred to, it should appear to me that the total voluntary contributions in support of UNFICYP are likely to be insufficient to cover all the costs for which the Organization might be responsible if the Force were to remain in Cyprus until December 26, 1964, I shall have no alternative but to inform the Council of the situation, and, whenever the financial situation makes it necessary, to withdraw the Force before the end of the three-month period.

The financial burden of stationing the Force in Cyprus has been carried until now by the supporting spirit and generosity of a limited number of Member states. I feel, therefore, that I must address a fresh appeal to all states Members of the United Nations to contribute toward meeting the costs of this peacekeeping operation and thus to demonstrate their effective support of the activities which this Organization has to undertake in the fulfillment of its paramount obligation toward the maintenance of international peace and security.

As regards the extension of UNFICYP for another period of three months, I wish to inform the Council that the Government of Cyprus has agreed to the extension of the mandate on the same basis and composition as heretofore. I therefore propose to request officially the continued participation in the Force of the countries now providing contingents. I wish to associate myself with the expressions of appreciation to these Member states which are contained in the resolution just adopted by the Council.

I am able to inform the Council that I have designated Ambassador Carlos Bernardes, the representative of Brazil, as my special representative in Cyprus to replace Mr. Galo Plaza who has now taken up his functions as United Nations mediator in Cyprus. I wish to express my deep gratitude to the foreign minister of Brazil, and through him to his government, for having responded promptly and favourably to my request for the services of Mr. Bernardes in this delicate position.

Mr. Bernardes needs no introduction to the members of this Council, in whose midst he sat until recently. His distinguished record of service is well known. In his capacity as permanent representative of Brazil to the United Nations, a post that he relinquished a short time ago, he represented Brazil in the Security Council and indeed played an important part in the deliberations of this body at the time when the United Nations Peacekeeping Force in Cyprus was established on March 4, 1964. I feel that we are fortunate in his willingness to serve as my special representative, and I am sure that the members of the Council share my feelings in this respect. Mr. Bernardes will arrive in New York on September 27, and I am confident that he will be able to depart for Nicosia soon thereafter.

Finally, I wish to refer briefly to the account of the fighting in Tylliria in early August which was presented by the representative of Cyprus during the recent debate in the Security Council. Since there seems to be a certain discrepancy between that account and the information recorded by UNFICYP in those distressing days, I intend shortly to make available to the members of the Council a more detailed account of the events in question as compiled from UNFICYP sources of information.

THE SITUATION IN YEMEN

AUGUST and SEPTEMBER

1. Text of Identical Messages to the Governments of Saudi Arabia and the United Arab Republic

NEW YORK   AUGUST 19, 1964

THE SECRETARY-GENERAL has the honour to approach the Government of Saudi Arabia [or the United Arab Republic] on the subject of the United Nations Observation Mission in Yemen.

The purpose of this communication is to determine the wishes of your government with regard to the Yemen mission, which will come to an end on September 4, 1964, unless specific action is taken to extend it once again. A communication identical to this one is being addressed to the Government of the United Arab Republic [or Saudi Arabia].

The mission to Yemen was established in July 1963, in response to the agreement between Saudi Arabia and the United Arab Republic on disengagement in Yemen. The mission, by the terms of reference defined for it in that agreement, has had a limited purpose and function, which it has discharged to the best of its ability for more than a year.

It will be recalled that the Secretary-General, in his report to the Security Council of July 2, 1964 (S/5794), indicated that on the expiration on September 4 of the present two months' extension of the mission, he would not be inclined to take the initiative in seeking a further extension in the absence of substantial progress in the fulfillment of the agreement between the two parties.

Clearly, the wishes of the two parties to the agreement should be a major determining factor in arriving at a final decision on the future of the mission. It will be very much appreciated, therefore, if the Govern-

Security Council Official Records, Nineteenth Year, Supplement for July, August, and September 1964, document S/5927, annex I.

ment of Saudi Arabia [or United Arab Republic] will inform the Secretary-General within the next ten days as to its wishes with regard to the United Nations Observation Mission in Yemen, that is to say, whether it wishes the mission to come to an end on September 4, 1964, or to be extended beyond that date on the prevailing basis.

The Secretary-General takes this opportunity to express to the Government of Saudi Arabia [or United Arab Republic] his appreciation of the cooperation it has never failed to extend to the mission.

2. Report to the Security Council

NEW YORK SEPTEMBER 2, 1964

1. IN MY LAST report on the functioning of the United Nations Yemen Observation Mission, which was submitted to the Security Council on July 2, 1964 (S/5794), I stated my intention to extend the mission for a further period of two months, that is, until September 4, 1964, and this has been done (see S/5794/Add.1). The mission has continued to operate over this latest period under the direction of Mr. Pier P. Spinelli, my special representative for Yemen, and whenever he was not in the area, under that of the chief of staff of the mission, Colonel S. C. Sabharwal. There has been during the period under review no significant change in the method of operation of the mission or in the deployment of its staff of twenty-five United Nations military observers. Caribou aircraft of the Royal Canadian Air Force continue to support the mission.

2. The formal mandate of the mission has continued to be to observe the implementation of the disengagement agreement between the governments of Saudi Arabia and the United Arab Republic, under the main provisions of which a demilitarized zone was established on the northern frontier between Saudi Arabia and Yemen; Saudi Arabia undertook to cease providing aid and support to the royalists of Yemen and to prohibit the use of its territory by royalist leaders for the purpose of carrying on

Security Council Official Records, Nineteenth Year, Supplement for July, August, and September 1964, document S/5927.

the struggle in Yemen; and the United Arab Republic agreed to carry out a phased disengagement of its troops from Yemen.

3. United Nations observers stationed on the northern frontier have continued to observe traffic crossing by the main routes, though with increasing difficulty because, inter alia, of less favorable climatic conditions and of problems of vehicle maintenance. Moreover, as indicated in previous reports, the control exercised by observers on a long frontier is necessarily far from thorough. A small, though increasing, traffic has been observed, but no military supplies have been discovered. However, observers have noted that royalists in one area not far from the frontier maintain a substantial dump of fuel, arms, ammunition, and rations. United Arab Republic military authorities have shown United Nations observers an appreciable quantity of weapons and ammunition allegedly provided to the royalists by Saudi Arabia and captured from them by United Arab Republic troops. It was observed that, according to the markings on the boxes, the ammunition appeared to have been made in the United States in 1963–1964 and delivered to Saudi Arabia. The Saudi Arabian authorities have emphatically denied that any such war material had been given by them to the royalists of Yemen.

4. As regards the disengagement of United Arab Republic troops from Yemen, the United Nations observers stationed at Hodeida have reported that during the period of this report some 6,700 troops departed by sea, of whom the great majority were in regular formations and were embarked with trucks and antitank guns. During the same period, some 4,300 United Arab Republic troops were observed to land at Hodeida, of whom about one-third appeared to be returning from leave and the remainder to be replacements. Taking into account movements by air, in which there is usually a net balance of troops leaving the country, it is estimated that there has been over the past two months a reduction of about 4,000 troops in the total strength of United Arab Republic troops.

5. Despite the reduction in United Arab Republic strength, there has been a substantial amount of military action directed against royalist strongpoints in north Yemen, in which Yemen republican troops, some of them trained in the United Arab Republic, and Yemeni tribesmen, have taken an increasing part. These operations seem to have met with some success and additional tribes appear to have rallied to the Government of the Yemen Arab Republic. The United Arab Republic authorities have, however, stated that the Yemeni units will continue to be supported by

United Arab Republic ground troops and the United Arab Republic air force. United Nations observers at Sada have reported that on several recent occasions operations in that vicinity were supported by aerial bombing and artillery fire.

6. The Saudi Arabian authorities have complained that on several occasions during August, United Arab Republic military aircraft have flown over Saudi Arabian territory east of Qizan. One of those reports has been confirmed by the United Nations observation mission. Representations were made to the United Arab Republic commander, who reiterated that his pilots have standing instructions not to fly over Saudi Arabia.

7. In my previous report I noted with regret that during its year of operation the mission in Yemen had been able to observe only a disappointing measure of disengagement, in particular as regards the withdrawal of United Arab Republic troops. I felt obliged, therefore, to appeal most urgently to the parties concerned to meet at the highest level in the near future with a view to achieving full and rapid implementation of the disengagement agreement. I also felt bound to advise the Council that if this new period of two months were to register no substantial progress toward fulfillment, or the firm prospect of imminent fulfillment, I would find it difficult to envisage a further extension of the mission in its present form, and with its present terms of reference and purpose.

8. The observations of the past two months have been somewhat more encouraging in that there has been a substantial reduction in the strength of the United Arab Republic armed forces in Yemen. However, it seems that this withdrawal is a reflection of the improved military situation in Yemen from the point of view of the United Arab Republic and of the increased participation by Yemeni republicans, many of them trained in the United Arab Republic, in the fight against the royalists, rather than the beginning of a phased withdrawal in the sense of the disengagement agreement. There are indications, moreover, that the Yemeni royalists have continued to receive military supplies from external sources.

9. My special representative visited the United Arab Republic, Saudi Arabia, and Yemen in the first half of August and held discussions with the authorities on the Yemen problem. However, the hoped-for direct high-level discussions between Saudi Arabia and the United Arab Republic with a view to further progress toward disengagement have not taken place, and there is no certainty that they will.

10. In the light of these circumstances, I addressed on August 19, 1964, identical notes to the two governments, in which, after recalling the remarks set forth in my previous report, I asked them to inform me of their wishes with regard to the termination of the mission on September 4, 1964, or its extension beyond that date on the prevailing basis.

11. In a reply dated August 26, 1964, the Saudi Arabian government, after noting that it had carried out its responsibilities as set out in the agreement faithfully and honestly but that the other party had not carried out its responsibilities, stated that it found itself unable to continue the payment of expenses resulting from the agreement and unable to abide by its terms after September 4, 1964. I was informed orally on August 31 that the Government of the United Arab Republic, in response to my note, had no objection to the termination of the mission on September 4.

12. In view of the expressed wishes of the parties to the agreement and in accordance with my own previously stated views, it is my intention to terminate the activities of the United Nations Yemen observation mission on September 4, 1964.

13. It is a matter of regret to me that the mission has been able to observe only limited progress toward the implementation of the disengagement agreement. In this regard, I must reiterate that the terms of reference of the mission were restricted to observation and report only, and that the responsibility for implementation lay with the two parties which had concluded the agreement and which had requested the establishment of the mission. My regret, however, is tempered by reason of the fact that the potential threat to international peace and security represented by the Yemen question has greatly diminished during the existence of the mission and, I believe, to a considerable extent because of its activities. The true measure of the mission, of course, is to be found in how it has discharged the limited responsibility and authority entrusted to it. In this respect, I think it can be said without question that the mission actually accomplished much more than could have been expected of it, in the circumstances; it certainly could have been much more useful had the definition of its functions been broader and stronger. It is clear, however, that during the fourteen months of its presence in Yemen, the mission exercised an important restraining influence on hostile activities in that area.

14. It is not possible to assess the likely effect of the withdrawal of the mission at this time. It is my hope that there will be no intensification of fighting, and that sincere efforts will be made by the governments of

Saudi Arabia and the United Arab Republic to settle their needless and now senseless dispute over the Yemen of today.

15. I have welcomed the reestablishment of diplomatic relations between Saudi Arabia and the United Arab Republic and hope that the differences of approach between them on the Yemen question may be reconciled. I remain convinced that a meeting between the two countries, at the highest level, would provide the best means for significant progress toward disengagement and toward peace and stability in Yemen and I hope that in the near future the opportunity for such a meeting will occur. I am, as always, at the disposal of the parties in the search for a peaceful solution.

16. I wish, in conclusion, to pay a tribute to those who served the United Nations in Yemen under very trying material and climatic conditions and at some degree of personal risk, whether as members of the Yugoslav military unit or the Canadian air unit, as military observers from the thirteen Member states which provided such personnel, or as members of the Secretariat. Their performance conformed to the highest United Nations standards. If, despite some incidents, there are no casualties to be deplored, this is to be attributed in part to good fortune and in part to the friendliness and consideration generally shown toward United Nations personnel by Yemenis of all factions.

From Transcript of Press Conference

NEW YORK   AUGUST 20, 1964

U THANT's August 20 press conference had special meaning since he had held private talks with a number of world leaders, including President de Gaulle, President Johnson, and Prime Minister Khrushchev, and also because of the worsening of the conflict in Southeast Asia. The Secretary-General acknowledged that he had "thought out loud" about the Vietnam war during the conversations in Moscow and Washington, but said he "did not present any formula or any proposals." While he did not consider it proper for him as Secretary-General to make proposals he noted that he was a national of a country close to the area and, as such, had "certain convictions." One was that the situation was deteriorating and another was that a solution could be found only through negotiation. Thant was particularly concerned about the incidents in the Gulf of Tonkin on July 31 and on August 2 and 4. He described these as "happenings of major significance." He did not mention the Gulf of Tonkin resolution, adopted by the United States Congress on August 7, which laid the foundation for full-scale United States military intervention as well as aerial bombardmemt of North Vietnam.

. . . .

THE SECRETARY-GENERAL: Actually, there is no immediate need for a press conference today; but I have been advised that many members of the press have expressed the wish to have it since my return from a rather extensive trip to Europe, Africa, and Asia.

I just want to mention very briefly one or two points by way of introduction.

The mediation effort in Cyprus suffered a cruel reverse when Mr. Sakari Tuomioja, the United Nations Cyprus mediator, was suddenly stricken last Sunday, August 16. I am sorry to say that reports from Geneva regarding the condition of Mr. Tuomioja are far from encouraging. The mediator's incapacitation came just at a time when he was about to start

UN Note to Correspondents No. 2966.

a new round of talks in the mediation process and when word from him indicated that, at long last, there seemed to be at least some ray of hope and encouragement.

Moreover, owing to the efforts of Mr. Galo Plaza and General Thimayya, and to the cooperation of the Government of Cyprus, there has been an improvement in conditions and a relaxation of tension on the island of Cyprus which will provide an improved climate for mediation.

Since it early became apparent that, at best, Ambassador Tuomioja would not be able to resume his duties for some time, I decided to request Mr. Spinelli to return to Geneva from Yemen in order to assume the responsibility, temporarily, of overseeing the office and staff of the mediator, whose headquarters are now in Geneva. Mr. Spinelli had just arrived in Sana in connection with his work as head of the United Nations Yemen observation mission; he arrived back at Geneva late yesterday afternoon.

The mediation effort in Cyprus will have to go forward, of course; and it is my intention to take such steps as future developments may require. As of now, I have made no move toward the appointment of either an acting mediator or a new mediator, although I know that all sorts of rumors about such actions are flying about. I am, of course, keeping a very watchful eye on the situation.

Our peacekeeping effort suffered another blow when, on Tuesday night, General Paiva Chaves, commander of UNEF in the Middle East, was stricken. Mr. Spinelli had said, in a telephone conversation after his arrival in Geneva, that he saw General Chaves in the hospital at Beirut yesterday and that he was in very serious condition. Naturally, we are hoping against hope that both these men will recover, for their own sakes and because we sorely need their valuable services.

Now I am ready to answer questions.

QUESTION: Could you kindly tell us the result—the success or otherwise—of your mission, particularly in the field of the United Nations peacekeeping force and the possibility of averting a crisis this fall?

THE SECRETARY-GENERAL: As I have stated on one or two previous occasions since my return from Europe, I brought up this question of the United Nations' financial position both in Paris and in Moscow. I found that the positions of both the French government and the Soviet government remained unchanged. I had said this in my press statements in Stockholm, I think, and also at the airport in New York. Then, on the 6th of this month, I went to Washington and had discussions with members of the government, including President Johnson, and among the topics discussed was the financial situation of the United Nations. I returned from Washington with a deep impression that the attitude of the United States government toward this problem also remains unchanged.

Of course, as you all know, it is not for me—at least, at this stage—to come out with some formula, since the positions of these Member states are very clearly defined and publicly stated. I very much hope that the working group of 21 will meet very early, perhaps early in September. Since my return from Europe, I have been in contact with the chairman of the working group, and I am confident that the group will look into this problem from all angles. Perhaps, if necessary, I may have to come out with some suggestions just before the commencement of the next session of the General Assembly.

. . . . QUESTION: Recently, of course, you visited Mr. Khrushchev, and also you visited your native Burma. You also had occasion to confer with President Johnson, and the newspapers said that you advised the president of the United States about the situation in Southeast Asia. Will you size up that situation for us, the United Nations correspondents?

THE SECRETARY-GENERAL: When I met some of the world leaders, naturally we exchanged views on several problems, including the situation prevailing in Southeast Asia. As I have made clear on previous occasions, I did not present any formula or any proposals. I just thought aloud, because in my position as Secretary-General of the United Nations I do not think it would be proper for me to come up with any proposals regarding the solution of the crisis in Southeast Asia. But, as a citizen of a country very close to the area and as one who has taken a very close interest in the developments in the area for about ten years I have certain convictions, and, as you are no doubt aware, we have to assess the situation in Southeast Asia primarily from one angle. We have to judge whether the situation is improving or deteriorating. I am sure you will agree with me that the situation is deteriorating, as I publicly indicated several months ago.

I became increasingly convinced that only the diplomatic and political methods of discussion and negotiation can perhaps lead to a lasting solution.

If we are to go back to particular incidents, I think it is worth remembering that three happenings of major significance took place recently on July 31, August 2, and August 4. To my knowledge, there has been no dispute regarding the developments on the two first cases, that is, July 31 and August 2, but regarding the happenings on August 4, there have been two different versions. This is known to you, and these versions were also presented to the Security Council as documents. So it is difficult for us, particularly for the United Nations, to know exactly what did happen on August 4, in the light of these conflicting versions. I feel increasingly convinced that the situation will continue to deteriorate if diplomatic and political means are not utilized.

. . . . QUESTION: There have been reports that the United Nations Force's activities on Cyprus have been defied, in some cases, close to the point of humiliation. Do you think that the United Nations peacekeeping activities can be maintained as a good image in the world if that defiance continues in similar situations in the future?

THE SECRETARY-GENERAL: Before I answer this question, I think it is very important to keep in mind certain aspects of the situation in Cyprus. In assessing the situation in Cyprus, we have to bear in mind the basic issue, involving two aspects: one aspect is the contention that the Government of Cyprus is a sovereign, independent Member of the United Nations. Another aspect of the problem is related to the contention that the agreements and treaties connected with the emergence of Cyprus to independent nationhood still hold good.

With respect to these two contentions, some Member states of the United Nations have come out with their own viewpoints, including the four big powers. The Security Council, in its several resolutions and decisions—on March 4, March 13, June 20, August 9, and in the August 11 consensus—did not attempt to define this particular aspect of the problem—understandably. This is one thought I want to put across.

Another thought is related to the use of force by UNFICYP. I think it is worth recalling some of the Security Council resolutions relating to the performance of ONUC in the Congo. You will no doubt remember that the United Nations Force in the Congo was authorized by the Security Council to exercise a requisite measure of force, if necessary, in certain situations. There was a specific authorization by the Security Council to the United Nations military force in the Congo to use a requisite measure of force, if necessary, in certain situations. But the United Nations Force in Cyprus has no such authorization.*

This is the distinction. It is also worth recalling that, within the framework of the Security Council resolutions, when the United Nations Force in the Congo exercised force in certain situations, there was a loud uproar of criticism and condemnation of the fact that the United Nations, as a peace Organization, should not resort to force. But now, in the absence of such an authorization by the Security Council in Cyprus, the very same quarters are advocating the use of force by the United Nations in Cyprus. At the same time, however, I am sure they are aware of the fact that the Security Council has not authorized the use of force by the United Nations Force in Cyprus.

Regarding the freedom of movement, I have to report that very perceptible progress has been made as a result of the negotiations between my special representative, Mr. Galo Plaza, and General Thimayya, on the one hand, and the Government of Cyprus on the other. There is increasing evidence of closer cooperation between the Government of Cyprus and the United Nations Force in Cyprus.

. . . .

*UNFICYP has, of course, the right of self-defense.

Statement to the Working Group of 21

NEW YORK   SEPTEMBER 9, 1964

THE MAIN TASK of finding a way out of the United Nations financial crisis was in the hands of the Working Group of 21, a special committee of the General Assembly which had been trying in vain since its establishment (originally as a group of 15) in 1961 to head off a United States-Soviet confrontation over peace-keeping assessments. When the group met on September 9, 1964, for a final try before the opening of the delayed nineteenth session of the General Assembly, the situation appeared to be hopeless. The atmosphere of gloom and urgency was reflected in U Thant's speech. Time, he said, was rapidly running out and it was up to the group to come up with a solution before the session opened. Actually, the deadlock was to become tighter than ever during the coming weeks as the United States and the Soviet Union submitted new memoranda to the group reaffirming their basic differences. These were several, but the main one was over the legality of Assembly assessments for the operation of UNEF and ONUC.

THE TASK before you and your colleagues is perhaps the most crucial one for the future of the United Nations. The magnitude of your task will not, I hope, deter you from striving with a renewed sense of urgency and determination to reach, within the letter and spirit of the Charter, such accommodations and arrangements as will assure the continued effectiveness of the United Nations.

I doubt that anyone who has followed recent events—and least of all members of this group—harbors any illusion as to the difficulties inherent in the problems you have been asked to examine or the importance, nevertheless, of overcoming them. It is perhaps easy and therefore tempting to be dramatic. Yet I am convinced by the experience of the past three years that a policy of drift, of improvisation, of ad hoc solutions, of reliance on the generosity of the few rather than the collective responsibility of all, cannot much longer endure. In fact, time, if I may say so, is rapidly running out. It is imperative, therefore, that your efforts in the

UN Press Release SG/SM/150.

weeks that remain between now and the nineteenth session of the General Assembly, be crowned with success.

It may be worth recalling, in this context, what I said in my report to the Security Council on June 15, 1964 (p. 578), with reference to UNFICYP financing. I stated that, although I well understood the reasons for it and realized that there is little or no possibility of change, the method of financing the Cyprus Force as defined in the Security Council resolution of March 4, is most unsatisfactory. Since funds are available only through voluntary contributions, there is a large degree of uncertainty about the resources which will be actually available, and therefore the planning and advance arrangements essential to an efficient and economical operation are sorely hampered.

Although the present outlook may seem far from encouraging, I am not without strong hope. As you know, I have had the opportunity since you last met, of full and frank discussion of the United Nations' financial and related problems in several of the world's important capitals. I have used every occasion, also, to review these same questions with many of the leaders of Africa, Asia and the Americas (including Canada), and of Eastern and Western Europe.

The first clear and definite impression I have formed as a result of these wide-ranging conversations is that all the leaders to whom I have freely expressed my concerns in all the countries I have visited, share one objective in common; that is, to see the United Nations strengthened. It is their common—and I am convinced, sincere—desire to see the Organization become a truly effective instrument for the performance of the functions outlined in the Charter. Unfortunately, this basic unanimity on objectives is accompanied by a very wide divergence of views as to the means of achieving them. I find it difficult to believe, however, that such divergency of views, albeit strongly and sincerely held, will be so inflexibly maintained as to jeopardize, if not nullify, the larger objective.

I am encouraged in this hope by the fact that a limited consensus on certain approaches and modalities seemed to be emerging as a result of this group's earlier deliberations. The report which it submitted to the General Assembly at its fourth special session, though admittedly of an interim and preliminary character, should serve, I believe, as a useful point of departure in your further examination of the questions that remain unanswered.

In this connection, I welcome the views expressed by the heads of African states at the recent Cairo meeting of the Organization of African

Unity. The meeting expressed concern in regard to the serious financial situation facing the United Nations arising mainly from its peacekeeping operations, and earnestly appealed to Member states to meet their obligations and to render the assistance necessary for the Organization to fulfill its role in maintaining international peace and security.

In the meantime, of course, there have been hopeful signs, in certain key quarters, of a willingness to explore the possibility of reaching some modus vivendi. These explorations, moreover, have apparently embraced such crucial issues, among others, as the need for a more explicit definition of the relative functions and responsibilities with respect to peacekeeping activities, of the Security Council, on the one hand, and the General Assembly, on the other.

I am conscious, too, of the fact that over the past several months there has taken place under the guidance of your distinguished chairman, Ambassador Adebo, much informal consultation and discussion between delegations and groups of delegations in an effort to broaden and to strengthen the consensus that had earlier been reached. If these patient and persevering efforts have contributed—and I am sure they have—to a better understanding of the problems to be solved and to their ultimate solution, the United Nations owes to all who have participated, its deep gratitude.

Mr. Chairman, in the light of these circumstances, it is neither my intention, nor my desire, to presume to offer, at this time, any thoughts or suggestions I may have as to how the United Nations' financial problems—past, present, and future—might be resolved. Responsibility for the initiatives that are called for properly rests with the Member states themselves. They have designated this group of distinguished representatives to exercise such initiatives, at least in the first instance, on their collective behalf.

If, at an appropriate later stage, it should be your feeling and mine that a more positive intervention on the part of the Secretary-General would be helpful, I will not be reluctant to respond. For the moment, however, I am content to await developments, inside and outside this working group, in the confident expectation that most governments—large, and small, east and west, north and south—wish to see reasonable accommodations emerge.

I do not wish to burden you at this time with detailed facts and figures pertaining to the Organization's present financial position and prospects. Information concerning receipts and disbursements, obligations and cash resources, the status of the bond issue, and of contributions and arrears—will be made readily available if and when you deem it useful for your purposes. For the moment, we need only note that while there is no occasion for alarm, there is certainly cause for serious continuing concern.

Having said this, may I venture to offer a few additional observations of a somewhat general character.

It seems to me that our concerns fall broadly under two headings: first, how to provide for the future; and second, how to take care of the past. Perhaps the order should be reversed, since failure to take care of the past may not leave us with much of a future. It is mainly to this aspect of the problem, therefore, that I shall briefly address myself.

The fact is that at the behest of the General Assembly or the Security Council, and under duly constituted financial authorization, obligations have been incurred in good faith but without adequate or assured means of meeting them. Voluntary contributions by some governments in cash and in kind have afforded a helpful measure of relief and, indeed, have made it possible for the Organization to play a significant role which otherwise would have been denied to it, in such crises as those associated with West Irian, Yemen, and now Cyprus.

But such arrangements, as I have said, cannot be properly regarded as a sound basis for providing the United Nations in the future with the sinews of peace. Nor can such appeals, including the bond appeal, be expected to close the gap between disbursements and receipts which has been occasioned by the failure of others—albeit for reasons of principle—to pay their due shares of assessed expenses.

It is not my purpose to seek to persuade any Member state to change, still less to abandon, any position of principle that it considers firmly based on its interpretation of the Charter. Indeed, it would not be proper for me, as Secretary-General, to try to do so. I have felt no compunction, however, about presenting the case as I see it.

In my judgment, the pressing need is to find a formula which will enable the United Nations to receive the financial support which alone can restore its strength and solvency; which will be consistent with the letter and spirit of the Charter; and which will not prejudice or compromise basic principles or policies to which any Member feels irrevocably committed.

That may seem a very tall order—the more so since I have had occasion to realize from recent visits that there is little, if any, immediate likelihood of past attitudes on certain issues being seriously reconsidered. Nevertheless, there are considerations which lead me to hope, and even to believe, that the order may not be altogether impossible of fulfillment.

One such consideration is that, while there are positions of political or juridical principle that must be taken into account, there is equally a question of moral commitment. I refer to the commitment which the Organization has accepted, in its collective capacity, toward those of its Members who have furnished the men and matériel for its successive peacekeeping operations—particularly those in the Middle East and the Congo.

These members, having incurred, in good faith, substantial additional and extraordinary expenditures by virtue of such participation are surely entitled to expect the United Nations to keep faith with them. By means of one expedient or another, and notably through the issuance of United Nations bonds, and with the patient understanding of the governments concerned, the United Nations has so far managed to do so. But we cannot by these same means indefinitely postpone a threatening payments crisis.

But the consideration which above all gives me hope for the future is the simple conviction that it is never beyond the capacity of reasonable men to reach a reasonable accommodation, if there is a will to reach one. It is on that note, Mr. Chairman, that I shall conclude these opening remarks—except to add that I shall follow your proceedings with the closest of interest and attention; and that you may count on the fullest assistance of the Secretariat.

I thank you, Mr. Chairman, for this opportunity of sharing with you my views on one of our major preoccupations and concerns. I hope your deliberations may be fruitful, because, as I said at the outset, so very much depends on the successful outcome of your labours.

Statement at the Unveiling of the Chagall Panel

NEW YORK   SEPTEMBER 17, 1964

THIS IS A DAY of solemn remembrance. Exactly three years ago Dag Hammarskjöld set out on his final flight. On the morrow, the whole world mourned his tragic death, and that of his gallant companions.

In a real sense, something of each one of us died with them, for the whole range of the Secretariat was represented on that flight—the substantive officers, the personal assistants, the secretaries, the field service, and the United Nations peacekeeping forces. Today, we remember their sacrifice, and we pay tribute to them and to all who have died in the service of the United Nations.

Now a great artist, one of the acknowledged masters of modern art, Marc Chagall, has created a living memorial to their memory; a superb work which takes its place among the historic treasures of this building. In shapes and colors, in symbolic forms and designs, Marc Chagall has sought to express the simplicity and the beauty of the ideals of peace and brotherhood which we all endeavor to serve.

I am deeply moved by his symbol of peace—a young child being kissed on the cheek by an angelic face which emerges out of a joyous mass of flowers. And there are other symbols of peace we shall find as we study and search out the varied significance of the glorious design before us.

In expressing man's yearning for peace and brotherhood, and his readiness to lay down his life in his search for these ideals, Marc Chagall has depicted that enduring spiritual reality which gives depth and meaning to human life and to all our efforts, both in the United Nations and outside it, to make this world a safer and better place for all.

In accepting this magnificent work of art, I wish to thank Marc Chagall and all the members of the staff whose joint gift it is. I wish to congratulate all those who had a share in it, particularly Charles and Brigitte Marq who translated Marc Chagall's visual poetry into glass, and I

UN Press Release SG/SM/153.

should also like to thank all those whose generosity has helped to make this event possible.

This beautiful memorial to Dag Hammarskjöld and to his companions becomes today a living part of our own awareness of the meaning and purpose of the United Nations.

From Address on the Occasion of Staff Day

NEW YORK   SEPTEMBER 25, 1964

. . . . THE CAPACITY of the Secretariat to act will ultimately depend on the quality of the men and women who have come to serve on it. Whether a candidate is or is not suitable for appointment as a staff member must remain within the good judgment of the Secretary-General. At the same time, it is our hope that, with the assistance and cooperation of the Member governments, we shall continue to obtain the services of persons of the highest efficiency, competence, and integrity, without sparing our efforts to recruit staff on as wide a geographical basis as possible.

Secondly, the effectiveness of the Secretariat rests on the experience its members have acquired in the handling of the varied and complex tasks assigned to them. Such experience is necessarily a function of long service. It is, therefore, my intention to preserve the highest proportion of permanent staff compatible with the requirements of the work program, and in the terms in which I have stated my views before the General Assembly. I also intend to seek longer periods of service in all cases where fixed-term appointments are considered desirable.

Thirdly, as part of our effort to safeguard the unity of the Secretariat, which I think is an essential prerequisite of its effectiveness, we have recently abolished the differences between permanent and fixed-term staff in the area of separation benefits.

Fourthly, it is my firm desire to ensure equitable treatment of all staff members. During the past twelve months, several steps have been taken in this direction. Salaries have been adjusted upwards for staff in the general service, manual workers and field service categories; authority has been obtained from the General Assembly to extend and improve the allowances for language proficiency. An advanced stage has been reached in the determination of the scope of an extended general service category, which I expect to see established in the coming year. Work is in progress on a review of the professional salaries, and also on the improvement of pension benefits.

UN Press Release SG/SM/157.

Lastly, I would like to see the futher development of the concept of an effective international civil service. As you know, we have recently consulted the International Civil Service Advisory Board on this very subject. The board, a body of eminent men of knowledge and experience in matters of public administration, have submitted a number of recommendations on the basis of which we in the United Nations propose to consult together with the agencies participating in the common system as to the best means of providing the assurance necessary to make the international civil service a firm and meaningful reality.

As we approach the coming year, the year designated as the International Cooperation Year, the year of the twentieth anniversary of the United Nations, I feel we shall all wish to reaffirm our faith in the purposes and principles of the Charter, in the ideals of international cooperation, in the destinies of the Secretariat as the servant of these ideals.

From Transcript of Press Conference

NEW YORK   OCTOBER 22, 1964

THIS PRESS CONFERENCE took place immediately after two important world events, the replacement of Soviet Premier Nikita Khrushchev by Alexei Kosygin and the explosion of a nuclear weapon by the People's Republic of China. U Thant expressed the belief that there would be no substantive change in Soviet policy. He concluded his comment with a statement that surprised many correspondents and diplomats. He not only praised Khrushchev for his efforts to implement a policy of coexistence but suggested that "it would be helpful and even desirable, if Mr. Khrushchev were able or inclined to make a public statement on the circumstances leading to his exit." On the question of Peking's nuclear test explosion, Thant said the action was regrettable in the wake of the signing of the partial test-ban treaty in 1963 but was not unexpected. He took the occasion to endorse the idea of a dialogue among the United States, Britain, France, the Soviet Union, and the People's Republic of China and suggested that it be held in 1965.

. . . . QUESTION: Mr. Secretary-General, would you explain the purpose of the present move to postpone the opening of the coming session of the General Assembly? What are its advantages?

THE SECRETARY-GENERAL: As you are no doubt aware, I have no strong views on this question. About two weeks ago I was asked what I considered to be necessary or desirable regarding the rumored moves about the postponement of the opening date of the session. I said at that time that if there were definite prospects of an agreed formula in the inter-regnum, then the postponement of the session of the General Assembly might be worthwhile, but not otherwise. I still hold this position.

But, of course, as you know, many delegations have been meeting in the last few days and considering the advisability of postponing the opening date of the session, and there are also rumors that December 1 is a possibility. All I have to say today is that, in any case, the General Assembly has to meet in December to dispose of certain important items,

UN Note to Correspondents No. 2991.

including the adoption of the budget, and elections to the Councils, and I have been informed that the Second Committee may wish to meet to consider the recommendations of the United Nations Conference on Trade and Development.

Of course, it is up to the Member states to decide on any line of action, and if I receive a request from a majority of the Member states, I shall have to postpone the opening date of the session accordingly. Even if I receive a proposal from the majority of Member states, I think that, as a matter of form and out of courtesy, I must poll the remaining Member states to get their positions on this issue for the record.

. . . . QUESTION: Since the two major powers have apparently hardened their positions with respect to financing, on the eve of the postponement—the very object of which is to get them together—would you still be prepared, in a critical moment, to intervene personally, as I believe you indicated some time ago that you might?

THE SECRETARY-GENERAL: At some stage I indicated that if the deadlock still persists by the time the General Assembly meets, I might perhaps come up with some ideas to break the deadlock. But the positions of the parties primarily concerned remain very rigid and I do not see any prospect of a conciliatory formula or an agreed formula to break the deadlock. In the circumstances, I do not intend to come up with any personal proposals.

QUESTION: Do you have any comment on Mr. Khrushchev's displacement and the method used? Would you, in the same way that President Eisenhower indicated, like to hear from him directly?

THE SECRETARY-GENERAL: Well, it is not proper, of course, in my position to make an assessment of situations like the one which we witnessed in the Soviet Union last week since they are primarily domestic matters. But if I may venture an opinion, after the change of leadership in the Soviet Union, I do not think that the Soviet government will pursue a foreign policy different from the one adopted by Mr. Khrushchev. Actually, last Friday Ambassador Fedorenko saw me and informed me of the change in the Soviet leadership and transmitted to me the line of the new government in the Soviet Union, that it would continue to pursue the policies of peaceful coexistence, disarmament, and the peaceful settlement of international disputes and the strengthening of the United Nations. So I do not think that there will be any material change in the Soviet policy regarding foreign affairs. But perhaps there is a possibility of a change in emphasis.

Incidentally, I happen to have known Mr. Brezhnev since 1955. I met him in Alma Ata at that time, when he was the head of the Communist party of Kazakhstan. When I met him again in 1962 in Moscow, and again last year on the occasion of the signing in Moscow of the partial nuclear test-ban treaty, I found him the same friendly, warm, and unaffected gentleman, with a deep knowledge of world affairs.

I also know Mr. Kosygin; I have met him several times. In my opinion, he is one of the most unostentatious men I have ever met. From all accounts he is one of the most respected leaders of the Soviet Union.

Of course, both Mr. Brezhnev and Mr. Kosygin have a realistic appraisal of the world situation, and it is unlikely that they will reverse the course of history by taking the Soviet Union back to the pre-1953 era.

As regards Mr. Khrushchev, I have, as you know, made my personal assessment on more than one occasion. I still believe that he will be long remembered as a man who tried his best to implement the principle of peaceful coexistence—and, if I may say so, he did so with some degree of success in that he had been able to convince a considerable segment of public opinion in the West of his sincerity. I think that it would be helpful and even desirable, if Mr. Khrushchev were able or inclined to make a public statement on the circumstances leading to his exit.

. . . . QUESTION: Have you any comments to make on the Chinese explosion of a nuclear bomb and on how that might affect China's membership of the United Nations?

THE SECRETARY-GENERAL: As regards the Chinese nuclear test last week, I must say that from the point of view of the United Nations, and particularly in the context of the General Assembly resolutions—specifically the resolution adopted in 1962 condemning all tests—the Chinese nuclear test is deplorable. In my view it is particularly regrettable in the wake of the signing last year in Moscow of the partial nuclear test-ban treaty, which was endorsed by the General Assembly by an overwhelming majority.

You will remember that I predicted last year that there was a probability of a Chinese nuclear test some time in 1964. I based that prediction on the available information that a nuclear reactor had been established in China as early as 1958. Although the Soviet Union had withdrawn its technical assistance from China in 1960, the Chinese were reported to have at that time at least ten nuclear scientists who had been trained abroad.

In that connection, there was an interesting news dispatch yesterday about a speech in Columbus, Ohio the day before yesterday, by an eminent American, Governor Landon, who was the Republic candidate for president in 1936. Of course, I do not agree with all that he said, but one aspect of his proposal, regarding the need for a dialogue between the present nuclear powers, has some merit. I feel that it could be very worth while if attempts were made to have a dialogue between the United States, the Soviet Union, the United Kingdom, France, and the People's Republic of China, perhaps some time in 1965. In my view, 1965 will be a more congenial year than previous years for the conduct of such a dialogue. Of course, there are protocol and diplomatic considerations, but I feel very strongly that they should be secondary. The primary consideration should be that of nuclear destructibility and radioactivity.

As you know, there are two duly constituted forums for the discussion of disarmament and a nuclear test ban: the General Assembly and the Eighteen-Nation Committee on Disarmament. Legitimately, all questions regarding disarmament, the banning of nuclear tests, the nonproliferation of nuclear weapons and nuclear weapon capabilities should be thrashed out either in the General Assembly or in the Eighteen-Nation Committee on Disarmament. However, the kind of dialogue proposed by Governor Landon can certainly supplement the work of the General Assembly and the Eighteen-Nation Committee on Disarmament.

Regarding the second part of Miss Pick's [Hella Pick, *Manchester Guardian*] question on the prospects of the admission of the People's Republic of China to the United Nations, I have this to say. It should be remembered that the problem has two aspects. I have made this observation on a previous occasion also. Some Member states maintain that the question is one of representation, not admission. Their argument is based on the premise that China is already a Member of the United Nations—one of the founding Members, one of the five permanent members of the Security Council. Therefore, China is already a Member of this Organization. The question, according to them, is one of representation: who should represent China? This is the attitude held by some of the Member states.

Another viewpoint is held by the vast majority of the Member states, who maintain that the question is one of admission. Of course, the General Assembly has taken up this question from year to year. The General Assembly decided by implication that it was a question of admission of a new Member, not representation. And this majority opinion prevailed. Of course, I have no means of knowing what will happen in the forthcoming session of the General Assembly regarding this question.

. . . . QUESTION: In view of what you call the rigid position of the major powers on Article 19, do you think that, as the chief executive officer of this Organization who bears the responsibility for the survival of this Organization, you can let the confrontation occur, if it has to occur, at the beginning of the General Assembly, or do you not think it is incumbent on the Secretary-General to maintain the viability of the Organization?

THE SECRETARY-GENERAL: I have tried my best privately in my meetings with many representatives, here and elsewhere, to take the necessary steps to avoid a direct confrontation on Article 19, so far without success. Of course, I will continue with my efforts in an unofficial and discreet manner to the best of my ability, but for the moment there appear to be no prospects of an avoidance of a direct confrontation. I understand many delegations are also thinking of certain measures on their own initiative to avoid such a confrontation. But, as I have said, in the face of the rigid positions taken by the parties primarily concerned, I do not propose to come up with any formal proposals to break the deadlock.

. . . .

Letter to the President of the Security Council Concerning the Mission of the Special Representative to Cambodia and Thailand

NEW YORK   NOVEMBER 9, 1964

IN MY LETTER of December 9, 1963, I informed the Security Council that at the request of the governments of Cambodia and Thailand it had been decided that the special representative of the Secretary-General would continue his activities for the calendar year 1964, under the same terms of reference as had been agreed to for 1963.

As I felt it necessary to provide at an early date for the future assignment of the staff detailed to the mission, I inquired in July 1964 of both governments whether they desired that the mission should be maintained in 1965 or should be terminated at the end of 1964.

On August 24, I was informed by the permanent representative of Thailand that, in the view of his government, the mission of the Secretary-General's special representative should not be continued beyond its appointed term at the end of December 1964. The Thai government however suggested that consideration be given to the devising of some other means by which the United Nations Secretariat might still be able to render its services in the normalizing of relations between Thailand and Cambodia. It was suggested that a high-ranking member of the Secretariat might be sent on ad hoc missions to the area at certain appropriate times to discuss the situation with the leaders of the two countries and to suggest to them such measures as might seem appropriate.

Subsequently, I have communicated with the Cambodian government regarding this suggestion and have received their concurrence although they have expressed some doubts as to the results that might be expected from such mediation attempts. Taking into account the views expressed, I have informed the two governments that I will address myself to them on this matter at a suitable time during 1965.

Security Council Official Records, Nineteenth Year, Supplement for October, November, and December 1964, document S/6040.

Meanwhile, the mission of the special representative will be withdrawn on December 31, 1964, or earlier if it is able to conclude the activities in which it is currently engaged.

In view of the nature of the action envisaged and the previous report I have made on this matter, I thought it appropriate to make this further report to the members of the Security Council.

U THANT
Secretary-General of
the United Nations

From Introduction to the Nineteenth Annual Report

NEW YORK   NOVEMBER 20, 1964

THE INTRODUCTION to the nineteenth annual report was delayed until November, because of the postponement of the nineteenth session of the General Assembly, and could thus cover developments almost up to the opening of the session on December 1. In a report to the Security Council on June 29, Thant had already announced the withdrawal of the last United Nations military forces from the Congo. Now he reported a serious deterioration in the internal security situation, resulting in widespread disorders, which he attributed mainly to "the spectacular failure" of the Congolese National Army to fill the vacuum left by the departing United Nations troops. He noted, however, that the Congolese government had not indicated any desire to have the United Nations forces remain beyond June and that this left the United Nations no choice except to go ahead with the withdrawal. He noted also an important political development, the return of Moïse Tshombé to replace Cyrille Adoula as prime minister on July 9. Thant's differences with Tshombé, while the latter was president of Katanga province, were well known, including the Secretary-General's description of Tshombé as "unstable" and his accusations of deceit and double-dealing against Tshombé. In the text below, Thant maintained that the United Nations attitude toward Tshombé had often been "falsely reported." He noted that although the Organization had thwarted the secessionist effort led by Tshombé, "it never failed to recognize Mr. Tshombé as President" of Katanga. Thant also reported that in Cyprus, the scene of another major United Nations peacekeeping operation, some progress had been made in reducing the dangers and discomforts facing the population but that the situation in Cyprus was, "by any measure, a grim and formidable one." He reported further that another United Nations operation, the Yemen observation mission, had been terminated on September 4.

    Sections III, IV, and V of this introduction, dealing with the peaceful uses of outer space, economic, and social problems and the International School, have been omitted because of lack of space. These subjects are covered to some extent in other parts of this volume.

I

THE INTRODUCTION to the annual report has been delayed considerably this year in view of the postponement of the General Assembly. I have taken advantage of the delay to bring the introduction up to date, al-

General Assembly Official Records, Nineteenth Session, Supplement No. 1A (A/5801/ Add.1).

though the annual report covers only the period up to June 15, 1964.

Since the last introduction, which was dated August 20, 1963, there has been some progress in disarmament, and also in our activities in the field of outer space. In the Congo, the military phase of the operations came to an end on June 30, 1964. However, the technical assistance and civilian operations still continue.

The major peacekeeping operation undertaken by the Organization during the period under review has, of course, been in Cyprus. Recent developments encourage me to hope that our efforts may assist in bringing about a peaceful solution of the various problems of this troubled island.

The most important event of the year in the economic field was the convening of the United Nations Conference on Trade and Development. The interest generated by this historic conference overshadowed all other developments in the economic field. I may point in this connection to the progress we have been making toward the merging of the expanded program of technical assistance and the special fund in a United Nations development program. I hope that the General Assembly will, before long, approve the establishment of this new unified program.

During recent months the financial crisis of the United Nations has been one of my major preoccupations, and I have no doubt this is true of delegations also. My detailed comments on the financial crisis are to be found elsewhere in the introduction. All Member governments seem to me to be agreed on the common objective of strengthening the effectiveness of the United Nations. If this objective is to be realized, I must reiterate that the financial solvency of the world Organization should be reestablished on a firmer and more stable footing.

II

Questions relating to disarmament continue to command serious attention and to have high priority on the international agenda. Although the expectations of the eighteenth session of the General Assembly have not been realized, the fact remains that more significant progress in achieving some measure of disarmament has taken place since the summer of 1963 than in all the years since the founding of the United Nations.

The partial test-ban treaty, the establishment of the direct communications link between Moscow and Washington, the resolution of the General Assembly to ban nuclear and other weapons of mass destruction from outer space, the unilateral reductions of the military budgets of the Soviet Union and the United States, and the mutual cutbacks in production of fissionable material for military purposes by these two countries and the United Kingdom, are all indications that a start may finally have been made to grapple successfully with the many difficult problems involved in putting an end to the arms race.

These first steps demonstrate the importance of using simultaneously a variety of diplomatic instruments and techniques. They include direct discussions through diplomatic channels, deliberations in regional and other conferences, detailed negotiations in the Conference of the Eighteen-Nation Committee on Disarmament, and the annual review in the General Assembly which provides support and guidance to these discussions and negotiations. The utilization of all these channels and organs provides an opportunity for a thorough consideration of the many political and technical problems of disarmament, encourages the great powers to bring to bear their major responsibilities on this field, and enables the other countries, all of which are vitally interested, to make their contributions toward finding solutions.

This past year has also seen the development of a new institutional approach or procedure, which involves what may be called "reciprocal unilateral action" or the "policy of mutual example." This avenue of progress permits the powers chiefly concerned to take new steps by independent or coordinated unilateral actions.

Despite these favourable developments, however, the year 1964 has not fulfilled the hopes generated by the partial test-ban treaty and the general improvement in international relations in 1963. The resolutions on disarmament adopted at the eighteenth session either by acclamation or by overwhelming majorities have remained unimplemented in important respects.

Although the eighteen-nation committee met for more than six months in 1964 in a good atmosphere, with several new and interesting proposals emerging from the discussions, it failed to make any concrete substantive progress. Despite a detailed discussion of a long list of collateral measures and an intensive debate on general and complete disarmament, the committee reported that it had thus far not been able to reach any specific agreement.

The treaty banning nuclear weapon tests in the atmosphere, in outer space, and under water remains neither universal nor comprehensive. Although more than one hundred states have become parties to the treaty, some states are conspicuous by their absence from the list of signatories. No progress has been made toward an agreement to ban underground tests, nor do the negotiations give the impression of having been conducted with the sense of urgency called for by the General Assembly. If it is agreed that both national and international security depend not on technical developments from continued underground nuclear testing, but on political and military restraint and the progressive curtailment and reversal of the arms race, a comprehensive test ban would be a logical next step. In this connection, the joint memorandum of the eight nonaligned members of the eighteen-nation committee may point the way to a practical solution.

Another area where progress is most urgent is in the prevention of the spread of nuclear weapons. It is almost three years since the General Assembly unanimously adopted a resolution calling on both nuclear and non-nuclear states to enter into an international agreement to prevent the wider dissemination of nuclear weapons. The dangers of dissemination have markedly increased during this time, with one more country joining the "nuclear club," and the failure to implement the Assembly resolution gives cause for genuine and growing concern. I am hopeful that all states will give this problem their most careful attention. This is an area where each country may make a specific contribution.

One measure which seemed to hold out some promise of agreement is the destruction of bomber aircraft. This question was discussed for the first time by the eighteen-nation committee during the current year and specific proposals were made by both the Soviet Union and the United States. Each of these powers has also indicated that there is some flexibility in its position and that it wishes to continue negotiations on the subject. It is hardly necessary to underline the fact that if an agreement could be reached on any concrete measure of real disarmament, even if only modest to begin with, it would symbolize the intentions of the great powers in the field of disarmament and would have most beneficial political, psychological, and moral results.

The reduction and elimination of vehicles for the delivery of nuclear weapons continues to be the key issue of general and complete disarmament. The eighteen-nation committee broke new ground by its concentrated effort to find an agreed basis for a working group to study the elimination of vehicles for the delivery of nuclear weapons. The committee has for the first time come within reach of an agreement on a procedure to examine jointly the technical and strategic problems associated with this vitally important measure, and I feel certain that Members will wish to encourage the mutual accommodation necessary for agreement on such new exploratory machinery.

Although both the Soviet Union and the United States favoured each of the foregoing measures, as indeed did all of the participants in the Conference of the Eighteen-Nation Committee, the disagreement between them on how to attain the desired objectives reflected a fundamental divergence in their approach to the respective measures. The efforts of the other participants to find mutually acceptable compromises did not succeed during the past session. Nevertheless, the intensive discussions at the conference once again served to clarify positions and to indicate in what areas and in what ways progress might be possible. By exploring the various problems in depth, the conference has also made it easier for the main parties to reach agreement more quickly when the requisite political decisions are taken by one or both sides.

That such further steps are necessary and that the time is ripe is, I believe, hardly open to question. Such steps would not only impose further limitations on the arms race, but would help to strengthen the agreements already achieved. They would also have a positive and far-reaching effect on the international political climate in general. Without such additional agreements, the momentum initiated by the partial test-ban treaty might be lost. Accordingly, I consider it to be of the highest importance that what was not achieved during the past few months be yet achieved at the forthcoming session of the General Assembly and during the next round of talks in the eighteen-nation committee in 1965. In addition, I hope consideration will also be given to the possibility of a dialogue among the five nuclear powers.

. . . .

VI

On June 29, 1964, I submitted a report to the Security Council which dealt with the withdrawal of the United Nations Force in the Congo, which had then just been completed, and the continuation of United Nations civilian assistance in the Congo. Little needs to be added here to what was said in that report beyond the observation that, immediately following the withdrawal of the United Nations Force, some of our worst fears for the Congo began to be realized and our apprehensions about that country's future were very great.

In view of the serious deterioration in the internal security situation in the Congo since the withdrawal of the Force, it is only natural that the question should be asked why the Force was withdrawn in the first place, since the course of events that might be expected to follow the withdrawal of the Force could have been anticipated. The answer is that there was no decision by the competent organs of the United Nations to extend the mandate of the Force, and there was no request from the Government of the Congo for any extension of the Force beyond the end of June 1964. Without such a request there could be no basis for any United Nations action involving the continued presence of the United Nations Force in the Congo after last June. The Force was sent to the Congo in the first place in answer to the urgent appeal of the Congolese government; it remained there for almost four years at the desire of that government; it could not remain there after June 30 without a further request from the government. Indeed, after December 1963 there was never any intimation from the Government of the Congo of any wish to have the United Nations Force stay on after June 1964.

I cannot say, of course, how the United Nations would have responded had there been a request from the government for a continuance of the United Nations Force in the Congo beyond June 1964 up to which date funds had been sanctioned by the General Assembly; but such a request most certainly would have been given serious consideration. There was, however, an evident feeling in some quarters that the United Nations could not maintain an armed force in the Congo indefinitely, and that far too much had already been expended for this purpose.

Much of the disorder in the Congo thus far has been due basically to the spectacular failure of the Congolese national army. There are other factors, of course, especially the lack of preparation of the Congolese people for independence in 1960. It will be recalled, however, that a major event influencing the future of the Congo occurred when, within a few days following the country's independence, the Congolese national army—one of the largest and best armed armies of Africa—mutinied and ceased to be a positive factor for security, law, and order in the country. This led to the reappearance of Belgian troops, and started the chain of events which caused the government, then headed by Mr. Kasavubu and Mr. Lumumba, to appeal to the United Nations for military and other assistance. The United Nations could not ignore that appeal without losing the confidence of most of the world. In responding to it, the United Nations served the interests of the peace of Africa and of the world, as well as those of the Congo, by preventing a power vacuum in the very heart of Africa which would have been extremely grave, with the inevitable risk of East-West confrontation as well as inter-African rivalry and conflict.

As I have reported previously, recognizing how vital it would be to the future of the Congo to have its army made effective and dependable through retraining and reorganization in order that it might regain a reasonable measure of discipline and morale, repeated efforts were made by the United Nations to induce the Government of the Congo to accept United Nations assistance in the retraining and reorganization of the army. Indeed, at one stage the personal approval of Prime Minister Adoula was given to me directly for the United Nations training plan, based mainly on assistance to be provided by other African countries—and we proceeded to make arrangements and even recruit personnel for that purpose—but I understand that the prime minister was unable to obtain the approval of the commander of the army, General Mobutu, for the project.

It would seem advisable also to clear up one more misconception about the Congo, which concerns the often falsely reported attitude of the United Nations toward Mr. Moïse Tshombé, who is now the prime minister. The United Nations Operation in the Congo, having been directed by the Security Council to seek, among other things, to preserve the territorial integrity of the country, to prevent civil war, and to eliminate mercenaries, was inevitably opposed to the attempted secession of Katanga. While sparing no effort to achieve a peaceful solution, it did what it could, in collaboration with the Government of the Congo, to prevent the attempted secession from becoming an accomplished fact. It succeeded in its objective. The attempted secession of Katanga was led by Mr. Tshombé, as president of that province. Although the United Nations operation thwarted the Katanga secessionist effort, it never failed to recognize Mr. Tshombé as president of the Province of Katanga, a position to which he had been duly elected.

The Government of the Congo has recently turned to the Organization of African Unity for assistance in helping it to reestablish peace, law, and order in the Congo. That organization acted on this appeal by setting up an ad hoc committee, under the chairmanship of the prime minister of Kenya, Mr. Jomo Kenyatta, with a view to assisting the Congo (Leopoldville) to normalize its relations with its neighbours, the Congo (Brazzaville) and Burundi in particular, and to exercising its good offices in an effort to secure a solution to the problem of the Congo by means of conciliation. I hope that this effort will prove helpful.

Although the prevailing picture of the Congo may be dark and un-promising, that country has demonstrated remarkable resilience through-out the troubles which have beset it since its independence. The resources of the country are rich. Surprises are frequent in the Congo, and it should not be excluded that the country, realizing that it no longer has a United Nations Force to depend upon for internal security, will in time muster the will and the ability to attain both security and political stability. For the sake of the Congo and its people, for the sake of the continent of Africa and for the cause of peace, I most earnestly hope that this will be so.

Meanwhile, it is worth recalling that, in its four years in the Congo, the United Nations operation reduced to a minimum the risk of East-West conflict there; it prevented the country from being engulfed in civil war, of tribal or other origins; it greatly helped to preserve the territorial integrity of the country; it was mainly responsible for restoring some semblance of law and order throughout the country; it eliminated completely the mercenaries of Katanga, some of whom have now reappeared in Leopoldville; and it provided, and continues to provide, a great amount of technical assistance. These are certainly achievements of lasting value.

It is sometimes forgotten that, although the United Nations Force has withdrawn from the Congo, the largest United Nations technical assis-tance/special fund operation anywhere in the world, at present consisting of approximately two thousand persons, is still found in that country. The main reason for the comparatively large size of this program is that the voluntary Congo fund, and various funds in trust, have made it possible until now to finance substantial extrabudgetary assistance programs under the aegis of the United Nations civilian operations in the Congo. Even though there have been some indications that a few countries might be prepared to make voluntary contributions to the Congo fund on a matching basis for the year 1965-1966, I do not intend, in view of the generally disappointing response to my appeal in 1964, to make a further general appeal to Member states to contribute to the fund in 1965.

Today, United Nations technical assistance is undertaking the functions of the civilian operations program in providing the backbone of many of the essential services and much of the public administration of the Congo. It is heartening to report that, despite the recent alarming situation in the Congo, many experts are still willing to serve there under the United Nations, and I should like to take this opportunity to pay tribute to the constancy, skill, and courage of the great many doctors, teachers, agricultural advisers, meteorologists, telecommunications experts, magistrates, airfield control staff, public works experts—to name only a few categories—who have continued their work in the Congo under very difficult, and often dangerous and highly unpredictable, conditions. Many of them, in addition to their regular work, have in troubled times provided a nucleus for rehabilitation in areas and towns where normal life had been seriously disrupted. The work of these devoted men and women is a matter for legitimate pride on the part of the United Nations and the specialized agencies.

VII

Since last March, the United Nations peacekeeping effort in Cyprus has been a major concern of the Organization, and I have been reporting on it in detail to the Security Council from time to time. The United Nations Force in Cyprus has already served twc three-month terms in the island and its mandate was extended for a third three-month term by the Security Council on September 25, 1964.

The mandate of the United Nations Force in Cyprus has been to prevent a recurrence of fighting and to contribute to the maintenance and restoration of law and order, and to a return to normal conditions there. The Force has done much more than might have been expected of it toward the fulfillment of that mandate. The commanders of the Force, General Gyani and later General Thimayya, the officers and men of the national contingents and the civilian members of the United Nations Secretariat associated with them have, in most difficult and complex conditions, performed their duties with signal devotion and effectiveness. I should also like to pay tribute to the valuable services of my special representatives, first Mr. Spinelli, then Mr. Galo Plaza, and now Mr. Bernardes.

The situation in Cyprus is, by any measure, a grim and formidable one, and it is sufficient here to recall that, in spite of the highly inflammable state of affairs which prevails in the island, there have been so far, while the Force has been in Cyprus, only two outbreaks of serious fighting, both of which were quickly contained and halted, the first of these in the St. Hilarion area in late April, and the second in the Kokkina area in early August.

Despite the great obstacles to a return to normal conditions in the island, and, indeed, to any quick solution of the problems of Cyprus, some progress has been made in reducing the dangers and discomforts under which some parts of the population of Cyprus have been living, and it is to be hoped that this progress will continue, with increasingly beneficial results.

As regards the efforts to resolve the long-term problems of Cyprus through the United Nations mediator, it is not possible at this stage to report any significant advance. The work of Ambassador Tuomioja, the first mediator, whose tragic death interrupted his painstaking and persistent attempts to find an acceptable solution, is now carried on by Mr. Galo Plaza, who brings to the task of mediator valuable first-hand experience of the situation in Cyprus from his service as my special representative there. It is certain that Mr. Plaza will spare no effort in seeking a peaceful solution, taking advantage of the relative quiet which the presence of the Force has produced.

The financial arrangements to support the Force, in accordance with paragraph 6 of the resolution adopted by the Security Council on March 4, 1964, have proved to be far from satisfactory. As I had occasion to state to the Council in my reports on the conduct of the Cyprus operation, the method of financing the Force has been inadequate and funds have been received in such manner, as regards both pledges and payment of pledges, as seriously to hamper the planning, efficiency, and economical running of the Force.

VIII

In the introduction to the annual report last year, I referred to the agreement reached with the governments of Cambodia and Thailand on the desirability of appointing a special representative in the area who would place himself at the disposal of the parties to assist them in solving all the problems that had arisen or might arise between them. The most immediate of these concerned the reactivation of the December 15, 1960 agreement on press and radio attacks and the lifting of certain air transit restrictions. It was hoped that in due time consideration might be given to the resumption of diplomatic relations. The expenses of this mission were to be shared on an equal basis by the two governments. In December 1963, at the request of the two governments, the appointment of the special representative was extended for another year.

During the period under review, the special representative has continued to serve as an intermediary between the two governments on a number of questions, such as the exchange of prisoners, and is at present assisting them in solving the problems that have arisen in connection with the closing of their respective diplomatic missions in Bangkok and Phnom-Penh. Meanwhile, however, the Government of Thailand has given notice that it is not in favour of continuing the services of the mission on a permanent basis, and has suggested that consideration may be given to dispatching a high-ranking member of the Secretariat on ad hoc missions to the area to discuss the situation with the leaders of the two countries and then make appropriate suggestions. Its views have been communicated to the Government of Cambodia which, while taking a different view of the value of such missions, has agreed to these suggestions in principle. The mission of the special representative will, therefore, be discontinued toward the end of 1964.

IX

One mission in the peacekeeping sphere, the United Nations Yemen observation mission, has come to an end. It had been set up in mid-1963 to observe the implementation of an agreement between Saudi Arabia and the United Arab Republic under which they had undertaken to disengage from their direct and indirect interventions in the prevailing civil war in Yemen. During its fourteen-month period of activities, the mission was restricted by the terms of its mandate to observation alone and was able to report only a limited measure of disengagement. It was terminated on September 4, 1964, when the two states concerned, which had met the full costs of the operation, informed me, one that it was not prepared to continue to do so, and the other that it had no objection to the termination of the mission. Despite its weak and inadequate mandate and its limited results, the mission did contribute to a reduction of international tension in the region of its operation and to some improvement in the internal security situation in Yemen. Moreover, it helped to keep the door open for further highest level discussions between the Saudi Arabian and United Arab Republic governments on the Yemen problem, which have finally, in fact, taken place with encouraging results.

X

In the introduction to last year's report, I referred briefly to the fact that I had sent a team of United Nations officials to carry out certain tasks as envisaged by the governments of the Federation of Malaya, the Republic of Indonesia, and the Republic of the Philippines. On August 5, 1963, these governments had requested me to ascertain, prior to the establishment of Malaysia, the views of the people of Sabah (North Borneo) and Sarawak within the context of General Assembly resolution 1541 (XV), principle IX of the annex, "by a fresh approach which in the opinion of the Secretary-General is necessary to ensure complete compliance with the principle of self-determination within the requirements embodied in principle IX." From the very beginning of 1963, I had observed with concern the rising tension in Southeast Asia on account of the difference of opinion among the countries most directly interested in the Malaysia issue. It was in the hope that some form of United Nations participation might help to reduce tensions in the area and among the parties that I agreed to respond positively to the request made by the three governments.

As is well known, the United Nations Malaysia mission expressed the opinion that "the participation of the two territories in the proposed Federation, having been approved by their legislative bodies, as well as by a large majority of the people through free and impartially conducted elections in which the question of Malaysia was a major issue, the significance of which was appreciated by the electorate, may be regarded as the result of the freely expressed wishes of the territory's peoples acting with full knowledge of the change in their status, their wishes having been expressed through informed and democratic processes, impartially conducted and based on universal adult suffrage." I accepted this view of the mission in my conclusions.

Unfortunately, the hope I had expressed that the participation of the United Nations might help to reduce tension has not been fulfilled. There have been continued incidents in the area, and accusations and counteraccusations have been exchanged, culminating in the complaint by Malaysia to the Security Council in September 1964. After a number of meetings, the Security Council was unable to adopt a resolution on this issue. Tension in the area, especially between Indonesia and Malaysia, continues to be a source of concern to me. I wish to express the hope that the endeavours of statesmen of the area to solve this difficult question peacefully will be steadfastly continued, and that the leaders of the countries involved will spare no effort to bring about a peaceful settlement of their differences.

XI

In the course of the year 1963-1964, a number of Member states have offered military units to the United Nations on a standby basis, that is, to be available to the United Nations when an acceptable demand is made by the Organization. Some other Member states have evinced interest in pursuing a similar course. I have welcomed the offers, but have been in no position to do much more than this, in the absence of any authorizing action by an appropriate organ of the United Nations, even though no expense to the Organization would be involved until a contingent was called into actual United Nations service.

There is much that could be done and needs to be done in the way of advance selection, training, and other preparations which would make the offered contingents more effective and which would in general ensure better, more efficient, and more economical peacekeeping operations in the future. It may be useful to have this question studied comprehensively in all its aspects, including manpower, logistics, and financing. Such a study may yield recommendations for consideration by the competent organs which may then authorize the Secretary-General to proceed along such lines as may be generally approved. I would accordingly welcome appropriate action by a competent United Nations organ which would authorize the undertaking of such a study.

XII

Decolonization continued to be one of the most important questions engaging the attention of the United Nations. Debates on this question in the General Assembly as well as in the other bodies concerned were held in the context of the Declaration on the Granting of Independence to Colonial Countries and Peoples, embodied in General Assembly resolution 1514 (XV).

During the eighteenth session of the General Assembly, several delegations expressed concern at the delay in the implementation of the declaration. The Assembly then requested the Special Committee on the Situation with regard to the Implementation of the Declaration on the Granting of Independence to Colonial Countries and Peoples to continue to seek the most effective and expeditious means for the immediate implementation of the declaration in all territories which had not yet attained independence. The Assembly also transferred to the special committee the functions previously performed by the former Committee on Information from Non-self-Governing Territories. With the disbanding of the Committee on Information, the special committee is now the only body responsible for matters relating to dependent territories, with the exception of the three remaining trust territories, for which the Trusteeship Council is responsible.

As in the two previous years, the special committee has been studying conditions in various dependent territories in order to determine the extent to which the administering powers are implementing the declaration. In a document prepared in April 1963, the special committee listed sixty-four territories to which the declaration is applicable. While I share the concern of Member states with regard to the delay in the implementation of the declaration, especially in relation to some of the larger territories in Africa, it is gratifying to note that Kenya, Zanzibar, Malawi (Nyasaland), Malta, and Zambia (Northern Rhodesia) have become independent sovereign States.

In spite of the many efforts that have been made to persuade Portugal to accept the principle of self-determination for the peoples of the territories under its administration, it continues to insist that the territories are parts of its "overseas provinces," and that the peoples of the territories have already been accorded "self-determination." The Portugese concept of self-determination has been rejected by the General Assembly as anachronistic, and it also conflicts with the concept of that term as defined in the Charter.

As the mandatory power for Southwest Africa, South Africa not only has continued to ignore the resolutions of the General Assembly, but also refuses to cooperate with those agencies of the Organization that have sought to render assistance to Southwest Africa. During the year the special committee considered the Odendaal Commission report, which was released by the South African government. The committee's view is that the recommendations of the Odendaal Commission are inconsistent with the responsibilities of the South African government as the mandatory power for the territory and that they should not be implemented.

The situation in Southern Rhodesia continues to give much cause for anxiety. The replacement of Mr. Winston Field by Mr. Ian Smith as prime minister in April 1964 reflected the ascendancy of those members of the Rhodesian front who favour a unilateral declaration of independence. Although in June 1964 Mr. Smith announced that there would be no unilateral declaration of independence, he continues to demand independence for Southern Rhodesia on the basis of the existing constitution and restricted franchise.

With a view to demonstrating to the United Kingdom government that this demand had the support of the majority of the population, his government proceeded to conduct a test of public opinion by means of consultation with local chiefs and headmen, in addition to a referendum of all registered voters; this method was rejected by the United Kingdom government as incapable of revealing satisfactory evidence of the wishes of the African population.

The United Kingdom government, in a statement issued on October 27, made clear to the Southern Rhodesian government the serious consequences of a unilateral declaration of independence. The statement has helped to clear any doubt as to the position of the United Kingdom government and has, at least for the time being, averted what would most certainly have been a crisis in Southern Rhodesia. The dangers still persist; and there is no evidence that the Southern Rhodesian government is prepared to accept the principles enunciated in various General Assembly resolutions concerning Southern Rhodesia. Nor is there any indication that the Southern Rhodesian government proposes to establish full democratic freedom and equality of political rights, and to convene a constitutional conference of all parties in Southern Rhodesia for the drafting of a new constitution based on the principle of "one man, one vote" and to prepare for an early independence of the territory.

In addition to the problems pertaining to the Portuguese territories, Southwest Africa, and Southern Rhodesia, to which I have just referred, there are two other important problems connected with decolonization to which I would like to make brief reference.

The first problem relates to the future of the smaller dependent territories. In my address to the opening of the special committee, on February 25, 1964, I referred to this problem as follows:

Although in the last two years a number of territories which were formerly non-self-governing have become independent sovereign states and are now Members of the United Nations, there are still some sixty dependent territories, many of which, though small in area and population, nevertheless come within the purview of the declaration on decolonization.

These small territories include many groups of islands in the Atlantic, Pacific, and Indian Oceans. The majority of them are sparsely populated and are spread over millions of square miles of ocean.

The special committee, during the present session, will be concerned with the questions relating to these small territories, and the committee will no doubt be faced with problems which it has not so far been called upon to resolve, namely, the most effective manner in which to enable the smaller territories to attain the objectives of resolution 1514 (XV). The task of the committee will not be an easy one, but I have no doubt that the experience which the members of the committee have gained during the last two years will prove helpful in the forthcoming deliberations of the committee.

It seems to me that this problem requires the attention of the General Assembly.

The second problem relates to the conflicting claims, by some Member states, to sovereignty over such territories as British Honduras, the Falkland Islands, Gibraltar, Ifni, and Spanish Sahara. It is my belief that these conflicting claims can be resolved only by goodwill and a willingness to give and take on the part of the various claimants. What is more, any solution should take into account the interests of the peoples of the territories concerned.

XIII

The period under review did not witness any improvement in the situation arising from the racial policies of the Government of the Republic of South Africa. On the contrary, the trend has been in the reverse direction and has been a source of heightened concern during the year, particularly in view of new legislative measures and the detention and trial of large numbers of persons for their opposition to the policies of apartheid. The Security Council devoted more time and attention to this problem than ever before and adopted four resolutions aimed at bringing about racial harmony based on equal rights and fundamental freedoms for all the people of South Africa.

In pursuance of the Security Council resolution of December 4, 1963, a group of experts was set up to examine methods of resolving the present situation in South Africa through full, peaceful, and orderly application of human rights and fundamental freedoms to all inhabitants of the territory as a whole, regardless of race, colour, or creed, and to consider what part the United Nations might play in the achievement of that end. This group, under the chairmanship of Mrs. Alva Myrdal, made a number of recommendations based on the essential principle that all the people of South Africa should be brought into consultation to decide the future of their country in free discussion at the national level. This principle was endorsed by the Security Council in June 1964.

Taking account of the composition of the population of South Africa and the present international context, there is a great danger that a continuation of the efforts to impose policies decided by one racial group in South Africa and the closing up of possibilities for a peaceful change may increasingly lead to violence which is likely to have widespread international repercussions. I can only reiterate the hope that the Government of South Africa will heed world opinion and the recommendations and decisions of United Nations organs, and take early steps to achieve racial harmony based on free consultations and respect for the human rights and fundamental freedom of all the people of the country. I also believe the United Nations should persevere in its efforts to persuade the South African government and people to seek a peaceful solution to the long-standing problem and thus reverse the unfortunate trends of recent years.

XIV

In May 1963, the General Assembly met in special session to consider, inter alia, the financial situation of the Organization in the light of a report of the Working Group on the Examination of the Administrative and Budgetary Procedures of the United Nations. At the end of the session, on June 27, 1963, it adopted a resolution in which it noted with concern the financial situation resulting from the nonpayment of a substantial portion of past assessments for the special account for the United Nations Emergency Force and the ad hoc account for the United Nations Operation in the Congo, and appealed to Member states in arrears in respect of these accounts to pay their arrears, disregarding other factors, as soon as their respective constitutional and financial arrangements would permit.

At that time, the arrears to the peacekeeping accounts totalled $99.7 million, the Organization had cash resources totalling $57.9 million, and its deficit was some $114 million.

Fifteen months later, on September 30, 1964, the arrears for the two accounts totalled $112.3 million, the Organization's cash resources totalled $24.8 million and its deficit was $113.3 million.

Thus, over a fifteen-month period, there has been virtually no improvement in the deficit position although in that period the Organization was able to apply in settlement of its debts approximately $50 million of nonrecurring income which derived from the sale of United Nations bonds and from the collection of assessments and voluntary contributions to the ad hoc account for the United Nations operation in the Congo.

While a further $15 million may be received for United Nations bonds, the present prospect in respect of the over-all financial position is that unless the deficit is to be further increased the Organization's cash resources will practically disappear within the next six months.

In this situation I found it necessary to say in my statement to the working group in September:

> . . . I am convinced by the experience of the past three years that a policy of drift, of improvisation, of ad hoc solutions, of reliance on the generosity of the few rather than the collective responsibility of all, cannot much longer endure. In fact, time, if I may say so, is rapidly running out. It is imperative, therefore, that your efforts in the weeks that remain between now and the nineteenth session of the General Assembly be crowned with success.

Since I addressed the Working Group in September, it has been decided further to postpone the opening of the nineteenth session to December 1, 1964. Meanwhile valiant efforts have been and are being made, both within and outside the working group, to find a solution for the financial crisis which may be acceptable to all sides. I would like to express my deep appreciation for these efforts, and I can only hope that such a solution may be found before the General Assembly meets.

XV

By resolutions 1991 A and B (XVIII), the General Assembly adopted amendments to Articles 23, 27, and 61 of the Charter to increase the number of nonpermanent members of the Security Council and to enlarge the membership of the Economic and Social Council. These amendments have so far been ratified by only thirty-two Members. They will come into force only when they have been ratified by two-thirds of the Members, including all the permanent members of the Security Council. As of today, none of the permanent members of the Security Council has done so. I sincerely hope that there will be greater progress in the ratification of these amendments in the near future, and that we may see the membership of both these principal organs expanded in 1965. I am sure that such expansion, which will make it possible to secure more adequate geographical representation in the two Councils, will contribute to the greater effectiveness of both bodies.

XVI

In July 1964, the second summit conference of the Organization of African Unity took place in Cairo. I was privileged to be able to attend this conference by invitation, and to address it. I was also able to exchange views with many African leaders whom I had been looking forward to meeting for some time. The proceedings of the conference confirm the optimistic view which I had expressed in the introduction to the annual report last year, and I am particularly grateful for the resolutions adopted by the conference, which were directed toward strengthening the effectiveness of the United Nations.

In October 1964, the Second Conference of the Heads of State or Government of Non-Aligned Countries took place, also in Cairo. Although I was unable to participate in this conference, I did send a message to it. Practically all the items on the agenda of the conference were also items under consideration by the United Nations. I hope that the conclusions reached at the conference will make a useful contribution to the discussion of related items on the agenda of the nineteenth session.

Steadily the Organization is continuing to make progress toward universality. Before long we will be welcoming Malawi, Malta, and Zambia into the world body. Some countries, which are not members of the United Nations but are members of specialized agencies, are represented in New York, and have also been participating in various activities undertaken by the world body, especially in the economic field. In addition, I believe that their presence in New York has helped them toward a better understanding of the international scene. Fully cognizant of the political difficulties involved, I cannot help but wonder whether the time has not come when other countries not at present represented in New York should be enabled to maintain contact with the world body and be able to listen to its deliberations. In this way, they too would obtain an exposure, now denied them, to the currents and crosscurrents of opinion in the world Organization. I feel that such exposure will have beneficial results which might well outweigh the political objections.

During recent weeks there have been changes in political leadership in two major governments, as well as in some others, while in a third recent elections have confirmed the present leadership for a further term with a reinforced popular mandate. I am confident that in 1965, which has been acclaimed as International Cooperation Year, these leaders, as well as the leaders of all other countries, will do their utmost to promote international understanding, to reduce tensions and to reach agreement on issues on which agreement seems so near. In particular, I would urge that in 1965 we should press forward to make progress toward disarmament and to reverse the arms race, especially the nuclear arms race. I also hope that we might see an end to the financial crisis which the Organization has faced in recent years, as I believe that the solution of this crisis will improve the international climate and usher in the International Cooperation Year under the most favourable conditions.

The General Assembly is due to meet on December 1, later than it has ever done before, in a hall which has undergone seating alterations and has been equipped with facilities for electronic voting. May I hope that the Assembly will also meet in an atmosphere of goodwill, which will be congenial to the realization of the purposes of the Charter.

U THANT
Secretary-General

November 18, 1964

ARTICLE 19 OF THE CHARTER

BY THE FALL of 1964 the potential application of Article 19 of the Charter had become a central issue in the Organization's financial crisis. This Article says: "A Member of the United Nations which is in arrears in payment of its financial contributions to the Organization shall have no vote in the General Assembly if the amount of its arrears equals or exceeds the amount of contributions due from it for the preceding two full years. The General Assembly may, nevertheless, permit such a Member to vote if it is satisfied that the failure to pay is due to conditions beyond the control of the Member." With total arrears of $54,768,188 on June 30—including disputed peacekeeping assessments of $15,638,166 for UNEF and $36,984,971 for the Congo operation—the Soviet Union was well over the cut-off figure. France was in arrears $17,752,565, enough to make her also subject to the penalty. As the time approached for the postponed opening of the nineteenth session of the Assembly on December 1, the question in everyone's mind was whether Article 19 would be invoked. The United States had taken the position that the loss of voting privileges for those sufficiently in arrears would be mandatory and automatic, requiring no decision of the Assembly. The Soviet Union, on the other hand, maintained that the peacekeeping assessments were illegal and could not be included in the total arrears figure. The Soviet Union, in addition, said it would consider any actions under Article 19 "as actions of those who do not care for the United Nations and who do not take into account the prospectives of its breakup as a result of such actions."[1]

At his August 20 press conference, U Thant reported that on his visits to Moscow, Paris, and Washington a short time earlier he had found the positions of the Soviet Union, France, and United States governments unchanged. Without mentioning Article 19 specifically, the Secretary-General said "perhaps, if necessary, I may have to come out with some suggestions just before the commencement of the next session of the General Assembly." In the introduction to his annual report, dated November 20, he said "valiant efforts have been and are being made" to find a solution which may be acceptable to all sides. These resulted in agreement among the United States, the Soviet Union, France, and the United Kingdom at the last moment on a formula which would permit the Assembly to transact limited and essential housekeeping business without formal voting. The president would simply ask if there were any objections to whatever was being considered and, if none was heard, he would declare the matter decided. For the scheme to work, it was essential for each Member state to acqui-

[1] Press Release No. 15, USSR Mission to the United Nations, March 21, 1964.

esce. One objection would have prevented action on any pending item of business. This was the situation when the Secretary-General made his statement on December 1 at the opening of the nineteenth session. The formula enabled the Assembly to get the necessary action on a substantial number of problems. It was able, for example, to admit three new Members—Malta, Malawi, and Zambia—and to fill vacancies on the Security Council and the Economic and Social Council, permitting those organs to continue functioning, and to adopt a budget for 1965.

The agreed procedure continued without formal challenge until February 16, when the Albanian representative, Halim Budo, declared that his delegation could not permit itself any longer to be "blackmailed" by threats of the United States to deprive certain Members of their voting rights. He submitted a request that the Assembly return to normal procedures without delay and asked for an immediate roll-call vote. The president, Alex Quaison-Sackey of Ghana, appealed to Budo not to press his proposal, but Budo refused. The president then adjourned the meeting until February 18 when he ruled that the procedures being followed had been accepted without objection on December 1 and that the Albanian proposal, therefore, was out of order. Budo challenged the ruling and asked for a roll-call on his challenge. The threatened confrontation was averted when United States Ambassador Adlai E. Stevenson told the Assembly he considered the Albanian challenge to be a procedural question and, for this reason, the United States would not invoke Article 19. The president's ruling was upheld by 97 votes to 2, with 13 abstentions. The nineteenth session was adjourned later the same day until September 1, 1965. By that time, Article 19 had ceased to be a cause for concern. Arthur Goldberg, who succeeded Stevenson as permanent representative of the United States, had declared on August 16: "The inevitable conclusion is that the Assembly is not disposed to apply the loss-of-vote sanction of Article 19 to the present situation." He added that the United States would not try to frustrate the will of the majority "that the Assembly should proceed normally."

1. Statement at the Opening Meeting of the Nineteenth Session of the General Assembly

NEW YORK   DECEMBER 1, 1964

IN VIEW OF the differences of opinion which have arisen among Member states regarding the conduct of the nineteenth session of the General Assembly, I have been in consultation with several delegations for the past week with the sole purpose of avoiding a confrontation. In this connection, I may mention that there is an understanding to the effect that issues other than those that can be disposed of without objection will not be raised while the general debate proceeds.

I hope that all delegations will agree with this procedure. As far as today's meeting is concerned, there is general agreement, I believe, that on the above basis we may proceed with the following items of business: first, appointment of the credentials committee; second, election of the president; third, admission of new Members to the United Nations.

I would recommend that the General Assembly proceed accordingly.

General Assembly Official Records, Nineteenth Session, 1286th plenary meeting.

2. Statement in the General Assembly

NEW YORK   DECEMBER 30, 1964

THE ASSEMBLY will recall the statement I made at the 1286th meeting of the Assembly, on December 1, 1964, and the understanding that was reached following my statement.

General Assembly Official Records, Nineteenth Session, 1314th plenary meeting.

There are two matters on which action has to be taken before the Assembly adjourns today, and in regard to which, I trust, a consensus exists.

First, I venture to assume that the General Assembly would wish to authorize the Secretary-General, pending decisions to be taken at the resumed session in 1965, to enter into commitments and to make payments at levels not to exceed, subject to statutory requirements, the corresponding commitments and payments for the year 1964 and, furthermore, pending such decisions, to continue existing arrangements and authorizations with respect to unforeseen and extraordinary expenses and the working capital fund. It is understood that the above-mentioned authorization will be without prejudice to the basic positions and objections of certain countries with respect to certain sections of the budget and to the budget as a whole.

Secondly, the Assembly will have noted from document A/C.2/224 that the Technical Assistance Committee at its 336th meeting on November 25, 1964, reviewed and approved the expanded program of technical assistance for the biennium 1965-1966, and authorized the allocation of the required resources to the participating organizations for the year 1965. Since the allocation of funds authorized by the Technical Assistance Committee requires the confirmation of the General Assembly, I trust it may also be assumed that such formal action is agreed to.

From Report to the Security Council on the Situation in Cyprus

NEW YORK   DECEMBER 12, 1964

ON DECEMBER 12, 1964, U Thant reluctantly asked the Security Council to extend for another three months the mandate of the United Nations Force in Cyprus, which had been operating since March 27. At the same time he warned that an indefinite stalemate could result if the parties came to rely on the presence of UNFICYP to maintain order and failed to press for a political solution.

. . . . 235. DURING THE PERIOD covered in this report on the activities of the United Nations Peacekeeping Force in Cyprus, the situation has much improved, and significant progress has undoubtedly been made. Fighting has largely ceased and, in general, the cease-fire is being observed in good faith. The easing of economic restrictions and restrictions on the freedom of movement of the population is reflected in a general relaxation of tension in most parts of the island and in a lessening of the hardship suffered by some sections of its population.

236. The improvement in the position of UNFICYP and the general recognition by all parties of its usefulness as a guardian of public safety, a go-between and a guarantor against the escalation of the conflict in Cyprus by the involvement of outside powers, constitute an encouraging development.

237. On the other hand, the efforts and achievements of UNFICYP (and here I express warm gratitude and admiration to the special representative, the Force commander, and their colleagues in UNFICYP) have clear limits, and it may well be that in a practical sense those limits are being approached unless existing attitudes change. The basic factors of the Cyprus situation remain essentially unchanged. Acute political conflict and distrust between the leaders of the two communities, and the passions stirred among the members of the two groups combine to create

Security Council Official Records, Nineteenth Year, Supplement for October, November, and December 1964, document S/6102.

a state of potential civil war, despite the present suspension of active fighting. This situation adversely affects the entire economy of Cyprus and causes some serious hardship for certain sections of the population, notably segments of the Turkish Cypriot community. The life and economy of the island remain disrupted and abnormal, and it would be unrealistic to expect any radical improvement until a basic political solution can be found.

238. In the meantime, while in certain areas controlled by Turkish Cypriots the government administrative and other services have no access, UNFICYP continues its complex task of providing good offices and acting as the link and channel of communication between two communities which arbitrarily and irrationally have cut themselves off from normal communication with one another.

239. In my opinion this task, in the absence of progress toward a political solution, will inevitably become an increasingly static one, and, in terms of a return to normal conditions, before long will begin to produce steadily diminishing results. The kind of stalemate which will surely result from such a situation will be the more undesirable for continuing to have within it the seeds of a relapse into chaos. It would be unfortunate, to say the least, if the present effectiveness of UNFICYP should become the pretext for failure to find a solution to the fundamental problem of Cyprus. An indefinite prolongation of UNFICYP would also present very serious problems to the United Nations itself. It is, therefore, in my opinion, essential that all concerned intensify their efforts to facilitate an early solution of the question of Cyprus which will have, among other positive results, the consequence of making the continued presence of UNFICYP unnecessary.

240. For the time being and in the immediate future, there seems to be no reasonable alternative to the continuation by UNFICYP of its functions in helping to keep the peace, supervising the cease-fire, and contributing to the maintenance of law and order and to a return to normal conditions. It is clear that UNFICYP's activities are at present indispensable, both for the welfare of the people of Cyprus and for the maintenance of conditions in which the search for a long-term solution can be further pursued. Having ascertained that all of the parties directly concerned, in the context of the Security Council resolution of March 4, 1964, that is, the Government of Cyprus and the Governments of Greece, Turkey, and the United Kingdom, wish the Force to be extended, I recommend the prolongation of UNFICYP under its existing mandate for a

further period of three months as from December 26, 1964, that is, until March 26, 1965. I do so on the assumption that the countries which have until now contributed to UNFICYP, providing either contingents or funds, will continue to give their generous assistance to the operation. I wish to take this opportunity to express to these countries the full measure of my gratitude for their support. At the same time, I urge all the states Members of the United Nations and of the specialized agencies to contribute to the financing of UNFICYP. In so doing, they would cooperate effectively with an operation which has helped to maintain international peace and security in a critical area of the world and would demonstrate, as well, their determination to uphold the peacekeeping ability of the United Nations.

Index

Sureck, David: Thant interview by, 383, 425, 432-41
Sweden: Congo Fund, 491-93; Congo operation, 84; exchange of messages with Thant on military build-up in Cyprus, 618-19; Thant message to: "The United Nations as a Force for Peace," 334-39

Tanganyika: independence for, 35
Tanganyika Concessions, 181, 191
Technical assistance: Expanded Programme, 141, 210, 406, 409-10, 511, 684; *see also* Congo, Republic of (Leopoldville); United Nations Technical Assistance Board
Technology, *see* Science and technology
Tension, world: causes of, 485-89
Thailand: Cambodia-Thailand border dispute, 16, 227, 288-90, 414, 490, 659-60, 670-71
Thant, U:
——biographical data, 3-11; accomplishments in office (self-evaluation), 436; appointed Acting Secretary-General, 3-4, 21, 23-25; association with Hammarskjöld, 21-22; Doctor of Laws degree from Carleton University, Ottawa, 120; elected Secretary-General (1962), 4, 19, 251-54; honorary degree from Williams College, 132; as journalist, 95-96; political philosophy, 8, 441; reactions to American culture, 438; religion and, 8-9, 441; "Two-Thant" doctrine, 10, 33, 39; views expressed prior to Secretary-Generalship, 5-7
——chronology of Thant documents dealing with Congo operation: **1961:** *Nov. 24,* statement in Security Council, on Security Council resolution of Nov. 24 reaffirming ONUC and Security Council Feb. 21 resolution, 51-54; *Dec. 8,* messages to Belgium, on Congo operation, 54-57; *Dec. 10,* statement (press release), on United Nations operations in Katanga, 57-59; *Dec. 14,* letter to United Kingdom, on Congo operation, 59; *Dec. 15,* letter to Belgium, on Congo operation, 60-64; *Dec. 16,* statement to Advisory Committee on the Congo, on implementation of Security Council Nov. 24 resolution, 65-67; *Dec.*

17, cable to Congo (Brazzaville), on ONUC transit and overflight facilities, 68-69; *Dec. 18, 19,* cables to Belgium, on ONUC and Katanga situation, 70-72; Dec. 30, *note verbale* to Portugal, on stationing ONUC observers in Angola, 72-73; **1962:** *Jan. 9,* statement to Advisory Committee on the Congo, on Kitona agreement, illicit traffic into Katanga, 80-82; *Jan. 17,* message to Adoula, on Gizenga's safety, 83; *Jan. 22,* letter to countries having troops in ONUC Force, on recent successes and need for more assistance, 83-84; *June 29,* statement to Advisory Committee on the Congo, on breakdown of Adoula-Tshombé talks, 154-55; *July 30,* letter to Adoula, on United Nations role in Congo, 159-60; *July 31,* appeal to United Nations Member states, to use influence to bring Congo factions together, 160-62; *Aug. 20,* report to Security Council, on efforts toward Congo reconciliation, 163-66; *Sept. 5,* statement to Press, on Plan for National Reconciliation in Congo, 166-67; *Dec. 13,* remarks to Advisory Committee on the Congo, on Plan for National Reconciliation, 272-74; *Dec. 31,* statement on improved situation in Elisabethville area, 274-80; **1963:** *Jan. 12,* letter to Nkrumah, answering charges against Thant's policy in handling Tshombé, 280-83; *Jan. 15,* statement on receipt of message from Katanga favoring implementation of Plan of National Reconciliation, 283; *Jan. 20,* letter to Nkrumah, reiterating substance of Jan. 12 letter, 284-86; *Jan. 22,* message to Gardiner and Guebre, on peaceful dissemination of United Nations Force throughout Katanga, 287; *Feb. 4,* report to Security Council, on phasing-out schedule for United Nations Force in the Congo, 291-304; *Mar. 20 and Apr. 23,* statements to Advisory Committee on the Congo, on modernization and training of Congolese Army (ANC), 305-7, 309-11; *Apr. 29,* letter to Adoula, on modernization and training of Congolese Army (ANC), 311-12; *Sept. 16,* letter to Adoula, on possible United Nations military presence in Congo following

Index by Lisa McGaw